School Counseling Principles

ETHICS AND LAW

FIFTH EDITION

Carolyn Stone, Ed.D.

The American School Counselor Association (ASCA) supports school counselors' efforts to help students focus on academic, career and social/emotional development so they achieve success in school and are prepared to lead fulfilling lives as responsible members of society. ASCA provides professional development, publications, resources, research and advocacy to school counselors around the globe. For more information, visit *www.schoolcounselor.org*.

1101 King St., Suite 310, Alexandria, VA 22314
(703) 683-ASCA, (800) 306-4722, fax: (703) 997-7572
www.schoolcounselor.org

ISBN: 978-1-929289-69-1

Dedication

School counselors, you inspire me every day. It is your wisdom and judgment that are found in the pages of this book. Your hard work, competence, dedication, and professionalism are without parallel. As ASCA Ethics chair for 20 years, it has been my honor to learn from you. This book is dedicated to you, Ashley Lawrence, you are an example of all that is right about the school counseling profession.

Acknowledgements

I would like to thank Sarah Beth Glicksteen, Greg Nuckols and Tracy Steele for their help with survey development. Thank you to the professionals who lent their voices to the In a Position to Know sections: Bob Bardwell, Katrina Beddes, Mary Bilboa-Waters, Christy Clapper, Mary Ann Dyal, Ken Elliott, Mary Hermann, Alexia Huart, Rob Lundien, Tammi Mackeben, Paul Meyers, Doug Morrissey, Theodore Remley, Wendy Rock, Russell Sabella, Rebecca Schumacher, Steve Schneider, Eric Sparks, Bob Tyra, Robert Weiss and Rhonda Williams. Bonnie Washick, thank you for your guidance with the LGBTQ+ chapter. Laurie Clark, Niegen Diggs and Denise Evans, thank you for your help with research. I would like to thank Kathleen Rakestraw, the editor of so many ASCA publications, for her support in getting this book to press.

Preface

Welcome to "School Counseling Principles: Ethics and Law." As all school counselors can attest, the profession offers many unique, interesting and often formidable legal and ethical challenges and responsibilities, primarily because we are working with minors in a school setting. School counselors live and work in an increasingly litigious society and are called to a high ethical standard. Professionals who work with minors are sensitive to the fact that issues for counselors who work with adults are far different. Each day school counselors have to consider the legal and ethical ramifications of their work in fostering academic, career and social/emotional development with students, while being faithful to their obligations to parents, administrators and the community.

This book is written for practicing school counselors and candidates for the profession. It is intended to raise awareness of legal and ethical issues and reduce the risk of unethical or unlawful behavior that might result in legal complications for school counselors. Although avoiding legal liability is a common thread throughout the book, the larger purpose is to enhance our obligations and responsibilities to students and not to provide legal counsel. Seek guidance from the legal arm of your district through proper channels. School counselors are rarely at the center of a lawsuit but daily are called on to act in the best interest of students and their families. Creating sensitivity to legal and ethical issues will heighten our awareness and help us examine the implications of our professional behavior for students.

Throughout this book we will examine the legal and ethical complications involved in working with minors in school settings, primarily through case studies. Case studies help school counselors reflect on possible consequences before they have to deal with real student situations, so that when in the throes of a dilemma, school counselors can ethically justify their courses of action. The case studies represent a wide range of circumstances and situations. They were developed from actual situations ASCA members posed to the ASCA Ethics Committee and from ethical dilemmas the author encountered when practicing as a middle school teacher, school psychologist, elementary school counselor, high school counselor and director of school counselors for Jacksonville, Fla. The more than 100 cases presented here will help the reader connect the reality of school counseling to critical federal and state statutes, the ASCA Ethical Standards for School Counselors (ASCA, 2022b), case law and school board policies that shape work with minors in schools.

The Organization of This Book

The chapter titled "Introduction to Legal and Ethical Issues" gives an overview of challenges and dilemmas school counselors face on a daily basis when working with minors in a school setting. As leaders and advocates, school counselors must choose the best path to support and assist students, and the ethical dilemmas and legal interpretations can at times make this feel overwhelming. This chapter presents key principles integral to ethical and legal understanding.

The remaining 13 chapters follow a template that will help you understand the concepts presented and will maximize effectiveness of the case-study format as a learning tool. Each chapter follows a similar outline:

- Objectives
- Ethical Standards Addressed in This Chapter
- Introduction
- Getting Started: What Would You Do?
- Working Through Case Studies
- Points to Consider
- In a Position to Know: A School Counselor Speaks
- Making Connections
- Quizzes
- Key Terms

Here is a brief description of these organizational items.

OBJECTIVES

The objectives section contains the intended learning outcomes the reader will take from each chapter. As an example, listed below are the book's overarching goals:

- Examine the legal and ethical obligations of the school counseling profession through application of case studies
- Raise awareness about and implications of professional behavior and professional actions
- Examine case law, court decisions and legislation that have an impact on practice
- Become familiar with legal and ethical terminology.
- Apply legal and ethical professional reasoning to concrete examples.

- Create sensitivity as to the difficulties and complexities of working with minors in a school setting
- Increase tolerance for ambiguity
- Lower the risk of legal liability in terms of professional practice

ETHICAL STANDARDS ADDRESSED IN THIS CHAPTER

Each chapter highlights the most salient standards addressing the ethical dilemmas presented. The ASCA Ethical Standards for School Counselors (ASCA, 2022b) provide direction to school counselors for answering the cases by applying the ethical standards. Discussion will also include reference to ethical standards, interpretations and practices formulated and promulgated by other professional organizations. However, the emphasis is on how to apply the ASCA standards to the resolution of cases.

INTRODUCTION

This section gives a brief overview of salient points that will be discussed in the chapter and sets the stage for learning.

GETTING STARTED: WHAT WOULD YOU DO?

This section presents an ethical dilemma to be answered at the end of the chapter by a practicing school counselor, school counselor educator, administrator or community member who has a special interest, understanding or experience. The intent is to generate interest and excitement for the material you are about to read and to have you develop your own resolution to the case before seeing how a colleague chooses to answer it.

WORKING THROUGH CASE STUDIES

The case studies are the heart of each chapter. In five or more case studies, this section presents common daily dilemmas school counselors face, as well as a few obscure legal and ethical pitfalls. In some cases, the answer can be found in the law. We will consider the Constitution, statutes, regulatory law and case law. Some cases involve school counselors who were charged with negligence under civil liability. Some of the cases presented will have both a legal and an ethical dilemma. The cases in the upcoming chapters are designed to challenge you and make you uncomfortable as you wrestle with problems that defy easy answers.

POINTS TO CONSIDER

Following each case presented, this section gathers court cases and legislation affecting the answer and allows you to apply some of the principles of ethics or law in context. It does not offer a black-and-white, right-or-wrong, concrete answer.

IN A POSITION TO KNOW: A SCHOOL COUNSELOR SPEAKS

This section provides you with a response from a practicing school counselor or someone who is in a position to know and understand how to approach the case in "Getting Started: What Would You Do?" School counselors, school counselor educators, administrators or community members respond to the case based on their own personal and professional experience.

MAKING CONNECTIONS

These questions give you an opportunity to extend your learning as you consider five to eight questions posed to help you apply what you learned in the chapter.

QUIZZES

Five-question, multiple-choice quizzes follow each chapter. School counselor educators wishing to use the quizzes in their classes may request an answer key from *asca@schoolcounselor.org*.

KEY TERMS

This section identifies the key terms and phrases used in the chapter, giving you a chance to review your understanding and reflect on what you learned.

Table of Contents

CHAPTER 3: CYBERSPACE

CHAPTER 4: STUDENT PRIVACY AND THE FAMILY EDUCATIONAL RIGHTS AND PRIVACY ACT

CHAPTER 5: NEGLIGENCE

CHAPTER 6: OBLIGATIONS TO SCHOOL BOARD POLICIES AND FEDERAL, STATE AND CASE LAW

CHAPTER 7: CHILD ABUSE

CHAPTER 8: INDIVIDUAL AND SMALL-GROUP COUNSELING

CHAPTER 12: BULLYING, CYBERBULLYING AND SEXTING

CHAPTER 13: VIOLENCE AND CRIMINAL ACTIVITY

CHAPTER 14: LEGAL AND ETHICAL ADVOCACY

Objectives

By the time you have completed this chapter, you should be able to:

- Define the difference between law and ethics
- Apply the ethics of the school counseling profession
- Discuss 13 of the most complicating factors of working with minors in schools
- Understand the courts' stance toward parental rights to guide their children

Introduction

A working knowledge of ASCA Ethical Standards for School Counselors (2022b) enables the professional to develop an understanding of the norms, customs and practices of the ethical school counselor. An understanding of laws, elements of negligence and principles established by courts informs school counselors as to the implications and consequences of their work with minors in school settings. An ability to reason ethically and to understand tenets of laws governing the school counselor's work affords us a greater comfort level with the ambiguous and situational dilemmas that are part of our profession. It is the hope that this book will guide school counselors toward strategies for handling the ethical and legal dilemmas that are part of a school counselor's daily life.

It is not the intent of this book to provide school counselors with concrete answers or legal guidance but to equip them with a working knowledge of certain principles of law and standards of ethical practice they can apply to their everyday work. By raising awareness, school counselors reduce their risk of backlash and develop a tolerance for ambiguity. Simple dogmatic solutions are seldom in the best interest of students, whose personal histories, developmental stages, family situations and problem-solving abilities are as complex as their conflicts. School counselors who consider the complications of their work with minors in schools appreciate the need to consider each ethical or legal dilemma in context. Always seek advice from the legal arm of your district when presented with legal concerns.

Law and Ethics

Ethical standards matter, which is why ASCA continues to revisit and update them. In 2016 and again in 2021, all ASCA state and territory school counselor associations were intricately involved in the revision process. In July 2021, the state/territory associations reviewed their assigned sections of the ASCA Ethical Standards for School Counselors and submitted their revisions in January 2022, at which time the ASCA Ethics Committee; the Diversity, Equity and Inclusion Committee; and the Position Statement Committee met and made further changes. The standards were sent out for public comment for one month, with the final step being a presentation to the Delegate Assembly in July 2022.

Ethics are ambiguous and contextual by nature. Ethics seldom provide black-and-white answers, nor should they. As frustrating as it may be for school counselors caught in a conundrum, there is always room for interpretation in each situation. Potter Stewart, associate justice of the Supreme Court, succinctly described the difference between law and ethics in one sentence. "Ethics is knowing the difference between what you have a right to do and what is right to do" (Stewart, n.d.). The ethical standards of practice are aspirational. School counselors strive to hold themselves to the highest standard.

The U.S. Constitution, federal and state statutes, and regulatory and case laws are based on precedence or common law. Common law is judge-made law. This type of law is based on legal precedents developed over hundreds of years. Common law also has been referred to as the "body of general rules prescribing social conduct" (Alexander & Alexander, 2019, p. 4). Because common law is not written by elected politicians but by judges, it can be referred to as "unwritten" law. The purpose of law is to codify a value or set of values. Law is the minimum standard society will tolerate. However, in the legal system, laws and their interpretation differ from one geographic location to another (Alexander & Alexander, 2019). Common law often contrasts with civil law systems, which require all laws to be written down in a code. Judges look for prior cases that have similar law and facts to the case at hand and render a judgment consistent with prior case law. "In the U.S. legal system, judicial opinions are probably the most frequently cited category of legal material. The articulated grounds of past judicial decisions are, in many instances, binding precedent for currently litigated matters. Under other circumstances, they are "persuasive authority" (Cornell School of Law, 2022, n.p.).

Ethics are agreed-upon values governing the conduct of professional members of an association and reflect the changing nature of the profession (Alexander & Alexander, 2019; Corey, Corey, Corey, & Callanan, 2018; Herlihy & Corey, 2015; Jacob, Decker & Lugg, 2022). Ethical standards and behavior are the result of values within a profession or organization and bind those who are members of the profession. Membership in school counseling professional organizations is critical to ethical behavior, but membership is not the deciding factor as to whether the ethical standards apply to the school counseling professional. The ethical standards apply to all members of the profession whether or not the person is an association member. Non-membership in professional organizations dents one's standard of care and calls into question if the professional holds to a high standard of care.

An ethical dilemma is not a clear-cut breach of the law but a complex situation from which positive or negative consequences can result, even when the problem is handled optimally. The nature of an ethical dilemma is that there is more than one right answer, thus the term "ethical dilemma." An ethical decision-making model empowers school counselors to make the best choices as they become more comfortable with ethical and legal ambiguity (Jacob, Decker & Lugg, 2022; Remley & Herlihy, 2019).

Cases presented throughout this book have both legal and ethical origins, specifically regarding the ethics of professionalism and confidentiality. Professionalism is the internal motivation to perform at the level of practice representing the ideals of the profession (Jacob, Decker & Lugg, 2022; Remley & Herlihy, 2019). Confidentiality issues can have both legal and ethical implications. For example, a state statute may require confidentiality but cite exceptions that render the issue an ethical one. Conflicts between the law and ethics are not uncommon, as we will see in several court cases presented in this book. In such cases, the law takes priority for school counselors. Remember, every decision a school counselor makes hinges on the context of a situation and deserves examination from multiple perspectives.

It is essential to keep in mind that school counselors do not practice in a protective bubble. A thorough knowledge of the laws, ethical standards, school board policies and prevailing community standards arms the school counselor with tools to make difficult decisions. This book endeavors to help school counselors not only accept their inability to eliminate risk but to learn how to reduce that risk.

The Complications of Working with Minors in a School Setting

The legal and ethical complications of any human-service profession are daunting; working with minors in a setting designed for academics only adds to the complexity. On any given day, a school counselor may navigate such charged, delicate subjects as abortion, harassment or suicide – sometimes doing this virtually. In addition, the school counselor's influence extends well beyond the student to include parents/guardians, teachers, administrators, the school district and the community. When you throw in legal and ethical complications and all these elements converge, school counseling can feel like walking a tightrope in a hurricane.

It might help to remember the acronym COMPLICATIONS as it applies to the difficulties school counselors face. The acronym will remind you of the following 13 factors that bear on your work in the legally and ethically complicated work with minors in the setting of schools.

Counselor's values
Obligations beyond the student
Minors' developmental and chronological levels
Privacy rights of minors
Legal status of minors
***I**n loco parentis*
Community and institutional standards
Academic instruction
Trusting relationship
Informed consent
Opacity of laws and ethical codes
Number of student-clients
Standard of care

Complicated legal and ethical work requires consideration of all the angles and a willingness to tolerate ambiguity. Exhaustive answers aren't possible in the context-dependent world of school counseling. Below are some guiding principles to consider in the context of your state and district laws, policies, procedures and the nature and culture of the individual school in which you work.

COUNSELORS' VALUES

We are our values; we cannot simply leave them at the schoolhouse door. Almost all individuals harbor biases against groups of people who they consider to be different from them. Such prejudices (racism, sexism, homophobic, ageism, ableism, etc.) are sometimes grouped together and referred to as "isms." Some people maintain isms as a conscious part of their value system, choosing to believe certain groups of people or behaviors are inferior; other people may have biases of which they are completely unaware. Isms sabotage objectivity and inhibit a school counselor's ability to work productively with all students. We outrank students in power and ability to influence. Of all the professionals in a school, we have to be able to affirm everyone with whom we work. As advocates for all students, it is essential that school counselors examine their isms and seek to eradicate them so as not to unconsciously or consciously oppress students who may already be marginalized.

Ethical school counselors examine their biases and seek to eliminate or at the very least soften them "through consultation, professional development opportunities, continuing education, exposure to others, introspection and deliberate self-examination. Mitigating isms is a critical component of the personal growth school counselors must seek as they position themselves to provide unconditional positive regard for all students" (S.B. Glicksteen, personal communication, Feb. 18, 2022).

Promoting a student's autonomy and independence is one of the moral principles of the school counseling profession (Kitchener, 1984). Imposing one's own values rooted in religion, culture, ethnicity, upbringing or personal worldview disregards the moral principle of autonomy. For example, if a school counselor is opposed to same-sex attractions, it is necessary to recognize and admit this as a personal bias and work to eradicate this bias so as to affirm and work responsibly with all students. Referring a student to another school counselor to avoid harming that student may be an appropriate ethical response in select cases, but because of our intensive work to eradicate or soften biases this should be the exception rather than the rule.

In a 2022 survey of 239 ASCA members by Stone, 84% of respondents strongly agreed or agreed with the statement: "Referring to another professional to avoid harming a student may be an appropriate ethical response in a few select cases, but this should be the exception rather than the rule" (Stone, 2022c).

School counselors must work to eradicate bias so students are not systematically referred to other school counselors to accommodate a litany of biases. School counselors cannot pick and choose their clients, so if school counselors believe abortion, same-sex attraction, premarital sex, etc. are wrong then they have to ask themselves if they are going to be leaving out large pockets of their charges. If your isms involve a person's identity, such as sexual identity, then a referral will likely feel like a rejection of who they are as a person, quite different from a rejection of a temporary situation such as a student's pregnancy. Certain school settings, grade levels or perhaps even the school counseling profession may not be the right choice for those who will be unable to work with different segments of the student population because their values will too often conflict with students' needs for support. For any professional career, people have to be honest and self-examine their suitability to that career, and this is never truer than the profession of school counseling as this work involves supporting vulnerable, minor clients.

In a 2022 survey of 239 ASCA members by Stone, 84.8% of respondents strongly agreed or agreed with the statement: "The school counseling profession is not an appropriate choice for someone who is unwilling to work with [LGBTQ+] students who request help with same-sex relationships" (Stone, 2022c).

South Shore Public School District had a high teen-pregnancy rate and moved to a comprehensive sex education program. Grossman, the school counselor, discarded school pamphlets teaching condom use. Grossman then ordered literature advocating abstinence. On two occasions, she prayed with distressed students. The superintendent allegedly informed Grossman that her prayer violated separation of church and state rules and that her promotion of abstinence was thwarting school officials' efforts to prevent additional pregnancies. The district chose not to renew her contract. Grossman filed a lawsuit against the district citing religious discrimination. In *Grossman v. South Shore Public School District* (2007), the 7th U.S. Circuit Court of Appeals barred Grossman from going forward with her Title VII religious discrimination claim against the district. The district did not renew Grossman's contract because of concerns that her promotion of prayer and abstinence was antagonistic to officials' efforts to prevent additional pregnancies and contends the firing was not because of Grossman's Christian values. Grossman failed to show that school district officials were reacting to her religious beliefs, rather than to her advocacy of prayer and abstinence, when they decided to cancel her contract.

OBLIGATIONS BEYOND THE STUDENT

The ASCA Ethical Standards for School Counselors (2022b) dictate that school counselors owe students loyalty and a trusting relationship. Students are a school counselor's primary clients; however, because school counselors are part of an educational community, their loyalty and obligation extend to parents/guardians, teachers, administrators, the school district and the community. The ASCA Ethical Standards (2022b) direct school counselors to "provide parents/guardians with accurate, comprehensive and relevant information in an objective and caring manner, as is appropriate and consistent with ethical and legal responsibilities to the students and parents/guardians" (B.1.j). The ASCA Ethical Standards include references to school counselors' responsibilities to other school professionals such as faculty, staff and administrators, specifying that school counselors "inform appropriate officials, in accordance with in accordance with federal and state law and school and district policy, of conditions that may be potentially disruptive or damaging to the school's mission, personnel and property while honoring the confidentiality between the student and school counselors to the extent feasible" (B.2.g).

School counselors respect students' confidences and balance minors' rights with parents'/ guardians' rights. Knowing when to invoke confidentiality at the exclusion of a parent's/ guardian's right to know is a daily struggle. Conflicts arise regarding information shared in counseling sessions because, historically, parents or legal guardians control the legal rights of their children, while the ethical standards extend confidentiality to all clients (ASCA, 2022b; Trice-Black et al., 2013).

Our courts are continually vesting parents/guardians with legal rights to guide their children (*Bellotti v. Baird* (1979); *H.L. v. Matheson* (1981); *Miller v. Mitchell* (2010). In *H.L. v. Matheson*, the U.S. Supreme Court said, "Constitutional interpretation has consistently recognized that the parents' and/or guardians' claim to authority in their own household to direct the rearing of their children is basic in the structure of our society." The Supreme Court emphasized that parents and guardians are the guiding voices in their children's lives, in part because of the peculiar vulnerability of minors to make life-altering decisions and a minor's inability to make informed, competent decisions, particularly under emotional stress.

In *Quilloin v. Walcott* (1978), the court expanded on this theme, "We have recognized on numerous occasions that the relationship between parent and child is constitutionally protected. The U.S. Supreme Court granted a stepfather the right to adopt a child born out of wedlock as the biological father had never made any attempts to be in the child's life. The courts allowed it was in the best interest of the child to remain with the family the child knew (*Quilloin v. Walcott*, 434 U.S. 246 (1978)).

In *Wisconsin v. Yoder*, the U.S. Supreme Court found that mandating Amish children to remain in school past the eighth grade was against parents' fundamental right to freedom of religion. The Amish church found that higher education is not necessary for their simple way of life and may hinder their salvation (*Wisconsin v. Yoder*, 406 U.S. 205, 231-233 [**1172] (1972)).

In *Meyer v. Nebraska* (1923), at issue was a Nebraska law restricting foreign-language education. During the case, the court said, "It is cardinal with us that the custody, care and nurture of the child reside first in the parents/guardians, whose primary function and freedom include preparation for obligations the state can neither supply nor hinder." We have recognized that parents/guardians have an important guiding role to play in their children's upbringing, which presumptively includes counseling them on important decisions (Bellotti II, supra, at 633-639).

In addition to parents'/guardians' extensive legal privileges, school counselors owe them an ethical obligation. Occasionally, parents/guardians express the obligation or right to know the contents of the school counselor's session with their child. In a survey by Stone (2017b), 34.9% of school counselor respondents reported that in the last three years students' family members regularly asked questions that would require a breach of confidentiality. This percentage is indicative of school counselors primarily being able to respect the confidentiality of the counseling relationship. Corey, Corey, Corey and Callanan (2018) noted the school counselor's ethical obligation: "If parents or guardians of minors request information about the progress of the counseling, the counselor is expected to provide some feedback" (p. 190).

School counselors seek to build collaborative relationships with parents/guardians. In doing so, they help parents/guardians better understand the school counseling program's role and the ethical issues involved (privacy, confidentiality and privileged communication), which are crucial in creating effective counseling relationships with students. Building collaborative relationships may require implementing activities to educate parents/guardians, such as brief discussions or programs at parent meetings. Creating these relationships may help increase their sense of trust that the school counselors will notify them when they need to be informed (Oehrtman, 2018).

Welfel (2016) indicated that positions validating minors' rights have increased since a 1967 Supreme Court ruling concluded that equal protection under the law granted by the 14th Amendment and the Bill of Rights, as a whole, was not solely for adults. State laws typically do not address questions related to school counselors' confidentiality with parents/guardians, requiring school counselors to use their professional judgment regarding when, how much and what information to share with them. Generally speaking, if parents/guardians insist on specifics and the school counselor is not able to dissuade them through generalities, in most states they have a right to this information. State statutes are unique, and it is always best practice to determine if students have protection in law for their confidences.

Parents'/guardians' desires, expectations and wishes regarding their children's welfare can be varied and diffused, complicating our work. The U.S. courts and laws give legal latitude to parents/guardians regarding their children's care and upbringing. The legal and ethical ramifications of this concept take on greater importance in those situations in which school counselors have to weigh minors' privacy rights with parents'/guardians' Supreme-Court-given right to be the preeminent voice in their children's lives (Stone & Zirkel, 2010).

MINORS' DEVELOPMENTAL AND CHRONOLOGICAL LEVELS

Minors' competency and developmental levels cannot be attached neatly to a chronological age. Not all seventh-graders, for example, will behave the same way in the same situation. These middle school students may present themselves developmentally as a mature 13-year-old one day only to surprise us the next day with behavior typical of a 9-year-old. A developmental approach, while more complex than a chronological approach, is based on characteristics and abilities of the students involved and the nature of their discussion with their school counselors. Based on developmental theories (e.g., Piaget), most school counselors would assume there is a stage at which the developing young person could better understand complex concepts (Koocher, 2008). Research indicates school counselors implicitly endorse such a developmentally based approach when faced with the dilemma of whether or not to breach confidentiality (Stone & Glicksteen, 2022).

To highlight these differences, consider the juvenile justice system. In February 2012, a 17-year-old high school student fatally shot three students and wounded two others at his school. This student, on the day of a shooting, wore a T-shirt with the word "killer" and admitted to the shooting. A psychiatric evaluation determined this student was competent enough to understand the case against him, and, therefore, he would be charged as an adult (Associated Press, 2012a). Three years younger and in the same developmental level according to his chronological age, a 14-year-old ninth-grader intentionally and fatally shot a classmate in February 2010. A psychiatric analysis found the student had the emotional makeup of an 8-year-old (Lawson, 2012). Although both the 17- and 14-year-old students should chronologically be in Piaget's formal operational stage, the difference between them is their cognitive functioning, and the 14-year-old may be categorized in Piaget's concrete operational stage for 7–11 years (Newman & Newman, 2012). School counselors' sensitivity to the unique and holistic picture of each student is an important consideration when dealing with developmental and chronological complications of working with minors in schools.

PRIVACY RIGHTS OF MINORS

Overall, although minor clients have an ethical right to privacy and confidentiality in the counseling relationship, the privacy rights of minors legally belong to their parents/guardians (Remley & Herlihy, 2019). The issue of students' privacy rights is a frequent topic of professional discussion because there are no easy answers to the questions typically raised by school counselors, who are concerned about students' ethical rights and parents'/guardians' legal rights. These conflicting legal and ethical obligations can create dilemmas for school counselors. Although, ethically, minor clients have a right to confidentiality, federal law does not protect school counselors who seek to keep information from the students' parents/guardians. In most states, school counselors who protect student confidentiality must negotiate with parents/guardians on ethical grounds as opposed to standing on legal grounds. Our guidance for this is found in federal statutes, primarily the Family Educational Rights and Privacy Act (FERPA, 1974) and the Protection of Pupil Rights Amendment, 1978 (PPRA). Some states extend even more privacy protection than the federal laws do, so school counselors must make themselves aware of their state statutes. States can extend more protections, but they cannot take away protection given to students and parents under federal law.

Further, the parents/guardians of minors have a legal right, except for limited exceptions, to control the professional services provided to their children and to be involved in planning those services. In general, if parents/guardians refuse the school counselor's individual counseling support for their child, we comply unless we can convince the parents otherwise or if our administration has reason to ask us to go forward.

A parent request to cease services sometimes comes after the parent has been reported for child abuse or is otherwise angry with the school counselor. Parents/guardians do not have the right to keep educators from checking on the welfare of their child, and we are especially vigilant in child abuse cases where parents/guardians want us out of the picture. However, our care usually comes in the form of teacher collaboration and other strategies adhering to parental requests.

In a survey with 427 ASCA members by Stone, 39.3% of respondents answered yes to the question: "Have you made a child abuse report in the last 36 months and then been contacted by the alleged perpetrator to discuss the report?"

In this same survey, 32.7% of respondents answered yes to the question: "In the past three years, have you experienced this situation: A parent/guardian about whom you reported child abuse found out you were the reporter and demands you not counsel their child?" The majority of respondents confirmed they would discontinue counseling the child but alerted teachers and others who came into regular contact with the student to keep a close eye out for signs of abuse. Surprisingly, 34.5% of the respondents would continue counseling (Stone, 2022a).

The parent, not the student, makes critical decisions about disclosure of personal information. Parents/guardians have the final word on who has access to certain details of their child's medical conditions, such as HIV-positive status. Unless an entity is exempt from FERPA, such as a private school not receiving federal funds, the parent, not the student, gives permission to release education records.

LEGAL STATUS OF MINORS

The legal status of minors is difficult to define. For example, the age at which a student can drive, marry and be held to legal contracts differs among states. Typically, 18 is considered the legal age of majority, unless otherwise designated. Minors, therefore, can legally be defined as those persons under the age of 18. The 26th Amendment (1971) to the U.S. Constitution established the right of 18-year-old citizens to vote and by extension has influenced the generally accepted age at which minors are extended other adult rights. For example, 18 is cited in FERPA as the age at which students as well as their parents can have the rights to records (1974).

All minors (unless emancipated) share the legal characteristic that they are unable to make decisions on their own behalf. Minors are "a group of individuals with few responsibilities, many restrictions and a complex legal status that maintains a dependency on adults for privilege and access to resources" (Sanger & Willemsen, 1992). The legal concept of the age of majority has implications for minor clients' rights to make choices about entering into counseling as well as their rights to privacy and confidentiality. The Supreme Court has upheld parents'/guardians' legal right to make critical decisions about their children (*Bellotti v. Baird* (1979)). Because counseling is considered to be a contractual relationship, minors are not afforded the opportunity to legally agree to counseling on their own (Remley & Herlihy, 2019). There are some exceptions in most states' statutes allowing minors younger than 18 to receive counseling or medical services without parental consent.

Additionally, most states have laws allowing minors to be declared "legally emancipated" from their parents/guardians, and a few states allow for minors to be deemed a mature minor and capable of understanding the ramifications of counseling (Alexander & Alexander, 2019). However, in a secondary school setting when a student turns 18, this student is not yet completely emancipated if he or she is still a dependent as defined under the federal income tax code. For example, even though adult students are now considered eligible to access their own education records under FERPA, the parents/guardians also still have access to their children's education records.

The lack of congruence among laws regarding minors adds to the difficulties of working with minors, because we are unable to rely on clearly stated principles of legal policy to guide us. Scott (2001) states, "The legal regulation of children is extremely complex. Much of the complexity can be traced ultimately to a single source – defining the boundary between childhood and adulthood. Thus, the question, "What is a child?" is readily answered by policy makers, but the answer to the question, "When does childhood end?" is different in different policy contexts. This variation makes it difficult to discern a coherent image of legal childhood. Youths who are in elementary school may be deemed adults for purposes of assigning criminal responsibility and punishment, while seniors in high school cannot vote, and most college students are legally prohibited from drinking" (pp. 562-563).

IN LOCO PARENTIS

Another complication of working with minors in a school setting is the interpretation of the common-law doctrine "*in loco parentis*," which at times allows school personnel to act in place of the parent. Common-law thinking on this issue has prevailed for many years. The Wisconsin Supreme Court recognized that educators must be able to address the diversity of expectations placed upon them and have sufficient control over the decorum and climate of the school to ensure learning can take place (*Burpee v. Burton* (1878)).

"Inherent in this thinking is the necessity that educators, by virtue of their positions, have the authority to govern school in a reasonable and humane manner. General education and control of pupils who attend public schools are in the hands of school boards, superintendents, principals, teachers and [school counselors]. This control extends to health, proper surroundings, necessary discipline, promotion of morality and other wholesome influences, while parental authority is temporarily superseded" (*Richardson v. Braham* (1933)). Educators have an ethical obligation to promote harmony in the school while simultaneously advancing and protecting students' interests.

Though "*in loco parentis*" translated to English means "in place of the parent," the courts never intended that school authorities, teachers or school counselors would fully stand in place of the parent in relationship to their children (Alexander & Alexander, 2019). The courts have recognized that although children's legal status is not identical to that of adults, they nonetheless are entitled to constitutional protection. Students also have an obligation to follow the laws and school rules, assume responsibilities and follow the commands of school authorities (Blokhuis et al., 2020)). Current thinking suggests it may be more appropriate to view the school as an extension of the state rather than as a substitute parent (Blokhuis et al., 2020).

Constitutional law that bears on the interests of students and protects their First and Fourth Amendment rights also reiterates the importance of *in loco parentis* in protecting children and charges school personnel with the responsibility to protect the rights of the child when the child is in their care, control and protection in the school environment. The Supreme Court, in *Bethel School District No. 403 v. Fraser* (1986), also reminded us of our obligation to protect children "from exposure to sexually explicit, indecent or lewd speech." The school counselor owes a special duty to exercise reasonable care to protect a student from harm and intervene if necessary. *In loco parentis* is also explored in Chapter 5 Negligence and Chapter 6 Obligations to School Board Policies and Federal, State and Case Law.

COMMUNITY AND INSTITUTIONAL STANDARDS

As difficult as it may be to accept, ethics are situational. Your ethical behavior is determined in large part by your school's location. This context-dependent nature of school counseling makes advocacy sometimes difficult. The prevailing community and institutional standards dictate to a large degree what school counselors can do to remain ethical. In some communities, the school counselor has the freedom to direct a student to a health clinic for contraceptives. In September 2012, the New York City Department of Education (NYC DOE) made the morning-after pill available to high school girls at 13 public schools in the Connecting Adolescents to Comprehensive Healthcare (CATCH) program. As of March 2022, the CATCH program was serving 90 high schools providing reproductive health education, information on sexually transmitted infection prevention, pregnancy testing (urine testing, no physical exam required), hormonal contraception (birth control), emergency contraception and condoms (NYC DOE, 2022). Students, not their parents, sign a consent form, but parents/guardians can opt their daughters out of the program. This is an example of community standards at work. In many schools across the country, school counselors would not even suggest to a student to obtain contraceptives as this may dramatically cross the line of the community's standards. This does not mean, however, that we sit idly by and accept the status quo; rather, we work responsibly to change community standards when they stratify students' opportunities.

Court cases have demonstrated that community standards can be an issue contributing to the outcome of a case. In *Grossman v. South Shore School District* (2007), the school counselor, alleging religious discrimination, worked in a district saturated with more than 800 churches, within 40 miles (Andrews and Beard Education Law Report, 2008). In finding in favor of the school district's right to fire her, the court said it was not her religious beliefs that were the problem, since the Christian school administrators who didn't renew her contract shared her beliefs. Rather, the court cited, it was her approach to the problem that was cause for concern (*Grossman v. South Shore School District* (2007)).

School counselors can learn about the internal and external community standards by questioning, listening and observing. Are you in an ultra-conservative part of the world, a bastion of liberalism, a middle-class suburb or an urban setting? Ask other educators, especially your fellow school counselors, about hypothetical and real cases and what the prevailing standard would be for handling sensitive, value-laden cases. School counselors have to understand what threads comprise the community's fabric to discern how to behave ethically in a particular environment.

It is the school counselor's responsibility to keep in mind how history factors into the lives of their students. In the case of disenfranchised minority students, the prior-established systems may perpetuate the inequality and inability to develop oneself due to their basis in fixed school goals reflecting the values of the community in which they are born into (Roche et al., 2020). By making those who they serve aware of the particular forces of oppression that they face in their environment, school counselors can play a significant role in breaking the cycle to foster growth and achievement.

It is important to have a feel for the local level of tolerance for school involvement in value-laden issues. Understand the prevailing written and unwritten standards of the community, school district and individual work site, and behave consistently within the parameters of those standards while working responsibly to change the ones detrimental to students. School counselors behave as change agents when community and institutional standards of behavior limit students' opportunities, at which point our ethical standards and codes give us a directive to act responsibly to try and change policies and practices impeding student success (ASCA, 2022b).

ACADEMIC INSTRUCTION

The setting in which school counselors work defines the student/school counselor relationship. Parents/guardians send their children to school for academic instruction, not individual counseling. When the school counselor enters the equation in personal counseling, there is the possibility of tension between parents'/guardians' rights to be the guiding force in their children's lives and children's rights to privacy. The definition of a counseling session is more complex because we are not in a formal counseling setting as are our colleagues in private or agency practice. School counselors interact with students virtually everywhere from the bus loading zone to the privacy of their offices.

TRUSTING RELATIONSHIP

Trust is an essential component in the development of helping relationships. School counselors regard the promise of confidentiality to be essential for the development of student trust. Most individuals seeking counseling services, by the nature of the relationship, assume what they divulge in counseling will be kept in confidence by their counselor, with limited exceptions (Kampf, McSherry, Ogloff & Rothschild, 2010). This is most likely true for children and adolescents as well as adults. Managing confidentiality when counseling minors, however, is more complex than when counseling adults, because school counselors must balance their ethical and legal responsibilities to students, parents/guardians and the school system (ASCA, 2022b). This complex balancing act is one reason the topic of maintaining the confidences and trust of students is raised in virtually every discussion of ethical and legal issues in school counseling.

The school counselor must provide a safe and secure environment in which trust can be established and maintained. Without the assurance of confidentiality, many students would not seek help or would censor what they tell the school counselor. Therefore, confidentiality is the foundation for meaningful and honest dialogue (Iyer & Baxter-MacGregor, 2010). School counselors must keep confidential information related to counseling services unless disclosure is in the student's best interest or is required by law (ASCA, 2018b; Remley & Herlihy, 2019).

INFORMED CONSENT

Informed consent is both a legal and ethical principle requiring school counselors to inform students about the purposes, goals, techniques and rules of procedure under which students may receive counseling (ASCA, 2022b). The ASCA Ethical Standards for School Counselors (2022b) tell us that at the beginning of the counseling session, the school counselor must tell students in terms the students can understand about the limits of their confidentiality so students can decide if they want to participate in the counseling session.

"Inform students of the purposes, goals, techniques, rules and procedures under which they may receive counseling. Disclosure includes informed consent and clarification of the limits of confidentiality" (ASCA, A.2.b., 2022b). "Recognize that informed consent requires competence, voluntariness and knowledge on students' part to understand the limits of confidentiality and, therefore, can be difficult to obtain from students of certain developmental levels and special-needs populations. The school counselor should make attempts to gain assent appropriate to the individual student (e.g., in the student's preferred language) prior to disclosure" (ASCA, A.2.c, 2022b).

School counselors work diligently to respect students' confidences except when there is serious and foreseeable harm for the student or others (ASCA, 2022b). One way to effectively approach the ethics of informed consent is to view it as an ongoing process rather than trying to cover every possible consideration in the first meeting. In addition, tailoring informed consent practices to a student's developmental level is critical. It is good practice to discuss examples in which the school counselor may need to disclose confidential information to the student's parents/guardians or to school personnel.

When feasible, obtaining parental permission for individual counseling that will extend beyond one or two sessions is considered best practice in the school counseling profession. Some school districts have policies or procedures requiring school counselors to obtain parents'/guardians' permission before counseling students. Just as the mathematics teacher can do his or her job, the school counselor can work with students individually in absence of a state or federal law or school board policy forbidding this. It is best practice, however, to seek not only the assent of students but also of their parents/ guardians (ASCA, 2022b).

OPACITY OF LAWS AND ETHICAL CODES

The multifaceted nature of working with minors in schools makes it difficult to develop law, ethical standards, written school board policies or procedures covering all the potential situations school counselors might face. Laws addressing malpractice, negligence and student privacy rights are complex and are often defined on a case-by-case basis (Alexander & Alexander, 2019; Rammell, 2019). Federal courts in each state can interpret the same law in different ways, and the interpretation will remain unresolved until a higher court can hear the matter, if ever. Although there is some legal guidance to be found in education law, state department regulations and local school board policy, school counselors often must practice in the absence of clear-cut guidelines. Thus, a tolerance for ambiguity is a good skill to develop, and the ability to research legal rulings is an even better skill to develop.

NUMBER OF STUDENT-CLIENTS

As leaders, advocates and change agents, we are charged with reaching every student, but the multiplicity of our role and the obligations we have to so many stakeholders considerably reduce the amount of supervision we can give to each student, the extent to which we can document what we have done and the effort we can undertake to see to each and every child's individual needs.

Although ASCA (n.d.) recommends a 250-to-1 ratio of students-to-school-counselors, the national average was actually 424-to-1 for the 2019–2020 school year. The demands placed on school counselors, including career and academic advising, paperwork and individual counseling, increases the importance of having lower student-to-school-counselor ratios to deliver services via the most effective, efficient and equitable means possible (ASCA, 2021f).

You can find your state mandates regarding the nature and function of school counseling, ratios, whether or not school counseling is legally required, and other information on ASCA's website, *www.schoolcounselor.org*.

Caseloads do not spell the difference between a school counselor who behaves professionally, ethically and legally and one who does not. However, caseloads influence the thoroughness school counselors can devote to a comprehensive school counseling program (ASCA, 2021a).

STANDARD OF CARE

Standard of care is defined as what the reasonably competent professional would do under similar circumstances (ASCA, 2021b). Remley and Herlihy (2019) argued that the best way for school counselors to defend their ethical decision making is to act as a reasonable school counselor would in a similar situation. Although helpful, the idea of "reasonable school counselor" potentially is subject to many interpretations, especially when it comes to breaching confidentiality with students and negligence. Negligence cases are founded on the assumption that the standard of care was not met. If you find yourself in legal hot water, your attorney will want to demonstrate you behaved as any other person in your profession would have behaved given the same or very similar circumstances.

The following criteria are just a few types of information your legal counsel will gather to show you behaved within the standard of care for your profession:

- Laws
- Ethical standards
- School board policy
- Case law
- Expert witnesses
- Length of career
- Professional development such as in-service training, professional conference attendance, books and publications read
- Membership and level of engagement in your local, state, and national professional organizations

Standard of care is explained more fully in Chapter 6 Obligations to the Courts.

Ethical Standards

All professional counselors are required to abide by the ethical standards of their particular professional organization. In the case of school counselors, this adherence is to the ASCA Ethical Standards for School Counselors (2022b). Ethical standards are established as a guideline to use and refer to in situations that create dilemmas or situations in which choices have good but contradictory reasons to take conflicting and incompatible courses of action (Kitchener and Anderson, 2011). The ASCA Ethical Standards for School Counselors (2022b) are an attempt by the profession to provide the profession's aspirations for the protection and best practice for students, parents/guardians, educators and school counselors. The Ethical Standards are a guide to help us meet the needs of individual situations but seldom are appropriate for rote application, as it is the context of a dilemma that determines appropriate action. Only the school counselor, in consultation with other professionals, can determine how to apply an ASCA Ethical Standard to further a student's best interest. Standards are guides or frameworks requiring professional judgment in context to make each standard meaningful. They are not intended to provide answers but are meant to guide.

ASCA's approach to ethical standards was considered a model by a task force of 11 prominent educational organizations that came together in 2015 to craft an ethical code for teachers. Troy Hutchings, subject-matter expert for the task force, explained, "Few teachers have been prepared at the pre-service or in-service levels in professional ethics, and the profession as a whole has not adopted a unified code of ethics to guide practitioner decision-making. The task force reviewed dozens of professional codes, and ASCA's Ethical Standards for School Counselors was clearly the gold standard. It connects the aspirations of professional ethics with the grounded, day-to-day realities of the profession in a thoughtful, practical manner. ASCA illuminated our journey. I cannot overstate how influential ASCA's ethics work was to the task force" (personal communication, Hutchings, Feb. 28, 2017).

2022 ASCA ETHICAL STANDARDS FOR SCHOOL COUNSELORS

At a glance, here are the basic concepts found in the ASCA Ethical Standards for School Counselors (2022b):

A . Responsibilities to Students

A.1. Supporting Student Development

This section discusses the school counselor's responsibilities to students. School counselors should not diagnose, but students should be provided with the appropriate support necessary to allow them to excel, which includes academic, career and social/emotional. It also emphasizes respect for families, including their belief systems, sexual orientation and values. This section discusses the awareness of laws affecting students and the maintenance of boundaries, including those of a sexual nature. Additionally, this section emphasizes advocacy for equitable, anti-bias policies.

A.2. Confidentiality

This section discusses the ethical standards and legal mandates regarding confidentiality. This includes informing students about the limits of confidentiality and recognizing the difficulty in achieving informed consent. The school counselor recognizes the competing interest between ethical confidentiality and the rights of parents/guardians to guide their children. School counselors protect the confidentiality of students' records in accordance with state and federal laws and adhere to these laws in conveying and transmitting highly sensitive information.

A.3. Comprehensive Data-Informed Programs

This section discusses collaborating with stakeholders around school-improvement goals, providing students with a comprehensive school counseling program that ensures equity and using data to determine interventions and assess the school counseling program's progress and effectiveness.

A.4. Academic, Career and Social/Emotional Planning
This section discusses collaborating with stakeholders to create a culture of postsecondary readiness. This includes advocating for students' rights to choose from existing options at the completion of secondary education, as well as providing students with the opportunity to develop the ASCA Student Standards: Mindsets & Behaviors for Student Success necessary to possess a strong work ethics and have a positive attitude toward learning.

A.5. Sustaining Healthy Relationships and Managing Boundaries
This section reminds school counselors to avoid dual relationships that might impair objectivity and increase the risk of harm to students. When this is not possible, they must implement some safeguards. They must maintain a professional relationship with students at all times. Where this boundary is extended, school counselors should document the nature of the interaction and include the rationale behind the interaction.

A.6. Appropriate Collaboration, Advocacy and Referrals for Counseling
This section addresses appropriate referrals for students to outside professionals and agencies. It highlights the process of how this should be done and emphasizes that school counselors should not impose their values on students when making referrals. Finally, the school counselor should provide the service provider with the necessary data needed to assist students and ensure there is no conflict of interest in the referral.

A.7. Group Work
This section discusses the standards behind group work. It emphasizes that school counselors should facilitate groups and inform parents about their child's potential group membership. School counselors measure the outcome of the group participation and provide necessary follow-up with group members.

A.8. Student Peer-Support Program
This section highlights school counselors' responsibility to supervise and safeguard students' welfare in peer-to-peer programs under the school counselor's direction. Also, they are responsible for appropriate skill development for students serving as peer support, emphasizing confidentiality.

A.9. Serious and Foreseeable Harm to Self and Others
This section emphasizes that school counselors should inform parents/guardians and appropriate authorities when a student poses serious risk to self and others. Before risk assessments are used, an intervention plan should be developed and in place. Also, students who are a danger to self and others should not be released until the student has proper support. Finally, school counselors should report to appropriate authorities and/or parents/guardians when students perpetrate or perceive a threat to their physical and mental well-being.

A.10. Marginalized Populations
This section highlights the role of school counselors in contributing to a school environment where all members of the school community demonstrate respect and civility, understanding that gender identity and gender expression should be respected. School counselors should identify resources needed to optimize education and collaborate with parents/guardians to ensure students' needs are met. This section underscores the need for school counselors to advocate for access to and inclusion in opportunities.

A.11. Bullying, Harassment, Discrimination, Bias and Hate Incidents
In this section, school counselors are to recognize the roots of bullying, discrimination, bias, hate and other forms of harassment. School counselors are to report suspected cases of child abuse and neglect to proper authorities and take precautions to protect students' privacy. Finally, school counselors are to be knowledgeable of state laws and school system procedure regarding reporting child abuse and neglect, as well as provide students who have experienced abuse or neglect with appropriate services.

A.12. Child Abuse
In this section, school counselors are to recognize the laws for mandated reporters and develop and maintain expertise in recognizing signs of abuse.

A.13. Student Records
This section discusses the handling and purging of both educational records and sole-possession records. It stipulates that school counselors should abide by FERPA, which covers who has access to educational records, and should inform administration of any inappropriate or harmful practices regarding educational records. Also, they must recognize that sole-possession records could be subpoenaed. Finally, they should establish a reasonable timeline for purging sole-possession records and case notes.

A.14. Evaluation, Assessment and Interpretation
This section emphasizes the use of only valid and reliable tests and assessments, with concerns for bias and cultural sensitivity, which also consider students' developmental levels. Also, school counselors should be mindful of confidentiality when using assessment instruments and provide interpretation of the results of the assessment to parents/guardians and students in a language they can understand. Finally, school counselors should conduct evaluations of school counseling programs.

A.15. Technical and Digital Citizenship
This section discusses the appropriate software application, with emphasis on confidentiality. School counselors should use only established and approved means of communication with students and should advocate for equity in access to technology for all students.

A.16. Virtual/Distance School Counseling
This section stipulates that school counselors should adhere to the same guidelines as in a face-to-face setting when implementing virtual/distance counseling. They must implement procedures for students to utilize when school counselors are not available and also sensitize students and parents/guardians to the benefits and limitations or virtual/distance counseling.

B . Responsibilities to Parents/Guardians, School and Self
B.1. Responsibilities to Parents/Guardians
This section covers the fact that school counselors must collaborate with students' parents/guardians as appropriate to facilitate students' maximum development. This must be done within the laws, local guidelines and ethical practice. In cases of divorce or separation, school counselors should follow the directions and stipulations of the legal documents.

B.2. Responsibilities to the School

This section discusses the school counselor's role to provide adequate support to staff, faculty and administration in schools. School counselors are to design and deliver a comprehensive school counseling program as well as develop and maintain a professional relationship and system of communication with faculty, staff and administration. Finally they must provide workshops and written/digital information to families to increase understanding and communication. Overall, they must work toward maintaining professionalism in the workplace.

B.3. Responsibilities to Self

This section emphasizes that school counselors must have a master's degree in school counseling as well as engage in ongoing professional development activities. They must maintain membership in a school counseling professional organization and adhere to the profession's ethical standards.

C. School Counselor Directors/Administrators/Supervisors

Directors, administrators and supervisors support school counselors by advocating for resources to implement a comprehensive school counseling program. They also provide for professional development in current research to school counselors. Finally, they monitor schools and organizational policies to ensure practices are consistent with ASCA recommendations.

D. School Counseling Practicum/Internship Site Supervisors

Field/intern site supervisors are licensed and certified school counselors who are also trained and educated to provide clinical supervision. Supervisors ensure supervisees are aware of policies and procedures related to supervision and evaluation, as well as ensure performance evaluations are conducted in a timely, fair and considerate manner. Supervisors communicate supervisees' limitations to the university/college supervisor and also contact the university/college supervisor to recommend dismissal when supervisees are unable to demonstrate competence.

E. Maintenance of Standards

This section serves as a guide for when serious doubts exist as to a colleague's ethical behavior. This outlines that the school counselor should consult with the colleague to seek resolution directly. If the matter remains unresolved, appropriate referrals may be made.

F. Ethical Decision-Making

This section stipulates that when faced with an ethical dilemma, school counselors and school counseling program directors/supervisors use an ethical decision-making model.

The standards demonstrate the scope and depth of the role of school counselors to school personnel, parents/guardians and students. School counselors can find a great deal of information about professional behavior by carefully reading the standards. Furthermore, professionals in schools can use the standards to improve effectiveness and help avoid ethical problems and legal entanglements.

The ASCA Ethical Standards guide school counselors in their ethical responsibility to students and parents/guardians but do not attempt to provide complete answers. Ethics are situational and must be considered in context of institutional and community standards, school board policy and individual circumstances. Ultimately, the school counselor has the responsibility to determine the appropriate response for students who put their trust in the security of the counseling relationship.

Even more so than laws, ethical standards are open to interpretation. Different professionals may implement varying courses of action in the same situation. Seldom is there is one right answer to a complex ethical dilemma. However, if you follow a systematic model, you can be assured you will be able to provide a professional explanation for the course of action you chose (Brown, et al., 2017). There are numerous approaches to making ethical decisions, and the professional is expected to use a credible model that includes consultation, documentation and weighing the risks and benefits to the student after identifying potential courses of action. ASCA has developed an ethical decision-making model, which is included in the ASCA Ethical Standards for School Counselors (2022b).

FIVE MORAL PRINCIPLES

School counselors also look to moral principles to make a sound ethical decision. Moral principles can be defined as beliefs or assumptions that are shared or agreed upon by professionals and guide their ethical reasoning (Ametrano, 2014; Remley & Herlihy, 2019). This is the foundation upon which the ethical standards are based. Kitchener's (1984) five moral principles borrowed and adapted from the health-care profession can serve as a guide to ethical decision making:

- Autonomy refers to promoting students' ability to choose their own direction. The school counselor makes every effort to foster maximum self-determination on the part of students.
- Beneficence refers to promoting good for others. Ideally, counseling contributes to the growth and development of the student, and whatever school counselors do should be judged against this criterion.
- Nonmaleficence means avoiding doing harm, which includes refraining from actions that risk hurting students.
- Justice, or fairness, refers to providing equal treatment to all people. This standard implies that anyone, regardless of age, sex, race, ethnicity, disability, socioeconomic status, cultural background, religion or sexual orientation, is entitled to equal treatment.
- Loyalty, or fidelity, refers to staying connected with your students and being available to them to the extent possible. School counselors often carry heavy caseloads, and loyalty takes on a different dimension in the school setting than at an agency. Loyalty for the school counselor does not necessarily mean 50-minute sessions once a week with students. Staying loyal may include connecting with students by encouraging them to stop by before and after school, visiting them at the bus-loading zone or briefly visiting their classrooms.

School counselors are confronted daily with ethical dilemmas requiring them to skillfully, and usually quickly, decide on an appropriate course of action. According to research and survey responses gathered by Sensoy and Ikiz (2019), school counselors were found to have the most issues ethically when confronting matters of confidentiality, the boundaries of their professional role and interactions between staff and parents.

Because of the complicated and multifaceted work associated with minors, an ethical decision-making model for school counselors must give special consideration to allow for the fact that our work setting is not intended primarily for individual therapy but for academic instruction.

The ASCA Ethics Committee during the 2022 revision blended the STEPS Ethical Decision-Making Model (Stone, 2005) model and the Intercultural Model of Ethical Decision Making (Luke et al., 2013) to address the ever-changing and unique circumstances for school counselors in the school setting. STEPS, an acronym for Solutions To Ethical Problems in Schools (2005), adapts the seven steps in the American Counseling Association model. The Intercultural Model of Ethical Decision Making by Luke et al. extends the conceptual and contextual applications. The results of this blending is the ASCA Ethical Decision-Making Model (2022), which addresses the emotional influences of a problem and considers chronological and developmental appropriateness as well as parental rights.

An ethical model helps school counselors negotiate the nuances of ethical dilemmas arising within an environment significantly different from those found in agency, community, private or hospital counseling settings. Counseling is another matter altogether when you primarily serve minors mandated by law to be in attendance in an environment designed for academic instruction and not for counseling.

Although the model is presented sequentially here, when tackling an ethical problem in the field it will be used in context and not always sequential.

1. Define the ethical dilemma.

- How do your emotions define this problem (your initial reaction)?
- What does your heart tell you should happen in this case? File this initial reaction away for later reference.
- How does your intellect define the problem unemotionally, objectively?
- What are the facts? Separate the hearsay, but remember rumors often inform.

It is important to acknowledge our first reaction to the problem. When a student in need comes through the door crying and in pain, our initial reaction generally is, "What can I do to help this student?" Our emotional reaction and supportive instincts are important because they help us protect our students' confidences. Because we care about our students, we don't want to discard the emotional reaction but use it to guide us along with a healthy combination of reason and judgment.

In defining the problem, school counselors are careful not to act on emotion without considering the other ethical decision-making steps. Make the necessary effort to gather the facts while weeding out innuendoes, rumors, hearsay and hypotheses. Remember, however, that in school settings we cannot rule out hearsay or rumors, as they are often a source for school counselors to discover the truth about situations involving their students.

2. Identify potential cultural, religious and worldview factors and power dynamics that are present within a potential ethical dilemma.

In this step, the school counselor identifies and predicts possible conflicts between their own and other district, family and community stakeholders' beliefs, religion, laws and culture to recognize the "intersection of multicultural concerns and ethical decision making" (Luke et al, 2013, p.189).

3. Apply the ASCA Ethical Standards for School Counselors and the relevant district policies and procedures.

Ask yourself whether your ethical standards or the law offer a possible solution to the problem. Ethical dilemmas are often complex, and we will not usually find a definitive answer in the standards or laws. The very nature of an ethical dilemma means there is more than one acceptable answer. Therefore, we must apply good judgment by proceeding with all steps of the ASCA Ethical Decision-Making Model and paying careful attention to steps six and eight, which emphasize seeking consultation supervision.

4. Consult with appropriate professionals (e.g., supervisors, other student service professionals, school counseling peers, cultural experts).

Discuss your case with an experienced fellow professional, preferably a supervisor, to help you illuminate the issues. As your colleague reviews the information with you, he or she may see other relevant issues, offer a new perspective or identify aspects of the dilemma you are not viewing objectively. Consult your state and/or national professional associations to see if they can help.

When caught in an ethical dilemma, it is sometimes difficult to see all the issues clearly. School counselors must often do their ethical problem solving on the run. It's not always feasible for school counselors to close their office doors, sit with paper and pencil and follow the decision-making model. Consultation is one step you should never skip.

In fact, consulting is such a critical part of ethical behavior that you should routinely and confidentially consult with a network of professionals when difficult situations arise. School counselors need to be constant consumers of legal and ethical information by seeking the counsel of colleagues, administrators, supervisors and school attorneys. When you routinely consult with other professionals, you will find the complexity of the legal and ethical world less daunting. More importantly, consultation can help school counselors provide increased safety and security for students.

5. Consider the student's chronological and developmental levels.

How does the student's developmental level affect the dilemma, and how will you approach it? This step is critical, yet it has been left out of decision-making models. A child's age, and the ability to show that he or she can make informed decisions, matters. Also, school counselors must remember that the younger and more immature the child, the greater our responsibility to the parents/guardians.

6. Consider parental/guardian and students' rights.

You must consider the rights of parents/guardians to be the guiding voice in their children's lives, especially in value-laden decisions. You must also honor parents'/guardians' rights to be informed and involved when their children are in harm's way.

Furthermore, you must consider the dilemma in the context of the school setting. Ethical dilemmas in a school take on a different meaning from ethical issues in other contexts. Students come to school for academic instruction, and when students enter into the social/emotional arena, school counselors should consider this will carry obligations to other educators and to parents/guardians.

7. Apply the moral principles.

Consider the basic moral principles of autonomy, beneficence, nonmaleficence, justice and loyalty (Kitchener, 1984), and apply them to the situation. Veracity was added to the moral principles. It may help to prioritize these principles and think through ways in which they can support a resolution. Decide which principles apply, and determine which principle takes priority for you in this case. In theory, each principle is of equal value, which means it is your challenge to determine the priorities when two or more of them conflict. Review the relevant professional literature to ensure you are using the most current professional thinking in reaching a decision.

8. Determine your potential courses of action and their consequences.

Brainstorm as many possible solutions as possible. Be creative. If possible, enlist the assistance of at least one colleague to help you generate options. Consider possible and probable courses of action. Write down the options, and discuss them with a colleague if you can. Examine the consequences of various decisions. Ponder the implications of each course of action for the student, for others who might be affected and for you. List the good and bad consequences of each decision.

Considering the information you have gathered and the priorities you have set, evaluate each option and assess the potential consequences for all the parties involved. Eliminate the options that clearly do not give desired results or cause even more problematic consequences. Then decide which combination of options best fits the situation and addresses the priorities you have identified.

Review the selected course of action to see if it presents any new ethical considerations. Stadler (1986) suggests applying three simple tests to ensure the decision is appropriate. In applying the test of justice, assess your own sense of fairness by determining if you would treat others in this situation the same way. For the test of publicity, ask yourself if you would want your behavior reported in the press, and if so, can you defend your behavior? The test of universality asks you to assess whether you could recommend the same course of action to another counselor in the same situation (Forest-Miller & Davis, 1996 as cited by ACA, 2012).

If the course of action you have selected seems to present new ethical issues, then you'll need to go back to the beginning and re-evaluate each step. Perhaps you have chosen the wrong option or identified the problem incorrectly (Forest-Miller & Davis, 1996 as cited by ACA, 2012).

If you can answer in the affirmative to each of the questions suggested by Stadler (1986), thus passing the tests of justice, publicity and universality, and you are satisfied you have selected an appropriate course of action, then you are ready to move on to implementation (Forest-Miller & Davis, 1996 as cited by ACA, 2012).

9. Implement the course of action, and analyze the outcome.

Go forward with your decision after you have considered the previous steps. Regardless of your decision there will be risk, but you will have made the best decision based on the advice and information you had at the time. School counselors cannot practice risk free, but we can reduce our risk and raise our support for students by using ethical reasoning.

You may find taking the final step in the ethical model disconcerting. In a real-life ethical dilemma, the final step never will be easy, but by strengthening your confidence through continuous professional development you will find it easier to carry out your plans. After implementing your course of action, it is good practice to follow up on the situation to assess whether your actions had the anticipated effect.

When following the ASCA Ethical Decision-Making Model, school counselors should keep up to date with ethical standards and state and federal laws, maintain a network of colleagues with whom to consult, educate parents/guardians and other stakeholders about school counselor's responsibilities when faced with issues such as student confidentiality, and establish procedures and alternatives for responding to delicate situations in advance. Such efforts will provide a foundation from which to respond and help to eliminate the stresses school counselors face as they walk the tightrope of legal and ethical dilemmas.

Ethics and laws are not clear-cut when dealing with issues of confidentiality. School counselors have the ethical obligation to respect the privacy of minor clients and maintain confidentiality. This obligation is often in conflict with laws related to minors because parents/guardians have the right to know and to decide what is in their children's best interest. School counselors must also take into consideration ethical standards, applicable statutes and policies of their local education agencies and their individual schools.

10. Identify any inconsistencies in school/district policy for potential revision.
See other ethical decision-making models:

- Intercultural Model of Ethical Decision Making, Luke et al., (2013)
- Solutions to Ethical Problems in Schools (STEPS), Stone (2005)
- Ethical Justification Model, Kitchener (1984)

Making Connections

1. Discuss your opinion of the premise that a thorough knowledge of the laws, ethical standards, school board policies and prevailing community standards better prepares school counselors to make tough decisions.

2. Why is the school counselor's job so much more difficult legally and ethically than that of fellow counselors in agency and private settings?

3. Discuss how you as a school counselor have the ethical imperative to promote the autonomy of your minor students.

4. Discuss each of the points the courts stress as reasons children should be guided by their parents/guardians:
   - The peculiar vulnerability of minors to make life-altering decisions
   - A minor's inability to make informed, competent decisions, particularly under emotional stress
   - The concept that parents/guardians are the guiding voice in their child's life

5. Why is it impossible to develop laws, ethical standards, written school board policies or procedures covering all the potential situations school counselors might face? How should we proceed, in light of the fact that we cannot always find guidance in laws, standards or policies for all the situations we face?

Chapter 1 Quiz

1) The purpose of the ASCA Ethical Standards is to:
   a. Provide a blueprint for ethical behavior for all educators
   b. Serve as a guide for the ethical practices of all school counselors, supervisors/directors of school counseling programs and school counselor educators
   c. Give a comprehensive list of legal requirements for school counselors
   d. Provide support and direction for parents to understand the ASCA National Model
   e. Serve as an exhaustive list of all ethical issues a school counselor might face

2) The ASCA Ethical Standards are:
   a. Not applicable to court proceedings but are used for administrative hearings when a school district is considering whether a school counselor's infraction warrants dismissal
   b. Considered irrelevant by state professional practice boards when a school counselor's certificate is in question of being revoked
   c. Used in court only if the school counselor defendant has not broken a law but has breached his or her ethical standards
   d. Used as applicable to establish standard of care for a school counselor in court, administrative and/or professional practice hearings
   e. Suggestions and therefore have no weight and cannot be used to establish the fate of any school counselor in any state, school district or court proceedings

3) You have established a positive relationship with an at-risk student who has not had a consistent adult in his life. He is troubled, and many credit you with the fact that he has not dropped out of school. He is a talented wrestler, and you plan to support him by attending his wrestling match, which is a three-hour drive away. You plan to go on Saturday, drive alone, sit in the stands and cheer this student and then return home alone. You will not take this student out for a victory lunch, dinner, etc. You simply intend to watch the match and return home. The ASCA Ethical Standards encourage you to approach this by:
   a. Letting this student know that a stronger self-esteem is possible if he wins the match and that you will be there to cheer him to victory
   b. Carefully considering the risks/benefits, precautions needed such as informed consent, consultation and supervision and documentation of the rationale and possible good and bad consequences
   c. Going forward with your plan and attending the wrestling event
   d. Abandoning this plan and any idea of this trip
   e. Helping the student add academic success to his athletic prowess

4) The ASCA Ethical Standards describe confidentiality as:
   a. Aspirational but legally nonbinding in all 50 states
   b. Impossible to respect in elementary schools because of the developmental levels
   c. Tied to informed consent, and therefore confidentiality cannot be breached
   d. A creature of statute and not ethical code
   e. Complicated, considered in the context of the circumstances and necessary to breach to prevent serious and foreseeable harm

5) The ASCA Ethical Standards:
   a. Recognize the difficulty of implementing data-informed school counseling programs and stress it is optional
   b. Expect school counselors to strive to collaborate with administration, teachers, staff and decision-makers around school improvement goals
   c. Recognize the political vulnerability of school counselors who use data to illuminate disparities that may exist related to gender, race, ethnicity and socioeconomic status
   d. Consider data-informed practice as moving too far away from process and perception data
   e. Admonish school counselors to avoid sharing data that does not place the school in a positive light with stakeholders

Key Terms

Autonomy
Beneficence
Case law
Chronological levels
Civil law
Common law
Community standards
Consequences
Counselors' values
Developmental levels
Dogmatic solutions
Ethics
Expert witnesses
Federal statutes
Informed consent
Institutional standards
Isms
Justice
Laws
Legal status
Loyalty
Moral principles
Nonmaleficence
Opacity of law
Personal bias
Potential courses of action
Precedents
Prejudice
Privacy rights
School board policy
Standard of care
State statutes
STEPS
Tolerance for ambiguity
Vested with rights

CHAPTER 2

Professionalism

Objectives

By the time you have completed this chapter, you should be able to:

- Define professionalism
- Discuss how professionalism is demonstrated in behavior, attitudes and beliefs
- Identify standard of care and the behavior of the reasonably competent professional
- Apply your ethical standards of behavior
- Discuss how personal behavior affects professional standing, and determine when your personal behavior has crossed the line of professionalism
- Reflect on your group membership and the additional responsibilities school counselors carry to be inclusive with all faculty and staff
- Define professional competence, and discuss how it should influence your behavior
- Identify the difference between defamation and qualified privilege
- Discuss dual relationships, professional distance and how to protect students from possible harm that can result from dual relationships

Ethical Standards Addressed in This Chapter

Professionalism means knowing your professional association's standards and adhering to them. The ASCA Ethical Standards for School Counselors (2022b) most germane to this chapter are the following:

School counselors:

- Engage in professional roles and relationships with students and stakeholders that foster wellness and student success. (A.5.a.)
- Recognize that establishing credibility, rapport and an effective working alliance with some students and stakeholders may be facilitated by developing relationships that extend beyond the school day and building (e.g., attending community events, advocating for community improvement for and with students and stakeholders, joining community enhancement organizations). (A.5.b.)
- Assess potential risks and benefits prior to extending relationships beyond the school building and school hours (e.g., attending students off-site extracurricular activities, celebrations honoring students, hospital visits, funerals). (A.5.c.)

- Document the nature of relationship extensions, including the rationale, potential benefit and possible consequences for the student and school counselor. (A.5.d.).
- Act to eliminate and/or reduce the potential for harm to students and stakeholders in any relationships or interactions by using safeguards, such as informed consent, consultation, supervision and documentation. (A.5.e.)
- Prevent potential harm to students and stakeholders with whom the school counselor's judgment may be compromised (e.g., family members, children of close friends) by helping facilitate the provision of alternative services or resources when available. (A.5.f.)
- Adhere to legal, ethical, district and school policies and guidelines regarding relationships with students and stakeholders. (A.5.g).
- Strive to avoid a conflict of interest through self-promotion that would benefit the school counselor personally and/or financially (e.g., advertising their products and/or services). (A.5.j.)
- Provide support, consultation and mentoring to professionals in need of assistance when appropriate to enhance school climate and student outcomes. (B.2.f.)
- Maintain membership in school counselor professional organizations to stay up to date on current research and to maintain professional competence in current school counseling issues and topics. (B.3.b.)
- Recognize the potential for stress and secondary trauma. Practice wellness and self-care through monitoring mental, emotional and physical health, while seeking consultation from an experienced school counseling practitioner and/or others when needed. (B.3.h.)
- Monitor personal behaviors and recognize the high standard of care a professional in this critical position of trust must maintain on and off the job. School counselors are cognizant of and refrain from activity that may diminish their effectiveness within the school community. (B.3.i.)
- Apply an ethical decision-making model and seek consultation and supervision from colleagues and other professionals who are knowledgeable of the profession's practices when ethical questions arise. (B.3.j.)

All the ASCA Ethical Standards apply to the professionalism chapter, but the standards were dispersed throughout all the chapters. The full text of the ASCA Ethical Standards for School Counselors is available at *www.schoolcounselor.org*.

Introduction

Professionalism is not easily defined. However, there are some core characteristics distinguishing professions from other occupations. Professionals have special skills and competence in the application of knowledge, and their behavior is guided by a code of ethics. This chapter focuses on some of the core characteristics of the school counseling profession and the behavior, attitude, beliefs and philosophy of school counseling that shape professionalism (Jacob et al., 2022; Remley & Herlihy, 2019).

The school counseling profession has the ASCA Ethical Standards for School Counselors (ASCA, 2022b). All school counselors have the responsibility to understand the ethical standards and to apply them to their work with peers, teachers, staff members, administrators, parents and students at their schools. These principles clarify the ethical responsibilities of the entire school counseling profession, whether or not the school counselor is an ASCA member. The ethical standards require adherence to school board policies and local, state and federal laws. When there is conflict, the law supersedes. At all times, school counselors work diligently to be both ethical and legal.

School counselors develop their principles of professional behavior through membership in professional organizations, reading and research, and attendance at professional development opportunities, such as conferences, regional meetings, district in-services, peer networking and training sessions. Greater ethical and legal knowledge leads to more sound ethical decision making. Being aware of the latest research, techniques and knowledge will help school counselors protect their professionalism, remain current and serve students' needs (Betters-Bubo, 2020; Levy & Lemberger-Truelove, 202; Wachter Morris et al., 2021).

Unprofessional behavior is usually handled through school districts' due process procedures, the courts, principals' annual evaluations of school counselors or other local procedures. Rarely are ethical violations brought to the ASCA Board of Directors; however, ASCA has developed a means to revoke membership when member have had their certificate revoked for cause or for violation of ASCA Ethical Standards. The procedures can be found in the ASCA Ethical Standards for School Counselors (2022b) in section E. Maintenance of Standards.

This chapter wrestles with the meaning of school counselors' professional conduct and how personal conduct can affect one's professional standing with fellow faculty members and the larger school community. At the heart of many case studies is the collaborative role of the school counselor with other educators, boundary issues with students, and legal and ethical communication. It is not possible to address all of the pitfalls and complications that can threaten professionalism, but this chapter addresses many of the guiding principles of professional behavior essential for effective school counseling.

Getting Started: What Would You Do?

The following case is answered at the end of this chapter by a school counseling leader. Before you read the response, formulate in your own mind how you would approach this ethical dilemma.

STANDARD OF CARE

Raney did not have a legal and ethical course in her school counseling master's degree program and is facing a tough situation in which a parent is suing Raney and the school district because the parent believes Raney acted illegally. Raney is not worried; she knows she is covered by vicarious liability as the school district (the deep pockets) will be the one sued. She also believes the standard of care is intact, as it was not her fault that she did not have the proper training in her master's program. Is Raney correct in her assumptions?

Working Through Case Studies

PROFESSIONAL COMMUNICATION: QUALIFIED PRIVILEGE

Greg was not promoted to ninth grade because he did "nothing," according to his eighth-grade teacher. His parents argue that he should be promoted because his failure to do work was the result of his disability (he has been diagnosed with mildly ADHD). Greg's parents, the principal, his teacher and you hold a joint conference. During the conference, you explain to Greg's parents that he is "lazy and interested only in his social life." Greg's parents file suit against you for defamation. How will the court rule?

Points to Consider

Qualified privilege protects educators when derogatory statements are made in good faith and without malice. Under this definition, it is clear that the communication must be made in good faith, without intent to harm, upon reasonable grounds. Also, it must be made with regard to assisting or protecting the interests of either of the parties involved in performing a duty to society. The educator's communication is qualified privileged if it is prompted by a duty to a student or to another and is made in good faith and without malice (Alexander & Alexander, 2019). The school counselor was legal if not ethical.

Legally, administrators and other educators may say unpleasant things about students, but only when it is necessary to fulfill their obligations to educate and care for students while the student is in their charge (*in loco parentis*). Legally, a school counselor may say a student is "lazy" and failed because the student did not complete work. Ethically, however, calling a student "lazy" creates defensiveness. The school counselor's words were legally tolerable since this was, in the school counselor's opinion, a true statement based on her observations. When this school counselor was named in a larger court case involving the retention issue, the case for defamation against the school counselor was thrown out with due speed because, as educators, school counselors have qualified privilege. This means they have the right to say things about students that are not flattering but necessary to fulfill their duties. School counselors may have to make unflattering statements, but do so only in the context of the situation at hand (Alexander & Alexander, 2019). Using terms like "lazy" can serve only to make parents and students angry.

Collaboration with parents cannot proceed effectively in a climate of hostility and defensiveness. Using "lazy" to describe the student might have been accurate, but it might also have been construed as mean-spirited. School counselors' word choices can be positive or negative motivating factors. Failure to recognize the power of words in conveying difficult information diminishes opportunities for growth and moves people away from the possibility of a good resolution. When conveying difficult information, school counselors should choose their words judiciously to maintain optimal communication lines with parents and students.

PROFESSIONAL COMMUNICATION: SENSITIVE INFORMATION

You are aware that Robert has been sexually abused. During a child study meeting in which exceptional student education is being considered for Robert, you become convinced it is in Robert's best interest if you reveal to the child study team that he was a victim of sexual abuse. His parents, who did not attend the child study team meeting, find out about this revelation and sue you and the school district. Were you legal? Were you ethical?

Points to Consider

Substantial interest is the key consideration in this case. In the case of *N.C. v. Bedford Central School District* (2004), social worker Reulbach and school counselor Mackie were at the center of a lawsuit that helped define and refine the limits of substantial interest.

N.C., the parents of the abused child, A.J., had a strong interest in keeping their child's abuse private. His parents feared, because of the nature of the offense, disclosure to his peers or other members of the community might cause A.J. more trauma. However, Reulbach and Mackie, in their respective responsibilities as social worker and school counselor, have a substantial interest in revealing relevant details about events, which likely affect the student's emotional well-being. All of the communications cited by the parents occurred during the course of the child study team evaluation, which was conducted at the parents' request. The communications took place only between the educators so they could adequately determine the student's need for exceptional student education.

The parents were upset because Reulbach was the only school district employee they had informed about the abuse. When Reulbach told Mackie, the parents said he relayed incorrect information about A.J.'s sexual abuse history. However, the court said the facts provided no basis to infer that Reulbach and Mackie were engaging in "gossip" rather than professional communication. No communications had occurred outside of a professional setting, outside of the scope of the psychological and emotional evaluation of the student or among individuals without a significant interest in communicating about the student's sexual abuse history. Therefore, the court found the defendant's' interest in professional communication for the student's benefit outweighed the student's and the parents' rights to confidentiality (*N.C. v. Bedford Central School District* (2004)).

We may often find it necessary to share information among other professionals in the same school or, as in this case, in the same school district. If the information about this child's sexual abuse had not occurred during professional discussions intended to help A.J., then the court might have ruled differently. We are cautioned to reveal such private and potentially prejudicial information in a formal setting and with parent permission if at all possible or only to educators who have the need to know and to be able to defend our actions as necessary to the student's well-being.

The social worker was legal. Was she ethical? Law and ethics can conflict, and when there is conflict, the law takes priority. The law is the minimum standard of care, and ethics are aspirational. School counselors must always be legal, but school counselors do not leave their ethical obligations behind just because they have managed to be legal. Holding ourselves to a high ethical standard is sometimes tough when the law conflicts with our ethics. This social worker could have remained ethical by encouraging the parents to tell the school counselor about their son's abuse, reminding them that the school counselor is a professional and will respect confidentiality. If the parents explicitly asked that the social worker not reveal the sexual abuse, then the onus would be on the social worker to try and convince the parents to engage other professionals.

PROFESSIONAL COMMUNICATION: DEFAMATION

At a faculty social gathering some colleagues are engaged in a heated debate about teenage pregnancy. You reveal that one of your students, Randall, has impregnated two girls, refused to accept responsibility and brags about his accomplishment. Your comments reach Randall. He and his mother seek legal counsel about whether or not you have committed slander (defamation that is orally conveyed). Have you committed slander?

Points to Consider

A communication is defamatory if it tends to harm the reputation of another person or to deter third persons from associating or dealing with him (Alexander & Alexander, 2019). In defamation, the plaintiff is not required to prove actual injury or out-of-pocket monetary loss but rather must merely show that the words were of such as to impair his or her reputation or standing in the community or to cause personal anguish, suffering or humiliation. The plaintiff need not prove that he or she suffered special harm or direct loss (Alexander & Alexander, 2019).

Gossiping about a student's behavior at a social gathering is not protected by qualified privilege or substantial interest and may fall under defamation. Information should not be conveyed to other teachers or administrators unless the motive and purpose is to assist and enhance the student's educational opportunities. Transmittal should be made in the proper channels and to persons assigned the responsibility for the relevant educational function. Gossip or careless talk among teachers not calculated to help the student may be shown to be malicious and not protected by the cloak of qualified privilege (Alexander & Alexander, 2019).

Qualified privilege is defined by the setting and circumstances in which we discuss a student, not by our job titles. It is unprofessional to mishandle information we have obtained in the course of doing our work. Social settings are the time to be especially discreet about sensitive, confidential information. School counselors only reveal sensitive information with great reluctance and care to make certain the recipients have a need to know and are in a position to benefit the student if they have the information we share (ASCA, 2018b; ASCA, 2018c).

COLLABORATION: GROUP MEMBERSHIP

You are trying to develop a place for yourself in a deeply divided faculty. Three faculty members control much of the group dynamics, deciding who will be accepted into the "in group" and who will be ostracized. Members of the in group have a great deal of fun together and take care of each other. However, a few teachers are treated as outcasts and appear to spend some lonely hours at the school. It is not apparent to you why some are accepted and others are not. It appears the leaders decide who will be included, and everyone goes along. You have been chosen to be included, and you love having the warmth and camaraderie of a large portion of the faculty. However, the fun you are having is tempered by the nagging voice that good people are being ignored. You have made a few suggestions about including the others without much response. You feel you are not being true to yourself by participating in a group that hurts others through social isolation. You view your behavior as weakness in not standing on your principles, but you fear being pushed out. What do you do?

Points to Consider

Group membership can be difficult, yet success as a group member is critical for school counselors to develop a place as collaborators and team builders. Collaborative skills are a building block for the development of leadership skills (Holman et al., 2019). Relationships with fellow educators and other critical stakeholders pave the way for an effective school counseling program. The title "school counselor" adds the additional responsibility to be inclusive of all faculty to the fullest extent possible.

A school counselor should reflect on the implications of having or not having membership in this group. A few questions to consider are:

- In an effort to fit in and not be ostracized, do you try to match the behavior of others even though it is against your better judgment and your own feeling of self-respect?
- Have you grown past peer pressure and the need to be accepted?
- Can you preserve your place with this group and still reach out to the ostracized faculty members?
- Do you believe your self-respect is your primary consideration in this situation?
- Can you fight through your own inhibitions and fears and learn to be a better group member?
- Do you have the ability to survey a person's situation and decide how best to support that person?
- Do you challenge yourself to step out of your comfort zone?
- Do you expend more energy trying to find the good in people than you do trying to point out their flaws?

This case can only be answered by individual professionals in the context of their own situation. There are no hard and fast rules of behavior that say a school counselor must abandon new friends. However, there is professional fallout when the school counselor is viewed as marginalizing part of the faculty. Guidance in ethical standards and a history of practice imply school counselors adhere to a higher standard of professionalism in interactions with fellow professionals. School counselors should aspire to the standard of demonstrating strong interpersonal skills and the ability to successfully move within and among the different "camps" that can be found in schools (Cholewa et al., 2020). Additionally, when school counselors show warmth toward the ostracized group, they strengthen their relationships with not only ostracized people but gain respect from quite a few of the in-group even if not the three bullies. School counselors invest in their relationships to yield results to advantage their students (ASCA, 2021d).

COLLABORATION: ADMINISTRATORS

Occasionally, the principal shares sensitive information with you. Last summer, he told you that he interviewed a recent graduate and hoped to hire her for a school counseling position. However, any surplus school counselors had to be placed prior to hiring the new graduate. He explained he was temporarily dropping the position out of the budget so he wouldn't have to hire a particular surplus school counselor who was considered weak and would reinstate the position after the surplus school counselor was placed at another school. At the 12-day count, the position is reinstated, and the new school counselor is hired. The teacher's union is filing a grievance and asks what you know about the entire situation. What should you do in this situation? Are you bound by your ethical standards to keep this confidential? Must you tell the union what you know?

Points to Consider

School counselors try to be neutral, and it is always a bad idea to be this entwined in the confidential workings of the administrative office. This situation has placed the school counselor in a difficult position.

The school counselor could explain to the union representative that this is an administrators' situation, and you are extracting yourself from it. If pushed, you could explain that sensitive information is discussed with the understanding between you and the principal that it will be kept confidential. This situation is no different than other conversations in which the principal's confidence has been respected (Geesa et al, 2020; Moyer et al, 2012). If more information is demanded, the school counselor should request on what legal grounds they are entitled to anything you and the principal share. There is no privity involved in this case. Privity is defined as having an interest in a transaction, contract or legal action to which one is not a party (Cornell Law, 2022). The school counselor does not have a legal obligation to tell the union the details of conversations with the principal; however, if school counselors are union members, they may have agreed to cooperate with union investigations as a condition of membership.

COLLABORATION: TEACHERS

You have, over the course of time, learned a great deal about different teachers' classroom management effectiveness. You believe certain students assigned to one particular teacher are suffering academically and emotionally because this teacher has chronic behavior problems. School administration seems to be unaware of her ineffectiveness with many students. What is your role in this situation?

Points to Consider

The school counselor cannot afford to come across as an informant or align too closely with anyone's "camp." The school atmosphere is not unlike the United Nations, and in cases where potentially divisive situations arise the school counselor is advised to remain neutral and nonjudgmental. Like a good ambassador, the school counselor's job is to develop relationships with administrators and teachers, listening to the concerns of each and helping warring factions arrive at compromises. Having a solid, professional relationship with the principal benefits the students, teachers and support personnel (Boyland et al., 2019; Elam et al., 2020). Regarding the above case in which a teacher's conduct may be a concern, the school counselor's role is not to spy and report to the principal but perhaps to share potential solutions with the principal without compromising confidentiality of sources or damaging the teacher's reputation (ASCA, 2020).

The key to success in difficult situations is to genuinely respect and support teachers. Think of teachers in terms of being trusted allies helping you advantage students. Study the faculty to determine who is functioning high on the social/emotional consciousness continuum, and use their talents to help you advantage students. Avoiding a "them" and "us" mentality will pay off for your students. Support teachers and the instructional program, as it pays huge dividends for students.

Also essential is to make the effort to build trust between the school counselor and principal, firmly establishing respect of confidences (Prasath et al., 2021; Arndt et al., 2020). It will be helpful for the school counselor to know how information will be used, to feel secure that it will be used to help the teacher make strides toward a better academic and social environment. If school counselors are uncertain the principal will deal deftly with a delicate situation, they might need another plan. Identifying allies early on, such as the assistant principal or someone else who will use compassion and a nonjudgmental approach to problem solving, will help during the throes of a dilemma. Remember, the best mentality for a school counselor to have is to think like an ambassador and to be neutral to the greatest extent possible (Prasath et al., 2021; Ruiz et al., 2018).

PROFESSIONAL BEHAVIOR: COMPETENCE AND PERFORMANCE

A colleague, Randolph, seems well-meaning and is good with students but indifferent to the paperwork involved in his job. Randolph's happy-go-lucky attitude is attractive to the students, but his lack of attention to detail has meant several of his students have almost missed graduation due to his failure in academic advising.

Randolph's inability to maintain solid record keeping is bound to catch up with him and cause a problem that can't be fixed. You aren't his boss, nor do you have any authority over him. As his colleague, however, do you have an ethical or legal obligation to do anything more to help Randolph or his students? Can the school district fire Randolph? Must the school district offer remediation for Randolph before firing him?

Points to Consider

In the case of *Carroll v. Rondout Valley Central School District* (1999), the school district in Ulster County, N.Y., fired a tenured school counselor of 19 years. The dismissal was a result of the school counselor's failure to maintain required records, to arrange required remedial assistance for students who failed the Regents Competency Test, to schedule students for required courses and for falsifying records. School counselors have an ethical and legal duty to maintain records on behalf of their students. School counselors are to some degree responsible for their colleagues' successes or failures. The ASCA Ethical Standards (2022b) give guidance as to how colleagues have to hold each other accountable for ethical behavior. The Ethical Standards state, "School counselors discuss and seek resolution directly with the colleague whose behavior is in question unless the behavior is unlawful, abusive, egregious or dangerous, in which case proper school or community authorities are contacted" (ASCA, 2022b, E.b.). Professionals work hard to portray the fraternity of education and to support each other to be competent school counselors. We are not entirely responsible for our fellow school counselors, but it is ethical to exhaust our options in trying to help colleagues.

PROFESSIONAL BEHAVIOR: SCHOOL DISTRICT POLICIES

You believe the school district's policy for calculating GPAs is unfair. If a student fails a course but subsequently retakes the course and passes, the original F is never removed, and 50 of your seniors will never make the 2.0 grade point to graduate because there is no grade-forgiveness policy. To get this policy changed, you have tried to go through the correct channels in the district, but no one seems to be listening. You resort to writing a letter to the editor of the local newspaper criticizing the policy, hoping public opinion will bring needed change. Does writing a letter to the editor constitute a legal or ethical concern?

Points to Consider

It is legal for educators to write a letter to the editor critical of a school district's practice or policy if it is a matter of public importance. The Supreme Court supported educators' rights to voice their opinion in the public forum of newspaper editorials in *Pickering v. Board of Education* (1968). Marvin Pickering was dismissed for writing and sending a letter to the editor that was critical of the superintendent and the Illinois Board of Education. The board said it could dismiss Pickering under Illinois statute because the letter was detrimental to the efficient operation and administration of the district's schools. The Supreme Court ruled in Pickering's favor; it said the statements in the letter were neither false nor recklessly made and that educators exercising their freedom of speech on issues of public importance is not a basis for dismissal from public employment (Imber et al., 2014; Alexander & Alexander, 2019). The test has been applied to protect Pickering as well as a teacher who had complained to her principal about racist hiring policies (*Givhan v. Western Line Consol. School District* (1979)) and a police dispatcher who expressed a negative opinion about the president to co-workers while on the job (*Rankin v. McPherson* (1987)). In *Connick v. Myers* (1983), the test did not protect an attorney who was fired for circulating a questionnaire about personnel matters; it neither posed questions of public concern (e.g., the department's transfer policy) nor was it sufficiently disruptive to office morale to justify a disciplinary response Hudson, 2020).

In most school districts, newspaper editorials are not considered an appropriate way for educators to voice their concerns about the district. In cases of public importance, they are probably legal, but are they ethical? Educators work extremely hard and are sometimes judged harshly by public opinion and the media. When a fellow educator criticizes the school district in a public forum, it can be disheartening or embarrassing to many in the school district. An alternative method might be to send an email to district-level administrators to continue to make your case internally. Taking the situation to the press is subject to public misinterpretation, and your colleagues and supervisors may afterward view you with suspicion.

An advocating school counselor will want to raise awareness of barriers adversely stratifying students' opportunities; however, knowing how to negotiate the political landscape is also critically important. Frustration with ridiculous policies is understandable, but failing to understand the political climate and acting in inappropriate ways to advocate is just as damaging as not advocating at all (Stone & Zirkel, 2010). Acting in an adversarial manner will almost certainly minimize the school counselor's effectiveness in all future dealings with certain school district officials. School counselors should use finesse and diplomacy to navigate the political landscape and to determine the least disruptive way to get what students need.

In the case study above, the school district is not doing anything illegal or unethical. School districts are allowed to establish a pupil progression plan, and it may include a forgiveness policy whereby a student can retake a course and receive the passing or higher grade. Professional behavior requires a school counselor to abide by the district policy while advocating appropriately for change.

Not since *Pickering* has a court case on First Amendment rights received so much attention as the court case of *Garcetti v. Ceballos* (2006). In this case, the Supreme Court held that "when public employees make statements pursuant to their official duties, the employees are not speaking as citizens for First Amendment purposes, and the Constitution does not insulate their communications from employer discipline." *Garcetti* is an important case for school counselors to know, as it limits First Amendment protection. The facts in brief are that Ceballos, a deputy district attorney in the Los Angeles County District Attorney's Office, determined that a sheriff misrepresented facts in an affidavit used to obtain a search warrant. In a memorandum to his superiors, Ceballos recommended that the case should be dismissed. The sheriff's department criticized Ceballos for his handling of the situation, and the district attorney sided with the sheriff and allowed the case to proceed. Ceballos asserts that, following these events, he was retaliated against by being transferred and denied a promotion. Ceballos filed suit, alleging the district attorney had violated his First and 14th Amendment rights. The Supreme Court heard the case and sided with the district attorney, ruling that a government employer can discipline an employee for job-related speech without offending the First Amendment. The Supreme Court left intact the tenets established by *Pickering v. Board of Education of Township High School District* (Hudson, 2020).

The Supreme Court emphasized that it found in favor of the district attorney because Ceballos wrote the memorandum pursuant to his duties and not as a citizen, which was the case for Pickering; so, the effect of the Ceballos case may be less significant than at first glance. At this point, the clearest message of the Ceballos decision is that employees who want to complain or express controversial opinions related to their job duties should do so as citizens (Hudson, 2020).

PROFESSIONAL BEHAVIOR: FALSIFYING RECORDS

You are a school counselor who works diligently on behalf of students. Your students have greater challenges than most students in your school system of 19 high schools, including a higher retention rate and few four-year university admissions. Your school's practice when a student retakes and passes a previously failed course is to change an F grade to the new grade. Therefore, many F's are permanently deleted from student transcripts. This is not a district practice or policy, but it has worked for your students and been silently blessed by the administration of your school. Your school's practice has resulted in more students being given an opportunity to graduate and/or attend a four-year university. Are there any legal or ethical concerns with the school's practice?

Points to Consider

School counselors are system change agents, but advocacy must be ethical. In the high-stress world of college admissions, where a university acceptance brings political capital to a high school and increased social status for parents and students, school counselors can feel the pressure to get students into Ivy League schools and provide the high school with more bragging rights. Sometimes, school counselors follow the unwritten rules and practices that have gone on before them to help a student secure a college admission or help an athlete comply with NCAA eligibility. Cases involving records manipulation have played out in administrative hearings, state professional practice commission hearings and the courts. Following are four cases that resulted in school counselors being fined, losing professional credentials, having their jobs taken away and ending up in court accounting for irregularities in transcripts.

Longtime school counselor Judith Meller, who worked at Fort Lee (N.J.) High School, was investigated for changing grades on transcripts sent to colleges. Dozens of college applicants had their grades boosted without their knowledge. The school district's website bragged about the success their students had in admissions into prestigious colleges: "The graduating class of 2007 surpassed our wildest expectations with the acceptance of students to five Ivies and 35 of the top 50 top-tier colleges in the nation." Indications were that part of the motivation to change grades was not just to help the students but also to enhance the school's reputation. The district found six altered transcripts for current seniors. Meller lost her job and her certificate to practice as a school counselor (Applebome, 2009).

Jolyon Raymond, Kory Kumasaka and Acie Dubose were accused of altering 200 grades during the 2002–2003 school at Franklin High School in Seattle, Wash. All three of the school counselors had glowing reputations and support from the internal and external community. Their advocacy was widely respected among the students, especially the senior class. Allegations arose when dozens of grades were changed that helped 55 students meet the necessary 2.0 grade-point average for graduation, but the changes were not properly documented or supported by written district policy. The school counselors were placed on leave during the investigation (Komo Staff & News Services, 2003). Students started a petition to reinstate the school counselors, and teachers and parents voiced their support. "If they did anything, it's because they care too much," said Lucy Gaskill-Gaddis, former chair of Franklin's site council (Bhatt, Vinh & Shaw, 2003, p1). Teacher Nan Johnson explains the reason six of her former students graduated from high school is that Raymond persuaded them to enroll in night classes and not give up. She said, "These three cared." The testimonials in support of these three school counselors were stellar. Following the investigation, all of the school counselors were allowed to return to the school (Roberts, 2003). Investigators found the practice of changing grades did not occur in isolation; in fact, hundreds of grades had been changed for students in 10 Seattle public high schools in recent years. Investigators deemed the school and district shared the blame as the practice of substituting F's for subsequent passing grades was well-known and part of the school's culture.

Sanzone was a high school counselor in the school his daughter attended. As part of his job, he was able to access course grades and could make grade changes when necessary. His daughter was in the running for valedictorian of her class, which allowed her access to many scholarships and would considerably soften the burden of financing her education. A transfer student became part of the same class as Sanzone's daughter. Sanzone was in charge of inputting the transfer student's grades into the school's computer system. Sanzone intentionally lowered several of the transfer student's grades, which lowered the student's overall cumulative average and class rank. He then raised some of his daughter's grades, securing his child's place as the valedictorian. Sanzone resigned from his position a year later and paid a civil penalty of $2,000 (Massachusetts State Ethics Commission, 1997).

Mellissa Krystynak was sentenced to six months in prison for a mail fraud scheme she executed while employed as a West Virginia high school counselor. She was also ordered to pay $13,750 in restitution to the victim scholarship organizations, and she was fined an additional $5,000. Krystynak inflated at least 34 of her daughter's grades to obtain scholarships (Department of Justice & U.S. Attorney's Office - Southern District of West Virginia, 2019).

Educators sometimes falsify records when the pressure to keep passing rates and graduation rates high. An East Oakland County California school counselor along with top school administrators and teachers were charged with a scheme to enhance their school's graduation rate or mask educational deficiencies by changing grades or giving credit for courses never taken (NBC, 2019).

A number of cases have involved National Collegiate Athletic Association eligibility. One such case involved a running back for Auburn University. In August 2012, a Memphis City Schools high school counselor resigned after admitting to creating a fraudulent transcript for an athlete at the school. Valerie Starks-Sykes made substantial grade changes for Javon Robinson, who went on to be an Auburn running back (Solomon, 2012). One week after the school district acknowledged the transcript manipulation, the NCAA ruled Robinson ineligible to play. Starks-Sykes admitted to making the changes and chose to resign (Veazey, 2012).

Most, if not all, of the school counselors involved in these cases were well-meaning, hard-working advocates who cared about making better lives for their students. It may be tempting to manipulate transcripts in favor of students, even when written policy does not support your actions; however, school counselors who seek to advocate for students should do so by advocating for changes to written policies. In the absence of supportive policies, falsifying records can lead to negative consequences for students. It can also lead to discipline for school counselors that includes forced resignation, firing and losing certification. Adhering to district policies can be especially difficult in situations where school counselors face pressure from others in the school, including administrators and supervisors, to alter grades or transcripts. School counselors must heed these cases as a warning; pressure from others will not lead to legal or political protection for their jobs. Falsifying records follows the warning that "the end doesn't justify the means."

PROFESSIONAL BEHAVIOR: PREVAILING COMMUNITY STANDARDS

Prior to becoming a school counselor, you were a teacher in four other school districts. You continue to be surprised by this school's hands-off approach to working with sexually active students. This district is so hands off even resources for pregnant students are out of the question. You have a student who has asked you for help, and you are considering giving her the phone number to Planned Parenthood. You are aware this action would be an affront to the community, but you intend to put your students' welfare above your own. Are you behaving ethically? Are there aspects of being a school counselor you are not considering?

Points to Consider

Ethics are situational. School counselors avoid the temptation to impose their own values on students, parents and the community. Community and institutional standards can differ significantly from school to school and community to community. It is difficult to accept that professional behavior varies according to the prevailing standards of the community, but our ethical imperative is to be aware and respectful of the school community's standards. It is acceptable behavior in certain communities for school counselors to refer pregnant students to Planned Parenthood; yet, in many other communities, this action would be considered a serious breach of ethics, infringing on family values and parents' rights to be the guiding voice in their children's lives.

School counselors acknowledge the prevailing standards of the community in which they are working, respectfully adhering to those standards; however, adherence does not mean that we unconditionally accept all community standards. If we believe a practice, policy or law of a particular school or community is detrimental to students, it is our ethical obligation to work in a responsible manner to try to influence a change so students are advantaged. School counselors are politically minded and work astutely with internal and external stakeholders, such as families, parents, guardians, administrators and teachers when change is needed. School counselors have an ethical responsibility to ask tough questions in a respectful way, and to encourage fellow educators to evaluate their stance on controversial topics (Havlik et al., 2019; Ratts, & Greenleaf, 2017).

PROFESSIONAL AND PERSONAL BEHAVIOR

You are a school counselor in a conservative small town. Your colleague at the high school has just finished writing a book and finds himself at the center of a firestorm. The book recounts sexually explicit details about acts, considered demeaning by many, that women should perform to please men. Promiscuity before marriage and female submissiveness are encouraged, and advice is given that young women with low self-esteem are the easiest sexual conquests. The book contains sexually explicit language throughout, and he gives his position as a school counselor as qualification that he knows women. He is fired. Has the school district violated his freedom of speech?

Points to Consider

"Congress shall make no law ... abridging the freedom of speech." The free speech clause of the First Amendment has been fiercely defended in the Supreme Court in cases of hate speech, flag burning, racist rants, parodies maligning people and anti-American hate speeches at military funerals. The Supreme Court protected: racist hate speech when it was "unlikely to incite violence" (*Brandenburg v. Ohio*, 1969), a parody of real people engaged in heinous acts as "no reasonable person would have interpreted the parody as factual claims" (*Hustler Magazine v. Falwell*, 1988) and the right to burn an American flag as the conduct was "an expression in a protest" (*Texas v. Johnson*, 1989).

Snyder v. Phelps (2010), one of the most highly publicized First Amendment Supreme Court cases, occurred in this decade. Westboro Church minister Phelps and his followers engaged in anti-American hate speech at military funerals to protest "America's tolerance of homosexuality." Typical signs were "God Hates the USA/Thank God for 9/11," "Thank God for Dead Soldiers," and "Don't Pray for the USA." Hate speech signs were displayed on public grounds across from the 2006 funeral for Marine Lance Cpl. Matthew Snyder, who was killed in Iraq in the line of duty. At Snyder's funeral signs read, "You're Going to Hell" and "God Hates Fags," among other hateful statements. The Supreme Court held that Phelps and his followers were "speaking" on matters of public concern on public property and, thus, were entitled to protection under the First Amendment.

With free speech protected in all of the above cases, will Bryan Craig prevail in his $1 million lawsuit against the school district for firing him from his school counseling job after writing "It's Her Fault," an explicit book about women pleasing men sexually? Let's examine how the courts treated Craig's free speech.

In September 2012, Brian Craig, a school counselor and girls' basketball coach at an Illinois high school, received a letter from the school district stating it had received concerns from community members regarding the publication of his book. The school board unanimously voted to terminate Craig, citing a violation of district policies: "Mr. Craig's conduct in this matter fell far short of our expectations and evoked outrage for me, members of this board and many others in this district who have come to expect the highest level of professionalism and sound judgment from the people they entrust with their children each day." The school district explained that Craig had caused disruption, concern, distrust and confusion among members of the school district community; violated a policy prohibiting conduct that creates an intimidating, hostile or offensive educational environment; and failed to properly comport himself in accordance with his professional obligations as a public school educator.

Craig filed suit, charging he was terminated in violation of his First Amendment rights, arguing the book was of public interest, meant to give women a road map to having the upper hand in relationships with men. The district court dismissed Craig's suit because his book did not address a matter of public concern and thus was not entitled to First Amendment protection. On appeal, the 7th Circuit Court of Appeals upheld the district court decision but for different reasons. The 7th Circuit agreed the book met the standard of public concern, as adult relationship dynamics is "a subject that interests a significant segment of the public." The designation of public concern entitled Craig's speech to special protection because of the long-held First Amendment value protecting public debate to be uninhibited, robust and wide-open with regard to public issues.

Since Craig's speech met the criteria of public concern, on what grounds did the 7th Circuit rule in favor of the district and against Craig? Having determined the speech was a matter of public concern, the 7th Circuit turned attention to the context and circumstances of the speech and evaluated what was said, when, where and how it was said and whether the school district's interests in restricting Craig's speech outweighed his First Amendment speech rights.

Craig linked the book to his place of employment, and he did so in a most disturbing way. Craig, in qualifying his expertise to write a book on instructing women in the techniques to please men, wrote in the introduction, "I coach girls basketball, work in an office where I am the only male counselor and am responsible for 425 high school students a year, about half of whom are females. Suffice it to say, I have spent a considerable amount of time around, and with, the fairer sex." Craig also thanked his students in the acknowledgements. Craig referred to his role as a school counselor in the book, talking about females in his counseling sessions and females on his basketball team. Craig's intertwining of his free expression to his employment was significant to the outcome of this case.

The school district's interest in Craig's ability to work effectively as a school counselor outweighed his First Amendment rights. The court noted that female students who knew about Craig's views in the book would be reluctant to seek his career, college or relationship advice. Craig's professed "inability to refrain from sexualizing females" might make some female students loath to get advice from him. If Craig fails to create the appropriate environment for his students, they will not approach him and he cannot do his job (*Craig v. Rich Township High School District*, No. 12-7581 (N.D. I11. Feb. 19, 2013).

Educators, especially school counselors, have First Amendment rights, but those rights are not absolute. Even speech determined to be a matter of public concern and entitled to special protection under the First Amendment is not unfettered when balanced against a school district's need to protect students. School counselors are held to a high standard of care and professionalism in working with minors in schools. Students are school counselors' primary clients; however, because school counselors are part of an educational community, their loyalty and obligation extend to parents and guardians, teachers, administrators, the school district and the community. School counselors must understand the community's prevailing standards and work within those standards. Craig ignored community standards; the fact that he was *in loco parentis* to students meant that his obligations to parents, the paramount need for the trusting relationship, and the expectation that someone who works with minors in a mandated set- ting such as schools held him to a very high standard. The 7th Circuit said, "The fact that Craig works closely with students at a public school as a counselor confers upon him an inordinate amount of trust and authority." The court found that the requisite trust and authority trumped his First Amendment rights (*Craig v. Rich Township High School District*, No. 12-7581 (N.D. I11. Feb. 19, 2013).

Discuss the following with other school counselors:

- Should school counselors be expected to exercise a higher standard of care than other educators given the uniqueness of their work in the personal and social/emotional arena?
- Consider the unique preparation of school counselors, which emphasizes confidentiality and the foundation of trust on which the profession is built. Does this place the school counselor in a heightened position of trust when it comes to protecting the social/emotional well-being of children in our care (even more so than the principal)?
- When you're in a professional position, especially one where you're interacting with children and parents, do you have to be above reproach?

FIRST AMENDMENT SPEECH THAT STRATIFIES JOB EFFECTIVENESS

Your school is 90% Hispanic. The students decide to stage a walk-out because of the way they were being portrayed as "thieves" and "rapists." You go on social media, and brag about how wonderful the day was without them. Students raise concerns that you should have had their back. You fire back, "Get over yourself." You are fired, but you file a lawsuit to get your job back. Will you prevail?

Points to Consider

Patricia Crawford, Jurupa Unified School District (Calif.) high school counselor, lost her job following Facebook comments to students who boycotted school to protest former President Trump's immigration policy (O'Brien, 2020). Students staged a "Day without Immigrants." Greer, a teacher, posted extremely derogatory words about the students, and Crawford commented in support and added that the cafeteria was much cleaner, there was less traffic on the roads, no discipline issues and said, give me "more, please." Students showed disappointment in her perspective, but Crawford continued posting, eventually writing, "Get over yourselves." Crawford's derogatory words about her students meant she could no longer do her job, as students lost all confidence in her abilities as a school counselor. The resultant outcry that followed her words was also found to be detrimental to the school district's mission and functions. More than 50 emails specifically naming Crawford were sent to the school district, and Greer and Crawford's post sparked a public outcry, resulting in a public hearing. Crawford was fired and in 2020, the Fourth Appellate District affirmed her firing, as conduct that is "immoral" and "evidently unfit for service."

This case caused such an outcry because as one student so aptly put it, "You are our counselor, you are supposed to have our back." School counselors are held to a high standard when it comes to student advocacy. Crawford added to and supported mean-spirited and racist comments. When school counselors exercise their free speech, but it results in them no longer being able to effectively do their job, they can be fired.

PROFESSIONAL BOUNDARIES: DUAL RELATIONSHIPS

You love being a school counselor, especially for a select group of students you describe as bright, engaging and accomplished. This group receives most of your time and attention. You attend select students' piano recitals, tennis tournaments and soccer games. You treat these students as your adult friends, encouraging them to call you by your first name, giving them your home phone number and your home email address. You go out of your way to be extraordinarily responsive to their parents, and you encourage their praise, gifts, invitations and personal favors. One parent who is an attorney helped you with your house closing without charging you. Are you behaving ethically and legally?

Points to Consider

School counselors work diligently to avoid dual relationships involving personal gains and unfair advantages. Examples of personal gain might include having a parent gift you free real estate services, but sometimes, as in this real case, it is boosting one's image with select parents and nourishing the belief that the school counselor is the only one in the school who is a student-centered advocate.

School counselors must continually examine their actions and ask the question, "Whose needs are being met by my behaviors?" If the answer is "only a select few students in my charge" or "I am feeding my own personal needs by my behavior," then the school counselor is in the throes of a serious ethical violation.

School counselors, more than any other group of educators, have a responsibility to ensure the emotional safety of minor students. It is a strongly recognized and respected tenet in the profession that school counselors should avoid dual relationships, as they have the potential for great harm. The power differential, between the school counselor and student, makes it impossible for students to give equal consent to the extraprofessional relationship. It is considered exploitation when a school counselor crosses boundaries to try to establish friendships (Remley & Herlihy, 2019). Violating professional distance suggests a school counselor is engaged in a dual relationship (ASCA, 2020b).

In a January 2017 survey of 1,038 ASCA members, 87.2% of respondents "strongly agreed" or "agreed" on a five-point scale with the statement: "I avoid dual relationships that might impair my objectivity and increase the risk of harm to the student (e.g., counseling children of friends/associates, family members, students on a team you coach, etc.). In the same survey, 93% of respondents "strongly agreed" or "agreed" with: "In circumstances where I have encountered unavoidable dual relationships, I reduce potential for harm through safeguards (e.g., informed consent, consultation, supervision, documentation, etc.) (Stone, 2017b).

Equity means you might accept an invitation to attend a special event for a show of support for a student who needs to know someone cares. Singling out a few on whom to lavish attention to the demise of the large majority is a quite different scenario, as this school counselor did. The students and parents who were popular and/or politically well-connected got his attention, and his emails showed how he dismissed help to those parents and students he did not like. Professional distance when appropriately applied will help avoid dual relationships that violate trust in the counseling relationship.

Currying favor with students or their parents, or establishing yourself as the hero for certain students as this school counselor did, is unethical. Although school counselors may convince themselves they are performing good deeds, the truth is that no one benefits from favoritism, especially the students who have been excluded from selective acts of altruism.

Heroism can be intoxicating, especially for the school counselor who craves attention and celebrity. In this case, the parents of the chosen few acted like fans, creating a loyal, vocal support system when the school district was trying to fire him for his favoritism. Inevitably, the school counselor who campaigns for allies will be indebted to these parents at the expense of others. What happens, for example, when the parent who provided free legal services asks the school counselor to pull strings for his son, the one who was just suspended from school for drug use?

Compromised school counselors lose their effectiveness. All students should receive our services; not just the select few. Yes, school counselors soften professional distance but are very vigilant to any possible negative impact when they do so.

PROFESSIONAL BOUNDARIES: THE COMMUNITY

You have lived in the same small, tight-knit community your entire life, and you know nearly every person in the town through religious affiliation and the fact that your father was a popular coach who always had a houseful of people. You worry you will never feel comfortable working with students on a personal or emotional level, as you will probably know too much about their parents and family history. Do you have reason for concern?

Points to Consider

School counselors should avoid dual relationships with students if possible, but in some instances, it is impossible. When a school counselor works in a small community where social circles are tight-knit, dual relationships may be unavoidable. The school counselor is responsible for taking action to eliminate or reduce the potential for harm. Such safeguards might include informed consent, consultation, supervision and documentation (ASCA, 2022b). Dual relationships also involve a differentiation in power, with the student seeking services from the more powerful school counselor; as such, there are possible negative ramifications that can occur.

The best practice is for school counselors to be vigilant about recognizing when they are engaged in a dual relationship and being prepared with steps to minimize negative implications. The personal relationships this school counselor has with many of the families and their children will sometimes require that the prudent professional refer students to others with a more objective eye. For example, if a friend's child asks you for help with a class schedule, and you are treating this child the way you would any other, then you have minimized any negative impact on this student or others. If the same child seeks your help during a relationship crisis with her mother (your close friend), then you will need more objectivity than you are able to deliver in this situation. Referring students to another school counselor, if possible, may be the most ethical response.

Some safeguards against dual relationships can be established in advance. For instance, a school counselor may want to stay clear of the teacher's lounge, where students and their families are often discussed. When it comes to dual relationships, school counselors must exercise caution and handle each situation on a case-by-case basis.

URGENCY TO CREATE CHANGE

It is late May 2020, and every child in your school has seen the footage of George Floyd's murder. You want your students of color to feel affirmed, to be treated with dignity and respect and to have a future free of inequality. How do you help your students?

Points to Consider

In May 2020, the nation was once again stunned and emotionally exhausted from another senseless killing. How do we explain George Floyd's murder to our students? We tell the truth. We must not dismiss his murder as an isolated incident done by bad people. Just as we must not dismiss the killing of so many other Black people. There is too much overt and covert killing of spirit, body and soul for our students of color to say this is not a widespread problem. Racism is a blight on the soul of our country. How do we, as school counselors, help eradicate this cancer?

School counselors are good people, but as ASCA's former board chair Tinisha Parker, Ph.D., said, "We have to be more than good people." School counselors have to be committed to the ethics of our profession, which implore us to advantage each and every student in our charge. Indeed, as written in the ASCA Ethical Standards for School Counselors (2022b) it is a nonnegotiable to close gaps, promote equity of opportunity, work on our own multicultural and social justice awareness, provide leadership for an inclusive school, ensure equity of resources, collaborate with others to ensure bright futures, provide culturally sensitive materials, engage with parents/guardians in a culturally responsive way and promote equity and access. We can use these ethical standards as leverage when others try to quiet our voices or tell us this isn't a school counseling issue.

We must become co-conspirators, sometimes leading the effort, sometimes being the good foot soldier but always in the thick of the urgency for change. Our fellow educators give school counselors much liberty to speak from a position of passion and heart; it is almost expected of us. It's time for us to all find our soapbox. The high standard of care we must exercise in our work makes us ideally situated and ethically bound to bring a call to action in our schools and communities. Let us be bold.

Action can take many forms. We can help build students who are better informed about what social justice really means. We can use our platform to help students understand and mutually respect each other. We can be a voice to provide inspiration and passion for a better school and community. Education in the form of classroom instruction can bring about needed change. Make your school an institution of social justice in action. Boldness has never been more needed and more critical for our students' future.

Bring new voices to the conversation through guest speakers, distinctively different career fairs, classroom lessons and parent exchanges. Facilitate dialogue on the topics of race, justice and equity. Provide culturally sensitive opportunities for parents to be engaged in creating a safe, respectful school environment.

Find people in your schools who have the same sense of urgency to create change. Build your ally base, but don't ignore those who resist change. They need our involvement, hard as it might be at times. Make connections with community members. Bring them in to discuss race relations in large groups or maybe to provide a safe place for small groups to vent their fears or frustrations about race relations. It's always risky when you bring in an outsider, regardless of if the message is as benign as how to grow a garden or as highly charged as racism. But it's better to take the risk than remain silent.

Will there be backlash or uproar if the message is offensive to some? Yes, and there are a few cases, *Parker v. Hurley*, 2007 and *Morrison v. Board of Education of Boyd County*, 2006, in which the court sent parents the message that they did not have a constitutionally protected right to tell the public school district what they could teach. Some parents, educators and community members might issue an outcry that students should not be exposed to the harsh realities of racism and that we should not tackle the subject. From an uncomfortable place can come growth. Students are already exposed, and it's far better for us to help them frame the message wrapped in solutions than to leave racism unaddressed.

PROFESSIONAL BOUNDARIES: GIFT TAKING

Dear School Counselor:
You are cordially invited to a two-day, all-expense-paid trip to Courterney University. Accommodations will be at a local bed and breakfast. The first day's activities will include golfing at the nearby Sunny Hills Country Club and a trip to the horse track, where you will receive $50 for wagering. On the morning of the second day, you will visit our university so you can speak with first-hand knowledge about the fine programs we have to offer your students. You will return home via commercial airlines the afternoon of the second day.
Sincerely,
Your College Admissions Representative

Is it unethical to receive perks with more than a token monetary value? For elementary and middle school counselors, consider a parallel situation. Can you accept gifts from parents whom you know want to influence you to gain advantage for their child, such as placement with certain teachers?

Points to Consider

This hypothetical case took an all-too-real twist when *The New York Times* ran the article "Wooing of Guidance Counselors is Raising Profiles and Eyebrows" (Winter, 2004). The article talked about school counselors receiving expensive perks such as trips to Vail, hockey tickets, nights at luxury hotels, spa treatments and other presents with monetary value in return for favorable or preferential treatment toward their universities. In the words of Mr. Davolt, a Denver College admissions representative who had been playing host to high school counselors, "It makes a huge difference as to how they're going to convey our university" (Winter, 2004). Although the writer interviewed only one school counselor at a private school, the article reads as if lavish trips were the norm. *The New York Times* implied that school counselors are willing partners in accepting perks designed to influence their college-advising role while also placing a focus on admissions representatives' questionable practices. There are ethical and, sometimes, legal considerations when accepting anything of monetary value if the expectation is to influence you to advantage one college over another.

This article did not represent the professional. School counselors visit colleges to develop relationships so they can advantage their students who might need a personal contact to help them. School counselors know so much more about a student than can be measured by an ACT or SAT score; relationship grooming is often the difference in being able to advocate that students who don't meet the school's profile be given a chance to prove themselves. School counselors learn first-hand information from stepping foot on a college campus. Being able to say to a student, "I have been there, and this is what I experienced" is quite different from talking to a student about a college in the abstract.

The overwhelming majority of school counselors would take college trips, learn about the school's offerings, place the information in their memory banks and use it only in appropriate and fair manners. School counselors will do what is best for students; the only advantage the college can expect is that, as a result of the visit to the campus and meetings with the college representatives, the school counselor will know more about the school. Previously, the college might have been only a name in a guidebook.

As Bob Bardwell, a Massachusetts school counselor, stated, "The problem with the given scenario is the extent of the gift. It would be one thing to simply invite the school counselors to the university, feed them and put them up overnight, but, to include golfing and money for gambling is excessive. In the past, I have been offered tickets to Broadway and professional sporting events, which I have declined because I considered them excessive. For a school counselor to visit a college, eat a meal, take a tour and leave with a college T-shirt – all while knowing he or she will not give that college an advantage when working with students – that is a different story" (personal communication, Jan. 3, 2021).

It is unethical to receive perks of more than a token monetary value, especially if the college is overtly trying to influence the school counselor. To ban school counselors (legally or ethically) from participating in such events to better get to know the institution, which in turn will likely help students, would be problematic. The key is to find a compromise in which the college gets its name and opportunities for students known to school counselors, for the school counselors to receive some incentive for their time and willingness to participate, and for school counselors to be careful to not cross a line as to unethically steer a student to a college that is not a good fit.

Steve Schneider, a Wisconsin high school counselor, wrote "Our ethical standards serve two important functions for our profession: First, to provide a basis for self-reflection on what motivates our practice and, secondly, to assure others where our motivation lies. Living by ethical standards requires honest reflection about why we do what we do. Reflecting on the following question could provide some direction: Do a lot of the students from my school attend this school, making it important for me to know more about it? Visiting schools to learn about programs is a good practice, especially local schools that pull large numbers of graduates" (personal communication, Dec. 22, 2021).

The reflective processes of determining when a perk becomes a conflict of interest is at the center of this situation. It is about being independent and knowing when lines are potentially being crossed. We expect professionals to understand when factors can lead to influencing private and personal interests. That is why school counselors training addresses metacognitive processes. In other words, we must have a reflective voice for any given situation, and we must have the courage to set boundaries of what we can and cannot accept. This extends to decision-making that equally considers avoiding the appearance of having a conflict of interest.

Typically, when a school counselor is in ethical trouble, their lack of discernment regarding the appearance of a conflict of interest is clearly at the heart of where things went very wrong. Usually, there is a rationalization process that preceded the decision. They justify... "I can still be objective," no matter what is offered. This rationalization ignores the fact that a loss of objectivity always prevents perception of when there is indeed a loss of objectivity.

In a Position to Know: A School Counselor Educator Speaks

The case presented at the beginning of the chapter is revisited here and answered by a school counseling leader Mary Waters-Bilbo, a school counselor educator. Read her opinion to see what you can learn. Compare her answer with your approach.

STANDARD OF CARE

Raney did not have a legal and ethical course in her school counseling master's degree program and is facing a tough situation in which a parent is suing Raney and the school district because the parent believes Raney acted illegally. Raney is not worried. She knows she is covered by vicarious liability, as the school district (the deep pockets) will be the one sued. She also believes her standard of care is intact, as it was not her fault she did not have the proper training in her master's degree program. Is Raney correct in her assumptions?

Raney appears to be unfamiliar with the ASCA Ethical Standards for School Counselors, which guide our work with minors in schools. Although she didn't take a legal/ethical course as part of her master's degree, that deficiency will not protect her; our profession expects school counselors to continue their studies. The Ethical Standards (2022b) clearly state that school counselors engage in routine, content-applicable professional development to stay up to date on trends and needs of students and other stakeholders and regularly attend training on current legal and ethical responsibilities.

Furthermore, ASCA's Standards for School Counselor Preparation Programs (2020a), states, "Candidates demonstrate ethical and culturally responsive behavior, maintain the highest standard of professionalism and legal obligation, and use consultation and ongoing critical reflection to prevent ethical lapses. (Standard 7).

This requirement to continue our professional development is reinforced through the ASCA School Counselor Professional Standards & Competencies. In particular, II-B-4H clearly states school counselors are expected to "continuously engage in professional development and use resources to inform and guide ethical and legal work."

These clear expectations point to an outcome not anticipated by the school counselor described in this case. Although her master's degree program did not have a separate legal and ethical course, the topic was almost certainly infused throughout the program. The ASCA Ethical Standards (2022b) and the expected competencies underline the need to be self-reflective and seek out professional development on a continual basis. Although Raney has representation from her district, she will have to explain her gap in knowledge to the courts if called to give a deposition or testimony. Professionals are expected to hold themselves to a high standard.

– Mary Waters-Bilbo, Ph.D., Assistant Professor, Northeastern State University

Making Connections

1. You are a school counselor who has a solid reputation as an effective professional. Your live-in boyfriend parties hard on weekends, and, along with a group of friends, you usually end up consuming large quantities of alcohol. Several times the police have come when the neighbors have complained about cars and loud music. Lately, the parties have been getting longer and wilder. Does your behavior pose an ethical question? Answer the case by discussing how your behavior is affected by standard of care (the behavior expected of the reasonably competent professional).

2. Your principal occasionally asks questions about the content of your counseling sessions. You worry about this principal's trustworthiness with information, as you have heard her repeat information others have told her, often embellishing the information to make herself look important. What do you do when the principal asks you for information? How would you use your ethical standards and qualified privilege to help you in this situation, without alienating your principal?

3. Grant money for career programs is currently plentiful, and your school is submitting a proposal; however, the equipment and expertise required to be in place at the time of grant submission are currently nonexistent. Administration tells you not to worry. If your school receives the grant, it will quickly gather the equipment needed and send you for training to acquire the needed expertise. Are there ethical violations here?

4. School climate is especially glum at your school. Your principal asks you to help her with the situation by conducting small focus groups with all grade levels to try to determine the causes. You are certain you will find that many faculty members are discontented with the principal. Faculty members constantly complain that the principal is inconsistent, shows favoritism and micromanages. Do you agree to hold the focus groups? If you do agree, what must you consider in advance before conducting the focus groups? What are the pitfalls and the possible advantages of agreeing to help in this manner? What parameters must you set with the principal in advance? Discuss how confidentiality and informed consent should play a role in this ethical dilemma.

5. Your principal wants you to conduct focus groups to evaluate a disciplinary policy that is drawing much fire from faculty as too permissive. Defend one of these two statements:
   - A school counselor is an appropriate person to lead a focus group of this nature.
   - A school counselor should always try to avoid running a focus group of this type.

6. You are concerned about a policy your school district has established for reporting students who express suicidal ideation. The policy requires that a three-part form be completed, with one part going in the educational record, one part going to the district-level and one part staying in the school counselor's office. You think the policy is an invasion of students' confidentiality and that it eliminates school counselor judgment. Discuss how you will address this situation. Who else needs to be involved? Who can help you advocate for change?

7. One of your students, 11-year-old Erin, lost a parent to cancer two months ago. Throughout her parent's illness, you tried to help Erin, but her grades continued to slip, and she lost her enthusiasm for playing soccer. You have a good relationship with Erin, and you continue to see her as often as you can. The last conversation you had with her surviving parent turned flirtatious, and you accepted a date. Are you involved in an ethical dilemma? Whose needs are being met?

Chapter 2 Quiz

1) Examples of avoidable dual relationships could be:
   a. Going to church with a student in your caseload
   b. Having a student's mother as a colleague
   c. Sharing a hotel room with a student's father while the student is in the adjoining suite
   d. Having the principal's child on your caseload
   e. Coaching a student in basketball and having her on your caseload

2) A boundary crossing is:
   a. Leaving school grounds without permission during the school day
   b. A departure from the verbal and physical distances normally maintained in a counseling interaction
   c. Speaking to a developmentally delayed student about the student's personal life
   d. A boundary violation
   e. More serious than a dual relationship

3) If a school counselor is in a dual relationship with a student, the school counselor:
   a. Explains to the student that he or she is limited in being able to serve the student
   b. Must make certain not to use his or her power differential to exploit the student
   c. Should always have the student moved to another school counselor's caseload
   d. Must never engage in a dual relationship
   e. Can rest assured that he or she is dealing with a mature-minded student and can count on this to protect both student and school counselor

4) Which best describes the school counselor's role?
   a. Always refer students to other school counselors to avoid a dual relationship
   b. Never enter into a dual relationship
   c. Try to avoid a dual relationship by changing your habits such as where you shop, eat out, go to church, send your children to school, etc.
   d. Recognize when you are in a dual relationship, and be prepared with steps to minimize negative implications
   e. Dual relationships are not an issue for school counselors, as we do not do therapy with students

5) A boundary crossing that moves school counselors too far outside of the role of school counselor is of concern because:
   a. A student might misinterpret the attention as other than advocacy
   b. Of the danger of countertransference, where the school counselor is meeting the school counselor's own needs ahead of the student
   c. A student who distorts in their mind why the school counselor is moving far outside of the scope and boundaries of the normal school counselor/student relationship puts the student at risk for disrupted attachments
   d. All of the above
   e. A and B above

Key Terms

Corporal punishment
Defamation
Dual relationships
Ethical standards
Falsifying student records
Maintaining student records
Monitoring your competence
Planned Parenthood
Prevailing community standards
Privity
Professional communication
Professional distance
Professionalism
Slander

Chapter 3

Cyberspace

Objectives

By the time you have completed this chapter, you should be able to:

- Discuss the influence technology has on the school counseling profession
- Identify the different aspects of the ASCA National Model related to the use of technology in school counseling
- Understand safety precautions students, school counselors and parents/guardians can take while interacting on social media websites
- Analyze the changes in school counseling as a result of the move to virtual school during the COVID-19 pandemic
- Reflect on the consequences of unprofessional behavior on websites
- Discuss policies and regulations regarding the use of technological devices in schools and the appropriate response taken in the case of a breach of those policies

Ethical Standards Addressed in This Chapter

The ASCA Ethical Standards for School Counselors (2022b) most relevant to this chapter are the following:

- School counselors advocate with appropriate school officials for acceptable encryption standards to be utilized for stored data and currently acceptable algorithms to be utilized for data in transit. (A.2.o.)
- School counselors avoid using software programs without the technological capabilities to protect student information based upon legal specifications and currently acceptable security standards. (A.2.p.)
- School counselor advocate for physical and virtual workspaces that are arranged to protect the confidentiality of students' communications and records. (A.2.q.)
- School counselors refrain from the use of personal social media, text and email accounts to interact with students unless sanctioned by the school district. Adhere to legal, ethical, district and school policies and guidelines when using technology with students and stakeholders. (A.5.h.)
- School counselors advocate for equal access to technology for all students. (A.15.a.)
- School counselors promote the safe and responsible use of technology in collaboration with educators and families. (A.15.d.)

- School counselors promote the benefits and clarify the limitations of various appropriate technological applications. (A.15.e.)
- School counselors understand challenges with confidentiality when using email and establish protocols and boundaries for responding to emails. (A.15.g.)
- School counselors advocate against alert tools or apps requiring constant monitoring by school personnel. These tools are not aligned with the nature and function of school counseling. (A.15.i.).
- School counselors adhere to the same legal and ethical standards in a virtual/distance/hybrid setting as in face-to-face setting (A.16.a.)
- School counselors recognize and address the limitation of virtual/distance/hybrid school counseling confidentiality, which may include unintended viewers or recipients. (A.16.d.)
- School counselors recognize the challenges in virtual/distance/hybrid settings of assisting students considering suicide, including but not limited to identifying their physical location, keeping them engaged on the call or device, contacting their parents/guardians and getting help to their location. (A.16.g.)

The full text of the ASCA Ethical Standards for School Counselors covers additional standards applicable to this chapter and can be found at *www.schoolcounselor.org*.

Introduction

Technology has influenced the school counseling profession, including fundamentally altering the way school counselors interact with students, school personnel, parents/guardians and school counseling supervisors. In 2013, 2017 and 2021, Steele, Nuckols and Stone conducted online surveys of ASCA members and affiliates on their professional use of online technologies and their beliefs regarding the role of technology in school counseling. The survey results reflect a striking change in attitudes and behaviors around technology coinciding with the COVID-19 pandemic. In March 2020, the vast majority of school counselors were suddenly thrust into online school counseling, and 50.8 million students had to rely on virtual learning (Savitz-Romer, 2021).

As might be expected, this health crisis accounted for the sweeping change in school counselors' comfort level with technology and their perceived compatibility with online tools for school counseling. For many school counselors, experimentation with virtual tools during the pandemic inspired changes to their delivery of services, even once students were back in person. Even if previously hesitant to use virtual tools, school counselors discovered that these tools can be effective for delivery and may better facilitate reaching all students with counseling support. Video conferencing improved markedly, allowing school counselors to deliver lessons more easily to multiple grade levels simultaneously or to visit classrooms online. (Steele, Nuckols & Stone, 2021).

The results of the 2013 Steele, Nuckols and Stone survey showed school counselors used technology primarily to access their district's student information management systems but not for other tools such as document sharing, social media or video conferencing. Less than a decade later in 2021, school counselors' technology use was significantly different. School counselors were using document sharing, and more than two-thirds were using video conferencing in their professional practice. Even school counselors who prefer delivering service in-person responded to the survey that they often use technology to design and develop their counseling programs and to track progress toward goals by analyzing data. In contrast, the use of social media to interact with students and families increased but was not widespread.

Additionally in 2021, school counselors, who in 2013 responded that online communication was not compatible with their program, reversed course with three-quarters responding that it could be useful in their role. Email communication and video conferencing increased access to parents and outside professionals. As a group, school counselors understand the effectiveness and convenience of video conferencing in helping them connect with parents while the approach with students still gets mixed reviews.

Do you feel online communication is compatible with your school counseling role?
Strongly agree *10.8%*
Agree *66.5%*
Disagree *17.4%*
Strongly disagree *4%*
Not applicable to me and my work *3%*
(Steele, Nuckols & Stone, 2021)

Additionally, this same survey asked the frequency with which respondents used nine devices or applications in their professional work with a rating of never, rarely, occasionally, moderate amount or a great deal. The percentages for the two highest-use ratings show an increase from 2017 and a sizable number of ASCA members are using technology in their work. Compare the difference between the 2017 and the recent 2021 survey.

Device or Application	**2017 Percentage who rated "moderate" or "a great deal of use"**	**2021 Percentage who rated "moderate" or "a great deal of use"**
Document sharing, e.g. Google Docs	82.7%	92.8%
iPhone/smart phone or other mobile device	45.8%	51.4%
School counseling department website	35.1%	50.1%
School counseling department blog, Twitter		6.1%
Facebook or other social media	17.7%	18.5%
Instant messaging	17.6%	23.1%
Video conferencing program, e.g. zoom, google meet	8.8%	69.1%

(Steele, Nuckols & Stone, 2021)

Email has significantly changed the way school counselors communicate with parents/guardians, students, teachers and administrators. Email is now a necessary part of school counselors' approach to implementing their program. In the survey, 92.1% of the respondents said they use email to communicate with students and/or families regarding meeting/scheduling, and 72.2% use email to discuss concerns regarding students' academic progress. School counselors are wired even during off hours. According to this same survey, 82.8% of respondents check their email regularly outside of work hours. Sixty-four percent of respondents have their work email connected to an iPad, personal phone or other personal mobile device. This same survey demonstrated that email is used as a way to communicate with students and/or families for academic planning (57.4%), college counseling (39.9%) and career counseling (36.2%). Email is also used to offer resources such as scholarship/program opportunities (62.7%). A sizable percentage of the work school counselors do with families, students and other staff members is through email, especially with other school staff (Steele, Nuckols & Stone, 2021).

How often do you use email to communicate with students and/or families?

	2017 Students/ families	**2017 School staff**	**2021 Students/ families**	**2021 School staff**
Schedule meetings	85.3%	94.3%	92.1%	96.0%
Discuss concerns regarding academic progress	65.5%	78.8%	72.2%	86.5%
Discuss social/emotional concerns	51.3%	68.6%	64.6%	76.4%
Share school or counseling information	57.2%	64.2%	63.2%	58.7%
Send information regarding your school counseling program	35.1%	45.8%	56.9%	69.3%

(Steele, Stone & Nuckols, 2017; 2021)

Face-to-face interaction is still the primary means of communicating with all stakeholders, but email supersedes phone calls as a means for school counselors to communicate with other educators (Steele, Stone & Nuckols, 2017, 2021). Respondents spending half or more than half their time in this mode of communication.

Within the time you spend communicating with students and families, what percentage do you use each of the following means of communication:

Communication method	**2017 Students/ families**	**2017 School staff**	**2021 Students/ families**	**2021 School staff**
Face-to-face	65%	63.4%	38.8%	42.2%
Phone	26.1%	15%	18.8%	7.1%
Email	23%	56%	28.1%	38.7%
Video conferencing	1.1%	1.3%	10.6%	7.2%
Instant messaging	1.1%	2.4%	1.3%	1.6%
Texting	1.4%	3.1%	2.5%	3.3%

School counselors are even able to access student data remotely (97.9%). One of the advantages of using technology within the school counseling practice is the access it affords as a common platform for communication and information dissemination. Technology is viewed as an essential component of life for students in today's schools. Integrating and using technological advancements such as electronic newsletters, audio files, webpages, and presentations show the school counselor is keeping up and trying to stay engaged with students and parents/guardians (Hassouneh & Alzoubi, 2019).

ASCA NATIONAL MODEL AND TECHNOLOGY

It is more efficient and effective to implement the ASCA National Model through the use of technology. The four components of a comprehensive school counseling program are: deliver, define, manage, assess. The delivery component is 80% or more of the ASCA National Model and is significantly aided by the use of technology (ASCA, 2019a).

Direct Student Services

Within the delivery component of the ASCA National Model are direct and indirect services. Direct services are in-person interactions between school counselors and students and include core curriculum, individual student planning and responsive services (ASCA, 2019a). School counseling delivery can include synchronous and asynchronous online delivery where one is not physically co-located with the student, thus, person-to-person rather than in-person.

Core curriculum: School counseling core curriculum is structured lessons built around competencies for students' developmental level. The core curriculum is delivered throughout the school's overall curriculum and is systematically presented by school counselors in collaboration with other professional educators in K–12 classroom and group activities (ASCA, 2019a). When asked how often, if at all, they deliver or perform school counseling instruction, individual or group counseling, appraisal/advisement, and indirect student services in an online setting, 378 ASCA members responded as follows:

Always 4.4%
Most of the time 6%
About half time 2%
Sometimes 43%
Never 41.8%
(Steele, Stone & Nuckols, 2021)

Individual student planning: Individual student planning is a systemic, ongoing set of activities to help students set and reach goals for their future plans. College and career readiness is just one area where school counselors are aided by technology in individual student planning. For school counselors to adequately equip students with valuable information about college and career readiness, they must access the same technology resources as students and parents and they can use that technology to conduct student assessments, including career inventories, personality questionnaires, disposition surveys, and progress checks (Goodrich et al., 2020).Promoting the use of technology allows increasing the communication and collaboration among parents, counselors, and students. Online career tools are often viewed as a resource of planning and support; allowing them to demonstrate to be valuable instruments to assist in career exploration and development. (Cerrito & Behun, 2020).

One technology we know teens use on a daily basis is text messaging. For many teens, texting is their dominant form of communication with their friends. The Pew Research Center notes that 88% of teens text their friends occasionally, while 60% do so daily (Anderson & Jiang, 2018). Therefore, school counselors can leverage texting to communicate proactively with their students in the area of individual student planning. Text messaging as a promising component of enhancing individual student planning includes timely reminders about tasks and deadlines and the ability to help students break down large projects into manageable tasks. The use of automated texts also frees up school counselors to focus on more individualized and unique support. Text messaging benefits might be more widely utilized in the various individual student planning capacities such as transitions from twelfth grade to college to offset the summer melt phenomenon or preparing eighth graders for high school.

	2021
Always	4.2%
Most of the time	3.7%
About half the time	4.4%
Sometimes	40.3%
Never	47.2%

Responsive services: Responsive services are activities designed to meet students' immediate needs and concerns. Responsive services include individual or small-group counseling or crisis response (ASCA National Model, 2019). According to this same survey (Steele, Stone & Nuckols, 2021), technology is now used at least occasionally for online remote delivery of responsive services by 52.5% of the 378 ASCA members responding.

How often, if at all, do you deliver or perform group counseling, referrals, psychoeducation, peer helping, consultation with other stakeholders (including parents, educators) using technology:

	2021
Always	5%
Most of the time	7.5%
About half the time	11.4%
Sometimes	50.3%
Never	25.8%

Indirect Student Services

Indirect services are provided on behalf of students as a result of school counselors' interactions with others. These services are delivered through strategies such as referrals, consultation and collaboration. ASCA member respondents indicated how frequently they used an online or remote setting for system support. In 2017, the most frequently used resources were ASCA, or local school district options, independent reading, and training provided by a degree or credentialing program. By 2021, counselors most often sought training with technology through online communities and peer collaboration. Interestingly, the use of training provided by credentialing or degree programs declined markedly over the same period. Technology seems to naturally lend itself to crowdsourcing, and often online communities or chat groups can point to novel apps or tools that have not yet found a place in structured training programs. The current state of the profession may be an opportunity for degree and credentialing programs to incorporate the use of technology more fully for school counseling into their curricula (Steele, Nuckols, Stone, 2021).

How often, if at all, do you use technology for system support (includes professional development, consultation, collaboration, program management, operations):

	2021
Always	5.%
Most of the time	7.5%
About half the time	11.4%
Sometimes	50.3%
Never	25.8%

In addition to technology contributing to the delivery component of the ASCA National Model, data use under the management component happens more efficiently with technology. A school counselor has access to computer programs to manage and analyze student data. Curriculum, small-group and closing-the-gap action plans are all positively affected by technology (ASCA, 2019a; Hayden, Poynton & Sabella, 2010).

Finding their technological voice helps school counselors with closing-the-gap action plans to demonstrate the discrepancies between those students who are advantaged and those students who are being left out of the success equation. Technology increases effective advocacy by helping school counselors connect students to challenging coursework, safety nets and opportunities.

In the assess component of the model, technology helps school counselors demonstrate the effectiveness of the school counseling program in measurable terms. School counselors analyze school and school counseling program data to determine how students are different as a result of the school counseling program. School counselors use that information to show the impact of the school counseling program on student achievement, attendance and behavior. The data are then used to guide future action and improve future results for all students. It is easy to see how school counselors can incorporate technology to improve this process (ASCA, 2019a).

School districts are equipped to maintain student information in database systems, unleashing the power of simple and complex data analyses to identify and track student outcomes. Districts and school counselors with data access can cross-tabulate data to look at more than one factor at a time. For example, data on the students with the highest number of discipline referrals can be cross tabulated with factors such as grades and attendance to discover factors for intervention and measure outcomes..

ASCA POSITION ON TECHNOLOGY

ASCA has issued a position statement, The School Counselor and Student Safety and the Use of Technology (ASCA, 2017), supporting school counselors in encouraging students to take full advantage of technological resources. The collaboration of school counselors, educators, parents/guardians and law enforcement officials is necessary to ensure students' protection and aid in disclosing possible risks of Internet use. Risks constantly increase as more students access and use the Internet. Hence, students must be taught to excel in an industrialized world where high-paying jobs and business growth are dependent on technology (ASCA, 2017). The ability to navigate technological devices determines how students survive and excel globally. As early as the postsecondary level, students must be able to use technology and be aware of their digital footprint, which allows them to be vulnerable to privacy invasion and may even jeopardize their safety (ASCA, 2017). Other behavioral, safety and privacy risks students may face due to technology are:

- online addictions
- invasion of privacy and disclosure of personal information
- inappropriate online communications
- easy access to inappropriate content and media
- cheating and copyright infringement
- cyberbullying/harassment
- sexual predators

(ASCA, 2017)

School counselors engage in professional development to improve and maintain digital literacy, which, coupled with expertise in human development, allows them to provide educators and families with guidelines for the appropriate use of technology by students (ASCA, 2017). School counselors must always consider actions that are in students' best interest when using and advising students about technology. Technology has many advantages for students in today's society, such as providing opportunities for growth, learning, exploration, communication, networking and collaboration (ASCA, 2017). However, students are especially vulnerable to the benefits and risks of technology. Therefore, school counselors, school personnel and parents/guardians can collaborate to promote Internet safety.

Getting Started: What Would You Do?

In a departure from the other chapters in the book, there will be four cases answered at the end of the chapter. A school counselor educator, the ASCA deputy executive director and a practicing school counselor who are experts in the field of school counseling and technology will weigh in on some critical issues. Before you read their responses, formulate in your own mind how you would approach this ethical dilemma.

Social/Emotional Counseling in a Virtual World

I've just been hired as a school counselor at a virtual high school. How can I meet students' social/emotional needs online?

Electronic Storage of Student Information

Alexis, a middle school counselor, has been working diligently to better integrate technology in her work so she can more effectively and efficiently help students. She has found Google Drive to be especially helpful. Are there precautions, uses and/or advantages to using Google Drive?

Confidentiality in a Virtual High School

The administration is looking to you for suggestions regarding procedures the school counseling department will use for the section of the server where all educators are to keep notes on every student. The notes section is to record summaries of emails, phone calls, text messages and face-to-face interactions. The principal explains it is not optional. Every faculty and administrative staff member must use this section so collaboration can happen to optimize each student's education. This means it will be visible to all educators at the school. You are uneasy about the fact that school counselors' notes will be there for all educators to see. What will you advocate for when you meet with the principal?

Online Counseling and Suicidal Ideation

Seth, a student in your online high school, has been in a tailspin academically and emotionally since his mother died a year ago. One of his friends forwarded some of Seth's electronic conversations about death to you. Seth's father feels his son is being overly dramatic and does not believe Seth would ever harm himself. Then, in a call to you, Seth describes using his father's gun or pills and ending it all. You keep Seth on the phone while you try to get his father on another line, but Seth informs you his father's cell phone is ringing right next to him as his father forgot to take it with him. He says he must go and hangs up the phone with you abruptly. What do you do?

Working Through Case Studies

TECHNOLOGY SKILLS TO OPTIMIZE YOUR OBLIGATIONS TO STUDENTS

Your colleague brags about her refusal to learn anything about technology. She does not access student data in determining program goals nor does she use online technology for even simple approaches such as email. This technology-free practice causes additional work for the office staff and her fellow school counselors. Are there legal and ethical implications for her behavior?

Points to Consider

Communication and information sharing through online technology are fast becoming integral components of school counselors' ethical practice. To be relevant and effective, school counselors have to work diligently to be competent and efficient with online communication and information technology. The ASCA Ethical Standards for School Counselors (2022b) encourage school counselors to "promote the benefits and clarify the limitations of various appropriate technological applications" (A.15.e.). The Council on the Accreditation of Counseling and Related Educational Programs requires preparation programs to ensure school counseling students are prepared to use technology to implement a comprehensive school counseling program. Online communication can offer school counselors a diverse set of effective modes of remote interaction to support professional development, networking and consultation.

In the 2021 technology survey by Steele, Stone and Nuckols, 378 ASCA members responded. About half of the respondents indicated using online technologies at least occasionally in delivering classroom lessons, events, activities and student planning tasks such as advising. Data-informed decision making, an important part of the school counselor's job, is enhanced by using technology to collect, disaggregate and report data. Important communication with students can be facilitated through online technologies rather than relying solely on infrequent, isolated, individual appointments or access to classrooms for lessons. Continually seeking professional development in technology to enhance capabilities is the standard of care and ethical practice required of school counselors.

PERSONAL LIFE AND ELECTRONIC PICTURES

The cameras are taking it all in as you celebrate a friend's bachelorette party. You end up drinking too much, and pictures surface on Facebook, where it looks like your hand is on the crotch of the male dancer hired for the occasion. In your words, you truly look "awful, drunk and vulgar." Someone forwarded the picture to your principal, who is considering taking action against you. Can you be disciplined or terminated for your behavior?

Points to Consider

In the past, school counselors found it easy to separate their personal and professional lives, but now, with the emergence of electronic media, the lines are easily blurred. Standard of care, the benchmark defining what the reasonable, competent educator would do, is a high standard for school counselors specifically and educators in general (see Chapter 2 Professionalism for more information). Through technology, some educators have been caught irreparably damaging their image in moments of lapsed judgment. Many educators have been terminated or reprimanded because of personal messages displayed on their social networking profiles. Dozens of cases demonstrate educators can and do lose their job over online comments and pictures.

Todd Erdman, a teacher at Umatilla Middle School for 12 years, was terminated when TikTok videos surfaced of him drinking a beer, cursing and joking that it was before school and he needed the alcohol because of the "idiots" he worked with, among other lewd videos (Postal, 2021). At Rubidoux High School, a school that is over 90% Hispanic/Latino, school counselor Patricia Crawford was fired after she made Facebook comments criticizing students who boycotted school to protest Trump's immigration policy (O'Brien, 2020). She responded to students' comments saying, "get over yourselves" after she claimed the day without them resulted in the cafeteria being cleaner, having less traffic on the roads and no discipline issues.

SOCIAL MEDIA AND SCHOOL COUNSELORS

You have always been told by other educators to refrain from having a professional Facebook site. Now many schools and school counselors are doing just that. You are always struggling with ways to increase outreach with students on critical timely information about career and college admissions. You have decided to develop a Facebook page. What are the legal and ethical advantages and potential pitfalls you need to address, if any?

Points to Consider

It comes as no surprise that educators are among the millions of users of Facebook and YouTube, with Instagram, Tok-tok, and Snapchat being most commonly used by adults under age 30 (Auxier & Anderson, 2021). Out of necessity and problem behavior, school districts are implementing policies and regulations controlling social interactions between educators and students. The Association of American Educators (2011) proposes that professional educators must "act with conscientious effort to exemplify the highest ethical standards (p.1)." ASCA members indicate they infrequently interact with students or families using social media, but when they do, it is often through Facebook.

If you interact with students and/or families on social media, which do you use for that interaction?

	2017	**2021**
Facebook	10.7%	29.3%
Twitter	13.6%	20.9%
Instagram	2.9%	18.0%
LinkedIn	0.7%	0.8%
Do not interact with students/families on social media	9%	47.3%

(Steele, Stone & Nuckols, 2017, 2021)

Missouri implemented the Amy Hestir Student Protection Act, now called the Missouri Facebook Statute, which prohibits public school teachers from utilizing any form of social media granting them exclusive access to students. This law followed after 75 Missouri educators lost their jobs because of inappropriate online posts with students. Louisiana and New Jersey have followed Missouri's lead by passing legislation requiring school districts to establish electronic communication policies between teachers and students (De Fina, 2020).

De Fina (2020) suggests school counselors do not friend or follow current students, parents or recent former students on personal social media accounts to protect students from grooming behaviors and staff from allegations of inappropriate behavior. Other recommendations by Jencius are to keep personal and professional Facebook and Twitter pages separate; reserve your professional name for messages sent through professional accounts; refrain from using inappropriate user names on personal accounts; provide students with a written policy regarding work hours and approximate response times; avoid frequent visits to students' Twitter or Facebook pages; and ensure school, agency or institution policies are followed regarding social media (personal communication, November 2012).

Do your students or families have access to your personal and/or professional social media accounts?

	2017	**2021**
Professional account	21.6%	34.0%
Personal account	1.4%	9.5%
Both professional and personal account	3.7%	7.8%
Students/families do not have access to my social media	73.2%	48.7%

(Steele, Stone & Nuckols, 2017, 2021)

It is helpful if school officials work together to ensure all students have access to and are knowledgeable about online educational outreach information. Students know, but it cannot be assumed they understand, that privacy on Facebook or other social media sites is often not secure. The privacy of anyone's posts cannot be guaranteed and a post can go viral at any time, even years from now (Sabella & Isaacs, 2018).

PROFESSIONAL DISTANCE AND CYBERSPACE

You are a technologically savvy school counselor, and you encourage your students to take advantage of your willingness to engage with them more frequently through technology. You find your tweets, Instagram stories and TikTok videos are more friendly, honest and less formal. You see this as a good communication mode. A group of parents/guardians has become concerned about some of the content of the postings, which are "way too familiar, more like student-to-student conversations than school-counselor-to-student." Are there legal and ethical concerns about your behavior?

Points to Consider

"Professional distance is the space professionals must keep between their professional relationship with another and any other relationship they have with that person" (Crehan, n.d., p.1). This space is necessary for school counselors to be able to fulfill their professional obligations in an impartial way, with a protective boundary between the student and the school counselor. This does not mean school counselors do not extend boundaries; rather, it means when you do extend boundaries you have to do a risk/benefit analysis. The ASCA Ethical Standards (2022b) state, "Recognize that establishing credibility, rapport and an effective working alliance with some students and stakeholders may be facilitated by developing relationships that extend beyond the school day and building" (A.5.b) and "Assess potential risks and benefits prior to extending relationships beyond the school building and school hours" (A.5.c.).

Spanierman v. Hughes (2008) is an example of the vigilance and judgment educators need to use with social networking. Jeffrey Spanierman, a nontenured English teacher, was terminated from his position at a high school in Connecticut. Spanierman tried to reach out to his students by creating a MySpace account to encourage communication (Belch, 2012). The school board fired him because Spanierman's communications with students were "peer-like" conversations that impeded the learning atmosphere. Spanierman filed a lawsuit (*Spanierman v. Hughes*, 576 F. Supp. 2d 292, Dist. Court, D. Connecticut, 2008) but lost in court when it was determined that the destruction of the learning process outweighed the educational value of the MySpace account.

The school counselor/student relationship is naturally an imbalance in power and requires vigilance on the school counselor's part to avoid exploitation. Professional distance provides a buffer space contributing to the safety of students and school counselors to lessen the possibility of exploitation. Consequences arise from crossing into the space between personal and professional relationships with minors in mandated settings such as schools.

The setting and the relationship between student and school counselor require a high standard of care. School counselors should avoid engaging students in peer-like conversations.

With today's social media platforms, it may be possible for students to view educators' content online. Unlike Facebook, which requires a mutual agreement to "friend" one another, apps such as Instagram, Twitter and TikTok allow content to be viewed and commented on without following or adding each other, unless users mark their account as private. Educators have used social media throughout the COVID-19 pandemic to create professional content students can connect to and foster a sense of community among other teachers (Hartung et al., 2022). Those who do engage in these types of social media with their students can maintain professional and personal boundaries by using appropriate language and music, using the apps outside of work hours and being aware that students and parents view these posts (Hartung et al., 2022).

People say and do things in cyberspace they would not ordinarily do in a face-to-face conversation. This is called the disinhibition effect (Wu et al., 2017). The online environment creates a feeling of invisibility and anonymity. This anonymity amplifies the disinhibition effect, resulting in people dropping their guard and revealing too much about themselves, such as secrets, fears or wishes. The sometimes-asynchronous effect (not interacting in real times, such as email and message boards) seems to contribute to the disinhibition effect. "Immediate, real-time feedback from others tends to have a very strong effect on the flow of communication and the amount of information people disclose about themselves" (Wu et al., 2017, p. 196). The appearance of authority is minimized in cyberspace, and the tendency and effect are that people are acting as equals, as in the case of Spanierman, who took on the role of peer and apparently dropped the role of teacher as role model. School counselors who engage in peer-like conversations with students have to ask themselves, "Whose needs are being met? Am I trying to meet my own needs in these familiar peer-like exchanges?"

STUDENT SAFETY ON THE INTERNET

Serena comes to you worried about her friend Althea, who plans to meet up with a boy she met online. However, Serena believes the boy is a man posing as a kid and may harm Althea. What do you do?

Points to Consider

This situation is one of those times when a school counselor will want to talk to the student to impress on her the danger she is putting herself in, and it is highly advisable that with few exceptions the school counselor will immediately alert the students' parents/guardians to possible harm.

Research from Kraut (2020) estimates that there are more than 500,000 active online predators, more than half of whom target children between the ages of 12 and 15. Instant messaging is the medium of choice or internet chatrooms, where it is estimated that this is where just short of 90% of these sexual advances occur. Predators ask for sexually explicit photos and 4% of targeted children have had the predator try to meet with them in person or over the phone. A contributing factor that aids the predators is that 40% of children remove privacy settings so as not to limit attracting more followers. Pedophiles create fake personas to hide their true age and identity, making it easier to connect with children and gain their trust. Dangerous apps are becoming more common and again, aiding the predators with access (The International Centre for Missing & Exploited Children, 2017).

BENEFITS OF ONLINE SCHOOL COUNSELING

You work in the state's virtual high school. You counsel students on various issues just as your brick-and-mortar colleagues do. What do you see as the benefits for your work as compared to that of face-to-face school counseling?

Points to Consider

The online environment has distinct qualities that draw students: accessibility, simplicity, convenience, flexibility and inexpensiveness are a few of the benefits. Online counseling is considered a satisfactory method to provide cost-effective and highly accessible mental health services. Students seeking sessions that don't require face-to-face interactions may find this appealing. Schools could effectively serve their communities by offering online counseling alongside face-to-face counseling to increase the usage of their services (Wong, 2017). Students may not have a need for persistent counseling sessions but may benefit from follow-up to track their progress. Online counseling facilitates a more flexible way to check in on a student's improvements by breaching barriers such as time, scheduling or location limitations (Fischer & Bloomfield, 2020). When dealing with time considerations, text messaging has been found to be useful; giving the counselor more space to better understand and respond to a student. Along with this, it also assists with any obstacles pertaining to language and stigmas associated with help-seeking (Gilly, 2020). The distinct response a school counselor provides to a student while texting is paramount to whether or not that student may return in the future for assistance (Gilly, 2020).

There are a number of research results on the benefits and disadvantages of online counseling via email, real-time chat or video conferencing. Steele, a school counselor at Stanford University's Online High School, recognizes a certain degree of anonymity holds true with the barrier of a monitor but believes it is less a factor for the students with whom she works because her online counseling is through video conferencing. "Granted, video conferencing is not in the flesh, but it is in many respects face-to-face because the school counselor and student can see each other through video conferencing real-time platforms. Video conferencing is certainly different from chat rooms, email or instant messaging, and it has proven to be a powerful medium for supporting my students. Counseling students online may seem paradoxical to support students' social/emotional lives virtually, but many aspects of such support may be easier and more effective within an online educational environment" (Steele, personal communication, March 2022).

In a 2016 study from Stanford University, researchers analyzed 660,000 text messages from 15,000 crisis counseling sessions that used text chat as the medium of support. Researchers identified several counseling skills associated with successful text sessions, including being able to personalize the discussion, getting to the root of the issue quickly and using words or phrases to steer the conversation in a positive and meaningful direction (Althoff et al., 2016). According to the Pew Research Center, 95% of teens have access to a smartphone, and among these teens, 45% say they are online on a near-constant basis (Anderson & Jiang, May 2018). These findings complement many of the goals of solution-focused counseling sessions that are effectively practiced in school settings and indicate that text- or chat-based sessions may facilitate this type of counseling practice" (Steele, 2022).

DISADVANTAGES OF ONLINE SCHOOL COUNSELING

The state's virtual school is assessing its online school counseling program, and you are in charge of improving it. What are some disadvantages of online school counseling the state can address?

Points to Consider

School counselors have always had ethical concerns when working with minors regarding confidentiality, informed consent and multicultural issues, but with virtual counseling services, additional considerations include using social media platforms, providing services online, keeping online records and communicating via email (King-White et al., 2019). Other legal and ethical issues school counselors face are protecting student confidentiality, maintaining rigor in the process of data collection for referrals, knowing and following the school crisis plan or policy, properly handling crises, reporting to children's services, dual relationships and parental rights (King-White et al., 2019).

Less than half as many school counselors in 2021 felt they faced barriers in online communication than in 2017. Technology improvements and a variety of new apps and platforms appear to be enticing school counselors to find tools compatible with their practice. Deficits in 2021 seem to wane as barriers such as time, professional development, technology access and interest dramatically bumped down.

What barriers do you face in using online communications?

	2017	2021
Lack of professional development in the area of online communications	70.3%	23.7%
Lack of time	67.1%	29.5%
Lack of access to online technologies	26.5%	9.2%
Little or no applicability to my role	23.3%	13.8%
Lack of interest	24.2%	10.0%

In this same survey by Steele, Stone and Nuckols (2021), ASCA school counselors responded to the level of technology training they have received indicating 44.4% have received "extensive" or "quite a bit" of training, 41.9% have received "some' training," and 13.7% have received "very little" or no technology training.

Respondents reported in which ways they received technology training.

	2017	2021
Attended webinar or sessions provided by the district or ASCA	66.7%	68.3%
Through independent reading, research on ethics and practice of counseling online	48.3%	64.3%
Received credentialing/certificate such as from NBCC, NCC	7.8%	11.6%
In a degree or credentialing program	30.7%	9.0%
Participating in blogging, communicating with other school counselors on Twitter, Google, Skype, etc.	4%	79.4%
Other	13.7%	10.3%

(Steele, Stone & Nuckols, 2017, 2021)

From a risk-management perspective, school counselors need to know the true identity and location of their students should an emergency arise. It is also important to know the community resources in the student's local area and to make plans for how to respond to an emergency situation during the informed-consent process at the outset of the professional relationship.

TELECOUNSELING IS GAINING MOMENTUM

You are being required to find a space for a student to have a Zoom telecounseling session, to set up the technology, see that the student is ready to go at the appointed time and to stand guard at the door in case the student has a need. Is this legal?

Points to Consider

This is a real case, triggering Steele, Nuckols and Stone (2021) to survey school counselors around this question, "Have any educators in your school been asked by an outside counseling entity to dismiss students from class during the school day to participate in mental health telecounseling?" Of the 380 respondents, 37% said "yes." When asked to comment, respondents had much to say. The comments spanned from how the school supported the efforts, to explain outside counselors were asking too much of the school; however, on balance the majority of respondents described how telecounselors are trying to be respectful and provide services in the least-intrusive way to respect both the educators and student's time.

Telecounseling is simply counseling services using technology such as videoconferencing, text, chat rooms and other internet-supported approaches. The positives are obvious, as school counselors in rural settings have always struggled with their students' access to outside counseling. Access has been a barrier regardless of the geographic setting for many school counselors whose students cannot participate in agency counseling due to transportation, scheduling issues and other barriers. COVID-19 has created an awareness of and an increase in mental health issues for our students.

Telecounseling may be an opportunity for school counselors to grow their reach by bringing agencies into the school through technology to help them meet students' needs. Much remains to be seen in the legal and ethical implications of this approach. One area is compliance with the Health Insurance Portability and Accountability Act (HIPAA) to protect client privacy. The technology used in schools and the barriers to secure, private settings may mean a breach of HIPAA compliance. The other legal and ethical issues to sort through is whose responsibility it is to ensure that technology works properly. Not everyone is comfortable with technology. The very nature of technology counseling makes some verbal and body language cues difficult to read, and in the case of text or phone counseling, these cues are nonexistent. School counselors also recognize how important face to face is for developing a relationship with a student. Can a school counselor do the same with a student if there is not face to face at all even for the first meeting? These and other questions are areas for research in the future.

ETHICS OF ONLINE SCHOOL COUNSELING

You are an online school counselor. You have just been thrown into the role as the state just came up with a virtual high school for students. No one has given you guidance in the ethics of online school counseling. Where do you go for help?

Points to Consider

The new modality of online school counseling brings with it previously undiscovered ethical concerns. Ethical standards are what separate the counseling occupation from other professions, and professional standards are needed for world of online counseling. Counseling and social work organizations have been proactive in developing Internet regulations. ASCA (2022b), the National Board of Certified Counselors (2016a), the American Counseling Association (ACA, 2014), the National Association for Social Workers (2021), the American Mental Health Counselors Association (2020) and the International Society for Mental Health Online (ISHMO) (2000) have all developed ethical standards for online counseling.

COVID-19 THRUST THE VIRTUAL WORLD ON ALL SCHOOL COUNSELORS

I never thought I would be a virtual counselor, but COVID-19 changed all that. The local university wants me to do a presentation around the lessons I learned in delivering virtual school counseling. What should I include?

Points to Consider

At the beginning of the move to virtual schools from the COVID-19 pandemic, many school counselors felt a burden to find ways to continue their work. School counselors were especially concerned about the technology platforms they were using. Our profession is based on the trusting relationship born out of confidentiality. However, it is too burdensome for school counselors to have to figure out all the encryptions and privacy protections of the school district platform and software. The school district, not the school counselor, is responsible for ensuring the software adheres to the federal laws governing privacy.

School counselors frequently voiced their concerns about respecting confidentiality as they learned to work in this new normal. School districts were providing directives more applicable to teacher success and, in some cases, disastrous to school counselor/student confidentiality. Confidentiality does not have the same meaning for administrators and teachers, and this has been very apparent. School counselors have been consulting and collaborating with their administrators to state their cases and make their needs known. An article in ASCA School Counselor magazine (Stone, 2020) reviewed for school counselors' areas to consider when working virtually. Some of the questions and answers follow:

Student Confidentiality

Is my written communication and video communication with students in platforms such as Google Hangout considered an educational record?
Yes, both written and video communications are educational records if we "maintain them," according to the Family Educational Rights and Privacy Act (FERPA). Anything we "maintain" that is directly related to a student is an educational record. If you erase the conversation, then it is not a record and not maintained, therefore, not an educational record. It must be maintained to be an educational record.

Can parents request access to any video recording I am using to virtually communicate with my students? Who else can have access to the video?
Yes. If the video is maintained, it is an educational record. It is easier to maintain confidentiality in a brick-and-mortar setting. If you are writing or recording conversations, check in advance if you'll be able to erase conversations after the session.

Use informed consent, and make sure students understand the limits of confidentiality in a virtual world. Anyone who is under contract and control of the district and has been designated as having legitimate educational interest (LEI) for a particular student's information can have access. In other words, if the administration has been deemed LEI for all students in the school, then they can have access to the video. The same goes if teachers or paraprofessionals are allowed to access records of students in their charge. Advocate for a limited number of educators to have LEI for your students' archived counseling sessions or, better yet, advocate that all counseling sessions be erased following the exchange.

Is it necessary for me to have each parent sign a consent form now that we have moved to virtual counseling?
No. If your district required this in your previous setting, you would continue the practice virtually, unless the district has softened or amended the policy. If the district enacts a new policy for parental permission for virtual school counseling, you must comply; otherwise, proceed without parental consent as you would have in person. Best practice is usually to inform parents/guardians when working with their child over time in individual counseling.

What are some things I can do to ensure confidentiality in the virtual world of school counseling?
Ask students to use a private room and headphones with a microphone if possible. Additionally, a white noise machine in the room will help further limit the risk of others overhearing the student's conversation.

I am being instructed to carry educational records and my case notes home. Is this even legal?
The Student Privacy Policy Office (SPPO), which governs FERPA, states there is no prohibition against teachers and school counselors taking home educational records, assuming

they are school officials with legitimate educational interests. However, be sure to protect the information you take home so others in your house don't have access to it.

My district is forbidding me from working one-on-one with a student and instructing everyone in the district that we must work with students in pairs or groups. They are citing FERPA. Can this be correct?
FERPA governs educational records and doesn't address access to students. However, the district has a right to determine access to students. Some states have statutes prohibiting educators from ever being alone with a student or out of sight of others when with one student. However, the very nature of school counselors' work is one-on-one, so this is another policy that doesn't take into consideration our unique need to work with students individually. Some states, such as Louisiana, prohibit educators from being alone with students but make an exception for school counselors.

If you cannot find legal muscle to support you, advocate and compromise until you find an agreeable solution. One possible compromise, and last resort, may be to agree to videotape the sessions and archive them should any future questions or accusations arise. However, you must follow district policy while advocating for what really needs to be in place so you can do your job.

I have been running small groups on social skills, and sometimes the conversations are of a personal nature. Can I continue my groups in the virtual school counseling office?
Legal and ethical complications are acutely present in small-group delivery in the best of circumstances but especially problematic in the virtual world. Confidentiality for groups in a brick-and-mortar situation is fragile because a school counselor can never feel secure in the fact that a student understands all the nuances of confidentiality and abides by it. We should always remember that whatever is said in the group can be tweeted, posted on social media or discussed in the hallways within seconds or minutes. This awareness heightens school counselors' vigilance as to what they allow one student to talk about in front of other students.

Ensuring confidentiality in a virtual world is even more difficult. You can't know who is listening in each student's household. It might be impossible for a student to seek a private place, have headphones or keep family members out of earshot. Informed consent is even more important for groups than individual counseling, as disclosing sensitive information happens in front of other students. The reality and safest approach when working with minors in groups is to come from the posture that confidentiality will be breached. The best approach in the virtual world is to stay with topics that have less likelihood of spinning off into the private world of students and their families. Stress the need for students to seek you individually if they have something of a personal nature they must share.

Technology

My district wants me to use one type of online conferencing technology, but I'd rather use a different kind. Is this okay?
It is far safer to use what the district suggests. The district has likely vetted the program to make sure it will interface and integrate with the district's system and security approach. It is not a matter of which program or app is superior but rather which online program offers the best layer of protection for all as determined by the district.

Do I have to use the computer the school issued me, or can I use my much superior laptop?
You must use the school-issued computer unless the district offers you an exception. Again, it is about safety and security. There are privacy settings that protect district computers that your personal computer may not have. Advocate for your equipment needs, but be careful not to go against school district dictates regarding equipment.

Does the platform I'm using have to be Health Insurance Portability Accountability Act (HIPAA) compliant? I have been receiving mixed messages about school counselors' obligation to ensure our platforms and software are HIPPA-compliant. Must they be?
HIPAA doesn't apply to elementary or secondary schools except in a few limited circumstances. Schools receiving federal funds are not a HIPAA-covered entity; the health information maintained on student records is educational records and covered by FERPA. Billing for health care services is when HIPAA applies.

Use the platform your district has assigned, as this is safest for you and students. You can find all the information you need about HIPAA and FERPA on the U.S. Department of Health and Human Services website.

My principal wants me to do suicide risk assessments over the phone when we have reason to believe a student might be at risk.
Requiring school counselors to conduct suicide risk assessments is problematic on so many levels, not the least of which is the fallibility of assessing suicidal risk. Add to this complication the fact that the virtual world puts a barrier between the school counselor and student; sometimes there are no verbal or nonverbal cues through a computer monitor. The standard of care for school counselors when being required by others to assess students for suicide is to employ these assessments with extreme caution, with a follow-up assessment completed by a mental health professional who can spend the amount of time needed to address more accurately what is happening with the student. Quantifying the risk (high risk, medium risk or low risk) based largely on student response is a dangerous practice; the information gleaned should be considered unreliable. To tell a parent the risk is low is to convey what you cannot possibly know with certainty.

Get in touch with the parents as soon as possible and tell them to seek professional help for their child. If a student expresses suicidal ideation while you are talking to him/her, proceed as you would in a brick-and-mortar situation. Stay with the student. Keep the student talking. Have the student "take you" virtually to his/her parent. If that isn't possible, alert the parent by another means. If you cannot reach the parents, have the police do a welfare check. Establish a protocol for virtual response to suicide ideology.

TECHNOLOGY CREATING ENDLESS WORKDAYS

Your district expects you to answer emails after school hours. You are concerned about the legal and ethical implications of being available 24 hours a day/seven days a week. Should you be concerned?

Points to Consider

Work/life boundaries can easily be blurred as school counselors use communication methods that serve both their personal and professional lives. Having the internet in the palm of one's hands with continuous access to email, social media, student information and web resources has the potential of extending the workday long past school hours. More than half of the respondents (64.5%) in the Steele, Stone and Nuckols survey (2021) responded that their email is connected to a personal mobile device (smartphone, tablet, etc.); 82.8% responded that they frequently check their email and 38.9% frequently respond to nonemergency messages received outside of regular work hours.

There are legal and ethical implications regarding student safety when creating for students, parents and administrators an expectation of being available electronically outside the normal workday. Thirty-one percent of respondents in the Steele, Stone and Nuckols (2021) study reported they have never received an electronic message after work hours from a student that triggered a safety concern. Of those who did receive such a message, 58.6% responded immediately and 6.3% responded within hours. Even though the majority of school counselors responded immediately, it is of grave concern that there are those who did not, as the consequence of the risk is too great.

It is a remote chance but a reality that an argument can be made in a court of law that a legal duty was owed by the school counselor who established a pattern of responding after work, broke that pattern, and an injury or death occurred. Case history tells us it is highly unlikely the school counselor will be found guilty of negligence in a student's suicide, but avoiding the dereliction of duty charge in the first place is best practice by not establishing a 24/7 pattern of availability.

The normal practice for school counselors when a student is suicidal is constant supervision, but outside the workday the school counselor cannot physically supervise a student while awaiting parental or resource help. For the protection of the school counselor and student, it is best practice to establish an "away-message" on emails clearly communicating available hours and including emergency resources such as a suicide hotline number. Any practice involving the potential of harm needs to be consistently implemented, and since it is unsustainable and unfair to expect a school counselor to be available all hours of the day, the next best thing is to give detailed after-hours resources. Hyper-alertness all hours of the day is the antithesis of downtime, which is necessary for school counselor effectiveness.

STUDENT FIRST AMENDMENT RIGHTS AND CYBERSPACE

Serena, the school newspaper editor, has a blog she runs from home in which she writes freely about the principal's "heavy handedness in controlling what goes into the newspaper." She says what a "narrow-minded bigot" he is and discusses his "homophobic editing of anything to do with gays." She says, "He is a major douchebag." The principal removes Serena as editor of the school newspaper. Serena sues for violation of her First Amendment rights. Will she prevail?

Points to Consider

Avery Doninger was junior class secretary and in charge of organizing school events. Doninger created and ran a blog from home in which she vented after a less-than-perfect battle of the bands event that the superintendent got "pissed off" and the school administrators were "douchebags." She also used other offensive language to further berate the school employees. The administrators reacted by barring Doninger from applying for senior class secretary. Her mother brought a lawsuit requesting the court implement a preliminary injunction that would allow her daughter to run for senior secretary. Her motion was denied by the District Court and 2nd Circuit Court (*Doninger v. Niehoff*, 527 F.3d 41 (2d Cir. 2008). After graduating, Avery Doninger became a plaintiff in her own case. She asked for damages from the court claiming her First and 14th Amendment rights were violated. Her case made its way through the court system from the District Court to the 2nd Circuit Court and ended up in the U.S. Supreme Court. The Supreme Court declared her offensive language revoked her First Amendment rights (Hader, 2009).

ILLEGAL SEARCH AND SEIZURE

A student is in trouble for bullying via text messages. The principal wants you to go through a student's phone and read him the text messages. Are there any legal or ethical concerns?

Points to Consider

A reasonable search of a student's possession by school officials occurs when school officials are suspicious of a student's activities and have reason to believe the student has violated school regulations and when a conducted search is directly related to the initial suspicion. The principal is drawing the school counselor into a disciplinary situation that could also be a situation of unreasonable search and seizure. To refuse is to appear uncooperative, but to oblige might mean you are now an unwitting party to an illegal search and seizure. As astutely as possible, school counselors will extract themselves from searching the phone's text messages. At the very least, the school counselor will want to discuss with the principal the ethical concerns regarding being placed in a disciplinary light with the student.

Unreasonable search and seizure has been the topic of many court cases involving school officials. One such case was *Klump v. Nazareth Area School District*. In this case, a teacher confiscated Klump's cell phone when Klump violated school rules and used it in class. The teacher and principal later accessed Klump's personal text messages, voicemails and made phone calls to classmates to inquire about drug activity. A drug-related text message was received while the officials were in possession of the phone. Officials consequently used this information to determine the student had violated the school's drug policy. Klump sued the district, stating his Fourth Amendment rights, which protect against unlawful search and seizure, were violated. The court agreed and ruled in favor of the student, stating the district "had no reason at the onset to suspect that such a search would reveal the [student was] violating another school policy" (*Klump v. Nazareth Area School District*, 425 F. Supp.2d 622 (E.D. Pa., 2006).

EDUCATORS' FIRST AMENDMENT RIGHTS AND CYBERSPACE

Your colleague makes disparaging remarks about Black Lives Matter. Your school is 72% African American and Black. Is she protected under First Amendment? Can she lose her job?

Points to Consider

With the recent protests against police brutality and institutional racism occurring across the country, some public employees have chosen to voice derogatory comments toward protestors and Black Lives Matter. Consider the following incidents that David Hudson, First Amendment Scholar, gathered that happened in just the month of June 2020:

- A Ladson Elementary School teaching interventionist in Charleston County, S.C., was placed on administrative leave after posting offensive comments about Black Lives Matter.
- A teacher at Palatine High School in Illinois made a controversial Facebook post critical of Black Lives Matter that led to an investigation and retirement by the teacher.
- A Staten Island, N.Y., assistant principal has been reported to the Department of Education for allegedly posting racist memes and comments about "the privilege" of being on public assistance.
- An assistant baseball coach at Battlefield High School in Prince William County, Virginia, lost his job after a Facebook post stated that he would put a knee on George Floyd too (Hudson, 2020, n.p.).

Educators have erroneously assumed that their personal speech is covered by the First Amendment, but when they post information that may dampen or hinder their ability to do their job they may find that their freedom of speech rights are not absolute (Hudson, 2020). Yes, educators do have First Amendment, rights as given to them by the U.S. Supreme Court *Pickering v. Board of Education* (1968). Marvin Pickering wrote a letter to the editor criticizing spending money on the football field instead of the academic program. However, fast forward four decades later and the Supreme Court, in *Garcetti v. Ceballos* (2006), held that speech related to one's official duties that harms one's employer can lead to discipline. In other words, a school counselor's post from an account that identifies him or her as a counselor at a particular school criticizing the district for their approach to the COVID-19 crisis may lead to discipline or termination if it is or could be damaging to the district. Educator's free speech is an even more complicated, fact-intensive, case-determinant area of law than student speech. Educators' First Amendment Rights can be solid grounds for dismissal if shown to interfere with the learning process.

CONFIDENTIALITY OF EMAIL COMMUNICATION

Teachers in your school routinely send you emails with sensitive details about students. Teachers are so busy you hate to burden them by asking them not to contact you about a student via email. You know you have to act, but you want to do so with support for the realities of busy teachers and school counselors while protecting student confidentiality. What is best practice?

Points to Consider

"School counselors take appropriate and reasonable measures to maintain the confidentiality of student information and educational records stored or transmitted through the use of computers, social media, facsimile machines, telephones, voicemail, answering machines and other electronic technology" (ASCA, 2022b, A.15.c.). Email is an accepted form of communication among educators; however, it may not be fully confidential. Maintaining students' privacy and confidentiality with online communications is a serious concern for school counselor practice and never more so than the common practice of sending or receiving identifying information about students in an email. In the Steele, Stone and Nuckols (2021) study, one in four respondents said they do not include any identifiable information in subject lines or in the body of an email. More than half (67.3%) of the school counselors in the survey reported they try to protect privacy with techniques such as using only initials in the subject line of the email.

School districts are putting policies into place about the use of the school district servers for emails. Language is appearing that says no identifying information can be used, such as this one from Philadelphia: "Users shall not reveal personal information to other users on the network, including chat rooms, email, social networking websites, etc. Personal information includes, but is not limited to, name, email address, home address, telephone number, school address, work address, pictures or video clips" (The School District of Philadelphia).

Also, policies often suggest informing students and parents about the limits of confidentiality in email communications and including it as a part of the email signature or footer.

SECURITY OF SENSITIVE INFORMATION

Amy's divorced parents have been incarcerated at various times. Amy alternately lives in a homeless shelter or her mother's car. This, and other sensitive information, is kept in Amy's electronic educational records. You wonder if there is anything you need to know to support your district's practice of managing the security of Amy's and other students' information?

Points to Consider

As technology evolves, districts need to continue to be proactive and predict and safeguard against possible privacy breaches. School counselors are not responsible for the security of student information management systems, but they can advocate effectively for privacy assurance for students. Technology products and websites have to meet state and federal student privacy regulations such as FERPA, the Children's Online Privacy Protection Act, the Protection of Pupil Rights Amendment and the Health Insurance Portability and Accountability Act. The iKeepSafe organization recently developed the California Student Privacy Assessment, a standard for education technology companies to demonstrate their products comply with federal and state privacy laws (iKeepSafe, 2022). A privacy assessment will likely become the norm for districts, which must reassure the public of their efforts to protect students' information. It is altogether appropriate for a school counselor who has doubts to question whether or not the district has had a privacy assessment.

In a Position to Know: School Counselors Speak

The cases presented at the beginning of the chapter are revisited here by a school counselor educator, the ASCA deputy executive director and a practicing school counselor in an online setting who are experts in the field of school counseling and technology. Compare their answers with your own approach.

SOCIAL/EMOTIONAL COUNSELING IN A VIRTUAL WORLD

I've just been hired as a school counselor at a virtual high school. How can I meet students' social/emotional needs online?

School counselors have been meeting students' social/emotional needs online since the advent of virtual schools more than 20 years ago. Although virtual schools served a small percentage of students throughout the U.S., the COVID-19 pandemic forced school counselors across the nation to pivot quickly online to meet students' social/emotional needs as well. School counselors employ a wide range of strategies, tools and methods to connect with students; build trusting relationships; and address student needs in an online environment. Similar principles, practices and frameworks that school counselors use working with students in brick-and-mortar schools can often be translated to an online environment. Whether through Zoom, Adobe Connect or another video conferencing platform, school counselors can meet individually with a student, hold workshops or teach advisory lessons. Counseling information can be offered to students through a school website or school counseling webpage, learning management systems such as Canvas or via student email or texts. For some students, working online with a school counselor can be preferable to working face to face. Research has shown that students suffering from anxiety and stress are particularly responsive to online counseling services (Barak, Hen, Boniel-Nissim, & Shapira, 2008). Students may feel safer disclosing personal information across the distance of a computer screen, and setting up counseling meetings in a virtual school can be more discreet and private than walking into a school counseling office on a physical school campus.

Although many benefits exist to online school counseling services, it is also important to consider the limitations of the virtual setting. As a school counselor working in a virtual high school, you will want to ensure you are using school- or district-sponsored platforms and applications. Most online video and text chat programs automatically keep records of communications, including full transcripts of text chats. Further, school counselors cannot guarantee that students are alone or cannot be heard when meeting privately. Therefore, it is recommended that online school counselors communicate with students and families about their confidentiality policy and the limitations of such a policy in a virtual world.

Holmes and Kozlowski (2016) studied the challenges inherent in offering online counseling services students. Findings from the study revealed students preferred to use only the chat feature of the online platform, did not use the video, and there was a high rate of attrition. Therefore, school counselors will want to consider using multiple modes of communication with their students. Many school counselors give students options on how they would like to meet. For some students, beginning sessions in chat first, and moving to audio and then video over time can help reticent students participate. However, as Holmes and Kozlowski report, some students may not show up at all or may be difficult to contact. Therefore, school counselors need to have a plan to respond in such cases. Often, school counselors can work with parents and school or district personnel to help follow up with such students to make sure they are fully supported.

The ability for a school counselor to respond effectively to students' urgent messages outside of work hours may prove difficult, if not impossible. Therefore, school counselors working with students online should develop protocols for students in urgent need. Providing a school or school counseling department webpage with after-hours resources directing students to 24/7 help can be vital for students in need of urgent assistance, particularly in an online school when a student may be operating in a different time zone than the staff. Because students are typically at home when attending virtual school, parents will often have most direct access and support to their child. School counselors will want to make sure to have parent contact information for all students available in case they should need to get in touch with a parent to ensure a student's safety.

School counselors are tasked to meet students where they are at – both figuratively and literally – including virtual schools and online settings. For students in virtual schools where access to peers and trusted adults may be more limited, school counselors can be particularly helpful. As students grow up in this new digital century, the opportunity to provide responsive services in cyberspace will continue to increase, and school counselors will have more opportunities to meet student needs both in person and online.

– Tracy Steele, Ph.D., director of student affairs, Stanford Online High School

ELECTRONIC STORAGE OF STUDENT INFORMATION

Alexis, a middle school counselor, has been working diligently to better integrate technology in her work so she can more effectively and efficiently help students. She has found Google Drive to be especially helpful. Are there precautions, uses, and/or advantages to using Google Drive?

Like other educators, school counselors use technology provided by their school districts to support much of their work. Presumably, a school district's electronic systems (e.g., student information and communications systems) protect information flow and storage using modern security methods. For example, schools may incorporate dual-factor authorization, point to point encryption, and robust cyber defenses to detect malware, reducing the risk of data breaches. School technology specialists typically work diligently to keep all software and hardware updated to ward off new threats launched every day.

School systems, however, are unlikely to provide all the technology tools that their staff needs. Beyond that which is provided, school counselors have many powerful apps from which to choose that can help them work more effectively, efficiently and make their jobs more enjoyable.

For example, Google Drive (or something similar such as Dropbox or Microsoft OneDrive) is a file storage and synchronization service that allow users to collaborate and share in real-time. When school counselors use Google Drive, they must be highly considerate of how doing so is consistent with school policies and in line with best practices for protecting student information and privacy. The same is true for any technology tools outside of the school district's purview.

School districts may purchase a license for a collaboration suite such as Google Drive (now known as G Suite for Education), which comes with many cost-effective advantages. G Suite for Education incorporates higher levels of security than does the free version or Google Drive. As of this writing, G Suite complies with various laws, including FERPA, COPPA, the Student Privacy Pledge introduced by the Future of Privacy Forum and ISO/ IEC 27018:2014 (Data standards) (Google, 2021). In this case, the school counselor can feel more confident and comfortable knowing the school supports the platform. The provider (in this case, Google) is taking reasonable data safety and security precautions. Still, the school counselor must follow any school policies and practices to make certain that a human error does not compromise or breach that security.

What if your school does not officially support Google Drive or another app, especially when the app operates in the cloud? Cloud computing raises questions about exactly who can access the data, what hosts such as Google can do with your data, and how this might conflict with rules or ethical practices about storing student information. So, how might our abilities to maintain ethical and legal standards be unwittingly compromised by using a given app or technology? In addition to Google's responsibility and efforts toward securing your data, school counselors also have a responsibility to protect their files' integrity and confidentiality. Your Google Drive is as secure as your Google account and file-sharing settings you apply. Some steps can be taken to reasonably mitigate any foreseeable risks. However, realize that taking one or more of these steps can only help you keep your data reasonably secure. That's not the same as invulnerable; no technology is 100% secure. What this does mean, however, is that anyone who wants the data in your account would have to use extraordinary measures to get it. Consider the following best practices:

Technological literacy: Technological literacy is the knowledge of when using technology is advisable and efficient in day-to-day counseling situations and when it is not. Technologically literate citizens make informed and critical decisions about which technologies to use in their work, under what conditions, for what purposes, and with what potential consequences/ impact. Before using any technology, the school counselor must understand how any data is secured and protected by the company or third party. If you have not already, consider making technological literacy an essential part of your ongoing professional development. School counselors should also consider maintaining an ongoing working relationship with their school's technology coordinator, media specialist or other educators with a track record in technology and media skills, especially when troubleshooting for situations when help is urgently needed.

Add account recovery options: Your recovery phone number and email address are powerful security tools that can be used to block someone from using your account without your permission, alert you if there's suspicious activity on your account and recover your account if you're ever locked out.

Turn on screen locks: Screen locks help protect your device from being used without your permission, especially your smartphones and tablets.

Log out when finished: If your device is easily accessible, make sure to either lock your screen or log out of your accounts before you leave your space.

Use strong, unique passwords only accessible to you: First, understand that it's risky to use the same password across multiple sites; everyone should use unique passwords for each account. Otherwise, if your password for one site is stolen, it could be used to gain access to your account on other sites. Second, your password should be difficult to guess, even for an artificially intelligent computer. A password manager (e.g., Password Safe, Keeper, Dashlane or LastPass) can help you generate and manage strong, unique passwords. Finally, do not write your password down and make it available to someone who might have access to your office. If your device is capable, you should consider using biometrics such as a fingerprint or facial identification to access your data.

Turn on two-factor authentication: Two-factor authentication (2FA) helps prevent hackers from getting into your account, even if they steal your password. 2FA is a method of establishing access to an online account or computer system that requires the user to provide two different types of information. The second credential (e.g., a code number) requires access to something that personally belongs to you, such as your smartphone.

Use school-issued devices. When possible, use a device (e.g., laptop, tablet, chrome book) issued by your school instead of a personal device. Schools typically take strong measures to keep devices updated, secure and private.

School policies: Another consideration for school counselors is how they may be unknowingly violating their school's technology policies.

Security and privacy: Educational institutions are responsible for maintaining and securing all types of information. Some of the information may be sensitive and highly personal, such as medical or disciplinary data. In the case of using Google Drive or any similar cloud-based productivity/collaboration suite, it is also important to know if your information may be accessed or used for purposes other than helping students.

Use antivirus and malware-protection software: A simple way to decrease the risk of a personal data security breach is to make sure your malware-protection software is up-to-date and running, and you have a strong password. There's a good chance your school-issued laptop, desktop or tablet is already running such software and keeping itself updated. G Suite takes care of this for its users. However, when using personal devices to access work-related information, it is your responsibility to make sure you are doing the same.

I applaud Alexis for working smarter by integrating technology she has determined to help her be more effective and efficient in her work. What we don't know in this case is whether she has taken reasonable precautions to protect her students' privacy and honor promised confidentiality. By keeping up with her technological literacy, practicing "safe computing," and staying up to date on school policies, laws and ethics, Alexis should be able to enhance her productivity and potential positive impact on the lives of students with fidelity, justice and nonmaleficence (Kitchener, 1984).

– Russell A. Sabella, Ph.D., Professor, Florida Gulf Coast University

CONFIDENTIALITY IN A VIRTUAL HIGH SCHOOL

The administration is looking to you for suggestions regarding procedures the school counseling department will use for the section of the server where all educators are to keep notes on every student. The notes section is to record summaries of emails, phone calls, text messages and face-to-face interactions. The principal explains it is not optional. Every faculty and administrative staff member must use this section so collaboration can happen to optimize each student's education. This means it will be visible to all educators at the school. You are uneasy about the fact that school counseling notes will be there for all educators to see. What will you advocate for when you meet with the principal?

There are limits to confidentiality and being in a cyber-setting will have an impact on those limits. A school policy requiring you to enter information in a notes section of a database is one limit of confidentiality. Although it may be tricky, I don't think the policy creates an unworkable situation. You can think of these notes in the same way as when, in a brick-and-mortar school, a school counselor sends a request to a teacher to send a student to his or her office or when a school counselor writes an excuse slip when a student returns to class. It is also common for school counselors to follow up with teachers, administrators or parents/guardians about a student concern after holding an individual counseling session with the student, so some information is naturally shared without breaching confidentiality when collaborating with other staff or parents/guardians. School staff members have a need to know some information but definitely not all information. On the positive side, the notes section of the database may be an effective way to communicate and collaborate with teachers, especially at an online school.

Advocate for a system where teachers and administrators can only see notes on students who are assigned to them. Also, advocate for school counselors to be allowed to keep generic notes in the notes section to avoid creating a major limit on confidentiality. Your notes could include dates and times you met with the student, contacted the parent or consulted with a teacher. Your notes could also include generic information such as academic discussion, college and career readiness, social/emotional issue, etc. These notes would be equivalent to what you might say to parents/guardians who question why you are meeting with their child if you were working in a brick-and-mortar school.

Once information is entered into the database, it becomes a part of the education record and will be included with the record if it is subpoenaed in a court proceeding. You will want to write any notes in a manner in which you would feel comfortable if that situation were to occur. You could then create more detailed personal case notes that are not a part of the education record based on FERPA.

It is critical in this situation to make sure students understand the limits of confidentiality. Be sure to include information about your school's policy in your informed consent so students can decide about how much information they are comfortable disclosing. After a particularly sensitive discussion, you could discuss with the student what information you would like to include in the notes section of the database and obtain the student's consent before entering it.

A school policy requiring school counselors to keep notes in the notes section of a schoolwide database may be tricky, but if you work with your administrators to help them clearly understand confidentiality and agree ahead of time as to what information will be included in the notes, you can turn this requirement into a workable situation that will help you collaborate for student success with other staff members.

– Eric Sparks, Ed.D. deputy executive director, ASCA, and former school counseling supervisor, Wake County Public Schools, N.C.

ONLINE COUNSELING AND SUICIDAL IDEATION

Seth, a student in your online high school, has been in a tailspin academically and emotionally since his mother died a year ago. One of his friends forwarded some of Seth's electronic conversations about death to you. Seth's father feels his son is being overly dramatic and does not believe Seth would ever harm himself. Then, in a call to you, Seth describes using his father's gun or pills and ending it all. You keep Seth on the phone while you try to get his father on another line, but Seth informs you his father's cell phone is ringing right next to him as his father forgot to take it with him. He says he must go and hangs up the phone with you abruptly. What do you do?

The main concern in this case involves Seth's safety. Given that the school counselor has information that Seth has discussed his desire to "end it all" in prior online chats with his friend and has been going through a difficult time, it is reasonable to suspect Seth may be at harm to himself. Given the presence of serious and foreseeable harm, the school counselor has a legal and ethical obligation to call Seth's father to inform him of the situation and to help him in seek help for Seth. If the parent/guardian cannot be reached, and the school counselor is unable to reach the student, the school counselor can call the police in the student's area to conduct a welfare check. When talking to the police, school counselors should let them know they worry the student may be suicidal, and the parent/guardian is unreachable. Often, the police may bring a social worker or psychologist to the house to perform an assessment of the individual's psychological condition and to provide resources for mental health assistance.

It will also be necessary for the school counselor to stay in touch with the father and to provide referrals to community agencies in the area. Seth's father should be educated about suicide risk in teens, and he should be strongly encouraged to seek professional help for Seth. Depending on the situation, the school counselor can support Seth in taking a health leave if he requires hospitalization and can assist in his return to school.

– Tracy Steele, Ph.D., director of student affairs, Stanford Online High School

Making Connections

1. During your classroom lessons, you usually take your students to the computer lab to assist them in researching prospective colleges and career options. Describe the websites you will have them research and why you have chosen these sites.

2. You are a school counselor at an urban school where few students have access to the Internet or computers at home. How do you help students access the information they need for future goals and plans?

3. Explain how ASCA eaddresss school counselors' use of technology.

4. The creative writing teacher wants to create a blog where students can share their opinions of books they read throughout the semester. She is apprehensive about using the Internet to communicate with students because of the many cases she has heard of where teachers have lost their jobs for inappropriate discussions with students. She has come to you for advice. What advice will you give her?

5. Discuss the ethical standards of online counseling.

Chapter 3 Quiz

1) A privacy assessment regarding student information management systems means:
   a. School districts are keeping some notes in educational records and putting some in locked file cabinets
   b. Educational records are to be kept in paper copy only
   c. Everyone who looks at educational records must do so only during school hours
   d. A standard for technology companies to demonstrate their products comply with federal and state privacy laws
   e. Only school counselors can see case notes

2) *Spanierman v. Hughes* (2008) is an example of:
   a. How critical it is not to engage in any social media
   b. The vigilance and judgment educators need to use when using social networking with students
   c. The false sense of security that comes when school counselors think students are paying attention to the critical, timely information they are putting on social media
   d. The reason school counselors need to keep abreast of technology and use it daily in their practice
   e. How easy it is to breach confidentiality while using social media

3) Online counseling is:
   a. To be avoided and never used
   b. Condemned by the American School Counselor Association
   c. A valid much-needed alternative for some students
   d. Dangerous
   e. Preferred over face-to-face counseling

4) Checking email during off school hours is:
   a. Proactive
   b. Okay as long as you still give yourself time for rest and relaxation
   c. A great way to reduce your workload during the workweek
   d. Establishing a pattern of behavior that cannot and should not be sustained
   e. Is required if parents are to appreciate school counselors' spirit of above-and-beyond

5) Students' cyber-behavior:
   a. Is a First Amendment right that can never be disciplined by school officials
   b. Can only be disciplined if they sent the message during school hours
   c. Can only be disciplined if they used a school computer to send the message
   d. Can be disciplined if the post causes a substantial disruption to the educational process
   e. Has been the subject of numerous U.S. Supreme Court cases

Key Terms

ASCA Scene
Blogs
Cyberspace
Digital footprint
Disinhibition effect
Facebook
Technologically literate
Twitter
Video conferencing
Webinar

CHAPTER 4

Student Privacy Laws

Objectives

By the time you complete this chapter, you should be able to:

- Discuss the exceptions and revisions to the federal statutes, the Family Educational Rights and Privacy Act (FERPA) and the Protection of Pupil Rights Amendment (PPRA)
- Define directory information and describe the precautionary methods to use when disclosing it
- Identify school counselors' role in protecting the privacy of students' education records and parents' rights to records
- Identify situations in which FERPA regulations can affect how school counselors perform their duties
- Adhere to FERPA's rights for noncustodial parents
- Understand students' privacy rights under PPRA
- Understand the complexities of students' First Amendment rights

Ethical Standards Addressed in This Chapter

Professionalism means knowing your professional association's ethical standards and adhering to them. The ASCA Ethical Standards for School Counselors (2022b) most relevant to this chapter are the following:

- School counselors abide by the Family Educational Rights and Privacy Act (FERPA), which defines who has access to students' education records and allows parents the right to review and challenge perceived inaccuracies in their child's records. (A.13.a)
- School counselors take appropriate and reasonable measures for maintaining confidentiality of student information and education records stored or transmitted through the use of computers, social media, facsimile machines, telephones, voicemail, answering machines and other electronic technology. (A.15.c)
- School counselors respect the rights and responsibilities of custodial and noncustodial parents/guardians and, as appropriate, establish a collaborative relationship with parents/guardians to facilitate students' maximum development. (B.1.b)
- School counselors provide parents/guardians with accurate, comprehensive and relevant information in an objective and caring manner, as is appropriate and consistent with ethical and legal responsibilities to students and parents/guardians. (B.1.j)

- In cases of divorce or separation, school counselors follow the directions and stipulations of the legal documentation, maintaining focus on the student. School counselors avoid supporting one parent over another (B.1.k)
- School counselors adhere to educational/psychological research practices, confidentiality safeguards, security practices and school district policies when conducting research. (B.2.n)

The full text of the ASCA Ethical Standards for School Counselors is available at *www.schoolcounselor.org*.

Introduction

The Family Educational Rights and Privacy Act (FERPA) of 1974 is federal statute governing education records and dictating how all written information regarding a student is handled and disseminated for the protection of students and their families (Alexander & Alexander, 2019). The statute is found at 20 U.S.C. § 1232g, and the regulations are found at 34 CFR Part 99. The U.S. Department of Education's Student Privacy Policy Office (SPPO) administers FERPA, which affords parents the opportunity to inspect and review their children's education records and have a voice in how that information is shared with others (FERPA, 1974). Managing the school's education records does not fall within the appropriate roles of a school counselor (ASCA, 2022b), but it is important to have a working knowledge of FERPA guidelines to advocate for the legal and ethical protection of a school counselor's case notes and any other written information kept on a student (ASCA, 2022b). Each school day represents multiple challenges school counselors and other educators must negotiate in complying with FERPA. The most frequent issues for school counselors are addressed in the cases throughout this chapter.

A term to know as you use this chapter is "personally identifiable information." FERPA and IDEA protect personally identifiable information, which is referring to identifiable information found in education records and includes direct identifiers, such as a student's name or identification number; indirect identifiers, such as a student's date of birth; or other information that can be used to distinguish or trace an individual's identity either directly or indirectly through linkages with other information. FERPA gives a complete definition of personally identifiable information specific to education records and examples of other data elements that are defined to constitute personally identifiable information. School counselors have a wonderful resource in all things personally identifiable information in SPPO's Privacy Technical Assistance Center (PTAC) (ED PTAC, 2014).

FERPA is not a static law. It has to change as society changes. SPPO issues frequent interpretations or changes based on court cases, legislation such as the USA Patriot Act, health/safety issues such as the COVID-19 pandemic and societal changes such as electronic media. For example, changes made in 2008 and again in 2011 involved attendance, peer grading, emergency situations and personally identifiable information. Attendance was redefined to include various forms of distance learning.

FERPA's primary purpose is to ensure parents' rights to view their children's education records, to seek to amend inaccurate information in the records and to decide, within certain parameters, which entities or individuals can access their child's records. Students who reach the age of 18 while in secondary school have access to their records (FERPA, 1974). According to FERPA, a parent or eligible student must provide written consent before personally identifiable information is disclosed from a student's education records. FERPA allows schools to disclose education records, without consent, to the following parties or under the following conditions (34 CFR § 99.31):

- School officials with legitimate educational interest
- Other schools to which a student is transferring
- Specified officials for audit or evaluation purposes
- Organizations conducting certain studies for or on behalf of the school
- Accrediting organizations
- To comply with a judicial order or lawfully issued subpoena
- Appropriate officials in cases of health and safety emergencies
- State and local authorities, within a juvenile justice system, pursuant to specific state law (FERPA, 1974)

FERPA affords parents and eligible students the right to seek to amend information in education records the parent or eligible student believes to be inaccurate or misleading. Once the request is made, the school must decide whether to amend the record as requested within a reasonable time after it receives the request. If the school decides not to amend the records as requested, it must inform the parents/guardians or eligible student of its decision. The parents/guardians/eligible student has a right to a hearing under FERPA. In a 2022 survey of ASCA members, 77% of the respondents said in the prior 36 months they had not been asked by a parent to amend their child's educational record, and 83% said this request had happened only one to two times in the prior 36 months (Stone, 2022b).

FERPA further allows for the dissemination of "directory information," without parent or eligible student consent. Directory information typically includes basic contact information about a student such as name, address and telephone number. However, FERPA allows school districts to determine the items they will consider directory information, within certain parameters. School districts can establish policies and procedures regarding the release of directory information, including having a limited directory information policy, and they may decide not to participate in releasing directory information at all. Parents also have the right to request their student's directory information not be released by opting out of the disclosure.

The Protection of Pupil Rights Amendment (PPRA) is another important student privacy law. If a school district wants to require students to reveal personal information about themselves or their family, the school must first obtain written parental consent. PPRA expressly requires schools receiving federal funding to obtain written consent from parents/guardians and non-federally funded schools to give notice before requiring minor students to participate in any "survey, analysis or evaluation" that reveals information concerning the following areas:

- Political affiliations
- Mental and psychological problems potentially embarrassing to the student and the student's family
- Sex behavior and attitudes
- Illegal, anti-social, self-incriminating and demeaning behavior

- Critical appraisals of other individuals with whom respondents have close family relationships
- Legally recognized privileged or analogous relationships, such as those of lawyers, physicians and ministers
- Religious practices, affiliations or beliefs of the student or student's parent
- Income (other than that required by law to determine eligibility for participation in a program or for receiving financial assistance under such program (PPRA, 1978, 2002)

PPRA applies to all educators, not just school counselors, and applies to instructional materials regardless of the format of the material: printed, audio-visual, electronic or digital. One exception was tried in court when parents insisted on viewing state tests in advance. In *Triplett v. Livingston County Board of Education*, KY Court of Appeals, 1997, the court stated, "Parents do not have the right to opt out of state tests, since none of the questions of those tests would trigger the protections of the PPRA."

In this chapter, we will primarily examine the many ways FERPA and PPRA legislation affect the school counselors' work. The cases presented here guide you through the primary tenets of FERPA and PPRA, but there is no substitute for consulting the legal arm of your district regarding these important federal laws. However, there are other laws governing student privacy but mainly related to administrators' work.

- **Children's Internet Protection Act** (CIPA) requires Internet safety policies, such as technology to block certain access, monitoring of access and programs to educate students on appropriate online behavior.
- **Children's Online Privacy Protection Act** (COPPA) ensures that children younger than 13 don't share personal information on the Internet without their parents' express approval.

CIPA and COPPA became school counselors' concern when COVID-19 led to virtual school counseling. As long as school counselors are using only district-approved platforms and equipment, they are fine, as these have been vetted by the district to meet federal standards.

States can expand PPRA requirements, but they cannot reduce PPRA requirements. For example, Louisiana expands PPRA-like collection to prohibit requiring students to reveal any of the information in PPRA plus the following unless voluntarily given by the parent/guardian:

- biometric information
- Social Security number
- gun ownership
- home IP address
- external digital identity (Sallay & Vance, 2020)

The information in this chapter and all others is not intended to represent legal advice but rather best practices based on the author's effort to research the applicability of federal and state laws. Consult your school district's legal counsel. SPPO also provides FAQs on its website: *https://studentprivacy.ed.gov/frequently-asked-questions*.

Getting Started: What Would You Do?

The following case is answered for you at the end of this chapter by school counseling administrators. Before you read their responses, formulate in your own mind how you would approach this ethical dilemma.

REPORTING STUDENT INFRACTIONS TO COLLEGES

You gave a student a strong letter of recommendation regarding character, service, leadership and academic record. The student, Mark, was accepted by his first-choice college, which subsequently received his midterm report showing all A's. In April, school officials discovered Mark and two others had exchanged papers during a test in the first semester of trigonometry. The school disciplined all three students, and once the zero grade was factored into the final grade, the result was a drop to a letter grade of B. Will you be breaching any legal or ethical obligation if you report the cheating incident to the college? How would you handle this dilemma?

Working Through Case Studies

DIRECTORY INFORMATION

Ms. Sheffield fled several cities away from her abusive husband and enrolled her fifth-grade son, Richard, in school without disclosing their situation to any of the faculty or staff. The school published a list of the honor roll students in the newspaper to include Richard. Mr. Sheffield saw Richard's name in the paper and started contacting his estranged wife. Ms. Sheffield is furious; she feels she must uproot her family once again and seek a new town in which to hide. She maintains the school acted inappropriately by publishing her child's name without her permission. Is she correct?

Points to Consider

Schools or districts are encouraged to designate specific information as "directory information" or information about a student that would generally not be considered harmful or an invasion of privacy if disclosed. Directory information may include:

- Name
- Address
- Telephone number
- Date and place of birth
- Dates of attendance
- Photographs
- Grade level
- Participation in officially recognized activities and sports
- Weight and height of members of athletic teams
- Degrees, honors and awards received (FERPA, 1974)

The school has to notify parents/guardians generally and provide them with an opportunity to opt their child out of the disclosure of directory information. It was legal for the school to print Richard's name in the newspaper to recognize his academic achievement if the school had given the mother a chance to opt out through their normal means of notification. FERPA allows for the publication of directory information, which includes the acknowledgment of honors or awards received (FERPA, 1974). Most school districts use best practice to safeguard privacy rights and prevent this type of situation from occurring by having parents/guardians sign a publicity release form agreeing that their child's photo or name can be used in the newspaper or other media. Parents/guardians always have the right to opt out of any and all directory information.

FERPA requires school districts to notify parents of their rights under FERPA each year (34 CFR § 99.7). As part of that notification, schools also include the required notification concerning directory information, including advising parents/guardians they can opt out of having their child's directory information made public. In other words, parents/guardians can keep their child's directory information private. Schools may use a variety of ways for this annual notification to parents/guardians, such as the student handbook, PTA newsletters, school calendars, special letters, email, websites or newspaper articles. Schools should offer parents/guardians or eligible students who wish to opt out of directory information a reasonable amount of time to respond. The American School Counselor Association states that school counselors should not be placed in charge of education records. In a 2022 survey of ASCA members, 65% of the respondents said the school counselors in their school were not in charge of receiving and sending education records (Stone, 2022b). Even though school counselors are not responsible, as a member of the school community they will want to know their school is complying with FERPA.

In the same survey, ASCA members responded to the question:

Which most closely describes your school's practice?
My school or school district complies with FERPA by annually giving each family their rights under FERPA through some written means such as a special letter, PTA bulletin, student handbook 62%

No, my school or school district does not comply with FERPA by annually giving each family their rights under FERPA through some written means 6%

I don't know 32%
(Stone, 2022b)

Richard's situation is especially sensitive because of the circumstances surrounding his personal life. Assuming the school district notified parents/guardians and eligible students of their right to opt out of the disclosure of directory information under FERPA and Ms. Sheffield did not take advantage of the opportunity to opt her son out of directory information disclosures, the school was not in violation of FERPA by publishing Richard's achievement. However, an overburdened parent/guardian like Ms. Sheffield may be too consumed with creating a safe home for Richard to read the fine print regarding FERPA. Additionally, if educators were made aware of the family situation, this would have provided an opportunity to discuss FERPA and its implications concerning directory information with Ms. Sheffield.

Another wrinkle in the case and not one the school counselor needs to fix is Ms. Sheffield might be breaking the law by hiding her children. The courts may not have severed Richard's father's rights. The school counselor might be able to help Ms. Sheffield with resources such as legal aid if she and her children are victims of domestic violence and need protection in the form of legal documents. The school counselor might also increase contact with Richard and check in with his teachers periodically. Keeping the lines of communication open with Richard can foster a beneficial comfort level between the school counselor and Richard, cementing a trusting relationship.

Most school districts have information on their website to help parents understand their rights under FERPA. School counselors may want to advocate that their school district establish a user-friendly website. There are dozens of states with helpful models.

ACCESS TO DIRECTORY INFORMATION

A local business owner, Mr. Atchison, was denied a request for the class lists, names and addresses of the students in the local high school for a targeted marketing campaign. He works for a cruise line that offers special cruises for graduating seniors. Mr. Atchison knows the local school district gives the information to cap and gown and class ring vendors, colleges and the military. He believes the school district is acting capriciously and arbitrarily in denying his request and that school officials do not have the legal right to deny him the information. Is the school district acting within FERPA guidelines?

Points to Consider

Although marketing campaigns like Mr. Atchison's may offer students relatively harmless products or opportunities, this may not be the case, and educators should not have to be in the position of figuring out which marketers are legitimate and which are not. Students are targeted by programs and services promising everything from a quick and easy high school diploma to helping provide for a fee support for filling out the Free Application for Federal Student Aid (US ED Federal Student Aid Department, 2022), taking advantage of students. FERPA permits schools to adopt directory information policies that limit the disclosure of directory information to specific parties or for specific purposes or both. Schools are not required to provide directory information to anyone and may pick and choose to whom they disclose, but state law may state otherwise. Class ring companies, yearbook companies and other entities considered necessary to the graduation process that have a history of not abusing class lists are usually provided information.

IDENTIFICATION BADGES AND DIRECTORY INFORMATION

A new student, Andrew Hall, was the victim of severe bullying at his previous school. His mother has opted him out of directory information and by extension wants him opted out of the school policy requiring all students to wear their name and photo ID badges. Ms. Hall fears friends of her son's bullies will now recognize Andrew and continue the bullying. Is Ms. Hall within her rights to demand that Andrew not be made to wear an ID badge?

Points to Consider

Information displayed on ID badges typically includes items usually considered directory information – a student's name, grade level and photograph – and parents can opt their children out of directory information. However, FERPA regulations state that opting out of directory information does not exempt students from school or district policies requiring students to wear or present identification cards or badges. Under FERPA, schools are not required to establish policies requiring students to wear ID badges, nor are they prohibited from having an ID badge policy (FERPA, 1974).

It is a common practice in schools throughout the United States to require all students to wear ID badges on campus. This allows intruders on campus to be more easily identified and is often intended as a measure to ensure student safety. As such, "The need for schools to implement measures to ensure the safety and security of students should not be impeded by a parent or student using FERPA's directory information opt-out provisions" (FERPA, 1974). The fact that Andrew would not be wearing a badge might bring more attention to Andrew than fellow students paying attention to the badge he wears.

LEGITIMATE EDUCATIONAL INTEREST

Your cousin coaches Little League baseball and would like information on one of your students, whom your cousin says cannot see. The child's parents dismiss the coaches concern with, "He is just uncoordinated." Your cousin would like you to look at the vision screening results in this child's education record to see if a problem has been noted and report back to him. Is there an ethical or legal dilemma here?

Points to Consider

FERPA guidelines delineate who may have access to education records without parental permission. School officials, including school counselors, who have "legitimate educational interest" as defined by the school, can access records (FERPA, 1974).

Legitimate educational interest generally means a school official may access an education record for the purpose of:

- Performing appropriate tasks within your job description
- Performing a task related to a student's education
- Performing a task related to discipline
- Providing a service or benefit related to the student or to the student's family such as counseling, health care or job placement

School counselors typically have legitimate educational interest, not by virtue of their title but in the context of their work. However, school counselors do not have unrestrained, unlimited access to education records. When a school counselor legitimately needs to access a record, it can be done without parental permission. Examining an education record out of curiosity, however, to figure out what that new next-door neighbor does for a living or to see how many people live in the house is not a legitimate educational interest. School counselors take great care to read records only if the action is within the parameters of legitimate educational interest. Furthermore, the regulatory requirement in section 99.7 of FERPA states, "A school must inform eligible students of how it defines the terms "school official" and "legitimate educational interest" in its annual notification of FERPA rights. A school official generally has a legitimate educational interest if the official needs to review an education record in order to fulfill his or her professional responsibility" (US ED, 2011c, p.3).

As the school counselor, you cannot give the coach information on the vision screening results, as this is outside the boundaries set by FERPA, unless the parents give consent for you to share this information. However, it is legitimate for you to take the information learned from the coach and review the student's education record to note if there are vision screening results and contact the student's parents if the student needs attention. Advocacy is important, but even hinting to the Little League coach, who is not a school employee, what you have learned is a FERPA violation. School counselors and other educators must access only those education records – paper or electronic – in which they have legitimate educational interests (Stone, 2022b).

POTENTIALLY VIOLENT STUDENTS: EDUCATION RECORDS

Clifton is a quiet, brooding young man almost void of peer interaction, who rarely speaks, and when he does speak, his comments are negative and dark. He views everyone as "incompetent." He has been known to become violent when he feels "pushed." Students say, "Don't mess with Clifton. He is crazy." You are alarmed when he names Lee as a student he would like to "take out." Where, if anywhere, do you go with this information?

Points to Consider

You never elevate confidentiality over a potential safety issue; the administration must know about Clifton's threat. School counselors often see signs and symptoms in certain students that cause them grave concern but experience uncertainty in determining where to go with the information. Beyond the support school counselors regularly exercise in trying to shepherd students like Clifton through the referral process to secure the most intensive counseling services, there should be absolutely no question that you must notify administration about Clifton's threat of another student.

When deciding the best course of action, many believe educators' hands are often tied due to federal statutes protecting students' privacy rights and antidiscrimination laws restricting how schools can deal with students who have mental health problems (Jones, 2012; Lewin, 2007). Caught between privacy rights and school safety, educators look for support from SPPO. "FERPA is not intended to be an obstacle to school safety" (US ED, 2007). In an emergency situation, FERPA permits school officials to disclose, without consent, education records, including personally identifiable information from those records, to protect the health or safety of students or other individuals. In 2008, this was expanded to move from "strict construction of a health and safety emergency" to a "rational basis test for disclosure of education records in an emergency." At such times, records and information may be released to appropriate parties, such as law enforcement officials, public health officials and trained medical personnel. This exception is limited to the period of the emergency and generally does not allow for a blanket release of personally identifiable information from a student's education records (FERPA 34 CFR § 99.31(a)(10) and § 99.36). FERPA empowers school officials to act decisively and quickly when issues arise (US ED/ SPPO, 2007).

Also, FERPA "does not prohibit a school official from disclosing information about a student if the information is obtained through the school official's personal knowledge or observation and not from the student's education records. For example, if teachers overhear a student making threatening remarks to other students, FERPA does not protect that information, and the teachers may disclose what they overheard to appropriate authorities" (US ED/ SPPO, 2007, p. 1). In the case of Clifton, administration will likely determine that his actions fit the health and safety emergency exception in FERPA. He has threatened another student's life. Administration will take the lead to determine next steps.

MEDICAL INFORMATION IN EDUCATION RECORDS

The school counselors in your district are increasingly concerned about the district's practice of housing mental health records that come from day treatment and inpatient settings. What are the pros and cons for housing the mental health admissions/discharge (and possible evaluation) in the educational record?

Points to Consider

The potential good that may come from having mental health records as part of the education records doesn't outweigh the great harm that can come from having this highly sensitive information accessible to many eyes. The litmus test must be whether or not there is a compelling reason to keep such information on a student who is not a threat to others. To maintain potentially prejudicial and highly sensitive information might seem desirable, but protecting a student's privacy should supersede keeping mental health records when a student is not a threat to other students. It is within a district's rights to include sensitive, private mental health records when they deem it appropriate to do so, but the question should be answered "toward what critical end?" Under FERPA, if the school is maintaining this information, the information is considered "education records" accessible to a parent's/ guardian's right to inspect and review.

PURGING EDUCATION RECORDS

A first-grader has just been adopted by her stepfather. The student's natural father agreed to the adoption. Her mother requests all information regarding the natural father be purged from the cumulative folder. The principal has appointed you to handle this situation. Can the record be purged?

Points to Consider

Records are not meant to be kept absolutely intact. FERPA allows for purging of records. If the entry on the record no longer has a legitimate purpose and the parent/guardian wants you to alter the record, then the designee can comply and amend the record. Maintaining the integrity of education records is important but not more so than respecting parents'/ guardians' right to advocate for the privacy and accuracy of their child's education record. The main point is that FERPA does not require a school to maintain any records, and records may be destroyed unless a parent/guardian or eligible student has an outstanding request to inspect and review the records or the records have been subpoenaed. In a related case, many transgender students are trying to change their gender on their education records with varying degrees of success depending on their state. See Chapter 10 LGBTQ+ for information on this subject.

There will be times, however, when parents/guardians or eligible students will have their request to have an item purged from an education record denied. FERPA states: "An educational agency or institution shall give a parent or eligible student, on request, an opportunity for a hearing to challenge the content of the student's education records on the grounds that the information contained in the education records is inaccurate, misleading or in violation of the privacy rights of the student" (1974, 34 CFR. 99.21). "If, as a result of the hearing, the educational agency or institution decides the information in the education record is not inaccurate, misleading or otherwise in violation of the privacy rights of the student, the parents will be informed of the right to place a statement in the record commenting on the contested information in the record or stating why he or she disagrees with the decision of the agency or institution or both" (1974, 34 C.F.R. 99.21).

CASE NOTES AND EDUCATION RECORDS

You have been seeing Stephen off and on for the first six months of the school year. His mother is in a battle with the school district about her son's educational opportunities. You have received a request from Stephen's mother for copies of your case notes. Are you legally required to provide her with your case notes?

Points to Consider

Parents/guardians have a right to inspect and review their child's education records. Therefore, if our case notes are not sole-possession records, meaning they meet the criteria for "education records" under FERPA, then we are legally required to respect the spirit and intent of FERPA and provide these case notes as education records to the requesting parent/guardian. Often, case notes simply record the student's name, time and a few details to jog the school counselor's memory. However, when we do write case notes, in the case of a child-abuse situation, a student who is self-mutilating or a student who has suicidal ideations, we take great care to write professionally and with caution because we know our notes can be subpoenaed in most states, and parents/guardians can access the case notes if they are demanded.

Not all the information collected and maintained by schools and school employees about students is subject to the access and disclosure requirements under FERPA. One of the six categories exempt from the definition of "education records" under FERPA is a record made by teachers, supervisors, school counselors, administrators and other school personnel that are kept in the sole possession of the maker of the record and are not accessible or revealed to any other person except a temporary substitute for the maker of the record. A sole-possession record is a record used only as a personal memory aid, not your official case records, and only personal memory aid records fall under sole-possession records.

The following examples are memory aids and are exempt from education records:

- Teachers or school counselors who observe a student and take a note to remind themselves of the student's behavior has created a sole-possession record, as long as they don't share the note with anyone else.
- You encounter Jeffrey in the hallway, and he asks you about a scholarship. You make a note on your to-do list that you have with you to meet with Jeffrey up the next morning.
- The principal catches you in the hall and asks you to meet with Seth and Len, who were friends but now seem to be at odds. You make a note to meet with them the next day.
- You have been talking to Callista's mother about needed interventions, and after observing her in a classroom lesson you presented you make a note of some of Callista's behaviors needing attention.

The following examples aren't exempt and are education records:

- After a counseling meeting with Karen, you write down her name, the date and two sentences about what you discussed and the recommendations you gave to Karen.
- You meet with Gary, and then put his name, the date and the words "same-sex relationships" to summarize his presenting problem.
- Doretha stops you in the hallway and explains her mother is very sick. You spend 15 minutes talking to her, walk her to her next class, slip a note to the teacher to let her know her tardiness is due to meeting with you and make plans with Doretha to see her the next day. You return to your office and write down her name, date and a couple of sentences to capture her presenting problem.
- Colin sees you to get out of a class he is failing. After you meet with him and do some solution-focused counseling, you go to your required electronic record keeping, where you record his name, the date and check the box on the drop-down menu titled "academic concerns," which then releases a more detailed menu in which you check "work is too difficult" and "student unable to understand the teacher's instructions."

Parents need to specify what records they want. SPPO's Protecting Student Privacy website and the sample notification of FERPA rights states, "Parents or eligible students who wish to inspect their child's or their education records should submit to the school principal [or appropriate school official] a written request that identifies the records they wish to inspect. The school official will make arrangements for access and notify the parent or eligible student of the time and place where the records may be inspected" (FERPA, 1974). School officials do not have to announce to parents what is in their child's education record, but they can't deny parents the right to see the record or make a request for all educational records.

School counselors with hundreds of students in their charge do not keep detailed case notes. In a January 2022 survey of ASCA members, only 8% of the respondents said they keep written case notes on the majority of the students they counsel, 66% of the respondents said they do not keep detailed notes, and 27% said they keep detailed notes on a few select cases that might be needed for legal reasons (Stone, 2022b).

AMENDING CASE NOTES

A parent just demanded your case notes on her son, and you complied. This incident has caused you to rethink all your notes and second-guess yourself on information you have kept in notes. You want to review and revise your notes for a number of students to remove information that may appear judgmental. Can you rewrite or purge case notes?

Points to Consider

In absence of a district policy, subpoena or court order (or the hint that one is coming), it is acceptable to review notes from the past and amend or delete the entire note. Again, if your case notes have been subpoenaed or you think they are about to be, you should not amend or purge your case notes on the case at hand as you would be interfering with a rule of evidence.

CASE NOTES KEPT OUTSIDE OF THE SCHOOL

You have been told that if you keep your case notes in the trunk of your car then they will not be considered education records as defined by FERPA. Is this true?

Points to Consider

"Education records may include materials that are physically located outside the school. For example, education records have been held to include documents in the possession of a school psychologist as in the case of *Parents v. Williamsport Area School District*, in the possession of a school district's attorney as in the case of *Belanger v. Nashua, N.H., School District* and in the home of a classroom teacher as in the case of *Warner v. St. Bernard Parish School Board*" (Hughes, 2001). In the *Belanger* opinion it was noted that, during the public comment period prior to the issuance of regulations for FERPA, there were many requests to replace the term "education records" with "school records," but the U.S. Department of Education instead stated that "[t]he statute does not provide for a differentiation between records ... based on the source of those records" (*Belanger*, 856 F. Supp.at 49). The location of an education record is not what defines it as an education record as it is any record a school district "maintains" on a student, with some exceptions such as records educators keep when they report child abuse. When schools are virtual, as often happened during the COVID-19, educators were allowed to carry records home with caution that they were to safeguard them from others' eyes.

PROTECTING GROUP MEMBER IDENTITY

Your case notes contain multiple names of children in your group. Reginald May's mother has requested your case notes on the group. You suspect she is gearing up for a nasty custody fight. Do you have to comply with Ms. May's request? Can you eliminate all the names of the other children before complying with her request?

Points to Consider

The school counselor should redact all identifying information pertaining to other students. Under FERPA, parents "have the right to inspect and review only such part of such material or document as relates to such student or to be informed of the specific information contained in such part of such material" (FERPA, 1974).

INDIVIDUALS WITH DISABILITIES EDUCATION ACT AND FERPA

Mr. Market is an attentive parent, whose child Shane is in exceptional student education (ESE). Shane has academic and social/emotional problems that are documented by the ESE teacher on the report card under "work habits and personal interactions with others." Mr. Market disagrees with the evaluations and wants them purged from the education record. The principal has denied the request to purge the report card record. Is the principal correct?

Points to Consider

Exceptional student education records also fall under FERPA and, therefore, are governed by FERPA. Additionally, the Individuals with Disabilities Education Act (IDEA), federal law for ESE administered by the Office of Special Education Programs, spells out parents'/guardians' and students' rights regarding ESE records. Therefore, ESE records are subject to FERPA. However, this scenario does not involve Shane's ESE records. Therefore, a due process hearing under IDEA is not necessary in this case, but parents can object to information in education records. There are procedures for handling this similar to due process in ESE, although FERPA does not address due process hearings. The work habit evaluation part of Shane's education record stands. Parental rights to challenge information are not unlimited. A school is not required by FERPA or IDEA to give parents the right to seek to change decisions made by school officials such as grades or other evaluations, including decisions regarding special education students (US ED/SPPO 2004, para. 4). If during a legitimate hearing, parents are denied the right to remove or change information, then each time the contested part of the record is given out, the parents can require that their statement of protest be attached (FERPA regulations, 34 CFR § 99.22(c)).

SECTION 504 AND FERPA

Over the past few years, you have noticed an increase in the number of students in your school with 504 plans. Are these plans considered education records?

Points to Consider

Under Section 504 of the Rehabilitation Act of 1973, students can receive aids and services if they "have a physical or mental impairment that substantially limits one or more major life activities, have a record of such an impairment or (are) regarded as having such an impairment" (US ED/OCR, 2011c, para. 20). A student's Section 504 plan is an education record and is protected under FERPA, as would be any other education records. Section 504 plans can be maintained anywhere and by anyone considered a school official and can be destroyed at any time after the student leaves the school or district, as long as there is not an outstanding request for the records. The Department of Education's Office for Civil Rights provides extensive information on Section 504.

STUDENT ACCESS TO EDUCATION RECORDS

One of your 17-year-old high school juniors comes in and asks to review her education records. Can you honor this student's request to review her own education records?

Points to Consider

FERPA permits, but does not require, school officials to share education records with a non-eligible student. (34 CFR § 99.5(b).) A request by students to view their records would most likely be addressed under a particular district's policies and procedures and, if allowed, would probably be conducted under adult supervision. Students who are 18 or older have the right to review their education records.

Under current regulations, all rights of parents/guardians under FERPA, such as the right to review education records and consent to disclosure of their child's education records, transfer to the student once the student has reached 18 years of age or attends a postsecondary institution at any age and thereby becomes an "eligible student." Current regulations also provide that, even after a student has become an "eligible student" under FERPA, postsecondary institutions (and high schools, for students over 18 years of age) may allow parents to have access to their child's education records, without the student's consent, in the following circumstances: the student is a dependent for federal income tax purposes (§ 99.31(a)(8) or the disclosure is in connection with a health or safety emergency under the conditions specified in § 99.36 (i.e., if knowledge of the information is necessary to protect the health or safety of the student or other individuals (§ 99.31(a)(10), US ED/SPPO, 2008, p. 4.) or other exceptions that may apply (99.5(a)(2).

MAINTAINED RECORDS ARE EDUCATION RECORDS

A teacher in your school has students grade each other's papers and call out the grade while she records them in the grade book. Is this teacher violating FERPA?

Points to Consider

Kristja Falvo had three children enrolled in Owasso Independent School District when she filed a lawsuit to ban peer grading (*Owasso v. Falvo* 534 U.S. 426 (2002). Ms. Falvo's children struggled in school, and their low grades contributed to embarrassment and bullying because peer grading often meant peers called out the grades aloud for all to hear as the teachers recorded them in their grade books. Ms. Falvo contended that the practice violated FERPA. In a summary judgment (a judge-made decision not a jury decision), the school district won because the court determined that grades put on papers by another student are not "maintained" education records. The Court of Appeals for the Tenth Circuit disagreed, but the case ended up before the U.S. Supreme Court, which reversed again saying FERPA does not prohibit peer grading. Following the Supreme Court's decision, the Department of Education made changes in FERPA, stating that grades on peer-graded papers are not education records until recorded in the grade book. The courts found the educators were legal, but in the words of Supreme Court Justice Potter, "Ethics is knowing the difference between what you have the right to do and what is right to do." Involved school counselors advocate for a respectful school with the elimination of policies and practices leading to student humiliation or embarrassment.

VIDEO IMAGES AND FERPA

A student is in trouble for bullying, and it was caught on a school security camera. Her mother is threatening to sue because she claims the video images are an invasion of her daughter's privacy under FERPA. Is she correct?

Points to Consider

The mother might be correct if the taping violates state law. However, according to FERPA: As with any other education record, a photo or video of a student is an education record, subject to specific exclusions, when the photo or video is: (1) directly related to a student and (2) maintained by an educational agency or institution or by a party acting for the agency or institution" (20 U.S.C. 1232g(a)(4)(A); 34 CFR § 99.3 1]. A key question to be considered is if the video is directly related to a student. The context must be considered when districts are determining directly related versus incidentally related, as FERPA does not define the difference. SPPO explains that some factors that may help determine "directly related" if the photo or video:

- Is for official purposes, such as disciplinary action as perpetrator or victim
- Depicts an illegal activity
- Shows a student getting injured, attacked, victimized, ill, or having a health emergency
- Is for ID photos or a student presentation

If the photo or video does not contain these factors and the student's image is incidental, such as background or part of school activities without any specific focus on the student, then it is not "directly related" (SPPO, 2022). Another key question is whether the school's law enforcement unit maintains the video or whether another office in the school does, such as the vice principal's office. If maintained by the school security office, was the video provided to the school administration and maintained there? See the video FAQs at *https://studentprivacy.ed.gov/faq/faqs-photos-and-videos-under-ferpa*.

VIOLATING THE PRIVACY OF EDUCATION RECORDS

You are making photocopies of a student's education record when you have to drop everything and get emergency medical help for a student. Twenty-five minutes pass before you are able to return to the copy machine, and you find another student reading this student's sensitive information. If this student's sensitive information gets out, can you be sued?

Points to Consider

FERPA does not give individuals the right to sue educational institutions that violate the law's provisions by divulging confidential student information. In a decision involving a lawsuit against Gonzaga University, the U.S. Supreme Court held that the original purpose of FERPA was not to give individual students and their families the litigious license to bring charges against educational institutions for violating the privacy of education records (*Gonzaga University. v. Doe* (2002)). Rather, FERPA was designed to protect the privacy and confidentiality of education records.

The justices held that FERPA intended that the U.S. Secretary of Education would enforce its privacy provisions, mainly by withholding federal funds to educational institutions that failed to change their policies to comply. Based on this Supreme Court case, the parents in the scenario above would not be able to seek damages for a breach in the confidentiality of their student's record (*Gonzaga University v. Doe* (2002)). The parent could file a complaint with SPPO alleging that the school violated FERPA. School officials should try to work with the parent and explain the situation.

NONCUSTODIAL PARENTS AND EDUCATION RECORDS

You alert Justina's mother and her noncustodial father, per Justina's request, about Justina's anxiety and depression. Justina's mother is furious and tells you to never again contact "Justina's deadbeat father" with any information about Justina. Were you right to call Justina's father even though she lives with her mother during the school week? Does Justina's father have the right to be included in parent-teacher conferences and to receive education records? Is the school obligated to notify the custodial parent before contacting the noncustodial parent?

Points to Consider

FERPA states: "An educational agency or institution shall give full rights under the act to either parent, unless the agency or institution has been provided with evidence that there is a court order, state statute or legally binding document relating to such matters as divorce, separation or custody that specifically revokes these rights" (34 CFR § 99.4).

You may contact and involve noncustodial parents in an academic or emotional issue. In an effort to preserve the relationship with the custodial parent, you may decide to inform the custodial parent that you have called the noncustodial parent. This is a judgment call that would depend on the context, history and the student experiencing the problem.

Consider the court case *Page, Petitioner, v. Rotterdam-Mohonasen Central School District* (1981). First-grader Eric Page lived with his mother, who was legally separated from his father. Mr. Page tried to meet with the educators in Eric's school and to review his son's education records so he could stay involved in his son's academic progress. However, Mrs. Page contended that the courts had awarded her custody of Eric and that, consequently, Mr. Page had "abandoned" any interest he had in Eric's education. She requested that the school deny Mr. Page's access to Eric's records, and the school followed Mrs. Page's directions.

The lawsuit against the Rotterdam-Mohonasen Central School District resulted in Mr. Page being given full access to Eric's teachers and also to his records, in accordance with FERPA, which allows inspection of school records by either parent, regardless of custody issues. According to the court, "Educators and school districts are charged with the duty to act in the best educational interests of the children committed to their care, and although it may cause some inconvenience, those interests dictate that educational information be made available to both parents of every school child fortunate enough to have two parents interested in his welfare" (*Page, Petitioner, v. Rotterdam-Mohonasen Central School District* (1981)).

All 50 states and the District of Columbia have adopted the Uniform Child Custody Jurisdiction Act in an effort to support both parents' involvement in their child's life. When deciding custody using the Uniform Marriage and Divorce Act, decisions in part favor the parent determined to be most likely to keep the other parent involved in the child's life (Uniform Law Commission, 2012).

PARENT INCARCERATED

The registrar tells you of a request from an incarcerated father for the educational records of Rob, his child. The registrar has already called Rob's mother, who told her not to give the father any information. The registrar is now concerned that she may not be able to honor the mother's request and asks your advice. What do you tell her?

Points to Consider

Unless there is a court order specifically severing the father's rights, then school officials cannot honor the mother's request. If the mother explains that Rob's father is incarcerated due to the abuse of his children, then the courts would have limited his rights. In this instance, the onus is on the mother to bring the school a court order. Districts may ask that it is not a copy but an original with a raised seal with an active date. If the mother explains plausible extenuating circumstances as to why she does not have a court order, school officials might consider helping her with a call to legal aid if she and her children need protection in the form of legal documents. Keeping the lines of communication open between Rob and his incarcerated father is something the court has to determine, and it is not for school officials to decide if Rob's father should be shut off from information about his son.

Federal support comes in the form of the Family Educational Rights and Privacy Act, which states: "An educational agency or institution shall give full rights under the act to either parent, unless the agency or institution has been provided with evidence that there is a court order, state statute or legally binding document relating to such matters as divorce, separation or custody that specifically revokes these rights."

ASCA Ethical Standards for School Counselors further support both parents' rights to be involved.

STEPPARENTS AND EDUCATION RECORDS

Joseph has just moved across the country after his mother sent him to live with his father and stepmother. You have worked with Joseph, but you have been much more successful getting his stepmother involved than his father. Can you involve Joseph's stepmother in parent conferences, progress reports, report cards and other education records?

Points to Consider

FERPA defines the term "parent" as "a natural parent, a guardian or an individual acting as a parent in the absence of a parent or a guardian." Additionally, in some cases, a stepparent may be considered a "parent" under FERPA if the stepparent is present on a day-to-day basis with the natural parent and child and the other parent is absent from that home. Conversely, a stepparent who is not present on a day-to-day basis in the home of the child does not have rights under FERPA with respect to the child's education records. A grandparent or other caregiver who is acting in the absence of the parent(s) may also be considered a "parent" under FERPA 34 CFR § 99.3."

RESEARCH INVOLVING STUDENTS

The discipline referral rate is high at Gracian Howell Elementary. You and a local university school counselor educator collected and analyzed aggregated data for the discipline referral rate for all students. Next, you identified the 12 students who represent the chronic discipline referrals and notified their parents that you would be working with them. You gave the school counselor educator the list without any personally identifiable information so students remained anonymous. Teachers who have the 12 students are tracking student behavior on a rating chart. In the final report, you will not identify students by name to the university. The university will never know the students' names. Have you followed FERPA laws?

Points to Consider

Yes, you followed FERPA when you completed these steps:

- All the data was collected and analyzed by you, the school counselor, in an effort to learn more about patterns of discipline referrals in your school to address the problem.
- All the data containing identifying information was absent from the file, and nonpersonal identifiers (Student A, B, C...) were used when given to the school counselor educator.
- The students' parents gave consent for the 12 students to have their discipline data collected and shared in a journal article without any student being identifiable.
- The school counselor gave the school counselor educator the list of students with all personally identifying information removed so students remained anonymous.

All universities have internal review boards established to approve research projects in advance, so human subjects are protected legally and ethically. Additionally, the school district probably has a research department with whom the school counselor would need to seek permission before starting the study. Also, the final report would pass the FERPA test if all other types of identifying information were also removed. For example, if the report discusses a 14-year-old Asian male in the sixth grade and there is only one student fitting that description, then the study has failed the FERPA test.

SCHOOL COUNSELORS AND STUDENT PRIVACY REGARDING EIGHT PROTECTED CATEGORIES

An increasing number of your students appear to have more mental health concerns since the start of the pandemic. You want to require all students to complete a survey about any mental health problems, suicidal ideation, counseling needs, psychological problems and family mental health issues they may have. Are there any legal and ethical considerations in conducting this survey?

Points to Consider

In addition to FERPA protection, there is the Protection of Pupil Rights Amendment (PPRA, 1978). PPRA protects student and family privacy. A model PPRA general notification is available on SPPO's website. PPRA (1978) has had a number of revisions since 1978, but school counselors and other educators have been unintentionally and unknowingly stepping on PPRA having no knowledge of it. Informed parents are starting to question the rights of educators to ask certain questions on surveys and needs assessments, and educators are becoming more aware that they cannot ask student information under eight protected categories.

Families' personal information in any one of the eight categories outlined in the introduction of this chapter is protected. The four categories that have often been violated on surveys are:

- Mental or psychological problems of the student and the student's parent
- Sex behavior or attitudes
- Illegal, anti-social, self-incriminating and demeaning behavior
- Critical appraisals of other individuals with whom respondents have close family relationships

Requiring students to respond about their own or their family's mental and psychological problems is prohibited unless you obtain written permission from parents for that particular survey. If the survey is required and is funded under an applicable program funded by the U.S. Department of Education, and it asks about any one of the eight protected areas, then parents must provide prior written consent for their child to participate in that survey. Other areas that often appear on surveys are questions about students' "Sex behavior and attitudes; illegal, anti-social, self-incriminating and demeaning behavior; and critical appraisals of other individuals with whom respondents have close family relationships." Income is often asked but it is not a problem if it is being asked to access financial assistance for a program (PPRA, 1978).

If a survey is anonymous, then it must just be research for the purpose of gathering information, perhaps to determine needed programs and interventions. If a survey does not identify individual students, then the survey should meet the criteria of research in schools.

This carries considerable legal safety nets for students and has its own unique and extensive set of rules. Consider personally identifiable information. Even if you think the survey is anonymous, if there is enough personally identifiable information gathered, the combination of which can be used to trace an individual's identity (parent name, student number, date of birth, address, telephone number), then the survey is not anonymous and carries the same PPRA rules as ones in which students reveal their name. Passive consent may be appropriate, but if the survey is actually research, follow U.S. Department of Health and Human Services requirements. For more information on research in schools, refer to the U.S. Department of Health and Human Services.

INDIVIDUAL COUNSELING AND PPRA

You are asking Joe questions about his mental well-being because you have been placed on notice by a peer that Joe is suicidal. Are you violating PPRA?

Points to Consider

This is not a violation of PPRA. FERPA clearly recognizes health or safety emergencies; however, they currently remain unresolved for PPRA. If a health and safety emergency involving a specific student has come to your attention, then you may ask the student about any suicidal thoughts. The purpose of the questions must be to get the student the appropriate services and to inform the parents/guardian of the need to seek help for their child.

These conversations are limited to individual situations in which you've learned a particular student might be suicidal. You must notify parents of any information obtained unless the parent is the reason for the suicidal ideation, and then you call child protective services. This questioning is appropriate to accomplish the goal of trying to keep the student safe, giving parents a chance to exercise custody and control over their child's safety, while still complying with PPRA. When feasible, it's appropriate to obtain written permission from parents in advance of asking their child about suicidal ideation.

PPRA PROTECTION OF PARENTS' EDUCATIONAL LEVEL

Can I ask my high school students if they are a first-generation college student? I want to help them with scholarships and opportunities available to first-generation college students.

Points to Consider

This seems appropriate and outside the intent of protected category five: critical appraisals of other individuals with whom respondents have close family relationships. Yes, parents might take offense that their education level (or lack thereof) was identified, but this seems far afield of the intent to protect families from having information revealed about them that is "negative." PPRA is not intended to thwart closing the information gap and other advocacy efforts. You may consider rephrasing the question with statements such as, "If you are a first-generation college student, please stop by the school counseling office to pick up a packet of scholarship materials and fee waivers especially for you." This of course depends on the student's advocacy instead of you reaching out, which can be problematic as many eligible students will not come forward. Consult your district person appointed to approve asking survey questions that may cross the line.

Case law has illuminated and given warnings about parental concerns and potential PPRA violations. The district needs to examine if a privacy-protected question really needs to be asked before putting it out to students. School districts often prevail in cases involving PPRA, but the expense and emotional take when fighting a court case should be considered. In *C.N. v. Ridgewood Board of Education, District Court, 2001*, the school system prevailed. The survey was voluntary and anonymous, but some parents sued under PPRA claiming they hadn't received adequate warning, despite letters from the school board to the parents stressing that the survey was voluntary and anonymous. In *Fields v. Palmdale School District, Ninth Circuit, 2005*, the school system once again prevailed. The school had informed parents of a voluntary and anonymous survey but failed to disclose the sexual nature of some of the questions. Some parents of elementary-age children sued under both federal and state claims because their children were asked about sexual topics, such as the frequency of "thinking about having sex" and "thinking about touching other people's private parts." The court found the district actions were related to the state's purpose of educating their citizenry.

In a January 2021 survey of school counselors, ASCA members who identified themselves as being in a federally funded school were asked, "In the last 10 years, have you given students the expectation or requirement to respond to a survey or needs assessment without written parental permission?" Of the 121 respondents, 75% had given a survey without parental permission (Stone, 2021b).

Conducting surveys without parental permission is not a problem in and of itself, except for when the surveys ask about protected categories. Of the survey respondents:

- 29% violated PPRA by asking questions about mental and psychological problems potentially embarrassing to the student and his/her family
- 3% asked about sex behavior and attitudes
- 4% asked about critical appraisals of other individuals with whom respondents have close family relationships
- 10% asked about illegal, anti-social, self-incriminating and demeaning behavior

Mistakes are easy to make when well-intentioned school counselors are trying to support students' mental health concerns. It is rare when a parent raises objections under PPRA, but parents are increasingly becoming educated about FERPA and PPRA. A recent case in point happened when a highly effective and well-respected school counselor was horrified to learn she had been violating federal law for a decade by gathering protected information each year while doing her classroom lessons. It is probably somewhat by chance that we haven't heard more over the years about PPRA violations.

ACTIVE VS. PASSIVE CONSENT

I need to obtain informed parental consent for a PPRA survey. What does this mean, and how must it be done?

Points to Consider

A school must have clearly written procedures that comply with a state's legal requirements for requesting consent and notifying legal guardians or students of the results of screening activities. These procedures should identify specific circumstances in which the information will be shared with other service providers. Schools should consider the following factors when implementing key steps of the screening process.

The school needs to:

- Explain that the tool can help identify if the student has a social/emotional challenge
- Inform the parents/guardians that if such a challenge is identified, they will receive help following up on the information
- Explain confidentiality
- Let parents/guardians know they and their students aren't required to complete the tool or answer any question they find objectionable
- Encourage parents/guardians to ask questions and express concerns about their student's social/emotional development.

If the parent/ guardian won't be present when the screening tool is administered, the school needs to obtain written, informed consent. Passive consent from parents/guardians may be obtained, if there is a provision for the parent/guardian and/or student to opt out of the screening. The following steps can help answer questions parents/guardians may have:

- Provide information about the tool, the process and follow-up assistance
- Provide a contact name for someone who can answer questions
- Make a copy of the screening tool available to the legal guardians

Properly executed passive consent procedures are appropriate at times. To stay PPRA compliant, avoid requiring students to respond to any surveys that include the eight protected categories, because obtaining written parental permission will be problematic and time-consuming, and it's unlikely you'll get a critical mass. If you do require such a survey, then you must follow the PPRA law. If you need to distribute your own survey or needs assessment that infringes on any of the eight protected categories, have it vetted by the district appointee who approves such surveys, and obtain the authorization in writing. Then follow PPRA requirements for parental permission. Be transparent with parents/guardians about any protected information that is to be collected from their child. If you see something going out that might be a violation, speak up. Above all, don't berate yourself if you were the one who violated PPRA. We learn, and we correct.

The HHS Substance Abuse and Mental Health Services (SAMSHA) provides the following "Principles Guiding Screening for Early Identification of Mental Health Problems in Children and Adolescents."

- First, do no harm.
- Obtain informed consent.
  - Informed consent for screening a student should be obtained from parents/guardians or the entity with legal custody of the student. Informed assent from students should be obtained. Screening should be a voluntary process, except in emergency situations precluding obtaining consent prior to screening. In these circumstances, consent should be obtained as soon as possible during or after screening.

- Clear, written procedures for requesting consent and notifying parents/guardians and students of the results of early identification activities should be available.
- Use a scientifically sound screening process.
    - All screening instruments should be shown to be valid and reliable in identifying students in need of further assessment.
    - Screening must be developmentally, age-, gender- and racially/ethnically/culturally appropriate for the student to the greatest degree possible, and use of results should be informed by potential limits to validity as indicated.
    - Early identification procedures and approaches should respect and take into consideration the norms, languages and cultures of communities and families.
    - Any person conducting screening and involved with the screening process should be qualified and appropriately trained.
- Safeguard the screening information and ensure its appropriate use.
    - Screening identifies only the possibility of a problem and should never be used to make a diagnosis or to label the student.
    - Confidentiality must be appropriately ensured, and limits to confidentiality must be clearly shared within the scope of obtaining informed consent/assent (e.g., when immediate steps must be taken to protect life in an emergency situation).
- Link to assessment and treatment services.
    - If problems are detected, screening must be followed by: notifying parents, students, guardians or the entity with legal custody; explaining the results; and offering referral for an appropriate, in-depth assessment conducted by trained personnel with linkages to appropriate services and supports (Early Identification Workgroup of the Federal/National Partnership for Transforming Child and Family Mental Health and Substance Abuse Prevention and Treatment, 2006, as cited in, SAMSHA, 2019, page 36)

Here is a summary of PPRA requirements.

Funded in whole or part by U.S. Department of Education and Student Participation is Required	**Covers eight protected categories**	**Opt in/Opt out**
Yes	Yes	Provide notice and parents must opt in for the student to take the survey
Yes	No	Provide notice and parents have the right to opt out
No	Yes	Provide notice and parents have the right to opt out
No	No	Provide notice only if the survey was created by a third party. In that case, parents have the right to opt out.

UNIVERSAL SCREENERS AND PPRA

Your district uses a universal screener developed by a third party that asks students about mental health concerns such as depression and suicide. Passive and active consent is not obtained, but the students are told the screener is optional. Is this PPRA compliant?

Points to Consider

Universal screeners gather information regarding behavioral and mental health issues by either reviewing existing data/input from educators or by asking questions directly of students. Schools receiving federal funding and using a universal screener asking any questions from the eight PPRA-protected areas must obtain active consent from parents if the survey is funded in whole or in part by the U.S. Department of Education and students are required to complete the screener. School obtain passive consent if the screener is voluntary (PPRA, 1978, 2002).

ELECTRONIC CASE NOTES

Your district has a new student information management system, and it has a section for school counselors to indicate who they are seeing and why. The "why" is captured on drop-down menus, and the school counselors click either academic, career or social/emotional and then a further drop-down menu gives general terms as to the presenting issues, such as "difficulty with peer relationships." Receiving schools can access the information for continuity of services. Should you be concerned about student privacy?

Points to Consider

With or without technology, a clear understanding of FERPA is essential for anyone working in a school. An excellent resource is the SPPO's Privacy Technical Assistance Center (PTAC), a one-stop resource for education stakeholders to learn about data privacy, confidentiality and security practices related to student-level longitudinal data systems and other uses of student data. FERPA makes no distinction between electronic and paper records, using the same standard for both and recognizing the difficulty of protecting records. There is no system for maintaining and transmitting education records, whether in paper or electronic form, that can guarantee they're safe from every hacker and thief, technological failure, violation of administrative rules and other causes of unauthorized access and disclosure.

Advocate that only educators who meet a narrow definition of "need to know" can access these electronic counseling notes. This narrow definition doesn't include every teacher who has the student and every administrator. It would require justification for why a particular educator needed to access the information to optimally provide an education for a particular student. Advocate that school counselor notes do not automatically transition to receiving schools. If there is a compelling need, such as child abuse or suicide ideation, for a school to know about an incoming student, then the current school counselor should call the receiving school counselor on the phone. It might seem innocuous for schools to receive electronic case notes, but a student's privacy should trump anything other than a compelling reason to transmit these notes. When there is a compelling reason, it would be best done in through personal contact.

LETTERS OF RECOMMENDATION

Evelyn is applying to a competitive university, and your letter of recommendation will be a critical part of her application to that school. Evelyn's freshman year was academically dismal due to depression. Evelyn has been a stellar student since, and you are considering explaining all this in your letter of recommendation. Legally and ethically, can you include this information in a letter of recommendation?

Points to Consider

School counselor respondents to a 2022 survey overwhelmingly said they would consider it a breach of confidentiality to put sensitive, confidential information in a letter of recommendation without a student's permission (Stone, 2022b). Most respondents said they would not put Evelyn in the position of having to make that decision but would write the letter to convey triumph without giving the details of her past and explain to Evelyn that she can write personal details in an essay. Even when it comes to confidential information that, if known, would benefit a student, school counselors would rather get the student's and/or parent's permission. Under FERPA guidelines, school counselors don't need to get parental permission to write a letter to a receiving school. School counselors hold to the approach that if information is sensitive, such as depression, and in many cases prejudicial, then it is not shared in a letter.

Typically, you write a letter of recommendation because the student or student's parent has asked you to do so. Legally, school counselors can include anything in a letter that is common knowledge and observable such as, "Kennard has never let the fact that he is wheelchair-bound keep him from being an active and high-profile school leader, engaged in numerous school activities such as…" It is best practice to get Kennard and his parent's permission to include his disability, as they might not want this known at this juncture.

Further, under 34 CFR § 99.12 of the FERPA regulations, a postsecondary institution may prevent a student from inspecting and reviewing "confidential letters and confidential statements of recommendation" if the student has waived his or her right to inspect and review the letters and statements under FERPA and the letter has to do with admission to an institution, application for employment or receipt of an honor or honorary recognition.

SIGNING LETTERS WRITTEN BY ANOTHER EDUCATOR

It is rumored that the only school counselor at Sebastian High School was fired. The colleges/universities where some of Sebastian's students are applying require a letter from the current school counselor. Sebastian's principal has decided the best way to handle this is to have teachers write the letters, and he has brokered an agreement with your principal for you to sign off as the student's school counselor.

Points to Consider

This is a real case that is obviously fraught with problems. The principal can send the colleges/universities a note that Sebastian does not have a school counselor but the students' teachers wrote the letters. The principal can provide a workshop to help teachers know what should be included to best position students and how to find information. As Mark Kuranz, retired school counselor, said, "I would never sign a letter of recommendation that I didn't write. I just don't think that it is appropriate. If I didn't know the students well, I would interview them and maybe touch base with some of the students' teachers to get some specific examples (I would cite that a teacher shared the information in the letter), but I would write the letter under my name" (personal communication, Feb. 5, 2017). There are numerous ways to address this situation so students are not penalized, but signing your name to another's letter of recommendation is not one of them.

In a Position to Know
School Counseling Administrators Speak

The case presented at the beginning of the chapter is revisited here and answered by two school counseling administrators. Compare their answers with your approach.

REPORTING STUDENT INFRACTIONS TO COLLEGES

You gave a student a strong letter of recommendation regarding his character, service, leadership and academic record. The student, Mark, was accepted by his first-choice college, which subsequently received Mark's midterm report showing all A's. In April, school officials discovered Mark and two others had exchanged papers during a test in the first semester of trigonometry. The school disciplined all three students, and once the zero grade was factored into the final grade, the result was a drop to a letter grade of B. Are you under any legal or ethical obligation to report the cheating incident to the college? Will you be breaching any legal or ethical obligation if you do report the cheating incident to the college? How would you handle this ethical dilemma?

Ethically, this is a case that must be decided by the individual school counselor, as there are no hard and fast rules governing what a school counselor should do. Legally, the school counselor is under no obligation to call or contact the university to inform it of changes in the status of students who have applied to the school. Knowing this doesn't necessarily help you do what is right. Following are some considerations to take into account.

The line of reasoning is that this student did not deserve the glowing letter and that it would be wrong to let the recommendation letter stand without adding the new information. However, if we follow this line of reasoning, where does it end? Is it then a school counselor's responsibility to inform potential employers, military recruiters, community colleges, career and technical schools, and other postsecondary placements of any new and potentially damaging information that came to light since the writing of any letter or evaluation? And, perhaps more importantly, is cheating the only offense that would trigger a report to any of these agencies? What does a school counselor choose to report or not report after an initial letter of recommendation or evaluation?

On the other hand, school counselors might respond that they do not believe it is their responsibility to notify the university. A school counselor believes the letter was written in good faith based on the information available at the time, and no obligation exists to voluntarily provide additional information to the university. The drop in the grade or any additional discipline issued by the school should be consequence enough without the incident of poor judgment affecting a student's entire future.

A potential downside to not informing the university is that many university admissions counselors believe they should be informed and could devalue future letters of recommendation written by the school counselor should this information come to light. This could adversely affect future college applicants who have letters of recommendation from this school counselor. Nevertheless, a school counselor's role is to be a student advocate, not a university gatekeeper.

School counselors may believe the grade change or cheating incident should be reported to the university in the belief that their own integrity will be called into question. Caution is needed, as this could be a problem with FERPA. Yes, according to FERPA 99.31 (a)(2), schools can send information to a school where a student is seeking to enroll, but an out-of-the-blue call to report a discipline infraction may be problematic. Instead, the school or school counselor might choose to send the disciplinary record as part of the final transcript or a transfer of record to the new school. All of this has to meet conditions of disclosure under FERPA. What is needed is careful consideration that parent and student rights are not being violated under FERPA. Through your administration, seek help from the school district's legal arm.

A third approach might work as an effective compromise. Upon the lowering of the grade, the school counselor sends the university a corrected transcript with no explanation. It is then the university's responsibility to call and inquire regarding the change of grade. If the university calls, the school counselor can truthfully explain the grade change. The school counselor should also inform the student that should the university call regarding the grade change, the school counselor is ethically responsible to tell the truth for the reason the grade changed. The student may make the decision to "do the right thing" and inform the university himself before the university inquires with the school counselor.

In any case, it would undoubtedly help the situation if the school district had a policy in place regarding letters of recommendation and updates. A short paragraph to be included with a recommendation form or evaluation could delineate the district policy. This would effectively inform both the student and any recommendation letter or evaluation recipient of the guidelines in place to protect all parties involved.

– Bob Tyra, consultant, Tyra Consulting, and retired Los Angeles County Office of Education project director, and Paul Meyers, superintendent, South Bay Union School District in Eureka, Calif.

On Feb. 3, 2017, a news article appeared giving reality to the hypothetical case answered here. A Stoughton, Mass., teacher was suspended for 20 days after reaching out to a college and telling them why she rescinded the letter of recommendation she wrote for a student. The student made a swastika during a class project and made an offensive comment. The school disciplined the student. The administration explained in a letter to parents that disciplinary action was taken including calling the police, who determined this was not hate speech or hate crime. The Stoughton Teachers Association president made the teacher's suspension public at the school board meeting, although the laws or policies broken were never made public (Boston 25 News, 2017). If the school district had a policy against releasing discipline records to receiving schools, this may have been the policy they used for the suspension. We can only speculate, but this example underscores how precarious it is when releasing a student's information when it may well be against FERPA or school board policy. But as Tyra and Myers noted in the previous example, "An out-of-the-blue call to report a discipline infraction may be problematic."

Making Connections

1. Based on your knowledge of a school counselor's role regarding education records, identify some personal changes you would make if you had free range.

2. Give examples of current practices by your school that potentially violate FERPA.

3. What is the current method your school uses to tell students and parents about directory information and their rights? Is this a good method? If not, what changes would you suggest?

4. A licensed mental health counselor, whom you know to be a reputable therapist, wants to write a book about student behavioral issues in middle schools. The mental health counselor asks you to identify common behavioral issues in your school and to supply notes about these behaviors for the book. What should you do? Give some examples of best practices.

5. A teacher in your school makes a habit of making her students' grades public in an attempt to motivate them to perform better. You realize this practice is quite hurtful to students and does not produce the aimed outcome. What can you do to advocate for these students?

6. A parent wants to change an "inaccurate" notation in her child's file regarding alleged behavioral issues. The parent wants this because she claims the teacher had personality conflicts with her child. You are the principal's designee for handling this matter. What are the due process procedures you must offer this parent?

7. A 14-year-old student tells you her biological father, whom she met for the first time recently, has suddenly appeared in her life and wants to be involved in her education. The father's name is on her birth certificate filed in her educational record. The student and the student's mother do not want him to be able to have any access to her education records or her teachers. Can you comply with their request?

Chapter 4 Quiz

1) FERPA's primary purpose is:
   a. To inform educators of the educational information that must be kept on all students.
   b. To give eligible students (i.e., 18-year-olds) complete control over their records.
   c. To protect medical records and to give students the opportunity to decide who will have their medical records.
   d. To establish noncustodial parents' rights to participate in teacher conferences.
   e. To ensure parents' rights to view their children's education records and to decide within certain parameters who will access their child's records.

2) In *Page, Petitioner, v. Rotterdam-Mohonasen Central School District (1981):*
   a. It has been clearly established that noncustodial parents do not have rights to educational records.
   b. It has been established that stepparents have rights to records.
   c. The school district prevailed because of governmental immunity.
   d. It was clearly established that parents cannot use FERPA as a basis for a lawsuit against educators.
   e. It has been clearly established that noncustodial parents also have rights to their child's educational records unless a court order has severed that right.

3) Stepparents:
   a. Do not have rights to their stepchild's educational records.
   b. Are entitled to their stepchild's educational records if they have been in the child's life at least five years.
   c. Are entitled to their stepchild's educational records if they are present on a day-to-day basis in the home with the child and the other parent is absent from that home.
   d. Are entitled to their stepchild's educational records only if the natural parent signs permission for them to view records.
   e. Have to legally adopt a child to view the child's educational records.

4) The FERPA law:
   a. Requires school districts to notify parents of their rights under FERPA each year.
   b. Only requires school districts to notify parents of kindergarteners and first-graders of their rights under FERPA.
   c. Does not speak to parental notification of rights under FERPA.
   d. Only requires parental notification of rights if educational records are requested by agencies or individuals without legitimate educational interest.
   e. Only requires districts to notify eligible students of their rights.

5) Directory information:
   a. Refers to the law requiring parents be given the contact information for their child teacher(s).
   b. Applies to the publication of athletes' achievements during sporting events and the resulting statistics.
   c. Is the 211 national hotline number for all students experiencing a crisis.

   d. Is information about a student that would generally not be considered harmful or an invasion of privacy if disclosed.
   e. Is a list of information school districts must keep on every student.

6) There is a distinction between Family Educational Rights and Privacy Act (FERPA) and Protection of Pupil Privacy Amendment (PPRA) in that
   a. FERPA is a federal law and PPRA is a state-by-state law should the state choose to enact it.
   b. FERPA only applies to surveys, and PPRA applies to all records we maintain on a student.
   c. PPRA can be extended in protection by states, but FERPA cannot.
   d. FERPA applies to anything we collect and maintain on a student, and PPRA applies to the future collection of material.
   e. None of the above.

7) Student privacy rights in school:
   a. Are nonexistent as students leave their privacy rights at the schoolhouse door.
   b. Are only in operation regarding physical examinations.
   c. Can be superseded by substantial interest.
   d. Are a state interest not a federal interest.
   e. Is a topic parents are informed about once during their child's elementary years then informed once during the secondary years.

Key Terms

Custodial parent
Directory information
Due process hearing
Family Educational Rights and Privacy Act
Student Privacy Policy Office
Individuals with Disabilities Education Act
Legitimate educational interest
Noncustodial parent
Protection of Pupil Rights Amendment Uniform Child
Custody Jurisdiction Act Uniform Marriage Act
Uninterrupted Scholars Act
USA Patriot Act

CHAPTER 5

Negligence

By the time you have completed this chapter, you should be able to:

- Define negligence as it pertains to school counseling
- Understand the definition of malpractice in school counseling
- Identify the components of standard of care
- Understand *in loco parentis*
- Identify the four elements of negligence
- Discuss practices that may lead to negligence in school counseling
- Discuss how to prevent negligence in academic advising, suicide prevention and other potentially difficult areas
- Apply the ethical standards governing competency in school counseling

Ethical Standards Addressed in This Chapter

The ASCA Ethical Standards for School Counselors (2022b) most relevant to this chapter include the following:

- School counselors are knowledgeable of local, state and federal laws, as well as school and district policies and procedures affecting students and families and strive to protect and inform students and families regarding their rights. (A.1.i.)
- School counselors maintain appropriate boundaries and are aware that any sexual or romantic relationship with students (whether legal or illegal in the state of employment) is a grievous breach of ethics and is prohibited regardless of a student's age or consent. This prohibition applies to both in-person and electronic interactions and relationships. (A.1.l.)
- School counselors act to eliminate and/or reduce the potential for harm to students and stakeholders in any relationships or interactions by using safeguards, such as informed consent, consultation, supervision and documentation. (A.5.e)
- School counselors inform parents/guardians and school administration when a student poses a serious and foreseeable risk of harm to self or others. This notification is to be done after careful deliberation and consultation with appropriate professionals, such as other school counselors, the school nurse, school psychologist, school social worker, school resource officer or child protective services. Even if the danger appears relatively remote, parents/guardians must be notified. The consequence of the risk of not giving parents/guardians a chance to intervene on behalf of their child is too great. (A.9.a)

- School counselors recognize the level of suicide risk (e.g., low, medium, high) cannot accurately be quantified. If required to use risk assessments, they must be completed with the realization that school counselors aren't able to accurately assess a student's level of risk for suicide. When reporting risk-assessment results to parents/guardians, school counselors do not negate the risk of harm to self even if the assessment reveals a low risk, as students may minimize risk to avoid further scrutiny and/or parental/guardian notification. The purpose of reporting any risk-assessment results to parents/guardians is to underscore the need for parents/guardians to act, not to report a judgment of risk. (A.9.b)
- School counselors adhere to federal, state and local laws; district policy; and ethical practice when assisting parents/guardians experiencing family difficulties interfering with their student's welfare. (B.1.g.)
- School counselors advocate for administrators to place licensed/certified school counselors who are competent, qualified and hold a master's degree or higher in school counseling from an accredited institution. (B.2.h.)
- School counselors accept employment only for positions for which they are qualified by education, training, supervised experience and state/national professional credentials. (B.3.c)

The full text of the ASCA Ethical Standards for School Counselors is available at *www.schoolcounselor.org*

Introduction

The fundamental basis for exploring legal concepts in this chapter is that school counselors live and work in a litigious society. People sue. Historically, the chances that school counselors would be sued in the course of doing their jobs have been slim (Remley & Herlihy, 2019; Zirkel, 2020).

"Even though various special-interest groups have contributed to skewed perceptions, objective research reveals K–12 education litigation, in terms of published court decisions, has gradually declined since the 1970s; the outcomes have continued to favor school district defendants; and the outcomes of the student suits, which are of primary concern to school counselors, have shifted significantly further in favor of school district defendants" (P.A. Zirkel, personal communication, Dec. 1, 2008). This fact may provide little comfort since the emotional and financial burden involved in defending against a lawsuit can be substantial. This chapter is designed to help familiarize school counselors with their obligations to students in issues involving the court system, specifically regarding negligence.

Constitutional law involves two major categories: criminal law and civil law. A criminal wrong is a crime against society. The degree of the crime can be categorized as either a felony or a misdemeanor, with a felony carrying a longer prison term (Alexander & Alexander, 2019). A civil wrong is a wrong against another person that causes physical, emotional or monetary damage and for which the plaintiffs can seek compensation. An individual can be exonerated of a crime, yet be found guilty of breaching the plaintiff's individual rights (Alexander & Alexander, 2019; Scheidegger, 2008). The government will prosecute a criminal act on behalf of the people, and the standard is beyond a reasonable doubt.

However, if a person is exonerated of a criminal act, they can still be sued for a civil wrong and the burden of proof is a lower standard of preponderance of the evidence. Probably the most famous case that demonstrates the difference is the O.J. Simpson case, in which he was found not guilty of murder in criminal court jury, yet in a civil court held responsible for the deaths of two people. In other words, the jury in the civil suit found it more likely than not (or a 51% chance) that he caused the death of Nicole Brown and Ron Goldman. A criminal jury was unable to find the higher standard of beyond a reasonable doubt. The outcomes are not contradictory (The Florida Bar, 2022). School counselors who find themselves in legal difficulty are frequently defending themselves in a negligence or civil wrong case. School counselors charged with job-related criminal activity are usually defendants in a case of sexual abuse of a minor student in their school or failure to call in child abuse.

This chapter focuses primarily on negligence and malpractice. Negligence is a civil wrong in which one person breaches the duty owed to another. Malpractice is the negligent rendering of professional services (Remley & Herlihy, 2019; Corey et al., 2018).

Negligence: As a general legal principle, civil liability for negligence accrues if a school counselor is found to owe a duty to another person, breaches that duty by not living up to expected standards and, as a result of the breach of duty, causes damages to another person. According to Prosser (1971), all four of the following elements must be present for negligence to be proven:

- The school counselor owes a duty to a student or parent/guardian of a student.
- The school counselor breaches the duty owed.
- There is sufficient legal causal connection between the breach of duty and the injury.
- The student or parent/guardian suffers an injury or damages, and an assessment is made.

Duty: Duty requires the establishment of a relationship whereby the defendant owes the plaintiff a duty to act reasonably (Cardi, J., & Green, M., 2008; Numngern, 2017). A school counselor who sponsors the Foreign Exchange Club and takes the members to the beach for their end-of-the-year party is acting *in loco parentis*. The school counselor owes a duty if a student enters the water and starts to drown, whereas a passerby does not in most states even if that bystander is Caleb Dressel, Michael Phelps or Mark Spitz. The stronger the duty, the greater the legal responsibility and concurrent legal liability if something goes wrong (Alexander & Alexander, 2019; Blokhuis et al., 2020).

Breach: The judgment as to whether or not a breach has occurred with regard to the duty owed is centered on the issues of reasonability and an agreed-upon standard of care. Reasonableness includes the precautions you take. When taking the students to the beach, did you have enough chaperones? Did you explain to the students they could not enter the water for any reason? Did you position yourself so you would know if any student wandered away? Did you take along someone trained in first aid? Another test of whether one has acted reasonably is the potential for harm and the possible magnitude of harm. There is significant likelihood of harm on field trips to locations with water, and the seriousness of harm, such as potential drowning, is great. School districts across the country have banned field trips to pools, beaches, rivers and lakes because of the likelihood of harm.

Reasonableness: This is difficult to define as it is person-specific and depends on an individual's background, education, profession, culture, nationality and experiences. The court system tries to answer the question, "What would the reasonably competent school counselor do in a similar situation?" School counselors, as defendants, would have to show they behaved with reasonable care. The ASCA Ethical Standards (2022b) provide us with standards, and our school districts provide us with written policies and procedures; out of this is born standard of care to help define the "reasonable person test" or how the reasonably competent school counselor would behave (Alexander & Alexander, 2019; Blokhuis et al., 2020; Remley & Herlihy, 2019).

Causal connection: There must be a causal connection between the school counselor's breach of duty and the injury suffered by the student. Liability in a negligence case hinges on causation. Proximate cause refers to the foreseeability of harm or whether the school counselor could have predicted the harm (Alexander & Alexander, 2019). Using the example of the educator who takes a student to the beach, this school counselor owed a duty to keep students safe, but another adult chaperone expressly there to watch the students decides to steal away to smoke a cigarette. The school counselor might have been negligent in not properly supervising the students, but if the second adult's job was only to keep a keen eye on the students, then that adult's percentage of fault would be greater. In some states, such as North Carolina, Tennessee, Virginia and Maryland, compensation to the injured party is denied in cases of contributory negligence because the injured party can only recover for injuries if the injured party did not contribute in any way. Comparative negligence, used by other states, balances the percentage of blame based on the school counselor's negligence with the percentage of blame assigned to others who contributed to the injury. Damages are then assessed by percentage of fault (Alexander & Alexander, 2019).

Injury suffered: Assessment refers to determining monetary damages needed to compensate for the harm an individual suffers, such as injury, lost scholarship or death. Nominal damages can be awarded in cases where actual cost cannot be determined. Punitive damages are awarded in cases where the intent is to punish the defendant and deter similar actions in the future (Blokhuis et al., 2020; Remley & Herlihy, 2019).

Student service educators, such as school counselors, make it even more difficult to prove negligence, as it is not easy to prove a school counselor deviated from accepted practices and that the school counselor's act or negligence caused the harm a client suffered (Remley & Herlihy, 2019). The courts have been reluctant to determine that school counselors owe a duty in areas such as suicide or academic advising. Generally speaking, since the courts are reluctant to find that school counselors owe a legal duty, liability for negligence against school counselors is infrequently imposed. Therefore, only a few court cases exist in which school counselors are the defendants in a jury trial involving negligence. Most of the cases in this book that involved a school counselor as defendant were settled out of court.

Educational malpractice: To prove malpractice, there must be a comparison between the acceptable standard of care for the school counseling profession and the specific act or conduct claimed to be malpractice. The testimony of an expert witness, another school counselor or someone well versed in school counseling often helps determine whether or not the defendant met the professional standard.

In addition to expert witnesses, the standard of care is established in a variety of other ways, including adherence to and participation in professional licensing and credentialing entities both locally and nationally, educational degree preparation and continuing education programs. For the school counselor, additional resources for establishing a standard of care include school board policies as well as participation with in-service opportunities on a local level. Using standard of care as the framework, the court will decide if the school counselor acted as the reasonably competent professional would have acted under the same or similar circumstances (FindLaw, 2018). Malpractice claims often result from dissatisfaction with services provided, breakdowns in communications between persons, anger with the professional, and retaliation or personal greed. Claims are not, generally, from substantiated grievances (Alexander & Alexander, 2019).

Historically, school districts have had governmental immunity or protection from civil or tort liability. In most states with regard to negligence, malpractice or civil liability, individual employees are protected from personal liability if they are not acting in a willful or wanton way (Alexander & Alexander, 2019). Most states have legislation declaring that public employers must defend, indemnify and hold harmless any employee who is named in a civil suit for an act of omission arising out of the employee's job (Alexander & Alexander, 2019).

There are limits and exceptions to governmental immunity. Malicious, willful and intentional torts occur when one acts in a determined way to harm another individual (Alexander & Alexander, 2019). Some intentional torts may also be crimes, such as assault, battery, wrongful death, fraud and theft. An example of a malicious, willful and intentional tort involving a school counselor is found in *Doe v. Blandford* (2000). The school counselor sexually abused a student, constituting a willfully harmful act or intentional tort. The student's parents brought a complaint against the school district, claiming the district was negligent in hiring, failing to supervise and failing to fire their child's abuser. In its decision, the court found that the intentional tort exception should be interpreted narrowly and that action in this case should be brought against the government.

Education malpractice has yet to be codified, but the term is failure to render professional service that reasonably should be expected from educators. States are hesitant to recognize educational malpractice. The courts have articulated five reasons. The standard of care for educators lacks specificity and is difficult to define. Financial harm to the complainant is difficult to determine. If a school counselor misadvised a student about a required prerequisite college course, causing the student to lose an awarded scholarship, should the student be awarded the cost of tuition for the first year or for all four years? Courts are aware the floodgates open for other suits when students and families win educational malpractice suits. The list would be long if students could sue for not getting into the college of their choice or they failed because of a bad teacher. The courts do not want to be in the position of making decisions regarding internal operations of schools.

A unique relationship exists between the school counselor and the minor in school settings. This unique and special relationship is *in loco parentis*, Latin meaning "in place of a parent," in which the person or entity takes on the standard of care attributed to a parent. A school has a duty to provide for its students' physical safety. Teachers and other certified employees may step in as a parent would to discipline and correct a child's behavior or, alternatively, to keep one child safe from another child or adult (*Gammon v. Edwardsville Community Unit School District* (1980)). In addition, a school board may stand in the place of a parent to ban sexually explicit material from the school library (*Bethel School District No. 403 v. Fraser* (1986)). A student's biblical condemnation of homosexual behavior and his assertion that he had a right to do so under freedom of speech was balanced against the school's responsibility to act as parent to protect the rights of other students (Doe and *Doe v. Greendale Baptist Church and Academy* (2003)).

Getting Started: What Would You Do?

The following case is answered for you at the end of this chapter by a school counselor educator. Before you read his response, formulate in your own mind how you would approach this ethical dilemma.

NEGLIGENCE IN EATING DISORDERS

Karen, one of your seventh-graders, has been a regular in your office for the last two years. She has serious problems. You can't get her father to respond, but you have implored Karen's stepmother to get her some help. Lately, you have good reason to believe Karen is suffering from bulimia. When you ask Karen about it, she does not answer but rather starts a long diatribe about how you cannot tell her father because he is ready to send her off to live with her birth mother, and this information will give him the ammunition he needs. Karen has all but admitted to you that she is bulimic, and you know her assessment of her father's reaction is probably accurate. You decide to try to help Karen without calling her parents. The unthinkable happens, and Karen suffers heart failure. You are sued for negligence. How do you believe the courts will react? Is it likely your school district will pay for your defense?

Working Through Case Studies

NEGLIGENCE IN ACADEMIC ADVISING

Bert was lured to your school by the basketball coaches. His school counselor was not able to match his courses from his previous school, and scheduling Bert was a challenge. The summer after graduation Bert learned he did not have enough English credits for NCAA eligibility. Is the school counselor liable?

Points to Consider

Before 2001, no jurisdiction had recognized that negligence could occur in the context of a school counselor giving academic advice to a student (Zirkel, 2001a). In reversing a lower court's decision and remanding the case to trial, the Iowa Supreme Court in *Sain v. Cedar Rapids Community School District* (2001) determined that a school counselor owed a duty in this situation to advise a student with due care and attention.

Bruce Sain, a senior in Cedar Rapids, Iowa, was a talented all-state basketball player. In 1996, he was awarded a five-year basketball scholarship to Northern Illinois University. However, in the summer prior to his freshman year, Sain was notified in a letter that he did not meet the NCAA regulations for incoming freshman athletes at Division I schools. The letter explained that he fell one-third credit short in the required English credits because his one-third English credit in technical communications was not on the list of classes his high school submitted to NCAA for approval. Sain lost his scholarship, and his family filed suit against the Cedar Rapids School District, citing the school district as negligent and the school counselor, Larry Bowen, as guilty of negligent misrepresentation in his role as an academic advisor (*Sain v. Cedar Rapids Community School District* (2001)).

In his senior year, Sain needed three trimesters of English. Dissatisfied with the second-trimester English course, he turned to Bowen, his school counselor at Jefferson High School, and asked Bowen to place him in another English class. Bowen suggested technical communications and explained to Sain that it was being offered at the school for the first time but that the Initial Eligibility Clearinghouse would approve the high school course. Without further concern, Sain completed technical communications and graduated in spring 1996 with the prospect of a five-year scholarship at Northern Illinois University. Then, the letter arrived from the NCAA Clearinghouse declaring Sain ineligible based on academic grounds. Sain and Jefferson High School requested reconsideration from the NCAA, but their request for a waiver was denied (*Sain v. Cedar Rapids Community School District* (2001); Zirkel, 2001a).

With his scholarship offer voided, Sain turned to the courts. He filed suit against the NCAA (a suit he dropped shortly thereafter) and the school district, but not the school counselor, claiming negligence and negligent misrepresentation. He alleged negligence occurred when the school counselor never submitted the course, technical communications, to NCAA for approval. The suitability of the course was not at issue, since technical communications had been approved for other schools as a core English course. The problem was it had not been approved for Jefferson High School because the school had not included it on the list annually submitted to the NCAA Clearinghouse for approval. Sain claimed negligent misrepresentation by the school district because Bowen gave out erroneous information by telling him technical communications would be an approved course (*Sain v. Cedar Rapids Community School District* (2001)).

The trial court initially rejected Sain's suit. In the past, courts have received a number of educational malpractice lawsuits, but they continually sided with school districts, rejecting the notion that school counselors owe a duty to a student to give competent academic advice. Courts recognize how difficult the role of academic advisor is for school counselors, who are routinely required to manage large numbers of students, constantly changing rules and regulations, and fluctuating admissions and financial aid criteria. Courts have therefore been reluctant to determine that school counselors owe a duty in the academic advising arena. Surprisingly, however, when Sain appealed to the Iowa Supreme Court, the court remanded the case for trial (*Sain v. Cedar Rapids Community School District* (2001)).

It is important to note that the Iowa Supreme Court did not determine whether the school district was negligent; that was left for the lower court to decide. Rather, the state Supreme

Court found the claim of "negligent misrepresentation" possibly had merit and should not have been dismissed by the lower court. "Never before had any court, let alone one in Iowa, considered the liability of a school counselor for the tort of negligent misrepresentation without the ability to rely upon a tort immunity statute that protected school districts" (Willis, 2004, p. 7).

The Iowa Supreme Court remanded the case to the lower court for trial on the count of negligent misrepresentation. Justice Mark Cady of the Iowa Supreme Court wrote for the 5-2 majority that school counselors could be held accountable for providing accurate information to students about credits and courses needed to pursue postsecondary goals (Parrott, 2001). The erroneous advice given by the school counselor was equated to negligent misrepresentation in professions such as accounting, the law and others whose businesses require they give accurate and appropriate information (*Sain v. Cedar Rapids Community School District* (2001); Zirkel, 2001a).

The court determined that school counselors have a similar type of business relationship and responsibility of giving accurate advice to students when the student has a need to know. The court explained that just as accountants and lawyers stand to gain financially from giving accurate advice, so do school counselors, since that is what they are paid to do. Therefore, negligent misrepresentation may be applied to the school counselor/student relationship when erroneous advice means a student loses a lucrative scholarship. This kind of lawsuit is more business-oriented than academic and, according to the Iowa Supreme Court, is a classic case of negligent misrepresentation (*Sain v. Cedar Rapids Community School District* (2001); Zirkel, 2001a).

The court found that school counselors must use reasonable care in providing specific information to a student when (a) the school counselor has knowledge of the specific need for the information, (b) the school counselor provides the information to the student in the course of a school counselor/student relationship and (c) the student reasonably relies upon the information in circumstances where the school counselor knows or should know of the student's reliance (Zirkel, 2001a). Bowen claims never to have had a conversation with Sain about NCAA course eligibility, which Sain disputes.

Justice Linda K. Neuman, speaking on behalf of the minority, wrote that the Iowa Supreme Court's decision "spells disaster for the law," explaining the decision will open the floodgates and could be applied broadly to students in a variety of situations and not just athletes who need counsel on NCAA rules (Reid, 2001, p. 3). Neuman noted that the decision exalts logic over experience; it might appear logical that school counselors should give correct advice, but the reality of the expectations placed on school counselors makes this logic impossible. School counselors cannot have a command of everything there is to know about colleges and universities, admissions requirements, NCAA rules, financial aid and scholarships and a multitude of other facts that change daily. Neuman wrote, "Instead of encouraging sound academic guidance, today's decision will discourage advising altogether" (Reid, 2001, p. 3).

The majority justices acknowledged that the ruling could have a "chilling effect" on academic advising by school counselors (Reid, 2001, p. 3). However, the court cautioned that the ruling should have limited effect, as negligent representation is confined to students whose reliance on information is reasonable (such as an inquiry as to whether a course meets NCAA eligibility). Additionally, the school counselor must be aware of how vital the information is to the student. This explanation was intended to reassure school counselors and to keep them from overreacting to the principles outlined by the *Sain* case (*Sain v. Cedar Rapids Community School District* (2001)).

Although the lower court never heard the case, the findings of the Iowa Supreme Court in remanding the case to trial serves as a caution to the school counseling profession about providing accurate advice that could have an impact on a student's future financial opportunities. It is unusual for a tort claim of this nature to proceed to court, but by breaking with tradition, the Iowa Supreme Court has reinterpreted the nature of the school counselor/student relationship (Parrott, 2001).

A court case in California, *Brown v. Compton Unified School District* (1998), further demonstrates the court's reluctance to impose the first element of negligence, a duty owed, against a school district. Brown enrolled in Manuel Dominguez High School as a senior with the express purpose of taking the required classes to satisfy the NCAA eligibility requirements and of participating in the Manuel Dominguez High School basketball program. School counselor Rae Bonner advised Brown to enroll in a particular science course, but the course did not meet the NCAA requirements. After Brown had enrolled at the University of Southern California, the university revoked his basketball scholarship. Brown argued in his lawsuit that a special relationship existed between him and the school district because the district induced him to transfer and assured him Manuel Dominguez High School would allow him to satisfy the NCAA requirements for athletic eligibility. Brown further contended that he relied on the promise that he would be placed in courses that satisfied NCAA requirements. Under governmental immunity, both Bonner and the school district were immune from liability. "Government Code n1 section 822.2 protects a public employee acting in the scope of employment from injury due to the employee's misrepresentation" (*Brown v. Compton Unified School District* (1998), p. 6).

Another case, in Wisconsin, made its way to the state's highest court, which ruled that school counselors and school districts may not be held liable for giving students erroneous information – even when that information costs a student a full four-year college scholarship. Ryan Scott, a student at Stevens Point Area Senior High, sued the school district after he was declared ineligible for an NCAA student-athlete scholarship. The negligence claim hinged entirely on whether the district was immune from liability for negligence under Wisconsin's governmental immunity statute. The Wisconsin Supreme Court dismissed (but not happily) the lawsuit because of governmental immunity. Although the justices were compelled to follow prior decisions, in their opinion their decision was an injustice. Justice Bablitch stated, "This court should revisit these past cases. …A doctrine of governmental immunity that has caused such injustice and inequity, in this case and others, cannot, and I predict will not, stand much longer. In light of these sentiments, which appear to have growing support in many state courts, school districts should keep a watchful eye on the seemingly unstable future of the state's government immunity law" (*Scott v. Stevens Point Area Public School District* (2003), n.p.).

RECOMMENDATIONS FOR ACADEMIC ADVISORS

The *Sain*, *Brown* and *Scott* rulings should not deter school counselors from career and academic advising, a role that has great opportunity for implementing a social-justice agenda and leveling the playing field for many students. Continue to offer academic advising sessions to students. School counselors can help close the information gap between those students who know what they need to do to successfully access postsecondary education leading to wider economic opportunities and those students who have not received even the most basic information. Students without a significant adult in their lives helping them understand how to access and be successful in postsecondary opportunities need the school counselor to be an advocate.

Following are recommendations for school counselors who are in the role of academic advisor.

- Act as the reasonably competent professional would. Hold yourself to a high standard-of-care test. The courts are not asking for extraordinary care, only reasonable care. Our ethical standards help professionals aspire to extraordinary care, but the courts do not demand this level. By exercising skill and care in every action taken as a professional, school counselors can demonstrate they are behaving as reasonably competent professionals.
- Stay abreast of information needed for competent academic advising. Demonstrate a working knowledge of procedures, policies, laws, ethical standards and the school district's policies. Seek professional development in the area of academic advising. Demonstrate a good faith effort to stay informed.
- Empower others to take responsibility for having and giving the right information. You can teach students to be their own advocates through school counseling curriculum lessons in the computer lab, where students can conduct online searches and locate information on their own. Widely publicize academic information for all students and parents/guardians. Make use of newsletters, form letters and email groups in your advising role, thus demonstrating a proactive stance to disseminating critical, timely information.
- Require students and parents/guardians to sign off when they receive critical information. When you give seniors their personal credit check for remaining graduation requirements, for instance, have them sign an acknowledgement that they have been told and understand what they need to do, and have parents/guardians sign, too.
- Have a statement on the schedule change form that asks the student to alert you if they are trying to meet NCAA eligibility standards and if they answer in the affirmative, require that they attach the courses that the school has on the NCAA approved list with the course they want to move into highlighted.

NEGLIGENCE IN WRITING LETTERS OF RECOMMENDATION

Mia, one of your seniors, asks you for a letter of recommendation. You have not worked with Mia other than a brief conversation over a schedule change. You asked a teacher who happened to be in the school counseling office what he thought of Mia. His opinion was that Mia excels academically (as confirmed by her transcript) and athletically but lacks character and is "always in it for herself, not a team player." This teacher appeared to know what he was talking about, so you sent the university a letter emphasizing Mia's self-centeredness. Are there any legal and/or ethical issues that may arise from this process?

A lawsuit was filed against a district when a student alleged that her school counselor and principal defamed her character and purposely caused emotional stress after her scholarship was withdrawn. Although the lawsuit was never tried in a court of law, it was tried in the court of public opinion. The accusation from the parents was that the school counselor wrote a "libelous and fabricated letter of recommendation." The school counselor's recommendation emphasized the student's deficiency in initiative, character, integrity, leadership and community service. The parents contended that the school counselor did not have any personal interactions with their child on which to base such claims.

The 2019 College Trends survey, by the National Association of College Admissions Counselors (NACAC), found that of the 218 respondents, 15% reported the school counselor recommendation has considerable importance, while 40% say these letters have moderate importance (NACAC, 2019). In NACAC's Pulse of College Admissions Report (2021), they found that 10% of colleges not requiring the college entrance exams said they will rely more heavily on letters of recommendation.

In a January 2022 survey, 122 ASCA members respondents said they write letters of recommendation. Of the respondents who work with students who need letters, 17% said, "I will only write a letter if I can write a strong letter," and 63% responded "I focus on a student's strengths but sometimes my letters are obvious that there are weaknesses (people can read between the lines)" (Stone, 2022b).

This same survey revealed school counselors might collaborate with other adults who know the students better or will focus on basic facts like GPA, honors courses, extracurriculars, etc. The above case informs the profession that if for some reason a school counselor feels compelled to include negative comments in a letter of recommendation, then it is imperative that personal knowledge and, ideally, more than one reliable source is needed to substantiate negative remarks.

In the same survey, ASCA members indicated they are, by and large, expected to write letters of recommendation for all students needing one. Letters of recommendation pose challenges for school counselors as they wrestle with how to be fair to a student while not saying anything the school counselor cannot stand behind. In this survey, 94% of the respondents said they work with students who need letters of recommendation, and 68% said, "It is the expectation that I write a letter for all students needing one" (Stone, 2022b).

These school counselors also described their letter-writing practice.

Regarding letters of recommendation, which of the following best describes your general practice:
Not applicable in my current role 6.5%
I write letters that also point out a student's weaknesses 0.8%
I will only write a letter if I can write a strong letter. 16.9%
I focus on a student's strengths but sometimes my letters are obvious that there are weaknesses (people can read between the lines). 62.9%
Other: 12.9%
(Stone, 2022b)

Some admissions officers say, "Be candid and comprehensive; include negatives if you are comfortable doing so" (College Board, 2016). However, the Stone 2022b survey revealed that school counselors are not comfortable including negatives in letters. Rather, they will stick to a student's strengths, but what their letters omit or say minimally conveys there might be some weaknesses simply by omission, e.g., the school counselor does not mention service or character as maybe these are not strengths. If a letter focuses on negative information instead of mentioning it in a minor point, then school counselors ask a student to seek someone else to write the letter.

THE SCHOOL COUNSELOR'S ROLE WHEN A STUDENT GIVES FALSE INFORMATION TO A COLLEGE

You are fairly certain a student has provided false information on a college application about having a nationally ranked position in rowing. You question the student, and her parents come roaring into the school and berate you for questioning their daughter's integrity. Is it your obligation to ferret out the truth and alert the college if you discover a student provided false information?

Points to Consider

More than 300 school counselors answered this question in surveys at five 2019 legal and ethical workshops for school counselors and college admissions officers. The majority of school counselors felt the onus is on students to ensure college admission applications contain honest information. Transcripts and application material generated by the school district must, of course, be accurate, but out-of-school activities aren't something school counselors should be required to verify. Students must be certain their application materials are accurate and must sign a disclaimer on their application stating the information is truthful.

Mossimo Giannulli and Lori Loughlin, parents of Olivia Jade, were accused of paying Rick Singer $500,000 to package their daughter as an athlete to the University of Southern California for the sake of side-door admissions. The college coach was also accused of conspiring with Singer, the mastermind of the Varsity Blues plot. Allegedly, the school counselor questioned Olivia Jade about the accuracy of her college application rowing claim. The school counselor was under no obligation to find conclusive evidence that Olivia Jade was a rower. Reportedly, Olivia Jade's school counselor contacted the University of Southern California after noticing Olivia Jade had been flagged as a crew recruit and said he had no knowledge of her being involved in the sport. The onus is squarely on the student's shoulders to report only truthful information. A school counselor may choose to research and/or reach out to admissions representatives with facts that can be substantiated. This is a professional decision made in context and should be respected, but it shouldn't be required. The school counselor in this scandal was on point for calling even though he probably knew parental wrath was heading his way. In 2020, both Loughlin and Giannulli were sentenced to prison for their roles in the massive nationwide college admission scandal (NBC News, 2020).

BRAG SHEETS AND THE SCHOOL COUNSELOR'S RESPONSIBILITY

You wrote a recommendation letter in good faith based on what was on the student's brag sheet. You later discover and the information the student provided you was blatantly false. Are you liable should a court case ensue surrounding the false claim?

Points to Consider

School counselors have to rely on students to self-report outside activities. These activities can't be found on students' educational records but help school counselors paint a picture of a well-rounded student. In another Varsity Blues scandal, a school counselor wrote that a student was a nationally ranked athlete only to find out later that the student had lied on the brag sheet, his father had paid hundreds of thousands of dollars to Rick Singer, who paid the tennis coach of Georgetown University to pretend the student was a recruit for the tennis team. Again, this school counselor behaved appropriately in relying on the student to give honest responses. It is unrealistic to think a school counselor can verify everything on a brag sheet. One technique some school counselors use is to have the students list a contact following each activity on the brag sheet. School counselors shouldn't be expected to personally speak with all the contacts, but this small accountability step may be enough to encourage student honesty and accuracy.

SUICIDE AND DUTY OWED

A student tells you her friend Jocelyn, one of your students, is threatening suicide. When you call Jocelyn into your office, she vehemently denies any consideration of suicide, scoffing at the idea that she would ever harm herself. You are convinced there is no basis for concern, and you drop the issue without discussing it with anyone else. Do your actions pose an ethical or legal dilemma?

Points to Consider

The law of negligence involves injury or damage to another through a breach of duty owed to that person. Duty owed is a legal responsibility one person has to another, such as a legal responsibility to drive with care so you do not injure another person (Alexander & Alexander, 2019). As we noted earlier, negligence requires the presence of four elements: (1) a duty is owed, (2) the duty owed was breached, (3) there is a causal connection between breach of duty and injury, and (4) an injury has occurred. Until the *Eisel v. Montgomery County Board of Education* court case (1991), courts consistently found that school counselors did not "owe a legal duty" to prevent a student's suicide. *Eisel* strengthened school counselors' legal obligation to students by satisfying for the first time the primary element of negligence, declaring school counselors have a special relationship with students and owe a duty to try to prevent a student's suicide.

The Maryland Court of Appeals in the *Eisel* case advised that school counselors had a duty to notify the parents of a 13-year-old student who made suicidal statements to her classmates and remanded the case back to the lower court to be heard. The appellate court did not find for guilt or innocence, but they found the case had merit and deserved a jury trial.

Nicole Eisel allegedly became involved in Satanism and told several friends and fellow students of her intention to kill herself. Some of these friends told their school counselor of Nicole's intentions, and this school counselor in turn informed Nicole's school counselor. The two school counselors questioned Nicole about the statements, and Nicole denied making them. The school counselors did not notify either the parents or the school administrators about these events. Shortly thereafter, in a public park, Nicole and a friend tragically consummated their suicide pact.

The court in the *Eisel* case cited as critical the *in loco parentis* doctrine. Furthermore, school counselors owe a special duty to exercise reasonable care to protect a student from harm and must use reasonable means to attempt to prevent a suicide when they receive notice of a student's suicidal intent. With the ruling, the court redefined the school counselor/student relationship and declared school counselors have a duty of care when placed on notice of a possible suicide. The court recognized the fact that school counselors hear a great amount of suicidal ideation and have the complicated task of trying to determine which threats are real. However, the court stated, "The consequence of the risk is so great that even a relatively remote possibility of a suicide may be enough to establish duty" (*Eisel v. Board of Education of Montgomery County* (1991), n.p.). In other words, the court stopped just short of declaring school counselors have an affirmative duty to notify parents in each and every case involving a suicidal threat.

The tenets established in *Eisel* set a precedent that school counselors now have a legal obligation to try to prevent suicide. School counselors should not be paralyzed by the *Eisel* ruling. Rather, the ruling should serve to help school counselors realize the importance of protecting students and giving parents a chance to exercise custody and control of their child. The *Eisel* case did not deliver the final word. Following the *Eisel* case, courts in at least five states have rejected these kinds of cases. An Illinois appellate court in 1997 absolved a school counselor of legal liability when the school counselor failed to tell the student's parents about the student's threats of suicide (*Grant v. Board of Trustees of Valley View School District* (1997)).

Where does a school counselor's legal liability end? More frequently parents are suing and not winning their cases in court but nevertheless tying up the district and school counselors in court battles that end in a settlement. Liability should end when the school counselor notifies parents and school authorities and provides resources and recommendations for outside counseling; however, parents are finding reasons to sue even when notified. I have served as an expert witness in a number of cases and school counselors have been sued not just because they did not call parents but because of different reasons for each case such as:

1. Did not follow the suicide protocol to the letter
2. Called parents and agreed with them that their child was fine
3. Thought an 18-year-old had autonomy and parents could not be involved
4. Used words such as impulse control instead of the word suicidal
5. Assessed and reported low risk and were wrong

However, the courts do not expect school counselors to do the impossible and prevent all adolescent suicides. Rather, the court's message is that the consequence of the risk in not involving parents is too great and that parents must be allowed to try to intervene.

A school counselor's ethical obligation to a student who is suicidal may extend beyond parental notification if the parents do not enroll the student in counseling. If they do not arrange counseling when the student is first identified, the probability of attempts and completion increases. School counselors must make every attempt to supply parents or guardians with counseling referrals until placement is secured for that student (Capuzzi, 2002; National Association of School Psychologists, n.d.). In most cases, the school counselor will need to notify child protective services of a possible neglect situation if the parents do not pursue counseling.

Ethical standards provide guidelines regarding protecting students and others from potentially dangerous situations, but it is ultimately the school counselor's responsibility to negotiate the rights and privileges of students and parents regarding issues of duty to care. The courts continually vest parents with legal rights to guide their children (*Bellotti v. Baird* (1979); *H.L. v. Matheson* (1981); American Bar Association, 2004) and parents need to exercise custody and control over their child and provide them with access to outside counseling if it is needed to save their child's life.

SCHOOL COUNSELORS REQUIRED TO QUANTIFY SUICIDE

Your district requires you to do a suicide assessment resulting in point scores based on a student's self-report and the points correspond to low, medium or high danger. This practice of quantifying suicide greatly concerns you, as it is so subjective and dependent on the student telling you the truth. Are your fears justified?

Points to Consider

In the school counseling world of gray, there is one truth that is a constant; school counselors know they cannot accurately quantify a suicide risk. School counselors want support students who present as suicidal or even the inkling that they may be suicidal, but to assess a student's level of suicide risk is to imply that we can peer into a child's head and heart. Medical professionals are themselves declaring in large numbers the danger, fallacy and inaccuracy of classifying a person for suicide. If the medical profession is questioning suicide risk assessments as untrustworthy, by reasonable extension those who require school counselors to assess a student's suicide potential do so at the risk of liability.

During the last decade, a growing body of research in the medical and mental health field on the predictive ability of suicide assessments has validated what school counselors have always known – suicide risk assessments are too inaccurate to be trusted. Medical and clinical researchers are examining the efficacy of assessments and concluding that despite substantial efforts, assessments have no predictive value. Risk stratification misses many cases with a very high false-positive rate. In 2017, research by Large, et al. examined 40 years of suicide risk assessment research. Ninety-five percent of patients assessed as high risk did not complete a suicide; however, 50 percent of patient suicides assessed in lower risk categories did complete a suicide. Large, et. al. found that there has been no improvement in the accuracy of suicide risk assessment over the last 40 years. They found no statistical method to identify patients at a high-risk of suicide in a way that would improve treatment. In another 2017 study by Berman, of the 157 patients who died by suicide, 67%

of the deceased had denied suicidal ideation during an assessment given within two days of their death (Berman, 2017).

As the medical and mental health professions continue to debate the efficacy and accuracy of their efforts to assess suicide, one thing is certain – school counselors should never be required to predict if a student is safe from suicide based on an in-school assessment. Many school counselors don't need research to tell them this truth, as they have first-hand, heartbreaking proof that school counselors aren't able to predict safety based on a student's self-report. School counselors rely on experts in the medical and mental health fields to use multiple means to attempt to unpack a student's future likelihood for suicide, and the debate would suggest that even these esteemed professionals are far from agreement that they can assess suicide.

Despite the dangers, school districts in America continue to impose on school counselors the impossible task of stratifying the lethality of suicide into the categories of low, medium and high risk based on a student's self-report. Yes, school counselors can gather information to convey to parents, but the risk of assessing and being wrong outweighs any advantages in saying a student is low risk for suicide. Explain to all those who would impose suicide assessments on you that to quantify a student as low risk is to abandon the norms of the profession. Explain the dangers of using an anemic tool in such a powerful and dangerous way. In addition to the principles established by the *Eisel* case, lessons learned from the *Mikell v. School Administrative Unit 33* (2009) and the *Rogers v. Christina School District* (2012) court cases have been included into the ethical standards as well, making it painfully clear the fallacy and danger of labeling a child's risk of suicide as low or nonexistent.

Suicide assessments by school counselors are inaccurate at best and dangerous at worst, especially for the few outliers in our profession who believe they can actually assess children and deem them low risk. An assessment should add to the body of gathered information and should not state or imply to parents their child's level of risk has been determined. School counselors who use suicide assessments to quantify a low risk are operating completely outside their competence, qualifications, ethical imperative and standard of care.

In isolation, an assessment is simply what the student chooses to reveal. Students often hide the truth or vacillate about whether to reveal the truth to the adults in their lives. There are many reasons why a student may deny self-harm. The competent school counselor would never conclude students weren't in danger simply because they said they are fine. The common-sense approach would be to dismiss all self-reports denying harm as untrustworthy.

School counselors have historically had an instant, deeply ingrained reaction to any potential suicide report, whether the source of those reports is self-report, peer report, rumors, staff/faculty or hearsay. Peer reports, unlike self-reports, are more likely to contain the truth, as adolescents tend to confide in peers more than adults as they move through puberty. If a peer tells you another student is possibly suicidal, ethical practice requires school counselors to put considerable weight on the report, provide the parents with an explanation as to how you came to be informed and emphasize the value of peer reports.

If after receiving a peer report and speaking with the student, alarm bells don't go off, don't trust it. Communicate with the student's parents and explain what precipitating events or persons led you to speak with their child. If it was because of a peer report, be certain to stress to parents that truth is often found in peer reports.

Peer pressure, social isolation and loneliness are areas to explore with the parents/guardians, as well as any stressors you know of that their child may be experiencing, such as high expectations, perfectionism, bullying, friendship woes, social media conflicts, indirect and/or direct threats, etc. Students who make suicide threats often give indirect indicators of suicide instead of directly saying, "I am going to kill myself." For example, "I wish I could float away and never come back" or "I am a horrible person, and I am going to do something about it" are examples of indirect threats. Ask parents to investigate their child's social media, phone, writings and/or room. Parents are in the best position to unpack clues in areas where you don't have access, and mental health professionals are in the best position to help the student in multiple sessions focusing on healthy and unhealthy coping mechanisms.

Give parents information and avoid the temptation to reassure them or minimize the risk. This is not the time to worry about what stress or alarm you may cause the parents; rather, it is a time to provide resources and information with the caveat that you are absolutely unable to tell them if their child is safe. Word choice and urgency are important. Parents need to hear the straightforward message of suicide, no couching in words such as "impulse control" or "hurt oneself."

If you have advocated against quantifying the lethality of suicide and lost the battle, win the war. Use politically astute language and refuse to negate the risk. Use any number of disclaimers in place of "low risk," such as "unable to assess"; "not enough information"; "unknown, as self-reports are invalid"; "student was not forthcoming"; "peer reports supersede student denial, and this assessment is not as valid as the peer report I received"; "I am not qualified to accurately assess, as it takes multiple approaches and means from the mental health and medical field"; or "my ethical response is to recognize and convey to parents my limitations in knowing what is in your child's head and heart. Seek outside mental health or medical help for your child."

School counselors have a very limited role in suicidal ideation. Receive and respond to the outcry, gather as much information to relay to parents as possible, notify parents, involve others to keep the student safe until parents arrive, provide resources, and try to determine if parents are taking the report seriously. Note, there is nothing here about predicting a child's future.

Even if the danger appears relatively remote, parents should be notified. School counselors do not wait for certainty, but rather the notion of a potential suicide places school counselors in a position to immediately notify parents/guardians. It is a well-known fact that students will often deny suicidal ideation to escape the gaze of adults while confiding their true intentions to their peers" (ASCA, 2020d).

PARENTAL RESPONSE AND RESPONSIBILITY TO SUICIDAL IDEATION

You often find it is more difficult to talk to parents about their child's suicidal ideation than it is to talk to their child. Parents so often want to minimize their child's potential harm and want you to agree. What is best practice?

Points to Consider

School counselors report risk assessment results to parents to underscore the need to act on behalf of their child's risk. The school counselor never assures parents their child isn't at risk; something a school counselor cannot know with certainty (ASCA, 2022b). Many parents will respond to a school counselor's report that their child has reported they want to kill themselves with the belief or the hope that their child was just using words. Parents will listen intently to the school counselor in the hopes of hearing a tone, words, cadence, tenor that might provide reassurance that their child is just talking and not at risk. Any time a school counselor finds reason to report to parents that their child is at risk, the approach should not be to reassure or lessen the parents' fear. The call is a warning not a conversational, nonchalant approach.

Parents are often at a loss as to how to help their child and will, therefore, listen and value what the school counselor has to say. In 2018, Czyz et al., studied the parents of 162 children who visited the emergency room for suicide-related concerns or attempts. Parents expressed considerable doubt in the following areas: in being able to recognize suicide warning signs in their child; in working with their child on a commitment to refrain from suicidal action; and, in the secure belief that their child would honestly disclose thoughts of suicide to them. School counselors have often experienced the danger of insecure parents clinging to the school counselor's recommendations; therefore, school counselors must overemphasize that they cannot reassure the parent their child is not in danger.

Avoid misplaced confidence. Even the most talented school counselors with dual licensure as a mental health therapist should never assume they can do therapy in school (2021d). The student who is suicidal needs an outside mental health therapist. With the help of a mental health professional, parents can explore their child's coping mechanisms and provide the time and skills needed to peel away and lay bare the complicated layers of their child's suicidality. School counselors rely on the skills of the mental health professional who can delve into the student's protective factors and the coping mechanisms the student is using to stay alive and determine how to help the child expand the healthy ones and eliminate the self-destructive ones. This is the time for action on the part of parents/guardians. Don't give parents an out by giving them a false sense of security and misplaced hope. Emphasize the urgency of parental action and provide resources.

The standard of care expected from school counselors in communicating self-harm reports to parents is not to label, but to provide resources to parents/guardians, and report negligence cases to CPS if parents don't take action. Parents do not feel confident to deal with their child's suicide. School counselors do not help them by easing the threat that their child is in danger; rather, they help parents/guardians by reassuring them they need to seek counseling for their child and for the family to learn how to help (Czyz et al., 2018).

PREADOLESCENTS AND SUICIDE

You are an elementary school counselor and don't have any experience with students threatening suicide – until this year. What do you do?

Points to Consider

The standard of care for school counselors is to avoid basing any conclusions of risk when asking "yes" or "no" questions. Rather, school counselors provide prompts to encourage talking with no intention of reaching a conclusion, but, rather with the goal of learning all they can about a child's thoughts and feelings. A series of questions that a student can give a "yes" or "no" response to: "Have you ever thought about suicide?" "Do you have a plan?" are all likely to be answered "no" by pre-adolescents. Interviewing preadolescent children about suicidality is different than discussing this topic with teenagers or adults (Doyle & Fite, 2021; Heise, York, & Thatcher, 2016). Preadolescents bring a different level of cognitive functioning.

Researchers in the medical field are trying to find appropriate ways to assess the preadolescent population of 5- to 12-year-olds, a cohort that differs from older students (Doyle & Fite, 2021; Heise, York, & Thatcher, 2016). With preadolescents, Tishler, Staats, Rhodes (2007) recommend gathering information with questions such as "Do you ever feel sad enough that it makes you want to go away and not come back?" "Do you feel like crying a lot?" and avoiding questions such as "Have you thought about killing yourself?" "Do you have a plan?" (p.814). Again, the standard of care is to exercise extreme caution in emphasizing answers to binary questions with all students but especially with preadolescents.

SUICIDE BOARD POLICIES AND STATE STATUTES

You are employed by a district that has a 14-step board policy for suicide prevention. Notifying parents, the most important step, is tucked into a dozen other steps, many of which are out of the school counselor's control to adhere to in each and every case. You absolutely call parents when placed on notice that a student might be suicidal, but you often miss some of the other board-approved steps in the protocol due to the unattainable and unrealistic nature of some of the steps. Should you worry?

Points to Consider

Yes, you should worry. The irony of our legal and ethical work in staying true to policies is that there are school board policies or rules that are at best unrealistic and at worst outright dangerous. Suicide prevention policies requiring school counselors to do what is not realistic each and every time should not be put to paper. Unless a board policy can be adhered to in its fullest intent in every instance, it leaves the school counselor open and vulnerable.

Some suicide policies are developed by those who have no understanding of the nature and function of school counseling. In one court case, it was the local health department that imposed the suicide policy on school counselors, requiring them to qualify the lethality of suicide and to move into other areas outside their competence level.

In one court case, the school board policy was at the center of the lawsuit in which a student was reported to be suicidal. The district was requiring the school counselor to obtain information from the outside therapist before readmitting any student who is suicidal into the public school. The school counselor was required to get written permission from the parents before they contacted the outside therapist. This was burdensome to the school counselor and the family. The board policy did not explain the purpose of this policy other than to say it's a requirement. This requirement might seem reasonable on the surface; however, in the reality of schools it is fraught with pitfalls. What are the implications if the school counselor fails to contact the therapist? School board policies must be followed, and a rigid policy of "musts" leaves school counselors unable to exercise judgment whether contacting the therapist is in the student's and family's best interest. Toward what end is the school counselor contacting the outside therapist? If it is to make a plan to transition the student back into school, then it is reasonable to expect that the therapist will contact the school counselor. It is up to the parents and students to decide how much they need to let the school know and if a transition plan is even needed. Outside therapists should contact the school counselor if they deem it to the advantage of the student. If there is a board policy and it is not followed, then it provides considerable fuel to the fire of any resultant lawsuit.

Policies that are unrealistic, cumbersome, intrusive and outside a school counselor's role and/or authority are written without the involvement of school counselors. However, once written, the school counselor must follow the policy. Regardless of what we think about our school board policies, school counselors must know the board policies governing their work and adhere to them. In several recent court cases involving school counselors, the lawyers were eager to demonstrate that the school counselors at the center of the suits did not follow a policy to the letter. In one of the cases, the school counselors could not possibly have followed a complicated multistep suicide prevention policy. Once sued, the district had to look at the policy through this new lens, and only then did the district realize how burdensome and unrealistic the policy was to implement. The district revised the policy from pages upon pages to one paragraph, which gave the basic and appropriate response, "Don't try to assess suicide or provide therapeutic counseling. Alert parents and provide parents with outside resources." It took a lawsuit to get a policy that made sense. Encourage your district not to wait for the lawsuit but until the district revises a policy that makes it possible to adhere to make certain you follow the policy to the letter and document why you could not when you did not.

Additionally, know your state statute. If the statute is not up to date or isn't appropriate, contact your state school counseling association to change it. State statutes can also be outdated and way outside the standard of care for the profession.

CHANGING AN UNREALISTIC BOARD POLICY

You want to change a complicated board policy on suicidal ideation, which is overly involved and includes many steps out of your control. How do you go about changing a dangerous policy?

Following are some suggestions for politically, correctly changing a burdensome school district policy that places students in danger. Approaching this with your district is context-driven response, but here are a few suggestions.

- Seek allies who agree with you and have the power to effect change.
- Point out the fallacies of the policy from a legal standpoint if possible.
- Find court cases that back your argument.
- Develop a "what if" scenario. For example, if your policy has you assessing suicide, discuss the issue with administration or others in a position of power, and walk them through the result if your assessment is wrong.
- Find the political leverage. Does a working group already exist to whom you can voice recommendations for policy changes? Identify school district policies that make sense, and provide them as examples. Find a political ally who can take the changes through the approval system.
- If you have a state statute that is against the standard of care for the profession, ask your state school counseling association to add it to their lobbying efforts. Sometimes school counselors or their organizations have asked for interpretations of existing statutes. California school counselors did this with a confusing state statute on confidentiality and student pregnancy.
- Provide professional development for the faculty on the existing policy in question. This would be an optimum time to get everyone's input as to how realistic or fraught with pitfalls the policy would be to implement.
- Keep written notes, however brief, on your efforts to change policy should the policy stand.
- Protect yourself and your students, and examine policies and state statutes for a symbiotic relationship to the role of school counseling. Get your state school counseling association to lobby for legislation that is appropriate for school counselor and student well-being.

INFORMATION-GATHERING TOOL

Your district is moving away from suicide assessments. You want to tell parents everything you have learned that might be pertinent to their child's mental health but not to mislead by quantifying risk. If you are not going to assess suicide, what might you use?

Currently there is an ASCA committee working to develop a tool for school counselors who are moving away from assessments and gathering information to relay to parents. The intent of this tool is to help school counselors take into consideration all the environmental/psychosocial factors that contribute significantly to a child's well-being and relay what is known to parents. These environmental/psychosocial factors include being bullied, suffering socially, difficulty making and keeping friends, academic stressors, family dysfunction, overachievement, etc. The judicious and safe approach is to dismiss as invalid any denial by a child and to gather information to relate to parents/guardians, including teacher input.

NOTIFY EVERY TIME

A student is frequently referred to you for suicidal ideation. You call parents every time but the last phone call you were met with a very irritated parent who said, "Stop calling me. She is a drama queen." What do you do?

This is a question frequently asked by practicing school counselors who find some parents do not want to hear about their child possibly being suicidal. This may very likely be a child neglect call. When you have continuously been in touch with parents and their child shows up often to talk of suicide, there is something wrong, even if not suicidal ideation. Parents/guardians have to exercise custody and control of their child and seek help. Make a plan with the parents/guardians as to how you will communicate and require that they respond that they have received the communication. Have them sign the agreed-upon plan of notification. Explain that you are legally and ethically required to notify them when their child is in harm's way, and it is outside your competence area to determine if a phone call is not needed and the child is just being a "drama queen." Document your notifications. Suicide and child abuse create conditions in which you have to document the when, what, and how of your notifications to authorities and/or parents.

In *Baab v Medina City BOE* (2019), the school counselor made multiple efforts to aid D.B., whose friends reported to the school counselor that he was cutting, talking of suicide and afraid of his father. On each occasion, the school counselor called the father and/or talked to D.B. about the peer reports. D.B. took his own life, and his father sued the school counselor because she did not report to the father that D.B.'s friend's mother said D.B. was telling her son he planned to take his own life. The school counselor had recommended counseling, D.B.'s father did take him to the hospital, but he was not admitted. The school counselor argued in the lawsuit that her actions were not reckless just because they were not perfect.

GOVERNMENTAL IMMUNITY AND SUICIDE

A student comes to you worried about her friend Jeff. "I think someone needs to check on him. Something is not right. He is not himself. He said he was sick and tired of life." You are pulled to do AP proctoring, and you did not have a chance to check on Jeff. His friend skipped school that afternoon and found Jeff dead from an apparent suicide. Your state has a strong governmental immunity law. Will you escape legal liability under governmental immunity?

Points to Consider

Andrew was a freshman at St. Croix Falls High School in January 1996. Mr. McMahons drove his son to school, but Andrew did not attend classes that day. A district policy provides that if a student is absent from school, the school will call the parents/guardians at home or work to verify the absence, but the school did not call the McMahons. A classmate, Jamie Stocker, told a school counselor that Andrew "was planning to skip school that day," that he was probably at her house and that someone should check on him or contact his parents. Stocker further said she thought Andrew seemed depressed and had said something to the effect that he was "sick and tired of this life." Stocker left school without permission that afternoon to check on Andrew at her home and discovered Andrew's body in her family's closed garage. Andrew had doused himself with gasoline and set himself on fire.

The McMahons' suit was dismissed, but they appealed their wrongful death suit against St. Croix Falls School District for their son's suicide. The McMahons argued the circuit court erred when it established that a school district has absolute governmental immunity for its negligent acts when a student commits suicide. The McMahons contend that, contrary to Wisconsin tort law, the circuit court erroneously established that, under no conceivable circumstances, no matter how egregious a school district's negligence, could a school ever be found liable for a minor student's suicide. They contended that the district breached its duty to call them and to follow up after a school counselor learned Andrew was despondent and absent from school. The district disputes the facts of Stocker's affidavit but states that it is of no matter as they are immaterial to governmental immunity. The appeals court agreed with the district that such facts would not change the results.

In *Fowler v. Szostek* (1995), the court found that school officials did not owe a legal duty to a student who committed suicide once she left the school campus. Brandi Nelson was suspended and had to face an expulsion hearing based on claims that she sold marijuana to two students while on school grounds. Brandi fatally shot herself on the eve of the suspension. Brandi's mother had implored school administrators to wait until after the impending Christmas holidays before disciplinary action, as the suspension would be a devastating blow to Brandi. The appellate court never reached the details of the negligence claim, because in Texas, as in many states, school officials are protected by governmental immunity except for actions of 1) excessive force in the discipline of students or (2) negligence resulting in bodily injury to students. In the court's opinion, this 1995 case did not rise to either exception (Fossey, R., & Zirkel, P., 2004).

DISCIPLINE AND SUICIDE

You worry that the overly punitive discipline at your school does not focus on helping a child learn and self-correct with help. You do not want to insinuate yourself in discipline but wonder if there is something you could do. Is there a role for school counselors in helping students self-correct?

No one would fault you if you did not put any effort or attention on the approach to discipline in your school with all that is packed into a school counselor's day. There is usually not enough time to complete your own job much less time to focus on anyone else's role. Discipline rarely results in a student's suicide, but it has happened. When it does, it reminds us of how important it is to approach vulnerable, developing minds with care. Suicide is rarely the result of a single cause, yet, we give pause when a growing number of discipline cases of seemingly well-adjusted, happy, future-oriented students are followed by suicides. Parents/guardians who have lost children to suicide following discipline are asking if discipline is intended to help their child self-correct and get back on track or is it instead simply punitive and creating despair. Some districts are moving toward restorative justice to reduce suspensions and move toward teaching lessons rather than punishing.

Nick Stuban's attendance record was almost flawless. He was on the football team, had good grades, and his history teacher described him as a model student. He was suspended after buying a capsule of JWH-018, a synthetic compound that is legal but not permitted on school campuses. His mistake and the consequences spiraled downward for 11 weeks, ending when Nick took his life. Two years earlier another football player in the district committed suicide the day before his disciplinary hearing (Washington Post, 2011).

School counselors are smart to avoid insinuating themselves into discipline issues. One of the risk categories is that 70% of completed suicides among youth are precipitated by a stressful event (McKean, et al., 2018). Knowing that a student will act on a precipitating event and understanding how scary a discipline event is for some students, a school counselor might want to be an advocate for initiating a restorative instead of punitive approach to discipline. School counselors can also advocate for individual students when placed on notice that a student is in trouble and the circumstances call for someone to speak up on the student's behalf. Our advocacy imperative might also be professional development for the entire staff on suicide triggers, lawsuits filed, the developing brain and other topics that raise educators' awareness that our youth need the educators to be teachers even in discipline.

SUICIDE: AN INTERVENING VARIABLE THAT BREAKS THE CAUSAL CONNECTION

Howard is very fragile. You have been unable to get his parents to seek outside counseling help for him, but you continue to call and to see Howard whenever you can. It has been three weeks since you have seen him, and you make a mental note to seek him out on Monday. Monday you are hit with the news that Howard committed suicide over the weekend. Howard's parents bring suit against the district and you, citing the depth of their child's distress and suicidal ideation was not told to them. What is the plausible outcome?

Points to Consider

In *Bogust v. Iverson* (1960), the Wisconsin Supreme Court dismissed a wrongful death action brought against a college counselor by the parents of a 19-year-old student who committed suicide six weeks after counseling was terminated. Bogust cited that suicide constitutes an intervening force that breaks the line of causation from the wrongful act to the death, and therefore the wrongful act does not render the counselor civilly liable (*Bogust v. Iverson* (1960)). The four major elements of negligence (one of which is the causal connection) are:

- duty owed
- duty owed breached
- causal connection between the breach and injury
- injury suffered

For negligence to be determined in the case scenario, there had to be a connection (the third element of negligence) between the school counselor's breach of duty (second element) and the injury suffered (fourth element). Most states follow the general rule that suicide is an intervening force. Regardless of what the school counselor did or did not do (the wrongful act) before, the suicide is the intervening variable that breaks any chain of causation.

Another ruling provided a similar result. In *Lezner v. Shaw and Gresham School District* (1990), Lezner, an emotionally disabled student, was suspended from school for smoking marijuana on school property. The school unsuccessfully tried to reach the parents by phone to let them know of the suspension, then gave a copy of the suspension papers to the student and mailed the original to his home. The student did not inform his parents of the suspension and committed suicide. The parents claimed the school was negligent by failing to notify them promptly of their son's suspension. Following the *Bogust v. Iverson* (1960) precedent, the court ruled that a delayed suicide was not sufficiently connected to any act of negligence.

Even though case after case throughout the country finds school officials and school counselors do not owe a duty to try to prevent suicide and that suicide is an intervening variable, school counselors take little comfort in the courts' reluctance to hold them to a legal duty. "Do no harm" means school counselors should always err on the side of caution when they think a student may be in danger. Call parents/guardians. The breach of confidentiality is a minor transgression, indeed is of no consequence at all, when weighed against the greater harm, the death of a child.

SUICIDE AND WILLFUL AND WANTON DISREGARD

Millie has made suicidal threats on three occasions this school year. The first time you called her mother, you were met with resistance, "You are just feeding into her bid for attention." The second time you called, there was a weak commitment to seek help for Millie. The third time Millie talked about suicide it was a veiled threat of, "No one understands how hard life is for me. Nothing works in my life so what is the point?" You question her, but she clams up. You knew that Millie's mother would hit the roof if you called her with Millie's statement as your evidence that Millie is still struggling with thoughts of suicide. Being absolutely worn down by the conversations you have already had with Millie's mother, you decide to wait for the next threat before calling her mother to check on Millie's outside counseling and to report subsequent threats. If this student follows through with her suicide threat, are you negligent?

Points to Consider

Parents/guardians have rarely succeeded in establishing liability for student suicide, and none of the known decisions have resulted in an educator being responsible. Certainly, there may be unpublished cases or settlements to the contrary, and the case law is subject to change in the future. Although the precedents to date strongly undercut any undue fear of school counselor liability, awareness of the legal reasoning behind the court decisions serves as guiding principles for school counselors as they make decisions that could prove lifesaving for students in the future.

In *Killen v. Independent School District No. 706* (1996), a ninth-grade student killed herself at home with a firearm. Although the school counselor had warned the parents that their daughter had expressed suicidal feelings and recommended counseling, the parents alleged the school counselor didn't inform them when their daughter subsequently made a more specific statement about committing suicide. The Minnesota appeals court upheld the lower court's dismissal based on governmental immunity provisions.

Similarly, in *Grant v. Board of Trustees of Valley View School District* (1997), a student's friends reported his suicidal ideations and drug use to the school counselor. The school counselor called the student's mother and urged her to take him to a hospital for drug treatment. Later that day, the student jumped to his death from a highway overpass. His mother alleged the school counselor failed to tell her about his suicidal expressions. An Illinois appellate court upheld the trial court's dismissal on the grounds that public schools and their employees have immunity unless their misconduct was willful or wanton.

Schools are acting responsibly when they have suicide prevention and intervention plans in place with regular in-service training sessions that prepare all educators to respond appropriately to suicidal threats. Training should include all school personnel: teachers, administrators, security guards, cafeteria employees, custodians, bus drivers, secretaries, paraprofessionals and student services staff. It is necessary to inform these colleagues of the appropriate procedure for referring students who are suicidal to resources, crisis teams or whatever the intervention plan entails. Although school counselors are not directly responsible for creating and implementing policies, as systemic change agents they advocate for policies and procedures that protect students' physical and mental health needs. Particularly, school counselors help ensure the suicide intervention plan includes contacting the parents/guardians of a student who is suicidal, not allowing the student to leave campus alone and contacting protective or emergency services if necessary.

Most states protect employees who are not willfully negligent; they often have legislation suggesting employers adamantly defend public employees who are in civil suits because of job omissions. Therefore, employees cannot be dismissed based on unintended acts they commit that may have negative consequences (Alexander & Alexander, 2012). However, there have been cases where school counselors, principals and even districts have been sued for committing actions that had foreseeable negative effects on students.

School counselors strive to be culturally sensitive when working with families to secure additional help. When school counselors and crisis team members meet with unresponsive parents/guardians, they may need to turn control over to other authorities such as CPS for possible neglect or, if the student is at immediate risk, police or emergency services.

School counselors, with their specialized training and *in loco parentis* status, have a high standard of care when a student's suicide is even a remote possibility. School counselors must always contact parents/guardians and refer them to appropriate resources that will allow them to seek help for their child. Confidentiality is trumped when weighed against the death of a child. Calling parents/guardians upholds school counselors' most significant obligation to students: above all, do no harm.

School counselors are clear with parents/guardians about a child's expressed or implied suicidal ideation. When a student makes veiled threats of suicide, school counselors avoid skirting the issue; rather, they ask the tough questions. Wanting their suffering, not their lives, to end, many students who are suicidal answer "no" when asked if they are considering suicide. However, this answer does not negate the risk. Use open-ended questions, such as "What do you think about life and death?" This approach can serve as the first step in getting necessary help for an at-risk student. Parents/guardians need to understand that expressions of suicide or other warning signs require vigilance.

In this particular case, a call to CPS is needed. As frustrating as it is for school counselors to add stress to this mother on top of having a child who is suicidal, school counselors are mandated to report neglect. School counselors should document they contacted the parents/guardians and wherever possible have a witness to the conversation. The principal or another administrator can add needed leverage and urgency to the conversation if parents/guardians are reluctant to act. School counselors use their best judgment in these emotionally charged situations and avoid putting documentation above the parents'/guardians' feelings and well-being. However, seek a signature from parents/guardians at the first appropriate opportunity.

NOTIFYING PARENTS WHEN THEIR 18-YEAR-OLD CHILD IS SUICIDAL

It has been reported to you that Chace, an 18-year-old senior at your school, is suicidal. Chace tells you not to tell anyone and that at 18 he has a right to his privacy. Do you comply?

Points to Consider

A school counselor in Loudoun County Public Schools (LCPS) in Virginia was named as the defendant in a lawsuit regarding one of his students, Jay Gallagher, an 18-year-old, who took his life. The allegations are that Jay's friend contacted his school counselor to explain that Jay was talking about suicide. "Last night was the most concerning due to the suicidal thoughts and the self-harm," Jay's friend wrote in an email to the school counselor. The school counselor called in Jay, who assured the school counselor he was not going to harm himself. The school counselor's lawyer, Judkins, stated that Jay specifically asked this school counselor not to tell his parents and, according to Judkins, because Jay was 18, he has the right to instruct his school counselor not to notify his parents. Do you agree? If this case makes its way through the court system, we will find out if a judge agrees with Judkins. The practice has always been for school counselors to act, regardless of the student's age, when they're placed on notice that a student may be suicidal. That action means parents/guardians are always to be notified. In a high school setting, when it comes to suicide the profession has never distinguished between minors and those who reached age of majority.

The student's family elected to sue the school counselor and not the district to avoid the district's shield of governmental immunity. The family sued the school counselor for "acts of simple and gross negligence," which they say caused their son's death. According to court documents, the school counselor allegedly violated LCPS' standard of care by diagnosing the teen as not at risk of harming himself, which is outside the scope of a school counselor's training. An additional violation is that LCPS' suicide prevention procedures require that parents/guardians be notified of suicidal ideation. According to the complainant, another student in this same school counselor's caseload committed suicide a year earlier. The school counselor was told by the student's friend that the student was at risk, and the school counselor met with the student who was suicidal but did not notify her parents (Balingit, 2016).

Call parents even if a student is 18. That said, it might be prudent to seek the backing of the legal arm of your district before calling. A distressed school counselor recently notified me that her district would not allow her to call the parents of an 18-year-old student who was suicidal. This district was adhering strictly to the belief that this 18-year-old is an adult, and his privacy could not be breached. It is hard to believe any court of law would hold educators responsible for a privacy breach when we are trying to save the life of a high school student, even if that student is no longer considered a minor in our society. The setting in which this student is in, that of a high school, should define what we do, and we call parents when there is even a hint that one of our students might be suicidal.

For 18-year-olds in college, there is even less liability for educators in suicide cases. In 2018, the Massachusetts Institute of Technology was exonerated for the suicide death of one of their students. The Supreme Judicial Court of Massachusetts said, "There is no duty to prevent another from committing suicide." Overall, universities "are not responsible for monitoring and controlling all aspects of their students' lives," the court wrote, and there is "universal recognition" that the age of *in loco parentis* is long over (Seelye, 2018, n.p.). However, pre-K–12 educators have a greater *in loco parentis* responsibility. Call parents. Call parents every time with the one exception; parents are abusing and causing the suicidal ideation, and then call CPS.

INTENTIONAL INFLICTION OF EMOTIONAL DISTRESS

A school counselor intern who chaperoned a middle school dance subsequently posted a picture of a girl at the dance, mocking the students' dress as ill-fitting and something she obviously made. In your opinion, should this intern be a school counselor?

This case, like so many others in this book, is based on a real case. I point this out for this case because it is unfathomable that this person is seeking to be a member of this profession. This person is an adult bully who used a child's picture and a mocking caption for her own and others entertainment. No, she shouldn't be a school counselor. She needs to seek a position that does not involved children who are mandated to be in her presence.

With half a billion users, Facebook can be a lawsuit in the making for educators who post students' information or images and especially those who make derogatory comments about a student. In one lawsuit, a mother created a hairstyle for her daughter's picture day that her child saw in a magazine and wanted copied using Jolly Rancher candies. The girl's computer teacher asked the child to pose for a picture and then put it on Facebook mocking the child. Her friends joined in to degrade the child, and the ridiculing made its way to the girl's mother who sued for intentional infliction of emotional distress (IIED).

IIED is conduct so terrible that it causes severe emotional trauma to the victim. A certain level of rudeness, maliciousness, harmful or offensive behavior is not IIED; however, when the conduct is truly reprehensible, then damages might be recoverable (Legal Information Institute, 2022). If the conduct exceeds all possible bounds of decency and there is a special relationship between the parties, then what might not be considered IIED otherwise would be IIED because of the special relationship, such as a school counseling intern and a middle school student. IIED can also be considered extreme if the actor knows that the victim is particularly susceptible to the type of insult. For example, a school counselor would know about the developmental stages of a middle school girl and how vulnerable she is likely to be to insults about her looks. The actor must intend to cause emotional pain or to know that emotional pain is likely to occur. If the suffering is something no reasonable person should have to endure, this would more than likely constitute IIED.

NO LONGER IMMUNE FROM LIABILITY

Your colleague Barbara flirts constantly with students, jumping on one kid's back to horseplay and putting her head down on the shoulder of another. You speak to Barbara about her behavior, but she dismisses you as someone who needs to "lighten up." You learn Barbara was dismissed from her last district for inappropriate behavior toward students. You decide to notify your principal, who says, "Let's give her a chance." Are there any legal repercussions for the district if and when this school counselor acts on her sexual flirtations?

Points to Consider

In *C.A. v. William S. Hart Union High School District,* C.A., a 14-year-old student, alleged that Hubbell, the head school counselor at his high school, sexually harassed, abused and molested him on a number of occasions. The district knew Hubbell had a history of engaging in sexually related conduct with minors and, despite this knowledge, the school district hired her and gave her unsupervised access to minors. In fact, in 2008, one year after C.A.'s alleged abuse by Hubbell, Hubbell was accused of improper conduct with two students and resigned. *The Signal*, a local newspaper, said she tried to check into a motel with an underage boy, not the plaintiff, and was required to register as a sex offender (Worden, 2012).

The lower court found in favor of the William S. Hart Union High School District. However, on March 8, 2012, the California Supreme Court noted, "Supervisory personnel have a duty to take reasonable measures to protect students from abuse, including abuse by teachers and school counselors when they know or have reason to know of the potential for such abuse" (*C.A. v. William S. Hart Union High School District*, 12 S.O.S. 1151). School officials "have a duty to protect students from harm, which includes an obligation to exercise ordinary care in hiring, training, supervising and discharging school personnel. An administrator who hires a known child molester as a school counselor and fails to provide adequate training, supervision or termination when faced with ongoing sexual misconduct has failed to perform the duties within the scope of his or her employment" (*C.A. v. William S. Hart Union High School District*, 12 S.O.S. 1151).

In a Position to Know: A School Counselor Educator Speaks

The case presented at the beginning of the chapter is revisited here and answered by a school counselor educator. Compare his response with your approach.

NEGLIGENCE IN EATING DISORDERS

Karen, one of your seventh-graders, has been a regular in your office for the last two years. She has serious problems. You can't get her father to respond, but you have implored Karen's stepmother to get her some help. Lately, you have good reason to believe Karen is suffering from bulimia. When you ask Karen about it, she does not answer but rather starts a long diatribe about how you cannot tell her father because he is ready to send her off to live with her birth mother, and this information will give him the ammunition he needs. Karen has all but admitted to you that she is bulimic, and you know her assessment of her father's reaction is probably accurate. You decide to try to help Karen without calling her parents. The unthinkable happens, and Karen suffers heart failure. You are sued for negligence. How do you believe the courts will react? Is it likely your school district will pay for your defense?

We can learn many lessons from this school counselor's unfortunate predicament. School counselors who want to make sure they are never sued for negligence could avoid such unfortunate experiences by always telling parents/guardians everything students tell them in counseling sessions. Of course, such school counselors might have to find other jobs at some point, because few students would seek them out for help when they realize the school counselors are informing parents/guardians of everything the students say. Every time a school counselor decides not to inform parents/guardians after students have disclosed something in a session that could possibly lead to the student or others being harmed, school counselors take a legal risk. However, if they refuse to take such risks from time to time, they could not possibly be effective school counselors.

In reality, school counselors have to decide on a regular basis when to inform parents/guardians of something students have told them in counseling sessions. When school counselors determine students may be at risk of endangering themselves or others, school counselors have an ethical and legal duty to inform parents/guardians. But when should school counselors tell parents/guardians, and when should school counselors take a risk and not tell them?

No one knows the answer to that question, and statutes and case law do not offer much help. The general rule is that if a reasonable school counselor with similar education and training in a similar community would have foreseen harm to self or others in a similar set of circumstances, then school counselors should disclose what they know from counseling sessions with their students to parents/guardians. Unfortunately, this is an "after-the-fact" test, and school counselors have to make their decisions on the firing line, often quickly.

The best advice for school counselors is to consult with other professionals if they are unsure whether they should disclose a student's confidence to the student's parents/guardians. The more colleagues school counselors discuss the situation with, the better. If a school counselor's decision not to inform parents/guardians is questioned later (as is the situation in this case study), and the school counselor consulted with others who agreed parents/guardians should not be informed, then the school counselor has met the legal test stated above, "What would a reasonable school counselor with similar education and training in a similar community have done?"

Most school counselors reading this case study probably will conclude that the school counselor should have told Karen's father of Karen's suspected bulimia because her condition was life-threatening, even though Karen's father was likely to react negatively in a way that would add more pressure to Karen's life. However, there might be special circumstances to this situation that could have led a reasonable school counselor and the people the school counselor consulted to decide not to inform Karen's father but instead to seek help for Karen in other ways. Telling the father of the school counselor's suspicion of bulimia would have relieved the school counselor of any finding of negligence, but would it have been the ethical, moral and professional action to take? Should the school counselor have taken a risk by not telling the father in this particular situation? No one knows for sure.

Will the school district pay for the school counselor's legal defense in this case study? Probably, yes. In this situation, both the district and the school counselor most likely will be sued. The insurance company holding a liability policy for the school will hire an excellent attorney who specializes in defending professionals in negligence cases to represent the school district. That same attorney probably will represent the school counselor as well, but only if the attorney believes it is in the school district's best interest to do so. In most states, public entities cannot be sued because of sovereign immunity, or there are limits to negligence suits because of the sovereign immunity doctrine. If the attorney believes he or she could get the school district dismissed from the lawsuit but could not get the school counselor dismissed, the attorney would have an obligation to do that.

Getting the school district dismissed from the suit would leave the school counselor in this case study legally and financially vulnerable. As a result, school counselors should always have their own personal professional liability insurance policies that would pay for their defense and any judgment rendered against them individually. If school counselors do not have such a policy as a benefit of their union dues, they should be sure to maintain their membership in the American School Counselor Association, which provides professional liability coverage at no cost to its members.

– Theodore P. Remley Jr., counselor educator, Old Dominion University

Making Connections

1. Discuss the differences between negligence and malpractice.

2. What are the elements of negligence? Why is it so difficult to find that a school counselor owes a duty to prevent suicide?

3. What is standard of care? Who is the reasonably competent professional?

4. What is foreseeability? How should this guide your behavior?

5. What is governmental or sovereign immunity?

Chapter 5 Quiz

1) The elements of negligence:
   a. Require proof of criminal activity
   b. Are duty owed, duty breached, causal connection and injury suffered
   c. Are proximate cause, causal connection and damages
   d. Are difficult to determine unless the defendant admits wrongdoing
   e. Were established to include governmental immunity, which means you cannot sue government employees

2) Injury suffered in a negligence case:
   a. Means the injury could be monetary, physical, emotional, loss of reputation or essentially any injury
   b. Applies to governmental immunity or protection from civil liability is not possible
   c. Happens only if the injury is physical injury and requires a hospital stay
   d. Does not apply to libel or slander accusations
   e. Adheres to the principal of "above all do no harm"

3) In the *Sain v. Cedar Rapids Community School District* (2001) court case, it was determined by the court that:
   a. A school counselor owes a duty to advise a student with due care and attention
   b. NCAA regulations for incoming freshman athletes at Division I schools were unreasonable, and NCAA had to change
   c. Students are completely responsible for seeing their own NCAA eligibility is satisfied
   d. The Iowa Supreme Court's erroneously dismissed the *Sain* case
   e. The advice the school counselor gave to the student was correct

4) If you take a group of your schools' national merit semifinalists to a celebratory event at a lake and a student defies your repeated warnings and enters the lake and is now in danger of drowning, why is it your duty to ensure his safety and not Michael Phelps, the Olympic swimmer who is walking by the lake?
   a. Governmental immunity
   b. Foreseeable harm

c. Clear imminent danger
d. Malpractice
e. *In loco parentis*

5) When a school counselor is placed on notice that a child is possibly suicidal, even if the suicide is a remote possibility, the school counselor must:
   a. Report to the principal to get an opinion as to whether the child is indeed suicidal
   b. Call the child in and make a determination as to whether or not the child is truly at risk
   c. Complete a suicide assessment and only call parents/guardians if the child has a plan to carry out the suicide
   d. Always call the parents/guardian and let them know about the suicidal ideation
   e. Report to child protective services within 48 hours

Key Terms

Addressing a known danger
Breach
Causal connection
Civil law
Constitutional law
Criminal law
Duty of care
Educational malpractice
Governmental immunity
Injury suffered
In loco parentis
Intervening, superseding cause
Malicious, willful and intentional torts
Malpractice
Ministerial negligence
Reasonableness
Willful and wanton disregard

Chapter 6

Obligations to School Board Policies and Federal, State and Case Law

Objectives

By the time you have completed this chapter, you should be able to:

- Understand that schools are governmental agencies and how this fact affects legal behavior for educators
- Discuss how the Constitution, statutes and case law form the legal foundation on which public schools are based
- Understand the difference between privileged communication and confidentiality
- Explain the difference between case notes and education records
- Determine what to do if you receive a subpoena
- Discuss how to advocate for your students without becoming involved in the court system
- Understand the circumstances in which you should be a witness for the courts

Ethical Standards Addressed in This Chapter

Professionalism means knowing your professional associations' ethical standards and adhering to them. The ASCA Ethical Standards for School Counselors (2022b) most germane to this chapter are the following:

- School counselors keep information confidential unless legal requirements demand confidential information be revealed or a breach is required to prevent serious and foreseeable harm to the student or others. Serious and foreseeable harm is different for each minor in schools and is determined by a student's developmental and chronological age, the setting, parental/guardian rights and the nature of the harm. School counselors consult with appropriate professionals when in doubt as to the validity of an exception. (A.2.f.)
- School counselors request of the court that disclosure not be required when the school counselor's testimony or case notes are subpoenaed if the release of confidential information may potentially harm a student or the counseling relationship. (A.2.i.)
- School counselors protect the confidentiality of students' records and release personal data in accordance with prescribed federal and state laws and district and school policies. (A.2.j.)
- School counselors adhere to legal, ethical, district and school policies and guidelines regarding relationships with students and stakeholders. (A.5.g.)

- School counselors follow the directions and stipulations of the legal documentation in divorce, separation or custody cases, maintaining focus on the student. School counselors adhere to clear boundaries and a position of neutrality when working with parents/guardians. (B.1.k.)
- School counselors adhere to the profession's ethical standards and other official policy statements such as ASCA position statements and role statements, school board policies and relevant laws. When laws and ethical codes are in conflict, school counselors work to adhere to both as much as possible. (B.3.d.)

The full text of the ASCA Ethical Standards for School Counselors is available at *www.schoolcounselor.org*.

Introduction

Public education is not a right granted by the constitution but "neither is it some governmental benefit indistinguishable from other forms of social welfare legislation" (Rivkin, 2008, p. 265). Schools are governmental agencies, and schools' legal authority is as diverse as the 50 states that enact laws to govern those schools. Even though the United States is composed of a union of states under one central government, America has a "unique education system that is governed by laws of 50 states, with component parts amounting to several thousand local school district operating units. Through all of this organizational multiformity and, indeed, complexity runs the basis for justice on which the entire educational and legal systems are founded" (Alexander & Alexander, 2019, p. 2). The basis of the states' responsibility for schools is the 10th Amendment, which states, "The powers not delegated to the United States by the Constitution, nor prohibited by it to the states, are reserved to the states respectively, or to the people. Therefore, under the "implied powers" of the 10th Amendment, state legislation provides the basis for public school law, and the courts, through litigation, interpret the laws. The Constitution, state statutes, judge-made law (case law) and administrative law (rules, regulations, applications, licenses, permits, available information, hearings, appeals and decision-making not usually found in statute) all combine to form the legal structure on which the public schools are based (Alexander & Alexander, 2019; Decker et al., 2017).

State legislatures give school boards authority to create their own rules and regulations. School boards must act in accordance with their own requirements (Alexander & Alexander, 2019), and school counselors must be aware of the nature of the school district's obligation to the judicial system. For example, a school district allowing first-time offender drug users to seek counseling instead of discipline failed to follow its own policy. The school counselor served as the hearing officer in this case, and the student was expelled. However, the courts overturned the recommendation because the school did not follow the school board's own policies stating that a first-time offender could seek drug counseling instead of being expelled (*Camlin v. Beecher Community School District* (2003)).

The courts have traditionally maintained and enforced the concept of separation of the different branches of power to enable each division of government to function freely within the area of its responsibility. In short, school districts are not often sued, and when they are, the lower courts are reluctant to rule against them.

According to the courts, statutes are the basis for "the most common litigation involving school operation" (Alexander & Alexander, 2019, p. 4). Courts determine the constitutionality of such legislation. If a statute can be interpreted in two ways, one of which will be constitutional, the courts will adopt the constitutional interpretation (*Bonvento v. Board of Public Instruction of Palm Beach County* (1967); *Hobbs v. County of Moore* (1966)).

The United States has court systems at both the federal and the state levels. This book includes court cases involving educators at both levels, although state courts decide most cases (Alexander & Alexander, 2019; Russo, 2021). The highest court in terms of this body of law is the supreme court of a state. The states' supreme courts are not considered lower courts, even in relation to the U.S. Supreme Court. State supreme courts follow the U.S. Supreme Court's ruling on the meaning of the U.S. Constitution, but the highest court in each state is free to interpret state laws or the state constitution in any way that does not violate principles of federal law (Alexander & Alexander, 2019).

The majority of the cases in this book involve school counselors as defendants or witnesses. In a survey of 874 ASCA members, 97% of the respondents said they had never been a defendant in a legal proceeding in the history of their career. Of the 3% who had been a defendant, 2% of them said it was for one occurrence (Stone, 2017c).

When a school counselor becomes a defendant in a case, it is often a civil case: a wrong against a student or a student's parents (see Chapter 5 Negligence). A criminal wrong might involve sexual misconduct with a minor student. Some of the most common cases in which a school counselor might become a defendant involve defamation and qualified privilege, abortion or birth control counseling, academic advising, failure to report child abuse or unauthorized disclosure of information (Stone & Zirkel, 2010; Russo, 2021).

In the same survey (Stone, 2017c), 22% of the respondents reported having been involved in a legal proceeding during the last five years as a witness.

Regarding your professional role as a school counselor, have you been asked to be a witness (not a defendant) in a court case or legal proceeding through a subpoena or a court order in the last five years? If so, how many times?
One or two times *83%*
Three to four times *14%*
Five to six times *2%*
Seven to eight times. *1%*

Court proceedings involving school counselors as witnesses for the court are usually cases of child custody, child abuse or disciplinary action (Hays, et al., 2009; Stone 2017b). School counselors overwhelmingly responded that custody issues and child abuse were the reason they were being asked to be witnesses in legal proceedings in the course of doing their job (Stone, 2017c).

The 22% of ASCA member respondents who said they have been asked to be a witness through subpoena or court order in the last five years reported the following:

Which statement best describes the reason you were subpoenaed or court ordered. Indicate how many times for each case. Indicate all that applies in the last five years.

Custody battle 59%
Child abuse or neglect 50%
Child abuse or neglect by a parent/guardian 38%
A student was sexually abused by a parent or stepparent 11%
A student was sexually abused by a relative 8%
A student was sexually abused by a neighbor, babysitter or friend of the family 8%
A student was sexually abused by live-in boyfriend or girlfriend 3%
Electronic communication on social media 2%
A student was sexually abused by a fellow educator or administrator 1%
A student was sexually abused by a stranger 1%

Negligence cases regarding academic advising (1%), falsifying records, failure to report child abuse and four other areas for whom school counselors were minimally engaged (0% to 1%) are discussed in Chapter 5 Negligence.

Percentages add up to more than 100% because respondents indicated all that applied to capture all reasons for witnessing in court proceedings (Stone, 2017c).

Generally speaking, school counselors are required to testify in a court proceeding. Although school counselors have confidentiality requirements, school counselors cannot deny the courts their testimony unless the students of school counselors are given privileged communication in state statutes.

The 874 ASCA member respondents who said they have been subpoenaed or court ordered in the last five years indicated their level of involvement as follows:

The case was settled without my testimony 52%
I had to give a deposition and testify in court 39%
I had to give a deposition only 38%
It ended up that I did not have to give a deposition or testify in court because my school district intervened 21%
I was able to explain to the attorneys that they did not want my testimony as it would likely damage their client's case. 11%

Percentages add up to more than 100% because some members were involved in more than one court case, and respondents were asked to indicate all that applied to them (Stone, 2017c).

Privileged communication is a creature of statute and only applies to court proceedings. Privilege is given to students, not school counselors, in a few states. Privileged communication allows the student and/or the student's parents to render the school counselor incapable of testifying in court about the student's confidential communications. Depending on the state statute, the student and/or parent(s) can give the school counselor permission to testify. In this same survey by Stone (2017c), 49% of the respondents were not sure about their state statutes and privileged communication. The question of privilege is one for the school district attorney and should be answered before a school counselor receives a subpoena, as it is helpful to know this information in daily work. Check your state statute.

In most states where statutes give privileged communication, there are many caveats about when a judge can decide that the needs of the state outweigh the right to privileged communication. There is judicial reluctance to extend the privilege to students of school counselors because of the age of their clients and the setting in which they work (Bodenhorn, 2006; Lazovsky, 2008). Another problem with privilege is the definition of what constitutes counseling. For school counselors, counseling takes place everywhere. Counseling can occur are the playground, in the bus-loading zone or in the hallways. A school counselor may believe that an exchange with a student in the cafeteria is counseling, intending all communication in that meeting to be counseling, and thereafter the student tries to invoke privilege. However, the judge may or may not rule that privilege applies in the situation. Whereas, if an attorney and client exchange any information anywhere – the subway, sauna, tennis court – every utterance is privileged. For the school counseling profession, the interpretation is much more confined. Very few states offer school counselor/student privilege, and in the rare cases where they do, there are exceptions in the statutes that usually says if a judge needs your testimony they can demand it. Check your state statutes.

All of the chapters in this book deal with statutes and school district policies that have an impact on the school counselor's role. This chapter focuses on statutes that are not covered in other parts of the book. If you don't find what you need in this chapter, it may well be elsewhere.

Getting Started: What Would You Do?

The following case is answered for you at the end of this chapter by practicing school counselors. Before you read their responses, formulate in your own mind how you would approach this ethical dilemma.

SCHOOL COUNSELOR'S ROLE IN CUSTODY BATTLES

Irene's parents are going through a bitter divorce, and Mr. Carter is calling you with what you believe is an ulterior motive of setting you up to testify in his favor. Mr. Carter continually calls and feeds you information against Irene's mother. You have negotiated these calls by cutting him off and bringing the conversation back to Irene. You stress outside counseling for individual family members, but you strongly suspect Mr. Carter's motivation is about you testifying in his favor. What do you do when a subpoena arrives to testify in the custody proceedings?

Working Through Case Studies

PRIVILEGED COMMUNICATION APPLIED

Richmond is in trouble and has a court date. The prosecuting attorney has sent you a subpoena. You live in North Carolina. Can Richmond keep you from testifying?

Points to Consider

Yes, Richmond can render you incapable of testifying about him in court in North Carolina. In North Carolina, school counselors cannot "testify in any action, suit or proceeding concerning any information acquired in rendering counseling services to any student ... and which information was necessary to enable him to render counseling services; provided, however, that this section shall not apply where the student in open court waives the privilege conferred" (North Carolina Gen. Stat., 2004, § 8-53.4).

You and Richmond live and work in Montana. His mother demands you testify. Can you refuse?

Maybe. In Montana, both the minor student and the parent must give permission to testify, or both must render you incapable of testifying. What if one parent says it is okay for you not to testify, and one parent wants your testimony? A thorough search failed to reveal a court case to give guidance; it stands to reason that the student's wishes would prevail if they coincide with the wishes of one parent as long as that parent's rights have not been severed by the courts. Because the Montana statute is designed to protect a student's confidence and one parent agrees to do so, then judges would most likely protect the confidence.

The answer to how the school counselor should behave in this case resides solely in the state statutes. In absence of a statute giving the school counselor's students privileged communication, school counselors legally owe the state their testimony. Ethically, the school counselor may continue to try and get out from under a subpoena, which is the topic of a case in the section, "Confidentiality When There is No Privileged Communication."

COURTS AND SCHOOL DISTRICT HEARINGS

A school counselor was accused of sexually abusing a student. The courts cleared him of any wrongdoing. Subsequently, the school district conducted a termination hearing. Can the school district fire an educator who was exonerated of wrongdoing by the courts?

Points to Consider

In a 2004 case, a school counselor was cleared in a criminal case for allegedly sexually abusing one of his students. The school board subsequently voted to dismiss him based on the same incident. Unlike criminal trials where prosecutors must overcome the much-higher reasonable doubt standard to secure a conviction, school boards may rely on "substantial evidence" to terminate employees (Shapira, 2005, p. 1). Additionally, evidence is permitted in a school district hearing that is not permitted in a criminal trial. For example, the results of a polygraph test showing deception were allowed in the school district hearing; however, the results were inadmissible in Virginia criminal courts. The board was also able to consider the discovery of pornography on the school counselor's school computer although this information was inadmissible in the court hearing because it was not possible to determine who had downloaded the material (Shapira, 2005).

FALSIFYING RECORDS AND SUING FOR REMEDIATION

Your colleague, Donna Hill, was fired for falsifying her daughter's transcript. Ms. Hill filed a court case against the district claiming breach of contract, as she was not given the contractual requirement to remediate before being fired. Will she prevail?

Points to Consider

In this real case, Donna Hill falsified her daughter's and other students' grades and was fired by the district on the grounds of moral turpitude and willful neglect of duty (*Hill v. Independent School District*, 2002). Hill posted a grade on a student's transcript for an advanced sociology course, a class not offered at Stilwell, and gave her daughter credit for two nonexistent courses and boosted her GPA by a point. The school board dismissed Hill, and she filed a lawsuit stating the board failed to give her due process, which requires the board to warn and remediate before firing.

The court found in favor of the school district. "While teachers who have remediable teaching performance problems that could result in dismissal for willful neglect of duty are entitled to admonishment, those whose dismissals are based on specific, irremediable instances of misconduct are not… . Given that Hill served as a school counselor at Stilwell High School, her dismissal was not based on teaching deficiencies or other remediable classroom problems. Rather, it was supported by discrete instances of misconduct, namely, altering students' transcripts. Hill's acts exhibited dishonesty, a lack of respect for the sanctity of school records and a tendency toward favoritism" (*Hill v. Independent School District*, 2002, pp.14-15). The court also agreed that there was sufficient evidence of moral turpitude. "Moral turpitude broadly defined is any conduct contrary to justice, honesty and good morals. Moral turpitude implies something immoral in itself regardless of whether it is punishable by law. Her conduct clearly fits the definition of moral turpitude. That conduct was also irremediable; the damage already done" (*Hill v. Independent School District*, 2002, p.16-17).

CONFIDENTIALITY WHEN THERE IS NO PRIVILEGED COMMUNICATION

You have built a bond with Hansen as his advocate as he has bounced from foster home to foster home. Hansen has a difficult time trusting adults, communicates only when necessary and is guarded and suspicious. His last foster parents are being investigated for dealing in stolen property. You receive a subpoena from the prosecution to give testimony about your confidential conversations with Hansen. Students in your state do not have privileged communication. Hansen has not told you anything about the accused foster family. What are your legal responsibilities to the court? What are your ethical responsibilities to Hansen?

Points to Consider

Ethically school counselors can try to protect their students' confidences and stay out of court. Legally, as explained in earlier discussion in this chapter, because this state does not extend privileged communication to students, the school counselor has to try to find other ways to keep students' confidences.

The school counselor should consult the school board attorney to see if the attorney can help by getting a motion to quash the subpoena. A motion to quash makes the subpoena null and void, therefore canceling the requirement to testify. The school counselor should inform the attorney who sent the subpoena that there is no information to help the case (if this is true). The school counselor should explain that his or her obligations are to the student. Cite ethical standards, which support the student's confidences, and stay out of court if possible. Advocate. Explain that the relationship is too fragile and too much at risk if you as the school counselor, like all the other adults in Hansen's life, cannot be trusted to stand with him and protect his confidence. Seek research on abandonment issues, foster care and other children in Hansen's situation if further work is needed. Draw attention to the fact that you, as the school counselor, should not be called on to breach Hansen's confidence.

Another approach if unable to get out of the testifying is to ask the judge to use only notes that are pertinent, thereby sealing documents and excusing you from the court proceedings or requesting an informal conference with only the lawyers and the court in chambers. Failing this approach, the school counselor must testify unless the student has privileged communication under state statute, rendering the school counselor incapable of testifying about him or her.

PROTECTING SOCIETY VS. CONFIDENTIALITY

A teacher asks you to talk to a student who is too preoccupied with sexual matters and displays overtly sexualized behavior. The teacher suspects this child has been or is being sexually abused, and your conversation with the child confirms the teacher's suspicions. You are subpoenaed in the alleged perpetrator's trial. Should you testify?

Points to Consider

Generally speaking, in custody matters and other court proceedings school counselors do not want their case notes or testimony in court. School counselors' loyalty is to their students, and they owe them confidentiality. School counselors advocate to protect their case notes and to be excused from testifying. However, there will be times such as child abuse situations in which school counselors will want to testify and share their records, as in this case. School counselors want to protect students' privacy as much as possible. However, the greater good to society and the protection of other potential victims far outweigh student confidence. See Chapter 4 Student Privacy for more information on case notes versus sole possession records.

COURT ORDER VS. SUBPOENA

You have been subpoenaed by the prosecution's attorney. Is a subpoena different from receiving a court order from a judge?

Points to Consider

A court issues a court order requiring a person to do a specified act, such as producing material or appearing in court (Kennedy, 2008). If a court orders a school counselor to provide it with information, the school counselor must provide the necessary documents or oral information unless the school counselor's students are protected by a privileged communication statute in that state. The government has the right to obtain a person's information by court order.

A subpoena *duces tecum* (Latin meaning "under penalty you shall bring with you") is a court order issued by a clerk of court, justice of the peace, notary public or lawyer, usually signed by a lawyer. It requires the recipient to perform a specified act, such as appearing in court to answer questions about something he or she has witnessed or heard or producing records as evidence (Kennedy, 2008). There are two different types of subpoenas. One is a subpoena to testify in the courts, and the other is to produce documents (Kennedy, 2008). Although both require a response from the school counselor, legal counsel may be more successful with a motion to quash a lawyer-signed subpoena than a motion to reverse a court order. Always seek help from the local school board attorney before responding to a court order or lawyer-signed subpoena. There are penalties for failing to respond to a subpoena or court order, so try to submit a motion to quash (Alexander & Alexander, 2019).

DUAL LICENSURE AND THE COURTS

Your colleague, Risty, is a licensed counselor practicing as a school counselor in a state that grants privileged communication for clients of licensed counselors but not for students of school counselors. Risty is called to testify regarding one of her students. If the student in question does not give Risty permission to testify, will she be able to successfully respect the student's privileged communications?

Points to Consider

Currently, there are no court cases that give the school counseling profession a clear answer as to dual license and how this will be used by a judge in deciding privileged communication. Risty is working as a school counselor, and her students are not granted privileged communication in her state. However, Risty holds a license as a mental health counselor, whose clients do have privilege. So, what is the judge to do? Risty argues she cannot be made to testify as her license as a mental health counselor grants her clients privileged communication. In absence of a court case conclusively answering this question, it seems intuitive that the role in which counselors are functioning defines the rules by which they must practice. Amy Colvin, Esq., said, "I would think a judge would not let a school counselor fall back on privileged communication as they are acting as a school counselor and not as a licensed counselor with a private client. If I were a judge in a complicated custody case and my whole decision rested on the testimony of the school counselor, I would not want to let them off the hook because I was unlucky enough to get the one school counselor who is also licensed. It is not fair to the justice system ... that some counselors do have to break confidentiality and some do not. The legislature should make these rules so it is fair to all" (A.L. Colvin, Esq., personal communication, January 2009).

J. Freidan, practicing school counselor, said, "I believe the role in which you are functioning defines the rules by which you must practice; this is the law. The law considers 'intent' when considering the truth of the matter." (J. Freiden, NCSC, LPC, personal communication, Jan. 13, 2005).

School counselors lean toward believing your job defines your legal imperatives but not by a sizable margin. In a February 2017 survey, 15% of the respondents said they hold dual credentials as both a licensed mental health professional and a certified school counselor (Stone, 2017d). In this same survey, a small majority of the respondents hold dual licensure (60%). These school counselors answered the following: "I believe the requirements of my certificate for my current job as a school counselor supersede my license in mental health, and I defer to the requirements of the certificate in the job I am actually performing. In other words, my school counseling certification credentials supersedes any requirements of my mental health license when there is a conflict." Forty percent of the respondents answered, "I believe the requirements of both my license and my certificate are applicable in my job as a school counselor, and when there is a conflict such as privileged communication, I can choose the license or certificate that best advantages my program or students and adhere to the tenets of that license or certificate" (Stone, 2017d).

INTERPRETING FEDERAL STATUTES AND SCHOOL COUNSELORS' OBLIGATION

The liaison officer for students who are homeless sent out a directive that all school counselors are to notify her office when they learn a child is living in a homeless situation. The homeless liaison officer explained the information is needed for children and their families to receive transportation, free meals, health care and other essential services. You agree her office should be notified to advantage students who are homeless, but you also appreciate that being homeless is highly sensitive information for some students. Is this one of the times in which confidentiality is superseded?

Points to Consider

The federal government defines homelessness as lacking a fixed, regular and adequate nighttime residence to include shelters, transitional housing, cars, campgrounds, motels or sharing temporary housing. The National Center for Homeless Education (NCHE) found the level of prevalence for children who are homeless and youth enrolled in U.S. public schools was 1,277,772 during the 2019–2020 school year. Even this disturbing number is likely a significant underestimate because the data collected represents only those children school officials were able to identify and report and does not include all preschool-age children. Eleven percent of children who were homeless were living in shelters, 77.5% were doubled up with others, 4% were living in motels, with the balance in unsheltered locations. It is estimated that the number of homeless youth unaccompanied by an adult is an additional 112,822 per year, representing runaways or those forced out of the home by parents (NCHE, 2020).

According to the National Association for the Education of Homeless Children and Youth (NAEHCY), these children are often living in precarious, crowded and unsafe conditions. For these children, school can be a lifeline, a place of safety, structure and opportunity. In addition to sometimes going unidentified and without services, children who are homeless face unique barriers to education including:

- Being unable to meet enrollment requirements (including requirements to provide proof of residency and legal guardianship and school and health records)

- High mobility resulting in lack of school stability and educational continuity
- Lack of transportation
- Lack of school supplies and clothing
- Poor health, fatigue and hunger
- Emotional crisis/mental health issues
- Lack of a parent or guardian in the case of unaccompanied homeless youth (NAEHCY, n.d.).

For these most vulnerable youth, how can school counselors respect students' confidentiality while also reaching out to the district's homeless liaison officer to support the student and family? This represents one of the complexities school counselors face on a daily basis with regard to respecting confidentiality while providing other educators with need-to-know information.

There is a legal imperative for reporting homeless youth to the liaison officer in the McKinney-Vento Homeless Assistance Act. The McKinney-Vento Homeless Assistance Act (2001) is federal legislation supporting children who are homeless to receive an equal, free, appropriate public education and all that this entails.

(A) DUTIES - Each local educational agency liaison for children who are homeless and youths, designated under paragraph (1)(J)(ii), shall ensure that ... (i) children who are homeless and youths are identified by school personnel and through coordination activities with other entities and agencies. (McKinney-Vento Homeless Education Assistance Improvements Act of 2001).

The Family Educational Rights and Privacy Act (FERPA) specifically allows the sharing of information with other school officials within the district or school who have legitimate educational interests (LEI). The homeless liaison officers have LEI. To do their jobs as directed by the federal government, they have to know who the children who are homeless are in their district. Additionally, school districts are legally required by the U.S. Department of Education to gather and report data on the number of students who are homeless in the district. To avoid duplication, the information collected must be personally identifiable and the nighttime residence given if known. The McKinney-Vento Homeless Assistance Act (2001) requires school districts to provide transportation so children have the option of staying in their school of origin regardless of how many times they move to different school zones. To comply with McKinney-Vento can be costly to districts. The required information collected for the Department of Education also allows many schools and districts to apply for grant money to provide additional programs and services, such as transportation aimed at meeting the needs of children who are homeless.

The McKinney-Vento Homeless Assistance Act does not provide immunity from normal school disciplinary provisions and guidelines; students who are homeless are subject to the same guidelines as their peers. However, the McKinney-Vento mandate implores school districts to develop, review and revise policies to remove barriers to the enrollment and retention of children who are homeless and youth in schools; there may be instances when leniency should be shown (NCHE, 2020). The legal support requirements for reporting children who are homeless are clear. However, the question of breaching the trust placed in us by students who request confidentiality still leaves many school counselors uncomfortable. Students might be deeply embarrassed by their plight, afraid they will be separated from their parents by social services, etc. There are many reasons why a child might appreciate or even plead for confidentiality. The profession acutely recognizes children's need for privacy and a trusting adult to whom they can share their confidences. The law supersedes ethics; however, this real scenario tests our skills to obey the legal imperative, while aspiring to also remain ethical.

At the end of the day, information must be provided to the homeless liaison officer, but prior to doing so the skilled school counselor will work with students who are homeless to help them understand why the breach is necessary. Relay what will be told to the liaison. If students are at a developmentally appropriate level, consider asking if they would like to be present or provide the information themselves. The test is to advantage students by collaborating with other educators in the school while keeping a trusting relationship.

ADVOCATING WITHIN YOUR FIRST AMENDMENT RIGHTS

In the summer of racial reckoning following the murders of George Floyd, Breonna Taylor and Ahmaud Arbery, an urgency was stirred in you to seize the moment to bring important conversations about respecting diversity to the students in your school. One of the things you do was to put up a Black Lives Matter flag in your office only to be told later that it is considered political by your district and must come down. Do your First Amendment rights protect you to leave the flag up?

Points to Consider

Generally speaking, school board policy carries the weight of law if the policy does not conflict with a state or federal statute. A number of districts have context-neutral policies banning political conversations, symbols, anything but spirit gear. Chapter 14 Legal and Ethical Advocacy has more information on First Amendment rights and advocacy. First Amendment rights enveloped inside the school environment have required special consideration from the courts for over five decades. The First Amendment says Congress shall make no law abridging the freedom of speech, or of the press; or the right of the people peaceably to assemble. Speech is not only written and verbal speech but also expressions such as the wearing of political clothing. There are many pitfalls and places where the exercise of the First Amendment can go wrong for an educator.

Court cases defining the freedom and limitations of the First Amendment in schools began with *Tinker v. Des Moines*. In December 1965, Mary Beth and John Tinker and Christopher Eckhardt were suspended for wearing black armbands to school to show support of a truce in the Vietnam War. The Tinkers' lost their freedom of speech court case in both the district court and the Eighth Circuit Court. The U.S. Supreme Court delivered the final opinion in favor of the students in a 7-2 majority. Justice Abe Fortas writing for the majority said that students and faculty do not lose their First Amendment rights to freedom of speech at the schoolhouse gate. In the decades to follow Tinker, courts have heard challenges to school speech such as the landmark case *Bethel School District v. Fraser*, 1986. This Supreme Court decision supported the district's decision to discipline high school student Fraser for delivering a lewd speech with sexual references to the student body during government nominations.

While there are obvious areas of speech that are not protected, such as the "vulgar" speech Fraser gave in the Bethel case, there are also limits to areas of speech usually considered protected speech. One test for protected speech for students and educators is whether or not the speech creates a substantial disruption. Speech can be limited if there is a good faith, reasonably founded belief that the speech will lead to a disruption or has led to a disruption. The standard for fettering student speech is very high. The administration cannot limit speech on a loosely held belief that the speech might disrupt; there has to be valid arguments to forecast such a disruption. For example, the administration can preemptively suppress expressive speech in the form of a confederate flag worn on a shirt if they can foresee a disruption with facts, such as the community considers the flag a symbol of racism (*Barr v. Lafron*, 2008) or the flag has caused disruption in the community or in neighboring schools (*Defoe v. Spivy*, 2010). The court in Defoe extended their opinion to also recognize a school district's substantial interest in helping students foster "both knowledge and democratic responsibility."

Content-neutral policies are being used by school boards to defensively limit speech. These policies usually dictate that no writing can be brought on campus in the form of clothing, banners, bumper stickers, etc., unless it is school spirit symbols. There are dozens of examples of educators being disciplined or fired for displaying symbols with Black Lives Matter in districts with content-neutral policies.

CRITICAL RACE THEORY AND SCHOOL COUNSELING CURRICULUM

A parent is complaining to your principal that you are teaching critical race theory (CRT). You are taken aback as your curriculum is built around the ASCA Student Standards: Mindsets and Behaviors for Student Success, which are basic skills everyone needs to master in a world where collaboration with others can make or break a person's success in life. What do you do?

Points to Consider

In communities where the anti-CRT movement is at fever pitch, educators are negotiating an ongoing minefield, facing challenges to innocuous lessons and professional development. The target in the attack on CRT is illusive, varies widely and is growing. Crenshaw, who along with others coined the term critical race theory, explains that it is "not a thing, it is a way of looking at race (2021). The primary argument against CRT is that it suggests that racial inequities are the result of bad choices made by people who were all equally positioned to achieve the American dream. Opponents negate that there are embedded systems difficult to change that stratify opportunities. Proponents view the attack on CRT as a strategy to "create a straw house to set aflame in order to draw attention away from not just its [the right's] incapacity but its outright refusal to address issues of cumulative, especially racial, injustice" (Goldberg, 2021, n.p.).

CRT has been defined by some as an approach to race relations that asks white people to consider their advantage within a historically racist system (Trilling, 2020). CRT has become a catchall target for opposition to equity efforts, affirmative action and "wokeness" in general (Jackson, 2021). The conversations were reignited during the Black Lives Matter movement during summer 2020.

CRT at its inception was to address racism in the law but the conversation now centers around CRT in K-16 education. CRT examines how race and racism affect society's policies and practices (Pottiger, 2021). The education system is identified by scholars of CRT as one of the worst systems to perpetuate racism (Gillborn, 2008; Gillborn & Mirza, 2000; Spring, 2004). Years after *Brown v. Board of Education* (1954), segregated schools persist (Bell, 2004). In addition to the harm of segregation, other contributions perpetuate the status quo, such as assessments that discriminate against students of color, curriculum that erases the contributions of students of color, discipline practices that affect children of color at a disproportionate rate, the overidentification of males of color for the emotionally handicap class, and school funding formulas that rely on property taxes.

School counselors, along with school boards, superintendents, principals and teachers continue to face questions about CRT, and there are significant disagreements even among experts about its precise definition as well as how its tenets should inform K–12 policy and practice. Public school districts are trying to find the best way to teach history in an honest way and to address current events, while those who oppose CRT taught in classroom lessons believe it is divisive. They cite racism as the work of a few bad individuals and that children should not be taught they are inherently privileged or racist because they are white. It is hard to determine to what degree K–12 educators are using curriculum materials or other tools or activities related to this concept (Sawchuk, 2021).

Even when CRT is replaced by diversity, equity and inclusion (DEI), the firestorm ignited by CRT carries over to DEI curriculum. In the epicenter of the CRT/DEI war, Southlake, Texas, has drawn battle lines with opposition saying CRT is reverse racism. After vile videos of racial rants by students surfaced, a diversity council of more than 60 parents, teachers and students developed a plan to make Southlake schools more inclusion and welcoming. The plan was met with outrage from mostly white parents. These opposing parents packed school board meetings to voice their strong opposition to a diversity designed to "fix a problem that doesn't exist… . They argued that the district's plan would instead create diversity and reverse racism against white children" (Hixenbaugh, 2021, n.p).

Rashawn Ray and Alexandra Gibbons of The Brookings Institute have found the following as of August 2021. Eight states (Idaho, Oklahoma, Tennessee, Texas, Iowa, New Hampshire, Arizona and South Carolina) have passed legislation banning the "discussion, training and/or orientation that the U.S. is inherently racist, as well as any discussions about conscious and unconscious bias, privilege, discrimination and oppression. Another 20 states have introduced bills or taken other steps that would restrict teaching CRT or limit how teachers can discuss racism and sexism. These parameters also extend beyond race to include gender lectures and discussions. State actors in Montana and South Dakota have denounced teaching concepts associated with CRT. The state school boards in Florida, Georgia, Utah and Oklahoma introduced new guidelines barring CRT-related discussions. Local school boards in Georgia, North Carolina, Kentucky and Virginia also criticized CRT. Nearly 20 additional states have introduced or plan to introduce similar legislation" (2021, n.p.).

The school counselor in this scenario never labeled her curriculum as CRT, and she could not see the connection. There are many approaches the school counselor could use such as:

- Develop parent allies. Get them to spread the word that what you are doing advantages their children.
- Develop administration allies. Share your curriculum and ask them to participate in a few lessons
- Present to parents in various ways how the curriculum will advantage their student now and in the future. Provide them with sample lessons.
- Consider using terms parents will understand, such as work force skills, job skills, life skills, career skills, collaboration and cooperation skills, etc.
- Voice that these standards come from the national organization for school counselors and are skills needed by productive citizens.
- Use your ASCA tools. The key to your advocacy efforts in forwarding diversity and singling out particular groups who need more attention lies in the ASCA Ethical Standards, ASCA Student Standards: Mindsets & Behaviors for Student Success, the ASCA National Model, the ASCA position statements and your knowledge of the school community and board policies.
- Hit the issue head on and talk about CRT. Before using this one you will need your administrator to support you, and be ready for the fallout.

DISTRICT POLICY AFFECTING ETHICAL BEHAVIOR

Your district has a policy that if students tell you they are transgender or questioning their gender identity you must call the parents and tell them. A blanket policy like this is dangerous in your opinion as it does not consider any context. What do you do?

Points to Consider

Policies that belie common sense place school counselors in an untenable position when they cannot meet the letter of the policy. Policies should not be put on paper unless they can be done every time. When working with students, context must always be part of any consideration. Sometimes well-meaning school boards or administrators craft policies without considering the context-dependent nature of the school counselor's work. When school boards and administrators hand down lockstep policies affecting school counselors' work with students' social/emotional needs, they ignore the fact that students range developmentally, have different support systems in place and have different track records for competency in making informed decisions.

Florida and other states are purportedly "giving rights back to parents" with controversial laws such as the Parents Bill of Rights, colloquially known as the "Don't Say Gay Bill" (Fla. Stat. § 1014.06). The bill restricts primary school teachers in Florida from discussing sexual orientation or gender identity with their students. The language is broad and leaves as many questions as demands. U.S. Secretary of Education Miguel Cardona released a statement: "Parents across the country are looking to national, state and district leaders to support our nation's students, help them recover from the pandemic and provide them the academic and mental health supports they need. Instead, leaders in Florida are prioritizing hateful bills that hurt some of the students most in need." Cardona also warned that, "The

Department of Education has made clear that all schools receiving federal funding must follow federal civil rights law, including Title IX's protections against discrimination based on sexual orientation and gender identity. We stand with our LGBTQ+ students in Florida and across the country and urge Florida leaders to make sure all their students are protected and supported" (Colarossi, 2022).

It is unreasonable to expect school counselors to adhere to a prescriptive policy that hurts children, yet, we have to obey school board policy so we "learn the rules to know how to break them properly" (author unknown). Unrealistic, cumbersome, intrusive policy should not go unchallenged.

What can you do if your school district has a burdensome, complicated policy that makes compliance difficult?

- Seek allies who agree with you and have the power to effect change.
- Point out the fallacies of the policy from a legal standpoint if possible. Find court cases that back your argument.
- Develop a "what if" scenario. For example, if your policy has you assessing suicide, discuss the issue with administration or others in a position of power, and walk them through the possible, unthinkable result if your assessment is wrong.
- Find the political leverage. Does a working group already exist to whom you can voice recommendations for policy changes? Identify school district policies that make sense, and provide them as examples. Find a political ally who can take the changes through the approval system.
- If you have a state statute that is against the standard of care for the profession, ask your state school counseling association to add it to their lobbying efforts. Sometimes school counselors or their organizations have asked for interpretations of existing statutes. California school counselors did this with a confusing state statute on confidentiality and student pregnancy.
- Provide professional development for the faculty on the existing policy in question. This would be an optimum time to get everyone's input as to how realistic or fraught with pitfalls the policy would be to implement.
- Keep written notes, however brief, on your efforts to change policy should the policy stand.

Policies may make some school counselors sleep better at night because their judgment is not required, but an easy decision is not what the vast majority of school counselors signed up for when taking on their role. Equity means determining what is best for a student based on all that is known and not always on a standard policy, which may only hurt and not help if applied in a lockstep fashion. Policies allow us to feel confident that we met the letter of the school board law, but did we meet the spirit of what needed to be done for a particular student on a particular day? Protect yourself and your students, and examine policies and state statutes for a symbiotic relationship to the role of school counseling.

In a Position to Know: School Counselors Speak

The case presented at the beginning of the chapter is revisited here and answered by practicing school counselors. Read their opinions carefully to see what you can learn. Compare their answers with your approach.

SCHOOL COUNSELORS ROLE IN CUSTODY BATTLES

Irene's parents are going through a bitter divorce, and Mr. Carter is calling you with what you believe is an ulterior motive of setting you up to testify in his favor. Mr. Carter continually calls and feeds you information against Irene's mother. You have negotiated these calls by cutting him off and bringing the conversation back to Irene. You stress outside counseling for individual family members, but you strongly suspect Mr. Carter's motivation is about you testifying in his favor. What do you do when a subpoena arrives to testify in the custody proceedings?

Middle School Counselor's Response

The child is always the primary client in the school setting. However, parents (both of them) are secondary recipients of care. My response to the father would be candid and honest about his voiced concerns. When he criticizes the mother, my response would be to validate his concern on behalf of the child and to invite both parents into the problem-solving process on the child's behalf. To that end, my efforts would be to engage them in assisting Irene's progress in school and getting her the emotional support needed through this turbulent period. I also would engage the school support process on the child's behalf (response to intervention, small-group counseling, etc.) to improve her progress in school and/or her emotional status. If called to testify, I can only speak to the child's performance in school; her observable affect and reports from teachers are all that can be discussed. I will endeavor to respect all other conversations, including any conversations with Irene, her father and her mother.

– Christy A. Clapper, Ph.D., school counselor (retired), Quaker Valley School District, Sewickley, Pa., ASCA School Counselor of the Year finalist, 2010

Elementary School Counselor's Response

As a school counselor, it is my obligation to work with students whose problems at home are affecting their school experience. There may be times, like a divorce situation, in which a parent might desire to use the knowledge gained from my responsive services to influence an outcome in a court case. Because of this danger, it is important to go over confidentiality with the student, who needs to know that if asked to share information from our sessions in a court of law I do not have the ability to decline. It is also important to remember that when sharing in a court case I should only relate examples of behaviors I have seen. It is up to the court to determine what these things mean because they will be able to more fully see the whole picture of the situation.

– Katrina Beddes, school counselor, Holt Elementary/Davis School District, West Point, Utah, ASCA School Counselor of the Year finalist, 2013

District Supervisor and Adjunct School Counselor Educator's Response
Following is a typical statement I have frequently made to parents appearing to alienate the other parent. "Mr. Carter, I am honored you would trust me with the details of your hurt over the divorce; however, I feel I need to be open and honest with you, as I have been with other parents going through similar difficulties. My role is to help you find additional help for your child. I want to provide you with a list of some wonderful counselors in the community who have received positive feedback from other parents who have sought their help. Based upon our collaborative history together when working with your daughter, I also feel a need to be honest with you about my professional ethics, which prohibits me from taking sides or forming opinions regarding divorce and parenting styles. My role is to be here for your daughter to provide excellent school counselor support and interventions and not become involved with family mediation issues."

– Ken Elliott, coordinator of testing services, director of the Violence Prevention Project, adjunct professor, University of Central Oklahoma; ASCA School Counselor of the Year finalist, 2012

Making Connections

1. Determine if your state extends privileged communication to students in schools. How does the statute giving your student privilege read? If your students do not have privileged communication in statute, is there any language that gives you confidentiality to protect their confidences?

2. Read and discuss the responses in the section, "In a Position to Know: School Counselors Speak." Which response do you particularly agree with and why? Which response do you disagree with and why?

3. Under what circumstances can school counselors deny the courts their testimony?

Chapter 6 Quiz

1) Confidentiality is
   a. Defined as privileged communication and only pertains to court proceedings
   b. A legal imperative rendering school counselors unable to testify about their student(s)
   c. The opposite of informed consent
   d. An ethical imperative for school counselors and a legal one in some states
   e. Only possible if parents sign a consent form when enrolling their child in school

2) The process of discovery in court proceedings
   a. Is given to the plaintiff in the case not the defendant
   b. Applies to oral or written depositions while other documents are under the heading "in-admissible in court"
   c. Is triggered by a judge in a summary judgment moving a case to court
   d. Requires the defendant to submit to a mental examination
   e. Happens prior to court with both attorneys fact finding through depositions, documents and other interrogatories such as mental or physical examinations

3) Subpoenas
   a. Do not require a response from school counselors, as all 50 states assign privileged communication to students in schools rendering school counselors mute in court proceedings
   b. Do not apply to school counselors, as their confidentiality means they have to testify without a subpoena
   c. Do not apply to school counselors who have been apprised that a motion to quash the subpoena was successful
   d. Do not apply to school counselors who have already testified once in a case, as this creates any further subpoenas for the same case null and void
   e. Do not apply to school counselors in appellant courts, only in trial court proceedings

4) School counselors' role in custody cases
   a. Is critically important and should command the school counselor's undivided attention
   b. Is to try to avoid being involved, and if this is not possible to speak to facts and not professional opinions or judgments
   c. Requires them to interview opposing parties (parents) to determine the facts to be a good witness
   d. Is to write letters to the judge explaining which parent should be awarded primary custody
   e. Is limited to their case notes, educational records and any other memory aids but not their testimony

5) The overwhelming majority of school counselors in an ASCA survey reported
   a. They have never been a defendant in a court case
   b. They have been a plaintiff in a court case
   c. They have been a defendant in a court case
   d. When subpoenaed in their professional role to testify ,the most common reason was sexual abuse of a student
   e. They have been the subject of a civil case

Key Terms

Case notes
Court of Appeals
Court order
Defendant
Deposition
Duces tecum
Federal court
McKinney Vento Homeless Assistance Act
Plaintiff
Privileged communication
Process of discovery
Separation of power
State legislature
State court
Subpoena
Testimony
Witnesses

Chapter 7

Child Abuse

Objectives

By the time you have completed this chapter you should be able to:

- Identify the signs and symptoms of child abuse
- Understand both short-term and long-term effects of abuse on students
- Discuss why suspicion of abuse is enough to establish duty to report
- Understand school counselors' legal and ethical obligations in child abuse reporting
- Understand good-faith reporting and how it protects school counselors
- Discuss laws and regulations regarding rape, statutory rape and child abuse

Ethical Standards Addressed in This Chapter

The ASCA Ethical Standards for School Counselors (ASCA, 2022b) most relevant to this chapter include the following:

- School counselors adhere to federal, state and local laws; district policy; and ethical practice when assisting parents/guardians experiencing family difficulties interfering with their student's welfare. (B.1.g.)
- School counselors promote equity and inclusion through culturally affirming and sustaining practices honoring the diversity of families. Recognize that all parents/guardians, custodial and noncustodial, are vested with certain rights and responsibilities for their children's welfare by virtue of their role and according to law. (B.1.c.)
- School counselors report to the proper authorities, as mandated by the state, all suspected cases of child abuse and neglect, recognizing that certainty is not required, only reasonable suspicion. School counselors are held to a higher standard regarding their absolute duty as a mandated reporter to report suspected child abuse and neglect. (A.12.a.)
- School counselors know current state laws and the school system's procedures for reporting child abuse and neglect and methods to advocate for students' physical and emotional safety following abuse/neglect reports. (A.12.d.).
- School counselors develop and maintain the expertise to recognize the signs of child abuse and neglect. Advocate for training to enable students and staff to have the knowledge and skills needed to recognize the signs and to whom they should report suspected abuse or neglect. (A.12.b.)

The full text of the ASCA Ethical Standards for School Counselors is available at *www.schoolcounselor.org*.

Introduction

Child abuse is not uncommon. Each year, thousands of children who are abused come through the halls of America's schools and interact with other students, teachers and school counselors. Many of these students are silent victims; educators do not know their pain. Child abuse is severely underreported. School counselors, using their observational skills and ability to deliver professional development, help all educators detect, report and prevent child abuse and neglect. This chapter will help school counselors recognize signs and symptoms of child abuse or neglect and understand the legal and ethical dimensions of this often-hidden problem.

According to the U.S. Department of Health and Human Services (HHS), child maltreatment includes all types of abuse (physical, emotional or sexual) and neglect. Minimum standards for what constitutes child abuse and neglect are defined in federal law, and the standard of what constitutes abuse is further stipulated in each state's statute (2021). The U.S. government has a website called *Childwelfare.gov* in which you can find state statutes defining what constitutes abuse or neglect, the statute of limitations, penalties for failure to report and other important information for your state.

Anyone who suspects child abuse or neglect of any kind can report it by calling the police, by contacting the Childhelp USA National Child Abuse Hotline at (800) 4-A-CHILD or by contacting a local child abuse hotline. Educators in all states are mandated to report suspected abuse under penalty of criminal charges. Federal law requires school counselors to report any reasonable suspicion of abuse, even in the absence of hard evidence. In most states, mandated reporters (such as school counselors) are immune from legal proceedings brought by parents or guardians who have been erroneously reported to child protective services (CPS). Good-faith reporting is assumed.

Eighteen states require all adults to be mandated child abuse reporters: Delaware, Florida, Idaho, Indiana, Kentucky, Maryland, Mississippi, Nebraska, New Hampshire, New Jersey, New Mexico, North Carolina, Oklahoma, Rhode Island, Tennessee, Texas, Utah and Wyoming (Child Welfare Information Gateway, 2019a). Forty-seven states, the District of Columbia, American Samoa, Guam, the Northern Mariana Islands, Puerto Rico and the U.S. Virgin Islands designate professions whose members are mandated by law to report child maltreatment. Individuals designated as mandatory reporters typically have frequent contact with children, i.e., educators. These states have laws similar to Florida's law: "Any person who knows, or has reasonable cause to suspect, that a child is abused, abandoned or neglected ... shall report such knowledge or suspicion to the department." The new law also makes reporting of child-on-child abuse mandatory. Children 12 and under who are deemed perpetrators will be referred for treatment and therapy, but those 13 and up will be referred to law enforcement (Fla. Stat. § 39.201- 1a (2012)).

Fifty states, the District of Columbia and Puerto Rico provided data to the National Child Abuse and Neglect Data System (NCANDS, 2019). Using this data, HHS released the 2019 report, which estimated that children who received an investigation or alternative response decreased 1.6% from 2018 (3,534,000) to 2019 (3,476,000) (US HHS, 2019). The number and rate of victims of maltreatment have decreased from 2018 to 2019 (US HHS, 2019).

Comparing the national estimate of victims from 2015 (683,000) to 2019 (656,000) shows a decrease of 4%. This decrease can be attributed to state-level changes in legislation and policies, as well as resolved investigations or assessment backlogs, new intake or screening processes, and more public awareness (US HHS, 2019). Three-fifths (61%) of victims were neglected only, 10.3% were physically abused only, and 7.2% were sexually abused only (US HHS, 2019). For 2019, a nationally estimated 1,840 children died of abuse and neglect at a rate of 2.5 per 100,000 children in the national population (US HHS, 2019).

As horrific as these numbers are, they probably do not tell the whole story. Research indicates that the official number of child maltreatment fatalities is underestimated (Michaels & Letson, 2021). Without question, school counselors know that the true level of incidence of child abuse and neglect is underreported for many reasons. Child Welfare Information Gateway (2021a) pulled together research on underreporting of child abuse and reasons. Retrospective reports from adults abused or neglected as children reveal that most cases were not reported to anyone. In these retrospective studies, the adults who did not tell anyone said they did not because they did not realize that they were actually victims of abuse, or they had fears about reprisals if they told anyone. There are many reasons why friends, neighbors, family who hear or observe abuse may not report. Reasons cited include fear of retaliation or rejection by the abuser, worse consequences for the child or family or uncertainty and they might be mistaken. Mandated reporters also fail to make reports at times citing as their primary reason the concern that CPS will actually make the situation worse. Often educators believe they can do a better job of intervening on behalf of a student than CPS. Also, a lack of clarity exists as to what constitutes reasonable suspicion as defined by the law. Neglect is especially difficult to define. Studies show that even professionals within the same organizations have variations and inconsistent assessments and decision making of what constitutes reasonable suspicion in child welfare situations (Bolton et al., 2021).

Another significant reason for underestimates of child abuse is that 40% of referrals to CPS get screened out and no investigation ensues (Child Welfare Information Gateway, 2021a).

In a 2022 survey, 427 ASCA members weighed in on their own child abuse reports. Nearly 40% of these school counselors reported making one to six child abuse reports in the last 36 months (Stone, 2022a). Abuse may take many different forms: physical, neglect, sexual, emotional, abandonment, parental substance use and human trafficking (Child Welfare Information Gateway, 2019b). More often than not, these types of abuse occur in combination with one another. Children who are physically or sexually abused often face emotional abuse and/or neglect at the same time (Child Welfare Information Gateway, 2019a). Individuals who are working or plan to work in schools should be prepared to recognize the signs of child abuse and neglect. Schools play a major role in the reporting of violence against children since the children are around those who typically notice and report signs of abuse (Petrowski et al., 2021). The presence of just one of these signs is not typically indicative of child maltreatment. Rather, alert professionals should consider abuse as a possibility when these signs occur repeatedly and in combination. The following are warning signs of physical abuse, neglect, sexual abuse and emotional abuse taken from the Child Welfare Information Gateway (2019a) fact sheet. Fifteen of these warning signs were recently added.

Consider the possibility of physical abuse when the child:

- Has unexplained burns, bites, bruises, broken bones or black eyes
- Has fading bruises or other marks noticeable after an absence from school
- Seems frightened of the parents and protests or cries when it is time to go home
- Shrinks at the approach of adults
- Reports injury by a parent or another adult caregiver
- Seems scared, anxious, depressed, withdrawn or aggressive
- Shows changes in eating and sleeping habits
- Abuses animals or pets

Consider the possibility of physical abuse when the parent or other adult caregiver:

- Offers conflicting, unconvincing or no explanation for the child's injury
- Uses harsh physical discipline with the child
- Sees the child as entirely bad, burdensome or worthless
- Shows little concern for the child
- Has a history of abusing animals or pets

Consider the possibility of neglect when the child:

- Is frequently absent from school
- Begs or steals food or money
- Lacks needed medical or dental care, immunizations or glasses
- Is consistently dirty and has severe body odor
- Lacks sufficient clothing for the weather
- Abuses alcohol or other drugs
- States that there is no one at home to provide care

Consider the possibility of neglect when the parent or other adult caregiver:

- Appears to be indifferent to the child
- Seems apathetic or depressed
- Behaves irrationally or in a bizarre manner
- Is abusing alcohol or other drugs

Consider the possibility of sexual abuse when the child:

- Has difficulty walking or sitting
- Experiences bleeding, bruising or swelling in their private parts
- Suddenly refuses to go to school
- Reports nightmares or bedwetting
- Experiences a sudden change in appetite
- Demonstrates bizarre, sophisticated or unusual sexual knowledge or behavior
- Becomes pregnant or contracts a venereal disease, particularly if under age 14
- Runs away
- Reports sexual abuse by a parent or another adult caregiver
- Attaches very quickly to strangers or new adults in their environment

Consider the possibility of sexual abuse when the parent or other adult caregiver:

- Tries to be the child's friend rather than assume an adult role
- Makes up excuses to be alone with the child
- Talks with the child about the adult's personal problems or relationships

Consider the possibility of emotional abuse when the child:

- Shows extremes in behavior, such as overly compliant or demanding behavior, extreme passivity or aggression
- Is either inappropriately adult (parenting other children, for example) or inappropriately infantile (frequently rocking or head-banging, for example)
- Is delayed in physical or emotional development
- Shows signs of depression or suicidal thoughts
- Reports an inability to develop emotional bonds with others

Consider the possibility of emotional abuse when the parent or other adult caregiver:

- Constantly blames, belittles or berates the child
- Describes the child negatively
- Overtly rejects the child

In a February 2022 survey, 427 school counselors responded to the type of abuse reports they had to make in the past 36 months (Stone, 2022a).

Reported injury by a parent or another adult caregiver. 45.8%
Student seemed frightened of the parents/guardians and protests or cries when it's time to go home. 45.6%
Student was frequently absent from school. 41.5%
Student had unexplained burns, bites, bruises, broken bones or black eyes. 40.1%
Student stated no one was at home to provide care. 34.7%
Student reported sexual abuse by a parent or another caregiver. 34.1%
Student was consistently dirty and has had severe body odor. 33.2%
Student lacked needed medical or dental care, immunizations or glasses. 28.7%
Student had fading bruises or other marks noticeable after an absence from school. . 26.1%
Student had attempted suicide. 24.9%
Student demonstrated bizarre, sophisticated or unusual sexual knowledge or behavior. 20.3%
Student showed extremes in behavior, such as overly compliant or demanding behavior, extreme passivity or aggression. 17.2%
Student ran away. 14.6%
Student lacked sufficient clothing for the weather. 14.3%
Student reported a lack of attachment to the parent. 13.5%
Student abused alcohol or other drugs. 10.0%
Student begged or stole food or money. 8.9%
Student was either inappropriately adult (parents other children, for example) or inappropriately infantile (frequently rocking or head-banging, for example)... 6.9%
Student was fearful at the approach of adults. 6.0%
Student was delayed in physical or emotional development. 5.4%
Student became pregnant or contracted a venereal disease, particularly if under age 14. .... 2.9%

THE IMPACT OF THE COVID-19 PANDEMIC

Research into how the pandemic has affected child abuse and reporting is still in the early stages. UNICEF estimates that 1.8 billion children were affected by the disruption of violence prevention and response services due to COVID-19. The most commonly disrupted services were case management services and home visits for women and children at risk of abuse (Petrowski et al., 2021).

School closings during the pandemic underscored how vital educators are to child abuse reporting. The data also shows that the suspension or disruption of child protective services has resulted in a decrease in the reporting of child maltreatment. State after state reported a significant decline in child abuse reports when educators did not have their eyes on students except virtually. For example, according to the Michigan Health and Human Services Department, reports dropped by 45% during the first month of virtual schooling from the same month the year before. The California Department of Social Services reported an 18% drop in referrals in March 2020 compared to the prior year. Georgia's Division of Family and Child Services reported a 50% decline in reporting of suspected child abuse or neglect since school closures, and the Texas Department of Family and Protective Services saw a 48% drop in reporting from the first to the last week of March 2020 (Petrowski et al., 2021). Although there has been a clear decrease in reports of child maltreatment, several studies found an increase in children's injuries as a result of maltreatment during COVID-19 (Katz & Fallon, 2021).

According to the World Health Organization, domestic violence tends to increase during epidemics, which can have an effect on child maltreatment and mental health. Experts believe children are at significant risk for maltreatment due to increased rates of poverty, food insecurity, unemployment and inequalities brought on by the health crisis (Katz et al., 2021).

With stay-at-home orders and social distancing guidelines, families spend more time with each other, which can translate into more opportunities for family conflict. Literature also shows that parents with less social support are at an increased risk of physical abuse and neglect. Statistics prior to the pandemic showed that parents with the lowest socioeconomic status are seven times more likely to neglect their children and three times more likely to physically abuse. More than 40 million Americans filed for unemployment within months of the announcement of the pandemic at rates that surpassed the Great Recession (Rodriguez et al., 2021).

Although reports show a decline in reporting in the early months of the pandemic, many child welfare agencies reported trends returning to pre-pandemic levels in summer and fall 2020. Due to the pandemic, child welfare agencies began providing virtual services that many states reported could continue in the future, such as case planning meetings, family time, caseworker visits, court hearings and telehealth visits (U.S. Government Accountability Office, 2021).

Child maltreatment has both long- and short-term consequences. Negative physical, cognitive, psychological and/or behavioral outcomes may appear at any time during an abused individual's lifespan. These effects range in consequence from minor physical injuries, low self-esteem, attention disorders and poor peer relations to severe brain damage, extremely violent behavior and suicide. Research consistently shows any and all forms of maltreatment increase the risk of lower academic achievement, juvenile delinquency, teen pregnancy, drug use and mental health problems (Child Welfare Information Gateway, 2019a). Such dire potential consequences emphasize the need for adults in schools to identify the symptoms of maltreatment and intervene appropriately. Early identification and intervention for these students may reduce the consequences of the abuse. There is an economic cost also. The total lifetime economic burden resulting from new cases of fatal and nonfatal child maltreatment in the United States is approximately $428 billion to $2 trillion (Peterson et al., 2018).

ASCA has a position statement on approximately 49 critical issues, none more important than our response to child abuse. The position statement on child abuse has been revised many times, most recently in 2021. The position statement can be found at *www.schoolcounselor.org/positionstatements*.

Unfortunately, child abuse persists in a cycle. Research indicates that children who experienced abuse or neglect do not automatically abuse or neglect their own children but are more likely to subject their children to maltreatment compared to children who were not maltreated (Child Welfare Information Gateway, 2019a). School counselors commit themselves to providing coping strategies and promoting healthy relationship skills to children who have been abused to help break the cycle of child abuse. School counselors can initiate appropriate behavioral changes and help students develop positive interpersonal relationships, which may reinforce appropriate parenting skills in the future.

When working with students for whom abuse is suspected, school counselors have an opportunity to use their facilitative counseling skills to make the students feel supported. It is paramount for school counselors to provide validation and encouragement to children who are maltreated. Listening attentively, reassuring students that the abuse is not their fault and explaining that reporting is what you have to do to protect them are all ways to use facilitative skills to comfort possibly abused students.

Being directed by law to report means being aware and alert to the potential of abuse, deciding whether abuse is present and being brave enough to take action. Some cases are simple, because the evidence is irrefutable and conclusive. Physical and sexual abuse can fall into this category. Professionals simply see it, hear about it and report it. Occasionally, cases fall into a gray area, where pinpointing neglect, mental or emotional harm, or threat requires the school counselor to consider any extenuating circumstances, the family and the sanctity of the home, the school counselor's own individual perceptions and beliefs, and how those beliefs will influence their choices. This due diligence does not mean school counselors ignore reasonable suspicion and their mandated reporting status; it simply means negligence is sometimes subjective so school counselors wrestle with the context of the situation to determine if they do have reasonable suspicion.

School counselors worry when making child abuse reports. In a 2022 survey of 427 ASCA members, 70.9% of the respondents reported feeling fear, anxiety or indecision while contemplating reporting abuse in the past three years (Stone, 2022a).

The reasons given for the feelings of fear, anxiety or indecision were as follows:

Child protective services would not properly investigate. *64.0%*
Child protective services would not take the report seriously. *59.7%*
Child protective services might take actions that would make the situation

far worse for the child. 56.4%
Breaking confidentiality with the child and harming our trusting relationship. 54.5%
Reporting abuse would harm the family's relationship with me or the school. 46.5%
I was unsure whether I had enough evidence to file a report. 39.9%
The family would move to another school, and the situation would worsen or stay the same for the child. 25.1%
The perpetrator would contact or harm me or someone else at the school 19.1%
Other. 7.6%

ASCA members responded that they felt "very prepared," "adequately prepared," "somewhat prepared," "not very prepared" or "not at all prepared" to make different types of child abuse reports. Regarding physical abuse, 66.5% of respondents felt very prepared to report. For sexual abuse, 51.5% felt very prepared, and 45.9% felt very prepared for neglect. The confidence level declined to 36.5% regarding reporting emotional abuse (Stone, 2022a).

State statutes vary slightly in language, but there are common themes in most state's statutes. Educators and school counselors are mandatory child abuse reporters, which means they:

- Have an absolute duty to report
- Do not have to be certain; suspicion is enough to establish a duty
- Have a duty that is not discretionary; it is inextricably clear
- Have an obligation to report within their state's specified time period
- Are protected, since good-faith reporting is assumed
- Understand there is not a statute of limitations on child abuse reporting

(Childwelfare, 2022)

The information reported to CPS generally includes the following: (a) the name and address of the child, (b) the name and address of the child's parents or other persons responsible for the child's care, (c) the child's age, (d) the conditions in the child's home environment, (e) the nature and extent of the child's injuries and (f) information about other children in the same environment (Child Welfare Information Gateway, 2017).

Getting Started: What Would You Do?

Two school counseling leaders' responses to the following case appear at the end of this chapter. Before you read their response, formulate in your own mind how you would approach this ethical dilemma.

RAPE, STATUTORY RAPE AND CHILD ABUSE APPLIED TO A STATE STATUTE

A 15-year-old tells you he is having sex with his 19-year-old girlfriend. A 14-year-old student tells you she is having sex with her 17-year-old partner. Is either scenario considered statutory rape in your state? Are you required to report in either scenario to CPS, the police and/or the sheriff? This is examined by leaders in the school counseling field as applied to their particular state.

Working Through Case Studies

FAILURE TO REPORT CHILD ABUSE

A student told you her father walked around the house naked. You told her to talk to her mother. She came back and told you her father touched her breast. Because she did not have breasts, you dismissed it and told her to tell her mother about things with her body that concerned her. She came back a third time and told you her father asked her to touch his penis. Again, you dismissed it because this student fabricates stories. Is there a legal or ethical problem with your behavior?

Points to Consider

In *Hughes v. Stanley County School District* (1999), an elementary school counselor was fired for not reporting alleged child abuse. M.B., a third-grade girl, told Mary Hughes, the school counselor, that in 1994 her father, G.B., walked around the house naked after a shower. In another conversation, M.B. told Hughes that G.B. "touched her in the area of her breast during a playful wrestling match," and in a third conversation Hughes learned that M.B. walked in on her father while he was masturbating. M.B., however, had a history of fabricating and exaggerating facts, so Hughes was unsure about how seriously to take the allegations. Accordingly, she spoke with the high school counselor to get a second opinion, and both felt Hughes should speak with the girl's parents. So, going against school policy to report suspicion of abuse, Hughes contacted the parents in an attempt to validate or dismiss the allegations. The parents told her the allegations were essentially true, and G.B. had taken steps to avoid reoccurrence in the future. While Hughes did check up on the situation with M.B. daily, she never reported the allegations to the authorities.

The failure to report came to light in July 1996 when the police questioned Hughes in connection with a complaint that G.B. had sexually assaulted a neighboring girl. G.B. pled guilty to the sexual assault charge with the neighboring child, and Hughes was fired for failure to report the previous allegations (Swinton, 2005).

On Aug. 15, 2016, a Florida mental health counselor was charged with waiting more than a week to report allegations of child sexual abuse. The counselor was babysitting a group of children when a 13-year-old told her he had sexually battered a 9-year-old. "It doesn't matter how she became aware of these allegations. Once this child told her of the alleged abuse, she was mandated to report that," said WFTV legal analyst Bill Sheaffer (WFTV News, August 2016).

The point in including this situation is to underscore that counselors are always mandated reporters whether they are babysitting or at work. According to the news article, the counselor defended herself to police saying she did not report the allegation earlier because she wanted to wait for the right time and had to collect her thoughts. She further explained that she was not in fear that the teen would abuse the younger child again because he promised he wouldn't. No state child abuse statute gives counselors discretion to "wait for the right time" or determine a victim is safe just because the perpetrator says they are safe.

JUDGMENT CALLS ARE NOT ALLOWED

Your principal wants to make the decision as to whether something meets the criteria of child abuse. The principal wants to build relationships with families by explaining to them what is considered unacceptable discipline of their child and avoiding calls to CPS. How should you respond?

Points to Consider

School counselors have reported this scenario or one like it enough to make it known that this frequently occurs. In the Stone survey (2022a), 5% of the 427 survey respondents stated that in the prior 36 months they had been asked by an administrator not to call in certain situations they suspected were child abuse – a frightening 21 times. This is illegal behavior. According to HHS, supervisors and administrators cannot impede or inhibit a report or subject the reporting person to any sanction. The warning is for administrators not to make it difficult or to cause problems for educators and staff to report child abuse. Educators whose administrators do not report may be held liable for the unreported maltreatment. Educators should not be put in a position of being vulnerable to legal sanctions or having to bypass the administrator (ISD HHS, 2021).

Share with the principal what has happened to other principals who did not report child abuse. The list is long of those who have been fired and/or charged with felonies and misdemeanors. You can find details of a few cases by researching the names that follow. Some of these cases involved the principal protecting the reputation of the school instead of protecting children.

Georgia principal Dority, Tapp Middle School, and school counselor Yatta Collins: Collins told Dority that a student had tried to hang herself, and the student's friend reported the reason was the student's stepfather sexually abused her. The school counselor did not call in the abuse, and the principal notified CPS past the mandated-reporting period. Both the principal and school counselor were arrested. The principal spent the night in jail, and they both lost their jobs. The principal admitted an error in judgment, and ironically, the school counselor may have saved both their jobs if she had reported to CPS instead of just her principal.

Other principals who have recently found themselves in jeopardy with their districts due to failure to report child abuse include: Georgia principal Donovan; Indiana principal Christopher Smith; Texas principal Kory Fancher Dorman; Texas principal Cindy Underwood; South Carolina principal Idasa Cobb; Nebraska principal Eric Nelson; Florida principal Abdulaziz Yalcin; Colorado principal Chad Broer, Virginia principal Yusef Azimi; and California principal Lyn Vijayendran.

CHILD ABUSE REPORTING AS A THREAT

Your school's social worker makes a blanket determination that parents of Asian students aren't likely to take their children for outside counseling. It is the social worker's practice to warn all parents of Asian students when he calls to report suicidal ideation that he intends to call CPS if they do not provide him with proof within 48 business hours that their child has an appointment or is in outside counseling. Many times, he sends a child to the hospital then calls parents afterward to meet them there. Are there any legal and ethical implications?

Points to Consider

This is the actual practice of a social worker in a school with a large Asian population. The social worker is lumping all parents into one category because of their culture or ethnicity, believing he can always predict their reaction. All of this may be well-meaning, but it is circumventing parental rights to exercise custody and control over their child. A school social worker or school counselor should not use an antagonistic approach with parents in what is already an extremely stressful situation for most families. Using CPS without context as a blanket threat without looking at each situation in context is an abuse of qualified privilege.

School counselors are careful to:

- Work with each suicidal child and family of the child in context.
- Educate parents as to the urgency and need to seek outside counseling.
- Recognize parents have the most investment regarding their child's long-term health and avoid believing you are a student's sole savior.
- Give parents credit that they may be in the best position to investigate areas the school counselor cannot, such as the student's social media activity, access to means of suicide, past indicators of suicidal ideation and current personal stressors of suicidal ideation.
- Recognize that short of child abuse as the cause of the suicidal ideation, parents have a right to be immediately involved when suicide is even a remote possibility.

There is a better way to support students who are suicidal than setting up conflict with parents from the first phone call. Help bring the parents along rather than from the outset creating barriers.

SCHOOL COUNSELORS WHO BREACHED THE CONFIDENTIALITY OF A CHILD ABUSE REPORT

Divorced parents have two children in your school. The mother has sole legal and physical custody. The father comes to you with examples of how his sons are being verbally and physically abused by their mother. You send in a child abuse report to CPS and then give a copy to the father. Do any of your actions create a legal or ethical problem?

Points to Consider

In *Cuff v. Grossmont Union High School Dist.* (2013) 221 Cal.App.4th 582, a school counselor was alerted by a noncustodial father that the mother of his two sons was physically and verbally abusing his children. The school counselor reported the accusation in a fax to CPS. CPS told her to call the police. Instead of calling the police, the school counselor gave the father a copy of the report and told him to take it to the police so his sons could be taken into custody. The mother subsequently sued the school district and school counselor for invasion of her privacy under the Child Abuse and Neglect Reporting Act (CANRA).

Once the school counselor heard of the alleged abuse from the father, her role and legal mandate was to call CPS and report what she knew. Any conversation about making the report or the contents of the report is a problem. The report may only be shared with appropriate law enforcement and child protection agencies. The lower court dismissed claims against the school counselor and district. However, on appeal the appellant court held the school counselor and the district could be liable for violating the confidentiality provisions of the CANRA statute. The court said governmental immunity does not immunize a mandated reporter's conduct that does not comply with the CANRA's confidentiality provisions. Any other result, noted the court, would invalidate the criminal provisions of CANRA. Based on this analysis, the court explained that the school counselor is not immune from her violation of CANRA and that the district may be vicariously liable for her actions. As such, the court reversed the trial court's ruling.

In a 2017 administrative hearing case, a school counselor ran afoul of his district when he shared with his fellow school counselors the contents of a child abuse report he had to make against another educator in his school who was accused by a student of sexually abusing her. The school counselor was not aware that child abuse reports are confidential and thought he was doing the right thing by alerting his fellow school counselors in preparation of any needs students might have should this information be revealed by the press. School counselors share their child abuse reports all the time with their administrators, and this rarely creates a problem. The difference in this case was that the district did not see that there was any compelling reason to start involving others in this highly sensitive matter when the correct players (CPS, the principal and the district) had been notified. The school counselor received a letter of reprimand in his file but not before facing the threat of dismissal (confidential personal communication, 2017).

Additionally, students have privacy rights. A school counselor lost her job after she told her entire department about the details of a child's sexual abuse at the hands of a relative after reporting it to CPS. The school counselor was told that the entire department did not need to know about this highly charged, sensitive information. Her argument was that they did need to know in case the student came in for help and she was out of the office for the day. Yes, we share sensitive information with others, but we have to be able to draw a very straight line as to why the recipients of highly sensitive information need to know that information. If the school counselor had been going out on maternity leave for 12 weeks and wanted to have the child hand pick the school counselor to whom she would be assigned and have the child (and parent in most cases) determine what if anything the interim counselor would know in advance, this school counselor would not be facing the loss of her job.

UNCERTIFIED SCHOOL COUNSELORS AND CHILD ABUSE REPORTING

You are not yet certified in your state to be a school counselor, but you are hired out-of-field as a school counselor. You are not certain of the child abuse laws or any other law governing schools, and you have one more year in your school counselor preparation program. Is there a legal or ethical dilemma for you or your preparation program in this situation?

Points to Consider

Principals and school counseling supervisors increasingly face the unfortunate choice between hiring an uncertified school counselor or leaving a position unfilled for months or, in some cases, years. Educators typically understand that hiring an out-of-field or uncertified person leaves the school district more vulnerable in the event of a breach of ethics or law. When a school district hires an uncertified school counselor, the school counselor, the school district and the university preparation program must ensure that the school counselor understands the duty to report child abuse. The school district is even more vulnerable if an uncertified school counselor commits an offense, as the school district lowered its standard of care by placing an uncertified person in a school counseling position. If you take a position for which you are not certified, it is in your best interest, and that of the school district, to do all you can to educate yourself about the law for mandatory reporting of child abuse, as well as school board policy and practice.

WHEN REPORTING DOESN'T YIELD RESULTS

A student comes to school with marks on his neck and severely bruised arms. The boy tells you his father picked him up by the neck and flung him against the wall. CPS wouldn't take action, saying they couldn't prove the father did this. What is your next step?

Points to Consider

This is an all-too-real case, and the school counselor spoke to the CPS supervisor, who reiterated that they were not willing to take the case. The school counselor found out the name of the director and contacted her and was given the same response, that the case did not meet the threshold of an investigation. The school counselor said the student remained scared to go home.

Keeping a close watch on the student can help allay your fears. If signs of abuse reappear, get your principal, a school nurse and teachers to all report the abuse, if possible with a phone call where everyone is on the call at the same time. Stress that you want it on record that you are frightened for this child. Explain to the supervisor that you are taking careful notes because you are afraid your notes may be needed one day in the event this child is severely hurt. Putting pressure on others to act is appropriate and necessary when you are concerned and must rely on CPS to intervene on behalf of the student's safety.

PARENTS DEMAND YOU STAY AWAY FROM THEIR CHILD

You recently reported a case to CPS. The case was deemed unfounded and closed. The parents easily figured out it was you who called, and they take issue with you for discussing "private, personal issues" with their child. They tell your principal they do not want you to ever work with their child again. Can the parents forbid you to work with their child?

Points to Consider

It is a violation of policy and illegal for CPS to reveal to parents/guardians who made the child abuse report, but parents/guardians can often surmise who the reporter was from details they are given or by simply asking their child whom he/she talked to about the abuse. This scenario is repeated many times in households across America, often placing the reporting counselor in a difficult position. School counselors should politically astutely refuse to talk to alleged perpetrators about the child abuse report, as it is an open case.

If the parents/guardians are in conflict with you over reporting, working with their child can be complicated. In many school districts, parents/guardians can refuse counseling services for their child even if the student still wants to come for counseling. Just as the math teacher and English teacher can do their jobs without parental permission, generally speaking, so can school counselors. However, since counseling involves the personal and social/emotional arena, it is considered best practice to have parental permission for individual counseling.

When parents/guardians expressly state they do not want counseling for their child, it is best not to dismiss their wishes. However, if you believe the child is in danger, and the parents/guardians are trying to hide their behavior by keeping you from having contact with their child, alert everyone to keep an eye out for signs of abuse. You can still work with the child if you think it is imperative to do so, but the fallout and strain on all may be too much. If the child needs help, implore the parents/guardians to allow someone else to help, perhaps by referring the student to another school counselor in the school.

NEITHER DENY NOR AFFIRM A CHILD ABUSE REPORT

The principal calls you to the conference room, and when you arrive the child's parents for whom you called in child abuse the day before are there with the principal. What do you do?

Points to Consider

The Child Abuse Prevention and Treatment Act is federal legislation addressing child abuse and neglect. CAPTA provides federal funding to states in support of prevention, assessment, investigation, prosecution and treatment activities and also provides grants to public agencies and nonprofit organizations, including Indian Tribes and Tribal organizations, for demonstration programs and projects. CAPTA recommends that we never affirm nor deny that we made a report to the alleged perpetrator and that we never discuss an open case. Although these cases may no longer be active cases, it stands to reason we should never breach confidentiality in such a sensitive situation. Federal and state laws are written to protect the educator's role in reporting child abuse. All states have laws requiring school counselors to report child abuse and all states provide immunity from criminal and civil liability in good-faith reporting. Educators should not have to face the alleged perpetrator and discuss or defend their report.

A typical state statute says a child abuse report is confidential, the reporter is to remain confidential, the reporter is not to be held criminally or civilly liable for good-faith reporting, an employer cannot hinder the employee reporting, and the reporter's employer cannot discriminate or retaliate against the reporter. Check to see if your state's statute has these elements. Regardless of the motive for the meeting, the principal has stepped on the intent of confidentiality for mandated reporters, who are to be protected and not subjected to having to justify their report or breach the victim's confidence. Parents often can correctly deduce who called CPS, but their suspicions should not be confirmed or denied nor should you discuss an open case with the alleged perpetrator. According to HHS, it is critical to remember that the educator should not reveal any information pertinent to the report made to CPS or law enforcement. Administrators shouldn't express or imply to the abuse reporter that a meeting with parents accused of child abuse is expected or even desired (2021).

As politically astutely as possible, the school counselor should request a private conversation with the principal, who then in turn explains to the parents that the meeting cannot go forward. If parents shift to asking for information outside the child abuse report, it is difficult to refuse, but do not allow yourself to cornered into listening to or discussing why the parents are innocent. It is completely counter to the spirit of the law to require the reporter to face the alleged perpetrator, especially when the reporter is asked to reveal any information pertinent to the report.

Many states have laws allowing the mandated reporter to receive feedback on the report. Check your state statute. Your local or state CPS administrators are a good resource and can provide school district administrators with clarification if they are engaging in practices contrary to the spirit of the law regarding confidentiality of reporters (American Bar Association Center on Children and the Law, n.d.). The fallout when reporters' confidentiality is trampled is to risk reticence in reporting. It stands to reason that an educator might think twice if past experience meant having to face parents and justify one's actions, breach a child's confidence, cause more trauma for the child and be placed in the light of an adversary not advocate.

LIABILITY IN CHILD ABUSE REPORTING

A teacher noticed a horrible slash mark across the back of a child's neck and saw that it extended far down the child's back. The mark closely resembled a belt mark. You report the incident to the CPS, whose investigation revealed a fall from a piece of playground equipment. The parents deduce the report came from you. The parents are threatening to sue you. Can you be sued?

Points to Consider

Good-faith reporting is assumed when a professional reports child abuse. "The term good-faith reporting refers to the assumption that the reporter, to the best of his or her knowledge, had reason to believe that the child in question was being subjected to abuse or neglect. Even if the allegations made in the report cannot be fully substantiated, the reporter is still provided with immunity. Immunity statutes protect reporters from civil or criminal liability that they might otherwise incur. This protection is extended to both mandatory and voluntary reporters" (Child Welfare Information Gateway, 2019b).

A mere suspicion of abuse is all that is necessary when reporting child abuse. By reporting the slash mark, the school counselor acted legally and ethically and earned immunity from all liability in most states. Every state and U.S. territory provides various degrees of protection from liability for persons who in good faith report suspected instances of abuse or neglect under the reporting laws. For a complete listing of state-by-state child abuse reporting laws, see the website for Child Welfare Information Gateway, at *www.childwelfare.gov*.

In *Zamstein v. Marvasti* (1997), the Supreme Court began an examination of this issue as it related to health care providers and determined safety from civil and criminal liability in its interpretation of the child abuse reporting statutes. In *Zamstein*, the child abuse report arose out of a bitter divorce and custody dispute in which Sharon Zamstein accused her husband, Jacob, of sexually abusing their children. Sharon Zamstein retained a psychiatrist for the express purpose of evaluating the children to determine whether or not the father had abused them. Custody of the children was granted to Sharon Zamstein. A criminal prosecution against Jacob Zamstein ended in an acquittal. He then sued the psychiatrist, Dr. Marvasti, claiming the prosecution against him and the alienation of his children only occurred because of the psychiatrist's report of suspected sexual abuse. The Supreme Court had no difficulty in deciding that, following the statutory guidelines, providers who make a report in good faith are immune from any liability, civil or criminal. Almost all health care attorneys will advise a client that it is far better to be faced with defending a civil action for reporting suspected abuse, rather than defending a civil action when a child is injured or killed after failing to make a report of suspected child abuse. Failure to report suspected child abuse can result in criminal and civil liability.

However, there has been a challenge to good-faith reporting. In January 2016, the U.S. Supreme Court declined to review a lower court's decision in *Schott v. Wenk* (2016). This was problematic because the lower court's decision had a chilling effect on good-faith reporting when the court determined a mandated reporter could be accused and found liable for reporting abuse in retaliating against parents. The principal reported the father was sexually abusing his daughter; the parents then sued. The accusation was that the principal was retaliating because the parents were in a fight with the administrator over an individualized education program for their child. Both a federal district court and a 6th Circuit three-judge panel rejected immunity for the administrator. "The decision imposes a Hobson's choice for mandatory reporters: either fulfill their responsibility under state law to report suspected or known abuse and risk federal litigation and potential personal liability; or fail to report and invoke the possibility of civil and criminal penalties for that failure" (Walsh, 2016, p. 2). The Supreme Court refused to hear the case and allowed the Sixth Circuit decision to stand. It is hoped that the *Wenk* case will not cause educators to hesitate to make a report since the reality is that there is a court that has allowed a report of a mandated reporter to end in liability.

ALERTING PARENTS YOU CALLED CHILD PROTECTIVE SERVICES

In most every case in which you report child abuse, you immediately call the parents to tell them you have had to file a report on them. You adamantly defend this because you have seen the results where this maintains the parents trust and you are able to continue a relationship with the parents. Is this good practice?

Points to Consider

This practice is coming from a well-meaning school counselor who is trying to be transparent and honest to preserve or grow a relationship with a parent. This case is not a hypothetical but a combination of a few real scenarios. Guidance comes from *ChildWelfare.gov*, who recommend that we do not inform parents when making a child abuse report because:

- If the parents are the perpetrators, the child might be in danger once the parents discover that the report was made.
- The parents might influence the child to change the story or lie when CPS interviews them.
- The parents could flee with the child, especially if they have even more to hide than child abuse, such as being in an undocumented status, a multiple child abuse offender, a drug user.
- The child may take on guilt for disrupting the family and harm themselves.

If the suspected abuse was perpetrated by someone other than the parents, a warning by the child abuse reporter might help parents know to keep the child away from the perpetrator before the CPS worker can address the situation. This seems like a perfectly logical response, but call your local CPS and obey their requirements regarding confidentiality. Regardless of our feelings about a parent who abuses, we treat parents with respect as this better serves the child in the long run.

PARENTS DEMAND TO SEE THE CHILD ABUSE REPORT

Parents are demanding a copy of a child abuse report you made accusing them of child abuse. Must you give them a copy of your report?

Points to Consider

FERPA and CAPTA both apply to this case, but CAPTA supersedes FERPA, so responsibilities under CAPTA and state law will be applied to this case. The school counselor would not release the report to the parents without the district's legal department requiring it. The legal department would only do so if there is a state statute that allows this; a grand jury or a court order; or a federal, state or local government entity, or agent of such, that needed the information to carry out its responsibilities under law to protect a child from abuse and neglect. There are other exceptions as outlined in the following excerpt from the CAPTA Manual. CAPTA requires that states have a state law or operate a statewide program that includes methods to preserve the confidentiality of all child abuse and neglect records and reports and provides for exceptions in certain circumstances. The statutory language states that such records shall only be made available to a specified list of persons and entities (US HHS, 2021).

It depends on the state as to whether the school counselor will be required to disclose the child abuse report to the accused. For example, Texas Family Code Section 261.201(k) states, "A governmental body may not withhold child abuse or neglect records from the parent, managing conservator or other legal representative of the child, if the parent, managing conservator or other legal representative is not accused of committing the abuse or neglect (2015).

Most states have similar statutes protecting reports to CPS. In general, CAPTA requires states to preserve the confidentiality of all child abuse and neglect reports, but there are some exceptions:

- State must provide otherwise confidential child abuse and neglect information to:
  - Any federal, state or local government entity, or agent of such, that has a need for such information in order to carry out its responsibilities under law to protect children from abuse and neglect
  - Child abuse citizen review panels
  - The public, in cases where child abuse or neglect resulted in a child fatality or near fatality
  - Child fatality review panels

States may provide otherwise confidential child abuse and neglect information to:

- The subjects of the report
- A grand jury or court, when necessary to determine an issue
- Other entities or classes of individuals who are authorized by statute to receive information pursuant to a legitimate state purpose
- States have the option of allowing public access to court proceedings that determine child abuse and neglect cases, so long as the state can ensure the safety and well-being of the child, parents and families

(CAPTA, 2019)

CHILD ABUSE AND STATUTE OF LIMITATIONS

You are a high school counselor. One of your students confides in you that five years ago she was the victim of sexual abuse by her mother's boyfriend. Four years ago, the perpetrator left the home and moved to another state. She tells you she never told anyone, not even her mother. She begs you not to tell anyone. What are your obligations?

Points to Consider

A statute of limitations is a law that sets the time within which criminal charges or civil claims can be filed and after which one loses the right to sue or make a claim (Child Welfare Information Gateway, 2019a). The statute of limitations of child abuse in most states is between five and 10 years. However, many states have recently extended their statute of limitations by several years, and some by 10 years or more (Katner, 2020).

The legal determination of the statute of limitations, however, is not part of the duty to report to which school counselors must adhere. If a situation of abuse is reported, the professional must contact the authorities, which will then pursue the matter and make the necessary legal determinations. In your advocacy role, you can and should support this student through any subsequent legal proceedings and help the student in any way possible, but you are not able to honor the student's request "not to tell anyone."

BREACH OF STUDENT'S PRIVACY RIGHTS

During his back-to-school speech for the entire school district, the superintendent used the narratives from the child abuse forms all educators are required to fill out and submit to the district office. Names were not used, but identifying information was, such as the child's grade level, gender and the school's name. The speech contained information about the abuse, and the child was identifiable to a few who knew the details of the abuse. His message was intended to inspire educators to be vigilant to signs of abuse, but you believe what he did was a breach of privacy. Are you wrong to be concerned?

Points to Consider

Personally identifiable information is protected as explained in Chapter 4 Student Privacy. Using a child's personally identifiable information is illegal, and using a child's most painful and sensitive information is unethical. It against the privacy protection of FERPA and CAPTA. If superintendents want to motivate, they must change all possible identifying information. It would still be an unethical if not an illegal practice to use any part of real reports generated on the students in the district.

STUDENTS WITNESSING DOMESTIC VIOLENCE

A teacher reports to you that one of her students is traumatized having witnessed her dad beating her mother the night before. You and the teacher are not sure if you need to report this as child abuse.

Points to Consider

Witnessing domestic violence can result in emotional difficulties similar to those of children who are direct victims of abuse. However, the statutes for reporting these types of incidences are aren't as clear as for other situations of child abuse. Approximately 26 states and Puerto Rico variously address in statute the issue of children who witness domestic violence in their homes (Child Welfare Information Gateway, 2021b). The legal system has begun to recognize that children who witness domestic violence are victims of child abuse.

The school counselor and teacher in this scenario will want to consult CPS and explain the situation and ask if it is reportable under state law. Nearly half the states (Alaska, Arizona, Arkansas, California, Connecticut, Delaware, Georgia, Florida, Hawaii, Idaho, Illinois, Indiana, Louisiana, Minnesota, Mississippi, Montana, Nevada, North Carolina, Ohio, Oklahoma, Oregon, Utah, Washington and West Virginia), have varying laws addressing the offense of perpetrating domestic violence in the presence of a child. Alaska offers an example, "A court may find that a child is in need of aid if the court finds by a preponderance of the evidence that the child has been subjected to conduct or conditions created by the parent ... that have resulted in mental injury to the child or has placed the child at substantial risk of mental injury as a result of exposure to [domestic violence] by a household member against another household member or repeated exposure to [domestic violence]" (Alaska, § 47.10.011 - 47.10.015, 2008).

In 13 states (Alaska, Arizona, Arkansas, California, Florida, Hawaii, Idaho, Louisiana, Mississippi, Montana, Ohio, Oregon, and Washington), additional sentencing penalties are considered when an act of domestic violence is committed in the presence of a child. In five states (Delaware, Georgia, North Carolina, Oklahoma, and Utah), committing domestic violence in the presence of a child is a separate crime that may be charged separately or in addition to the act of violence. Illinois, Louisiana and Nevada require domestic violence perpetrators to pay for any counseling a child victim may require. Indiana requires that visitation of a noncustodial parent who has been convicted of domestic violence in the presence of his or her child be supervised for at least one year and not more than two years following the act of domestic violence (Child Welfare Information Gateway, 2021b).

Laws aside, ethically there is much that school counselors can do to support children who witness domestic violence. Supporting children of domestic violence at school, helping families find resources and connecting the child with an understanding teacher or school mentor are just a few of the ways school counselors can provide these children with a safe haven. The Department of Justice is but one of dozens of resources to help school counselors find ways to support children who witness domestic violence.

The case of *Nicholson v. Williams* (2001) challenged the practice of New York City's Administration for Children's Services. This service was removing the children of battered mothers solely on the basis that the children saw their mothers being beaten by husbands or boyfriends. Judge Weinstein ruled the practice is unconstitutional, and he ordered it to be stopped. Even when witnessing domestic violence does harm, removing the child from the nonoffending parent can be more harmful. As one expert witness in the case testified, "[It] is tantamount to pouring salt on an open wound" (*Nicholson v. Williams* (2001)). Another witness testified, "When a child is separated from a mother because of domestic violence, the separation is even more traumatic, because the child "'is terrified that a parent might not be OK, may be injured, may be vulnerable. ... They feel that they should somehow be responsible for the parent, and if they are not with the parent, then it's their fault'" (*Nicholson v. Williams* (2001)).

Especially cruel is when siblings are treated differently with abusers targeting one child and not another. A child who observes parental mistreatment of a sibling fears for that sibling, worries about getting the same treatment and may feel survivor's guilt if they do not experience that treatment (Tucker et al., 2021). The Childhood Domestic Violence Association (2014) researched the impacts of domestic violence on children. Key findings include:

- Five million children witness domestic violence each year in the United States.
- Children from homes with violence are much more likely to experience significant short- and long-term psychological problems.
- Children who've experienced domestic violence often meet the diagnostic criteria for post-traumatic stress disorder, and the effects on their brain are similar to those experienced by combat veterans.
- Domestic violence in childhood is directly correlated with difficulties learning, lower IQ scores, deficiencies in visual-motor skills and problems with attention and memory.
- Children in homes with violence are physically abused or seriously neglected at a rate 1,500% higher than the national average.

- Those who grow up with domestic violence are six times more likely to commit suicide and 50% more likely to abuse drugs and alcohol.
- Children who grow up witnessing domestic violence are 74% more likely to commit a violent crime against someone else.
- Children of domestic violence are three times more likely to repeat the cycle in adulthood, as growing up with domestic violence is the most significant predictor of whether or not someone will be engaged in domestic violence later in life.

(Childhood Domestic Violence Association, 2014)

FAILURE TO REPORT CHILD ABUSE

Brianne comes to you and ask for your help in telling her mother "something serious." When her mother arrives, Brianne reveals to you both that her uncle (her mother's brother) is sexually abusing her. After a lengthy discussion, it is decided that Brianne's mother will be the one to call CPS and the police. Three days later a teacher tells you about calling CPS for Brianne, and you learn that Brianne came to her because her mother never reported the abuse. Will you lose your certificate for not reporting? Your job?

Points to Consider

This all-too-real situation recently happened with a veteran educator/school counselor. The school counselor knew his legal obligation, but he got emotionally involved with the family and lost his objectivity. He could see how distraught this mother was for her child and miserable in the knowledge of what her child had endured and how this was going to tear the family apart. When the mother convincingly explained it would be better for the child if she saw her mother taking charge and handling the situation with authorities, the school counselor acquiesced.

State statutes mandate educators in all states to report suspected abuse under penalty of criminal charges. Federal law requires school counselors to report any reasonable suspicion of abuse, even in the absence of hard evidence. For a mandated reporter to behave otherwise is to risk spending time in jail, lose one's certificate and/or pay a fine.

CHILD NEGLECT REPORTING

You are concerned about a 12-year-old student who appears to be underweight, and about half of the time comes to school wearing dirty clothes. You arrange a conference with the student and his parents. When the parents arrive, you notice a strong smell of alcohol on their breath. What do you do?

Points to Consider

Child neglect is lack of care that risks or causes harm to a child, including lack of food, clothing, supervision or medical attention. Neglect is sometimes more difficult to describe to CPS and to make a strong case for an investigation. Neglect can sound subjective. It is never wrong to call the abuse hotline and discuss your concerns with one of the supervisors or caseworkers for an opinion. Err on the side of caution. It is better to have an angry parent than to let a child in danger escape your attention. It is important to remember that a mandated reporter does not have to prove that abuse or neglect has taken place; reasonable grounds for suspicion are sufficient. Your state statute can describe your mandated status and whether or not you need to secure permission from anyone else before making a report.

SCHOOL COUNSELOR REQUIRED TO BATHE A NEGLECTED CHILD

Your administrator is asking you to bathe a 3-year-old who came to school with a strong odor. Several reports have been recently made to CPS about the neglect of this child. However, he once again comes to school with soiled clothing that obviously did not happen on the way to school, rather, he was put on the bus this way. You explain how this is a dangerous boundary crossing and how someone else, perhaps a medical person, should be the one to bathe the child. The principal will not hear you and says, "bathe this child." What do you do?

Points to Consider

In this very real case, the school counselor is being asked to fix a negligence situation that has already been reported. If parents cannot be reached to pick up the child and if the situation is so dire that someone needs to take off a child's clothes without parental permission and bathe a child, then it is time for an emergency call to CPS. If parents could not be reached, then the child continues his education until parents can be reached or someone from CPS arrives. If the odor is such that the child cannot be in the classroom, then the child needs a protective place until CPS can address the case. If this had been a one-time situation where the child happened to soil himself on the way to school and parents could not be reached, then educators could help the child clean himself up in the normal way that a 3-year-old would who goes to the bathroom and cleans himself or herself with adult help.

It is unconscionable that the school counselor is being made to perform dangerous and unadvised behavior, running the risk of the wrath of parents, a lawsuit, unemployment and revocation of certificate. It is highly unlikely any of this befalls the school counselor, but the act of bathing someone else's child at school is trauma in and of itself for the school counselor and potentially for the child. A departure from normal behavior, such as bathing students at school, is too risky.

Even CPS has to follow protocol before asking a child to remove clothing. CPS investigators may ask a child to remove clothing if they think there is a hidden injury, but investigators would not do this if they know a child will soon be examined by a doctor or if this upsets the child. Investigators would not ask older children or children of the opposite sex to remove clothing. Without question, educators should not be asking students to remove clothing that leaves private areas unclothed.

REPORT MULTIPLE TIMES AS NEEDED

You and three of your colleagues reported Gregory as being severely underweight and hungry. CPS reported that the child was underweight due to a medical condition and not neglect. For the next 12 months, the four of you continue to email about how hungry Gregory is, how he looks to be losing even more weight and how he is afraid of his stepmother. The student was later found to be in critical condition due to starvation. You and your colleagues did call in a second report. Have you fulfilled your mandated reporting obligation?

Points to Consider

A principal, teacher, special educator and school counselor all pled "no contest" to failure to report child abuse and were sentenced to probation, fines and community service. The evidence against the educators included two years of email exchanges showing a 12-year-old student's safety and well-being was a topic of conversation among them as they discussed his safety with expressed concerns such as: he is 10 to 20 pounds lighter than the previous year; he is afraid of his stepmother; he is hungry all the time; he never stays home even when he is sick; he appears to have poor nutrition. CPS did investigate physical abuse of the boy during the middle of the two-year period but did not substantiate abuse. The educators were still discussing concerns including weight loss following this investigation but did not reach back out to CPS. In 2016, the student ran away from home and was found bruised, dehydrated, weighing 47 pounds, with a cut lip and old cigarette burns. Educators daily saw the stark contrast for this child when compared to his peers. A physician confirmed his condition was life-threatening, having endured forced starvation and abuse. An investigation led to felony child abuse/torture charges against the boy's father and stepmother, each of whom received a lengthy prison sentence. Call frequently. Get people like a nurse, the principal or others to back you, but you are allowed to make multiple calls.

HEARSAY AND SECONDHAND INFORMATION

Two girls come to you saying their parents told them to come talk to you about their friend Shania. The girls tell you that they think Shania's stepfather is sexually molesting her. They tell you that Shania says "things," but she has never come right out and told them she was being molested. What will be your next step?

Points to Consider

School counselors often receive possible child abuse reports second hand, often with sketchy information. Authorities, such as the police and CPS, caution educators against investigating child abuse reports because we may inadvertently ask leading questions of the student, thus hindering the investigation or subsequent trial of alleged perpetrators. However, the courts support us in asking questions of Shania and others such as her teachers. In *Picarella v. Terrizzi* (1995), the court concluded that a student's constitutional rights were not violated when school officials questioned the student about suspected abuse (LaMorte, 2001; *Picarella v. Terrizzi* (1995)). Likewise, in *Landstrom v. Illinois* (1990), courts supported school officials who had a student remove her dress and underwear to examine her buttocks for signs of abuse. Know your state statutes and whether your state has granted mandated reporters immunity from liability in cases of more-intrusive investigation. It is also appropriate to make the call to CPS without any investigation or consultation. If you have reasonable suspicion, certainty is not required, and you have enough to call in a report to CPS.

A recent court case involved a school counselor who allegedly told a student to "stop lying" and go back to class when she reported to the school counselor that her teacher, Michael Alexander, was touching her inappropriately. "The teacher, Michael Alexander, pleaded guilty in July 2012 to taking indecent liberties with a child and first-degree sex offense with a child" (Marsh, 2013, p 1). He is serving a 40-year sentence. Court documents indicate that abuse by Alexander to the students of his classes probably went on for more than 10 years. Alexander copied videos of young girls having sex with each other and with adult men, the documents revealed, and he was caught when one of the pictures was of a child wearing a T-shirt printed with Alexander and the child's school's name (Marsh, 2013). We never ignore a report from a student. We take additional steps to have authorities investigate. How many other students may have reported incidences and were ignored? Nonmaleficence means, above all, do no harm.

In *Jane Doe v. Unified School District, School Counselor and Elementary School Principal* (2003), a mother alleged that school personnel negligently failed to report information concerning the suspected sexual abuse of her child. Three classmates told the school counselor that Doe told them of alleged abuse by her stepfather. The school counselor told the school principal, but neither reported the allegations of abuse.

PARENTAL SUBSTANCE ABUSE AND CHILD ABUSE

You are unsure if you have a child abuse report or a police report or neither. A 7-year-old student described to his classmate how his parents make methamphetamine at home on the stove.

Points to Consider

The federal government does not provide a definitive law on parental substance abuse and whether or not to treat it as child abuse. States, however, have the option of establishing their own laws, and 23 states and the District of Columbia include prenatal substance exposure in their definition of child maltreatment in civil statutes, regulations or agency policies (Child Welfare Information Gateway, 2019a). State statutes may consider maltreatment to include manufacturing a controlled substance in the presence of a child; selling, distributing or giving drugs or alcohol to a child; or using a controlled substance that impairs the caregiver's ability to care for the child. You do not have to know with certainty the law for your state to make a call to CPS, as they can advise you about your state's stance on the intersection of parental drug use and child abuse.

Parental substance use is included in the definition of child abuse or neglect in many state statutes. Some common language in state statutes outlining abuse include the following:

- Exposing a child to harm prenatally due to the mother's use of legal or illegal drugs or other substances

- Manufacturing methamphetamine in the presence of a child
- Selling, distributing or giving illegal drugs or alcohol to a child
- Using a controlled substance that impairs the caregiver's ability to adequately care for the child

State statutes are available at *https://www.childwelfare.gov/topics/systemwide/laws-policies/state/*.

EDUCATORS AND STATUTORY RAPE

You are a school counselor, and it comes to light that your 23-year-old colleague, who is new to the school counseling profession, has been having a three-month sexual relationship with one of her 17-year-old students. Will she be criminally charged with statutory rape?

Points to Consider

From October–December 2009, a Florida high school counselor was engaged in a sexual relationship with a 17-year-old student. Once discovered, she was immediately fired. However, the school counselor was not guilty of statutory rape. Florida, like the vast majority of states, deems a 17-year-old to be within the age of consent. In Florida, a 23-year-old can legally enter into a sexual relationship with a 17-year-old. The school counselor was 23 years old, so the difference in age was not enough to trigger a statutory rape charge (Sanders, 2010). For some states, specific laws have been passed to criminalize educator-student relationships, even when the students are at the age of consent. Alabama, Arizona, Connecticut, Ohio, New Hampshire and Texas all have specific laws aimed at educators who prey on students. For example, without equivocation, the Texas statute makes it clear that educators cannot have sex with their students regardless of the student's age.

Texas Statute: § 21.12. Improper Relationship Between Educator and Student: (a) An employee of a public or private primary or secondary school commits an offense if the employee engages in sexual contact, sexual intercourse or deviate sexual intercourse with a person who is enrolled in a public or private primary or secondary school at which the employee works. (b) An offense under this section is a felony of the second degree.

Perhaps if Florida had a specific statute like Texas, then there would have been a law with which to charge the 23-year-old perpetrator. Instead, she was able to leave one district and secure a job in a counseling agency, which repositioned her into a high school, so within weeks she was back working with minors. The school counselor was eventually arrested and charged under a more-difficult-to-prosecute Florida statute regarding government employees who have sexual relations with a minor over whom they have custody and control. Advocate through your state school counseling association to lobby legislators for a law making it a felony when educators have sex with a student in their school.

CHILD ABUSE IN A COUNSELING SESSION

Your colleague appears to be too familiar with students. Students have shared a few comments he has said to them, and you believe he is walking a narrow line with some of the topics he addresses during individual counseling sessions. Today a girl tells you he asked her about her menstrual periods and her sexual relationship with her boyfriend. You are stunned. Is this child abuse?

Points to Consider

The differential in power between school counselor and student is considerable. Although school counselors have influence over their vulnerable minor students, they rarely abuse this power. Occasionally, school counselors abuse their position of trust. Although it may or may not be a reportable offense by child protective services, it is grounds for dismissal.

A 28-year-veteran Maryland high school counselor is not the first school counselor to be dismissed because of inappropriate sexual comments to students. Circuit Court Judge David Bruce said that the school counselor went far beyond acceptable limits by asking the junior about her sex life with her freshman boyfriend, whom the student complained "treated [her] like crap." Judge Bruce noted the school counselor had a legal obligation to determine if the girl was a victim of sexual abuse, but the school counselor stepped far beyond the limits when he asked her how many times she and her boyfriend had sex, which sex acts she liked, whether certain sex acts hurt her and whether she knew any gay or lesbian students in the school (Capital-Gazette Communications, 2004). Students do not leave their privacy rights at the schoolhouse door.

SCHOOL COUNSELOR COMMITS CHILD ABUSE

You have observed your colleague allowing students to sit on his lap. Is this abuse?

Points to Consider

A school counselor allegedly tried to show a fifth-grade girl personal attention by letting her sit on his knee while they talked, and he hugged and stroked her when she cried on his shoulder. On one occasion, she complained of a lump on her hip, and the school counselor felt the lump both inside and outside her pants. The school counselor denied he had any sexual contact with her. Although supported by a number of teachers and former students who testified on his behalf, he was dismissed for taking indecent liberties with a student, using highly improper counseling techniques to the detriment of the students and demonstrating immoral and unprofessional conduct resulting in irreparable loss of confidence in his ability to perform his duties as a school counselor.

On appeal, the appellate court reversed the circuit court's judgment and held that the board of education for the Tonica schools did not have good cause for dismissing the school counselor. Although the school counselor's conduct was unethical and unprofessional, the court did not consider it a criminal activity (*Board of Education of Tonica Community High School District v. Adelbert E. Sickley* (1985)). Even though this school counselor was exonerated, his conduct violated boundaries and was unethical.

PERMISSION FROM PARENTS TO IGNORE AGE OF CONSENT

A 16-year-old student tells you she lives at home with her parents and her 21-year-old boyfriend. Do you have to report this?

Points to Consider

Age of consent and close-in-age laws differ by state. In some states, the age differential of three or more years for minors makes sexual relationships a crime, such as a 16-year-old and the 19-year-old having a sexual relationship. In some states, it is illegal for two minors to have a sexual relationship. Depending on the state, an adult who is 18 or older having a sexual relationship with a minor of certain ages is statutory rape. The age of both victim and perpetrator are variable depending on the state. Even when parents/guardians are aware and blessing a union, this is still considered statutory rape if one party is an adult and the minor is under a certain age. Some educators believe that if parents/guardians know, then it is not our place to report illegal sexual relations. However, law enforcement agencies and CPS do not agree. To find how your state statutes describe age of consent go to the website Age of Consent at *www.ageofconsent.us.*

There is contradiction in the literature as to whether school counselors have to report statutory rape, but err on the side of caution and report. It is a misunderstanding in the counseling field to think that reporting statutory rape is a choice. Bernard James, Ph.D., professor of constitutional law at Pepperdine University, states, "In law, a codified statute controls the question under discussion and reshapes common law (as well as professional guidelines for a field of endeavor such as counseling). Reporters, including counselors, are given immunity purposefully to emphasize the point that discretion (and possible failure to report) is not to be exercised by the reporter. Only a federal law would place counselors above the law of the states on this matter" (personal communication Sept. 12, 2012). To determine if a specific situation constitutes statutory rape, contact your school board's legal counsel, CPS, the sheriff's office and/or police headquarters. A school counselor who is in a position of trust cannot ignore something as serious as a student being victimized by a perpetrator who, according to the law, is committing statutory rape.

HUMAN TRAFFICKING IS CHILD ABUSE

While packing up from delivering classroom instruction, you overhear a student say she wants a fellow eighth-grader to be her boyfriend. Regina, her 13-year-old friend, says, "Not me. I already have a boyfriend. He's 23-years-old, and he has money." What, if anything, is your legal and ethical obligation?

Points to Consider

In this real case, the school counselor did not immediately react, but later that day she had a sinking realization that she may have overheard potential child abuse/statutory rape and maybe even a case of human trafficking. The school counselor spoke to the student not to determine certainty but to get more information. Regardless of what she learned, she was going to call in a child abuse report, per the reasonable-suspicion mandated reporting law. The school counselor discussed the student's spotty attendance, academic issues and worked toward her weekend and afterschool activities. After some time and relationship building, the school counselor asked her about her "boyfriend." Regina was guarded with answers that seemed scripted, rehearsed and contradictory in detail. Regina refused to make eye contact, and her nonverbal behavior told a different story than her verbal denials. When the school counselor finally asked her directly about a 23-year-old boyfriend she overheard being discussed, Regina showed obvious discomfort and evasiveness. The school counselor called in the report, she conveyed these intangible warning signs as well as more concrete information she knew about the child's circumstances, which made the student more vulnerable to exploitation and abuse.

Intangible warning signs are difficult to describe and are weak compared to tangibles such as bruises and admissions. However, as a trained observer and expert in human behavior, a school counselor's suspicions should carry increased weight, and we cannot be afraid to provide these intangible warning signs even when they may sound weak. Even more concerning is the school counselor's knowledge that this student was also a prime target for manipulation and exploitation into sex trafficking. A much-older boyfriend is a dangerous sign.

Although there is not one profile, the Polaris Project (2022) has found when disaggregating more than 32,000 reports of being trafficked that they are overwhelmingly from lower socioeconomic status, people of color and from dysfunctional homes. Regina's parental influences were limited and often nonexistent, meaning an older man could fill a parental figure void. Regina was needy for attention and often drove herself into social isolation from her peers. Therefore, it wasn't a leap for the school counselor to worry this child might be involved with a 30-year-old who was grooming her for sex trafficking.

In *United States v. Kozminski* (O'Connor & Supreme Court of the United States, 1987), which involved two mentally challenged men enslaved to work on a dairy farm, it became clear that better laws and support were needed to protect people and to prosecute human traffickers. January 2020 marked the 20th anniversary of the Trafficking Victims Protection Act of 2000. There are two major categories of human trafficking: labor and commercial sex. The Trafficking Victims Protection Act defined sex trafficking as the recruitment, harboring, transportation, provision or obtaining of a person for the purpose of a commercial sex act in which a commercial sex act is induced by force, fraud or coercion or in which the person committing the commercial sex act is under the age of 18 (U.S. Department of Justice, 2017). Federal law makes any minor under the age of 18 engaging in commercial sex a victim of sex trafficking, regardless of the presence of force, fraud or coercion (National Human Trafficking Hotline, n.d.).

It is estimated that 25 million people are currently being abused at the hands of commercial human traffickers. In 2018, the National Human Trafficking Hotline identified more than 23,000 human trafficking victims in the United States. Of these victims, 65% were women, and one in five were children. Sex trafficking is not limited to race, gender or socioeconomic status; however, some demographics are more often represented. Higher rates of victimization are found in children of color, children of poverty, sexual minorities, victims of childhood trauma and those who are socially isolated. Children whose home life is unstable are more susceptible to the grooming process. Human traffickers understand the risk factor of not having a strong parental influence, and they use this knowledge to prey on potential victims who:

- Are troubled youth looking for a sense of belonging
- Receive insufficient affection in the home
- Lack supervision in the home
- Lack family structure
- Experience physical or sexual abuse in the home
- Have drugs or alcohol in the home
- Are involved in the juvenile justice system
- Are in foster care

According to National Human Trafficking Hotline and the Polaris Project (2020), educators should recognize the primary signs of human trafficking. A student:

- Doesn't attend school regularly, has unexplained absences and/or is considered a truant
- Runs away from home regularly
- Talks about frequent travel to other cities
- Has bruises or other physical trauma, is withdrawn and seems depressed or afraid
- Doesn't seem to have control over her/his own schedule or identification documents
- Shows signs of poor hygiene, malnourishment and/or fatigue
- Shows signs of substance abuse or addiction
- Demonstrates a sudden change in clothing, behavior or has expensive items a child usually cannot afford
- Makes references to sexual situations that are unusual for a child of that age
- Has a "boyfriend" who is noticeably older (10+ years)
- Uses language that is beyond his/her normal age or terms that are used in the commercial sex industry, engages in promiscuous behavior and may be labeled "fast" by peers
- Is fearful, anxious, depressed, submissive, tense or nervous/paranoid
- Shows signs of physical and/or sexual abuse, physical restraint, confinement or torture
- Is frequently monitored
- Is not allowed or able to speak for himself/herself (a third party may insist on being present and/or translating)

The National Human Trafficking Hotline cautions that this list is not exhaustive, represents only a selection of possible indicators, and no one indicator should be considered in isolation but in context. As educators we spend a considerable percentage of our students' lives with them and are in a good position to notice warning signs and to practice preventive education. As a school counselor, what might you have done with a student claiming to have a 30-year-old boyfriend? You can call CPS and report. You can also first have a conversation with the student. Research the student's attendance patterns, grades, teachers' observations and transiency history. A review of the educational records and discussions with people in a position to observe the student might provide clues that can be probed.

If your school district has a protocol, you must follow it. Some protocols send the school counselor immediately to an administrator and/or the student resource officer. Beyond a school district's protocol there is not a script. Call CPS, who will guide you. You will probably be instructed to call the police if it is an emergency. This is not intended to be a blueprint for how to interact with a student you suspect may be a victim of human trafficking. There is no one size fits all, but as a minimum, what you overheard cannot be ignored. It is not the school counselor's job to fully investigate, but you are allowed to ask questions of the student when you are just not sure of what you heard. You have a legal imperative to follow up the seemingly offhand comment Regina made to her friend, and in context you will determine what, if any, questions you should ask or if you should go right to the child abuse authorities or sheriff's office. In almost every circumstance, you would also talk to your administrator.

In a Position to Know: School Counselors Speak

The case presented at the beginning of the chapter is revisited here and answered by two school counseling leaders.

RAPE, STATUTORY RAPE AND CHILD ABUSE APPLIED TO A STATE STATUTE

A 14-year-old tells you he is having sex with his 19-year-old girlfriend. A 13-year-old student tells you she is having sex with her 17-year-old partner. Is either scenario considered statutory rape in your state? In either scenario, are you required to report to CPS, the police and/or the sheriff? This is examined by leaders in the school counseling field as applied to their particular state.

The legal age of consent in Texas is 17 years of age. However, in the state of Texas there is a statutory provision called the Romeo and Juliet Law. This is the term used that can make sexual conduct between persons close in age noncriminal or provides substantially reduced punishment. Sexual assault in Texas has an affirmative defense if: (1) the person engaging in sexual conduct with a minor is not more than three years older than the minor; (2) the person, at the time of the sexual conduct, was not required to register for life as a sex offender and did not have a reportable conviction or adjudication for an offense and (3) the child was 14-years-old or older, and the offender and child did not commit bigamy. However, if the actor is 17-years-old or older and the other child involved is at least 14-years-old and not more than three years younger than the actor, one should always report the incident to the CPS and law enforcement and let the agencies take whatever action they deem necessary. The agencies will determine if the Romeo and Juliet Law applies. In the state of Texas, sex with a child younger than 14 is always illegal.

In scenario number one, the girlfriend is 19 and therefore above the age of consent. However, the boy is 14 and not the age of consent. In this situation the Romeo and Juliet Law does not apply, because the 19-year-old is more than three years older than the minor. This case is considered statutory rape/sexual assault. This case must be reported to the CPS and law enforcement.

In the second scenario, a 13-year-old student is having sex with her 17-year-old partner. This case is also considered statutory rape/sexual assault two reasons. First, in Texas, children less than 14-years-old are unable to consent to sexual acts regardless of the partner's age. Secondly, 17-years-old is the age of consent, but there is more than a three year age difference. This case must be reported to child protective services and law enforcement.

– Tammi Mackeben, director of guidance and counseling, Socorro Independent School District, El Paso, Texas

Missouri consent laws state that it is legal for a person to have sex with someone who is under the age of consent, age 17, as long as both parties are at least 14 and under 21 years old.

In the first situation, the boy is 14 and the girl is 19, and it would be considered a legal activity, as long as it was a consensual between both. Because of this, no report would be made to the police or CPS. I would try to get more information from the student to be sure it was consensual. If so, then I would counsel the student about the risks involved with the behavior as well as the importance of making good choices. I would encourage the student to talk with his parents about his activities.

In the second situation, the female student is under 14, and it would be considered illegal, even if it were consensual. Upon getting the information from the student, as a mandated reporter, I would call the Missouri Child Abuse Hotline and a make a report to the Missouri Children's Division. If they deem it necessary, they may dispatch a local Department of Family Services investigator and/or police to complete a thorough investigation. Depending upon the results of their investigation, criminal charges could be filed and legal actions possibly taken.

– Rob Lundien, retired high school counselor, and 2016 ASCA School Counselor of the Year finalist

Making Connections

1. The perpetrator shows up at your office the next day after you reported him for child abuse. What will you do? This is not a person you fear but someone who is angry and confused about why you would consider her "discipline" as child abuse.

2. You are a school counselor in a school where child abuse and neglect are prevalent. You want to develop programs to inform parents/guardians, teachers and students about child abuse and neglect, but your principal does not support your endeavor. What can you do to get your principal on board?

3. You need to make a child abuse report, but your principal wants to call the parents/guardians in and talk to them about better approaches to discipline. Write up how you would make your principal feel heard and supported and yet at the same time meet your mandatory obligations.

4. Call CPS in your area and inquire whether they consider witnessing domestic violence to be child abuse for your state. Gather resources they suggest might help if you have a student in this situation.

5. Visit the state statutes search at https://childwelfare.gov/topics/systemwide/laws-policies/state/, and write a summary of the information about child abuse and reporting that applies to your state. What constitutes abuse? Who are the mandated reporters? How are they protected?

6. Although a CPS investigation did not yield any evidence of abuse, you are still uncomfortable about the way Jacob comes to school. He is unkempt and never eats lunch. His parents refuse to allow him to get free lunch, and he never has lunch money. The other students shun him, and he is a frequent target of bullying at the school. Besides contacting CPS again if necessary, what other strategies might you employ to assist Jacob and his family?

7. A student comes to you to discuss her sexual relationship with her boyfriend. He is 16, and she is 14. Their relationship is unsanctioned by their parents. Do you know the law regarding statutory rape in your state? What would be your advice to this student?

Chapter 7 Quiz

1) School counselors absolute responsibility in child abuse is:
   a. To make certain abuse has actually happened before calling in abuse and turning a family life into a nightmare.
   b. To consult with the administration to get a consensus as to whether or not abuse has happened.
   c. To make parents aware an abuse report has been made.
   d. To be the sole provider of abuse workshops for faculty.
   e. To report to child protective services if there is reasonable suspicion that abuse has happened.

2) Which of the following is accurate when it comes to child abuse reporting? It is best:
   a. In the case of sexual abuse by a family member to protect the student by telling another family member who can protect the child and then make your report to child protective services.
   b. To wait and report just prior to when your state's reporting period ends (most states is 24 hours or 48 hours) in the event you learn more information between the first abuse outcry and the report.
   c. To negotiate with the child protective services worker the terms under which the case should be investigated.
   d. To never affirm or deny to the alleged perpetrator that you have made a child abuse report.
   e. To consult with the school nurse, social worker or school psychologist before making a sexual abuse report.

3) Which statement is correct?
   a. If you take a position before you are certified and fail to report child abuse, the school district is not monetarily responsibly should a court case ensue because you took a job for which you were not certified.
   b. When a school counselor fails to report child abuse, the courts will dismiss any case against the district and allow a case against the school counselor to proceed.
   c. It is best not to discuss with the alleged perpetrator of abuse the particulars of an abuse report you made because you may interfere with the investigation.
   d. Neglect has to be validated by the school nurse or a physician before a school counselor can call in a neglect case to child protective services.
   e. Reasonable suspicion in reporting abuse means beyond a shadow of a doubt.

4) Which of the following statements are true? Child protective services workers:
   a. Are required to tell alleged abusers who made the child abuse report as abusers are protected to face their accuser.
   b. Are not to tell the alleged abuser who made the report, but the abuser can often figure out who made the child abuse report.
   c. Are not allowed to talk to the alleged abuser about the report but must only talk to the child.
   d. Are required to interview the school counselor every time the school counselor makes a report.
   e. Are not allowed to talk to the educator who made a child abuse report.

5) If a child reports to you he or she was sexually abused five years ago and the perpetrator has since moved out of the home:
   a. You do not have to report this to child protective services or to the police because the child is no longer in danger.
   b. The statute of limitations has likely expired so no report is necessary.
   c. You must report this to child protective services and/or the police as directed by child protective services.
   d. The damage done to the student in having to relive the abuse trumps the need to report so it is best not to report.
   e. Once the danger is removed you only need to talk to the parent about making certain the perpetrator stays away from the child.

Key Terms

Child abuse
Child neglect
Child maltreatment
Child Protective Services
COVID-19
Domestic violence
Emotional harm
Expert witness
Human Trafficking
Immune from liability
Mandated reporter
Nonmaleficence
Reasonable suspicion
Statute of limitations
Statutory rape
Threat of harm
Pandemic

CHAPTER 8

Individual and Small-Group Counseling

Objectives

By the time you have completed this chapter, you should be able to:

- Describe the meaning and limits of confidentiality in individual and small-group counseling
- Define the process of informed consent
- Apply the ASCA Ethical Standards for School Counselors (2022b) for individual and group counseling
- Understand the responsibility of group leadership for small-group counseling
- Adhere to appropriate individual counseling in schools

Ethical Standards Addressed in This Chapter

Professionalism means knowing your professional associations' ethical standards and adhering to them. Following are some of the ASCA Ethical Standards for School Counselors (2022b) most relevant to this chapter.

School counselors:

- Inform students of the purposes, goals, techniques, rules and procedures under which they may receive counseling. Disclosure includes informed consent and clarification of the limits of confidentiality. (A.2.b.).
- Are aware that even though attempts are made to obtain informed consent, it is not always possible. When needed, school counselors make decisions on students' behalf that promote students' welfare. (A.2.d)
- Develop a plan for the transitioning of primary counseling services with minimal interruption of services. Students retain the right for the referred services to be conducted in coordination with the school counselor or to discontinue counseling services with the school counselor while maintaining an appropriate relationship that may include participation in other school support services. (A.6.d)
- Refrain from referring students based solely on the school counselor's personal beliefs or values rooted in one's religion, culture, ethnicity or personal worldview. School counselors maintain the highest respect for student cultural identities and worldviews. Pursue additional training and supervision when their values are discriminatory in nature (e.g., sexual orientation, gender identity, gender expression, reproductive rights, race, religion, ability status). School counselors do not impose their values on students and/or families when making referrals to outside resources for student and/or family support. (A.6.e)

- Offer culturally sustaining small-group counseling services based on individual student, school and community needs; student data; a referral process; and/or other relevant data. (A.7.a)
- Provide equitable access to participation in groups, including alleviating physical, language and other obstacles. (A.7.b)
- Use data to inform group topics, establish well-defined expectations and measure the outcomes of group participation. (A.7.f)
- Communicate the aspiration of confidentiality as a group norm, while recognizing and working from the protective posture that confidentiality for students in small groups cannot be guaranteed. (A.7.h)
- Select topics for groups with the clear understanding that some topics are not suitable for groups in schools (e.g., incest survivorship, eating disorders, dating violence) and accordingly take precautions to protect members from harm as a result of interactions with the group. (A.7.i)
- Practice within their competence level and develop professional competence through training and supervision. (A.7.k)

Many other standards apply. Read the full text of the ASCA Ethical Standards for School Counselors (2022b) at *www.schoolcounselor.org.*

Introduction

The legal and ethical complexities of working with minors in schools require school counselors to remain vigilant about the rights and responsibilities of students and their parents/guardians, as well as the implications of these rights on school counselors' work (ASCA, 2019a; ASCA, 2020a; Berger, 2018; Erford, 2019). The numerous responsibilities school counselors have in schools and the complexities of delivering individual and group counseling services in a setting designed to deliver academic instruction further complicate the legal and ethical realm of school counseling (King-White et al., 2019; Oehrtman & Dollarhide, 2021). There is additional concern in group counseling, where confidentiality cannot be guaranteed, and sensitive information about the private world of students and their families is often discussed (Corey et al., 2018). The tenuous nature of confidentiality in groups is even more concerning in virtual groups, as you do not know who is sharing the room or within earshot. Groups reach more students and are an essential method for school counselors and other human service personnel (Finnerty et al., 2019).

The astute school counselor will use caution to guard what is said in the group to prevent students from harm due to a breach of confidentiality. In Stone's January 2017 survey exploring 1,038 ASCA members' practices in individual and group counseling, 95.1% of respondents agreed or strongly agreed that they review confidentiality and its limits with students before beginning small-group counseling. Eighty-seven percent indicated they notify parents/guardians before beginning small-group counseling with their child, and 76% require a parent/guardian to sign a permission form for their child to participate in small-group counseling (Stone, 2017b). The 2022 Ethical Standards for School counselors state, "School counselors inform parents/guardians of student participation in and the purpose of the small group" (ASCA, 2022b, A.7.d.).

Confidentiality, which is addressed in Standard A.2 of the ASCA Ethical Standards, means school counselors provide informed consent, i.e., disclosing the terms at or before entering the counseling relationship or at the beginning of counseling sessions to provide counselees the purposes, goals, techniques and rules of procedure under which they may receive counseling. The school counselor explains the meaning of confidentiality in developmentally appropriate terms and helps students understand school counselors will try to keep confidences, except when the school counselor determines serious and foreseeable harm is present. The use of serious and foreseeable is a shift from the previous idea of "clear and imminent" danger, which, after several incidents, was found to be insufficient to cover situations in which school counselors may know of a danger that could not be classified as "clear and imminent" but still needs to be addressed. Therefore, the term "serious and foreseeable" was adopted to provide a larger blanket of protection for students and school counselors.

In brief, confidentiality in school settings is complicated because of the school counselor's competing interests and obligations that extend beyond the students to parents/guardians, administrators and teachers. Working with minor clients always poses special considerations with the client's parents/guardians, but never more so than when the minor client is a student in a setting designed for academic instruction rather than clinical counseling. In some instances, parents/guardians may demand and obtain "maintained" information on their child including case notes (see Chapter 4, Student Privacy and the Family Educational Rights and Privacy Act). In *Parents v. Williamsport Area School District* (1991), a psychologist could not use his professional confidentiality as a basis for refusing to reveal to parents/guardians what was said in an individual counseling session and recorded in individual case notes.

Other court cases have supported the school counselor's confidentiality to the greatest extent possible; however, the courts tell us to be ready to defend our behavior and to show we are competent to address sensitive subjects with students in isolation from their parents/guardians. Generally, school counselors should feel free to discuss relevant but controversial issues with students, such as drug and alcohol abuse, pregnancy, abortion and birth control. However, when counseling a student about these sensitive topics, we must carefully consider the student's developmental and chronological levels and the legal status of minors, as well as parents'/guardians' rights to be the guiding voice in their children's lives, especially when it comes to value-laden issues.

School counselors recognize that individual and group counseling in schools is not a therapeutic, clinical approach and that when students require long-term counseling or therapy, school counselors make referrals to appropriate community resources (ASCA, 2018b; ASCA, 2019a; ASCA, 2021d; Goodman-Scott et al., 2021). ASCA's position statement on group counseling states, "School counselors do not provide therapy or long-term counseling in schools to address psychological disorders. However, school counselors are prepared to recognize and respond to student mental health crises and needs. School counselors address those barriers to student success by offering instruction that enhances awareness of mental health and short-term intervention to include small-group counseling until the student is connected with available community resources. When students require long-term counseling or therapy, school counselors make referrals to appropriate community resources and maintain collaborative relationships with providers to align service coordination" (ASCA, 2020c).

In a survey of 1,038 ASCA members, 99.4% reported they refer students to professionals and/or organizations when the students' needs go beyond the scope of what the school counseling program can provide (Stone, 2017b). Refer to the case *Smith v. The School Board of Orange County Florida* (1994) in Chapter 5 Negligence, in which a school counselor provided only one name of an outside resource, who turned out to be a pedophile and who abused the referred student. When giving parents a list of referral resources, make certain you add a disclaimer at the bottom such as this one from Arlington Public Schools in Arlington, Va.:

> *This list is of known providers of a particular service. The providers on the list are from a variety of sources. The list is being provided as a courtesy, for information only, and the user should understand that no assurances or guarantees regarding the providers on the list are being made by providing this list. Arlington Public Schools neither endorses, approves, nor recommends any specific provider listed below. This list is not inclusive of all community agencies, services or organizations that provide the particular service, and the omission of an agency, service or organization from this list does not imply disapproval. It is the responsibility of the users of this list to determine whether any of the content is of value to them and whether or not the agency, service or organization meets their specific needs* (personal communication, Aug. 29, 2016).

In December 2021, U.S. Surgeon General Dr. Vivek Murthy issued an advisory about the nation's youth mental health crisis, outlining the unprecedented impact the pandemic has had on the mental health of America's youth. Mental health challenges existed long before the pandemic, but there is an alarming increase in the number of young people with feelings of helplessness, depression and suicidal ideation (Murthy, 2021). In fall 2021, a coalition of the nation's leading experts in pediatric health declared a national emergency in child and adolescent mental health (American Academy of Pediatrics, 2021).

"The Surgeon General's Advisory on Protecting Youth Mental Health outlines a series of recommendations to improve youth mental health across 11 sectors, including young people and their families, educators and schools, and media and technology companies. Topline recommendations include:

- Recognize that mental health is an essential part of overall health.
- Empower youth and their families to recognize, manage and learn from difficult emotions.
- Ensure that every child has access to high-quality, affordable and culturally competent mental health care.
- Support the mental health of children and youth in educational, community and childcare settings. And expand and support the early childhood and education workforce.
- Address the economic and social barriers that contribute to poor mental health for young people, families and caregivers.
- Increase timely data collection and research to identify and respond to youth mental health needs more rapidly. This includes more research on the relationship between technology and youth mental health, and technology companies should be more transparent with data and algorithmic processes to enable this research.

Surgeon General's Advisories are public statements that call the American people's attention to a public health issue and provide recommendations for how it should be addressed. Advisories are reserved for significant public health challenges that need the American people's immediate attention (Murthy, 2021).

The U.S. Department of Education data suggests that schools all over the country are trying to play their part. A federal survey of 170 schools in September 2021 found that 97% are taking some steps to support student well-being now that they are back to teaching in person. This includes one or more of the following:

- 59% are offering specialized professional development to existing staff members so they can support students in turn.
- 42% have hired new staff, such as school counselors and school social workers.
- 26% have added student classes to address topics related to social/emotional or mental well-being.
- 20% have created community events and partnerships.
  (Institute of Educational Sciences, 2021)

This chapter gives us an opportunity to revisit and highlight some of the basic principles of legal and ethical issues for individual and group counseling. In this chapter we will discuss confidentiality, informed consent, best practice for group leadership, parents'/guardians' rights, administrators' and teachers' need to know, serious and foreseeable harm and no-harm contracts.

Getting Started: What Would You Do?

The following case is answered for you at the end of this chapter by a school counselor educator who is a past president of the Association of Specialists in Group Work. Before you read her response, formulate in your own mind how you would approach this ethical dilemma.

SMALL-GROUP COUNSELING: SCREENING POTENTIAL MEMBERS

You develop a small group in response to complaints from seventh-grade teachers who say some students are having difficulty getting along with their peers and are interrupting classroom lessons. The teachers also say they believe the behavior is affecting the students' grades. You establish a set of goals for the group that includes learning ways to get along with others while improving group members' own grades. The teachers recommend eight students for the group. The principal asks you to include two other students, who are repeatedly in trouble for fighting. After you secure parental permission, you conduct your first meeting to discuss the ground rules, confidentiality and group goals. By the third session, bickering escalates. The two students the principal recommended are not benefiting from the group and are fueling the group's negativity by making threatening comments to the other members. Are there ethical issues with the small group?

Working Through Case Studies

INFORMED CONSENT: IS IT ATTAINABLE WITH STUDENTS IN SCHOOLS?

A mother asks you to work with her daughter, an incest survivor, when the perpetrator's court-ordered, financial support for the victim's counseling ended. You are already working with another survivor of incest. You know of a third student who's an incest survivor, and you decide to form a group. You hold individual student conferences, and all three girls sign the informed consent document to participate. The consent form and your initial conversations before and during each group session stress confidentiality, and you are confident the students understand the trust that has been placed in them to protect each other. Have you received informed consent?

Points to Consider

All professional ethical standards in the health, social and counseling fields require informed consent for clients and patients, and in many states, it is a legal obligation in professional practice statutes. Informed consent comes from the medical principle of *primum non nocere*, "first do no harm." Competence, voluntariness and knowledge are necessary elements of informed consent. Although informed consent is one of the most represented values in the helping professions, many of the ethical standards, including ASCA's, recognize informed consent is difficult and sometimes impossible to attain.

Informed consent requires competence, voluntariness and knowledge on the part of students to understand the limits of confidentiality and, therefore, can be difficult to obtain from students of certain developmental levels, English-language learners and special-needs populations. If the student is able to give assent/consent before school counselors share confidential information, school counselors attempt to gain the student's assent/consent (ASCA, 2022b, A.2.c.).

In a 2017 survey of 1,038 ASCA members, school counselors indicated a faithfulness in reviewing the limits of confidentiality when working with students. Eighty-five percent of respondents indicated they review confidentiality and its limits with students before ongoing individual counseling (Stone, 2017b).

Informed consent for students in schools requires that the student has knowledge of all the components of informed consent, is voluntarily engaging in the counseling services provided and is competent to understand the positive and negative implications for engaging in the counseling. Informed consent is not an event but a process that is repeated as needed in developmentally appropriate terms as to the goals, limits of confidentiality and how students can voluntarily terminate or participate. Competence means the student is able to rationally appreciate the facts, breadth and consequences of entering into counseling. Just as school counselors must come from the posture that confidentiality can never be guaranteed, so too must they come from the stance that informed consent is largely unattainable with students in schools. Even when school counselors believe a student is developmentally mature, has solid reasoning ability and understands all the nuances of informed consent, it is best practice for school counselors to question their confidence. Informed consent from a minor in a school setting is the rare exception, not the rule.

Setting aside all the other alarming issues in this all-too-real scenario (e.g., school counselor's skill level, confidentiality, appropriateness of school group topics, parental involvement), it is informed consent that should rally the school counseling profession to better delineate how fragile and infrequent this ethical imperative is to achieve. Did the school counselor actually get informed consent when she talked to the students individually and obtained their signature prior to the group? In the case of the incest group, the students put their trust in the school counselor with a level of confidence often unmatched with other educators. In many cases students will assume if the school counselor is asking them to do something, then they will be safe and it must be okay. These students probably never considered the potential for harm; yet, it happened. Upon hearing her private world discussed in the hallways, one of the group members refused to return to the school and was granted a special assignment to a distant school where she hoped to regain her privacy.

The Association for Specialists in Group Work also addresses the complexity of guaranteeing confidentiality in group work setting: "Group facilitators define confidentiality and its limits (for example, legal and ethical exceptions and expectations; ... inability to ensure confidentiality by other group members)" (ASGW, 2021, C.6.c.). Confidentiality can never be guaranteed in groups in schools; therefore, school counselors are careful to try and orchestrate what is likely to be discussed or revealed in a group. Extra precaution is needed to the extent possible, to watch and control what students say in front of each other so as not to give students access to each other's private, sensitive information or worse, to give students material or ammunition to use against each other. Emotional safety comes before encouraging students to reveal personal information in front of each other. Stress confidentiality, but protect students by not allowing them to reveal information in front of their peers that they may later regret (ASCA, 2022b, A.7.h.).

Given minors' mercurial behavior of changing friends and loyalties, there is an increased risk of breach. School counselors have to be the guardians of informed consent, safeguarding, protecting and proceeding on behalf of students who cannot actually act on their own behalf. Being the guardian of informed consent means:

- Continuing to fight for time to run groups in schools. Groups are a critical tool in the efforts to advantage all students.
- Recognizing and honoring that the current reality of informed consent in schools falls far short of its stated goals.
- Foregoing services when the potential risks outweigh the benefits.
- Honoring the elusiveness of informed consent, while diligently trying to obtain it.
- Enhancing students' ability to give informed consent and providing many opportunities for students to ask questions and to check for understanding.
- Avoiding a mechanistic, routine approach and finding developmentally appropriate words and opportunities to explain informed consent.
- Protecting voluntariness. If an educator or parent/guardian asks for services a student does not want, avoid coercion and persuasion.
- Continuing to obtain written or oral permission from a parent or guardian for counseling services but still assuming the responsibility to protect the student. Repeating with each student revelation, "this will be in the hallways" will heighten your vigilance to monitor what students say in front of each other.

- Recognizing the tenuous nature of confidentiality of groups in a virtual setting as there is no control over who is sharing the space in the home or who is within earshot. When possible have the student use a private space in the home, a headset and a noise machine to increase protection of confidentiality (Stone, Rock, & Steele, 2020)
- Attending to the role that language, cultural background and other elements of diversity play in the informed-consent process.
- Reminding yourself often that informed consent is not an event but a process to help students move toward self-governance.
- Evaluating and considering other approaches to help such as generic groups on school success issues to support students when a theme or topic group may possibly place them in harm's way.

COUNSELING AS A CONDITION OF SCHOOL ATTENDANCE

You are a public school counselor who questions the legality of a practice by your principal, who routinely tells the parents of students for whom suicidal ideation is a concern that they must provide proof that their child is seeing an outside therapist in order to return to school. Is the principal's practice legal?

Points to Consider

The legal question is whether school attendance can be made conditional for a student who is suicidal and not homicidal. When such an attendance requirement is made, can the district be responsible for paying for the outside services? The answer will be different for regular education students and students identified as disabled under the Individuals with Disabilities Education Act. School districts may not charge parents of qualified students for related services that have been determined to be needed and placed on individual education plans. The list of related services is extensive and may include psychological services, counseling services, parent counseling and training, to name a few.

Some public school administrators are requiring proof of outside counseling before a student who is suicidal and isn't a danger to others is allowed back into their school. A public school district who is withholding education for a child and it is not a discipline issue, they do so at their own peril. Parents would have a strong case that the school district must provide reimbursement for required counseling if their child is not a danger to others. If outside counseling is a recommendation or suggestion and not a requirement of school attendance, it is unlikely parents would be successful in requiring the school district to pay for such services. If parents aren't providing treatment for their child who is suicidal, educators call child protective services about the negligence.

There is nothing in the constitution that guarantees citizens an education. However, there are plenty of federal laws prohibiting discriminating against categories of citizens. The history of public education began in the 1830s when early leaders of this country recognized the need for an educated citizenry to preserve democracy. A formal and unified system of publicly funded schools was proposed, charging the states with forming an education system. Horace Mann, a Massachusetts legislator and secretary of that state's board of education, began to advocate for the creation of public schools that would be universally available to all children, free of charge and state-funded. The federal government provided support for establishing public schools through federal land grants with the requirement that a portion of the land be set aside for public schools.

Throughout U.S. history, groups have been discriminated regarding public school attendance. *Brown v. Board of Education* was a pivotal case and declared state-sponsored segregation of public schools to be unconstitutional (Alexander & Alexander, 2019; Neem, 2017). Many court cases have followed, and public schools receiving federal funds cannot discriminate against any one group or class of students and make school attendance conditional. This includes students who are considered suicidal but who are not considered homicidal. Discipline, of course, can result in students being excluded from education and expelled or suspended, but we do not expel or suspend students because they are suffering from suicidal ideation.

COUNSELING YOUR STUDENTS IN YOUR PRIVATE PRACTICE

You are a school counselor in a rural community with limited community social services and counseling support. In addition to being the school counselor of the sole K–8 school, you and your wife are two of the few licensed counselors in the community. Can you counsel your own students and/or refer them to your wife?

Points to Consider

The complications of such a dual relationship are numerous and, therefore, have long been recognized by the profession. It is important to minimize the risk of harm to the student/school counseling relationship. The possibilities of harm are glaring. A dual relationship is to be avoided when possible, and if not possible, school counselors take pains to minimize the potential for harm to their students. It is not a valid argument to say that you must provide the service or the student will not receive help. It is a serious problem when the community offers few options for counseling, but this does not mean the police chief can also act as the trial attorney and the judge because of a shortage any more then you can be all things related to counseling for the community. The obligation of the moral principle by which the profession stands is to do no harm. Additionally, ensure there is not a conflict of interest in providing referral resources. The ASCA Ethical Standards (2022b) are clear that school counselors should not counsel their own students in private practice.

CLEAR AND IMMINENT DANGER OR SERIOUS AND FORESEEABLE HARM

You are working with a student you suspect might be clinically depressed. In your professional judgment, this girl is in trouble, but you hesitate to breach confidentiality and tell her parents as clear and imminent danger is the threshold you use to determine if you should breach confidentiality. You have never defined any circumstance except suicide as triggering a breach under the clear-and-imminent-danger test. Are you behaving within the profession's standard of care?

Points to Consider

School counselors' test for breach is not that of the proverbial uplifted knife poised to plunge in the heart. In 2016, the ASCA Ethical Standards for School Counselors replaced clear and imminent danger with serious and foreseeable harm, as did the 2014 American Counseling Association Code of Ethics (Kaplan, 2006).

What is a clear and imminent danger for a minor who is in a setting designed for academic instruction and in most cases is mandated to be there? Webster defines imminent as about to happen, looming. Clear and imminent danger has always been a concept that was defined by most school counselors as broader than looming, as they are acutely aware their obligation extends beyond their minor students to the parents/guardians who have the right to be the guiding voice in their children's lives. Is clear and imminent danger a 7-year-old smoking cigarettes? A 17-year-old smoking cigarettes? If you substitute the concept of clear and imminent danger with serious and foreseeable harm, does this help you make the decision as to whether or not to notify the 7-year-old student's parents/guardians or the 17-year-old student's parents/guardians?

Serious and foreseeable harm also describes a concept used in negligence (tort) law to limit the liability of a party to those acts carrying a risk of foreseeable harm, meaning reasonable people would be able to predict or expect the ultimately harmful result of their actions. The legal and ethical complications of any human-service profession are daunting, but on any given day a school counselor puts into play the reasonable-person approach and navigates such charged, delicate subjects as abortion, harassment and suicide. School counselors exercise professional judgment when a reasonable person would know a student has reached the limits of being able to negotiate a situation in isolation from parental involvement.

Serious and foreseeable harm is more appropriate in the case of a student in a downward spiral into a dangerous zone. No, we cannot say with conclusiveness that this situation is clear and imminent danger and that this student is going to succumb to the temptation of suicide today. However, if it is evident that it is serious and foreseeable harm, then the school counselor will want to consult, seek supervision, work with this student to involve the parents and, if need be, make the decision to call the parents. In a 2017 survey, 95% of 1,038 ASCA member respondents indicated they regularly consult with professionals and/or organizations to optimally do their job (Stone, 2017b). The Association of Specialists in Group Work states, "Group workers process the workings of the group with themselves, group members, supervisors, co-facilitators or other colleagues, as appropriate" (2021, D.9).

Trust is a crucial hallmark of the school counseling profession. The ASCA Ethical Standards (2022) emphasize the balance that must happen between minors' rights and the rights of their parents/guardians. The school counselor's primary obligation and loyalty is to students, but it does not end there. Our setting dictates responsibility beyond the student. School counselors should always feel off balance when negotiating between the rights of parents/guardians and those of students, as it is a tug of war we must skillfully negotiate with the help of our partners in consultation – colleagues and supervisors.

Confidentiality and the efforts to respect the trusting relationship are compounded by the seriousness of the presenting problem and the students' developmental levels. When asked which issues provided the greatest challenges to maintaining a student's confidentiality, ASCA members replied:

Suicidal ideation *27.3%*
Student victims of abuse or neglect *19.6%*
Students who are engaging in self-injurious behaviors
(e.g., cutting, burning). *18.4%*
Student victims of bullying *10.6%*
Pregnant students *4.2%*
Students using drugs *3.9%*
(Stone, 2017b)

CONFIDENTIALITY AND A TEACHER'S NEED-TO-KNOW

Mr. Frazier, one of the school's teachers, stops you in the hall and launches in with, "Why is Roberto out of my class all the time? He has been out four times in the last two months. What can be so important that he has to miss my class when he is barely hanging on to a D?" What is your response?

Points to Consider

Mr. Frazier's concerns are legitimate, although the method of relaying his frustration could have been more collaborative than accusatory. It may be tempting to respond in-kind and to jump right into defending yourself, but it is more important to set aside ego and figure out how to keep the lines of communication open. A good place to start is by honoring the teacher's frustrations with an acknowledgement that you should have staggered the times you are seeing Roberto so he would not be missing the same class. An offer to come by later during his planning period would be helpful to discuss what he has been observing with Roberto. It might be necessary to find a private spot immediately and get the teacher to talk about what he has been observing.

The benefit to using this technique is that if Mr. Frazier is talking, then you do not have to, so confidentiality is respected, and you can skirt the pressure to give the teacher information that should be kept confidential. There are many times when teachers need to know what is going on with one of their students. They should know at least enough information to be able to optimize this student's education and well-being. Two professionals working to advantage a student is not a breach when, if informed, the teacher can be a more powerful support to the student. Providing information to the teacher in general terms will sometimes be enough, but the judgment is on the school counselor to determine need-to-know information and how much to involve the teacher in a student's confidential communications. The test is always to balance how to advantage the student by collaborating with other educators in the school while keeping a trusting relationship. Sometimes teachers are just curious. School counselors try to determine the teacher's motive for knowing the information. In a 2017 survey, 41.3% of school counselors responded that teachers and staff members regularly ask questions regarding contents of counseling sessions that would require breaking confidentiality (Stone, 2017b). School counselors usually know better than anyone which teachers are operating high on the social/emotional consciousness continuum and will easily discern between a caring teacher's need to know and pure curiosity. If in doubt as to the teacher's motives, the school counselor errs on the side of keeping the information confidential.

INDIVIDUALIZED EDUCATION PROGRAMS AND SCHOOL COUNSELORS

You are a school counselor who has developed a program for all students. The new individualized education program (IEP) team has begun to write you in for weekly 30-minute, yearlong counseling sessions. When you question the practice, there is indignation from team members with a retort, "These kids need help." What do you do?

Points to Consider

There is a growing phenomenon that threatens comprehensive school counseling and it is quietly taking hold in a number of communities. The Education for All Handicapped Children Act of 1975 and the subsequent Individuals with Disabilities Education Improvement Act (IDEA) of 2004 are being misinterpreted in such a way as to hold school counselors responsible for counseling sessions being written into IEPs with very prescriptive parameters of how many minutes per week a student is to receive counseling, often for the duration of the entire school year or the IEP active period. When school counselors are given such a defined schedule, this is akin to mental health counseling and threatens to erode a comprehensive school counseling program.

The U.S. Department of Education Office of Special Education Programs (OSEP), which governs the Education for All Handicapped Children Act of 1975 and IDEA, responded to my inquiry (personal communication Jan. 30, 2017). An official from OSEP's national office provided his expertise and welcomed me to share the information with the school counseling profession. He stated that IDEA is "individual," and children who show emotionality on a psychological examination do not automatically have a counseling need. He strongly questioned the practice of having a school counselor work in yearlong counseling, which he described as a "therapeutic role." Additionally, ASCA staff, ASCA Board members, and I met with OSEP officials in November 2021 and expressed the need to remove school counselors from the list of related services. We stressed the fact that school counselors are being written into IEPs to teach social skills in individual counseling when school counselors and teachers need to teach social skills in classroom instruction (advantaging all students in the schools). In a 2021 survey by Stone (2021a), 24.8% of the 435 respondents said they were required to deliver counseling services to students based on an IEP. Of those who deliver counseling service via an IEP requirement, they said they spend the following percentage of the workweek delivering those services:

Percentage	
5%- 10%	*62.4%*
11%-20%	*15.1%*
21%-30%	*6.5%*
> 30%	*16.1%*
Total	*93*

When asked about the duration in months or years that the IEP counseling must occur this was the result:

One year (approx. 9 months) 40.9%
Two years (approx. 18 months) 7.5%
Three years (approx. 27 months) 10.8%
Other. Please specify: 19.4%
Unsure 21.5%
Total 93
(Stone, 2021g)

ASCA's position statement The School Counselor and Students with Disabilities (2022h) encourages a comprehensive school counseling program. School counselors recognize their strengths and limitations in working with students with disabilities. School counselor responsibilities may include, but are not limited to:

- providing school counseling curriculum lessons, individual and/or group counseling to students with special needs within the scope of the comprehensive school counseling program
- providing short-term, goal-focused counseling in instances where it is appropriate to include these strategies as part of the IEP… . Inappropriate administrative or supervisory responsibilities for the school counselor include but are not limited to: ... providing long-term therapy (ASCA, 2019a).

The School Counselor and Student Mental Health (2020c) position statement invites school counselors to aspire to recognize and educate others to mental health warning signs, provide short-term counseling and crisis intervention, provide referrals to school and community resources that treat mental health issues, and recognize and address barriers to accessing mental health services. Further, the position statement challenges school counselors to deliver curriculum that proactively enhances awareness of mental health; promotes positive, healthy behaviors; and seeks to remove the stigma associated with mental health issues.

The ASCA National Model (2019a) details appropriate and inappropriate activities. Under the inappropriate activities category is listed, "providing long-term counseling in schools to address psychological disorders." ASCA's Ethical Standards for School Counselors (2022b) state, "School counselors provide culturally responsive counseling to students in a brief context and support students and families/guardians in obtaining outside services if the students need long-term clinical/mental health counseling. School counselors advocate for a school counseling program free of non-school-counseling assignments identified by The ASCA National Model: A Framework for School Counseling Programs."

School counselors need not fear coming across as uncaring or unsupportive when they push back from being written into IEPs. School counselors fight for a program for all students and the practice of relegating the school counselor to work with just a few students not only erodes the school counselor's time but the students are having to miss class time, the very place where the classroom teacher can reinforce or extinguish behavior in the authentic context of the classroom.

WHEN PARENTS/GUARDIANS OPPOSE CURRICULUM

As part of your classroom instruction on celebrating differences, you use the book "King and King," which depicts same-sex marriage along with many other examples of diversity. Two sets of parents have come to the principal to state they want their child to opt out of all future curriculum you offer. Must the principal comply?

Points to Consider

Parents/guardians may ask that their child not be included in classroom instruction for fear they will be exposed to what they view as objectionable material. Usually this happens around lessons involving sexual orientation, gender expression or sex education. Astute school counselors will educate themselves about the institutional and community standards and learn to predict and negotiate the political landscape. An undemocratic response can lead to mistrust and conflict, with students as the losers. The school counselor as advocate will work to find a way to address concerns but avoid bending to the will of a few. It helps to review potentially controversial material with administrators to ensure their support and to plan a response to parents should concerns arise.

Although school districts and school counselors can make allowances and exemptions for parents/guardians who do not want their children to participate in certain topics, schools are not legally obligated to do so. As discussed in Chapter 10 in the court case *Parker v. Hurley*, 2007, two families objected to their elementary-school children's curriculum, which used a book depicting single-parent families, a family with two dads, one with two moms and the book "King and King," a story depicting a wedding scene between two princes. When the school refused to provide prior notice and refused to allow the parents to exempt their children from "instruction recognizing differences in sexual orientation," the two sets of parents sued the school district. In dismissing the case, Judge Wolf, wrote, "Parents do have a fundamental right to raise their children. The Parkers and Wirthlins may send their children to a private school … . They may also educate their children at home… . However, the Parkers and Wirthlins have chosen to send their children to the Lexington Public Schools with its current curriculum. The Constitution does not permit them to prescribe what those children will be taught" (*Parker v. Hurley*, 2007). That dismissal was unanimously upheld in the U.S. Court of Appeals (*Parker v. Hurley*, 2008).

In a separate case, parents were not allowed to opt their children out of a court-ordered anti-harassment training that the parents viewed as violating their religious rights. The training was judge-ordered because of widespread anti-gay harassment in the school. U.S. District Judge David L. Bunning wrote that students and staff have no religious right to opt out of such training, since the training did not force students to change their religious views.

School counselors respect parents' right to ask questions about curriculum work, but it is up to the school district/administration in collaboration with the school counselor to determine if it is imperative to the overall well-being of all students in the school that each child participates in the lessons. It becomes a more difficult decision to refuse a parent's request when it involves value-laden issues; therefore, securing administration support ahead of the lessons is a critical step.

Districts may require parental notification or written permission for some topics. Notification may simply mean the school counselor is giving notice of what will be taught, and if parents have concerns then they can contact the school counselor to request more information or to opt out.

CONFIDENTIALITY AND PROTECTIVE PARENTS/GUARDIANS

You are working with Esther in a small group on school success skills. You informed the parents in advance and, after many questions, they seem satisfied. However, despite your explanation that you would give them a periodic update as to Esther's progress, they call every week wanting to know how she did in the group. What do you do?

Points to Consider

Parents/guardians often ask questions about the contents of school counseling sessions. School counselors' primary loyalty is to maintain students' confidentiality as outlined in the profession's ethical practices and standard of care. School counselors want to protect student privacy to the extent they are able to do so while negotiating the political landscape with parents/guardians who request information from individual counseling sessions. In a January 2017b survey of 1,038 school counselors, 34.9% of respondents indicated students' family members regularly ask questions that would require breaking confidentiality.

Iyer and Baxter-MacGregor (2010) recommend school counselors always remind both parents/guardians and students about confidentiality and its limits. This approach helps give parents/guardians comfort that they will be informed if there is serious and foreseeable harm to their child and may help them maintain realistic expectations when making requests of their child's school counselor.

Maintaining positive relationships with parents/guardians is important as this enhances the school counselor's ability to provide services to students (ASCA, 2022b). Parents/guardians are protected by statute and the courts to be the guiding voice in their children's lives, and school counselors support parents/guardians in this role to the greatest extent possible. "The conflict for school counselors is that parents/guardians need to be an integral part of a student's educational experience, yet students expect they can talk freely with a school counselor without the fear that the information will be shared. Finding a balance between protecting the information shared and collaboratively working with parents/guardians and other educators to do what is best for the student is a key issue for professional school counseling program success" (Huss, Bryant & Mulet, 2008, p. 362). Although confidentiality must be breached in cases where there is serious and foreseeable harm to the student, such as in the cases of students who are suicidal or those suffering from eating disorders, situations such as this one have many more gray areas.

In some cases, it is not appropriate to break confidentiality, even at the parent's request. Again, while allowing parents/guardians to be the guiding voice in their child's life is important, your primary obligation is to the student. However, there are appropriate actions school counselors can take in these situations to help both the student and the parent while still maintaining their ethical and professional obligations.

In Esther's case some general responses might be enough: "She is working hard in the group" or "She is making progress." You can back up statements with facts by allowing Esther to take her completed work home to share what she did with parents/guardians, opening up conversations and allaying concerns.

CONFIDENTIALITY AND A PARENT'S/GUARDIAN'S NEED TO KNOW

Two teachers approach you and share their concerns about Katie, whom they believe is suffering from an eating disorder. You have only worked with Katie a few times, usually around scheduling issues, but you do know that she is cautious about sharing personal information and seems closed-off emotionally. You have no medical proof Katie has an eating disorder, but based on the teachers' reports and your professional observations during counseling with Katie, you believe she is in trouble. Katie vehemently denies having an eating disorder and, in so many words, asks you to stay out of her life. What do you do?

Points to Consider

You may be wrong in your assessment, but err on the side of caution. It is better to be wrong and have a student mad at you than to turn a blind eye simply because you cannot be certain she really has an eating disorder. Do not ignore it and hope someone else will address it (Smith et al., 2012). You will want to contact Katie's parents. School counselors cannot assume Katie's parents are aware of her behavior or that they even know what an eating disorder is. Don't worry about being right or wrong, as this is a medical issue. The important response is to alert parents to the possibility. Several factors complicate confronting a student about having an eating disorder. On one hand, a person's weight and eating habits are considered private and personal. Generally speaking, students with eating disorders are often secretive or ashamed of their behavior; hence, school counselors usually hear about eating disorder issues from concerned friends (Carney & Scott, 2012). Regardless, these students may not always welcome what they consider interference with their lives.

Insist that the student involve his or her parents/guardians and offer your help in telling them. Make the student aware of your concerns, and get in touch with the parents. Too much hangs in the balance. Given the highly sensitive nature of eating disorders, the student will likely become upset, or the parents/guardians may become angry and complain about you to administration. However unpleasant the consequences and fallout to your relationship with this student, not involving the parents/guardians poses a greater risk to the student. Only in an extraordinary circumstance where more harm than good comes from involving the parents/guardians would the school counselor choose not to contact them. Bardick, et al., (2004) stress making "honest, objective statements defining the behaviors of concern followed by insistence on obtaining the opinion of a trained professional" (p. 170) in situations such as notifying parents/ guardians of their child's potential eating disorder. Telling students that you care about them but believe they need help is the brave thing to do. Even if the parents/guardians are also in denial, you have forced them to discuss the situation and perhaps have planted some seeds so they will at least consider the possibility their child is not well.

Can you be charged with negligence for not acting? There are no court cases at this point charging a school counselor for negligence in not reporting a student's suspected eating disorder. It would be hard to charge a school counselor with negligence for not reporting a student with anorexia. In the case of a bulimic student, there is more tangible evidence you might observe, such as purging. Anorexia is harder to determine. This situation is really less about avoiding a lawsuit and more about bravely facing the fallout by refusing to look the other way when you think a student may be in danger.

INFORMING PARENTS/GUARDIANS WHEN CLINICAL COUNSELING IS NEEDED

You have a student who has been cutting for several years. You have spoken to her parents on numerous occasions about this behavior, and they have the student in counseling. The student is doing well without an incident for months but just had a slip up and engaged in the behavior again recently. Do you need to continue to contact the parents every time the student reports to you that she cuts?

Points to Consider

In this real scenario, the key piece of information is that both the parents and the school counselor have been working together. The student knows the school counselor may well call the parents, but she reveals the cutting anyway. Her motivation might be that she hopes the school counselor will talk to her parents. I would advise calling the parents, perhaps with the student in the room or having the student call while you are in the room. You are not being asked to carry this student around on your back but a schedule of contact with parents might be the appropriate answer to repeated incidents.

ADMINISTRATORS AND THE NEED TO KNOW

Your principal has asked you to keep him informed about all the students you see, including their presenting problem. He is a strong child advocate and a good administrator, but on this directive you disagree. You do not believe he means any ill will, but you have not been successful in getting him to understand how his insistence on knowing all "the issues our students bring to school" is causing you an ethical dilemma. Can you legally and ethically refuse to cooperate?

Points to Consider

This is a familiar scenario for many school counselors. Administrators, more than teachers or parents/guardians, want to know the contents of counseling sessions. In a January 2017c survey, 36.5% of school counselor respondents indicated they had been asked regularly by administrators for content of their counseling sessions that would require breach of confidentiality.

School counselors fulfilling both ethical principles and negotiating political landmines face challenges not easily solved, as demonstrated in the case of *Woodlock v. Orange Ulster B.O.C.E.S.* (2006/2008). In this case, a school counselor found herself in a conflict with her principal that ended with the loss of her employment and a federal civil rights lawsuit. N.W., a school counselor at a special education center, tried to advocate with her administrators for gym and certified art instructors for her students as indicated on their individualized educational programs. Administration did not respond to her calls and faxes, so she started keeping a log of her attempts and eventually went over her principal's head to the district's pupil services administrator. The principal responded by sending N.W. a letter of reprimand for "going out of process." In what appears to have morphed into a full-blown power struggle, the principal subsequently sent N.W. two disciplinary letters for performance problems, which N.W. contended were unfounded. The principal recommended against N.W. receiving tenure, and N.W.'s response was to file a civil rights suit in federal court alleging adverse administrative actions that violated her First Amendment freedom of expression. The Second Circuit Court of Appeals eventually ruled in favor of the school district.

The Supreme Court's ruling in *Garcetti v. Ceballos* (2006), a separate case, was peripherally related to N.W.'s case. The Supreme Court held in *Garcetti* that First Amendment freedom of expression does not protect statements public employees make pursuant to their official duties, as compared to those they make as citizens on a matter of public concern. The Second Circuit Court of Appeals concluded that N.W.'s repeated communications were made pursuant to her official duties as a school counselor at the special education satellite center and therefore did not fall under protection of her First Amendment rights.

The case shows how legal protection does not necessarily accompany ethical imperatives. The responsibility is on the politically astute school counselor to minimize the conflict between political compliance and ethical behavior, as the option of legal recourse is not a promising one. Negotiating the politics with administrators can at times be complex or even fruitless work but adhering to ethical standards requires school counselors to find alternate routes to compromise without going to battle with administrators.

N.W. was trying to be an advocate for her students, but she approached the administration in what resulted in a self-defeating way. School counselors use their best political and collaborative skills to demonstrate respect for the position of authority that has been entrusted to school administrators, while carefully determining the most effective way to adhere to the school counseling profession's obligation to protect and advocate for students.

So, what is the answer to the question posed at the beginning, "Can you legally and ethically refuse to cooperate?" The balance of power is in the principal's favor, and courts tend to rule in the favor of school districts when administration and other educators collide in the legal arena (Gavin & Zirkel, 2008). School counselors engage in both political acumen and legal awareness to effectively advocate.

SIGN-IN LOG FOR THE SCHOOL COUNSELING OFFICE

My principal wants the school counselors to use a sign-in/sign-out log for the counseling office. This came about because of COVID-19 and the requirement to do contact tracing. I am worried that this breaks confidentiality to have students write their name and time in/out on a log where everyone can see who has visited the counseling office. Students would be able to see who had been in the counseling office that day.

Points to Consider

There are many ways to handle contact tracing on visitors to the school counseling office without risking a confidentiality breach. School counselors have a legitimate concern, and principals have demands on them also to know where each student is at all times, especially in contact tracing. Electronic sign-in, kiosks, digital sign-ins all used by some doctors' offices can be used by school counseling offices but probably pose more problems than they solve depending on equipment availability, student age and other issues. If the electronic or digital approaches are not possible, then perhaps individual school counselors can keep track of who visits them or have students fill out an individual sign-in card, with the cards stored in a box and collected each day in the event they are ever needed.

CLASSROOM CURRICULUM AS COUNSELING

A teacher asks you to help the class deal with the terminal illness and imminent death of one of their classmates. You have had limited training in grief counseling. What do you do?

Points to Consider

There will be times when everyone in the class could use counseling. In this actual case, the teacher asked the school counselor to help with the impending death of a student. The school counselor offered support to individuals who wanted extra help and also found a specialist who had intensive training, research and experience in children's grief, who provided parents/guardians techniques for helping their child at home. This school counselor also sought the help of her local hospice organization, which agreed to come in and provide classroom instruction on several occasions before and after the student's death. The school counselor knew she could seek training and probably conduct the lessons, but hospice staff's skill level was, in her judgment, far superior. Ethically she felt it was only right to reach out for more expertise where she lacked it while still staying involved and connected to the work being done in the classroom. Because of the sensitive nature of the lessons/discussion, best practice might be to notify the parents/guardians about the upcoming lesson and provide them with suggestions on how to follow up with their child at home.

Students exposed to traumatic life events need the legal system and a caring school community to negotiate the horror and helpless feeling that comes from victimization. The legal landscape for child victims of trauma is complex and not always favorable. Federal and state laws are increasingly providing protection to meet the needs of one of America's most vulnerable populations. The list of trauma-inducing life events is long. This book deals with the state and federal laws supporting children in the following situations:

- Witnessing domestic violence
- Homelessness or inconsistent housing
- Physical abuse, sexual abuse, abandonment and/or neglect
- Bullying
- Incarcerated parent

ASCA adopted an updated position statement The School Counselor and Trauma-Informed Practice in 2022, which recognizes school counselors can be key players in promoting a trauma-sensitive school environment (ASCA, 2022). In the U.S., 46 million children witness violence, crime, and physical and psychological abuse every year (Listenbee et al., 2012). Research has shown trauma significantly increases the risk of mental health problems, difficulties with social relationships and behavior, physical illness and poor school performance (Gerrity & Folcarelli, 2008). School counselors strive to understand the impact of adverse childhood experiences to promote students' physical, emotional and mental health. School counselors advocate to create conditions allowing students to thrive and succeed by:

- Recognizing the signs of trauma in students
- Understanding traumas need not predict individual failure if sufficient focus on resilience and strengths is present
- Avoiding practices that may re-traumatize students
- Creating connected communities and positive, trauma-sensitive school climates to keep students healthy and in school and involved in positive social networks
- Implementing effective academic and behavioral practices, such as positive behavioral interventions and supports and social/emotional learning
- Promoting safe, stable and nurturing relationships

ASCA encourages school counselors to collaborate with school staff and community partners to create a trauma-sensitive framework that establishes a safe school climate for all students (ASCA, 2022j).

TEACHERS AND ADMINISTRATORS AS ALLIES IN INDIVIDUAL COUNSELING

During individual counseling, Marcus brings up Sarah, a classmate, with chilling anger, "All she does is talk, talk, talk," he said. "I intend to take her big mouth and shut it once and for all. I am done with listening to her." You have been able to make progress with Marcus, but you know if you breach his confidence he will turn his back on the progress you have made. However, Sarah may be in danger. What do you do?

Points to Consider

Safety supersedes confidentiality. The school counseling profession is built on trust, and the professional guards confidentiality with great care, but this is a threat and it is not your responsibility to determine if it was a real threat. Marcus' comments indicate the possibility of serious and foreseeable harm to Sarah and administration has to be alerted so they can make plans to protect Sarah.

NO-HARM CONTRACTS IN INDIVIDUAL COUNSELING

Heather has been referred to you because she was overheard saying she was going to take her dad's gun and blow her brains out. Much ensued, including alerting the parents, providing resources and developing a no harm contract. You had Heather write on the contract the name of a friend she could turn to if she ever felt like harming herself. She listed another student in your school. Are there any legal or ethical concerns in your handling of this case?

Points to Consider

No-harm contracts are controversial practices in suicide prevention in school settings and for more than a decade have been considered ineffective. No-harm contracts are simple, and many school counselors believe the contracts will help them avoid lawsuits, which results in an over-reliance on them. However, little empirical evidence supports the effectiveness of these contracts (Centre for Suicide Prevention, 2002; Goin, 2003; Leenaars & Wenckstern, 1995). Additionally, use of a suicide contract in some parents'/guardians' minds might imply the school counselor is ensuring the student's safety. The word "contract" can give the impression of a binding agreement. However, a suicidal person is in no way trustworthy to uphold the promise made in signing a contract due to the delicacy of the person's mental and emotional state. If a school counselor believes it is necessary to have the student put something on paper, a better approach might be to ask the student to identify personal goals, write hopeful comments, list what is going right or what adult the student can turn to for help.

In some cases, well-intentioned school counselors may recruit a student's friend as a helper and name the friend as someone a suicidal student can turn to for help when having suicidal thoughts. However, doing so burdens a peer with too much responsibility for another minor's life or death. It would, however, be a wise decision to make all students aware of what to do when a classmate shares suicidal thoughts with them (King & Smith, 2000). Few students know what to do, yet students reported being more likely to report suicidal ideations to a friend than to an adult (American Association for Suicidology, n.d.; American Foundation for Suicide Prevention, n.d.; American Psychological Association, 2018; Trevor Project, n.d.; Society for the Prevention of Teem Suicide, n.d).

LEGAL AND ETHICAL ISSUES IN REFERRALS TO MENTAL HEALTH PROVIDERS

You have referred students to one particular counselor in the community who came to your attention through a parent who raved on the help he provided for her incorrigible teenager. You routinely give out just his contact information for students with similar problems. You have given little thought to the fact that he was not on the district's vetted list for outside counselors. Are there any legal and ethical issues with your practice?

In *Smith v. The School Board of Orange County, Florida* (1994), the parents of 14-year-old K.W. sued the school district because a school counselor was required to give a list of multiple district-approved resources and allegedly gave only one resource, Ron Markham. Markham ran an outpatient treatment center licensed by the Department of Health and Rehabilitative Services, but his name was not on the school district's approved list, nor was he licensed for in-patient care. K.W's mother immediately had misgiving when Markham insisted he be given 24-hour custody of her child and sought more information from a school employee who said if the school counselor thought Markham was "okay" then he must be "okay." Unknown to K.W.'s mother and apparently to the school counselor, Markham "placed" K.W. in his own home, and for two-and-a-half months sexually abused her. The Florida Court of Appeals dismissed the complaint, but a dissenting justice issued the opinion that the case should have been allowed to proceed to a jury trial.

"The foreseeability of K.W.'s injury – sexual battery by Markham – is a jury issue. In my view, the school had at least a threshold duty to make a referral only to 'approved' programs. ... Further, K.W.'s mother's specific inquiry about Markham, after meeting him, should also have triggered a follow-up by the school counselor, which was not done in this case" (Smith v. The School Board of Orange County, 1994).

The Smith case underscored:

- It is best practice to always gives multiple resources and never just one resource.
- If a district provides a list of resources, it should be basic information that the resource is currently licensed or certified by the state licensing board. Other basic information might be provided such as whether the resource uses a sliding fee scale so parents can make an informed financial decision.
- The need for caution if a district does not provide a vetted list and school counselors have to develop a list on their own. A disclaimer is needed to stress the list is not exhaustive nor is it an endorsement.
- The need to advise parents to also check references and current licensure and to discontinue the relationship if they feel there is something troubling or ineffective about the counseling or counselor.

Arlington Public Schools (Va.) provides this disclaimer for their vetted list of resources:

> ***Private Mental Health and Psychological Services Providers***
> *This list is of known providers of a particular service. The providers on the list are from a variety of sources. The list is being provided as a courtesy, for information only, and the user should understand that no assurances or guarantees regarding the providers on the list are being made by providing this list. Arlington Public Schools neither endorses, approves, nor recommends any specific provider listed below. This list is not inclusive of all community agencies, services or organizations that provide the particular service, and the omission of an agency, service or organization from this list does not imply disapproval. It is the responsibility of the user of this list to determine whether any of the content is of value to them and whether or not the agency, service or organization meets their specific needs.*

ASCA's Ethical Standard A.6.b. drives home the point: "School counselors provide a list of resources for outside agencies and resources in their community to students and parents/guardians when students need or request additional support. School counselors provide multiple referral options or the district's vetted list and are careful not to indicate an endorsement or preference for one counselor or practice. School counselors encourage parents to interview outside professionals to make a personal decision regarding the best source of assistance for their student."

OBLIGATION TO A STUDENT USING DRUGS

One of your students gives the appearance of being under the influence of drugs or alcohol. She admits to you she smoked marijuana on the way to school but tries to assure you she is not impaired. In your district, she is breaking the student code of conduct. Must you report her to the administration for her code of conduct violation?

Points to Consider

In some school districts, it is written into the student code of conduct that even the admission of the use of alcohol or drugs is a code of conduct violation regardless of whether the substance is currently in the student's system. School counselors in these districts may be contractually required to report student code of conduct violations and even if not contractually required to do so may choose to report the infractions.

For example, Duval County Public Schools in Jacksonville, Fla., states that employees must uphold the student code of conduct and that drug and alcohol use is a Class III violation. "The use or possession of any drug, narcotic, controlled substance or any substance when used for chemical intoxication. Use means the person is caught in the act of using, admits to use or is discovered to have used in the course of an investigation." School boards are given the right to establish policies and laws, and in absence of a conflict with a state or federal statute, school board policy stands as law. Therefore, in this district all school personnel are required to uphold the student code of conduct by reporting the infraction to the administration. The school counselor must also determine if parent/guardians should be notified. As stated earlier, the school counselor is trying to determine serious and foreseeable harm, often an impossible task as the struggle is real when determining if confidentiality should be breached. The type of drug, the student's age, the student's family support and the frequency of drug/alcohol use are legitimate considerations when determining if and when parents should be informed. If there is doubt, err on the side of caution regarding students' health and safety, and call parents/guardians so they can watch over their child.

CASE NOTES AND STUDENT DRUG USE

You have recorded in a student's case notes that he has admitted to past drug use. He does not admit to and you have no way of knowing if he is still using. His parents have requested access to your case notes, and you are now questioning why you wrote in your notes about his past drug use. You are worried about breaching the student's confidentiality. Do you purge the notes before giving them to the parents? An additional question might be needed if he admits to using. Can you counsel a student about drug use and not involve his parents?

Points to Consider

Parents have a right to access their child's educational record, which includes case notes unless the notes are sole-possession records, a difficult category to achieve (see Chapter 4). In seeking guidance from three agencies, the Student Privacy Policy Office, which governs FERPA; SAMHSA's Student Assistance Program office; and the Healthy Students Group, Office of Safe and Healthy Students (OSHS), U.S. Department of Education, there appears to be no laws or regulations superseding FERPA's requirement that parents be provided access to their children's educational record upon request. There is an exemption in the definition for counseling records when they are written as a memory jogger, not shared or accessible, created solely by the maker for his or her eyes only and containing only professional opinion. Again, this is a difficult criteria to achieve. School officials do not have to announce to parents what is in their child's educational record, but they can't deny parents the right to see the record or make a request for all educational records.

The answer about whether school counselors can maintain confidentiality when counseling students about their drug use is more complex. OSHS' mission is to provide "useful and timely information that will enhance your knowledge of safe and supportive schools; health, mental health, environmental health and physical education; drug-violence prevention; character and civic education." When I spoke with an OSHS representative about whether there was anything in federal statutes or regulations addressing a student's right to seek confidential help from a school counselor for drug or alcohol use, the OSHS representative said there wasn't anything in federal language providing guidance on the issue (personal communication, Oct. 22, 2012). So where does this leave school counselors who are trying to determine best practice?

Federal Statute 42 CFR Part 2 protects the records of students and patients "who have applied for, participated in or received an interview, counseling or any other service from a federally assisted alcohol or drug abuse program." School counselors have wrestled with these questions, especially regarding whether Federal Statute 42 CFR Part 2 extends to school counselors' students (Substance Abuse and Mental Health Services Administration & U.S. Department of Health and Human Services, 2010). Public education receives federal funds, but school counselors do not offer federally assisted alcohol or drug abuse programs. Once again, it appears in absence of federal guidelines this complicated issue rests on school counselors' shoulders to consult and exercise judgment to determine when, how and if to involve parents/guardians. Drug and alcohol use requires counseling outside the purview of the school counselor's role. We must address each individual case in the context of the student's developmental levels, the student's family support, the type and frequency of drug/alcohol, and parental rights. School counselors involve parents when a student is engaged in serious and foreseeable harm. Err on the side of caution. Confidentiality does not supersede students' health and safety. Consult, seek supervision and, in the vast majority of cases, give parents the chance to exercise custody and control over their child.

Norris Dickard and Paul Kesner of OSHS were subsequently contacted with this question: "If a student comes to a school counselor for help with alcohol or drug use and wants the school counselor's help but does not want his or her parents/guardians to know, is there anything in federal statute or regulations addressing a student's right to seek confidential help from a school counselor for drug or alcohol use? Again, the question is not about a written case note, just about a school counselor having the knowledge that a student is using drugs and the student is requesting confidentiality. Does this student have a right to confidentiality in federal statute?" Kesner responded, "To the extent that we know, there is nothing in federal language that gives guidance to the issue we've been presented" (personal communication, March 18, 2013).

The National Institute on Drug Abuse (NIDA) sponsored the University of Michigan to conduct the annual 2021 Monitoring the Future survey. This is a survey of substance use by eighth-, 10th- and 12th-graders. 2021 saw the most significant decrease since NIDA started the survey in 1975. There has been a continued long-term decline in the use of many illicit substances among adolescents previously reported by the Monitoring the Future survey. "We have never seen such dramatic decreases in drug use among teens in just a one-year period. These data are unprecedented and highlight one unexpected potential consequence of the COVID-19 pandemic, which caused seismic shifts in the day-to-day lives of adolescents," said Nora Volkow, M.D., NIDA director. "Moving forward, it will be crucial to identify the pivotal elements of this past year that contributed to decreased drug use – whether related to drug availability, family involvement, differences in peer pressure or other factors – and harness them to inform future prevention efforts" (National Institute on Drug Abuse, 2021, para. 3). Opiate use, including the misuse of prescription pain medication, has seen a drop among high school students, with a 45% decrease over the last five years.

It is not time to relax, as there are still major concerns about drug use among youth. One in 16 12th-graders reported daily use, the highest usage from states with medicinal marijuana laws. High school seniors are smoking marijuana more than cigarettes. By 12th grade, about half of all students have at least tried drugs or alcohol, with 35% of seniors admitting drinking alcohol within the previous month along with 21% having used marijuana. One in six high school seniors report binge drinking daily (National Institute on Drug Abuse, 2021). School counselors who know the risk factors can be an educated voice for schools to have substance abuse prevention programs and to improve protective factors in schools.

INDIVIDUAL COUNSELING AS ENTRAPMENT

Mr. Kline asks you to talk to his daughter Gabby, whom he has caught storing and using alcohol. Mr. Kline worries Gabby will fall victim to what he describes as the family's predisposition to alcoholism. Mr. Kline hopes you will gain his daughter's trust and share back with him how much alcohol Gabby is consuming, where she is getting it since they don't keep it in the house and how often she's drinking. How do you respond?

Points to Consider

Our professional standards dictate that, "School counselors have a primary obligation to the students, who are to be treated with dignity and respect as unique individuals" (ASCA, 2022b, A.1.a). Mr. Kline has a legitimate concern, and he needs help. According to the National Institute on Alcohol Abuse and Alcoholism, "Alcohol use disorder (AUD) research shows that genes are responsible for about half of the risk for AUD. ... Environmental factors, as well as gene and environment interactions, account for the remainder of the risk." School counselors would agree that it is not ethical to establish a relationship with Gabby simply to become an informant. Substantiating or refuting information is not an end goal of counseling, but helping Gabby is altogether appropriate. The approach is context-dependent, but it might include helping Gabby's father understand that it is best if you are upfront with Gabby about her father's concerns. Connecting Gabby and her father to an outside agency specializing in alcohol use and abuse should be a consideration as Gabby is consuming alcohol, and her father is right to be concerned, especially given his description of the family's predisposition to alcoholism. Deceit really has no place in the counseling setting, but seizing the opportunity to help Gabby and her father confront the issue is a worthy undertaking and also lets the father know you hear and validate his concerns as a parent.

MULTICULTURAL CONSIDERATIONS AND SMALL-GROUP COUNSELING

You are running a school success skills group, and you have carefully planned out your group by looking at school data on who is in danger of failing for the second year in a row. You have pre-screened participants, determined appropriate techniques and resources, obtained parental permission and are ready to go. One group member, Lilith, lived in a refugee camp for 17 months before being resettled in America. All students will need consideration, but what do you need to know or consider about Lilith's refugee status in particular?

Points to Consider

The Association for Specialists in Group Work (ASGW) in its 2021 guiding principles document states. "Group specialists screen prospective group members appropriate to the type of group being offered and the modality being used. Group facilitators identify group members whose needs and goals are compatible with the goals of the group" (ASGW, 2021, C.7). "Group facilitators apply and modify knowledge, skills and techniques appropriate to group type, modality and stage, and to the unique needs of various group members' identities, developmental level and needs (e.g., age, cultural values, religious practices, ability-specific needs, etc.) (ASGW, 2021, D.3.).

Adequate and thorough preparation time when building a small group allows the school counselor to learn as much as possible about Lilith's background in compliance with ASGW statement, "Seek to possess specific knowledge and information about the life experiences, cultural heritage and socio-political background of group members who have been displaced as a result of trauma, violence and/or other overt forms of oppression with whom they are working (ASGW, 2012, p.1) and "consider the purpose and membership of the group and select activities and interventions that are culturally informed" (ASGW, 2021, D.5.).

One solution to aid Lilith's comfort and feeling of belonging to the group is to add a group member or two who shares Lilith's background or situation. ASGW states, "Determine if group membership needs to be expanded or altered to allow for a greater level of connection and support for group members who are isolated in the group due to one or more dimensions of multicultural identity or experience. This collective strength helps validate and reframe members' experiences to foster their resilience" (Chen et al., 2010, p. 256). "Group workers ensure a framework exists for members to feel supported for their diversity in the group" (ASGW, 2012, p.1). Promoting multiculturalism in small groups is to design and facilitate a support group for newly immigrated students. "In this group the school counselor helps members recognize their individual and collective strengths by validating and reframing members' experiences to foster their resilience, which they have demonstrated in continuously overcoming educational, psychological and social barriers against a challenging, if not harsh, social backdrop" (Chen et al., 2010, p. 256).

PARENT PERMISSION IN SMALL-GROUP COUNSELING

There are five students in your school who have come to your attention as being isolated from their peers, and it is affecting these students in different ways such as attendance, class participation and/or academic success. You think a small group would be a good intervention. You completed pre-screening interviews with students, and they are all interested in participating. However, parental involvement is an issue at your school, and getting parents to get permission forms back would be time-consuming. Do you need to get written or oral permission from parents before starting this group?

Points to Consider

School counselors want to build, not erode, credibility and maintain a strong working relationship with parents/guardians. This mission is forwarded when school counselors include parental permission for students to be a group member.

The ASCA Ethical Standards (2022b) direct school counselors to inform parents/guardians of student participation in and purpose of the small group (A.7.d.). Parents/guardians send their children to school for classroom academic instruction. Some parents/guardians may view small-group counseling as moving away from classroom instruction to a social/emotional focus; therefore, it is required that school counselors inform parents/guardians. The Association for Specialists in Group Work agrees. In its publication "ASGW Guiding Principles for Group Work 2021" it says, "Specialists in group work engage in the appropriate informed consent/assent processes for work with minors and other dependent group members including the provision of both oral, written and technology-facilitated information" (ASGW, 2021, C.6.c.). This parental notification gives school counselors a chance to explain the connection small groups has to school success, and it gives parents/guardians a chance to opt out.

A review of the 2022 ASCA Ethical Standards (2022b) reminds school counselors of the importance of involving the family, acting in the best interests of students, working collaboratively with parents/guardians, adhering to laws and local guidelines and obtaining consent when working with minors.

GROUP WORK WITH DISCIPLINE REFERRALS

You are conducting a small group with five students accused of sexual harassment. The principal is responsive to issues of bullying and harassment and believes these five students have the potential to change their behavior and hopes they will be able to provide testimonials to other students about how sexual harassment harms victims. Is it appropriate to run a group designed to correct a discipline problem? If so, what are some things you may want to consider before starting the group?

Points to Consider

Smead (1995) states, "Counseling is a voluntary effort to improve oneself. Change and personal growth cannot be legislated" (p. 14). It is a risky move to involve oneself in discipline issues. If a school counselor agrees to conduct groups in accordance with administrator-identified discipline issues, then the school counselor may be viewed as an arm of the administration and identified as a disciplinarian.

The principal and school counselor would want to make certain they agree that students have to be voluntarily involved in small groups created by the school counselor. The danger would come if a student chose not to be involved and the alternative for that student is discipline. This forced participation would not meet the criteria of voluntariness. Competence, voluntariness and knowledge are necessary elements if students are to give us informed consent to participate in a group. The conflict is positioned that, "Because of increased student misconduct in academic institutions, school counselors have had to use traditional voluntary counseling models with involuntary disciplinary clients" (Kiracofe & Wells, 2007, p. 259). Even though school counselors are being asked to work with involuntary students, it is the ethical and astute school counselor who carefully moves through this landmine with administration to ensure students have the option. An option would be to let the students try the group for a time or two, and then if they make the decision not to continue, the principal would not use an alternative discipline against the students.

As addressed in other cases in this chapter, confidentiality cannot be guaranteed, so the school counselor must stress, but never rely on, participants not to breach confidentiality (see the section Confidentiality in Group Counseling). School counselors can help students by informing them about the principal's belief that the students can make positive change, stressing that for change to happen students must come prepared to work and to take ownership of their behavior. Some school districts, such as Duval County Public Schools in Jacksonville, Fla., have special programs for drug abusers where they can attend lessons and small groups for a first-time drug offense. "The in-school suspension may not exceed 10 school days and shall end upon both the parent/guardian agreeing to enroll in the Nighttime Substance Use Prevention Counseling Education Program" (Duval County Public Schools, Student Code of Conduct, 2011, p. 16). This group cannot be viewed as a voluntary group, but it has a place in the complicated world of trying to help students succeed.

SENSITIVE INFORMATION REVEALED DURING A LESSON

A school counselor's classroom instruction took an unexpected turn when students were asked to talk about a time when they felt sad. Cedric offered, "My dad just killed my mom and then killed himself." The school counselor asked Cedric if he would like to share his story, at which time he graphically described for the school counselor and his classmates his parents' murder/suicide. What is your reaction to this situation?

Points to Consider

In this real situation, it is probable but unfortunate that the school counselor did not know that Cedric, new to the school, had recently suffered such an unfathomable trauma. School counselors have to be ready with skillful responses when highly sensitive information is shared with peers and be able to divert the conversation without dismissing or devaluing the student's response. Quickly the school counselor must honor Cedric with a sincere acknowledgement of how very sad he must be and then skillfully move the conversation to another student or topic. Cedric was not developmentally able to understand the implications of sharing his story in front of his classmates. To do more than acknowledge Cedric opens him up to the possibility of bullying, curiosity seekers, isolation and/or regret that he shared his life so openly. Clearing the calendar and quietly bringing Cedric to the office for unconditional positive regard, helping him safely share his story and connecting him with resources for ongoing support would be important next steps.

Given the age and developmental levels of Cedric's classmates who heard his story, it is a strong possibility that some of his peers might need support. The school would initiate a preconceived plan to contact the parents/guardians and let them know what transpired with suggestions on how to support their child. Follow-up might also include helping the class understand how best to support Cedric.

Predicting questions and spotting potential land mines is part of the overall preparation school counselors undertake when organizing their classroom instruction.

MULTITIERED SYSTEM OF SUPPORTS AND CLASSROOM CURRICULUM

You have been receiving referrals from quite a few teachers, each complaining of two or three students who are not completing work. You want to address their concerns, but with 17 students at issue coming from just two grade levels your schedule is squeezed. Can classroom instruction help?

Points to Consider

The multitiered system of supports (MTSS) includes three levels of intensity. Individual counseling is a Tier 3 intervention, and small-group counseling is a Tier 2 approach. When school counselors use research-based classroom instruction to improve academic outcomes, they are engaging in Tier 1 interventions (ASCA, 2021e). An MTSS Tier 1 approach is aimed at benefiting all students and is an appropriate way as a first response to addressing the 17 chronic offenders. Tier 2 is more intense, such as a behavior management program or small-group counseling and is probably more appropriate for the 17 underachieving students. However, casting a wider net around all students in classroom instruction is efficient and may well reduce the number of chronic offenders from 17. For students who do not respond to Tier 1 or Tier 2 an even more individualized approach, such as one-on-one counseling, a Tier 3 intervention, may be needed.

CONFIDENTIALITY AND CLASSROOM INSTRUCTION

You set up class rules to include respecting confidentiality before conducting classroom instruction, but you still worry about some of the inappropriate and sensitive material students blurt out. Are your concerns legitimate?

Points to Consider

Working with minors in classroom lessons in which students talk in front of each other requires the full realization that whatever is said in the classroom will be repeated on social media or in the hallways within minutes. School counselors take precautions to monitor what they allow one student to talk about in front of other students. School counselors come from the posture that confidentiality will be breached in the fluid social world of schools where minors frequently change friends and loyalties. This provides a lens through which they can run classroom topics they intend to introduce to determine potential landmines.

Empathy training for large groups of students (entire grade level or entire school) is happening in many schools across the country. This event asks students to cross a line marked on the floor if certain events have happened to them, such as drug or alcohol abuse in their family, victimization of bullying, isolation, taunting for "acting like a girl." These situations are often emotional, and in the heat of the moment students will reveal personal information because all around them their peers are being supportive. Students may later regret what they revealed when peer support wanes or when walking the halls and knowing the entire school knows about their struggles. For students to give informed consent, they have to understand the implications of revealing private information. Developmentally, they may not think about the fallout that might come from their revelations. Because the event pulls strongly on a student's emotion, counseling is supposed to be available at the end of the experience. Some children may need counseling for many weeks long after the exercise is over, and the school counselor is left trying to provide support to all who may need it. Considerable caution is needed before allowing students to discuss issues in front of their peers exploring family troubles or personal issues. School counselors must ask themselves if the potential emotional cost to students and their families is worth the potential gains.

In a Position to Know: A School Counselor Educator Speaks

The case presented at the beginning of the chapter is revisited here and answered. Read the school counselor educator's opinion carefully to see what you can learn. Compare her answer with your own approach.

SMALL-GROUP COUNSELING AND SCREENING POTENTIAL MEMBERS

You develop a small group in response to complaints from seventh-grade teachers who say some students are having difficulty getting along with their peers and are interrupting class lessons. The teachers also say they believe the behavior is affecting the students' grades. You establish a set of goals for the group that includes learning ways to get along with others while improving grades. The teachers recommend eight students for the group; the principal also requests you also include two other students who are repeatedly in trouble for fighting. This brings your group to 10 students. After you secure parental permission, you conduct your first meeting to discuss the ground rules, confidentiality and goals for the group. By the third session, bickering escalates. The two students who were recommended by the principal are not benefiting from the group and are fueling the group's negativity by making threatening comments to the other members. Are there ethical issues with the small group?

This school counselor's membership on the school leadership team is exemplary for all school counselors to replicate. And, that the teachers and administrator recognized the role of the school counselor to help with what clearly is a significant concern and in need of resolution is a testimony to the credibility of this school counselor. Although the school counselor's plan for this group is clearly "to facilitate short-term groups to address students' academic achievement, postsecondary and career exploration, and social/emotional well-being" (ASCA, 2022b, A.7.e.), and despite the well-intended plan of the school counselor to address the social/emotional issue of bullying, this group is fraught with ethical issues.

School counselors are the front-line professionals responsible for creating and facilitating an experience that ultimately fulfills the goals for the group and for each member. Screening prospective group members is an ethical standard (ASCA, 2022b, A.7.c.) and an essential first step to providing an effective learning experience for students. In this case, the school counselor relied on teacher referrals and complied with the principal's request, which is acceptable if then screening is done to ensure members understand the purpose of participating in the group, confidentiality and have a clear understanding that some topics are not suitable for groups in schools and accordingly take precautions to protect members from harm as a result of group interactions (ASCA, 2022b, A.7.i.).

Membership in this case was unfortunately based on others' perceptions of which students might benefit from the small-group experience, rather than the school counselor adhering to best practices (Erford, 2015) and following ethical practices for group leaders (ASCA, 2022b). The school counselor's expertise was ignored. In this case study, the school counselor did not meet with group members until the first session, thus sidestepping advance assessment to ensure suitability of each student for group participation and formulating individual goals with each student. The school counselor missed the opportunity to explain to each student the group purpose, acceptable and expected behaviors, benefits and outcomes, answer questions and overall elicit buy-in and commitment from each student. Consequently, feeling trust and security, dynamics needed early in the life of a group, were not present to begin development of group cohesion. By the fourth meeting, the group was unraveling.

Typically, the more preferred method of screening is an individual interview. While individual meetings may be dismissed because of time constraints, school counselors need to remember that screening is an ethical practice for conducting small groups in schools and will contribute to the effectiveness of the group experience (Sink et al., 2012). Smead (1995) suggested individual meetings (a) afford the group leader the opportunity to discuss the purpose and goals of the group, (b) confirm the student's willingness to participate, (c) check for compatibility with other group members and (d) check that the student is indeed interested in and committed to participating in the group. Sink et al. suggested that screening need not be considered a lengthy, formal process and offered suggested questions that may be completed informally and in a reasonable time frame. In this case, students were drafted as members of the group and only in the first meeting can we assume that expectations were adequately discussed.

A second issue related to screening is the selection of members and the number of members for a group. Typically, a group size for this age level in school would range from six to eight members. This group had 10 members, all of whom were in the group because of unacceptable and aggressive behaviors. Because of the homogeneity of the group, the potential for appropriate modeling behaviors between group members significantly decreased. The size and composition of this group potentially pose challenges for any group leader. Mixing ages, grade levels and gender are acceptable, but mixing of this nature should be done with precise attention and consideration to developmental appropriateness. For this group, having two groups would increase the likelihood for an effective group experience and positive results.

Third, some schools and districts require parental/guardian written permission; some schools and districts do not. Irrespective of your district policy, the ethical standard A.7.d., clearly instructs us to inform parents/guardians of students' participation in small groups (ASCA, 2022b). The school counselor in this case followed ethical practice and informed the parents/guardians.

A fourth issue in this case relates to confidentiality. It is mentioned that the school counselor discussed confidentiality with the group in the first session, but it is unclear if the parameters of confidentiality were addressed. Did the group members hear and acknowledge understanding that it is acceptable to talk about they say or do in the group, but it is not acceptable to talk about what others say and do? Did the school counselor talk about what to do if someone accidentally breaks confidence? The ethical standard for confidentiality is significant to adhere to and a delicate factor to facilitating groups. Discussing confidentiality during screening and again in the first session is an essential step to facilitating a group, regardless of age and grade. Related to confidentiality is naming a group. While seemingly harmless to name a group, extra caution is needed to not have the group name ultimately label the students participating in the group. To protect members from being labeled by the group title, it is advisable to refer to the group as simply "group." If asked about the group, the school counselor can describe the group as instruction for school and life success. By keeping the name of the group simple, labeling is avoided, and there is no risk that you as the school counselor inadvertently imply confidential information about a student.

A fifth ethical standard lacking in this case is the use of data to identify the needs and define expectations for a group (ASCA, 2022b, A.7.f.). Before leaping into a small group based on teacher and administrator requests, the school counselor would want to review and try to determine the extent of bullying in the school more objectively. It would be good practice to first review the aggregate data on grades and the discipline referrals and disaggregate the data by grade and gender. What do the grades show? What are the grades of students in the different subjects? Disaggregating the data frequently provides more insights into an issue. How to determine objective data about bullying in the school? One strategy is a survey-like version whereby students identify where and when bullying occurs within the school. Using different colors to represent degrees of feeling safe within the school and symbols for different times of the day, students color in the floor plan of the school where and when they don't feel safe (Borba, 2016).

A sixth issue with this situation is how will the outcomes of the group be measured? The stated goal for this group, to increase safety and respect among students, is not measurable. This goal needs to be revised to quantify how much to increase safety and respect among students and what in observable, measurable terms is "safety" and "respect." Only by re-crafting this goal will the school counselor be able to measure the group outcomes. (ASCA, 2022b, A.7.g.)

Creating a safe and respectful climate in a school requires everyone within the school to participate. Rather than singling out "some students" for small groups, the school counselor might find it beneficial to conduct classroom instruction, using the same goal developed for the small-group counseling. It is reasonable to consider that every student can benefit from learning how to develop positive relationships and the use of empathy. By delivering classroom lessons on the skill of forming positive peer relationships and use of empathy skills for better working relationships, the school counselor contributes to the school learning climate and teaches life skills for these students.

Small-group work is a complex and difficult process and, unfortunately, far too frequently dismissed as a powerful strategy to use in a school counseling program. Yet small groups have the potential for effectively helping students in schools and teaching critically important skills for adulthood. The first step for school counselors is the responsibility to be informed and knowledgeable of group work's ethical, legal and professional standards. Developing knowledge and skills for leading groups with children and adolescents is a continual process that calls for experience running small groups, professional development and supervision (ASCA, 2022b, A.7.k.).

– *Rebecca A. Schumacher, Ed.D., assistant professor, University of North Florida*

Making Connections

1. You are considering running a small group for children of alcoholics. Are there any ethical issues you should consider regarding this topic?

2. You are considering running a small group for children whose parents/guardians are going through a divorce. Are there any ethical considerations you must consider regarding this topic?

3. You would like to enlist a group of parent volunteers to help you follow through on a behavior management program for a group of seven students who are having difficulty finishing their work every day. The volunteers will stop by five classrooms and check to see if the participants have finished their work and, if so, bring them to the school counselor's office to put stickers on their charts. Are there any legal or ethical issues you must consider before involving parent volunteers in this behavior management program?

4. When is it best practice to get parental permission for individual and group counseling?

5. If parent want to know what their child is saying in individual counseling sessions with you, must you share the information? What are some techniques for making parents feel included without breaching a child's confidence?

Chapter 8 Quiz

1) School counselors adhere to the ASCA Ethical Standards in recognizing that small groups:
   a. Are an excellent way to deliver clinical therapy in schools
   b. Are safe for confidentiality if confidentiality is explained to students properly
   c. Hinge on the understanding that each group member must participate equally
   d. Are at risk for breaches of confidentiality, but the ethical school counselor still communicates the aspiration of confidentiality, as a group norm
   e. Can only be delivered to middle and high school students as elementary students are not developmentally ready for groups

2) When school counselors are asked by parents to counsel their child on a clinical, therapeutic topic requiring specialized training, best practice would be to:
   a. Explain it is in their child's best interest to be seen by someone who specializes in the area and provide resources
   b. Immediately sign up to receive specialized training and within six months make certain you are up to the challenge
   c. Carve out 50-minute sessions for at least six weeks to work with the student
   d. Explain to parents you are way too busy to deliver clinical help to their child
   e. Explain that they will need to bring their child to you off hours for private therapy as this is not in the school counselor's role

3) Informed consent:
   a. Requires competence, voluntariness and knowledge on the part of the student to obtain informed consent
   b. Requires a state statute specifically rendering school counselors unable to testify
   c. Is a legal principle only applying to students' medical records
   d. Supersedes the Health Information Portability Privacy Act
   e. Originated from the constitutional principle of "In God We Trust"

4) School counselors have to be the guardian of informed consent, safeguarding, protecting and proceeding on behalf of students who cannot act on their own behalf. Being the guardian of informed consent means:
   a. Recognizing and honoring that the current reality of informed consent in schools falls far short of its stated goals.
   b. Resting assured that after you have stated the limits of informed consent you can always proceed with confidence you have fulfilled your ethical responsibility
   c. Weighing the potential risks of having a student in a group yet proceeding with caution even when the risks outweigh the benefits
   d. Adhering to a mechanistic, routine, standardized approach to explain informed consent
   e. Recognizing that informed consent is not a process but an event

5) In the *Parker v. Hurley*, 2007 court case:
   a. The courts ruled for the parents stating that school counselors should have adhered to the prevailing community standards when deciding curriculum
   b. The Parkers were allowed to opt their children out of what they considered controversial curriculum promoting homosexuality

c. The court said parents have a fundamental right to decide public school curriculum
d. The court said the Constitution does not permit parents to prescribe what children will be taught in public school education
e. The court sided with the Parkers because to do otherwise the court feared any possible benefits would be outweighed by the damage done to parent/educator collaboration

Key Terms

Anorexia Bulimia
Classroom lessons
Clear and imminent danger
Confidentiality in group counseling
Serious and foreseeable harm
Group counseling sessions
Informed consent
Multiculturalism
No-harm contract
Parental permission
Screening members
Suicide assessment
Trauma-informed
Unconditional positive regard

Chapter 9

Sexually Active Students

Objectives

By the time you have completed this chapter, you should be able to:

- Discuss the complications of confidentiality regarding sexually active students
- Define your own values regarding sexually active students
- Recognize when and if your values interfere with your ability to work effectively with students
- Understand the rights of pregnant students
- Understand how the school setting complicates school counselors' efforts to respect confidentiality
- Understand parents' and/or guardians' rights to be the guiding voice in their children's lives in value-laden issues
- Discuss the prevalence of sexual activity among teens

Ethical Standards Addressed in This Chapter

Professionalism means knowing your professional association's ethical standards and adhering to them. The ASCA Ethical Standards for School Counselors (2022b) most germane to this chapter are the following:

- School counselors acknowledge the vital role and rights of parents/guardians, families and tribal communities. (A.1.g).
- School counselors inform students of the purposes, goals, techniques and rules of procedure under which they may receive counseling. Disclosure includes informed consent and clarification of the limits of confidentiality. (A.2.b).
- School counselors recognize that informed consent requires competence, voluntariness and knowledge on students' part to understand the limits of confidentiality and, therefore, can be difficult to obtain from students of certain developmental levels and special-needs populations. The school counselor should make attempts to gain assent appropriate to the individual student (e.g., in the student's preferred language) prior to disclosure. (A.2.c).
- School counselors keep information confidential unless legal requirements demand confidential information be revealed or a breach is required to prevent serious and foreseeable harm to the student or others. Serious and foreseeable harm is different for each minor in schools and is determined by a student's developmental and chronological age, the setting, parental/guardian rights and the nature of the harm. School counselors consult with appropriate professionals when in doubt as to the validity of an exception. (A.2.f).

- School counselors recognize their primary ethical obligation for confidentiality is to the students but balance that obligation with an understanding of parents'/guardians' legal and inherent rights to be the guiding voice in their children's lives. School counselors understand the need to balance students' ethical rights to make choices, their capacity to give consent or assent, and parental or familial legal rights and responsibilities to make decisions on their child's behalf. (A.2.g).
- School counselors collaborate with and involve students to the extent possible and use the most appropriate and least-intrusive method to breach confidentiality if such action is warranted. The child's developmental age and the circumstances requiring the breach are considered and, as appropriate, students are engaged in a discussion about the method and timing of the breach. Consultation with professional peers and/or supervision is recommended. (A.2.h).
- School counselors inform parents/guardians and school administration when a student poses a serious and foreseeable risk of harm to self or others. This notification is to be done after careful deliberation and consultation with appropriate professionals, such as other school counselors, the school nurse, school psychologist, school social worker, school resource officer or child protective services. Even if the danger appears relatively remote, parents/guardians must be notified. The consequence of the risk of not giving parents/guardians a chance to intervene on behalf of their child is too great. (A.9.a).

The full text of the ASCA Ethical Standards for School Counselors is available at *www.schoolcounselor.org*.

Introduction

This chapter deals with the highly sensitive and value-laden issue of sexually active students. The consequences of student sexual activity can place school counselors in vulnerable positions with students and parents/guardians. Through a series of case studies, this chapter examines the difficulties of working with minors around this delicate topic.

School counselors regularly face ethical dilemmas of confidentiality for which there are few definitive answers. The ASCA Ethical Standards for School Counselors (2022b) provide guidelines for ethical behavior, but it is ultimately the school counselor's responsibility to negotiate the rights and privileges of students and parents/guardians in regard to disclosing information to parents/guardians. Parents'/guardians' legal rights to guide their children, community standards, a school counselor's personal values, school board policy and the school setting all contribute to the complex nature of working with sexually active students. Difficult decisions involving value-laden issues must always be made against the backdrop of parental rights. School counselors have the complicated task of figuring out when it is time to involve parents/ guardians so they can exercise their right to guide their children.

Court decisions give school counselors some guidance in issues involving abortion counseling. However, the answers to complex questions involving sexually active students are context-dependent in absence of clear-cut school board policies. Sexually active students pose some nail-biting, tense moments regarding confidentiality. As a school counselor, sometimes your best defense is to seek supervision and consultation with other professionals who are in a position to understand the context-specific world in which you are operating, including the prevailing community standards and school board policies.

Sexual activity trends among adolescents have shown a reduction in rates of teen pregnancy, births and abortions and a drop in the number of adolescents engaging in sexual activity. However, unintended pregnancy and sexually transmitted infections (STIs) among teens and young adults remain higher in the United States than in other developed nations and are considerably higher among certain racial and ethnic minorities and in different geographic regions in the nation. Statistical analysis of adolescents' sexual activity, contraceptive use, pregnancy, prevalence of STIs and access to reproductive health services among teens calls attention to school counselors and educators on how to best communicate with adolescents in relation to their sexual behavior (Kaiser Family Foundation, 2018).

According to the 2019 Youth Risk Behavior Surveillance survey, 38% of all high school students report having had sexual intercourse (CDC, 2019). Nationwide, 27% of students from ninth to 12th grade reported being sexually active (had intercourse during the three months before the survey, i.e., currently sexually active) (CDC, 2019). Among the 27% of currently sexually active students, the prevalence of males using condoms during last sexual intercourse was higher (60%) than female (49.6%) students (CDC, 2019).

The National Survey of Family Growth analyzed students' perceptions of sexual behaviors they identify as "sex" or "abstinence." Results from the survey highlighted that slightly less than half of males (44%) and females (42%) reported they had given or received oral sex (National Survey of Family Growth, 2021). This is a slight decrease from previous studies, which also demonstrated that smaller percentages (38% of males and 39% of females) said they had given oral sex (Child Trends, 2015). Although most men and women have not yet given or received oral sex by the time they turn 18, research shows students may not understand the possible consequences of this behavior. Results from this study show adolescents consider oral sex to be more acceptable and generally expect fewer negative consequences, including physical, emotional and social consequences. A substantial minority of teens are completely unaware of any health risks associated with oral sex and cite the most common reasons for engaging in oral sex were for pleasure, to be popular, to improve their relationship and to protect their reputation (Child Trends, 2015).

Casual relationships are not uncommon among sexually active students. Although the majority of sexually active teens, (73% of females and 58% of males) reported their first sexual experience was with a steady partner, cohabiters, fiancé or spouse, a sizeable minority (16% of females and 28% of males) report their first sexual encounter was with "someone they had just met or who was just a friend" (Guttmacher, 2022).

Teenage pregnancy is a significant contributor to high school dropout rates among teen girls. The National Conference of State Legislators (NCSL) reports that 30% of teenage girls who drop out of high school cite pregnancy or parenthood as a primary reason (2016). The rate for Hispanic and African American or Black teens is at 36% and 38%, respectively. In 2019, the birth rates for Hispanic teens (25.3 per 1,000) and non-Hispanic Black teens (25.8/1,000) were more than two times higher than the rate for non-Hispanic white teens (11.4/1,000). The birth rate of American Indian/Alaska Native teens (29.2/1,000) was highest among all race/ethnicities (Martin et al., 2019).

Nationally, only about half of all teen mothers earn a high school diploma by age 22. And among those who have a baby before age 18, about 40% finish high school and less than 2% finish college by age 30 (NCSL, 2016). In 2018, fewer babies were born to women aged 15–19 years, with a birth rate of 16.7 per 1,000 women in this age group (Centers for Disease Control, 2019). A study by the CDC and National Center for Health Statistics (NCHS) presented preliminary data to show 230,000 girls ages 15–19 gave birth in 2015, which was an 8% decrease from 2014. The birth rate in this age group has been falling sharply since 2007, and between 2013 and 2014, there was a record decrease of 9% (CDC, 2015). Although reasons for the declines are not clear, more teens may be delaying or reducing sexual activity, and more of the teens who are sexually active may be using birth control than in previous years. Still, the U.S. teen pregnancy rate is substantially higher than in other western industrialized nations, and racial/ethnic and geographic disparities in teen birth rates persist (CDC, 2019).

Getting Started: What Would You Do?

The following case is discussed for you at the end of this chapter by a school counselor educator. Before you read her response, formulate in your own mind how you would approach this ethical dilemma.

DEVELOPMENTALLY DELAYED, PREGNANT STUDENT

Sharon is slightly developmentally delayed. Chronologically, Sharon is 14, but developmentally she is more like an 11- or 12-year-old. Sharon is pregnant, and her mother is aware of the pregnancy. Sharon has long been a concern of many in the school. She is unkempt and explosive at times. Her developmental problems mean she is always out of sync with her age group. Her peers avoid her because they are afraid of her. Sharon seems incapable of taking care of herself, and you fear for the welfare of her child. She tells everyone that having this baby will bring the father of the baby back to her. She says her mother plans to help her raise the baby. Do you have any role in this case?

Working Through Case Studies

HELPING A STUDENT GET CONTRACEPTIVES

Jessica comes to you distraught over a fight she had with her boyfriend and during the conversation she reveals they are sexually active. She asks you to help her get birth control, explaining it is out of the question for her to ask her parents for help and she refuses to visit the school nurse. You are convinced that without your help and transportation Jessica will never visit a clinic. Can you transport her to get birth control?

Points to Consider

It is beyond the scope of a school counselor's role to take students to clinics for birth control. In this real case, the school counselor had already done this and then reached out to me when she thought better of her behavior. In many American communities, taking Jessica to get birth control would be considered stepping on family values. Transporting a student to get any kind of nonemergency medical attention is out of the question without parental involvement. Yet, students are not accessing contraceptives as their primary birth control method. In a 2015–2017 study of birth control methods among teenagers, only 3% of the female respondents who were sexually active had ever used a condom, and their most common method of birth control was withdrawal (65%), followed by the pill (53%) (Martinez & Abma, 2020). Work with Jessica to help her figure out if she can involve her parents. As you counsel Jessica, keep in mind any relevant school board policies regarding sexual activity.

With the exception of four states, there are statutes giving students guidance as to whether or not they can seek contraceptive help in absence of parental involvement. Guttmacher conducted a study of the state statutes involving minors and contraceptive information (Guttmacher, 2021). In summary, "21 states and the District of Columbia explicitly allow all minors to consent to contraceptive services. Twenty-five states explicitly permit minors to consent to contraceptive services in one or more circumstances (Guttmacher, 2021). Three states allow minors to consent to contraceptive services if a physician determines the minor would face a health hazard if not provided with contraceptive services. Twenty-one states allow a married minor to consent to contraceptive services. Eleven states allow a minor to consent if the minor meets other requirements, including being a high school graduate, reaching a minimum age, demonstrating maturity or receiving a referral from a specified professional, such as a physician or member of the clergy" (p.1).

NOTIFYING PARENTS/GUARDIANS WHEN THEIR CHILD IS SEXUALLY ACTIVE

Rachel confides in you that she and Bradley, both 17, are having unprotected sexual relations. Are you required to notify the parents/guardians of students who are engaged in sexual activity?

Points to Consider

At 17, is Rachel prepared to understand the potential repercussions of having unprotected sex? Perhaps, a place to start is to find out what she believes her future should hold and help her think through the roadblocks and barriers that could derail her future aspirations. Encourage Rachel to involve her parents/guardians.

The 2015–2017 National Survey of Family Growth showed that nearly 84% of females and 82% of males ages 15–19 have received formal instruction before the age of 18 on how to say no to sex (CDC, 2017). More than two-thirds of male teenagers and almost four-fifths of female teenagers had spoken with their parents/guardians about at least one of six sex education topics, which included how to say no to sex, methods of birth control, STDs, where to get birth control, how to prevent HIV/AIDS and how to use a condom (Martinez et al., 2010). In general, the younger the child, the more rights are vested in the parents/ guardians – a concept that applies to both physical maturity and, in a court of law, also mental maturity.

You can avoid scrambling in a crisis by being prepared. Know your community's prevailing opinions about minors and pregnancy, as these opinions have an impact in some respects on how you will respond. In some communities, the school counselor has the freedom to direct a student to a health clinic for contraceptives. As discussed in the Introduction chapter more fully, New York City public schools include reproductive health education, information on STI prevention, pregnancy testing (urine testing, no physical exam) and hormonal contraception (birth control), including emergency contraception and condoms. This is an example of community standards at work. In many schools, school counselors would not even suggest students visit a local clinic for contraceptives as this would dramatically cross the line of community or institutional standards. This does not mean, however, that we sit idly by and accept the status quo; rather, we work responsibly to change community standards when they stratify students' opportunities.

Know which resources in your community can help your students with issues involving their sexual activity. ASCA's position statement of The School Counselor and Prevention of Sexually Transmitted Infections (2018) outlines school counselors' educational efforts related to HIV, AIDS and STDs and collaborates with students, families, staff and the community to prevent infection and the spread of these diseases. As adolescents explore multiple facets of their identities, they may engage in risky behaviors jeopardizing their health. School counselors address STIs by helping students understand the causes and potential consequences of sexual behaviors and experimentation. The STI education curriculum includes instruction for students, families and staff promoting healthy living and responsibility to self, family and society.

Specific elements may include general information about HIV/AIDS/STDs, including knowledge of:

- Behaviors putting people at risk
- Methods of transmission
- Health risks to self and others
- Related nondiscrimination policies and confidentiality policies
- Prevention efforts
- Accurate information dispelling myths and stereotypes
- Referral information for health clinics providing testing and treatment

Essential to establishing a network of support is developing a relationship with the school principal and staff members, including teachers, the school nurse, cafeteria workers, janitors and secretaries. One of the secrets of being an investigative reporter in the world of journalism, for example, is to cultivate sources on the front lines; these are the people who see and hear everything and can be the most useful to you. Teachers and other educators can be your front line if you empower your "investigators" to responsibly gather and use sensitive information to help you support students. You can widen your influence by delivering professional development around topics such as suicidal ideation, signs of abuse and available community resources and help each educator be an extension of the school counseling program.

The following are recommendations for the school counselor when counseling students in the area of sexuality or abortion:

Know your school board policy: School counselors can sometimes find guidance in school board policy and must adhere to the stated policy. School counselors behaving as advocates work appropriately to change policies they believe have an adverse impact on students.

Know your state's age-of-consent laws: The Romeo and Juliet law was first created in Florida during the 2007 legislative session to address concerns about high-school-age youth being labeled as sexual offenders or sexual predators as a result of participating in a consensual sexual relationship. The pedophile registry provides no clear distinction between the young sex offenders who had consensual sex and the offenders who harm children. Texas and other states have used a petition process for sex offenders to clear their name and to get off the pedophile registration if they were charged as sexual offenders having engaged in consensual sex with a close-in-age partner. States set up what the close-in-age partner is, and this is often labeled a Romeo and Juliet law.

Consider developmental issues. If Rachel had been 14 you would act with greater caution for her well-being in possible risky behavior. It is especially important to consider the developmental level to determine whether an intervention is needed and how much is required. School counselors promote the autonomy and independence of a minor by carefully considering how much to support students in making their own decisions without interference or breach of confidentiality. Primary to the school counselor's decision-making is the seriousness of the minor's behavior, his or her developmental level and the minor's history of making informed decisions.

Consider the impact of the school setting and parental/guardian rights. Parental/guardian rights are complicated since parents/guardians send minors to school for academics, not for personal counseling. Therefore, when a minor seeks counseling in a value-laden area such as abortion, which may be related to the parents'/guardians' morals or religious beliefs, consideration must be given to the wishes of parents/guardians and their rights to be the guiding voice in their children's lives. The onus is not on the school counselor to know the religious beliefs of all the students and their families. However, if a student confides that religion is at issue or if the school counselor learns this information from another source, then it is appropriate to consider this information when determining how to proceed with the student.

Consider diversity issues: Each decision must be made in context and must consider a minor's ethnicity, socioeconomic status, gender, race and sexual identity.

Consult with a supervisor or respected colleague, examining the good and bad consequences of each course of action: Strive to minimize the risk to the student while respecting parents'/guardians' inherent rights. It is ethical, lawful and beneficial to inform and consult with supervisors and colleagues. After the school counselor implements a course of action, it is important to process the results to strengthen the probability of making appropriate decisions in the future.

Know yourself and your values: School counselors should understand their own values in sensitive areas such as abortion and teen pregnancy and understand the impact of those values on their ability to act in their students' best interest. Professionals know they cannot divorce themselves from their values and exercise caution when their values could inappropriately interfere with promoting a student's autonomy. School counselors will want to refer students to a colleague when they can no longer be objective.

Avoid involvement in a student's medical care: Referring students to birth control clinics should be avoided, and a school counselor should never agree to take students for any kind of medical procedure, especially a procedure as controversial as abortion.

PARENTAL NOTIFICATION POLICIES AND STUDENT PREGNANCY

Your school district was challenged by an angry parent who felt her daughter's school counselor should have informed her when her daughter sought counseling about her pregnancy. In response, the district has issued a new written policy saying school counselors must try to get students to inform their parents/guardians about their pregnancy, and failing to accomplish this the school counselors themselves must inform parents/guardians. Are there any legal or ethical concerns regarding this policy?

Points to Consider

The majority of school counselors work tirelessly to try and help students find a way to inform their parents/guardians in a situation like this. School counselors understand sometimes they have to let the student take the lead in deciding what is best.

Parental involvement can be supportive and beneficial; however, it can also be punitive, coercive or abusive (Hasselbacher, Dekleva, Tristan, & Gilliam, 2014). It is the unpredictability of parental reaction that makes it impossible to develop a hard and fast rule on school counselor behavior in parental notification of student pregnancy. School counselors also cite incidences in which students have valid reasons or legitimate fears preventing them from involving their parents/guardians. Studies show minors who choose not to discuss their abortion decision with their parents/guardians cite one or more of the following reasons for not confiding: fear of rejection, fear of disappointing their parents/guardians, fear of violence at home, fear of being forced to leave home, wanting to spare their parents/guardians from the problem, wanting to handle it on their own and/or fear their parents/guardians will force them to have an abortion (Hasselbacher et. al., 2014)). In cases where such fears are legitimate, parental notification policies stand to cause physical and psychological harm to girls who are already highly vulnerable.

In a March 2017 survey of 749 ASCA members, school counselors were divided about whether or not they think students accurately predict their parents' reaction to their pregnancy.

In your experience, do your students accurately predict their parent/guardians' reaction to their pregnancy?

Yes *52.7%*

No *47.3%*

(Stone, 2017e)

In this same survey, the majority of school counselors who have worked with pregnant students responded they work diligently to get the student to involve her parents.

Respondents indicated the statement that most closely matched their practice.
I do not inform her parents, but I always work diligently to get her to inform her parent/guardians *48.4%*
I will sometimes make the decision to inform her parent/guardians if she does not *21.9%*
I let the student take the lead as to whether she wants her parents to know *11.4%*
I never inform parents about a student's pregnancy (under any circumstances) *2%*
I have never worked with a student regarding pregnancy *16.3%*
(Stone, 2017e)

A district policy eliminates school counselors' capacity to help students weigh the facts, grapple with the issues and determine when, how or whether to involve parents/guardians. A one-size-fits-all policy reduces the school counselor's role to a trigger to be pulled regardless of circumstances and is not in keeping with the intent, nature and function of school counseling. School counselors avoid quick, easy answers in the form of policies but rather rise to the challenge of supporting students and wrestle around the issues in context of students' personal circumstances, fears, developmental levels and parents'/guardians' rights.

In 2002, New York's Port Washington School District enacted a written policy requiring educators to inform parents/guardians of a student's pregnancy. In 2005, the district's teachers association failed in court to get an injunction to stop the implementation of the policy (*Port Washington Teachers' Association v. Board of Education of the Port Washington Union Free School District* (2005)). It was hoped that the messiness of the Port Washington court case would dissuade other districts from policy making around pregnancy and minors' confidentiality rights. The courts ruled in favor of the district but not without serious concerns about how the policy affects federal law. Unfortunately, districts do not seem deterred; similar policies continue to surface in other districts.

On the surface, parental notification policies might appear as a reasonable approach to protecting minors, their parents/guardians and unborn children. In practice, however, such policies are too drastic as they completely eliminate the discretion needed for caring educators to work in context on behalf of individual students. Notification policies treat each student the same whether she is a competent, mature 17-year-old or a developmentally delayed 14-year-old.

A districtwide notification policy is likely meant to protect the district from angry parents/guardians should they threaten to flex their legal muscles when not informed about their child's pregnancy. Other proponents of such a policy hold the view that parental notification requirements will result in parents/guardians persuading their children to carry their baby to term when studies show the opposite appears to be true (Blum, Resnick & Stark, 1990; Prober, 2005). One-fifth of minors whose pregnancy was revealed by a third party were forced by their parents/guardians to have an abortion, and more than 90% of the parents/guardians expressed the stance that an abortion is in their minor child's best interest (Henshaw & Kost, 1992; Prober, 2005). Minors whose pregnancy was revealed by a third party were more likely to report physical violence between them and their parents/guardians or concerns there might be such violence (Henshaw & Kost, 1992).

Whatever the motivation for such policies, legal opponents view them as a violation of students' federal and state rights and explain they work against the public interest by deterring students from using school-based medical and mental health care providers for confidential counseling and information (Prober, 2005). When school policies protect students' confidentiality, they encourage students to voluntarily involve surrogate parents/guardians or trusted adults in the school in their abortion decision. Blanket notification policies scare students away from taking advantage of school-based resources (Prober, 2005).

In the Port Washington case, the court examined whether the policy was constitutional in light of the fact that in New York a minor has a right to an abortion without parental involvement. The court drew a distinction "between notification of pregnancy and consent or notification for abortion." It reasoned such parental notification "does not intrude on the student's right to ultimately seek an abortion or to carry her fetus to term" (*Port Washington Teachers' Association v. Board of Education of the Port Washington Union Free School District* (2005)). With consideration of judicial bypass, the argument becomes even stronger. Judicial bypass is a process in which minors can get state approval to have an abortion without parental involvement in states requiring parental involvement. School notification policies render the intent of judicial bypass ineffective as it takes away the minor's option to keep parents/guardians from knowing about her pregnancy. All states that have parental consent or parental notification requirements for abortions must allow for a minor to have access to judicial bypass, following the Supreme Court case *Bellotti v. Baird* (1979). "Minors must be afforded the opportunity to go before a neutral, detached decision-maker to seek an abortion free from any sort of parental involvement. Thus, policies that require parental notification of a student's pregnancy, yet do not provide the student with the required judicial bypass procedure, effectuate an unconstitutional regime because they take away the ability of the student to seek an abortion without the involvement of a third party" (Prober, 2005, p. 4).

What does *Belotti v. Baird* have to do with school counselors' daily lives? It strengthens school counselors' argument that not only do they have an ethical imperative to negotiate the difficult task of supporting pregnant students but also the legal imperative to support students' constitutionally protected rights. It would hold to reason that policies involving minors' reproductive health are made in consultation with the district's legal department. Ethical standards carry clout in court, and school district attorneys understand this. However, school board attorneys are rightfully more concerned with ensuring the district's policies safeguard students' constitutionally protected rights. When school counselors need to advocate against district policies requiring an automatic parental notification, they should speak not only in terms of their ethical imperative but also of the constitutionality of parental notification. Ask the district to carefully weigh the possibility that a challenge to the policy might cause the next big court case.

School counselors do what they have always done: encourage and support students to involve their parents/guardians but with the freedom to use their judgment when it is time to let mature minors make their own decisions. School counselors function best when given the freedom to exercise their responsibility to negotiate the rights and privileges of students and parents/guardians about disclosing information regarding pregnancy. Difficult counseling decisions involving value-laden issues must always be made against the backdrop of parental rights and the trusting relationship and not quick-and-easy policies eliminating all judgment. It would be far easier for the school counselor to have a policy, but resist such, as it takes away the wonderful, messy, confusing, troublesome job of helping a student move toward independence and autonomy by wrestling with the nuances of what is best for each student on each day given the context of that student's life. School counselors choose this messy role not because it is easy but because it makes a difference in children's lives, even those children carrying children.

It is still the exception and not the norm for school districts to establish policies requiring school counselors to inform parents/guardians of a student's pregnancy, and the majority of school counselor respondents in a 2017 survey do not think it is a good idea for district to implement policies dictating they must call parents.

In a survey of 749 ASCA members (Stone, 2017e), respondents were asked if their school or school district has a policy requiring school counselors who learn of a student's pregnancy to inform the student's parent(s)/guardian.

Yes, the district has a written policy 6.5%
No, there is no policy 81.9%
It is not a written policy, but it is verbally conveyed that the expectation is to inform parents.................................... 11.6%

Does the policy allow for exceptions in which not all situations require a parental or guardian notification of pregnancy?
Yes 8.4%
No.................................... 10.3%
Not applicable/no policy.................................... 81.4%

In your opinion, should all school districts have policies requiring school counselors to call parents/guardians if a student reports being pregnant?
Yes 27.7%
No.................................... 72.3%
(Stone, 2017e)

State statutes and confidentiality for pregnant students can also be ambiguous. California gives an excellent example of how an attorney general can bring clarity to a state statute. School counselors were especially concerned about Education Code section 49602(c), a confidentiality statute for students in schools, and then-California attorney general Kamala Harris gave an interpretation on Dec. 29, 2011, in answer to the following questions: Under Education Code section 49602(c), is a school counselor required to disclose pregnancy-related or abortion-related personal information received from an unemancipated student ages 12 or older to the student's parents or school principal when the school counselor has reasonable cause to believe disclosure is necessary to avert a clear and present danger to the student's health, safety or welfare? And, to the extent that the statute allows disclosure of a student's pregnancy-related or abortion-related information to be made under any circumstances, is it invalid on its face as violating the student's constitutional right to privacy?

Harris rendered an opinion on Dec. 29, 2011: "Education Code section 49602(c) permits, but does not by its terms require, a school counselor to disclose personal information (including pregnancy-related or abortion-related information) received from an unemancipated student ages 12 or older to the student's parents or school principal when the counselor has reasonable cause to believe that disclosure is necessary to avert a clear and present danger to the student's health, safety or welfare. The statute does not, on its face, violate a student's constitutional right of privacy." Your state school counselor association can ask your state's attorney general for interpretation of any ambiguous statutes affecting your work.

PREGNANT STUDENTS AND ADMINISTRATORS' REQUEST FOR INFORMATION

Your assistant principal comes to you and asks you for a list of all students in the school that you know are pregnant. He explains he wants to notify these students about an alternative school for pregnant and parenting teens and encourage them to go there. Do you have any concerns about this request? Must you comply with this request?

Points to Consider

In a 2002 California court case, *Holt v. Bellflower Unified School District*, school counselor Mary Beth Holt filed suit against the district for wrongful termination. The school's vice principal ordered Holt to disclose the names of students who were pregnant so they could be transferred to another school specifically designed to handle pregnant students' circumstances. Holt explained the information was confidential, having been disclosed during private counseling sessions and protected under California statute for school counselors and confidentiality. Holt contacted the state department of education about the situation. The district then informed her that her employment would not be continued the following year. She was told there was "no cause" for her firing.

Holt sued the school district, the principal, the vice principal and each member of the Bellflower Board of Education. The case was initially dismissed. On appeal, it was ruled Holt could proceed with her complaint in the lower court. The results of the lower court's decision are not published and may have been settled.

Holt's willingness to put her students above the system is admirable. However, once an educator takes employment in a system designed for academic instruction there needs to be a recognition that the rules are more complicated than in a system designed exclusively for counseling. The best approach is to avoid a power struggle with your administration. Perhaps, tell your principal you will consult with the students and seek their permission to be included on a list to administration. There are a number of other techniques to get the job done, protect confidentiality and avoid going to war with administrators. The bottom line is that confidentiality is much harder to respect with the competing interests in a school setting. The case took place in California, one of the states where it is easiest to keep confidentiality. Digging in your heels with administrators is one of those no-win situations. School counselors need to balance promoting respect for students' autonomy while also showing administrators they are listening to administration's requests. Holt sounds like a student-centered school counselor, and it is always unfortunate to lose good people because a compromise could not be found.

ABORTION COUNSELING AND THE COURTS

Regina is 16 and pregnant. She comes to you seeking help as she considers getting an abortion. Regina tells you she really needs to explore her options with an adult who is "outside of her family." Can you discuss with Regina her pregnancy and her options, including abortion? Does this scenario automatically trigger for you the need to inform Regina's parents/guardians about her pregnancy?

Points to Consider

Respecting students' confidences requires school counselors to balance the rights of minors with the rights of their parents/guardians (Isaacs & Stone, 2001; Kaplan, 1996). ASCA Ethical Standards for School Counselors (ASCA, 2022b) offers suggestions and guidance in the complexities of confidentiality. However, it is ultimately the school counselor's responsibility to determine the appropriate response for individual students who put their trust in the security of the counseling relationship. School counselors need to be advocates and a source of strength for the individual students who come to them for help in confronting and navigating areas such as sexual activity and pregnancy.

To avoid ambiguity when counseling students and to delineate the limits of your pledge to preserve confidentiality, you must give informed consent to students, letting them know when you believe they are in danger you may need to contact their parents. You should also inform students of any district policies requiring you to contact their parents, whether or not you feel they are in danger. You have a strong ethical responsibility to Regina at a time when she may be most vulnerable.

Your choice of words, body language and tone carry enormous weight as Regina decides what to do about her pregnancy. If possible, encourage Regina to confide in her parents or a close relative, explaining that discussing her problem with loved ones can benefit her. Assist Regina in exploring her options without imposing your own views or giving her advice. Generally speaking, it is best practice to let her suggest possible courses of action and the good and bad consequences of each. If you supply her options, you may inadvertently be blessing a choice that until now she had considered completely out of the question, such as abortion. Maybe abortion is not one of her considerations because of religious values or family pressure, and you just planted the idea that it should be a viable option for her.

A school counselor who is vehemently opposed to abortion could not work ethically with a minor in the throes of an abortion decision. The ethical and responsible course of action would be to refer Regina to another school counselor if at all possible. Sometimes an outside agency or a school nurse will be a good choice to help her with the medical questions she may have.

Although school counselors may not voice their opposition to abortion, values may be revealed in voice tone, a raised eyebrow, a heavy sigh or a diverted glance. Such nonverbal cues can inadvertently impose a school counselor's values on a vulnerable student. The influence a school counselor can have on a pregnant minor cannot be understated. The compounding factors of the school counselor's authority over the student, the student's inexperience or lack of awareness of her rights, the student's lack of confidence in her own beliefs and the emotions she may be experiencing related to the pregnancy can result in a heightened state of vulnerability for the student.

Students who do not want their parents/guardians to know about their pregnancy frequently have substantial fears of abuse. This same population demonstrates a strong overlap with students who were victims of incest, in which case notifying parents/guardians might mean notifying their rapist or rapist's partner or relative (Prober, 2005).

Under what circumstances could a school counselor be held liable for giving abortion advice? In *Arnold v. Board of Education of Escambia County* (1989), Jane and John, two high school students, filed suit along with their parents/guardians against the School District of Escambia County, Ala., alleging the school counselor, Kay Rose, and the assistant principal, Melvin Powell, coerced and assisted Jane in getting an abortion. Further, they accused Powell of paying someone $20 to drive Jane to the abortion clinic and Powell and Rose of hiring Jane and John to perform menial tasks to earn money for the abortion. John, the baby's father, and Jane claimed their constitutional rights were violated, including involuntary servitude and free exercise of religion. Their parents/guardians claimed their privacy rights were violated when the school counselor and assistant principal did not inform them Jane was pregnant and when school officials urged the students not to tell their parents/guardians. The trial court dismissed the suit and plaintiffs appealed (*Arnold v. Board of Education of Escambia County* (1989); Zirkel, 2001b).

The U.S. 11th Circuit Court of Appeals partially reversed the trial court's decision and found Jane's privacy claim and both students' religious claim as worthy of further consideration by the courts. In other words, if Jane and John's religion prohibited abortion and Rose and Powell coerced Jane and John to proceed with Jane's abortion, then their constitutionally protected right of freedom of religion might have been violated. Further, Jane's constitutionally protected right to choose to carry or abort a pregnancy had been violated if she was coerced into having an abortion. Jane's parents/guardians claimed their privacy rights were violated when the school counselor and assistant principal coerced Jane into having an abortion and urged her and John to refrain from discussing her options with a parent. The case was remanded back to the lower court for a trial to take place (Zirkel, 2001b).

In fact-finding, the trial court found Jane visited a physician who confirmed she was pregnant and provided her with abortion information upon her request. John and Jane told Rose they did not want their parents/guardians to know about the pregnancy as they were not supposed to be seeing each other, and Jane left home because she was being abused by her stepfather. Rose presented various alternatives, but the students rejected all alternatives except abortion. Rose repeatedly urged Jane and John to consult with their parents/guardians. Rose reported the alleged abuse by the stepfather to the Department of Children's

Services Resources, which sent a representative to meet with Jane. The representative urged Jane to consult with her mother and offered alternatives such as foster care and adoption. When Jane rejected all alternatives, the representative assisted Jane in trying to obtain financial assistance and Medicaid. Jane and John said they felt pressured to have an abortion by Rose when she asked them how they planned to care for the baby and where they were going to take the baby. During the process of discovery, Jane admitted Rose's questions were valid. She conceded that she alone made the decision to have an abortion and that she was not coerced by Rose or Powell. John admitted he had chosen not to tell his mother. The trial court concluded the students were not deprived of their free will, had chosen to obtain an abortion without telling their parents/guardians and that there was no coercion on the part of school officials (*Arnold v. Board of Education of Escambia County* (1989); Zirkel, 2001b). School counselors must be prepared to argue they behaved as the reasonably competent professional would have. Coercion and imposing one's values on a minor student would not be appropriate actions of a competent school counselor (Stone, 2004a).

After the Arnold ruling, the question remains: Can school counselors be held liable for giving abortion advice to pregnant minors? School counselors may assist students with value-laden issues such as abortion if they are competent to give such advice and if they proceed in a professional manner. School counselors must consider their responsibilities extend beyond the student to parents/guardians and take great care in abortion counseling. Fischer and Sorenson (1996) stated: "If an immature, emotionally fragile young girl procures an abortion with the help of a school counselor, under circumstances where reasonably competent school counselors would have notified the parents/guardians or would have advised against the abortion, liability for psychological or physical suffering may follow.

The specific facts and circumstances must always be considered" (p. 60).
Are school counselors providing students with information about acquiring an abortion? The results of a March 2017 survey revealed that 23.4% of the respondents said they do give information to students on abortion.

Which best describes your practice? If a student seeks your help to obtain information about acquiring an abortion:
I support, listen, but I do not provide them with information 39.1%
I support, listen and give accurate information about how to obtain an abortion 23.4%
I do not listen 0.3%
None of the above 29%
(Stone, 2017e)

Consider if Jane had been 13-years-old. Would the school counselor in the Arnold case have responded differently? Stadler's (1990) test of universality is a good gauge because the test asks professionals to consider the advice they would give to a colleague in the throes of a similar ethical dilemma. If school counselors would advise a colleague to take a different path, then this is a sign they should further examine their proposed actions. Perhaps the school counselor is planning action that is too conservative, too risky or outside the bounds of what the reasonably competent professional would do.

JUDICIAL BYPASS INFORMATION AND THE NEUTRAL STANCE

One of your students, Jenny, and her boyfriend come to you and tell you she is pregnant and they fear for their safety if her parents were to find out. Jenny has heard that in your state medical personnel are required to notify parents before performing an abortion on a minor. Jenny doesn't know about judicial bypass. Would you tell her about the judicial bypass option? What if you, personally, don't approve of abortions? Would you tell her about judicial bypass then?

Points to Consider

Judicial bypass is a process in which minors can get state approval to have an abortion without parental involvement. Of the 38 states requiring parental involvement in a minor's abortion all but Maryland have an alternative process known as judicial bypass in which a judge can approve a minor's abortion bypassing parental involvement. Seven states (Arizona, Arkansas, Florida, Kansas, Kentucky, Ohio, and Texas) require judges to use specific criteria, such as a minor's intelligence or emotional stability, for deciding whether to waive parental involvement. Fifteen states require judges to use the "clear and convincing evidence" standard to determine whether the minor is mature and the abortion is in their best interest when deciding whether to waive parental involvement. Generally speaking, minors seeking judicial bypass must demonstrate maturity, an understanding of the health risks, a consideration for alternatives and an awareness of the psychological and emotional consequences that may occur as a result of the abortion (Guttmacher, 2022).

In a survey (Stone, 2017e), school counselors were asked the following:

If your state requires parental involvement in a minor's abortion, would you tell a student she can avoid involving her parents with a judicial bypass?
Yes 32.7%
No. 67.3%
(Stone, 2017e)

Can a school counselor explain judicial bypass and maintain a neutral stance in a value-laden decision such as abortion? In April 2016, a high school counselor in New Hampshire, which requires parental notification for an abortion, was reinstated in her job by the New Hampshire Supreme Court (*McKaig v. Farmington*, 2016). The school counselor's legal team successfully argued that the nonrenewal of the school counselor's contract was retaliation because the school counselor obtained a restraining order on the student's behalf to prevent the principal from telling the girl's mother her daughter was pregnant. Additionally, the school counselor informed the student about how to avoid the state's parental notification law by getting a judicial bypass. The ACLU said the school counselor was "courageous" for helping the student, but the district's superintendent disagreed, believing the family should be involved because of the state's parental notification law. "On April 7, 2016, the New Hampshire Supreme Court sided with McKaig and the ACLU-NH, holding that the Farmington School Board's decision to not renew McKaig's employment was inappropriate" (ACLU, 2016, p.1).

Working with pregnant students can lead to tense moments regarding the trusting relationship, student confidentiality and the need to respect parents'/guardians' legal rights to guide their children in value-laden issues. Additionally, school counselors are negotiating the issue through the lens of community standards, school board policies and the school counselor's own personal values. Difficult decisions involving value-laden issues must always be made against the backdrop of all of these elements and most especially with regard to parental rights. School counselors want parents/guardians to be involved but understand this isn't always possible in such a complex situation.

The courts continually vest parents/guardians with legal rights to guide their children in value-laden issues. In *H.L. v. Matheson* (1981), the U.S. Supreme Court said, "Constitutional interpretation has consistently recognized that the parents'/guardians' claim to authority in their own household to direct the rearing of their children is basic in the structure of our society" emphasizing three reasons:

- The peculiar vulnerability of minors to make life-altering decisions
- A minor's inability to make informed decisions
- Parents rights to be the guiding voice in their child's life especially in value-laden issues (n.p.).

The school counselor in the *McKaig v. Farmington* case had to determine whether she would be putting the student in jeopardy of abuse/neglect if she breached confidentiality. Parental involvement can be supportive and beneficial; however, it can also be punitive, coercive or abusive. School counselors have the complicated task of figuring out if and when they can safely involve a pregnant student's parents if a student expresses fear of potential abuse. School counselors have a huge responsibility to protect students, especially when it comes to a student's health or safety, and if child abuse/neglect is suspected, they are mandated to report it.

The goal is always to have students involve their parents, but sometimes we have to recognize our main goal cannot be achieved for all. When students tell the school counselor they're afraid for their physical and/or emotional safety, the school counselor must work with the student to try and find out why the student is expressing fear of potential abuse.

We are our values; we cannot leave them at the schoolhouse door. Abortion is a value-laden issue. The school counseling position is not a platform to forward values or beliefs rooted in one's religion. School counselors strive to stay within the neutral zone of abortion, supporting pregnant students while skillfully checking to ensure they are not edging the student toward one decision over another. Are school counselors moving too far out of the neutral box if they help a student obtain a restraining order against the principal to prevent the principal from informing parents about a student's pregnancy? Are school counselors in or out of the neutral zone when they provide a student with judicial bypass information?

Breaching confidentiality requires school counselors to try and find the least-intrusive way to breach confidentiality that supports the student's developmental and chronological levels. It can be difficult to make judgments about the student's problem-solving ability and the likelihood a student will have family support. The continuum of breach may simply be a role play to help the student figure out what to say to her parents, or it may move down the continuum of breach to a more intrusive, yet supportive, way to breach such as offering to facilitate the conversation with parents. Providing neutral resources can help pregnant students obtain the information they need without having to provide it yourself.

School counselors' work is influenced by community standards as well as school board policy, local and state laws. For example, although many school districts in the United States have abstinence-only sex education that forbids teaching of contraceptives, some public high schools in New York are able to provide contraceptives to female students. State laws on contraceptive services and abortions, while not directly dictating how school counselors will behave, certainly influence their approach. School counselors who are in a state that allows minors to make medical decisions about their reproductive life will find their work with minors different than in a state or community that believes parents/guardians should decide if a child takes birth control or has an abortion. The school counselor's best defense is often to seek supervision and consultation with other professionals who are in a position to understand the context-specific world in which a school counselor operates.

Students today are being confronted with adult situations earlier in life, requiring school counselors to deal with more value-laden issues such as pregnancy. School counselors need to have the space and latitude to work with students on these issues while constantly reminding themselves to remain as neutral as the circumstances will allow. A student might have a valid reason preventing her from involving her parents/guardians.

With student abortion, the school counselor is facing the ethical dilemma of confidentiality for which there are few definitive answers. It is ultimately the school counselor's responsibility to negotiate the rights and privileges of students and parents/guardians with regard to disclosing information. Parent responses to abortion can be varied and diffused, complicating our work. It is the unpredictability of parental reaction that makes it impossible to develop a hard and fast rule on school counselor behavior in parental notification of student pregnancy. The U.S. courts and laws give legal latitude to parents/guardians regarding their children's care and upbringing. The legal and ethical ramifications of this concept take on greater importance in those situations in which school counselors have to weigh minors' privacy rights with parents/guardians' Supreme Court-given right to be the pre-eminent voice in their children's lives in value-laden issues.

HELPING A STUDENT GET AN ABORTION

One of your counselees is pregnant, distraught and unwilling to involve her parents. She turns to you for help. You believe your relationship is such that you can support the student to acquire the abortion she desperately wants. You have worked with this student to help her realize her dreams of a college education, and now she is uncertain if she can take the scholarship and go forward. You give her all the information she needs to have this procedure in a neighboring state, as your state requires parental consent. Have you done the right thing?

Points to Consider

A couple in the Hatboro-Horsham School District in Pennsylvania sued their daughter's high school counselor after their daughter revealed her school counselor advised her to obtain an abortion, a violation of Pennsylvania state law (Sanchez, 2000). The school counselor allegedly advised the student to get the abortion, helped to excuse her from school for the procedure, cashed the checks written by her boyfriend for the abortion and created a map to an abortion clinic in the neighboring state of New Jersey. Pennsylvania state law requires the consent of a parent or guardian before a minor can undergo an abortion procedure; New Jersey does not. The parents' suit centered on their right to be the guiding force in matters of family life and the upbringing of their children (U.S. Const., amend. XIV). The Hatboro-Horsham School District was named as a co-defendant in the suit, and the parents/guardians sought to prevent the school district from counseling students about abortion or helping students obtain medical procedures or information without parental consent.

In a similar case, *Gordon v. Hunterdon Educational Service Commission* (2006), the school counselor was accused of coercing a student into having an abortion after her parents came to the school and discussed with the administration how their child had decided to carry her child to term. The school counselor was also accused of providing the pregnant teen with money for an abortion and driving her to an abortion clinic in New Jersey. The school counselor was fired, and the parents sued the district, citing a violation of the teen's constitutionally protected right to privacy, her First, Fifth and 14th Amendment rights to raise a child without state interference, and the permanent damage to her and her family. The case settled out of court.

PERSONAL PRIVACY RIGHTS

A school counselor hears a rumor that a certain student is pregnant. The school counselor calls the student in and asks her to confirm or deny the rumors. The student said she was unsure but thought she might be pregnant. The school counselor provided a pregnancy test and strongly urged the student to take it in the staff restroom, which the student did. Is this school counselor's behavior problematic?

Points to Consider

Discretion and judgment are vital to school counselors' daily lives, and if a school counselor gives a pregnancy test to a student, then the school counselor failed to use either. In the actual court case, *Gruenke v. Seip* (2000), the culprit was a coach who suspected one of his swim team members was pregnant and required her to take a pregnancy test while at practice.

This teacher abused his power and intruded on the student's privacy in a way that violated her Fourth Amendment rights (unreasonable search and seizure) and her familial and personal privacy rights (*Gruenke v. Seip* (2000)). It would have been even worse had the actual intrusion been at the hands of a school counselor, which has happened because school counselors are held to a higher standard of care. This school counselor in this fictional case needed better instincts to steer her away from doing something that is truly violating the standard of care for the profession.

In *Villanueva v. San Marcos CISD*, a school nurse in San Marcos, Texas, administered a pregnancy test, and the question was whether or not it would be reasonable to assume that a student in that situation would likely feel that she had no choice but to submit and would be a case of illegal search and seizure a violation of the Fourth Amendment. The court found that the nurse's behavior was reasonable and that the student was not coerced into submitting to the test (*Villanueva v. San Marcos CISD*, unpublished and unreported, 5th Cir. 2007). Intent and reasonableness matter. It probably made a difference also that in the Villanueva case the defendant was a nurse attending to a medical issues, unlike Gruenke in which the defendant was a coach.

PREGNANCY AND TITLE IX

Your administration asked you to convince Erika, a pregnant student, to attend the alternative school for pregnant and parenting students. You have a relationship with Erika, and you have been helping her stay on track, as she is often absent due to her morning sickness. One teacher in particular is condemning her absences and refusing to give make-up work. Erika has expressed a desire to stay in her current school. Does Erika have protection under Title IX?

Points to Consider

Title IX affords students protection from discrimination based on their "actual or potential parental, family or marital status" and based on a student's "pregnancy, childbirth, false pregnancy, termination of pregnancy or recovery there from." All public schools and private schools must comply with Title IX if they receive even $1 of federal funds. School officials must treat pregnant and parenting students as they would treat all able or disabled students and "provide equal access to school for pregnant and parenting students and treat pregnancy and all related conditions like any other temporary disability."

School officials:

- Cannot require a doctor's note for pregnant students to participate in activities unless the school requires a doctor's note from all students who have conditions requiring medical care.
- Must excuse absences due to pregnancy or childbirth for as long as the student's doctor deems medically necessary and provide make-up work or opportunities for catching up.
- Must reinstate students to the status held when the leave began.
- Must ensure that any separate programs or schools for pregnant and parenting students are voluntary and offer opportunities equal to those offered for non-pregnant students.
- Must avoid encouraging students to attend inferior programs.
- Must provide access to homebound instruction if medically necessary (National Women's Law Center, 2017).

It is in the best interest of Erika, her child and the community if Erika is supported and encouraged to finish high school. As Erika's school counselor and advocate, empower her to make her decisions based on her and her child's future needs and not a decision based on efficiency or convenience for the school. It is unethical to use our influence to persuade students to abandon their home school if this is not what they want to do.

The USDOE OCR (2013) wrote a publication and included school counselors as key in preventing pregnant and parenting students from dropping out. They made the following recommendations:

School counselors:

- Recognize that pregnant and parenting students are more likely to drop out of school than are other students. Advise them of the importance of staying in school. Let them know of any school assistance that may be available to them for this purpose.
- Work with pregnant and parenting students individually and come up with a graduation plan tailored to each student's needs. This plan may include an academic credit-recovery component for pregnant and parenting students who have fallen behind.
- Contact pregnant and parenting students who have dropped out of school to see if you can offer them advice and encouragement to return.
- Whenever possible, conduct follow-up counseling with pregnant and parenting students after they drop out of school, providing them information about programs, services and support that will help them return to school.
- Encourage the establishment of school policies and programs for pregnant and parenting students, particularly those at high risk of dropping out of school. Take a leadership role in determining what policies and programs can address students' various needs.
- Set up support groups to help pregnant and parenting students stay in school.
- Advise librarians, teachers, and pregnant and parenting students of books and materials that may be useful for keeping their education on track.
- Advise pregnant and parenting students of the availability of programs and services to help them stay in school and maintain their educational progress.
- Provide parents with information regarding the availability of programs and services that help all students stay in school and maintain their educational progress regardless of pregnancy or parenthood (n.p.).

EDUCATORS AND STUDENTS: NEVER CONSENSUAL SEX

Your school district is being sued by a student whose math teacher sexually abused her. The district is trying to establish that this was not abuse but consensual sex. Is this a viable defense?

As already discussed in the sexual harassment chapter and the negligence chapter, consensual sex between a student and a teacher is not recognized as a student cannot consent to sex with someone in a position of authority such as a teacher. The Los Angeles Unified School District (LAUSD) came under fire when it allowed its attorneys to argue that a 14-year-old student was mature enough to consent to sex with her middle school math teacher. District officials defended their legal strategy, saying they needed to rebut the student's claim with evidence that she was a willing participant who had a prior history of sexual activity. Many legal experts question the actions, saying it is impossible for a middle school student to consent to sex with adults, especially with teachers and others who have authority over them and can easily manipulate them. Legal experts decry the use of a 14-year-old's sexual history as evidence and explain it should not have been permitted and would not have been allowed in most courtrooms. A jury found LAUSD not liable for damages. However, there was an outcry for the school district to fire the attorney who argued a 14-year-old could consent to sex with a teacher (Watanabe, 2014). There are far-too-many cases that could have been the subject of this scenario. Too many school counselors have committed the grievous harm of taking advantage of their position of trust with students and sexually abusing them.

PREGNANT STUDENTS AND DISCRIMINATION BY ADMINISTRATION

Two students in your school are being denied induction into the National Honor Society based on what administration describes as their "lack of character" because both students are unmarried and pregnant. Are there legal implications for the administration's decision?

In *Chipman v. Grant County School District* (2014), Somer Chipman and Chasity Glass were denied membership into the Grant County High School Chapter of the National Honor Society (NHS). Both students exceeded the minimum requirements for NHS induction. These two students were the only students denied membership, and the reason was based on their character. Both students had a baby in their junior year. The NHS Committee decided premarital sex reflected on their character, and therefore, they were denied admission. No other students were asked about their sexuality when applying for membership, and no males were asked if they had fathered any children. The ACLU, on behalf of these students and their parents, sued Grant County School District for violating Title IX of the Education Amendments of 1972. The court decided the students were members of a protected group and the policy had an adverse impact on them. The court ordered the students to be admitted into the Grant County High School's NHS chapter.

SAFE-HAVEN LAWS

To protect newborns, most states have passed laws allowing birth mothers to leave their newborns at hospitals, fire stations, police stations and other select safe havens for abandoned babies, relinquishing any legal rights to the child. You want to include this law with other important laws you tell students about, but you are not sure if you should. You wonder if you are sending the wrong message.

Points to Consider

Each state has some form of safe-haven laws to prevent abandonment of newborns. These laws, sometimes called "Baby Moses laws," allow the birth mother or agents designated by the birth mother to leave an infant in designated "safe places" (such as hospitals, churches, police or fire stations) anonymously, mostly with no questions asked and mostly with no legal repercussions (Child Welfare Information Gateway, 2010). More information on state-specific state laws is available at the National Safe Haven Alliance website (*https://www.nationalsafehavenalliance.org/safe-haven-locations*). That alliance also operates a confidential toll-free crisis hotline, (888) 510-BABY.

Research, delicate diplomacy and probably a collection of compromises could help school counselors inform their students about this law. A school district advocating an abstinence-based curriculum makes thorough sex education a battle; the issue has ignited arguments between community groups as well as the international scientific and religious communities. Even when limited by district policy it is the school counselor's responsibility to work with administration and the community to develop programs in students' best interest (ASCA, 2022b). Gather information from local and national organizations, such as the Guttmacher Institute, Planned Parenthood, the Centers for Disease Control and Prevention and the National Women's Law Center, that provide statistics concerning teenage pregnancy and the practice of abandoning unwanted children in your area. Maybe you can invite a local nurse, emergency medical technician or firefighter to share a success story in which a child was saved because of the safe-haven law.

The goal of such laws is not to encourage teenage pregnancy or irresponsibility but to protect the life of a newborn in the event of a mistake. Perhaps public-service posters detailing the safe-haven law would be an appropriate way to inform students. A think tank composed of health care workers, district officials, educators, parents/guardians and school counselors could put your mind at ease that this is proactive and not encouraging irresponsible behavior.

In a Position to Know: A School Counselor Educator Speaks

DEVELOPMENTALLY DELAYED, PREGNANT STUDENTS

Sharon is slightly developmentally delayed. Chronologically, Sharon is 14, but developmentally she is more like an 11- or 12-year-old. Sharon is pregnant, and her mother is aware of the pregnancy. Sharon has long been a concern of many in the school. She is unkempt and explosive at times. Her developmental problems mean she is always out of sync with her age group. Her peers avoid her because they are afraid of her. Sharon seems incapable of taking care of herself, and you fear for the welfare of her child. She tells everyone that having this baby will bring the father of the baby back to her. She says her mother plans to help her raise the baby. Do you have any role in this case?

Legal, ethical and clinical issues related to teenage pregnancy are problematic for school counselors. Sharon's case is particularly challenging because of her chronological age compounded by her developmental delay. Furthermore, a school counselor would be likely to have concerns about how Sharon's violent tendencies may create an unsafe environment for the baby and how Sharon will care for a baby if she seems incapable of caring for herself.

Staying mindful of the evidence that a baby in the care of this student may be in danger, it is still important to explore one's own values related to teen pregnancy. It is often difficult to separate one's values from the clinical, legal and ethical issues involved in these cases. However, the ASCA Ethical Standards for School Counselors (2022b) state school counselors "respect students' and families' values, beliefs and cultural background, as well as students' sexual orientation, gender identity and gender expression, and exercise great care to avoid imposing personal biases, beliefs or values rooted in one's religion, culture or ethnicity" (A.1.h). The standards clarify that a school counselor's primary obligation is to the student and that each student is to be treated with respect (A.1.a). Thus, even though a school counselor may be concerned about Sharon being responsible for a baby, the school counselor has an ethical duty to address the issues presented by the student's pregnancy and act in the student's best interest without making value judgments.

The fact that Sharon's mother knows about the pregnancy and is willing to help raise the child eliminates the dilemma of whether or not to breach confidentiality and tell a parent about the student's pregnancy. Thus, in this situation, respecting a student's ethical right to privacy while balancing parents'/guardians' legal rights is probably not as challenging of an issue. Yet Sharon's mother's rights still need to be considered.

In Sharon's case, discussing the pregnancy, the reality of raising a child and options with Sharon and her mother may be an appropriate course of action. As previously indicated, such an intervention should be approached with care and consideration of the values of the student and her mother.

If the school counselor decides to meet with Sharon and her mother, the school counselor may want to express concerns about Sharon's view of parenthood. Sharon has little idea of what caring for a baby really involves. Furthermore, her idea that the pregnancy will bring the baby's father back to her is a common belief among pregnant teenagers that usually is not based in reality.

Several other issues could be addressed in a conversation with Sharon and her mother. A school counselor may want to explore if Sharon's unkempt appearance could be indicative of depression. Her lack of grooming could also be linked to an inability to take care of herself. Her violent tendencies could put the baby at risk. Sharon's age and developmental delay will make caring for a child difficult. Involving Sharon's mother may help Sharon and her mother make an informed decision about whether keeping the baby is in Sharon's and her baby's best interests. If Sharon and her mother decide Sharon should keep her baby, discussing these types of issues could help Sharon and her mother create a plan for caring for both Sharon and the baby.

Many schools are implementing groups for teenage parents/guardians; thus group counseling may be another option for students like Sharon. From an ethical standpoint, the school counselor is expected to screen each potential group member and ascertain whether the student would benefit from the group and be an appropriate fit for the group (ASCA, 2022b, A.7.c.). The school counselor would have to assess if Sharon's violent tendencies might be exhibited in a group session and pose a danger to other group members. The school counselor would also want to consider if Sharon's lack of peer support would have a negative impact on the group process. Yet, if the school counselor decides Sharon would be an appropriate group member, attending such a group could help Sharon become better aware of the realities of raising a child. Group settings also provide additional support from peers who are struggling with the harsh realities of teenage parenthood.

The school counselor's legal duty is to act as a reasonable school counselor would act under similar circumstances. Sharon's mother is aware of Sharon's pregnancy and has agreed to help take care of the child. However, school counselors need to remain cognizant of their legal duty to report suspected child abuse. Accordingly, a school counselor needs to determine if Sharon's unkempt appearance is indicative of abuse or neglect. Furthermore, if Sharon keeps her baby and the school counselor suspects the baby is being neglected or harmed, the school counselor would be legally required to report that suspected abuse as well.

Stone (2002) provided guidelines for school counselors who are counseling students in situations like Sharon's. Stone suggested school counselors look to school board policy for guidance, consider the student's developmental level when providing interventions and remain cognizant of parental rights and values. Stone also recommended consulting with a colleague or supervisor when faced with issues related to a student's pregnancy. Finally, Stone cautions school counselors to avoid involving themselves in a student's medical care.

Sharon's case presents yet another example of the legal, ethical and clinical complexities of working with minors in school settings. Attending workshops and other continuing-education opportunities on legal, ethical and clinical issues is vitally important in remaining competent, practicing in an ethical manner and minimizing legal liability. And, because school counselors face such challenging issues in a litigious society, school counselors are wise to maintain professional liability insurance.

– *Mary A. Hermann, J.D., Ph.D., associate professor, Virginia Commonwealth University*

Making Connections

1. Do you believe you have an obligation to tell parents/guardians that their child is pregnant if the child refuses to involve her parents/guardians?

2. Under what circumstances, if any, would you help a pregnant student get medical care of any kind?

3. How do your state statutes read regarding minors and abortion?

4. How do the standards of your state and community affect your behavior regarding pregnant students?

5. How do your state statutes read regarding age of consent? What are the implications of your state's age-of-consent laws for you as a school counselor?

Chapter 9 Quiz

1) Title IX provides supports for pregnant students to:
   a. Have their absences excused and make up work provided if it is medically necessary for them to be out of school
   b. Remain in their school if they so choose

c. Be given accommodations as any other student would be given who had a temporary disability
d. Receive homebound instruction if medically necessary
e. All of the above

2) *Arnold v. Board of Education of Escambia County* taught us:
a. School counselors should never agree to meet with a student who wants to discuss her pregnancy.
b. If a child's religion prohibits abortion and school counselors use their influence to convince the student to have an abortion, this could be a violation of freedom of religion.
c. School counselors have a right to exercise their religious freedom if a student's decision goes against the school counselor's religious beliefs.
d. School counselors must be ready to report pregnancy to administrators.
e. Because of parents' privacy rights, school counselors must always notify the parents if the school counselor knows of their child's pregnancy.

3) Title IX can be applied to all but which of the following:
a. Bullying
b. Pregnancy
c. Dating violence
d. Domestic violence
e. Sexual harassment

4) *Holt v. Bellflower Unified School District* informed us that:
a. Regardless of what the administration needs to know or wants to know about your private conversations you never breach confidentiality.
b. School counselors have to first quiz administrators about why they need to know information before breaching confidentiality.
c. School counselors politically astutely negotiate a request from an administrator for information without setting up a power struggle between the administration and the school counselor.
d. Pregnant students have a right to remain in their school and cannot be sent to an alternative school.
e. Administrators will most likely lose their job or be demoted if they require a school counselor to breach a student's confidentiality regarding pregnancy.

5) Fourth Amendment rights were applied in the *Gruenke v. Seip* case because:
a. An administrator illegally searched a student's cell phone when a school counselor reported the student was cyberbullying another student.
b. The school counselor illegally searched a student's backpack when the student reportedly had stolen the journal the school counselor and another student were sharing.
c. An educator required a student to take a pregnancy test.
d. A school counselor required a student to log on to her Facebook account to prove they were not cyberbullying.
e. A school counselor required a student go to the nurse to determine if she was pregnant.

Key Terms

Abortion
Age of consent
Contraceptives
Developmentally delayed
Judicial bypass
Safe-haven law
Sexually active students
Teenage pregnancy
Value-laden counseling

Objectives

By the time you have completed this chapter, you should be able to:

- Discuss your leadership and advocacy role in creating a safe and inclusive school environment for students who are lesbian, gay, bisexual, transgender and queer (or questioning) and others, hereafter referred to with the acronym LGBTQ+.
- Report the cost of dangerous school climates to LGBTQ+ students
- Discuss case law, statutes and federal guidelines that can influence a safe school climate for LGBTQ+ students
- Apply specific strategies for acting as a systemic change agent to improve school climates
- Identify the legal and ethical ramifications for school counselors and school districts that do not intervene on behalf of LGBTQ+ students who face harassment or bullying

Ethical Standards Addressed in This Chapter

Professionalism means knowing your professional association's standards and adhering to them. The ASCA Ethical Standards for School Counselors (2022b) most relevant to this chapter are the following:

School counselors:

- Foster and affirm all students and their identity and psychosocial development. (A.1.b).
- Respect students' and families' values, beliefs and cultural background, as well as students' sexual orientation, gender identity and gender expression, and exercise great care to avoid imposing personal biases, beliefs or values rooted in one's religion, culture or ethnicity. (A.1.h.)
- Refrain from referring students based solely on the school counselor's personal beliefs or values rooted in one's religion, culture, ethnicity or personal worldview. School counselors maintain the highest respect for student cultural identities and worldviews. School counselors pursue additional training and supervision when their values are discriminatory in nature (e.g., sexual orientation, gender identity, gender expression, reproductive rights, race, religion, ability status). School counselors do not impose their values on students and/or families when making referrals to outside resources for student and/or family support. (A.6.e).

- Recognize that bullying, discrimination, bias and hate incidents rooted in race, gender, sexual orientation and ethnicity are violations of federal law and many state and local laws and district policies. (A.11.a).
- Develop knowledge and understanding of historic and systemic oppression, social justice and cultural models (e.g., multicultural counseling, anti-racism, culturally sustaining practices) to further develop skills for systemic change and equitable outcomes for all students. (B.3.g.)

The full text of the ASCA Ethical Standards for School Counselors is available at *www.schoolcounselor.org*.

Introduction

School counselors are committed to facilitating and promoting the fullest possible development of each individual by reducing the barriers of misinformation, myth, harassment and discrimination based on sexual orientation, gender identity or gender expression (ASCA, 2022b). School counselors promote equal opportunity and respect for all individuals regardless of sexual orientation, gender identity or gender expression. School counselors recognize the school experience can be significantly more difficult for students with marginalized identities. School counselors work to eliminate barriers impeding LGBTQ+ youth, including lesbian, gay, bisexual, transgender, queer, nonbinary, two-spirit and intersex youth's development and achievement. Recognizing the unique responsibility of school counselors for students' social/emotional well-being, this chapter seeks to inform school counselors of the particular vulnerabilities of LGBTQ+ students and the legal muscle to advocate for these students when working with school administrators or on school policies. Research data related to academic achievement and case law discussed in this chapter seeks to inform and to strengthen the advocacy of school counselors working in environments where emotional language appealing may fall short.

School counselors acting as advocates know there are many ways to have an impact on school conditions for vulnerable students, but having a legal base to stand on considerably strengthens the effort. "School counselors are often students' first resource for addressing social/emotional issues, particularly regarding relationships and identity. For children and adolescents, exploring gender and sexual identity is difficult enough without the additional burden of restrictive school policies that tend to impede rather than support their growth," said Jill Cook, ASCA executive director. "Students cannot perform to their highest levels when the school environment creates barriers to learning. All students, regardless of race, ethnicity, religion, age, economic class, gender or sexual identity, deserve a safe and supportive school climate that fosters their academic achievement, social/emotional well-being, and college and career readiness" (personal communication, September 21, 2021).

During the past several years, there have been major shifts in terminology toward the LGBTQ+ community. The LGBTQ+ acronym is increasingly used to describe a community of people who identify as nonheterosexual and noncisgender. (Cisgender describes individuals whose gender self-perception matches the sex they were assigned at birth.) LGBTQ+ in this chapter is used to refer to all sexual and gender minority people, including those whose LGBTQ+ identities are not named in any one explanation of an acronym that is used as a shorthand for the community. This acronym has grown longer in recent years, to include young people who increasingly question binary descriptions of gender and sexuality. Variations on this acronym might include an "I" for "intersex," an umbrella term used to describe individuals born with variations in sex characteristics (InterAct, 2021). Queer used to be a derogatory slur, but the LGBTQ+ community has reclaimed that word. "Q" can stand for "questioning." An "A" stands for "asexual," which describes someone who experiences an absence of sexual and/or romantic attraction (GLSEN, 2022) and 2S for "Two-Spirit," an umbrella term for people who identify as having both a masculine and a feminine spirit. The plus sign includes pansexual, nonbinary, agender, genderqueer, bigender, gender variant and pangender.

GLSEN's Model Local Education Agency Policy on Transgender and Nonbinary Students defines gender nonconforming as "a term sometimes used to describe people whose gender expression differs from social expectations, such as "feminine boys," "masculine girls" and people who are perceived as androgynous in some way. Being gender nonconforming is distinct from being transgender, although some trans people may consider themselves to be gender nonconforming. For example, a cisgender woman who has short hair and likes sports might consider herself gender nonconforming but may not identify as transgender" (2020, n.p.).

Homosexuality and homosexual are biased terms and should not be used. In 1973, the American Psychiatric Association (APA) removed the diagnosis of "homosexuality" from the second edition of its Diagnostic and Statistical Manual (DSM). "APA's 1973 diagnostic revision was the beginning of the end of organized medicine's official participation in the social stigmatization of homosexuality... . As a result, cultural attitudes about homosexuality changed in the U.S. and other countries as those who accepted scientific authority on such matters gradually came to accept the normalizing view" (Drescher, 2015, p. 7).

School counselors can make the school counseling program feel more inclusive to LGBTQ+ students simply by using language accurately and respectfully. The best ways to do this is to include using gender-neutral language when speaking about relationships and attractions and asking individuals which identity terminology and pronouns they use. School counselors can also model inclusive best practices, such as sharing the pronouns they use along with their name when introducing themselves. Finally, school counselors can advocate for and support the development of comprehensive policies, including anti-bullying policies and policies on transgender and nonbinary students. For example, a school counselor could assist in creating a template for a confidential support plan for transgender and nonbinary students that can address sensitive questions such as whether the students are out to their friends, teachers, family and guardians; whether they would like support in coming out; and what other supports they need. (GLSEN, 2019b).

GLSEN, the leading national education nonprofit organization on LGBTQ+ issues in K–12 schools, was founded in 1990 by educators seeking to foster safe, welcoming learning environments for LGBTQ+ youth. For more than two decades, GLSEN's biennial National School Climate Survey of LGBTQ+ secondary students in U.S. schools, has demonstrated that four key supports – supportive educators, peer networks of support, comprehensive school and district policies, and curriculum that includes positive representations of LGBTQ+ people and history – contribute to a range of positive educational attainment and well-being outcomes for LGBTQ+ youth, including fewer reports of missing school, fewer reports of feeling unsafe and greater academic achievement (GLSEN, 2019c). GLSEN's Research Institute has also conducted surveys of educators and school mental health professionals, including a report conducted in collaboration with ASCA (GLSEN, 2019b). This research informs GLSEN's advocacy and policy resources.

GLSEN's 2019 National School Climate Survey shows that LGBTQ+ students commonly experience hostile school climates (GLSEN, 2019). Of the 16,713 secondary school students surveyed aged 13 to 21, more than eight in 10 (81%) reported they were verbally harassed because of their sexual orientation, gender expression or gender identity, and more than a third (35.1%) reported they were verbally harassed often or frequently. More than one in three (34.2%) LGBTQ+ students were physically harassed (e.g., shoved or pushed) because of their sexual orientation, gender expression or gender identity. One in seven (14.8%) LGBTQ+ students were physically assaulted (e.g., punched or kicked) because of their sexual orientation, gender expression or gender identity. Students who hold multiple marginalized identities commonly report victimization across these identities. At least two in five LGBTQ+ youth who are students of color reported bullying based on both their sexual orientation and their race. Four in 10 (40.2%) LGBTQ+ students avoided physical education or gym classes because they felt unsafe or uncomfortable; 27.2% were prevented from using locker rooms aligned with their gender identity; and 10.2% were prevented or discouraged from participating in school sports because they were LGBTQ+.

A fair and inclusive education is not possible for a student whose physical and emotional safety is routinely compromised. School climates can have an adverse impact on educational opportunities for LGBTQ+ students by being, at best, indifferent to the vulnerability of this at-risk minority and, at worst, hostile and dangerous (GLSEN, 2019c). When someone with the authority of a teacher describes the world and you are not in it, there is a moment of psychic disequilibrium as if you looked into a mirror and saw nothing (Rich, 2017). Additionally, the frequent societal condemnation of sexual and gender minorities contributes to LGBTQ+ students' identity confusion and often influences them to keep their identities a secret. This results in a tendency to hide nonheterosexual feelings and the negative emotions associated with them, such as guilt, fear of stigmatization and fear of rejection (Mayer et al., 2014).

Transgender and nonbinary students experience more hostile school climates than their cisgender lesbian, gay, bisexual and queer peers. The majority reported that they were harassed or assaulted based on their gender identity and gender expression. More than three-fifths (59.1%) reported feeling unsafe at school because of their sexual orientation, and about a third (32.7%) skipped a day of school in the past month because of feeling unsafe (GLSEN, 2019c).

School-based bullying and harassment research most often places the focus on physical or overt acts of aggressive behavior, but relational bullying is equally as damaging. Relational aggression manifests itself in rumors, strained peer relations and intentional inclusion by peers (90.1%). More than two-fifths (44.9%) reported experiencing some form of electronic harassment (cyberbullying) in the past year (GLSEN, 2019c). Cyberbullying is addressed further in Chapter 12 and Chapter 13.

Policymakers have an opportunity to improve school climates. Comprehensive bullying and harassment policies should specifically include language affirming all students' rights, regardless of sexual orientation, gender identity or gender expression. Although a majority (79.1%) of students were aware of an anti-bullying policy at their school, only 13.5% of students reported their school had a comprehensive policy (i.e., that specifically enumerates sexual orientation, gender identity and gender expression) (GLSEN, 2019).

In 2021, the U.S. Department of Education released a Dear Educator Letter informing schools of protections for LGBTQ+ students under Title IX and has since issued factsheets. The department made it clear that Title IX's prohibition on sex discrimination covers students who are discriminated against or harassed either for exhibiting what is perceived as a stereotypical characteristic for their sex or for failing to conform to stereotypical notions of masculinity and femininity (USDOE, 2021c).

State and local laws may prohibit discrimination and bullying on the basis of sexual orientation and gender identity. As of 2021, 21 states and Washington, D.C., have anti-bullying laws that specifically protect students who are harassed based on sexual orientation and gender identity, and two states have laws prohibiting schools from specifically protecting LGBTQ+ students. Many states, however, continue to allow discrimination in employment, housing and public accommodations. Although there are more states every day that strive to pass laws to protect their citizens from discrimination, many legislatures sponsor bills that invoke religion, preempt local protections and target transgender people to allow discrimination. Six states have proposed legislation that will preempt any local protections provided by cities and local government entities (ACLU, n.d.) The American Civil Liberties Union (n.d.) updates its legislation affecting LGBTQ+ rights across the country every Monday. Review updated legislation at: *www.aclu.org/other/legislation-affecting-lgbt-rights-across-country.*

The National School Boards Association has issued several resource documents to help school leaders address legal issues surrounding students' sexual orientation and gender identity. Aimed at school policymakers and administrators yet a valuable resource for school counselors, the guide, "Protections for LGBTQ+ Employees and Students after *Bostock v. Clayton County*," provides practical guidance on the legal rights of lesbian, gay, bisexual and transgender students (National School Boards Association, 2020a).

Between March 2020 and February 2021, 11 states banned transgender students from sports. Twenty-eight states have now introduced anti-trans sports ban with Idaho passing the most restrictive and intrusive sex-testing bill for student athletes. LGBTQ+ students across our nation's schools are being targeted in legislation. "LGBTQ+ youth, like all youth, deserve to be safe and supported in school spaces, from locker rooms to soccer fields to overnight field trips, and these new resources are designed to give coaches, teachers and families the tools they need to ensure all students are able to fully participate" (GLSEN, 2021b).

In March 2022, ASCA and approximately 25 other child association, such as the National Association of Secondary School Principals and the National Association of Social Workers, issued this statement: "LGBTQ+ youth are already at a heightened risk for violence, bullying and harassment. In addition, students who would be affected by these bills are among our most vulnerable to experiencing depression and engaging in self-harm, including suicide. These bills exacerbate those risks by creating an unwelcoming and hostile environment in places where students should feel the safest and most supported. Research has shown that when transgender youth have access to gender-affirming services, competent care and affirmation, their risk of depression, anxiety and other negative mental health outcomes is greatly reduced. We stand in opposition to proposals that harm LGBTQ+ youth, including limiting access to medically necessary, best-practice care, forbidding students from using the restroom at school consistent with their gender identity and preventing transgender youth from playing sports alongside their peers. On behalf of our members and communities, we call on legislators across the country to reject these harmful measures."

Under the Biden administration, the U.S. Department of Education's Office of Civil Rights issued a Notice of Interpretation in June 2021 regarding Title IX. This notice affirms that Title IX's prohibition of discrimination on the basis of sex encompasses prohibiting discrimination on the basis of sexual orientation and gender identity and represents a step toward full implementation of the U.S. Supreme Court decision in *Bostock v. Clayton County* (2020) that discrimination on the basis of sexual orientation or transgender status constitutes illegal discrimination on the basis of sex. The notice acknowledges the application of the court's ruling on education programs and activities that receive federal funding (USDOE, 2021c).

"Negative treatment by others, such as bullying, is a strong and consistent risk factor for youth suicide, and LGBTQ+ youth experience bullying at significantly greater rates than their straight and cisgender peers." (The Trevor Project, n.d.). The Trevor Project launched 23 years ago to support LGBTQ+ youth in crisis by providing 24/7 counseling via phone, text or chat. The organization has become a leading resource for research on LGBTQ+ youth, advocates for protective and inclusive legislation and trains educators to improve mental health support for these students. Through their work, The Trevor Project researchers have learned that students who attend schools with affirming cultures are much less likely to attempt suicide (The Trevor Project, n.d.). They provide training on being an ally to LGBTQ+ youth as well as suicide prevention and mental health training specifically for educators and counselors who serve LGBTQ+ youth. To learn more visit *thetrevorproject.org*

IMPACT OF COVID-19

According to the Office of Civil Rights (OCR), LGBTQ+ youth are among those disproportionately affected by the COVID-19 pandemic. For some LGBTQ+ youth, school closures and activity restrictions meant more time in unsupportive or abusive environments, and many experienced disruptions or diminished access to school-based supports, such as gay-straight alliances or gender-sexuality alliances (GSAs) (OCR, 2021). LGBTQ+ youth are also overrepresented among students experiencing homelessness, another student group that OCR identified as disproportionately affected by the COVID-19 pandemic. Surveys conducted showed that 50% of LGBTQ+ youth aged 13–17 and 65% of transgender and nonbinary youth aged 13–17 reported that the pandemic had an impact on their ability to express their sexual identity, and 81% of these youth said the pandemic made their living situation more stressful than before (OCR, 2021). Other surveys showed that 83% of LGBTQ+ students reported experiencing more problems that affected their schoolwork or well-being than the year before, compared with the 69% of their heterosexual peers (OCR, 2021). Another survey showed that of nearly 35,000 LGBTQ+ youths ages 13–24, 48% reported they were unable to access mental health care when they wanted it during the pandemic (OCR, 2021). Eighty-five percent of transgender and nonbinary youth reported that COVID-19 negatively affected their mental health (OCR, 2021).

Getting Started: What Would You Do?

The following case is discussed at the end of this chapter by a school counseling candidate. Before you read her response, formulate in your own mind how you would approach this ethical dilemma.

A SCHOOL COUNSELOR'S BELIEF

Alexia Huart had been taught in religious training and at home that being gay is a choice, and people who make the choice to be gay are misguided. She never really questioned her beliefs, and she thought as a school counselor in training it really did not matter how she felt about gay people. Huart's preparation program pushed her to examine her biases. Must school counselors continually take inventory and confront their own prejudices and beliefs about others regarding diversity issues such as sexual orientation and gender identity?

Working Through Case Studies

HARASSMENT OF LGBTQ+ STUDENTS

A 15-year-old student who identifies as gay asks you to help stop the daily harassment she has been enduring from other students. She tells you she receives approximately 25 anti-LGBTQ remarks a day and at least twice in the last five months she has been kicked and punched while on school grounds. She tells you the harassment is especially bad in Mrs. Smith's class, where students call her a "she-he," but Mrs. Smith pretends not to hear. She tells you she has gone to the assistant principal for support and provided the names of the students who have verbally and physically attacked her. What do you do?

Points to Consider

OCR requires schools to provide an educational environment free from harassment and discrimination on the basis of sex, sexual orientation or gender identity (USDOE OCR, 2021b). School counselors can be at the forefront of diversity training for students and staff to raise awareness of the LGBTQ+ population. Raising awareness in the school community by facilitating classroom lessons, seminars, assemblies or other functions can go a long way toward creating the type of environment in which all students can learn and feel safe. Indeed, the school counselor might implement effective yet simple measures like prominently posting rights and responsibilities of students as citizens of the school to help one another learn and grow in an accepting climate (ASCA, 2022e; 2022i). By creating and delivering anti-bullying programs and inviting speakers who have overcome bullying to present at assemblies, school counselors can convey the message that the school community will not permit intolerance for any group within it (ASCA, 2022e; ASCA 2022l; Stone & Isaacs, 2002b).

In the case of *Walsh v. Tehachapi Unified School District* (2011), the Department of Justice and the U.S. Department of Education found Seth Walsh's school did not fulfill its duty to protect him after two years of anti-gay harassment led to his suicide in 2010. The school district's settlement included the implementation of a series of specific policies, procedures and training designed to better protect students from sexual harassment and harassment based on gender stereotypes (ACLU, 2011). This case helped to bring about the 2012 Seth's Law, which requires California schools to "specifically address harassment based on sexual orientation, gender identity and gender expression in their antidiscrimination policies" (Seth's Law, 2012).

Heterosexist climates certainly have contributed to the degree to which LGBTQ+ students are harassed and the degree to which they internalize this harassment. These climates are found to increase sexual harassment and are associated with negative psychosocial and mental health outcomes (Kaltiala-Heino et al., 2019). Different from but related to homophobia, heterosexism refers to a system of attitudes, biases, assumptions and discrimination in favor of opposite-sex relationships and attractions. A study found that a combination of LGBTQ-focused programs and policies improve school climates and are effective for addressing bias-based bullying (Day et al, 2020). Students from schools with more inclusive programs and policies reported less frequent anti-LGBTQ+ harassment. Being sensitive to heterosexism is important since heterosexism is manifested in various ways in school. Heterosexism is seen when LGBTQ+ issues, history and culture are not included in school curricula; school rules or policies regarding name calling, harassment or bullying are not enforced for anti-LGBTQ+ incidents; students' rights, laws or policies do not include sexual orientation as a protected category; school functions are organized around assumptions of heterosexuality; and same-sex displays of affection in school are not tolerated or are treated differently than opposite-sex displays of affection (Kjaran & Jóhannesson, 2013).

Homophobic behavior displayed by students toward those identifying as or perceived to be LGBTQ+ might include bullying, verbal or physical aggression, ostracizing, ignoring or gossiping about LGBTQ+ students. This type of behavior is not exclusive to just students; adults in schools sometimes make homophobic comments. School counselors are aware of the implicit, covert and unintentional demonstrations of homophobia and heterosexism that surface through presumptions of heterosexuality. When this occurs, the result is that LGBTQ+ students, many of whom desperately need the school counseling program and its services, become alienated from it (Strear, 2017).

ASCA's position statement The School Counselor and LGBTQ+ Youth (revised, 2022) states, "School counselors promote equal opportunity for all individuals regardless of sexual orientation, gender identity or gender expression. School counselors recognize the school experience can be significantly more difficult for students with marginalized identities. School counselors work to eliminate barriers impeding LGBTQ+ student development and achievement."

The school counselor works with all students through the stages of identity development and understands this development may be more difficult for LGBTQ+ youth. It is not the school counselor's role to attempt to change a student's sexual orientation or gender identity. School counselors provide support to LGBTQ+ students to promote academic achievements and social/emotional development (ASCA, 2022e, 2022l).

School counselors:

- Counsel students with feelings about their sexual orientation and gender identity as well as students' feeling about the identity of others in an accepting and nonjudgmental manner
- Advocate for equitable educational and extracurricular opportunities for all students regardless of sexual orientation, gender identity or gender expression
- Provide a safe space for LGBTQ+ students, including by serving as an advisor to student-led gay-straight alliance or gender-sexuality alliance (GSA) clubs
- Promote sensitivity and acceptance of diversity among all students and staff to include LGBTQ+ students and diverse family systems
- Identify LGBTQ+ community resources for students and families and assess the quality and inclusiveness of these resources before referring to such resources

(ASCA, 2022)

Considering that LGBTQ+ youth are not typically raised with parents/guardians, siblings and extended family members who share their marginalized identity, these youth are left with little support, experience and wisdom to draw upon from their family regarding how to navigate this identity within a heterosexist and gender-normative culture. In many schools, this leaves these youth intensely isolated with minimal resources. School counselors can become powerful advocates and begin to actualize social justice advocacy for their LGBTQ+ students by taking incremental, tangible and concrete steps toward supporting these students (Bidell, 2011; Neighmond, 2020).

SCHOOL COUNSELOR'S DANGEROUS ADVICE

Reggie comes to his school counselor about his harassment. Reggie has started wearing rainbow pins on his bag to express his identity. The school counselor suggests Reggie tone it down. "Your classmates understand that you're gay," she tells him. "Why don't you make it easier for them to accept you by not flaunting it in their faces all the time?" Are there legal or ethical concerns with her advice?

Points to Consider

In 2002, The Washoe County School District in Nevada settled a lawsuit with Derek Henkle for $451,000 for bullying and physical attacks he experienced in two district schools. The settlement also required the district to adopt a new anti-harassment policy including sexual orientation and to train staff and students on sexual harassment and intimidation. Although school officials were aware of the ongoing, severe harassment and physical assaults, they repeatedly told Henkle to keep his sexual orientation private. This case says, "Students have a constitutional right to express their sexual orientation in school without harassment or discrimination" (NCLR & GLSEN, n.d., p. 6).

In 2003, a school district in Arkansas settled a lawsuit with an openly gay student whose school disciplined him for discussing his sexual orientation and, later, for talking about his punishment. Fourteen-year-old Thomas McLaughlin claimed teachers and school officials violated his rights to free speech, equal protection, privacy and freedom of religion by outing him to his parents without his permission, preaching to him and forcing him to read from the Bible as punishment. In a settlement, the school paid $25,000 in damages and attorney's fees, expunged McLaughlin's disciplinary record, formally apologized and implemented new district policies to protect student speech, student privacy and discrimination on the basis of sexual orientation (The New York Times, 2003).

Numerous court cases, such as *Doe, et al. v. Anoka-Hennepin School District No. 11*, et al. (2012), found the district inadequately responded to persistent physical and verbal harassment based on real or perceived sexual orientation. This school district's sexual orientation curriculum policy required staff to remain neutral on issues of sexual orientation, which has been argued to attribute to the lack of educator's response to the harassment of LGBTQ+ students (Baca, 2012; *Doe, et al. v. Anoka-Hennepin, et al.*, 2012; Eckholm, 2011; Karnowski, 2012; Wooledge, 2012). LGBTQ+ students did not feel safe at school because they were not affirmed for who they are; one high school teacher said students began to internalize the policy to mean being gay is shameful and wrong. Students saw adults in schools adhering to the policy and repeatedly failing to address anti-gay bullying (Karnowski, 2012). In 2010, the Justice Department began a civil rights investigation into the district after eight local students committed suicide in less than two years. Of them, four were either gay or perceived to be gay and reportedly bullied by other students (Baca, 2012; Eckholm, 2011; Wooledge, 2012). The Justice Department found sex-based harassment in the district and said it contributed to a hostile environment, as teachers and administrators failed to protect students (Karnowski, 2012).

In 2014, *Hatcher v. DeSoto County Board of Education, et al.* was resolved by the school board's decision to revise their anti-harassment code and policies to include sexual orientation and gender identity and to establish a new freedom-of-speech policy for the district aligned with the First Amendment (Lambda Legal, 2014). This suit was filed after Amber Hatcher was denied permission by her principal to observe the National Day of Silence, in which students remain silent to call attention to the silencing effect of anti-gay bullying and harassment in schools. Backed by the superintendent, who denied Hatcher's request for a meeting, the principal also repeatedly threatened "ramifications" and "consequences" if she moved forward without permission (Lambda Legal, 2014).

Going beyond anti-bullying and harassment policies, students and civil rights activists are addressing more ways in which schools fail to be inclusive and affirming to LGBTQ+ students by challenging school policies pertaining to bathroom use and sports participation. In 2017, a federal district court judge ruled in favor of three students who filed a suit against the Pine-Richland School District after the school board adopted a new policy following pressure from anti-LGBTQ+ groups that denied students the right to use bathrooms that align with their gender identity, even though they had been using their preferred bathroom for three years (Lambda Legal, 2017). In *Adams v. The School Board of St. Johns County, Florida* the St. Johns County school board appealed a similar ruling in the lower courts, and lost, with the 11th Circuit Court ruling that schools must treat transgender students equally in restrooms (Lambda Legal, 2020). There are also several open cases in which suits have been filed against school districts by transgender students who were denied participation in sports teams aligned with their gender identity, many of which are in response to a slew of anti-LGBTQ+ bills adopted by state legislatures as recently as 2021 to deny these students access, such as *B.P.J. vs. West Virginia State Board of Education* and *L.E. vs. Lee* (Lambda Legal, 2021a, May 26, November; Brassil, 2021).

COMMUNITY STANDARDS AND PARENTS'/GUARDIANS' RIGHTS

You want to support GLSEN's A Day of Silence to kick off your program to create a safe and respectful school climate for all students. You are confident any program aimed at reducing bullying will be supported and respected by your administrators, teachers, parents/guardians and community. What criticism could a bully-proofing program encounter, and how might you be informed and prepared to respond and combat the criticisms?

Points to Consider

Brubaker, Harper and Singh reviewed strategies for school counselor advocacy at the intersection of multiculturalism and social justice for the LBGTQ+ community and encouraged counselors to (a) learn about audiences, (b) communicate with respect, (c) identify what people have in common, (d) use language that brings people together, (e) develop primary messages supported by secondary messages, (f) reframe conversations about stereotypes, (g) challenge inaccurate information, (h) share personal stories and (i) prepare beforehand to share with others who possess different viewpoints (Simons et al., 2017). Singh, Urbano, Haston & McMahon (2010) present seven overarching strategies school counselors use as social justice advocates: a) using political savvy to navigate power structures, b) consciousness raising, c) initiating difficult dialogues, d) building intentional relationships, e) teaching students self-advocacy skills, f) using data for marketing and g) educating others about the school counselor role of advocate. Additionally, political savvy (knowing when and how to intervene) serves as a prerequisite for and is an integral part of each of the strategies.

Schoolwide and districtwide programs such as Day of Silence (GLSEN, 2021a) can have a strong impact on school climate and culture, helping students with marginalized identities feel safe at school. Implementing inclusive programming expands the school counseling program's reach to involve all students and takes a proactive approach instead of a reactive approach to potential harassment. The chart at the end of this case describes several programs school counselors can introduce in their schools, along with some notes on pushback other communities have faced.

As advocates, school counselors educate themselves about the prevailing community standards, and they learn to predict and skillfully negotiate the political landscape. It is easy for school counselors to feel so strongly about the work of advocacy that their responses might be undemocratic; however, these responses lead to mistrust, distrust and stalemates that do nothing but maintain the status quo, with students getting lost in the process (Savage & Harley, 2009). It helps to review materials with administrators to ensure their support and to anticipate possible concerns – and be prepared to address them – should they arise.

APPROPRIATE PRONOUNS FOR TRANSGENDER AND NONBINARY STUDENTS

A teacher in your school refused to use the correct pronouns for your student, a transgender boy, meaning he was assigned female at birth and has transitioned to male. After repeated warnings from the administration to use the right pronouns, the teacher was dismissed. He filed a lawsuit against the district saying his religion will not allow him to lie. Will he win?

Points to Consider

In *Vlaming v. West Point School Board*, high school teacher Peter Vlaming refused to use male pronouns when referring to John Doe. The school administration made it clear several times that Vlaming was to use John's correct masculine pronouns, but he refused. The school district fired Vlaming under its nondiscrimination policy in 2018. Ten months later, Vlaming sued the district, claiming his constitutional right to free speech and free exercise of religious freedom were violated. On June 7, 2021, the Virginia state court dismissed Vlaming's claims that his constitutional rights were violated (National Center for Lesbian Rights, n.d.). GLSEN's Pronoun Guide (updated 2020) provides guidance on gender-neutral terminology and pronouns and can be found at *www.glsen.org/activity/pronouns-guide-glsen.*

OUTING STUDENTS TO THEIR PARENTS/GUARDIANS

John has stuffed his desk to overflowing with papers, library books, supplies from the teacher's closets and more. His teacher turns the desk on its side, empties the contents and proceeds to sort through the pile. Some of John's papers catch her eye, and she starts to read his words describing his pain over accepting his sexual orientation and expressing his love for another boy in the school. The teacher immediately brings six papers to you to read. You are convinced this child is in a great deal of pain and at risk for self-harm. How will you proceed in this situation?

Points to Consider

The school counselor in this complex case will need much sensitivity. A child is in pain and possibly suicidal. John's parents need to know their child needs help, but do they need to know about his writings? *Eisel v. Board of Education of Montgomery County* (1991) has shown that if we have any reason to suspect this child might be suicidal, we have a duty to warn parents. However, this duty to protect John from harm does not give us the right or duty to "out" him to his parents. Minors in schools do have a right to privacy with respect to their sexual orientation, and they have the right to decide when and if they will come out to their parents/guardians.

LGBTQ+ individuals are one of the only cultural minority groups to typically grow up in families outside of their cultural group. Often there are only few, if any, LGBTQ+ people visibly available to aid these youth in learning how to cope with the societal realities of having a marginalized sexual or gender identity. The school counselor cannot know with certainty if the family will be supportive. Address the suicidal ideation but be careful not to diagnose why you think this child might be suicidal.

The development of sexual identity is a natural process, but it can be much more stressful for children and adolescents questioning their sexual orientation because of the way society views sexual minorities (The American Psychological Association, 2021). Adolescence, as difficult as it is, frequently requires LGBTQ+ students to negotiate the daily challenges of hiding their sexual identities, resulting in problems of isolation, depression and real or imagined fear of discovery or rejection by their families and friends (Villines, 2021).

There is a potential danger for John. Statistics have shown LGBTQ+ students have a higher rate of depression and are more likely to consider suicide than other students (American Academy of Child & Adolescent Psychiatry, 2006; National Education Association, 2006). A study by Klein and Golub (2016) found that transgender youth who experience high levels of family rejection about their gender identity were associated with three and half times the odds of suicide attempts and two and half times the odds of substance misuse, compared to those who experienced little or no family rejection. Some may believe parents/guardians have the right to know the content of the letters. However, what is most important is protecting the student's legal privacy. It is impossible to know how the adults at home will react. Maybe the parents/guardians will react negatively to their child's sexual identity. The child is experiencing pain and confusion because he is afraid his parents will reject him if they find out (American Academy of Child & Adolescent Psychiatry, 2006; Heatherington & Lavner, 2008).

Allen (2021) found that those who shared their sexual identity with their parents/guardians revealed it had a positive and healthy effect on their mental health, parent-child relationships, their personal self-esteem and their willingness to express openly sexual desires. Sexual identity is also often disclosed earlier and more frequently to mothers than fathers (Allen, 2021).

To support John, the school counselor will need to establish a relationship with him to address the pain he is experiencing. Let John know you are there for him to talk to and share his feelings with. Without labeling him, drop clues that you are prepared to address these issues by saying phrases like "gay and lesbian" or "sexual orientation" as part of your conversation. Ask for, use and affirm whatever language and pronouns John uses to describe himself. Some state statutes are forbidding this support.

After you form a counseling relationship with John, you could inquire how he believes his parents would react to finding out that he identifies as gay, bisexual, questioning or another identity. For students who seek your help in coming out, consider whether they are developmentally able to make that decision. Allow students to explore their parents' likely reaction, and help them generate strategies for talking to their parents and worst-case scenarios.

Although studies of LGBTQ+ youth show they recognize their sexual orientation between ages 8 and 11, the age at which they come out is between 15 and 17, indicating that for many years they may feel too afraid to be honest about the issue. But the fact is that many students are increasingly coming out while still in high (or even middle/junior high) school, making it more imperative that school counselors consider how to support students (Elias, 2007; James, 2008; Kramer, 2011; Lobron, 2007; National Education Association, 2006; PFLAG, 2005). The decision to share one's sexual orientation with others and the experience of doing so varies greatly from person to person and can depend hugely on the individual's systems of emotional support, both inside and outside of school. In 2011, *The New York Times* published "Coming Out," an interactive feature on its website, telling the stories of youth all over the country in various stages of coming out (Kramer, 2011). It is available at: *www.nytimes.com/interactive/2011/05/23/us/20110523-coming-out.html?ref=us.*

Unfortunately, in many cases students' reluctance to disclose their sexual orientation to family has a basis in real and rational fear. LGBTQ+ youth represent a disproportionate percentage of the homeless youth population. According to the National Coalition for the Homeless, LGBTQ+ youth represented up to 40% of the homeless youth population (National Coalition for the Homeless, 2017). The most commonly cited factor leading to homelessness was family rejection on the basis of sexual orientation and gender identity, with 68% of clients reporting they ran away because of family rejection, and 54% reporting a history of family abuse (National Coalition for the Homeless, 2017). Research has found that parent and family rejection among lesbian, gay and bisexual youth is linked to poorer health outcomes, such as depression, substance abuse, homelessness and sexual risk-taking (Grossman et al., 2021). Ryan, Huebner, Diaz and Sanchez (2009) found that "young adults who reported higher levels of family rejection during adolescence were 8.4 times more likely to report having attempted suicide, 5.9 times more likely to report high levels of depression, 3.4 times more likely to report illegal drug use and 3.4 times more likely to report having engaged in unprotected sexual intercourse, compared to peers from families with no or low levels of family rejection" (p. 349-350). Their study concluded, "helping families identify and reduce specific rejecting behaviors is integral to helping prevent health and mental health problems for LGB young people" (p. 350).

In a GLSEN study, students were asked about their level of comfort talking one-on-one with various school personnel about LGBTQ+ issues. Students reported they would be most comfortable talking with school counselors or social workers and teachers. Approximately half of the students reported they would be somewhat or very comfortable talking with a school counselor or social worker (51.8%) or a teacher (41.8%) about LGBTQ+ issues (2019, p. 62). LGBTQ+ students with 11 or more supportive staff in school have an average GPA of 3.34 compared to schools with 0 to 5 supportive staff with average GPAs of 3.14 (GLSEN, 2019c).

CONVERSION THERAPY

A school counselor and a student are talking just outside the school counselor's door. As you walk by, you see the school counselor hand the student a copy of the book "You Do Not Have to Be Gay" and hear her say to the student, "I know where you can go to get better. You do not have to go through life like this." You strongly suspect the school counselor is talking to this young man about conversion therapy. What do you do?

Points to Consider

Conversion therapy, referred to by some proponents as "reparative therapy," refers to interventions aimed at changing an individual's sexual orientation, gender identity or gender expression. Conversion therapy is based upon the assumption that being gay or transgender is a mental disorder, rather than normal, healthy human diversity with respect to sexual orientation, gender identity and gender expression. The UCLA Williams Institute in 2019 reported data on the prevalence of conversion therapy. They estimated that 16,000 LGBT youth (ages 13–17) will receive conversion therapy from a licensed health care professional before they reach the age of 18 in the 35 states that have not banned licensed professionals from conducting conversion therapy. In addition, religious leaders and advisors will try and convert 57,000 youth (ages 13–17) before they reach the age of 18 (Mallory et al., 2019).

Few practices are more dangerous for LGBTQ+ youth than attempting to change their sexual orientation or gender identity through conversion therapy. All major professional psychological associations in the United States, including the American Psychological Association, American Psychiatric Association and the American Academy of Child and Adolescent Psychiatry, have taken public positions against the use of conversion therapy (Cordero & Carlisle, 2019).

Ipsos/Reuters (2019) found that 56% of U.S. adults believe conversion therapy by mental health practitioners should be illegal as compared to a minority (18%) who think it should be legal. Twenty states and the District of Columbia have passed laws banning licensed practitioners from using conversion therapy with minors. California was the first state to ban the practice in 2012. As of October 2018, 42 municipalities, the majority of them located in states that do not yet have a ban on conversion therapy, passed their own ordinances prohibiting the use of conversion therapy. Every leading medical and mental health organization rejects this practice as dangerous to children's well-being. Likewise, in *Tingley v. Ferguson* (2021), a legal group filed a lawsuit against the state of Washington in response to its 2018 law prohibiting state-licensed therapists from using conversion therapy on children under 18 years of age. The legal group was challenging the law on behalf of Brian Tingley, a therapist who wanted to use conversion therapy. Tingley's challenge to the law was rejected in August 2021 by the federal district court for the Western District of Washington.

It is necessary for someone in a position of authority admonish the school counselor to cease this behavior and to help the school counselor understand that her behavior is bordering on child abuse. It may also be illegal in your locale. The school counselor's behavior is unethical, and it is potentially damaging to students. The school counselor is using her school counseling office as a platform to forward her religious beliefs. There are parents/guardians who would sue quickly if they knew she was imposing her religious beliefs on their child. The school counselor must cease ever discussing conversion therapy with a child or their parents/guardians. Your colleague is inviting legal trouble for the school district and herself. If your school's administration will not address the school counselor's behavior with her, then give them the abundance of research as to why this is a legal and/or ethical violation and the dangers it poses to children. It is a difficult position to be in to try and correct a colleague's behavior, but this behavior cannot go unaddressed. As uncomfortable as it might be to discuss or confront your colleague, you cannot turn a blind eye to this kind of abuse.

In a related case, *Hamilton v. Vallejo City Unified School District* (2009), a school counselor required Hamilton to attend a special weekly support group for gay students. Within this group, the school counselor allegedly berated students for "choosing" to be gay and tried to convince them to change their sexual orientation or gender expression (ACLU, 2009a). This Northern California school district reached a settlement in which the district agreed to adopt a clear policy explicitly prohibiting discrimination and harassment based on sexual orientation or gender identity, develop a specific procedure for harassment and discrimination complaints and provide mandatory training for all teachers and other staff who interact with students in how to identify anti-gay harassment and discrimination (ACLU, 2009a). Silence and minding one's own business are not options when you see a colleague harming a child in this way.

EQUAL ACCESS AND GSA CLUBS

Johnston, a junior in your high school, asked for your advice on starting a gender-sexuality alliance club. Before he talks with the administration he wants to know if you think it is legal. He explains that seven years ago when his brother tried to form the club this same administration told him he could not because it would put him and the other students in danger and substantially disrupt the school. What is your response?

Points to Consider

Banning gay-straight alliance (GSA) clubs also known as gender-sexuality alliance is a relic of the past. Administrators are becoming more aware that you cannot deny a GSA club that follows the same rules that apply to other clubs in the school. This dilemma presents an opportunity for you to use your knowledge of court findings and legislation to benefit a minority student population. Legal efforts to ban GSAs have been struck down by federal court rulings based on the protections afforded in the Equal Access Act of 1984, as well as the First Amendment of the U.S. Constitution (Mercier, as cited by Bidell, 2011). The case *Colín v. Orange Unified School District* (2000) marked the first time the Equal Access Act was invoked to order a school to allow a GSA to meet on campus. Courts have found that the Equal Access Act requires schools that receive federal funds to provide LGBTQ+ clubs the same access to school facilities other student groups enjoy. This means that, for example, if your school requires parent/guardian consent for students seeking to join a GSA, they must require consent for all clubs and extracurricular activities.

These student clubs must be student-initiated. In other words, the Equal Access Act dictates community members outside the school community may not direct, conduct, control or regularly attend activities of student groups. Guests may occasionally attend student meetings, and school faculty and staff may regularly attend and supervise meetings. If a school staff member is provided to monitor extracurricular student clubs, a staff member should be assigned to the GSA as well (Equal Access Act, 1984).

Certain limitations apply regarding equal access. For example, a limitation would apply if the school denied access based on a substantive possibility that it will interfere with the orderly conduct of educational activities within the school. In cases of equal access and freedom of expression, the burden tends to fall on schools to prove the disruption significantly interfered with education (B. Littrell, personal communication, Oct. 26, 2012). A complete guide on the Equal Access Act can be found at *www.justice.gov/crt/about/cor/byagency/ed4071.php*.

Efforts have not been met with court favor when school districts have tried to finesse legal definitions to defeat GSAs or other clubs addressing LGBTQ+ issues. In a Georgia district, students attempting to form a GSA were met with resistance, and eventually, the district announced a ban on all noncurricular clubs for the next academic year. Students sued, and a federal judge found that the ban on noncurricular clubs was an attempt to discriminate against Peers Rising in Diverse Education and forced the school to grant them and all other student groups equal access and the opportunity to meet on school campus (*Pacer v. White County School District* (2006)).

In the case of *Yasmin Gonzalez v. School Board of Okeechobee County* (2008), a U.S. District Court judge rejected the school's claim that the GSA was by definition a "sex-based" club and that it violated the school's abstinence-only policy (ACLU, 2008b). The list of cases rolls on and on. The school administration has the legal responsibility of allowing Johnston to form a GSA club. As the school counselor, you have an opportunity to advocate by talking to the administration about the Equal Access Act to avoid a legal misstep. Your advocacy role would serve two purposes: to position you as supporting administration by drawing attention to the appropriate federal legislation and to provide support for Johnston and other students who would benefit from a GSA club.

The American Civil Liberties Union (ACLU) has a chronology of court cases titled GSA Court Victories: A Quick Guide for Gay-Straight Alliances. Download this from *www.aclu.org*, and provide it for your administrators if they are hesitating about a student led GSA club.

DISCRIMINATION IN DISCIPLINE AND PRIVACY RIGHTS OF MINORS

Your principal has recently brought in several same-sex couples and called their parents/guardians for code of conduct violations for public displays of affection. You notice heterosexual couples are treated differently. You are considering discussing this with him. Are you overstepping your boundaries by involving yourself in disciplinary actions?

Points to Consider

The courts are more frequently hearing cases involving gay students, who feel they have been discriminated against. In one such court case, *Nguon v. Wolf* (2007), a federal judge in Los Angeles ruled that a high school does not have the right to reveal a student's sexual orientation without the student's permission. The ACLU brought the lawsuit on behalf of Charlene Nguon, a senior in Orange County's Garden Grove Unified School District, who claimed the principal violated her privacy rights by telling her parents she was a lesbian after he disciplined her for being affectionate with her girlfriend (ACLU, 2005; ACLU, 2006; ACLU, 2007). The school sought to have the lawsuit dismissed, but Judge James Selna of the U.S. District Court in the Central District of California allowed the suit to move forward. "We are pleased that the court recognized that the school does not have the automatic right to disclose a student's sexual orientation just because that student is out of the closet to his or her friends at school," said Christine P. Sun, a staff attorney for the ACLU. "Coming out is a very serious decision that should not be taken away from anyone, especially from students who may be put in peril if they live in an unsupportive home" (ACLU, 2005, para. 4).

In September 2007, a California federal district court ruled that the principal, Ben Wolf, had not violated Nguon's privacy rights by disclosing her sexual orientation to her parents because it occurred within the context of the official's legal duty under the California Education Code to inform parents/guardians of disciplinary measures being taken against their child (*Nguon v. Wolf* (2007)). However, the case is still viewed as important by those fighting for LGBTQ+ rights as the case was allowed to proceed because educators do not have an automatic right to infringe upon students' privacy rights.

In the light of *Nguon v. Wolf* (2007) and similar cases, informational privacy as it relates to minors has recently received attention. Cullitan (2011) proposes that informational privacy afforded to minors "should be expanded to better serve the particular vulnerabilities of children" (p. 460). Courts considering such cases, Cullitan (2011) writes, should consider whether the state had a compelling interest to intervene and, if so, whether they utilized the least-intrusive means to violate a minor's informational privacy.

LGBTQ+ youth are at greater risk for substance abuse, suicide and homelessness and are often targets of physical, verbal and psychological abuse; therefore minors have a lot at stake regarding their informational privacy in the context of the family (Cullitan, 2011; Ludeke, 2009; Roberts, Rosario, Corliss, Koenen & Austin, 2012; Potoczniak, Crosbie-Burnett & Saltzburg, 2009). The application of this strict scrutiny to children's informational privacy rights does not mean they are granted more rights concerning their sexual behavior or conduct; it simply means children will be provided the assurance that their private information will remain confidential when expressing themselves in ways that are legal for minors (Cullitan, 2011; Ettinghoff, 2014).

If Cullitan's (2011) proposal were in place, Nguon's outing would have been unconstitutional, in that she considered school to be insulated from home, a reasonable expectation of privacy, and even if the school had a compelling interest in outing Nguon, it would not be able to demonstrate it had employed the least-intrusive means available for achieving that interest.

We do not want to be disciplinarians and insinuate ourselves into areas administrators should handle. However, equity is always our business, and it is the politically astute school counselor who will figure out how to let administration know LGBTQ+ student rights are an increasing topic of court cases. Political astuteness can go a long way in supporting equitable learning environments for all students.

SCHOOL COUNSELORS, PERSONAL VALUES AND AFFIRMATION OF LGBTQ+ STUDENTS

A student confided in his teacher he was gay and that he was having a difficult time negotiating a same-sex relationship. The teacher asked the student if he would be comfortable talking to the school counselor about his relationship difficulties. The student said he would. Your colleague informed the teacher that, due to a conflict in her values, she would be unable to provide counseling services to this student. Are there any legal and ethical concerns regarding your colleague's behavior?

Points to Consider

Julea Ward, a student preparing to be a school counselor at Eastern Michigan University (EMU), was dismissed from her counseling program after she refused to counsel a gay client who requested help with his same-sex relationship. Ward, citing her religious beliefs, said she needed to refer this client as she could neither validate nor affirm homosexual behavior. Ward filed suit against EMU in 2009, citing her constitutional rights to religious freedom were violated. The university said she was dismissed for not following the American Counseling Association's (2014) code of ethics and not for religious expression. After a failed attempt in federal court, the Alliance Defense Fund helped Ward appeal to the U.S. Sixth District Court of Appeals. Ward won the right to a jury trial, and the case was remanded to a lower court to be heard, but a jury trial never ensued. On Dec. 10, 2012, EMU settled with Ward for $75,000. The university president stated, "Eastern Michigan University has made the decision that is in the best interest of its students and the taxpayers of the state of Michigan to resolve the litigation rather than continue to spend money on a costly trial. ... The faculty retains its right to establish, in its learned judgment, the curriculum and program requirements for the counseling program at EMU" (Kraft, 2012).

Are there those school counseling candidates whose "isms" should cause them and their preparation program to rethink their suitability for the school counseling profession? Can you have religious beliefs that match with Ward's and still seek and become an effective school counselor? ASCA members were asked to give their opinion on the issues raised in this case, specifically around referring students to other school counselors when school counselors believe their religious values will impede their effectiveness or when they believe they may harm a student. The survey also explored the question raised by the court case as to whether those with certain deeply held convictions biasing them against segments of their student population were suitable for the school counseling profession.

In a March 2022 survey, 239 ASCA members responded to 11 opinion prompts using a five-point Likert scale: strongly agree, agree, neutral, disagree, strongly disagree. Their responses give some insight into how school counselors see their profession as it relates to personal, religious and moral values around sexual orientation.

Referring to another professional to avoid harming a student may be an appropriate ethical response in a few select cases, but this should be the exception rather than the rule.
Agree or strongly agree: *80%*

A blanket practice of referring all known same-sex attracted students to other school counselors because conversations may turn to their same-sex relationships is appropriate.
Disagree or strongly disagree: *77.2%*
(Stone and Glicksteen, 2022)

Prejudices (racism, sexism, ageism, ableism, etc.) and the multiple prejudices faced by LGBTQ+ students face (including intersecting marginalization experienced by LGBTQ+ students of color and LGBTQ+ students with disabilities) are sometimes grouped together and referred to as "isms." Some people maintain isms as a conscious part of their value system, choosing to believe certain groups of people or behaviors are inferior. Other people may have biases of which they are completely unaware. In a profession such as school counseling, biases and isms are especially troubling because school counselors are assigned a caseload, and students do not choose their school counselor. Ward professed she was unable to work with students around issues of unwanted pregnancies, sexual activity out of wedlock ("fornication") and homosexuality. Referring becomes burdensome when colleagues have to take on the referrals of school counselors whose biases continue to inhibit the provision of unconditional positive regard for segments of their caseload. Troubling is how unrealistic referring can be when there are no other school counselors in the school to whom a student can be referred.

Compounding the issue of the referral approach is a student may come in with a presenting problem that is a safe topic, such as academics, to test the school counselor for trust and acceptance before broaching the real presenting issue of same-sex attraction. Working with students only to pull up short to refer to another school counselor would likely read to students as a rejection of who they are as a person. To reject (by referring) a student based on pregnancy or having sex out of wedlock is grave, but this is a rejection of the student's conduct not a rejection of who the student is as a person. Rejecting a student based on sexual orientation, gender identity or gender expression is to reject the student as a person, carrying with it far more potential for grievous harm.

Lambda Legal (2012) wrote an *amicus* brief (an opinion for the court to consider, provided by someone not a party to the action but invested in the outcome) for the *Ward v. Wilbanks* (2012) court case. "Abundant empirical research attests to the vulnerability of LGBTQ+ youth in school and the potentially devastating consequences, including youth suicide, which may result from repudiation and rejection by school officials." In asking the state to support EMU, the *amicus* brief stated, "...especially in light of the harm that a counselor could cause to LGBTQ+ youth if a counselor expressed disapproval of or refused to counsel such a student in a school setting."

If a practicing school counselor/school counseling candidate has a bias against LGBTQ+ people or other marginalized identities, then it is appropriate to refer a same-sex attracted student to another school counselor.
Agree or strongly agree: *79.1%*
(Stone and Glicksteen, 2022)

"Above all do no harm" (Kitchener, 1984). What about the 100,000 school counselors already in the field, some of whom may have deeply held biases that mirror Ward's beliefs? We are our values; we cannot simply drop our values on the way through the schoolhouse door to retrieve them at the end of the day. ASCA members see the value of referring to avoid harming (79.1%), but that this should be the exception not the rule (80%) (Stone & Glicksteen, 2022). School counselors frequently counsel students who exhibit behavior they do not condone, such as cursing at the teacher, refusing to cooperate with faculty and staff, and disrespecting their parents/guardians. In the same survey, 99.2% (238 respondents) of ASCA members identified that they must work within their students' value systems without imposing their beliefs on their students (Stone and Glicksteen, 2022). School counselors work through these conflicts in values with students, making sure they accept the student if not the behavior. Referral is a drastic step and should be done only as a last resort to avoid harming a student, but the real work needs to happen with school counselors examining their own isms and biases. The onus is on the school counselor to eradicate or soften biases, so students are not systematically referred to other school counselors to accommodate a litany of topics the school counselor is unwilling to help students negotiate. Certain school settings, grade levels or even the profession itself may not be the right choice for those who are unable to work with segments of the student population because their values will too often conflict with students' need for support.

Survey respondents primarily work with high school or middle school students (67.1%). Think about how many of your students you would not be able to counsel if you denied services to anyone having sex out of wedlock, struggling with an unwanted pregnancy or grappling with sexual orientation or gender-identity issues. Even elementary school counselors have students with these needs. School counseling is a position that has power to promote good or do harm to vulnerable minors. Practicing school counselors have to hold themselves accountable with honest, self-examination of their biases and isms and work so their standard of care is to support all students with unconditional positive regard. Ethical school counselors engage in intentional self-examination, professional development opportunities and pointed opportunities for exposure to other opinions and viewpoints.

If a school counselor/school counseling candidate is generally unwilling to work with students who request help with same-sex relationships, then the school counseling profession is not an appropriate choice for this person.
Strongly agree or agree: *84.8%*

A school counselor should be willing to counsel a student if he or she requests help with same-sex romantic relationships.
Strongly agree or agree: *94.1%*

School counselors/school counseling candidates are entitled to religious or other beliefs about sexual identity.
Strongly agree or agree: *84.5%*

With respect to all students, the school counselor's role is to assist all students in a non-judgmental manner as students clarify feelings about their own sexual orientation/gender identity and the identity of others.
Strongly agree or agree: *99.2%*

Sexual orientation refers to a personal characteristic within an individual, not merely a pattern of behaviors.
Strongly agree or agree:. *69%*
(Stone and Glicksteen, 2022)

Because school counselors act as door openers for their pre-K–12 students, the profession bristles at the idea of gate keeping. However, school counselor educators have the unenviable but critical ethical imperative of gatekeeping to guard who goes into the profession, making sure to prepare school counseling candidates to be door openers for all pre-K–12 students (ASCA, 2020a). Is this gatekeeping in the spirit of the profession of school counseling whose tenet is advocacy for all? Absolutely. School counselor educators realize their primary responsibility is not to the school counseling candidate but to this person's future vulnerable students. Students are mandated to be in the school setting, without legal autonomy over their lives, struggling with identity issues and at the mercy of the adults they should be able to turn to for help, the school counselor they've been assigned to based on identifiers such as their last name or grade level. All these variables and more make it critical that professionals in the field be aware of their power for harm or good and avoid consciously or unconsciously oppressing students. Isms and biases can sabotage objectivity and inhibit a school counselor's ability to work productively with all students. Professionals who harbor biases preventing them from working with segments of their population have work to do. Self-awareness work of ethical school counselors should never end in a profession built on advocacy for all students.

Legislators are introducing bills that conflict with ASCA's Ethical Standards such as Florida's Parents Bill of Rights HB 241, and similar bills have been introduced or passed in Utah, Iowa, Indiana, Alabama, Wyoming, South Dakota, Colorado and the list goes on. Some of these bills have negated the ethical standards requiring school counselors to provide services and to avoid discriminating against a student based on "age, culture, disability, ethnicity, race, religion/spirituality, gender, gender identity, sexual orientation, marital/partnership status, language preference, socioeconomic status, immigration status or any basis proscribed by law" (ASCA, 2022b, p.1). ASCA has a strong policy/government affairs team and continually advocates for an inclusive, affirming school environment for each and every student. ASCA signs onto *amicus* briefs to support our LGBTQ+ youth when they are fighting for their rights in court. For example, ASCA was a signature supporter of an amicus brief for Gavin Grimm in his court battle to use the restroom of his identity.

PROM AND SCHOOL-SPONSORED EVENTS

A student comes to you seeking advice about whether or not she will be able to bring a same-sex date to the prom. Before she approaches the administration, she wanted your thoughts. Can the student legally bring a same-sex date to the prom?

Points to Consider

In a 1980 decision by a U.S. District Court in Rhode Island, a judge found a student's First and 14th Amendment rights were violated when school officials attempted to stop him from escorting another young man to his senior prom (*Fricke v. Lynch* (1980)). Aaron

Fricke, a senior at Cumberland High School, requested permission to attend the senior reception with a male date, and Lynch denied his request, citing his prime concern as fear of violence against the couple. Lawyers for the school argued this was "speech activity" and Fricke had chosen an inappropriate time and place for his speech activity. Judge Pettine recognized Fricke sought to express a political message in a social setting; however, he differentiated Fricke's desire to attend and participate in the dance with leafleting or speech making, which might legitimately be banned at a dance. He found that Fricke's expression took a form "uniquely consonant with the setting he wishes to attend and participate like everyone else" (Fricke v Lynch, 1980, p. 4).

Judge Pettine wrote, "After considerable thought and research, I have concluded that even a legitimate interest in school discipline does not outweigh a student's right to peacefully express his views in an appropriate time, place and manner. To rule otherwise would completely subvert free speech in the schools by granting other students a "heckler's veto," allowing them to decide through prohibited and violent methods what speech will be heard. The First Amendment does not tolerate mob rule by unruly school children" (*Fricke v. Lynch* (1980), p. 5). Fricke and Guilbert were allowed to attend the dance together. The school provided increased security, and the dance was otherwise unremarkable (Associated Press, 1980).

Since 1980, same-sex couples banned from attending their school's prom and other school-sponsored events have used the precedent set by *Fricke v. Lynch* to negotiate permission to attend. In many cases, school districts allow same-sex dates without incident. In one high-profile Mississippi case, Constance McMillen, a lesbian student, was forbidden from wearing a tuxedo to her school's prom and bringing her girlfriend. School officials told her only boys could wear tuxedos and circulated a memo saying all prom dates had to be opposite sex. When the ACLU filed a complaint on her behalf, the school board withdrew their sponsorship from the prom, effectively canceling the event. McMillen sued the Itawamba County School District (*McMillen v. Itawamba County School District, et al.*, 2010), and a federal court agreed in a preliminary ruling that McMillen's constitutional right to freedom of speech was violated. The school board encouraged parents/guardians to organize a private prom, which was represented to be the official prom for most of the student body. However, parents/guardians also organized a second "decoy" prom, which McMillen, her girlfriend and seven other students attended while most of their classmates partied at a private prom 30 miles away.

The ACLU amended their complaint to highlight the humiliation McMillen faced both on prom night, during the school day and at home, as her classmates treated her with hatred and animosity. The court awarded monetary damages to McMillen and required the school district to establish inclusive policies. McMillen's case played out in the national media, and she appeared on several national television shows, including the Ellen DeGeneres show, where she received a $30,000 college scholarship (ACLU, 2010b; ACLU, 2010c; CNN Wire staff, 2010; Johnson, 2010; Jonsson, 2010; Joyner, 2010).

DRESS CODE AND STUDENT EXPRESSION

A student showed up at school with a T-shirt that said, "Gay Pride." The principal made her turn the shirt inside out to hide the message. Was the principal's action legal?

Points to Consider

Heather Gillman sought help from officials at her Florida school when other students were harassing her because she is a lesbian. The principal, David Davis, lectured her that being gay is wrong and outed her to her parents (causing her father to threaten to kick her out of the house). When Gillman missed school the following day, a rumor circulated in the school that she had been suspended because she was gay. To show their support, numerous students wrote "GP" or "gay pride" on their bodies and wore T-shirts supporting gay rights. Davis interrogated 30 students about their sexual orientation, prohibited students from wearing rainbow belts and from writing "GP" or "gay pride" on their arms and notebooks. He required students with such writings to wash them from their arms and hands and lifted the shirts of female students to see if there were writings on their bodies.

Less than two weeks later, Davis suspended 11 students for five days each for their involvement in the gay pride movement. Gillman and her cousin approached the school board with legal counsel asking for guidance on which phrases and symbols were permitted in school. They asked to display rainbows, pink triangles and slogans such as, "Equal, Not Special Rights," "Gay? Fine By Me," "Gay Pride," "I Support Gays," "I'm Straight, But I Vote Pro-Gay" and "Sexual Orientation is Not a Choice. Religion, However, Is." The school board responded that such speech would "likely be disruptive" and ruled the symbols and slogans indicated students were part of a "secret/illegal organization," which was forbidden by school board policy. Gillman sued the Holmes County School Board and Davis. The U.S. District Court ruled in favor of the students, agreeing their First and 14th Amendment rights were violated. The court said the student expression in question was not "vulgar, lewd, obscene, offensive or violent" but instead it was "pure, political and expresses tolerance, acceptance, fairness and support for not only a marginalized group but, more importantly, for a fellow student." The court explained that political speech on controversial topics such as equal rights for gays was likely to lead to debate, and high school students, many of whom are old enough to vote, shouldn't be left out of that national dialogue (*Gillman v. Holmes County School District* (2008); ACLU, 2008a; ACLU, 2009b; Volokh, 2008).

In 2013, the ACLU also fought for and won a student's right to wear a shirt with anti-gay imagery. Seth Groody was banned from his Connecticut high school for wearing a shirt depicting a rainbow with a slash through it, a man and woman holding hands and the words "Excessive Speech Day." He wore it on a designated day of awareness toward harassment of LGBTQ+ people. The Connecticut ACLU said it vehemently disagreed with Groody's views on same-sex marriage but that he was "absolutely correct about his right to express his opinion." As the ACLU prepared a federal lawsuit, a lawyer from the school contacted it to say the student could wear the T-shirt (Associated Press, 2012b; Associated Press, 2013a).

Schools have struggled in recent years with how to address student dress that defies gender stereotypes (Hoffman, 2009). There is substantial case law to caution schools against creating and enforcing dress code policies discriminating on the basis of gender, gender identity or sexual orientation. Katrina Harrington, a seventh-grade transgender student in Brockton, Mass., faced discipline from her principal for wearing skirts, hair accessories and makeup. Harrington, who was assigned male at birth and known in court documents as Pat Doe, had to report to the principal's office daily by the eighth grade to have her clothing approved. If the principal disapproved, he sent her home. This practice forced Harrington to miss so many school days she could not pass the grade, and she eventually quit going to school altogether. Represented by Gay and Lesbian Advocates and Defenders (GLAD), Harrington sued the Brockton School Department for violating her First and 14th Amendment rights for preventing her from attending school wearing her choice of clothes. The Superior Court in Massachusetts ruled a middle school may not prohibit a transgender student from expressing her female gender identity and stated, "Exposing children to diversity at an early age serves the important social goals of increasing their ability to tolerate differences" (GLAD, n.d.a). The school had to allow Harrington to wear any clothing the school dress code allowed, feminine or otherwise (*Doe v. Yunits* (2001); GLAD, n.d.a; GLAD, 2000; NCLR & GLSEN, n.d.).

In 2009, graduating senior Ceara Sturgis posed in a tuxedo for her senior photograph. School officials refused to publish her photo in the yearbook with the other seniors and excluded her name from her senior class. Traditionally, female students at the Mississippi high school wear drapes (to give the appearance of a blouse or dress) and male students wear tuxedos. Sturgis, an honor student who was active in band and soccer, habitually dressed in boy's clothing at school and was openly gay. She hadn't previously had any problems at school and said nobody at school ever made her feel weird or like an outcast. Represented by the ACLU, Sturgis filed a lawsuit against her school, saying it discriminated against her based on her sex and gender expression. After two years, the school settled the lawsuit. Although Sturgis could not be retroactively placed in her yearbook, the high school will include it in her class picture in the school library. The school also agreed to require all students to wear caps and gowns in their senior portraits, instead of gender-specific outfits (ACLU, 2011b; Eng, 2011; Hoffman, 2009; Sturgis, 2011). This is an important point of advice for dress codes. Regulations should ideally be written in gender-neutral language, such as "tops" and "bottoms" without having specific acceptable articles based on gender or perceived gender.

Some state departments of education have issued their own guidance for supporting transgender students. It is the inherent responsibility of school counselors to educate themselves about the laws and policies of the states and districts in which they practice.

INCLUDING TRANSGENDER STUDENTS IN ANTI-BULLYING LEGISLATION

Your state but not your school district has an anti-bullying policy, but the law does not speak to transgender and gender-nonconforming students as protected students. You know at least two of your students who would be better protected with a stronger state and district policy, but you are told the state policy covers what is needed. You think it would be helpful if your district has an anti-bullying policy. Are you right?

Points to Consider

Yes, you are right. In the Hatzenbuehler and Keyes (2013) study, the researchers found that environments in which LGBTQ+ students are embedded can shape their mental health, independent of individual characteristics (ASCA, 2020c). All states have an anti-bullying law, something unheard of just three decades ago. The progress made in anti-bullying legislation is a direct result of the correlation between bullying and school success. In July 2015,

GLSEN released the study From Statehouse to Schoolhouse: Anti-Bullying Policy Efforts in U.S. States and School Districts. State anti-bullying laws appear to influence policy at the local level. From 2008–2011, GLSEN assessed the existence of anti-bullying policies in all 13,181 public school districts from all 50 states and the District of Columbia. Policies existed for 9,296 (70.5%) districts. Of the 70.5% of U.S. school districts with anti-bullying policies, only 14.1% enumerated protections for students based upon their gender identity and/or gender expression. Only 3% of district policies included all three elements recommended by GLSEN (LGBT enumeration, professional development requirements and accountability stipulations).

GLSEN's 2019 National School Climate Survey provides a chilling snapshot of the experiences of transgender students in school. As reviewed in this report, 69.5% of transgender students felt unsafe at school because of their gender expression; 44.9% reported being unable to use the name or pronoun that matched their identity; and 82.1% reported avoiding bathrooms, which can lead to significant life-long health problems (GLSEN, 2019c).

The school counselor in this scenario was right in advocating for a stronger state and district policy that gives explicit protection to students based on sexual orientation, gender identity and gender expression. The 2019 GLSEN National School Climate Survey (2019c) suggests that LGBTQ+ students who believe their schools have policies inclusive of LGBTQ+ students experience better school climates, feel protected and are more likely to report incidents of bullying when they occur. These policies make it possible for LGBTQ+ students to arrive ready to learn each day.

EDUCATIONAL RECORDS AND TRANSGENDER YOUTH

Sam, formerly Samantha, is a middle school student who was assigned female at birth but transitioned to male with the full support of his parents and school staff. Sam wants to wipe his educational records clean of having ever been a female. Can the school comply?

Points to Consider

Privacy of the student's educational records will be a key component to a successful transition. Students should not live-in fear that they will be identified. Educational records as defined by FERPA are legal documents and must include a student's legal name and gender marker. In most states, a court order will be required to change a student's name and gender marker on these records. In some states, such as Massachusetts, school districts can change official records without a court order (Massachusetts Department of Elementary and Secondary Education, 2013). California, in the Gender Recognition Act (2017), allows one to change their gender on their birth certificate without the declaration of a physician and instead asks for an affidavit.

Documents not requiring a student's legal name and gender use the student's preferred name and gender. For example, Sam's identification badge is not a legal document and can be changed from Samantha to Sam. GLSEN suggests the district adopt policies and practices above and beyond the usual compliance to ensure this information is protected. A court order is not needed to address students by a name and pronoun matching their gender identity even if it does not match their educational record.

INVOLVING PARENTS/GUARDIANS IN GENDER IDENTITY AND PROTECTING STUDENTS

You have been working with a student who is struggling with expressing his gender to his world. He is certain of his gender identity, which does not match with "female" as assigned at birth. He wants to be embraced by his family, but he knows this is an impossibility right now as his parents and religion preach against transgender people. He knows it will be years, if ever, before he can involve his parents. He talks to you about his struggles. Are you breaking the law by listening to him and encouraging him to stay strong?

In March 2022, the state of Texas issued a directive requiring the Department of Family and Protective Service (DFPS) to investigate parental abuse if a parent is working with medical professionals to provide any medically necessary treatment such as hormone therapy in support of their transgender child. At the time this book went to press, the Texas ACLU and Lambda Legal were able to secure through the courts a temporary halt to the DFPS investigations, but there was an immediate appeal to halt the halt from the Texas Attorney General. School counselors are not medical purveyors, but I bring this to your attention as just one example of the dozens of laws and court cases across the nation that are directed at LGBTQ+ youth, especially transgender youth. It is not just the medical profession being challenged but educators, including school counselors, are being limited or eliminated in their ability to listen and support transgender and LGBTQ+ students. Currently, two court cases are underway in Florida. The school counselor is at the center of these lawsuits because the claim is the school counselors talked to their students about their struggles with gender identity and failed to notify the parents, who believe it was their right to be informed. Child & Parental Rights Campaign Inc., (CPR-C) a law firm out of Georgia and Virginia, filed the lawsuits against Clay County Schools on the parents' behalf. CPR-C states, "As a nonpartisan, nonprofit public interest law firm, the Child & Parental Rights Campaign Inc. was founded to respond to a radical new ideology overtaking families and threatening the well-being of children and the fundamental right of parents. Children are being led to believe a powerful untruth – that they could be "born in the wrong body." It is our mission to defend the rights of children and parents against this dangerous ideology and to restore the rights of parents to direct the care, education and upbringing of their children. Together we must fight to engage the culture in meaningful ways in order to secure the future of our children and families" (Lambda Legal, 2022, n.p.).

Florida just passed the Parents' Bill of Rights, colloquially known as the "Don't Say Gay" bill, ostensibly to protect the rights of parents and legal guardians to "direct the upbringing, education, health care and mental health" of their child. The bill will limit school counselors support of LGBTQ+ students and threaten to create liability for school counselors and other educators who are acting in good faith to help students negotiate difficult developmental issues.

In a press release March 8, 2022, U.S. Secretary of Education Miguel Cardona stated, "Parents across the country are looking to national, state and district leaders to support our nation's students, help them recover from the pandemic and provide them the academic and mental health supports they need. Instead, leaders in Florida are prioritizing hateful bills that hurt some of the students most in need. The Department of Education has made clear that all schools receiving federal funding must follow federal civil rights law, including Title IX's protections against discrimination based on sexual orientation and gender identity. We stand with our LGBTQ+ students in Florida and across the country and urge Florida leaders to make sure all their students are protected and supported" (USDOE, 2022b).

PARENTS UNAWARE OF THEIR CHILD'S GENDER EXPRESSION

Jackson is a 17-year-old who wants to transition from female to male at school and is adamant that he believes his parents will reject him or worse if they know. Should the school support him to transition in isolation of parental involvement? What if Jackson were 12? Or 9?

Points to Consider

In *D.T. v. Christ* (2020), Doe and Roe are transgender children who wanted to change their birth certificates, but Arizona required reassignment surgery to get a new birth certificate. This is the first such challenge on behalf of children in schools. The disposition of this case is pending. Another more recent case was filed on behalf of three plaintiffs: an adult, and two minors (Campos v. Cohen (2021). Plaintiffs were born in North Carolina but are unable to obtain a birth certificate accurately reflecting their identity. "Birth certificates are essential and foundational identity documents critical for people navigating life. North Carolina's policy explicitly requiring transgender people have surgery to affirm their identity is not only discriminatory but arbitrary and inconsistent with standard medical practice. This discriminatory requirement presents a significant barrier, sometimes insurmountable, to many transgender people, particularly those who may not be able to afford gender-confirmation surgery, or who may not want or need it," said Omar Gonzalez-Pagan, senior attorney and health care strategist at Lambda Legal" (Lambda Legal, 2021b). California and other states are supporting transgender people to change their identity without surgery or hormone therapy. Families and schools working together is a powerful alliance for a safe, respectful school for students' well-being. Parents/guardians of elementary-age children ideally and typically approach educators for support in their child's transition or nonconforming-gender expression.

When parents/guardians are not aware or seem not to be addressing a struggling child's need for support, the educators must decide how to tip the balance in the student's favor, and that can only be done in context. When students are in middle or high school, the decision is easier as students can be consulted and can shed light on many of the issues surrounding parent/guardian notification, such as how safe they feel in involving their parents/guardians.

Even with middle and high school students, a child's developmental level is a crucial consideration and one very much in the forefront when making decisions about an elementary-age child. Err on the side of caution by respecting the child's privacy when struggling for an answer as to whether or not to inform parents/guardians, as there should be an overriding and compelling reason to do so. Avoiding the wrath of parents/guardians who says they should have been informed is not a compelling reason. It can be dangerous for gay or lesbian children to be outed to their parents, and likewise, transgender students can also be vulnerable to homelessness, rejection or abuse. Proceed with great caution and if possible, student involvement.

Every educator can appreciate how critically important support from parents/guardians is for transitioning students. The hard part for educators is when they know that transgender students want desperately to be able to express their deeply held sense of their own gender but don't feel emotionally or physically safe letting their parents/guardians know. Like so many issues we face as school counselors, this one is context-dependent without a hard and fast answer, but there is some guidance.

What we do know through laws applied in court cases is that transgender and gender-non-conforming students have the right to express their gender identity openly at school. What is not clear is how educators apply parents'/guardians' rights to be the guiding voice in their children's lives when students are in the throes of this complex issue and want to negotiate it without parent/guardian involvement. The context of this scenario is that the student told educators he might be in harm's way if his parents are called. A skilled educator such as the school counselor could work with the student to uncover any additional information that might shed light on his fear of involving his parents and to help the student consider possible scenarios and implications if his parents accidentally learn of his transition. This conversation should not discourage the student from moving forward but should help him weigh the impact of telling his parents at this point in time and possibly serve to help him become empowered so he will allow the educators to support him in involving his parents.

The primary goal is to help the student have a safe place to learn while expressing authentic identity, and school might be the only place the student feels safe. A strong secondary goal is to help the student's family accept his gender identity. The publication "Schools in Transition: A Guide for Supporting Transgender Students in K–12 Schools" (Gender Spectrum, 2015) helps educators better serve students who decide to transition alone with best practices, such as using the student's legal name and corresponding pronoun when contacting parents.

Educators who help students transition in school in absence of parental involvement will likely bring on parents'/guardians' wrath if they believe the school overstepped their authority to help their child transition at school. In Leon County, Fla., parents filed a civil lawsuit against the school board claiming the school created a support plan to socially transition their child without parental involvement (*Littlejohn v. School Board of Leon County*, 2021). Court documents' accusation is that the "defendants have violated plaintiffs' fundamental rights by, inter alia, implementing a protocol which explicitly circumvents parental notification and involvement in critical decisions affecting their children's mental, emotional and physical health, i.e., the children's assertion of a discordant gender identity and accommodations to facilitate asserting the discordant gender identity at school" (*Littlejohn v. School Board of Leon County*, 2021, p.1).

Helping students transition in isolation of parental involvement carries risk that educators have to strongly consider. Many will weather the risk when they see students suffering and express fear should their parents/guardians know. Educators cannot practice risk-free but in context weigh the greater good for the student against the potential fallout for the district. Community standards play into how educators will choose to respond. The tug of war for educators is that we would not want to place students in harm's way, nor can we disallow them to express their gender identity. Proceed with as many facts as you can and with as much guidance as the student is developmentally able to give you. It could be that parents' negative reaction might come from worry that their child will be mistreated or have a difficult life. Educators can help allay those fears through literature and resources.

TRANSGENDER STUDENTS AND PHYSICAL FACILITIES

Gabe used the boys' restroom without incident for several years, until a group of parents found out he was biologically assigned female at birth and made an outcry that he be stopped. The district pulled his rights to use the restroom coinciding with his gender identity. Does Title IX protect him?

Points to Consider

Research underscores the damage to transgender youth when they are unable to live consistently with their gender identity. This disaffirmation of a child's identity can have dire consequences (Pullen Sansfaçon et al, 2019). Pronouns, dress, chosen names and facilities all matter profoundly for transgender children.

For Gavin Grimm, Aug. 25, 2020, was a victorious day after a five-year battle to get recognition that he should have been allowed to use the restroom for the gender in which he identified. The Fourth Circuit Court of Appeals ruled it is a violation of Title IX to segregate transgender students from their peers for restrooms. In June 2021, the U.S. Supreme Court allowed the lower court's decision in support of Gavin Grimm to stand, signaling a victory for all transgender youth.

Grimm's long journey to victory included an ill-fated trip to the Supreme Court in 2017, when the Trump administration pulled the support transgender students were given under Title IX just prior to his case being heard. Title IX of the Education Amendments of 1972 states, "No person shall be subjected to discrimination in any educational program or activity based on sex." Undefined in Title IX is sex, but before February 2017, Title IX was being applied to transgender youth. During the Trump administration, gender was defined as binary, taking away protection for transgender youth under Title IX.

The Gavin Grimm case coupled with another case, *Bostock v. Clayton*, led to a significant change in the way transgender students are viewed. In June 2020, the Supreme Court ruled in favor of three workers in the Bostock case who were fired because they were transgender. The court stated, "It is impossible to discriminate against a person for being homosexual or transgender without discriminating against that individual based on sex." This landmark Supreme Court civil rights case held that Title VII of the Civil Rights Act of 1964 protects employees against discrimination because of their sexual orientation or gender identity.

The clear message that transgender is about sex means discrimination against transgender students is about gender, and Title IX is about gender discrimination.

The justices giving the majority opinion in the Bostock case acknowledged the decision will extend beyond Title VII to other federal or state laws that prohibit sex discrimination or invalidate sex-segregated bathrooms, locker rooms and dress codes. The court reiterated that the only issue it was deciding was that an employer who fires someone simply for being homosexual or transgender has violated Title VII. However, these two court cases are widely celebrated by those seeking opportunities for transgender youth. The findings of these two critically important court cases have to affect how OCR interprets and handles violations of transgender rights under Title IX.

Paul D. Castillo, Lambda Legal counsel and students' rights strategist, stated, "This is an incredible victory for Gavin Grimm and transgender students' right to be themselves at school. There should be no doubt that federal law requires schools to protect all students. Courts all over the country, as well as the federal government have made [it] crystal clear that LGBTQ+I+ students are protected by federal law and have a right to an equal education, to be protected against harassment and discrimination and to a school environment where they can be their authentic selves" (Castillo, 2021). Under the Biden administration, the Department of Justice and the Department of Education have affirmed these court decisions in a newly minted Dear Educator Letter (USDOE OCR, 2021a).

The controversy is not over. At the time this book went to press, a coalition of 20 states filed a complaint against the Biden administration over the administration's support of transgender youth to use the restroom of their identity, participate on sports teams and be identified using pronouns that correlate to their identity (Mattise, 2021). In *Parents for Privacy v. Barr* (2020), a group of parents lost their challenge to their school district's policy of allowing transgender students to use the restroom consistent with their gender identity. The District Court dismissed the parents' suit saying the policy did not infringe on the rights of nontransgender students. The parents appealed, but in 2020, the Ninth Circuit Court of Appeals upheld the lower court's decision (*Parents for Privacy v. Barr*, 2020).

In another case that has had a long and winding road through the courts, Drew Adams is fighting for his right to use the boy's restroom. In *Adams v. School Board of St. John's County*, in a summary judgment (judge-made not jury-made judgment), Judge Corrigan ruled that the school's restroom policy violated Title IX. The school district appealed to the 11th Circuit Court of Appeals, which ruled in 2020 that the trial court's ruling stands under Title IX and the Equal Protection Clause of the U.S. Constitution. The school board filed a request for a rehearing *en banc* meaning that the district is asking that the full circuit court hear the case in an effort to overturn a decision reached by the 11th Circuit three-judge panel. That request is still pending and awaiting a final decision (*Adams v. School Board of St. John's County*, 2021). On June 14, 2021, in response to the motion for reconsideration by the entire 11th Circuit, the three-judges reconsidered their opinion and ruled for Drew without using Title IX but using a more-narrow approach under equal protection. St. Johns School District policy allows transgender students who register to use the restroom of their identity but not those who transition after registering. The court said their policy is unconstitutionally arbitrary. On Aug. 4, 2021, the school again asked the full 11th

Circuit to reconsider the appeal. The school district's motion was pending at the time this book went to press. The Drew Adams case again highlights the complications transgender students face just to use the restroom.

School counselors contribute to the efforts to create a safe, respectful school climate for transgender youth and gender-nonconforming students. All students must have a learning environment that affirms their gender identities. Progress has been made, but the legislators and the courts will continue to refine and define law that gives educators guidance in this area. Keep up to date on changes, and consult the legal arm of your district. Find valuable resources at GLSEN intended to help educators affirm all students (GLSEN, 2019a). The scenarios and points to consider in this chapter are not intended to be the final word or legal advice, as transgender youth are still fighting in many states for their right to be an equal participant in the education process.

The June 2021 Department of Education fact sheet, Supporting Transgender Youth in School, instructs school districts to support transgender youth. "Discrimination based on sex – including sexual orientation and gender identity – isn't just wrong, it's prohibited in America's schools. For transgender students in particular, this discrimination can threaten students' well-being and ability to thrive or even participate in school… . There are many ways for schools to ensure that all students, including transgender students, are safe… . Here are examples of policies and practices:

- Using welcoming and inclusive language
- Ensuring that school policies clearly affirm students' right to be free from discrimination based on sexual orientation or gender identity.
- Adopting policies that respect all students' gender identities, such as using the name a student goes by, which may be different from their legal name, and pronouns that reflect a student's gender identity.
- Adopting policies or model plans to guide school staff on how to support students and communicate with families.
- Facilitating opportunities for students to find support with peers, teachers, faculty and staff, such as student-led organizations, and identifying safe spaces on campus.
- Providing professional development opportunities for educators on equitable and supportive treatment of historically marginalized students, including LGBTQ+ youth, and taking steps to promote increased diversity among educators.

RESOURCES AND ADVOCACY TOOLS

Numerous resources, position statements, webinars and advocacy tools to support LGBTQ+ students are available on the ASCA website at *www.schoolcounselor.org*.

Additional resources are available from:
APA Office on Sexual Orientation and Gender Diversity
www.apa.org/pi/lgbt

The Bisexual Resource Center
www.biresource.org

Children of Lesbians and Gays Everywhere (COLAGE)
www.colage.org

GLSEN
www.glsen.org

Welcoming Schools
www.welcomingschools.org

Lambda Legal Defense and Education Fund
www.lambdalegal.org

Parents, Families, and Friends of Lesbians and Gays (PFLAG)
https://pflag.org

Point Foundation
www.pointfoundation.org

In a Position to Know: A School Counseling Candidate Speaks

The case presented at the beginning of the chapter is revisited here and discussed further by a practicing school counseling candidate. Compare her thoughts with your approach.

A SCHOOL COUNSELOR'S ATTITUDE

Alexia Huart had been taught in religious training and at home that being gay is a choice, and people who make the choice to be gay are misguided. She never really questioned her beliefs, and she thought as a school counselor in training it really did not matter how she felt about gays. Huart's preparation program pushed her to examine her biases. Must school counselors continually take inventory and confront their own prejudices and beliefs about others regarding diversity issues such as sexual orientation and gender identity?

I never had to confront my values or what I thought of others' values prior to entering the school counseling program. The more courses I took, the more my values, biases and prejudices were challenged. At first, my reaction was, "So, what's the big deal? My thoughts and opinions are mine and should not matter or affect my ability to become a successful school counselor."

But I began to realize confronting my values was of extreme importance. I learned that when it comes to a student's issues and situations, what I think, my nonverbal behavior (i.e., my reactions: empathy, shock, horror, concern or indifference), as well as what I say, could make a crucial difference in the student's life. I think about students who could be spared pain or brought back from the brink of suicide just by a caring look, empathy or unconditional support from an educator.

My entire life I believed I was trying to be vigilant in respecting beliefs and cultural differences. I had a great desire to learn more about others, regardless of race, ethnicity or religion. Now the professors in my school counseling preparation program were adding to the pot sexual differences. I had no idea as to the challenge it would bring to my doorstep. Now I have to look into myself and address my beliefs and biases [concerning lesbian and gay people]. I felt I respected the rights of others to be different from me, but did I really? Did I ever consider their actual pain? Not until I watched "The Laramie Project," the moving story of Matthew Shepard (Baldwin & Kaufman, 2002).

Matthew was beaten, tied to a fence and left for dead because he was gay. After watching "The Laramie Project" and seeing Matthew's father give his impassioned speech during the sentencing phase of the trail, I was changed. Anyone who has a heart would realize it doesn't matter about Matthew's skin color or sexual orientation. He was a son, a classmate, a neighbor, a friend, a person – a human being. This man and his family suffered pain and devastation, like so many who've experienced the cruelty of hatred, prejudice and ignorance, which will never go away.

After much pondering and soul searching on my own, I have concluded that there is a plethora of qualities a counselor should possess to do an adequate job in his or her field. Chief among them are fairness, loyalty, and a tolerance and appreciation for diversity. In the world in which we live, one must do a personal inventory of where he or she stands in view of these most necessary attributes. There are some things that cannot be acquired from a book. One can study forever and still not possess the qualities needed to work with people successfully or compassionately. This takes personal effort and determination to improve your character and view of the world at large. I'm determined to grow daily through my interactions with others regardless of race, creed, ethnicity or sexual orientation. It's not a pat on the back by any means, just a "charge to keep" to myself, personally.

– Alexia Huart, retired staff development teacher at P.S. 224 in Brooklyn, N.Y.

Making Connections

1. Develop 10 strategies you would like to implement to reduce harassment of and actively affirm LGBTQ+ students in your school. Consider what changes you can advocate for including school policy; LGBTQ+ visibility in school celebrations and assemblies; professional development for administrators, faculty and staff; creating supportive clubs, etc. What actions can you take to increase awareness of these issues and to strengthen your intervention and support?

2. What are the human costs to LGBTQ+ students in dangerous school climates? Cite some statistics to show their peculiar vulnerability. How do these statistics relate to the students at your school? Consider conducting GLSEN's Local School Climate Survey of your students to better gauge their realities of LGBTQ+ students in your school. Go to *http://localsurvey.glsen.org*

3. View the HBO film "The Laramie Project," or attend a local production of the documentary play. What is your reaction? Pick a character in the movie and write your

reaction about the barriers or contributions that person made to acceptance of diversity. There are recent revelations from the defendants that Matthew Shepard may not have been a victim of a hate crime but a target for robbery; does this change the impact of the re-enactment for you?

4. What are your personal beliefs about sexual orientation, gender identity and gender expression? How will your attitudes and beliefs be manifested in your work? Is this a problem? If so, what will you do to minimize harm to your students?

5. Why is it particularly important for school counselors to promote diversity and respect for all students?

Chapter 10 Quiz

1) Heterosexist climates are a system of attitudes, biases, assumptions and discrimination in favor of opposite-sex relationships and attractions and should:
   a. Be encouraged in schools as students suffer discrimination if they identify as gay
   b. Be promoted because students need to be developmentally and legally able to make their own decisions before they identify openly as gay
   c. Intentionally demonstrate heterosexism is the expected norm in America, and schools should reflect the values of a society
   d. Be intentionally eradicated as LGBTQ+ students need to be able to feel safe and be knowledgeable that their school environment is inclusive of them
   e. Be encouraged to avoid outing LGBTQ+ students who might experience violence, bias and harassment

2) Which of the following statements is not correct?
   a. LGBTQ+ individuals are the only cultural minority group to typically grow up in families outside of their cultural group.
   b. The societal condemnation of sexual minorities contributes to the internal struggle faced by LGBTQ+ students and often influences them to keep their identities a secret.
   c. When educators out students to their parents/guardians (tell parents/guardians of students' sexual orientation or gender identity) they may be placing them in a position of being rejected or worse if they live in unsupportive homes.
   d. It is appropriate to post signs in schools that signify rights and responsibilities of students as citizens of the school to help one another.
   e. The American Psychiatric Association supports reparative therapy as an appropriate action by professionals in working with LGBTQ+ youth.

3) Diversity training in schools should:
   a. Convey the message that the school community will not permit intolerance for any group
   b. Convey the message the school community will not permit intolerance for any group but should leave out LGBTQ+ youth as too controversial
   c. Only occur in high schools because of the developmental levels of middle- and elementary-age students

d. Challenge and encourage students to come out of the closet and reveal themselves as gay so they are free to be themselves
e. Stay focused on only the ethnicities present in the school so as to advantage these students

4) In the court case *Hamilton v. Vallejo City Unified School District,* a school counselor required a student to attend a special weekly support group for gay students. Why was this problematic?
a. Small groups have no place in schools.
b. The school counselor used her role to forward her own religious beliefs and to attack a student's identity.
c. There was a clear policy in the school district that students were never to identify as gay; therefore, a support group for gays should not have been possible.
d. The school counselor had not been trained on running a support group for gays.
e. The students in the group did not tell their parents/guardians about the true nature of the group.

5) Gay-straight alliance clubs:
a. Are permitted in schools and protected by the Equal Access Act of 1984
b. Were banned by the U.S. Supreme Court as against parents' rights to be the guiding voice in their children's lives in value-laden issues
c. Set LGBTQ+ students up to be the subject of increased harassment and bullying
d. Are permitted only if parents/guardians sign permission slips due to the club's sensitive nature
e. Are permitted only if outside agencies or institutions direct, conduct, control and attend to the activities of the club

Key Terms

Amicus brief
Biological sex
Bisexuality
Cisgender
COLAGE
Coming out
Community standards
Conversion or reparative therapy
Equal Access Act
GLSEN
Gay-straight alliance club
Gender-sexuality alliance club
Gender-expansive
Gender expression
Gender
Gender identity
Gender nonconforming
Heterosexism
Homophobia
Intersex
Marginalized identities
Nonbinary
PFLAG
Physical and emotional safety
Privacy rights of minors
Questioning
Relational aggression
School climate
School culture
Sexual orientation
The Safe Schools Coalition
Title IX of Educational Amendment of 1972
Transgender
Trans man
Trans women
Trevor Project

Sexual Harassment

By the time you have completed this chapter, you should be able to:

- Discuss the role of the U.S. Department of Education Office for Civil Rights in sexual harassment and dating violence
- Discuss the legal implications of ignoring sexual harassment
- Explain the emotional cost to victims of sexual harassment
- Develop strategies preventing repeated occurrences of sexual harassment
- Understand the elements of a sexual harassment policy and how a policy can be put into practice

Ethical Standards Addressed in this Chapter

Professionalism means knowing your professional association's ethical standards and adhering to them. The ASCA Ethical Standards for School Counselors (2022b) most relevant to this chapter are the following. School counselors:

- Maintain appropriate boundaries and are aware that any sexual or romantic relationship with students (whether legal or illegal in the state of employment) is a grievous breach of ethics and is prohibited regardless of a student's age or consent. This prohibition applies to both in-person and electronic interactions and relationships. (A.1.i.)
- Report to administration and/or appropriate authorities (e.g., law enforcement) when a student discloses a perpetrated or a perceived threat to another person's physical or mental well-being. This threat may include but is not limited to verbal abuse, physical abuse, sexual abuse, neglect, dating violence, bullying or harassment. The school counselor follows applicable federal and state laws and school and district policy. (A.9.e.)
- Actively work to establish a safe, equitable, affirming school environment in which all members of the school community demonstrate respect, inclusion and acceptance. (A.10.b.)
- Understand and advocate for all students right to be treated in a manner that honors and respects their gender identity, gender expression, sexual orientation, language and ability status, and to be free from any form of discipline, harassment or discrimination based on their identity and expression. (A.10.e)
- Report all incidents of bullying, dating violence or harassment to administration, recognizing these behaviors may fall under Title IX of the Education Amendments of 1972 or other federal and state laws as being illegal and require administrator interventions. (A.11.d.)

- In developmentally appropriate ways and in the context of the incident, support victims, encourage growth and provide tools for accountability and change (e.g., restorative practices) in perpetrators and promote healing in the school community while deferring to administration for all discipline issues or any other violation of federal and state laws or district and school policies. (A.11.g.)

The full text of the ASCA Ethical Standards for School Counselors is available at *www.schoolcounselor.org*.

Introduction

The Biden administration announced in October 2021 that the Trump administration's interpretation of Title IX as applied to sexual harassment will receive a major overhaul by April 2022 (date is not binding). This is welcome news for victims of sexual harassment, as the new regulations should provide more protective for victims. Eighteen attorneys general filed suit when the Trump Administration unveiled its interpretation of Title IX as it pertains to sexual harassment. The Biden administration promised to roll back the changes. Throughout this chapter there will be notations of areas expected to be overhauled under the Biden administration. However, presented throughout this chapter are school counselors legal and ethical imperative that will not change regardless of which presidential administration is interpreting Title IX; when in doubt, refer to the latest regulations post-April 2022.

The U.S. Department of Education Office for Civil Rights (OCR) governs the implementation of Title IX. Sexual harassment has been the focus of much discourse and debate within the context of social and educational policy. Understanding what constitutes sexual harassment and how to respond to it is now as much a part of being an educator as teaching the alphabet. Sex discrimination, especially regarding the influence of gender in educational opportunities, was outlawed by Title IX, enacted by Congress in 1972 (Title IX of the Educational Amendments of 1972). OCR defines sexual harassment as conduct that is sexual in nature, is unwelcome and denies or limits a student's ability to participate in or benefit from a school's education program (USDOE OCR, 2022).

There are two types of sexual harassment in schools: hostile environment and *quid pro quo*. Hostile environment is any sex-based or gender-based intimidation. "Sexual harassment does not always have to be 'sexual.' It can also look or feel like teasing, intimidating or offensive comments based on stereotypes (e.g., about how certain people "are" or should act) or bullying someone based on their sex, gender identity (man, woman, trans, intersex, nonbinary, two-spirit) or sexual orientation (queer, bisexual, lesbian, gay, asexual, pansexual, etc.). There is no requirement that the sexually harassing person or persons derive any sexual pleasure from their acts or that they are sexually attracted to their victims" (Equal Rights Advocates, 2022).

Quid pro quo sexual harassment means something for something, where benefits are conditioned upon the grant of sexual favors. *Quid pro quo* is when a school employee causes students to believe they must submit to unwelcome sexual conduct to participate in a school activity or that the employee will make an educational decision based on whether or not students submit to unwelcome sexual conduct (USDOE OCR, 2022). In a school setting, student benefits can include grades, admission to a program, scholarships and grants in exchange for sexual favors" (Perry & Marcum, 2008).

Males and females often look at sexual harassment in different ways. Regardless of which gender or educational institution is defining sexual harassment, three elements are present: the behavior is sexual in nature or at least related to the person's gender, the behavior occurs in an unequal relationship where one person has more power over another (physical, psychological, authoritative or other), and the behavior is unsolicited or unwelcome (Espelege et. al., 2016).

OCR provided examples of sexual conduct within the school system. Some examples are: making sexual propositions or pressuring students for sexual favors; touching of a sexual nature; writing graffiti of a sexual nature; displaying or distributing sexually explicit drawings, pictures or written materials; performing sexual gestures or touching oneself sexually in front of others; telling sexual or dirty jokes; spreading sexual rumors or rating other students as to sexual activity or performance; or circulating or showing emails or websites of a sexual nature (USDOE OCR, 2021c).

Title IX ensures students are not sexually harassed during any activities associated with schools such as academic, educational, extracurricular, athletic and other programs regardless of where programs take place. OCR believes a single act of sexual harassment can create a hostile environment in schools and hinder academic achievement (USDOE OCR, 2021c). When school officials are aware of student-on-student harassment, Title IX mandates schools take immediate action to eliminate further instances, prevent recurrences and address issues that may arise. School must also have a published nondiscrimination policy and a grievance procedure all employees are trained to implement. (US ED OCR, 2021c).

In a 2018 study by Grigentyte and Lesinskiene, 200 16- to 19-year-old students relayed their experiences with sexual harassment. Sixty-five percent of the girls and 35% of the boys indicated they had experienced one of the three forms of sexual harassment (verbal, gestures or physical). Girls were significantly more likely to experience unwelcome sexual behavior. Half of the victims reported that sexual harassment had some impact on their mood, with 11% reported having sleep disturbances and 9% experienced a change in eating habits.

Espelege et. al. (2015) conducted a two-year study that found middle school students who bully as children are more likely to perpetrate sexual harassment in adolescence. Sexual harassment at younger ages is not typically about sex itself but about gender identity (Hill & Kearl, 2011; Espelege et. al. 2015). Young, Allen and Ashbaker (n.d.) explained boys and girls experience different types of sexual harassment. "Girls are more likely than boys to be physically harassed and are also more likely to be harassed by adults. Girls are more likely to be touched, grabbed, pinched or brushed up against in a sexual way (Young, Allen & Ashbaker, n.d.). Girls are more likely to report boys as perpetrators, and boys are more likely to report other boys and close friends as their perpetrators (Espelege et. al., 2016). The National Women's Law Center (2021) also addressed the issue of sexual harassment in schools. It found "56% of female and 40% of male students in grades 7 through 12 had been sexually harassed at school in ways that interfered with their lives." (p. 1). Students continue to avoid telling an adult in the school. "Fewer than one in four students in grades

7–12 who are sexually harassed report the incident to a teacher, guidance counselor or other school employee. A minuscule 2% of girls ages 14–18 who are kissed or touched without their consent report it to their schools. Many students choose not to report because of shame or self-blame, fear that no one will help them, fear of retaliation, fear of being disciplined by their school or fear of police or immigration officials. Other students do not report sexual harassment because they simply do not know that their schools can help them." (National Women's Law Center, 2021, p.2).

School counselors in their role as advocates for students serve as anchors and sources of strength for individual students in dealing with issues of sexual harassment in schools. Educators promote a safe and respectful school climate for all students by providing students with the knowledge and support they need. School counselors are part of that imperative. As leaders within school settings, school counselors can participate in efforts to raise awareness among students and fellow educators as to the problem of sexual harassment. Confidentiality is superseded by the legal imperative to report when students are the target of illegal behavior.

Court rulings have given school counselors support for raising awareness and making positive change for victims of sexual harassment. One important court case is the U.S. Supreme Court decision in *Davis v. Monroe County Board of Education* (1999), based on a violation of Title IX. Davis demands advocacy against known sexual harassment. In the Davis, case a fifth-grade girl and her mother, Mrs. Davis, repeatedly complained to teachers and the principal for five months regarding sexual abuse behaviors by another student, G.F., but they received no relief of any kind. In desperation, Mrs. Davis filed a complaint with the Monroe County, Ga., Sheriff's Department, and G.F. pled guilty to sexual battery. Mrs. Davis' subsequent lawsuit under Title IX's prohibition of sex discrimination in schools ended with a Supreme Court decision in her favor. Justice Sandra Day O'Connor emphasized a relatively stringent standard of proof for plaintiffs. Liability may be imposed if the harassment is so severe, pervasive and objectively offensive that it deprives a student of an equal educational opportunity. Additionally, school officials must know of and be deliberately indifferent to the sexual harassment. The Davis case decidedly supports school counselors in exercising their leadership and advocacy role to help students victimized by their peers (*Davis v. Monroe County Board of Education,* 1999).

Teacher-on-student sexual harassment also takes place in America's schools. The important U.S. Supreme Court decision in *Franklin v. Gwinnett County Public Schools* (1992) established a legal precedent by drawing a parallel between teacher-on-student sexual harassment and supervisor-to-subordinate harassment in the workplace (Zirkel, 2001b, 2002). Teacher-on-student sexual harassment was extended to student-on-student sexual harassment in subsequent court cases (Alexander & Alexander, 2019).

Schools may respond to alleged sexual misconduct that does not meet the definition of sexual harassment in the 2020 amendments as Title IX is not the exclusive remedy for sexual misconduct or traumatic events that affect students. "A school has discretion to respond appropriately to reports of sexual misconduct that do not fit within the scope of conduct covered by the Title IX grievance process… . Put simply, Title IX's sexual harassment regulation need not replace a school's more expansive code of conduct and does not prohibit a school from enforcing that code to address misconduct that does not constitute sexual harassment under the 2020 amendments. OCR encourages schools to develop and enforce their codes as an additional tool for ensuring safe and supportive educational environments for all students" (USDOE OCR, 2021a, p 6-7).

The purpose of this chapter is to explore through case study the legal and ethical implications of deliberate indifference to sexual harassment, the emotional cost to youth and the financial cost to school districts if we do not act on students' behalf.

Getting Started: What Would You Do?

The following case is discussed for you at the end of this chapter by a school counselor educator. Before you read his response, decide how you would approach this ethical dilemma.

CYBERSEXUAL HARASSMENT

Using computers at both the school and her home, Ashley has been sending Kenneth provocative pictures of herself and long love letters, not seeming to care he has asked her to leave him alone. Ashley has emailed her communications to Kenneth and to her friends, who have also sent them to other friends. She is texting people about every move Kenneth makes, what he wears and what his afterschool activities are each day. All this attention across electronic media feels creepy to Kenneth. Ashley has made such an issue of her "love" for him, Kenneth feels he has become the object of ridicule. Despite his embarrassment, he feels frustrated he does not seem to have any recourse with Ashley and must simply endure, continuing to tell her he is not interested. Is this harassment? Could this be sexual harassment? Could Ashley be breaking any laws or school board policies? What recourse, if any, does Kenneth have?

Working Through Case Studies

SEXUAL HARASSMENT AND CONFIDENTIALITY

Samantha, a 14-year-old girl, is continually harassed by her classmate Devin, who keeps asking her to meet him for sex, along with descriptions about what he would do to her. She feared retaliation if she told on him, so she has kept quiet until now. She confides in you, begging you not to tell anyone. Is your primary obligation to protect Samantha's confidentiality or to inform administration?

Points to Consider

Samantha fits the profile of the harassed student. She uses avoidance techniques and wants to be free of the harassment but endures it rather than risking becoming known as an informant or having Devin take his revenge out on her for reporting him. Once regarded as harmless, flirtatious or playful, sexual harassment is now widely understood to be destructive, illegal and damaging. Must you report the sexual harassment to school administration? Absolutely.

School counselors are required by law to report sexual harassment to school officials otherwise OCR calls it deliberate indifference, regardless of the reasons why we did not report the harassment. Confidentiality is superseded by the need to report under Title IX. Once a school has notice of possible sexual harassment of students, they must take immediate and appropriate steps to begin the process of remediating the harassment by following Title IX's regulations. A school has actual notice of sexual harassment if an agent or responsible employee of the school receives notification (U.S. Department of Education, Office for Civil Rights, 2022). In elementary and secondary school settings, a school must respond whenever any school employee has notice of sexual harassment. This includes notice to a teacher, teacher's aide, bus driver, cafeteria worker, school counselor, school resource officer, maintenance staff worker, coach, athletic trainer or any other school employee. (USDOE OCR, 2021c)

OFF-CAMPUS DATING VIOLENCE

Mia was sexually harassed by Alex at a party last weekend, and they share geometry together. She asked to move to another geometry class, and she finally tells you why. What do you do?

As discussed in the previous case, you are not allowed to keep her assault confidential; you must tell the administration. Under the Obama administration, school districts had to investigate sexual harassment regardless of where it occurred if it created a hostile environment for a student, such as this one for Mia. Both students are in the same school and, in this case, the same class, and the hostile environment is stratifying the victim's (complainant's) education. The Trump administration changed this to remove the hostile environment if the harassment did not occur during a school-sanctioned event; however, the student code of conduct can step in where Title IX leaves off and support Mia. The Biden administration is revisiting the Trump administration changes and will most likely return to the Obama approach. Regardless of where the regulations land, districts "should offer supportive measures to a complainant who reports sexual harassment that occurred outside the [school's] education program or activity, and any sexual harassment that does occur in an education program or activity must be responded to even if it related to, or happens subsequent to, sexual harassment that occurred outside the education program or activity. When a school finds a respondent responsible for sexual harassment under its Title IX grievance process, the school must provide remedies to the complainant that are designed to restore or preserve equal access to the [school's] education program or activity. These remedies may include the same individualized services that the school provided to the complainant as supportive measures, additional services or different services. These remedies can be disciplinary or punitive and can burden the respondent. Schools are required to [d]escribe the range of possible disciplinary sanctions and remedies or list the possible disciplinary sanctions and remedies; however the preamble clarifies that this requirement is not intended to unnecessarily restrict a [school's] ability to tailor disciplinary sanctions to address specific situations" (USDOE OCR, 2021a, n.p.).

In other words, schools can offer supportive measures to Mia, the complainant, (alleged victim) and can discipline the respondents (alleged perpetrator), it is just not an Office for Civil Rights violation under the Trump administration, but it may well once again become a Title IX violation under Biden.

DANGEROUS AND ILLEGAL WORDS

Kayla comes to see you about her discomfort with a group of boys who are sexually harassing her in English class, but when she told the teacher she responded "just ignore their foolishness. I will watch out and catch them." Is the teacher acting illegally?

Points to Consider

Yes, the teacher is setting the school district up for a possible OCR violation. The words "just ignore their foolishness," "boys will be boys," "she is just trying to get your attention," "enjoy the flirt," are dangerous words. School officials are not legally allowed to ignore sexual harassment. Kayla is in a hostile environment according to the OCR. The perpetrators are affecting Kayla's ability to participate in the educational program. Title IX is the equal-access law, meaning students education cannot be stratified based on their gender (US ED OCR, 2022). The imperative to act that comes from the Supreme Court in *Davis v. Monroe County Board of Education* supports school counselors to advocate that Kayla be helped. If a school determines sexual harassment has occurred, it should take reasonable, timely, age-appropriate and effective corrective action, including steps tailored to the specific situation.

DISCIPLINE FOR THE VICTIM OF SEXUAL HARASSMENT

One of your students was sexually assaulted by another student in the stairwell. The victim ended up being disciplined for indecency. You are shocked and feel there must be a law that supports the victim not to be victimized twice. Are you correct?

Jane Doe was suspended by her Georgia high school after reporting that she was assaulted by a classmate. Doe was forced to engage in a sexual act at school, and instead of treating it like an assault, school administration treated it as sexual misconduct and indecency. The case the student brought against the district was settled out of court but not before many advocacy groups brought an *amicus* brief to the appellant court. The *amicus* brief argued that the district's response undermined the purpose of Title IX and "puts students at risk of further traumatization. And by chilling reporting of such incidents, unfair discipline leaves student survivors – particularly students of color – without protection or recourse. *Amici* implore the Fourth Circuit to make clear that, to protect students' equal access to educational opportunities, Title IX requires schools to protect, not punish, student survivors like Jane Doe" (NWLC, 2022, n.p.).

YOUNG CHILDREN AND SEXUAL HARASSMENT

A mother comes to you and complains her kindergartener is being sexually harassed by another student. The mother explains that a male student kissed her child on the cheek several times last week. Can young children engage in sexual harassment?

Points to Consider

OCR addresses the issue of sexual harassment among minors by stating, "School personnel should consider the age and maturity of students in responding to allegations of sexual harassment. When determining whether a young child has committed sexual harassment, it is important for teachers and school administrators to use good judgment and common sense" (USDOE OCR, 2008, p. 7). OCR depicts the issues that may be of concern in this area in the following scenarios: "On one occasion, a first-grade student kisses another first-grade student on the cheek in the playground" (USDOE OCR, 2008, p. 8). This situation is not sexual harassment. This other situation is: "On numerous occasions over a period of several months, a fifth-grade student inappropriately touches another fifth-grade student and makes overtly sexual comments and gestures to that student" (USDOE OCR, 2008, p. 8). The perpetrator's conduct is only considered to be sexual harassment when it is unwelcomed by the victim and affects the victim's performance in school activities. 2020 amendments to Title IX place even more emphasis on schools' legal responsibility to respond to complaints of sexual harassment by establishing protocols and educating students of all ages on their rights to report incidents of sexual harassment (USDOE OCR, 2021c).

TEACHER ON STUDENT SEXUAL HARASSMENT

A teacher is having a sexual relationship with a student who is at the age of consent for her state. Is this illegal?

Points to Consider

It is outrageous, and in many states it is not only outrageous but a possible felony charge, as it is illegal when educators have a sexual relationship with students in their school, even if the student is at the age of consent. The position of trust and the differentiation in power means there is never consensual sex between educators and students in their school. See the Chapter 7 Child Abuse for more details, as this is child abuse and sexual harassment all rolled into one.

STUDENT INCAPABLE OF IDENTIFYING SEXUAL-HARASSMENT BEHAVIOR

You are walking down the hall, and you see Meri pulling away from Marvin, who is trying to kiss her. From the look on her face, it is obvious she wants no part of his show of affection. He blocks her by pushing his shoulders into her, and with quick steps and small shoulder pushes, he keeps her from wiggling around him. Is this sexual harassment?

Points to Consider

If the conduct is unwelcomed by Meri, she did not request or invite it, and she considers Marvin's conduct to be undesirable or offensive, then she is being sexually harassed. Regardless of Meri's past willingness to kiss Marvin, the subsequent kiss is considered unwelcome. If you speak to Meri and she says the advances were unwelcome, "I broke up with him, and he just will not leave me alone," then you have a sexual harassment situation. OCR explains sexual harassment in its scenario, "A female high school student willingly kisses a male student on one occasion. When the student subsequently attempts to kiss her again, she objects, but he kisses her anyway" (US ED OCR, 2008, p. 5). "A student's submission to the conduct or failure to complain does not always mean that the conduct is welcome. This scenario clarifies a special situation of unwelcome advances" (US ED OCR, 2008, p. 5).

Sometimes the student's age, the nature of the conduct and other relevant factors affect whether a student was capable of welcoming the sexual conduct. Consider a change in the scenario. The student in question is in fourth grade and is developmentally delayed; she is functioning more on a 7-year-old level. Her age and developmental level make it unlikely she is capable of identifying this behavior as sexual harassment. Again, a student does not have to object or report for a situation to be considered unwelcome and sexual harassment. This scenario describes what OCR would label an unequal relationship, where one person has more power over another (in this case physical and probably status in the school), may be unable to give consent due to an intellectual or other disability, and the behavior is unsolicited or unwelcome (USDOE, OCR, 2021c).

SEXUAL HARASSMENT AND SCHOOL COUNSELORS

Your colleague frequently puts her hands all over male students in a suggestive way. It is an understatement when you say your colleague's behavior is way out of line. Administration has seen her do this and has heard complaints but always responds that "touching is how she conveys warmth." Administration seems unwilling to deal with it. What do you do?

Points to Consider

Legitimate nonsexual touching or conduct generally will not be considered sexual harassment. However, it may rise to that level if it takes on sexual connotations. This example from OCR further clarifies the difference: "A high school athletic coach hugs a student who makes a goal. This by itself is not considered sexual conduct. However, a coach's hugging of a student could be considered sexual conduct if it is unwelcome and occurs under inappropriate circumstances" (USDOE OCR, 2008, p. 4).

In this scenario, administration has been warned and is now deliberately indifferent under Title IX. It is miserable when one has to report a colleague, but it is one's legal and ethical obligation to first and foremost look out for a child's well-being. A federal district court in *Doe v. Fournier* (2012) WL 591669 refused to dismiss Title IX and other claims against Palmer Public Schools stemming from a male school counselor's sexual relationship with a female high school student. The plaintiff alleged that, prior to the school counselor's sexual affair with her, school officials had notice of allegations that he had had sex with another student and were concerned about his tendency to get "too cozy" with students. Yet, he was not disciplined or supervised in any way to protect female students. The only actions school officials did take were stopping a female student from placing her legs on his, directing him to remove pictures of female students from his office wall and "contemplating – but never effectuating– transferring him to the middle school" (*Doe v. Fournier* (2012) WL 591669 (D. Mass. Feb. 22, 2012)).

In contrast, a federal district court in *Doe v. Coleville School District* held school officials did not have notice and were not deliberately indifferent to signs a school counselor posed a risk to students prior to having molested the plaintiffs. The child's lawyers argued that school officials should have been on notice of this risk because they knew the school counselor had once taken a student away from school during lunch (with the parent's permission). The court said even if true this, in and of itself, would not be evidence that school officials had actual notice the school counselor was or could become a child molester (*Doe v. Coleville School District* (2012) WL 554430 (E.D. Wash. Feb. 21, 2012)).

SEXUAL HARASSMENT DENYING EQUAL ACCESS

A student confides in you that her chorus teacher is promising her the lead in the spring musical. She says every time he mentions giving her the lead it is always after he gets her alone after class, and he brushes up against her. She tries never to be caught alone with him because she feels he is coming on to her and that he wants something in return for her having the chorus lead. What do you do?

Points to Consider

Quid pro quo is one form of sexual harassment that occurs when a teacher or other school employee makes an educational decision or benefit conditional on the student's submission to unwelcome sexual conduct. If this occurs, it does not matter if the student resists and suffers the consequences or submits to avoid the threatened harm (Meinick, 2020). An example would be if a teacher promised a spot on the debate team in exchange for sexual favors.

SCHOOL COUNSELORS AS ADVOCATES FOR A SAFE, RESPECTFUL SCHOOL CLIMATE

The principal insists every faculty member serve on a committee. This year, as your service, you would like to form a committee to raise awareness about sexual harassment on the campus. Is this an appropriate role? What will be some of your considerations?

Points to Consider

Sexual harassment is illegal behavior and belongs to administration to discipline. However, playing a role in fostering a school climate free of fear and intimidation is a worthwhile leadership endeavor for the school counselor. School counselors can serve as another set of eyes and ears as they put into place preventive measures to reduce harassment in the school environment before it starts (ASCA, 2019d). School counselors have to report rumors, hearsay, a student's self-report or any report that they discover. Students will often fail to report incidents of harassment and those that do often see no effective action taken by school officials. Therefore, it is important that staff members who observe inappropriate behavior among students and/or staff members report their observations so an investigation and action may be taken. Listed below are several recommendations to help your committee get started.

Have the committee develop a school policy protecting all students from sexual harassment. A sexual harassment policy should include the following elements:

- Provide sexual health education for all students
- Train all staff on sexual harassment
- Remove police from schools
- Invest in social workers and non-law-enforcement adult helpers in schools
- Abolish dress codes
- Respect transgender and nonbinary students
- Collect climate survey data
- Make it easy to report sexual harassment
- Provide supportive measures to students who report sexual harassment
- Protect – don't punish – students who report sexual harassment
- Ensure prompt and equitable investigations
- Offer a restorative process as an option

(National Women's Law Center, 2021)

In a Position to Know: A School Counselor Educator Speaks

The case presented at the beginning of the chapter is revisited here and answered by a school counselor educator. Compare his answer to your own approach.

CYBERSEXUAL HARASSMENT

Using computers at both the school and her home, Ashley has been sending Kenneth provocative pictures of herself and long love letters, not seeming to care he has asked her to leave him alone. Ashley has emailed her communications to Kenneth and to her friends, who have also sent them to other friends. She is textting people as to every move Kenneth makes, what he wears and what his afterschool activities are each day. All this attention across electronic media feels creepy to Kenneth. Ashley has made such an issue of her "love" for him Kenneth feels he has become the object of ridicule. Despite his embarrassment, he feels frustrated he does not seem to have any recourse with Ashley and must simply endure, continuing to tell her he is not interested. Is this harassment? Could this be sexual harassment? Could Ashley be breaking any laws or school board policies? What recourse, if any, does Kenneth have?

Generally, online harassment is defined as experiencing one or more online behaviors, including offensive name-calling, purposeful embarrassment, stalking, physical threats, harassment over a sustained time period and/or sexual harassment (Duggan, 2017; Pew

Research Center, 2021). Sexual harassment occurs when online communications or information dissemination leads to unwanted sexual attention, creates a hostile environment or becomes *quid pro quo* harassment.

Hostile environment harassment occurs when unwelcome conduct of a sexual nature is so severe, persistent or pervasive it affects a student's ability to participate in or benefit from an education program or activity or creates an intimidating, threatening or abusive educational environment. A hostile environment can be created by a school employee, another student or even someone visiting the school, such as a student or employee from another school (Gillander et al.,2019; Levesque, 2019).

Quid pro quo harassment occurs when a school employee causes students to believe they must submit to unwelcome sexual conduct to participate in a school program or activity. It can also happen when an employee causes a student to believe the employee will make an educational decision based on whether or not the student submits to unwelcome sexual conduct. When a school counselor threatens to withhold an important benefit (e.g., a recommendation letter) unless the student agrees to a date, it is *quid pro quo* harassment. *Quid pro quo* harassment can also occur between two or more students when there is a power imbalance. For example, when one student offers to help another student pass an important exam in exchange for sexual favors. In the case described in our scenario, *quid pro quo* sexual harassment could occur if Ashley promises to stop the online sexual harassment if Kenneth were to go on a date with her or perhaps even "hook up" (see Office for Civil Rights *https://www2.ed.gov/about/offices/list/ocr/docs/sexhar00.html*).

Is Kenneth experiencing online harassment? I think yes. His unpleasant emotions resulting from the persistent and now pervasive comments from Ashley is a key indicator. Is sexual harassment occurring in the scenario involving Ashley and Kenneth? Probably yes, because his experience seems to meet all the needed criteria under the definition of sexual harassment. In particular, Ashley's actions are preventing him from participating in or benefiting from his education.

Ashley is hurting Kenneth with her unwanted sexual words and actions, although what she may not realize is that she may also be hurting herself and putting her friends at risk. For instance, each school typically has an acceptable use policy specifying what a student (or staff member) can or cannot do while using technology, such as the school's Wi-Fi. Increasingly, schools throughout the country have also chosen to deal with online harassment among their students as part of the student code of conduct, even when the harassing behaviors originated off campus. In particular, sexual harassment of students is also prohibited by Title IX of the Education Amendments of 1972 (Department of Education Office for Civil Rights, 1997).

Being harassed, sexually harassed, or stalked is a horrible experience by definition and has proven to be a problematic issue to prevent. Being online seems to exacerbate the prevalence, incidence and intensity of these offenses in several ways.

The issue of sexual harassment is controversial, sensitive and sometimes unpleasant to discuss. However, it is a problem that is now recognized to affect students at a young age, not just adults. Students can be emotionally and physically traumatized, which seriously hinders the developmental and educational processes. The injurious effects of sexual harassment can span from the classroom to the courtroom. The destructive nature of sexual harassment compels action, especially in the form of risk-reduction. School counselors can help students better understand the nature of sexual harassment, what supports are available to them and what they can do about it – both from the perspectives of the victim and the perpetrator(s) (American School Counselor Association, 2018; Rowell et al., 1996; Sabella, 1997).

– *Russell A. Sabella, Ph.D., professor, Florida Gulf Coast University*

Making Connections

1. How can you help determine the extent and prevalence of sexual harassment in your school? What are some of the strategies you can suggest to reduce sexual harassment for your students?

2. See if your school has a sexual harassment policy. Read the policy and highlight parts you think the school could strengthen as well as sections the school is successfully implementing.

3. Sexual harassment is emotionally costly to students. In what other ways does it take its toll on students and schools?

4. How does Title IX support students who are being sexually harassed? Why does the Office for Civil Rights recommend you keep the identity of the victim confidential?

5. Discuss why sex between a teacher and a secondary student is not recognized by boards of education and state statutes as being consensual sex.

Chapter 11 Quiz

1) Roberta is very developed for someone 12 years old. She refuses to go to her locker and carries her books around all day or goes without books, as a group of boys who hang in her locker area between classes make comments about her breasts. Roberta is:
   a. In a *quid pro quo* situation
   b. In a hostile environment
   c. In neither a *quid pro quo* or hostile environment because the comments do not interfere with her education
   d. Deliberately indifferent so no sexual harassment exists
   e. In violation of Title IX because students have to report harassment to school officials

2) Once students confide to a school official they are being sexually harassed this requires:
   a. the school to take responsibility to correct the situation
   b. law enforcement be notified and must come to the school to investigate
   c. harassed students must to write a lengthy detail of the harassment as required under Title IX
   d. Administration to ask students if they provoked the harassment
   e. the perpetrator to be suspended

3) A sexual harassment policy should include all but which of the following elements:
   a. Clearly defined disciplinary consequences for sexual harassment behavior
   b. A promise of complete confidentiality for the victim of sexual harassment
   c. Identification of specific sexual harassment behavior
   d. Provision of a contact person to whom the victim can report incidents
   e. Process for grievance procedures

4) When abusive harassment is based on race, color, sex, national origin or disability and creates a hostile environment, it violates students' civil rights. Statutes protecting these civil rights may include all of the following, except:
   a. Title VI of the Civil Rights Act of 1964, which prohibits discrimination on the basis of race, color or national origin
   b. Title IX of the Education Amendments of 1972, which prohibits discrimination on the basis of sex
   c. Section 504 of the Rehabilitation Act of 1973
   d. Title II of the Americans with Disabilities Act
   e. First Amendment rights

2) *Davis v. Monroe County Board of Education* was a critical court case because:
   a. It placed school districts on notice that they cannot be deliberately indifferent to sexual harassment
   b. The courts finally gave a definition of substantial disruption in cyberbullying
   c. It involved a supervisor and subordinate and defined sexual harassment in the workplace
   d. School districts learned they cannot be expected to address sexual harassment
   e. The Supreme Court refused to hear the case and let the lower court's ruling stand in favor of the district

Key Terms

Breach of trust
Deliberate indifference
Hostile environment
Liability
Office for Civil Rights
Title IX
Quid pro quo harassment
Sexual harassment
Sexual harassment policy
Student-on-student sexual harassment
Teacher-on-student sexual harassment

CHAPTER 12

Bullying, Cyberbullying and Sexting

Objectives

By the time you complete this chapter, you should be able to:

- Discuss the prevalence of bullying in schools
- Classify the different forms of bullying and the different ways others can be included
- Discuss school counselors' roles regarding discipline as it pertains to bullying
- Describe how bullying can violate a student's civil rights
- Describe a bullycide incident
- Cite court cases where the victim's identity is protected
- Identify anti-bullying policies in schools, and explain how they are implemented
- Describe cyberbullying as it relates to First Amendment rights
- Identify the complications of substantial disruption
- Define sexting and its negative consequences

Ethical Standards Addressed in This Chapter

Professionalism means knowing your professional association's ethical standards and adhering to them. The ASCA Ethical Standards for School Counselors (2022b) most relevant to this chapter follow; refer to the full document at *www.schoolcounselor.org*.

School counselors:

- Report to administration and/or appropriate authorities (e.g., law enforcement) when a student discloses a perpetrated or a perceived threat to another person's physical or mental well-being. This threat may include but is not limited to verbal abuse, physical abuse, sexual abuse, dating violence, bullying or harassment. The school counselor follows applicable federal and state laws and school and district policy. (A.9.e).
- Recognize that bullying, discrimination, bias and hate incidents rooted in race, gender, sexual orientation and ethnicity are violations of federal law and many state and local laws and district policies (A.11.a).
- Advocate for schoolwide policies, protocols and training centered in safety, belonging and justice for response to bullying, harassment and bias incidents. (A.11.b).
- Advocate for accessible, effective tools for students or community to report incidents of bullying, hate or bias. (A.11.c).

- Report all incidents of bullying, dating violence or harassment to the administration, recognizing these behaviors may fall under Title IX of the Education Amendments of 1972 or other federal and state laws as illegal and require administrator intervention. (A.11.d)
- Recognize that bias incidents are not only potentially traumatizing for students but can lead to significant damage and disruption of the school environment. Facilitate and monitor schoolwide prevention of bullying, harassment, discrimination, hate and bias through active practices that support a positive school climate, culture and belonging. (A.11.e)
- In response to a hate or bias incident (e.g. discrimination, explicit bias, hate speech), collaborate with administrative teams to ensure safety, provide support for targeted students, facilitate effective communication, provide education, connect students to resources and promote healing and recovery within the school community. (A.11.f)
- In developmentally appropriate ways and in the context of the incident, support victims, encourage growth and provide tools for accountability and change (e.g., restorative practices) in perpetrators and promote healing in the school community while deferring to administration for all discipline issues or any other violation of federal and state laws or district and school policies. (A.11.g).
- Actively respond to incidents of bias or hate, demonstrating a commitment to equity and promoting a safe, inclusive school community. (A.11.h).

Introduction

Title IX and Title VI apply to bullying if the bullying is based on race, color, national origin or sex/gender (U.S. Department of Justice, 2021). A variety of federal laws prohibit such discrimination and harassment, although the authority to enforce those laws is divided among different federal agencies. For example, the Department of Education and Department of Justice both enforce Title VI of the Civil Rights Act of 1964, which prohibits discrimination on the basis of race, color and national origin by any entity (public or private) receiving federal financial assistance. 42 U.S.C. § 2000d. Even though Title VI doesn't expressly prohibit discrimination based solely on religion, discrimination against persons belonging to religious groups violates Title VI when the discrimination is based on the religious group's actual or perceived shared ancestry or ethnic characteristics, rather than solely on its members' religious practices. The Department of Justice enforces Title IV of the Civil Rights Act of 1964, which prohibits discrimination on the basis of race, color, national origin and religion by public schools and colleges, 42 U.S.C. § 2000c-6, and the Equal Educational Opportunities Act, which prohibits discrimination on the basis of race, color or national origin by public schools, 20 U.S.C. § 1703.

The Office for Civil Rights recently conducted a civil rights violation of a California school district when the children who are Sikhs and wore a turban were continually bullied with acts such as having the turban pulled off. There is no federal law that specifically applies just to bullying, but laws overlap when it comes to attacks based on who a person is. You can directly apply a federal law when bullying is based on race or ethnicity, color, national origin, sex, disability, religion or sexual harassment, and schools are legally obligated to address it (ASPA, 2021).

School counselors contribute to students' academic success by fostering a positive school climate. A comprehensive school counseling program includes bullying, harassment and violence prevention, as well as interventions such as conflict resolution.

ASCA's revised position statement, The School Counselor and the Promotion of Safe Schools through Conflict Resolution and Bullying/Harassment Prevention (2022f) states "The school counselor includes prevention programs as a part of the comprehensive school counseling program and ensures these programs include training in key skills in peacefully resolving issues such as:

- communication skills
- conflict-resolution skills
- decision-making skills
- development of cultural competence
- acceptance of differences
- intervention strategies for bullying/harassment
- recognition of early warning signs of violence
- prevention/intervention services
- crisis response
- appropriate use of technology and social media
- community involvement
- parent/guardian and faculty/staff education
- evaluation of program effectiveness
- building positive staff and student relationships
- mental health awareness training
- bystander training" (ASCA, 2022f)

Bullying in middle schools appears much more common than at other levels, with 27.9% of middle school students reporting bullying occurred at school daily or at least once a week, compared to 8.7% of primary and 15.8% of high school students (Robers, Zhang, & Truman, 2020). A higher percentage of males (10%) than females (8%) reported being physically bullied, such as being pushed, shoved, kicked or spit on (Robers, Zhang & Truman, 2020).

Technology has expanded teenagers' social lives but also offers more opportunities for student-to-student bullying and harassment. Bullying is no longer confined to the lunchroom or face-to-face contact, as cyberbullies are online around the clock. Students have taken cyberbullying to new heights, often not realizing the implications of their actions.

Technology has brought a disturbing, dark side to bullying because it allows a student to inflict pain with anonymity or perceived anonymity, sometimes even without being forced to see the effect of bullying on the victim. Power balances are different from those in traditional bullying, since such factors as physical strength, energy and courage take on a lesser importance (Sabella, 2022).

Findings from the National Center for Education Statistics' (NCES) (2019) "Student Reports of Bullying: Results from the 2017 School Crime Supplement to the National Crime Victimization Survey" illuminate the bullying issue. NCES data shows 20.2% of students ages 12 through 18 were bullied at school in the 2016–2017 school year.

Approximately, 6,189 public and private school students grades 6–12 self-reported the following for the 2016–17 school year:

- 20.2% reported being bullied at school.
- 15.5% reported being cyberbullied, either online or via text.
- Bullying decreased as their grade level increased from 29.5% in sixth grade to 12.2% in 12th grade.
- Bullied students more frequently reported being afraid of being attacked on the way to or from or at school (12.7%) compared to students who weren't bullied (2.1%).
- The percentage of students who reported being electronically bullied in 2017 was higher for female students than for male students (20% vs. 10%); higher for white students (17%) and students of two or more races (16%) than for Black students (11%) and Asian students (10%) and higher for white students than for Hispanic students (12%); higher for gay, lesbian or bisexual students (27%) and students who were not sure of their sexual orientation (22%) than for heterosexual students (13%); and higher for ninth-graders than for 12th-graders (17% vs. 13%).

(National Center for Education Statistics, 2019; Wang et. al., 2020)

In a March 2017 survey, 527 ASCA members responded that they see bullying as a problem in their school. The positive news is that the 82.8% of the respondents felt their school's approach to handling bullying was intentional, methodical and that their school administration was responsive to bullying acts (Stone, 2017a).

	Strongly Agree or Agree	Neutral	Disagree or Strongly Disagree
Bullying is a problem at my school.	41.7%	32.5%	25.8%
My school has a practical, well-thought- out, research-based protocol to handle bullying.	51.7%	22.1%	26.1%
My school administration is responsive to acts of bullying.	82.8%	11.2%	5.9%

In this same survey, 63% of the 527 respondents responded that cyberbullying is a problem in their school. More than a quarter of the respondents (28%) thought their administrators' approach to handling cyberbullying was effective.

	Strongly Agree or Agree	Neutral	Disagree or Strongly Disagree
Cyberbullying is a problem at my school.	63%	22%	15%
My school district has a policy addressing cyberbullying.	67%	18%	15%
My school district's policy on cyberbullying is effective.	28%	48%	24%

(Stone, 2017a)

Cyberbullying is difficult to describe in succinct, concrete terms; however, some of the most common cyberbullying tactics include:

- Posting mean, hurtful or embarrassing comments or rumors about someone online.
- Threatening to hurt someone or telling them to kill themselves.
- Posting a mean or hurtful picture or video.
- Pretending to be someone else online to solicit or post personal or false information about someone else.
- Posting mean or hateful names, comments or content about any race, religion, ethnicity or other personal characteristics.
- Creating a mean or hurtful webpage about someone.
- Doxing, an abbreviated form of the word documents, is a form of online harassment used to exact revenge and to threaten and destroy the privacy of individuals by making their personal information public, including addresses; Social Security, credit card and phone numbers; links to social media accounts; and other private data (ASPA, 2019).

It is rare for cyberbullying to occur without the presence of in-person bullying. According to a Boston University study of Google search terms, bullying and cyberbullying decreased significantly from March 2020 to February 2021 when many schools were closed and students either attended remotely or experienced extremely structured socially distant in-person learning with limited free time in hallways and cafeterias (Sparks, 2022). Overall searches related to bullying were 33% lower than previous years (Sparks, 2022). Despite the increase in time spent online, searches related to cyberbullying were also 27% lower during the pandemic than previous years (Sparks, 2022). However, schools that returned to in-person learning in 2021 also saw the return of searches related to cyberbullying at a faster rate than searches pertaining to in-person bullying (Sparks, 2022).

The courts continue to offer disparate judgments and confusion in cases of cyber-speech. "It is exceedingly difficult for a school or court to parse out which bullying happened off campus (and can be ignored so as to protect the bully's First Amendment rights) and which bullying happened on campus" (National School Board Association, 2011). Administrators have the daunting job of determining when cyber-speech represents a substantial disruption to the educational environment. However, the courts have not provided an operational definition of substantial disruption (National School Board Association, 2012). The lower court rulings are mixed, and the muddiness continues in determining when off-campus speech creates a substantial disruption to the learning environment. School district officials are obligated under federal laws to seek to remedy bullying and harassment that is severe, pervasive and objectively offensive. These statutes do not distinguish between whether bullying happened on or off campus. The responsibility to act is clear, yet substantial disruption is not clear or in any way standardized.

Three student cyber-speech cases were jointly presented to the U.S. Supreme Court, *J.S. v. Blue Mountain School District*, *Layshock v. Hermitage School District* and *Kowalski v. Berkeley County School District*, but the Supreme Court announced it was unwilling to accept the cases and allowed the lower courts' decisions to stand (Huffington Post, 2012). Six education associations filed a friendly brief (*amici curiae*) in hopes a Supreme Court ruling would result in standards administrators could follow in addressing off-campus cyber-speech affecting the on-campus learning environment.

In 2020, the Supreme Court agreed to hear an off-campus cyber-speech case. The court decided in *Mahanoy Area School District v. B.L.* that a student's off-campus, profane Snapchat rant was protected by the First Amendment and her public high school overreached its authority in removing her from the cheerleading squad (Hudson, 2021).

The National School Boards Association (NSBA) filed an *amicus* brief in the case urging the Supreme Court to "overrule a troubling lower court decision that would limit public school officials' ability to address online student speech originating off-campus. NSBA believes the physical location of a student's speech is irrelevant in today's socially distanced and social-media-fueled world, adding that schools will be hampered in their duty to address harmful online speech – including bullying – if such a limitation remains" (NSBA, 2020b).

Mahanoy Area School District v. B.L. provided some clarity on student's free speech. Brandi Levy sent a Snapchat with an expletive about her school and cheerleading. The cheerleading coach was sent a screenshot of her rant and ruled it was a violation of the code of conduct for cheerleaders and benched Levy for the year (Hudson, 2021). District employees at all levels supported the cheer coach. The case made its way through the courts to the Supreme Court. The court felt the need to answer the question as to whether the disruption standard applies to off campus as well as on campus speech. Levy won the battle, but in the words of Joy Baskin, director of legal services, Texas Association of School Boards, school districts across the nation won the war (2022). School officials have long needed a more definitive answer to disruption that starts off campus. The substantial-disruption standard applies to off-campus speech, but school officials have a much-diminished position of authority to punish for off-campus speech that is not a safety issue (Johnson, 2021). It is a sliding scale of regulatory authority that begins to diminish with parental authority taking over off-campus, out-of-school time communication. However, the Supreme Court upheld that administrators have a right to intervene in safety issues including bullying.

The case was important because it recognized that students have First Amendment rights and that parents have a role to play when educators' *in loco parentis* status goes away. Standards and codes created by coaches must apply to legal expectations, and conduct (drinking while in the school's cheer uniform) is different from a message and requires a different response. Many asked if the outcome would have been different if Levy were wearing her uniform at the time she flipped the bird and said four expletives on Snapchat to her friends. While in the act of being a cheerleader as a uniform member of that group you are subject to the schools' authority to edit such behavior such as profane speech. You certainly look more like you are a representative of the school when wearing the uniform "but the uniform does not make it decisive" (Joy Surratt Baskin, 2022 n.p.). However, the answer is not an easy one. In *Matthews v. Kountze ISD*, cheerleaders painted scripture verses on cheer banners to share what they believed to be positive messages for their team. The Wisconsin-based Freedom From Religion Foundation (FFRF) complained, and the case was heard by the Ninth District Court of Appeals, which issued its ruling in favor of the cheerleaders" (Joy Baskin, 2022). Safety issues justify fast, prompt action. When it is not a safety issue but speech that causes discomfort, then tempo must slow way down (Baskin, Zeigler, & Negron, 2022).

Administrators are given tremendous grace when it comes to student safety; however, addressing bullying, especially verbal bullying, can prove to be difficult for educators. A current case, *C1.G. ex rel. Son v. Siegfried*, underscores the challenges. In the first federal appeals court case since the Supreme Court issued its ruling in the Levy case, a student posted a vile, anti-Semitic comment on Snapchat and was expelled. C.G. posted a picture wearing hats in a thrift resembling WWII military garb and captioned it, "Me and the boys 'bout to exterminate the Jews." He immediately apologized and was later visited by the police, who deemed there was not a real threat. He was expelled on the grounds that he violated school conduct and that the district could regulate "behavior on or off school property which is detrimental to the welfare, safety or morals of other students or school personnel," according to the lawsuit. The case was dismissed, but it is now in the 10th Circuit Court of Appeals.

This case, the first since the Levy case, regarding off-campus speech and discipline will be watched closely. Alan Chen, a Denver University law professor who specializes in First Amendment cases, stated, the Supreme Court ruling said that the less a student's off-campus speech is connected to school, the more their First Amendment rights are equivalent to that of an adult (Julig, 2021, n.p.). *Mahanoy* instructs that discipline should be left to a student's parents, not to the government, and C.G.'s parents did punish their son and allowing him to return to is unlikely to cause a substantial disruption to the school environment (Sheth, Shapiro, and Berry, 2021).

Cyberbullying is especially problematic due to the disinhibiting effect of hiding behind a screen. Also, victims and perpetrators frequently know each other and attend the same school. Pictures and posts are repeated and shared and provide recurring trauma. Normally we think of bullying as an imbalance in social, physical, emotional or academic power. Cyberbullying allows for a power shift based on possession of an embarrassing picture, technology used to wound (Hinduja & Patchin, 2021).

States are doubling their efforts to address bullying and cyberbullying by passing state laws. An example comes from North Carolina, which has a detailed law describing what constitutes cyberbullying and the consequences: "A student who is convicted under G.S. 14-458.2 of cyberbullying a school employee shall be transferred to another school within the local school administrative unit… (§ 115C-366.4. 2012-149, s. 9.) Seth's Law in California went into effect on July 1, 2012. Seth's Law strengthens existing state anti-bullying laws to help protect all California public school students. Seth's Law specifically contains the following requirement: "If school personnel witness an act of discrimination, harassment, intimidation or bullying, he or she shall take immediate steps to intervene when safe to do so." (Seth's Law, 2012).

Bullying is illegal and no longer considered just something children have to learn to stand up to. Many suicides and school shootings can be traced to bullying. In *Malone v. Moss Point Mississippi School District* (Public Justice, 2019), the discoveries said Malone died of injuries "sufficient to trigger the onset of a fatal health crisis involving his heart." He had an undetected heart problem, and the stress of being bullied was blamed for his death. He was regularly teased because of his size, clothing looks, and because he practiced his religion by handing out crosses, pictures of angels and anti-bullying slogans. His bullying was reported on multiple occasions.

Getting Started: What Would You Do?

The following case is discussed at the end of this chapter by a school counselor. Before reading her responses, formulate how to approach this ethical dilemma.

SCHOOL COUNSELORS AND BULLY PROOFING

The discipline referral rate for bullying in your school is high. You conduct an anonymous schoolwide survey and learn bullying is a problem for many students in fourth and fifth grade. What might you do to try and create a safer school climate for students?

Working Through Case Studies

SUBSTANTIAL DISRUPTION AND CYBERSPACE SPEECH

Rachel, a student, comes to you distraught that she was being called a "slut with herpes" online by Joan, a classmate. Joan asked others to join her in humiliating Rachel. You take it to the principal, who expresses concern for Rachel and promises to call in Joan and her parents, but she says her hands are tied as far as being able to punish Joan because the cyber-speech did not cause a disruption to the educational environment, and a future disruption is not predicted. Is your principal correct?

Points to Consider

As discussed earlier, *Mahanoy Area School District v. B.L.* sent a clear message that punishment for off-campus speech should be looked upon with great skepticism unless there is a substantial disruption to the educational process or very likely to be such a disruption. The Supreme Court set a high bar in this case, and unless the speech is a disruption or a safety issue, educators should proceed with great caution before punishing off-campus speech. In *C1.G. ex rel. Son v. Siegfried*, the case doesn't meet that high bar, and the Tenth Circuit should reverse his expulsion. The Fourth Circuit court cited *Tinker v. Des Moines Independent Community School District* (393 U.S. 503, 1969), which supported the school district's discipline of the cyberbully. *Tinker*, a U.S. Supreme Court case, defined the First Amendment rights of students in public schools and supports the conclusion that public schools have a compelling interest in regulating speech interfering with or disrupting the work and discipline of the school, including discipline for student-on-student harassment and bullying. Court rulings are not consistent, creating a difficult situation for school administrators to manage as to when they are able to discipline off-campus speech and when discipline will infringe on a student's freedom of speech.

ADMINISTRATORS INVOLVING SCHOOL COUNSELORS IN DISCIPLINE

Your administration continually involves you in bullying cases, asking you to provide conflict resolution between the bully and the bullied. What, if anything, can you do?

Points to Consider

All 50 states have statutes making bullying illegal. Bullying is a discipline problem, and conflict resolution is not an appropriate intervention when a student's action is actually bullying. In an April 2017 survey with 527 respondents, school counselors confirmed that they are involved in discipline for bullying. When asked if their school administration asks them to provide conflict resolution when the problem is actually a bullying situation, 26% agreed or strongly agreed. When asked if they are willing to work with students on conflict resolution but refer to administration if they discover it is bullying, 66% agreed or strongly agreed (Stone, 2017a).

School counselors struggle with the predicament of administrators involving them in discipline (Bryan, Day-Vines, Griffin & Moore-Thomas, 2012; Bryan, Young, Griffin, & Holcomb-McCoy, 2017). Often this involvement is as a valued member of the school with specialized skills and abilities to participate in the overall effort to evaluate behavior and/or remediate behavior as part of the effort to stop bullying. In this same survey by Stone (2017a), 41% said their school administration involves them in working with bullies as part of the disciplining of bullying.

School counselors help teachers with disruptive students to support students needing school counselor intervention before the teacher has to resort to disciplining students. School counselors help remedy disruption or unproductive behavior through membership on discipline committees, behavior modification programs, mediation, parent conferences, classroom guidance lessons, individual counseling and small-group counseling, just to name a few. Discipline is a role school counselors try to avoid as it can change the nature of the student/school counselor relationship from nonthreatening to threatening. Trust is an underlying factor in counseling, and it can be shaken with this role confusion. School counselors are not disciplinarians but facilitators of growth (2019b). School counselors have specialized training and skills in promoting appropriate student behavior and preventing disruptive student behavior. School counselors are not disciplinarians but should be a resource for school personnel in developing individual and schoolwide discipline procedures. School counselors collaborate with school personnel and other stakeholders to establish policies encouraging appropriate behavior and maintaining safe schools where effective teaching and learning can take place. (ASCA, 2019b)

The National Parent Teacher Association (PTA) also recommends school counselors be involved in behavior modification to try and replace discipline action: "By addressing behavioral issues on an individualized basis – instead of in the context of a pre-arranged set of sanctions – principals, teachers, school counselors and other school officials have the ability to address each student with a proactive plan for behavior modification instead of punishment... . Ensure adequate access to and retention of school counselors, school social workers and school psychologists to implement school-based interventions that promote positive school discipline" (PTA, 2016).

Respondents of the Stone (2017a) survey indicated just how much their specialized skills are used in proactive methods to try to prevent bullying. Individual counseling (83.1%) was on par with school and classroom rules (89.2%) as a proactive means for administrators to rely on in addressing bullying.

Which of the following proactive methods does your school currently use to prevent bullying (Check all that apply):

School and classroom rules	89.2%
Individual counseling for students	83.1%
School counseling core curriculum lessons	63%
Schoolwide assemblies	43.3%
Group counseling	43.5%
Teacher in-services/professional development	41.7%
Classroom meetings	41.7%
Parent meetings	32.1%
My school doesn't use any proactive methods to prevent bullying from taking place	2.7%

(Stone, 2017a)

As part of Public Justice's Anti-Bullying Campaign, jury decisions involving bullying are tracked. From 2000 to 2019 The Public Justice Campaign tracked approximately 250 jury verdicts and settlements in bullying and harassment cases filed against school districts in federal and state courts throughout the country (Public Justice,2019).

THREATS OF BULLYING AND IMMEDIATE RESPONSES

You receive an e-mail from a student expressing fear of another student, describing incidents of being punched by this student and asking you for ideas to help him cope with the bullying. You were in the middle of state testing and needed to proctor a test. You fully intended to get back to the student immediately, but one interruption led to another, and it was two days later when it hit you that you had not responded to this student. Are there any legal and ethical issues here?

Points to Consider

Sawyer Rosenstein was a middle school student at Eric Smith Middle School and was being continuously bullied by another student. The bullying was so incessant that Sawyer emailed his school counselor asking for coping mechanisms. Sawyer also emailed the assistant principal stating he would like to have his bullying instances on file. Three months later, Sawyer was punched in the stomach by his bully. This injury resulted in a blood clot, 19 surgeries and paralysis from the waist down. In the ensuing lawsuit, Sawyer stated that school officials knew about his attacker's violent tendencies and revealed other punching instances his attacker had with other students. The Ramsey Board of Education settled with Sawyer for $4.2 million (Leitsinger, 2012).

Shannon Sugg was a freshman in Albuquerque Public School District when a fellow student, Alicia Andres, allegedly began tormenting her. Sugg sought her school counselor's help. The school counselor allegedly told Sugg to work things out and also spoke with Andres about the situation. Later, Andres and a group of girls threatened Suggs with a knife. Suggs' parents tried to intervene with the school, but administration could not find the perpetrator because of a misspelled last name. Administration told Sugg and her parents they would need the exact spelling of the student's name to proceed. When Andres stabbed

Sugg in the left shoulder, Sugg's parents filed a claim against Albuquerque School Board members, administrators and the school counselor. Governmental immunity kicked in, and the case was dismissed (*Sugg v. Albuquerque Public School District* (1999)).

It can be difficult to drop everything and act when so many people depend on school counselors and pull at them in so many different directions. However, the risk of harm meant Rosenstein and Sugg's situations needed attention as soon as possible. If the school counselor in the Sugg case had brought the situation to the principal's attention, then this administrator would have at least had Andres' full name, as the school counselor knew it. Regardless, the administration needed to dig deeper to find the perpetrator. This response may not have made any difference, but it would certainly have demonstrated a higher standard of care on the school officials' part. Bullying incidents brought directly to the school counselor's attention should be reported to administration. *In loco parentis* requires we act in place of the parents and can be considered negligent if a student is harmed.

Bully Police USA (2022) provides a website with links to the specific laws and regulations against bullying for each state at *www.bullypolice.org*. The Education Commission of the States is also a good source for information about state anti-bullying statutes at *www.ecs.org*.

CONTROVERSIAL ANTI-BULLYING PROGRAMS

During a schoolwide anti-bullying program, the premise of which was to develop empathy in students, one of your 10th-graders, in the heat of the emotional moment, revealed he was gay. His peers rallied to his side and gave him much support. However, days later he experienced even worse bullying. He comes to you distraught that he was foolish enough to reveal his personal pain. Are there any lessons learned from this situation that you should share with administration?

Points to Consider

In 2016, the West Allegheny School District had to face a barrage of angry parents threatening legal action against the school district over an anti-bullying program. The parents reportedly have retained the services of a Pittsburgh attorney to pursue a class action lawsuit claiming administrators infringed on students' rights. Students were asked questions and then grouped together with other students who answered similarly. Some of the questions were:

- You have been affected by drugs or alcohol.
- You have been called fat or made fun of.
- You or someone close to you identifies as gay, lesbian or transgender.
- You have been affected by mental challenges or learning disabilities.
- You or your family has ever worried about not having enough money
- You or someone close to you has been imprisoned.
- You have been raised by a single parent. (Gable, 2016)

One irate parent said, "There is now so much damage done to these children, and there is no way to go back and make this better for them." Another parent added, "I asked them [administrators] to do the same thing they asked the kids to do: Stand in a circle, put a mask on and step in the circle and say all your problems." (Gable, 2016). Parents believe the exercise gave the bullies ammunition.

According to NCES' 2017–2018 School Survey on Crime and Safety, there is no definitive profile of a student who bullies others. A youth who bullies may be either socially well-connected or marginalized, and many bullying victims can exhibit bullying behaviors themselves (USDOE NCES, 2018). Bullying behavior may be learned or be a mode for manipulation. More than 50% of victims reported they believed the person who bullied them had more social influence and the ability to influence other students' perceptions of the victim (USDOE NCES, 2018). Victims can be either classified as chronic (always victims) or acute (targeted based on an action), characterized by low self-esteem, social awkwardness, high anxiety and high risk for suicide (Copeland, et al., 2013). Witnesses are students who are aware bullying is taking place, do their best to avoid it and, because they are empathetic, suffer when they know it is happening.

Channing Smith, a 16-year-old boy, died by suicide after his intimate messages to another boy were leaked and posted on Instagram and Snapchat. He discovered them late at night, and by morning he was dead. "My brother couldn't face the humiliation of cyberbullying, so he chose to commit suicide," Joshua Smith wrote on Facebook. Channing hadn't publicly expressed interest in a same-sex relationship prior to the explicit messages being leaked, his family members said. But a classmate reported that Channing was already bullied at school because he sometimes "talked in a girly voice and walked with sass." It sounds like Channing had reason to believe he would not be able to face his classmates' attacks (Stevens, 2019).

PARENTAL RESPONSIBILITY AND LIABILITY FOR CHILD'S BULLYING BEHAVIOR

A group of female students took harassment to a new level, threatening students outside their group no matter how much the school district tried to intervene. The parents were combative when asked to intervene with their children's behavior. Can parents be held liable for their child's behavior if someone gets hurt?

Points to Consider

This scenario of stubborn discipline problems is a reality. Student offenders and their parents are sometimes unwilling to acknowledge the existence of the harassing behaviors and tend to blame everyone else. A safe environment is a basic need for all children in schools, but educators need parents to step up and help them in some of these stubborn cases.

"Lawsuits against the parents of alleged bullies are rare, since school officials are usually the first to be accused of not doing enough to stop bullying. But *Shaposhnikov v. the Pacifica School District* and *John Roes 1-10* may be part of a new approach to finding legal fault, and somebody to pay financial damages, when bullying goes unchallenged, experts say" (Wykes, 2005, p. 1). In this case, a group of parents settled a lawsuit filed by Mark Shaposhnikov, whose son, a competitive dancer, was taunted with homosexual slurs for two years in middle school. Shaposhnikov says he met many times with school officials and that nothing changed until he filed the lawsuit. The suit used a legal principle called vicarious liability meaning the parents are responsible for the emotional distress their children are inflicting on others... Six of the parents of alleged bullies named in the suit settled, but terms of the deal are confidential (Wykes, 2005, p. 1).

Parental responsibility for their children's delinquent acts has long been recognized in the United States. Parents may be held civilly or criminally liable for their children's acts of juvenile delinquency. Such envisaged crimes perpetrated by children include the causing of physical or psychological harm such as damage to property, bullying, assault, sexual assault, the infringement of dignity and privacy, gun-related offences, defamation and even murder (Van der Bijl, 2018) Another approach that has been successfully used is negligence cases. As in the Shaposhnikov case, parents are being sued and settling under their home-owner's insurance policies (Writer, 2011). Parents have also been charged with paying juvenile court fees and community service when they fail to stop their children from committing commit crimes or other delinquent acts.

At the time this book went to press, the parents of Ethan Crumbly, the Oxford High School (Mich.) student who killed four of his classmates, are going to trial for the crimes their son committed. The judge decided after the preliminary examination that there was enough evidence to continue to hold the Crumbly parents and to send them to trial explaining that it could have been apparent to an ordinary person that Ethan was a troubled person, and the parents were neglectful in not addressing his troubles and instead buying him a gun (Frye, 2022).

One powerful example comes from Marbletown Elementary School, where the school counseling team sponsors a series of efforts to engage students and staff in activities designed to create a safe and respectful school climate. The events are developed and planned by a committee of second- and third-graders (Freeman, 2022).

BULLYING BASED ON RACE, COLOR, SEX, NATIONAL ORIGIN, DISABILITY, HARASSMENT AND CIVIL RIGHTS

Aalia, a new student from Tunisia, is the first student in your memory who has come to this school wearing a hijab, a headdress often worn by Muslim women to meet religious requirements for modesty. You wonder if the fact that her dress is different will bring any kind of harassment or bullying but decide to take a wait-and-see approach. Several days after Aalia arrives at school, you check in with her and, as feared, find she is experiencing verbal and physical harassment. Aalia had her hijab pulled off and thrown to the ground with taunts about her religion and nationality. Several students came to her aid and spoke up on Aalia's behalf, but some students pretended not to notice the harassment. What are your obligations in this situation? Are Aalia's civil rights being violated?

Points to Consider

Some bullying instances may fall under federal civil rights statutes and regulations enforced by U.S. Department of Education Office for Civil Rights (OCR) (2022). School staff should be aware that when abusive behavior based on race, color, sex, national origin or disability creates a hostile environment, it violates students' civil rights. Statutes protecting these civil rights include (1) Title VI of the Civil Rights Act of 1964, which prohibits discrimination on the basis of race, color or national origin; (2) Title IX of the Education Amendments of 1972, which prohibits discrimination on the basis of sex; (3) Section 504 of the Rehabilitation Act of 1973; and (4) Title II of the Americans with Disabilities Act. Section 504 and

Title II prohibit discrimination on the basis of disability (U.S. Department of Education Office for Civil Rights, 2010). These statutes require schools to respond directly to such discriminatory harassment to protect students' civil rights.

OCR also has received an ever-increasing number of complaints concerning bullying students with disabilities and the effects of that bullying on their education, including on the special education and related services to which they are entitled. This concerning trend highlights the importance of OCR's continuing efforts to protect the rights of students with disabilities through the vigorous enforcement of Section 504 and Title II. It also underscores the need for schools to fully understand their legal obligations to address and prevent disability discrimination in school. When a school knows or should know of bullying conduct based on a student's disability, administration must take immediate and appropriate action to investigate or otherwise determine what occurred. If a school's investigation reveals bullying based on disability withheld or limited a student's ability to participate in or benefit from school services, activities or opportunities, the school must take prompt and effective steps reasonably calculated to end the bullying, eliminate the hostile environment, prevent it from recurring and, as appropriate, remedy its effects. Therefore, OCR would find a disability-based harassment violation under Section 504 and Title II when: (1) a student is bullied based on a disability, (2) the bullying is sufficiently serious to create a hostile environment, (3) school officials know or should know about the bullying and (4) the school does not respond appropriately (U.S. Department of Education Office for Civil Rights, 2014).

BULLYING BASED ON RELIGIOUS EXPRESSION

Abeer wears his Sikh turban to school to signify his adherence to his faith. In Sikhism, the turban is worn to celebrate a male's coming of age. Abeer experiences continuous verbal harassment about his turban, and on more than one occasion a peer tried to remove it. Are Abeer's civil rights being violated?

Points to Consider

The USDOE OCR explains that some instances of bullying fall under federal civil rights statutes and regulations enforced by OCR. School staff should be aware that when abusive behavior is based on race, color, sex, national origin or disability, it violates a students' civil rights. As expressed in Aalia's case above, none of the laws that OCR enforces expressly address religious discrimination. However, the law OCR enforces protects students of any religion from discrimination, including harassment, based on a student's actual or perceived shared ancestry or ethnic characteristics, or citizenship or residency in a country with a dominant religion or distinct religious identity. For example, OCR can investigate complaints that students were subjected to ethnic or ancestral slurs; harassed for how they look, dress or speak in ways linked to ethnicity or ancestry (e.g. skin color, religious attire, language spoken); or stereotyped based on perceived shared ancestral or ethnic characteristics. Hindu, Jewish, Muslim and Sikh students are examples of individuals who may be harassed for being viewed as part of a group that exhibits both ethnic and religious characteristics.

OCR has investigated a number of cases based on religious discrimination. One such case was against the Fremont School District. In 2010, The Sikh Coalition shared student survey results indicating the district had the highest rate of reported harassment of Sikh students among San Francisco Bay Area school districts. According to the report findings, the harassing conduct toward Sikh students took the form of physical and verbal harassment regarding students' outward appearance, including clothing related to articles of faith, and perceived race, color, national origin or cultural background.

OCR's review resulted in the district implementing several proactive efforts to address the harassment and provide a nondiscriminatory educational environment for Sikh and Middle Eastern students including: strengthening the district's anti-harassment policy, engaging in outreach among Sikh and Middle Eastern communities, bringing in community-based organizations to increase cultural awareness and competency; creating parenting workshops for parents of Afghan heritage and mentorship opportunities for Afghan students, creating anti-harassment curricular tools, launching anti-harassment initiatives, scheduling training for staff and students on understanding harassment and promoting respect and appreciation of all cultures.

A variety of federal laws prohibit such discrimination and harassment, although the authority to enforce those laws is divided among different federal agencies. For example, the Department of Education and Department of Justice both enforce Title VI of the Civil Rights Act of 1964, which prohibits discrimination on the basis of race, color and national origin by any entity (public or private) receiving federal financial assistance, 42 U.S.C. § 2000d. Even though Title VI does not expressly prohibit discrimination based solely on religion per se, discrimination against persons belonging to religious groups violates Title VI when the discrimination is based on the religious group's actual or perceived shared ancestry or ethnic characteristics, rather than solely on its members' religious practices. In addition, the Department of Justice enforces Title IV of the Civil Rights Act of 1964, which prohibits discrimination on the basis of race, color, national origin, and religion by public schools and colleges, 42 U.S.C. § 2000c-6, and the Equal Educational Opportunities Act, which prohibits discrimination on the basis of race, color, or national origin by public schools, 20 U.S.C. § 1703.

PROTECTING POTENTIAL VICTIMS

Marsha tells you she heard Stevie plans to beat her up. You know Stevie well, and you are worried as she is a volatile student. You send for Stevie to meet with Marsha and review with them school board policies related to student fighting. Your impression is that Marsha is scared, and when you get her alone she says she doesn't even know why Stevie hates her. Is there anything more you must do as the school counselor?

Points to Consider

School counselors are often the first members of the school staff to become aware a student might be at risk for harm. As of April 2017, all states have anti-bullying legislation (Bully Police USA, 2022). Therefore, bullying is illegal in all 50 states. This makes it a discipline issue, which requires administration to act. The potential for harm trumps confidentiality as the school counselor's efforts shift to protecting the student from harm as well as protecting the student from being identified as the one who told about the bullying. Students will endure great harm to avoid the worst fate of retaliation should it become known they told on their peers.

A school counselor was at the center of a court case that involved bringing the bully and the victim together for conflict resolution. The problem is the well-meaning intervention on the part of the school counselor was misguided and ended disastrously (*Gammon v. Edwardsville Community Unit School District* (1980)). An eighth-grade student was warned by her peers that another student who was making threats against her wished to see her in the restroom. The student went to her school counselor for help. The school counselor testified she had worked extensively with the offending student and had established a good rapport with her. The school counselor brought in the threatening student to give the two girls a chance to air their differences. The school counselor testified that the threatening student's considerable anger was apparent and did not diminish as a result of the joint counseling session or later when the school counselor met privately to warn her suspension would result if any fighting occurred. The school counselor subsequently conferred with the apprehensive student and recommended she avoid any encounter with the other girl. The student continued to express her fears and indicated her difficulties with the aggressor were not over. The school counselor did not notify the administration or playground supervisors. Both girls were on the playground at the same time later in the day, and the aggressor struck the victim in the left eye with her fist, producing a skull fracture so serious it required corrective surgery (*Gammon v. Edwardsville Community Unit School District* (1980)).

The victim's mother contended that the school's response to a known threat of violence on school premises was inadequate under the circumstances. The school counselor was aware of the offending student's prior conduct, and there was evidence school officials knew of prior fighting on her part. The victim's mother argued immediate steps should have been taken following the morning counseling session to discipline the student who threatened her daughter (*Gammon v. Edwardsville Community Unit School District* (1980)).

The court cited the school counselor, as a school official, had *in loco parentis* status: "In all matters relating to the discipline in and conduct of the school and the school children, they [educators] stand in the relation of parents and guardians of the pupils. This relationship shall extend to all activities connected with the school program and may be exercised at any time for the safety and supervision of the pupils in the absence of their parents or guardians" (Illinois Rev. Statute, 1977).

School counselors must recognize the imbalance of power and unequal emotional responses associated with bullying and treat such cases differently from conflict-resolution cases. The minute this school counselor learned she was in the midst of a bullying situation and not conflict, she should have sought out administration and made sure all parties knew of the potential for harm to the victim. School counselors would not bring a bullied student together with the bully unless in that very rare situation a mature student would ask to face her tormentor in the safety of an adult who could facilitate. Again, this would be handled by administration not the school counselor. Bullying is illegal behavior, and a prudent school counselor would proceed carefully, assessing the victim's developmental level before supporting a student's decision to face his or her attacker. This approach can quickly backfire and be dangerous.

PROTECTING THE VICTIM'S IDENTITY

Phillip confides in you he is being bullied by a group of boys. Phillip begs you not to do anything and says he just wants to be moved to another class far away from the boys. He tells you if you tell anyone and it gets back to the boys, bullying will be worse, and no one will be able to protect him. Your instincts tell you to follow Phillip's instructions. You are looking into his eyes, and you see the fear and pain. However, you know that in your state bullying is illegal, and you have to notify administration. How do you negotiate honoring your student and staying legal?

Points to Consider

Shea Albers was bullied by three students while in seventh grade. He complained to his parents, who then contacted the school. The principal wanted to know the students' names, but Albers and his mother would not disclose the information for fear of retaliation. A social worker, Breen, was then brought in to talk with Albers. Albers disclosed the names to Breen, who in turn told the principal. The principal told one of the bullies Albers had accused him of bullying him. To avoid harm, Albers transferred to a new school and filed suit against the social worker and the principal. The circuit court and the appellate court dismissed the case (*Albers v. Breen*, 346 Ill.App.3d 799, 806 N.E.2d 667 (4th Dist. 2004)) on the basis of protections for school personnel under the state's Tort Immunity Act. The court understood the difficulty school principals have in trying to make discretionary decisions in dealing with bullying, stating, "Certainly the way that a principal handles an instance of bullying in his school falls within the definition [of a discretionary act]; any student who has been sent to the principal's office could attest that he has broad discretion in how to handle such situations."

Even though the Albers case did not result in a ruling in the student's favor, revealing a student's name and complaint to the bullies should be avoided. To behave otherwise victimizes students like Albers twice and can inflame the situation, resulting in emotional distress for the bullied that could end up being worse than the bullying itself. Confidentiality presents a difficult dilemma. Supporting Phillip will be an ongoing process made more complicated by the fact that, whether his name is used or not, the bullies may well conclude Phillip told, and the reality is we cannot protect Phillip at all times. The fear of retaliation is often the reason students do not confide in educators. Even if educators can protect students from further bullying at school, students know we cannot protect them from being bullied outside of school or, worse, the cruelty of social isolation that may follow when students alert administrators to their peers' behavior. Even though bullying statutes and federal legislation prohibit retaliation, school officials will do well to work to reassure students that their confidentiality will not be breached, especially to the perpetrator.

Phillip has an advocate in the school counselor, who hopefully does not just report his bullying but also works with administration to minimize the additional trauma an investigation could have on him. The school counselor's role is to encourage administration to act to provide a safe and nondiscriminatory environment for all students. School counselors should encourage administrators to allow Philip to change his schedule so he feels safe at school; of course, it is better to change the bully's schedule rather than the victim's schedule as the bully should be the one who is inconvenienced. However, sometimes educators just need to follow the student's lead; students know the players and the circumstances better than the school officials ever could. Administration has to weigh the request for confidentiality and schedule changes against the seriousness of the bullying. Optimally, it is better to catch the bullies in the act. If possible, remedy the bullying and prevent its recurrence without naming Phillip or giving him away as the one who told. The bullied and the bullies should never be brought together except in those rare incidents when the bullied wants to face his or her tormentor in a safe place. Again, this approach is a risk to the bullied; it should be the rare exception for a developmentally able student with involvement by his or her parents and conducted by the administration with the school counselor in a supportive if in a role at all.

BULLIED STUDENT WANTS TO TRANSFER TO ANOTHER SCHOOL

Ryan struggles with feelings of inadequacy. Ryan's parents are asking the district to allow their son to go to a different high school to get away from bullies who have followed him for the last two years. Despite their efforts, school officials have not been able to stop the bullying. The principal will not agree to this special assignment, saying this just teaches children to run away from their problems. What, if any, might be your role in this situation?

Points to Consider

Shore Regional High School Board of Education v. P.S. (2004) ruled that a school district's failure to protect a student from bullying constituted a denial of a free, appropriate public education required by the Individuals with Disabilities Education Act (1990). P.S., a New Jersey ninth-grader, had been teased and bullied throughout elementary school, to the point where he displayed suicidal tendencies and became eligible for the emotionally handicapped class. His parents wanted him to go to a different high school than the assigned one so he could avoid being with the same children who had previously emotionally and physically abused him.

Despite repeated complaints, the school administration failed to remedy the situation. After the district refused to place P.S. at the requested high school, the parents decided to take him to an out-of-district high school and requested a due process hearing to obtain reimbursement for the cost of having to go out of district. The new high school's plan was to mainstream P.S. for all his classes. The plan also included a program intended to combat bullying through discipline and diversity seminars. Court testimony described how P.S. thrived both academically and socially at the new high school. The plaintiffs presented testimony that the home high school could not provide P.S. with a free, appropriate public education, as required by IDEA. The administrative law judge ordered the school district to reimburse the parents for the out-of-district placement.

School counselors have a limited role in discipline but not in student advocacy. School counselors may have been able to influence administration to relent and allow P.S. to attend the new high school due to his well-documented problem that needed an out-of-the ordinary response. Special assignments for students are frequently made for far-less-critical reasons. The principal's comment about how the move simply teaches children to run away from their problems provides gasoline on the fire in court cases.

ASCA encourages school counselors to collaborate with others in the school and community to promote safe schools and confront issues threatening school safety. School counselors encourage the development of local policies supporting a safe school environment, and they provide leadership to the school by assisting in the design and implementation of schoolwide prevention activities and programs. School counselors also advocate for state and national policies supporting these efforts. Additionally, school counselors recognize differentiated interventions are needed for bullying and resolving a conflict. Comprehensive anti-bullying/anti-harassment/violence-prevention and conflict-resolution programs require data-driven decision making, coordination, instruction and program evaluation" (ASCA, 2022f).

CYBERBULLYING

Three girls come to you hysterical as they have become the target of what they guess is about 50 hate text messages that have been flying around today. They know the contents as many of their peers have shown them the messages. The girls do not want to go back to class, and they want you to help them. What can you do?

Points to Consider

The school counselor in this scenario should involve administration. The administrator has the job of balancing a school's obligation to keep students safe against respecting students' rights to freedom of speech (Baskin, 2022). Cyberbullying is intentional, oftentimes retaliatory, with the perpetrator seeking power, belonging or fun. It may take the form of trolling, attacking, outing (making personal information public), excluding, impersonating, stalking, baiting or blackmailing to name a few (Sabella, 2021; UNICEF, 2022). Estimates of the pervasiveness of cyberbullying vary widely, depending on the definition of cyberbullying and the age group studied. The Cyberbullying Research Center defines cyberbullying as when someone "repeatedly makes fun of another person online or repeatedly picks on another person through email or text message or when someone posts something online about another person they don't like." The Cyberbullying Research Center conducted a survey of 1034 randomly selected 9-12 year-olds. Twenty percent of these preadolescents identified as a victim of cyberbullying at some point in their life (Patchin, 2020). Six percent had been cyberbullied many times, while another 8.5% were cyberbullied once or twice. Few admitted to cyberbullying others (3.2%). Nearly 70% said it affected their feelings about themselves, about one-third said it affected their friendships, 13% said it affected their physical health, and 6.5% shared it influenced their schoolwork. Preadolescents will seek help for cyberbullying. Blocking the person worked for 60%; turning to their parents for help worked in 50% of the cases. Few survey respondents turned to the school for help (11.8%).

The bullies in online situations often remain anonymous, making it difficult for administration to take down certain websites because it takes away the students' rights to free speech (Li, 2007). In New York, a student sent a threatening email to his teacher depicting an image of a gun being aimed at the teacher's head. The student said the message was sent from an off-campus computer and that the school was violating his free-speech rights. Administrators felt they reacted due to their concerns for safety and were right in suspending the student because the student's communication could potentially disrupt the school. Courts found in favor of the school district, saying the email was a true threat to the teacher (Walsh, 2008).

CYBERBULLYING AND ZERO-TOLERANCE POLICIES

You are part of a committee charged by administration to develop a zero-tolerance policy for cyberbullying on or off campus. What are the legal and ethical implications of such a policy?

Points to Consider

Zero-tolerance policies started with the passage of the Gun-Free Schools Act of 1994, which required expulsion of students who bring a gun on school property, but the law allowed for a case-by-case determination (Thomsen, 2019). States took the kernel of the act and expanded it. The result has been an extraordinary increase in suspensions and expulsions for minor infractions and behavior that is obviously not threatening. According to Curran (2019), some claimed the guidance may have made things worse – and even contributed to school shootings – by discouraging schools from reporting problem behavior. During the 1990s, proponents of zero-tolerance discipline saw it as a solution for school violence. They also saw it as a way to ensure unbiased discipline by removing discretion from school staff. For example, in 1995 Albert Shanker, then-president of the American Federation of Teachers, stated: "The way to make sure that this is done fairly and is not done in a prejudiced way is to say, look, we don't care if you're white or Hispanic or African American or whether you're a recent immigrant or this or that, for this infraction, this is what happens." To the contrary, however, studies have found that zero-tolerance policies can increase suspensions and exacerbate racial disparities in discipline. They may also yield little benefit in terms of improved school climate (Curran, 2019).

A student with a rubber ax was suspended even though he had on his firefighter costume for Halloween. An honor student with a kitchen knife for his science experiment was suspended. A 16-year-old who was helping his family move was suspended when a security guard roaming the parking lot found kitchen utensils on the student's car floorboard. The list goes on and on. Over the last 15 years, it has become apparent that zero-tolerance policies do not work, and there is a call for them to be banned (Kang-Brown et al., 2013). The American Bar Association, which has passed a resolution opposing zero tolerance, says these are "policies that have a discriminatory effect, or mandate either expulsion or referral of students to juvenile or criminal court, without regard to the circumstances or nature of the offense or the student's history" (McAndrews, 2001). "The results of zero tolerance are more harm than good, and it has to stop," says Harvard University's Civil Rights Project. "The exclusion of students from the educational process is a crisis of epidemic proportions; it has long-term implications not only for the students affected but also for our society as a whole," according to Opportunities Suspended: The Devastating Consequences of Zero Tolerance and School Discipline Policies (EdWorld, 2022).

The underlying theory behind zero-tolerance policies is that small rule violations (or crimes) necessarily lead to larger infractions. By acting swiftly and harshly when a violation is first committed, larger problems can be avoided. Zero-tolerance policies do not consider the circumstances surrounding an incident or the disciplinary history or background of the person who committed the violation.

Advocates for restorative justice in education taking the place of zero-tolerance policies point to major problems with zero tolerance and exclusionary discipline in schools:

- They are largely ineffective. Suspensions and expulsions often result in poorer academic performance and lower school engagement.
- They disproportionately target students of color. Structural racism and the implicit bias of some teachers and administrators leads to students of color being overrepresented in exclusionary discipline measures (ASCA, 2022a).
- They can be overly harsh. Expulsions and suspensions are often for nonviolent actions.

Students who are suspended or expelled often feel ostracized, undervalued and misunderstood. They are at greater risk for dropping out of school, and students who are not in school are at greater risk of coming into contact with the criminal justice system. The phenomenon of harsh school disciplinary policies resulting in students becoming criminals is known as the school-to-prison pipeline (MILLS, 2020).

Revisit the case of Substantial Disruption and Cyber-Speech at the beginning of this chapter. Students in Kentucky left school by the dozens to avoid what they perceived as a real threat to their safety. Two Bullitt Central High School freshmen threatened a middle school student on MySpace, one with a picture of himself holding a gun. The school district decided to implement a new no-tolerance policy addressing both on- and off-school cyber-speech that was bullying. The Kentucky Chapter of the American Civil Liberties Union reminded the school district that students have a right to free speech under the First Amendment and all policies have to carefully define how free speech will be regulated only if it forecasts a substantial disruption. Administrators and school districts are simply not able to write blanket zero-tolerance policies regarding cyberbullying. If taken to court by students and their parents, then the court will want to know how the speech substantially disrupted the school (National Association of Secondary School Principals, 2008). Zero-tolerance policies disproportionately suspend and expel children of color (Losen & Martinez, 2013; Skiba & Williams, 2014; Skiba et al, 2014), and they do not work according to mounting research. A 2000 study conducted by the Justice Policy Institute reveals that many cases of unjust punishments thrown at innocent children have garnered national attention (Chen, 2021):

- In Louisiana, a 12-year-old diagnosed with a hyperactive disorder warned her peers not to eat all of the potatoes, or "I'm going to get you." This simple statement led to a two-day suspension, citing that the student had made "terroristic threats" toward others.
- In Texas, a 13-year-old boy was required to write a scary story for a Halloween-based assignment. His story involved a character who shot students at a school. Consequently, the teenager was arrested and spent six days in jail before the police confirmed no crime was committed.
- In Florida, a 14-year-old student with special needs was referred to the police after the principal discovered the child allegedly stole $2 from a classmate. The child was charged with "strong-armed robbery" and was held in an adult jail for six weeks. When a CBS "60 Minutes" news crew arrived to report this case, the charges pending were fortunately dropped.

Although these cases are certainly severe and uncommon examples, many individuals are still being punished for even seemingly smaller infractions. In fact, there have been widespread cases involving children bringing toy guns to school, unaware their toy guns would be an offense to schools' zero-tolerance rules. Specifically, one 10-year-old Georgia student was faced with potential expulsion and long-term juvenile detention after bringing a toy gun to school. According to the student, he brought the toy gun to class because it reminded him of pictures from his history textbook, as the class had been studying various wars, soldiers and leaders from the past. Yet, despite the criticism of zero-tolerance rules, according to data from the U.S. Justice Policy Institute and the Department of Education, crime and violence have decreased by 30% in all public schools since 1990. Furthermore, less than 1% of all violent incidents involving younger teens or adolescents occur near or on school property (Chen, 2021).

SEXTING LEADING TO BULLYING

A student comes to you distraught because she sent her boyfriend a sex text, and he forwarded it to a friend who promised to keep it private. From there the picture spread widely. She is reaching out to you for help. What, if anything, can you do?

Points to Consider

Although people have been taking sexually explicit self-portraits for longer than most adults would care to admit, technology has advanced in such a way that these images now spread more quickly than ever. "Sexting" is the exchange of explicit sexual messages or images by mobile phone. A 2012 study revealed a low prevalence of sexting among participants aged 10–17, with 2.5% and 7.1% of predominantly older youth sending and receiving sexts, respectively. That study had notable strengths, including a nationally representative sample, an explicit definition of sexting, and a wide age range. However, several methodological limitations likely resulted in the underreporting of sexting, including the use of landlines to conduct the survey and interviews with youth in the presence of parents. Recent studies reveal that sexting is an increasingly common practice, with the prevalence increasing each year until youth reach the age of 18 years. Moreover, the increase in prevalence rates with age is commensurate with older youth having greater access to and/or owning smartphones compared with younger youth. That said, there is a growing trend for tweens to have access to smartphones; in 2016, the mean age of first smartphone possession was estimated to be 10.3 years. (Madigan et al., 2018). Pictures of girls spread rapidly more frequently than those of boys because the sexual double standard leads to "slut-shaming" of girls by other girls and because homophobia prevents boys from forwarding pictures of other boys (Boyd, 2011b).

The school counselor can support the student in this scenario in a number of ways. Do her parents know about the bullying, and will she freely agree to allow the school counselor to involve them? If she is reluctant to involve her parents, the school counselor needs to convince her it is in her best interest to let her parents know because this is a crime against their child, and they should be involved from the onset (National Association of Secondary School Principals, 2008). Administration has to be contacted because this is illegal behavior. The administration is in the difficult position of having to protect this student while also protecting the bullies' free-speech rights. Since this is widespread and has even had national exposure, administration is probably safe in labeling this bullying as creating a substantial disruption to the educational process, meaning administration can punish and take action against the bullies. Conducting periodic climate surveys will help assess the environment and what is going on in cyberspace that is hurting students. (See the chapter on Student Privacy and PPRA before conducting any surveys).

SEXTING AND PEDOPHILE CHARGES

You are on a committee to develop an assembly to help students understand the dangers of sexting. You are considering using the alleged information that sexting is illegal and those students who forward nude photos of themselves or others might be charged with distributing child porn. Would you be accurate in telling students that sexting is illegal?

Points to Consider

Margarite, an eighth-grader in Lacey, Wash., was a victim of a sexting ordeal that escalated into child pornography. In fall 2009, Margarite sent Saiah, another eighth-grader, a nude picture of herself. Saiah then forwarded the picture to a former friend of Margarite's, who distributed it widely. The juveniles were all to be charged with the dissemination of child pornography and spent the night at the county juvenile detention center. The district attorney struck a deal with the students, charging them with telephone harassment and requiring them to complete community service. The case was dismissed.

Miller, et. al. v. Skumanick (2010), a pivotal case in Pennsylvania, involved the threat of child pornography charges against three girls. The girls had taken provocative pictures of each other during a sleepover in 2008. Teachers later discovered the pictures on male classmates' cell phones. The county district attorney threatened the girls and other students who had stored the pictures on their phones with child pornography charges unless they participated in an educational and counseling re-education program, intended to teach them "what it means to be a girl in today's society." At the parents' request, the American Civil Liberties Union helped sue the district attorney, arguing that the re-education program violated the 14th Amendment, which guarantees parents' rights to raise their children as they see fit. They also argued that he violated the girls' First Amendment right to freedom of expression. After two years of legal proceedings, the Third Circuit Court of Appeals ruled in March 2010 that the teens could not be prosecuted under child pornography laws solely for appearing in the images. (McLaughlin, 2010, p.1).

Many states are rewriting their legislation in attempts to avoid an overlap between teen sexting and child pornography. The laws currently in place, some argue, were meant to protect children, but these laws incriminate children in some sexting cases to the detriment of their futures. New laws should protect voluntarily sexted images under the First Amendment, advocates say. Others argue that relaxing these laws could put more children at risk by hindering prosecution of adults who possess and distribute child pornography. For example, 10 states have felony provisions for sexting. Meanwhile, 10 other states have legal provisions to treat sexting as a violation. In these less-punitive states, judges order a fine, counseling or community service. When sexting occurs between two minors, state law varies in how to prosecute these cases. Generally, however, the laws treat sexting between minors with more levity than in child porn cases. For example, some states do not require sex offender registration, as is the case in Rhode Island, Vermont and Nevada. Consent can be a defense to sending or receiving sexts but generally only when it occurs between two adults. A handful of states allow this defense, including Florida, Louisiana, Nebraska, New Jersey, New Mexico, North Dakota, Oregon, Utah, and Vermont. Of these, only Nebraska treats consent as an affirmative defense if the sexting occurred between two minors. Otherwise, as with statutory rape laws, minors cannot provide consent (Zapal, 2021).

Theoharis (2020) explains how the states that have adopted sexting laws have specifically targeted images sent between or among teenagers. For example, Connecticut's sexting law targets teens (13–17) who either transmit or possess nude or obscene photos of either themselves or another teenager. The Connecticut law also makes distinctions between the age of the sender and the recipient, penalizing senders aged 13–15 who send pictures of themselves and recipients aged 13–17 who receive any images.

However, state laws differ significantly. Louisiana, for example, prohibits anyone under the age of 17 from sending or keeping explicit photographs, while Texas allows an exception for sexting if a minor sexts with another minor who is no more than two years older or younger and the two are dating. It's important to note that even though sexting laws apply to teenagers, this doesn't mean that people over the age of 16 or 18 who send sex messages are free from committing a crime. For example, a 19-year-old who sends or receives and keeps an explicit image of a person under the age of 18 may be charged with child pornography or similar crimes. Sexting laws are designed to target teens who send explicit images to other teens, making the crime less significant than a child pornography charge, which would otherwise apply if the people involved were adults (Theoharis, 2020).

Given the new and unique dangers associated with sexting, schools should create opportunities to educate teens about safe digital etiquette and about potential social, legal and professional consequences to risky behavior. As the school employee charged with students' social/emotional and career aspects, school counselors can take the lead in developing digital safety curricula within a school. Students should learn about the laws surrounding sexting. They should also learn that, although the laws may change, social and professional consequences are always a risk.

As school counselors and educators, it is also important to listen to teens and understand sexting behavior from their perspective. Hinduja (2020) explains how despite efforts to dissuade youth from sharing intimate images, some teens continue to participate in sexting. Anecdotally, many teens who sext explain sexting is a harmless, normative behavior that is done for various reasons: foreplay, experimentation, a prelude to hooking up, to increase intimacy, as a form of sexual expression, because that's what you do when you love someone else, because they're proud of their body and it's their right to show it off, because it's exciting and enjoyable.

Given many teens' desire to be intimate with their partners and the potential consequences of doing so using technology, along with the ineffective efforts to stem participation in these behaviors, it is time to reconsider our approach to teen sexting.

Patchin and Hinduja's 2016 research found that 12% of U.S. middle and high school students had sent a nude photo or video of themselves to someone at some point in their lifetime (Patchin & Hinduja, 2019). About 19% said they had received a nude photo from someone else. Newly collected (unpublished) data from a national sample of nearly 5,000 youth aged 12–17 years in April 2019 found that 14% had sent and 23% had received sexually explicit images. These figures represent an increase of 13% for sending and 22% for receiving from 2016 data. Although some indicators of teen sexual behavior are trending in the right direction, sexting is not. As such, something new needs to be done.

Adopting a harm-reduction framework to educate those inclined to sext will help minimize the worst of the possible outcomes that could occur. Such a philosophy should include strategies for youth to use to reduce the likelihood their images can be directly linked to them or that the images will be shared beyond their original target (Hinduja, 2020).

Although many teens recognize the potential negative outcomes associated with sexting, they may need some help from educators to urge them toward safe digital communication. Understanding your school's culture can be paramount to building trusting relationships with students and building an effective preventive education program. Small groups and classroom instruction can be excellent forums for teaching resiliency skills and healthy relationship skills. In addition, school counselors should collaborate with administrators and teachers to crack down on name-calling and bullying behavior they see. Digital safety should be a part of every student's health or life skills coursework. The Cyber Civil Rights Initiative provides a 24/7 crisis hotline reachable at (844) 878-CCRI.

Revenge porn is defined as the act of distributing intimate photography through different means without the individual's consent. While revenge is not always the motivating factor, this act seems to be increasingly used by the perpetrator as retaliation for romantic relationships going south and is becoming more prominent with the growing popularity of sexting (Hinduja, 2016). To date, 34 states have laws against nonconsensual porn (and six have pending legislation). For example, Florida's law makes the act a first-degree misdemeanor and third-degree felony for repeat offenders (Hinduja, 2016).

Revenge porn happens when one person shares private explicit photos online or with others as payback. Revenge porn also can lead to sextortion, a serious crime that occurs when someone threatens to distribute these images if you don't do what they say. This can include paying money, performing illegal acts or even sending more explicit photos. Many states explicitly consider revenge porn illegal, and these laws can apply to both minors and adults. States with no laws to address revenge porn treat it as a crime under child pornography, harassment and other laws (Zapal, 2021).

California has specifically outlawed revenge porn. In California, it is a crime to post or otherwise electronically distribute a digital image of another person to harass, cause fear in or lead to injury of that person. Revenge porn, sometimes called cyber exploitation, is a form of nonconsensual pornography (NCP). Although disgruntled exes are frequently the revenge porn perpetrators, strangers also commit NCP by hacking into others' accounts or devices and then posting images they find. As of 2021, California is one of 42 states and the District of Columbia that explicitly outlaw nonconsensual pornography.

But even states that do not specifically address NCP often have existing criminal laws that cover NCP (England, 2022).

In a Position to Know
A School Counselor Speaks

The case presented at the beginning of the chapter is revisited here and answered by a school counselor. Compare her answer with your own approach.

SCHOOL COUNSELORS AND BULLY PROOFING

The discipline referral rate for bullying in your school is high. You conduct an anonymous schoolwide survey and learn bullying is a problem for many students in fourth and fifth grades. What might you do to try and create a safer school climate for students?

Being an elementary school counselor for more than 1,000 students, I was outnumbered. To tackle the bullying problem at my school, I involved all the resources I could muster from inside and outside the school. I established a committee primarily of parent volunteers, and we set our sights on reducing the number of discipline referrals that involved fighting, name-calling, verbal harassment and other forms of bullying. Support and teamwork came from every part of the school: teachers, paraprofessionals, custodians and the principal.

Classroom teachers were especially active, and their buy-in for a bully-proofing program was strong because they could immediately see the program resulted in reduced conflict among students. The teachers were consistent in implementing various conflict-resolution strategies, such as teaching the students to identify bullying behavior and charting it as a class, until they extinguished the behavior. Navy pilots helped mentor students with a history of discipline referrals for conflict. The art, music and PE teachers and the media specialist coordinated with others and me in the bully-proofing program and made their lessons and activities coincide.

At the end of the year, the efforts reduced the number of discipline referrals from 183 to 98, almost a 50% reduction. I believe ethical school counselors use their time and talents to help create a safe, respectful school climate so all students can come to school and not feel abused by others. Bullying is a form of child abuse, just at the hands of other children instead of adults. I believe by working with others who want to see bullying reduced we can make a difference.

– Mary Ann Dyal, Jacksonville, Fla., retired elementary school counselor and a consultant for anti-bullying programs

Making Connections

1. Bullying in your school has become so prevalent that your principal wants you to correspond with the neighboring schools to develop interventions or strategies that can lower bullying instances. List five interventions, and discuss how they relate to bullying statistics.

2. A group of students at your school are chronic bullying offenders. Discipline referrals, pleading and behavior modification have worked only as long as someone is watching these students. You want to change their attitudes and beliefs about their right to bully those who are less able to defend themselves. What approach do you use?

3. Principals and teachers often send students with disruptive tendencies to the school counselor's office. As a school counselor, what is your role in working with these students?

4. Michael is an excellent student who excels in extracurricular activities. Recently, you've noticed Michael has started to remove himself from afterschool practices, and his grades have started to decline. Michael has been to your office many times to speak to you about an older student who keeps bullying him. You have reported the occurrences to the principal, but she has failed to react. How can you advocate for Michael without losing your job?

5. You have recently noticed an increase in sexting at your school. Students often send nude pictures to each other as a form of flirting without realizing the possible implications of this behavior. What would you like to see happen to address this problem?

6. You have noticed an increase in student complaints about classmates bullying them on social media sites. What can you do to advocate for these students?

7. Discuss how the First Amendment affects students' rights online.

8. Write up a proposal to present to administration advocating for anonymous reporting of bullying in your school. Include statistics and facts to support your proposal.

Chapter 12 Quiz

1) Which of the following statements is true?
   a. The U.S. Supreme Court heard three cases, *J.S. v. Blue Mountain School District*, *Layshock v. Hermitage School District* and *Kowalski v. Berkeley County School District* to clearly standardize what is meant by substantive disruption.
   b. School districts are ethically but not legally obligated to seek to remedy bullying and harassment that is severe, pervasive and objectively offensive.
   c. The courts continue to offer disparate judgments and confusion in cases of cyberspeech, making it difficult for school officials to know what they can discipline and what would be a violation of a student's First Amendment rights.

d. Cyberbullying must result in a physical injury before it can be addressed by school officials.
e. Any off-campus speech is protected by First Amendment rights and students cannot be disciplined unless school district equipment was used.

2) Which is not an appropriate response when students tell a school counselor they are being bullied?
a. Report the bullying to administration.
b. Recognize and act in loco parentis and protect the student from harm
c. To the extent possible, keep the student's identity confidential but always report to administration.
d. If not severe and pervasive bullying, tell students to try and work things out with the people bullying them.
e. Help the student talk about the abuse.

3) In *Albers v. Breen* school officials prevailed but were reminded that:
a. Administrators need to bring the bullied and bullies together to seek a resolution.
b. Administrators should seek school counselors' help in conflict resolution with the bullied and bullies.
c. Administrators must have the bullies sign an agreement not to retaliate against the student who reported them for bullying.
d. It is not possible to victimize a student twice.
e. Revealing bullied students' names to the bullies they reported should be avoided.

4) Traits and characteristics of bullies and bystanders according include all except:
a. Bully aides are students who actively encourage the bullies.
b. Bully supporters are students who laugh when bullying is taking place.
c. Defenders are students who guard the victims by actively stepping in to stop the bullying.
d. Dodgers are students who actively seek to hide to keep from being bullied.
e. Witnesses are students who are aware bullying is taking place and do their best to avoid it as it causes them to suffer to see others hurt.

5) *Tinker v. Des Moines Independent Community School District* is a critical court case for educators because it:
a. Defined the First Amendment rights of students in public schools.
b. Underscored that public schools do not have a compelling interest in regulating student speech, including speech disrupting the discipline of the school.
c. Defined *quid pro quo*, student-on-student harassment and bullying.
d. The court explained when school officials have the power to regulate off-campus student speech.
e. Made bullying illegal in all 50 states.

Key Terms

Amici curiae brief
Bullying
Bullycide
Cyberbullying
Cyber-speech
Discriminatory harassment
Immunity
In loco parentis
Jessica Logan Act
Revenge porn
Sexting
Slut-shaming
Social bullying

Objectives

By the time you have completed this chapter, you should be able to:

- Discuss the prevalence of school violence
- Identify forms of peer-on-peer aggression
- Define and describe bystander behavior
- Understand the *Tarasoff* ruling and duty to warn
- Understand foreseeability and how it affects educators
- Define risk factors, protective factors and threat assessments
- Discuss the implications for educators to act and the federal mandates requiring action
- Describe effective strategies to support a safe and respectful school climate
- Describe the role of anonymous reporting in providing students with a safe environment
- Define dating violence and the Office for Civil Rights' Mandates to Educators
- Understand state statutes on involuntary mental health hospitalizations

Ethical Standards Addressed in This Chapter

Professionalism means knowing your professional association's ethical standards and adhering to them. The ASCA Ethical Standards for School Counselors (2022b) most germane to this chapter are the following:

- All students have the right to privacy that is honored to the greatest extent possible, which at times may be limited by school counselors' balance of other competing interests (e.g., best interests of students, the safety of others, parental rights) and adherence to laws, policies and ethical standards pertaining to confidentiality and disclosure in the school setting (preamble).
- All students have the right to a physically and emotionally safe, inclusive and healthy school environment, both in-person and through digital platforms, free from abuse, bullying, harassment, discrimination and any other forms of violence (preamble).
- School counselors inform parents/guardians and school administration when a student poses a serious and foreseeable risk of harm to self or others. This notification is to be done after careful deliberation and consultation with appropriate professionals, such as other school counselors, the school nurse, school psychologist, school social worker, school resource officer or child protective services. Even if the danger appears relatively remote, parents/guardians must be notified. The consequence of the risk of not giving parents/guardians a chance to intervene on behalf of their child is too great. (A.9.a.)

- School counselors report to administration and/or appropriate authorities (e.g., law enforcement) when a student discloses a perpetrated or a perceived threat to another person's physical or mental well-being. This threat may include but is not limited to verbal abuse, physical abuse, sexual abuse, dating violence, bullying or harassment. The school counselor follows applicable federal and state laws and school and district policy. (A.9.e.)
- School counselors advocate for policies, protocols and training for schoolwide response to incidents of bullying, harassment and bias that are centered in safety, belonging and justice (A.11.b)
- School counselors, in response to a hate or bias incident (e.g. discrimination, explicit bias, hate speech), collaborate with administrative teams to ensure safety, provide support for targeted students, facilitate effective communication, provide education, connect students to resources and promote healing and recovery within the school community. (A.11.f.)
- School counselors, in developmentally appropriate ways and in the context of the incident, support victims, encourage growth and provide tools for accountability and change (e.g., restorative practices) in perpetrators and promote healing in the school community while deferring to administration for all discipline issues or any other violation of federal and state laws or district and school policies. (A.11.g).
- School counselors actively respond to incidents of bias or hate, demonstrating a commitment to equity and promoting a safe, inclusive school community. (A.11.h.)
- School counselors respect the privacy of parents/guardians in accordance with the student's best interests. (B.1.i.)
- School counselors provide parents/guardians with accurate, comprehensive and relevant information in a caring manner as appropriate and consistent with legal and ethical responsibilities to the students and parents/guardians. School counselors exercise due diligence in a timely, efficient manner to communicate concerns that affect the students' safety and welfare. (B.1.j.)
- School counselors inform appropriate officials, in accordance with federal and state law and district policy, of conditions that may be potentially disruptive or damaging to the school's mission, personnel and property, while honoring the confidentiality between the student and the school counselors to the extent possible. (B.2.g).

The full text of the ASCA Ethical Standards for School Counselors is available at *www.schoolcounselor.org*.

Introduction

This chapter should need no revision, but, tragically, each year brings a new school shooting and new laws and research in a desperate attempt to curtail violence in schools. Violent deaths in school used to be rare events, but the tragedies of Oxford High School on Nov. 30, 2021, and the Marjory Stoneman Douglas High School on Feb. 14, 2018, are just two in a long list of recent school shootings. Parents, students, educators and other stakeholders expect schools to be safe havens for children to learn, and any violence is unacceptable. Other forms of violent victimization, such as rape, sexual assault, robbery and aggravated assault, decreased between 2001–2017 (Frederique, 2020). However, both covert aggression and overt violence remain significant concerns.

A joint effort by the National Center for Education Statistics (NCES) and Bureau of Justice Statistics examines crime occurring in school as well as on the way to and from school. The report, "Indicators of School Crime and Safety," provides the most current detailed statistical information to inform the nation on key crime trends in schools. The latest report is for the 2017–2018 school year:

- Students ages 12–18 experienced 33 nonfatal victimizations per 1,000 students at school and 16 per 1,000 students away from school.
- Eight percent of male students in grades 9–12 reported being threatened or injured with a weapon on school property within that year, compared to 4% of female students.
- About 71% of public schools recorded one or more violent incidents, 21% recorded one or more serious violent incidents, and 33% recorded one or more thefts.
- Twenty-three percent of students in grades 9–12 reported they had been in a physical fight anywhere during the previous 12 months, and 8% reported they had been in a physical fight on school property during this time period.
- Six percent of students reported they avoided at least one school activity or class or one or more places in school during the previous school year because they feared being attacked or harmed.
- Twenty-three percent of students in grades 9–12 reported they had been in a physical fight anywhere during the previous 12 months, and 8.5% reported they had been in a physical fight on school property during this time period.
- Eighty percent of public schools recorded that one or more incidents of violence, theft or other crimes had taken place, amounting to an estimated 1.4 million incidents.
- During the 2017–2018 school year, there were 3,482 incidents where students brought firearms to or possessed firearms at U.S. schools, and the average rate of firearm possession incidents was seven in 100,000 students.
- About 4% of students ages 12–18 reported they were afraid of attack or harm at school during the school year. Similarly, 2.7% of students ages 12–18 reported they were afraid of attack or harm away from school during the school year.
- Twenty-one percent of public schools recorded one or more serious violent incidents in 2017–2018. However, the percentage of public schools reporting one or more incidents of violence, theft and other crimes was lower in 2017–2018 than any other school year from 1999–2010.
- In the 2017–2018 school year, 20.2% of students ages 12–18 reported being bullied at school. This percentage has been steadily decreasing since 2007 (US ED, NCES, 2016).

The U.S. Secret Service and U.S. Department of Education's Safe School Initiative, studied targeted violence, which they characterized as a premeditated act an attacker commits when he/she chooses a target before the attack. Previous incidents of targeted school violence were studied so pre-attack behaviors could be detected and future attacks prevented. Educators would find the results counterintuitive in one critically important area; there simply was not a clear profile of a school shooter. After comprehensively studying 37 instances with 41 perpetrators from 1974 to 2000 in the United States, some generalizations have emerged. The generalizations allow for more preventive measures to be taken, but they cannot be used as the only markers of an attacker as each previous attack had its own particularities. Here are the key findings from this study by Vossekuil, Fein, Reddy, Borum and Modzeleski (2004):

- School attackers do not act on sudden impulse but methodically plan their attack.
- Schools are chosen in advance by the attacker for a reason such as a specific person(s) is targeted.
- The target is often someone in an authoritative position over the attackers such as an administrator, teacher or faculty member, and attackers feel as though they have been wronged by these people. Many of the targets did not have any knowledge they were the targets or had caused any grievance from attackers.
- Most of the attackers are successful in finding their targets as the planning and premeditation allows the attacker to know the victim's whereabouts.
- Generally speaking, the attackers are Caucasian males between the ages of 13 to 18, come from two-parent households with at least one biological parent living with them, have grades of A's and B's, seem socialized with the mainstream of the student body, participate in organized social activities both in and out of school, are rarely in trouble and do not have evidence of violent or criminal behavior.
- Although they did not display violence, a majority of school attackers showed interest in violent books, movies and video games. The attackers showed signs of suicidal thoughts and suffered from depression. One-fourth of the attackers studied abused alcohol and/or other substances. These attackers had access to weapons prior to the attacks, and most had used the actual weapons before the attacks. The weapon was in their personal household or that of a relative. The attackers used mainly handguns; they used one weapon during that attack but had many other weapons on their person.
- The attackers were victims of long-standing and severe bullying by others.
- Fully 98% of the attackers experienced a major loss or failure prior to the attack. Major losses or failures included job layoff, terminal illness in the family or a relationship break up.
- Each of the attacks lasted no more than 15 minutes and was stopped by an educator or the attackers themselves. Only 27% of the attacks were stopped by law enforcement.
- Forty-four percent of the attackers were influenced by others who either dared or encouraged the attackers to carry out their plans (pp. 11-12).

The Federal Bureau of Investigation has released the report "A Study of the Pre-Attack Behaviors of Active Shooters in the United States (2018)," which compiles evidence of active shooter cases from 20002013. The FBI warns that developing a profile of a typical school shooter may seem reasonable, but it is dangerous because such a list can unfairly label and there is not a reliable profile. Students' motives for violent and aggressive behavior are difficult to understand and challenging to assess.

The FBI utilizes the Secret Service's 11 key questions in threat assessment:

- What are the student's motives and goals?
- Have there been any communications suggesting ideas or intent to attack?
- Has the student shown inappropriate interest in school attacks, weapons and/or mass violence?
- Has the student engaged in any attack-related behaviors? Does the student have the capacity to carry out an act of targeted violence?
- Is the student experiencing hopelessness, desperation and/or despair?
- Does the student have a trusting relationship with at least one responsible adult?
- Does the student see violence as an acceptable/desirable way to solve problems?
- Is the student's version of events consistent with the student's actions?

- Are other people concerned about the student's potential for violence?
- What circumstances might affect the likelihood of an attack? (FBI, n.d.)

The U.S. Department of Education and Office of Safe and Healthy Students (2021) advises schools to collaborate with their local government and community partners to take steps to plan for potential emergencies through the creation of a school emergency operations plan (EOP). A threat assessment team can be formed to develop and revise the school's EOP, and it's recommended that districts and individual schools compare existing plans and processes against the content and processes outlined in the "Guide for Developing High-Quality School Emergency Operations Plans" (US ED, 2013).

The U.S. Secret Service National Threat Assessment Center (NTAC) found the bystander effect occurred in these school attacks and was documented by the Safe Schools Initiative study. The study found that 100% of attackers demonstrated disconcerting behavior prior to the attack (NTAC, 2019). This statistic suggests observance can be essential in circumventing attacks. In a good number of cases, the attacker told someone what was going to occur. A majority of informants were told within two days (54%) or two weeks of the attack (66%), and 77% of attackers threatened their target or shared their intentions to carry out an attack. Most of these informants were friends of the attackers. The youth who did come forward immediately with information were in positive relationships with adults and felt as though they could trust adults to skillfully handle the information. Informants had parental influence to guide them to inform the administration of the plans.

Bystanders who knew but did not approach with the information felt as though it was attention-seeking behavior, a mere joke or misjudged the immediacy and the seriousness of the attack. One bystander reported he had identified disconcerting behavior from the shooter that made him uneasy. He even chose to disclose his feelings to a trusted adult, who assured him there was no reason to tell anyone. He also had other reasons for not reporting his friend to the authorities. The bystander said it was hard to believe someone could carry out a school shooting. He and his friends had discussed school shootings and how they could have been improved, but he assumed they were joking like he was. Another student expressed that he thought the school officials were "too judgmental," which probably made it harder for him to disclose information to them. Another bystander stated he was certain school officials knew about the shooter's "violent temper and direct threats." The shooter shared his allure of bombs and killings with classmates and teachers through writing and was also penalized for taking a gun to school. Because of the shooter's outlandish behavior, the bystander thought school officials "had everything under control" so he had no need to disclose additional information about threatening statements the shooter had made (Pollack, Modzeleski & Rooney, 2008, p. 13). This data highlights the imperative and ethical obligation of teaching staff and, more importantly, students, the value of speaking up when situations feel uneasy.

Relationships are important, as demonstrated by two school counselors who very likely prevented a school shooting. In February 2022, a school counselor learned from a small group of students that a fight was planned between two middle schoolers and that one of the students had a gun. The seventh-grader told friends during breakfast service that he had a gun, and the friends went straight to their school counselor. School staff recovered the gun from the student's locker. Another school counselor, Molly Hudgens, handled a potentially volatile situation like the professional she is. In 2016, Hudgens talked a 14-year-old middle-schooler into handing over his gun to her. The student planned to kill teachers and a policeman. He went to see his school counselor, later explaining that he knew she could dissuade him. Hudgens instinctively knew something was amiss, as she knew this young man and could read him. The conversation triggered Hudgens to ask the student if he had a gun, and he showed her a loaded pistol. Hudgens stayed calm, and after 45 minutes convinced the student to give up the gun. Cheatham County Sheriff Mike Breedlove said, "Had she not been there, it could have been very different. ... It was Ms. Hudgens that diffused the whole situation." Hudgens seemed reluctant to accept praise for her actions, but she did say her training in de-escalation helped her persuade the student in need to hand over the weapon (Hawkins, 2016).

Not every school counselor has such a dramatic end to involvement in thwarting a school shooting, but the relationships school counselors form are critically important to school safety. ASCA's position statement The School Counselor and Prevention of School-Related Gun Violence (revised 2019) lays out rationale through three tiers of recommended practices. ASCA's position statement The School Counselor and Safe Schools and Crisis Response (revised 2019) outlines additional resources and response methods for school counselors and school staff.

It is impossible to prevent all incidents, but the U.S. Secret Service (2019) implores schools to create a comprehensive prevention plan and review security procedures to identify gaps to reduce the likelihood of a violent attack occurrence. Even though this comprehensive plan should be administrator-driven, it is important for school counselors to be aware of the facets of a comprehensive prevention plan, which include:

- Step 1: Establish a multidisciplinary threat assessment team of school personnel including faculty, staff, administrators, coaches and available school resource officers who will direct, manage and document the threat assessment process.
- Step 2: Define concerning behaviors, including those that are objectively concerning or prohibited, which should trigger an immediate intervention (e.g., threats, violent acts or weapons on campus), and other lower-level concerning behaviors (e.g., depressed mood, interest in violent topics or conflicts between classmates).
- Step 3: Establish and provide training on a central reporting system, like a smartphone application, an online form or a dedicated school email address or phone number. Ensure it provides anonymity to those reporting concerns and is monitored by personnel who will follow up on all reports.
- Step 4: Determine the threshold for law enforcement intervention especially if there is a risk of harm to self or others.
- Step 5: Establish threat assessment procedures that include practices for maintaining documentation, identifying sources of information, reviewing records and conducting interviews. The assessment should be guided by an understanding of the thinking and behavior observed in past school attackers, as described in Protecting America's Schools: A U.S. Secret Service Analysis of Targeted School Violence.
- Step 6: Develop risk management options to enact, once an assessment is complete. Create individualized management plans to mitigate identified risks. Notify law enforcement immediately if the student is determined to pose an imminent risk of harm to self or others. Take steps to ensure the safety of potential targets, create a situation less prone to violence, redirect the student's motive and reduce the effect of stressors.

- Step 7: Create and promote a safe school climate built on a culture of safety, respect, trust and emotional support for students. Encourage communication, intervene in conflicts and bullying, and empower students to share their concerns.
- Step 8: Provide training for all stakeholders, including school personnel, students, parents and law enforcement.

This is an intentional approach to evaluating threat levels and the immediacy of the threat. In a January 2022 survey, roughly half of the ASCA members responding reported their school had an intentional and methodical approach to evaluating risk assessment and a protocol when a threat is posed (Stone, 2022a).

My school has an intentional and methodical risk assessment to evaluate threat level and the immediacy of the threat.
Strongly agree 31.7%
Agree.......... 34.5%
Unsure 8.4%
Disagree 18.9%
Strongly disagree.......... 6.4%

My school has a practical, well-thought-out, research-based protocol when a threat is posed that protects educators and students.
Strongly agree 23.9%
Agree.......... 36%
Unsure 14.2%
Disagree 19.4%
Strongly disagree.......... 6.5%

My school uses an informal approach to evaluating threat levels and the immediacy of the threats.
Strongly agree 12.1%
Agree.......... 35.5%
Unsure 8.9%
Disagree 27.4%
Strongly disagree.......... 16.1%
(Stone, 2022a)

School attacks make headlines, but dating violence brings far less attention. The Department of Justice defines dating violence as "violence committed by a person who is or has been in a social relationship of a romantic or intimate nature with the victim and where the existence of such a relationship shall be determined based on a consideration of the following factors: the length of the relationship, the type of relationship and the frequency of interaction between the persons involved in the relationship (2022, n.p.). Physical abuse includes hitting, punching, slapping, shoving or kicking. Emotional abuse can be threats, name-calling, screaming, yelling, ridiculing, spreading rumors, isolation, intimidation, stalking and, more recently, using technology to harass or intimidate by texting, calling and/or bullying or monitoring via social networking sites. Sexual abuse is unwanted touching or kissing, forced or coerced engagement in sexual acts.

Data on dating violence comes from the CDC's 2019 Youth Risk Behavior Surveillance System, a national survey sent to 13,677 students grades 9–12. Two-thirds of students reported having dated during the 12 months before completing the survey. A large number (8.2%) had been physically hurt on purpose (hit, slammed, injured with an object or weapon) by someone they were dating or going out with one or more times during the 12 months before the survey. The report also highlighted the prevalence of physical dating violence being higher among female (9.3%) than male (7%) students. Nationwide, 8.2% of students had been forced to do sexual things they did not want to do by someone they were dating or going out with one or more times during the 12 months before the survey (CDC, 2019a).

Dating violence has long-term effects. Victims are more likely to experience violence in future relationships, more likely to experience symptoms of depression and anxiety, engage in unhealthy behaviors and/or exhibit antisocial behaviors and have thoughts of suicide (CDC, 2016d). The CDC outlines factors that increase risk for harming a dating partner to include the following:

- Belief that dating violence is acceptable
- Depression, anxiety and other trauma symptoms
- Aggression toward peers and other aggressive behavior
- Substance use
- Early sexual activity and having multiple sexual partners
- Having a friend involved in dating violence
- Conflict with partner
- Witnessing or experiencing violence in the home (CDC, 2016d)

To learn more about promoting healthy teen relationships or to get help:

- CDC's Dating Matters: Strategies to Promote Healthy Teen Relationships
- National Domestic Violence Hotline 1-800-799-SAFE (7233)
- National Sexual Assault Hotline 1-800-656-HOPE (4673)

The Chapter 9 Sexually Active Students has additional information on dating violence.

Getting Started: What Would You Do?

The following case is discussed for you at the end of this chapter by a school counselor educator. Before you read the response, formulate in your own mind how you would approach this ethical dilemma.

SUPPORTING A SAFE AND RESPECTFUL SCHOOL CLIMATE

Your student, Beth, came into your office with a letter from her best friend, Jane. In the letter, Jane was descriptive about the violence she wanted to inflict upon another girl, Samantha, who had "stolen her boyfriend." You know Jane fairly well and believe she would not act on her angry words. However, a threat was made. Do you have to tell the administrator? This information was supposed to be confidential.

Working Through Case Studies

SCHOOL COUNSELORS' ROLE IN THREAT ASSESSMENTS

The principal has assigned you to be in charge of completing a risk assessment with students who have presented themselves as a potential threat to others. You are uncomfortable with this assignment and expressed your concerns that this responsibility should not fall on any one person to try to predict if a student might be violent. You are trying to convince the administration to make you part of an administrative-led team and not the leader and/or sole assessor. Are you alone in your thinking, or do other school counselors feel the same way?

Points to Consider

Each school day, our nation's schools are entrusted to provide a safe and healthy learning environment for approximately 55 million elementary and secondary school students. In January 2022 town hall meeting, NTAC joined forces with ASCA, the National Association of School Psychologists and the National Association of Secondary School Principals to discuss threat assessments. The ASCA stance is that school counselors' role in threats should largely be preventive and proactive given the nature and function of a school counselor's role in delivering a developmental, comprehensive school counseling program. In a January 2022 survey, school counselors strongly indicated (91.4%) that if school counselors are involved in threat assessments, it should be in collaboration with other professionals specifically trained in violence assessment (Stone, 2022d).

Families and communities expect schools to keep their children safe from threats and violence. The NTAC, the U.S. Department of Education and Office of Safe and Healthy Students, and the FBI, all stress to school officials that there needs to be a multidisciplinary team approach when a student presents as a potential threat to others. School counselors should not be asked to go it alone in threat assessments. Advocate for your proactive, prevention role and to be but one voice in a sea of voices assessing and developing interventions and support for those who may pose a school community threat.

According to a January 2022 survey by Stone, school counselors do believe they have a role to play in threat assessments, with 79.1% of respondents saying they share this responsibility with the administration. Over half the respondents (53.2%) reported they conduct formal threat assessments on individual students (Stone, 2022d). There was total agreement (100%) that school counselors should not lead the threat assessment team. Respondents believed they are part of a collaborative but not the driver or leader of the team.

School counselors should be involved in threat assessments but only in collaboration with other professionals specifically trained in violence assessment.
Strongly agree 50.2%
Agree.. 41.4%
Unsure 3.6%
Disagree 4.4%
Strongly disagree.. .4%
(Stone, 2022a)

If involved at all, school counselors are a member of an administrative-led team with other educators and experts sitting in the decision-making chair. Administrators must be involved and lead the team, as they have the authority to call law enforcement, search lockers and backpacks, suspend or expel students. School counselors do not have any of these tools. It is unwise of the district and school administration to ever place the burden on a school counselor or any one person to determine the inexact science of predicting a person's potential to level harm on the school community. This responsibility falls on administration's shoulders, with school counselors as contributors and consultants to the team approach.

The school counselor in the scenario is right to work diligently to convince administration it would be dangerous for only one person to be the sole determinant. Bring supportive research to the conversation if administration will not relent. ASCA's position statement The School Counselor and Suicide Risk Assessment" (2020) encourages school counselors to interact and consult with school staff, particularly when they believe a student may be at risk of violence to others. A school counselor's role is to keep students safe when others or the students themselves are in danger. In this same January 2022 survey, school counselors agreed (91.6%) that risk assessments should not be the school counselor's responsibility in isolation but rather as a team member who is knowledgeable about violence and how to report any warning signs or activity. Information on establishing a threat assessment program can be found at the U.S. Secret Service National Threat Assessment Center website.

Borum, Lodewijks, Bartel, and Forth (2021) share risk factors of adolescents who commit violence.

History factors include: (a) history of violence or nonviolent offending, (b) early initiation of violence, (c) past supervision/intervention failures, (d) history of self-harm or suicide attempts, (e) exposure to violence in the home, (f) childhood history of maltreatment, (g) parental/caregiver criminality, (h) early caregiver disruption, (i) poor school achievement.

Social/contextual risk factors include: (a) peer delinquency, (b) peer rejection, (c) stress and poor coping, (d) poor parental management, (e) lack of personal/social support, (f) community disorganization.

Individual/clinical risk factors include: (a) negative attitudes, (b) risk taking/impulsivity, (c) substance use difficulties, (d) anger management problems, (e) lack of empathy/remorse, (f) attention deficit/hyperactivity difficulties, (g) poor compliance, (h) low interest/commitment to school

Protective factors include: (a) prosocial involvement, (b) strong social support, (c) strong attachments and bonds, (d) positive attitude toward intervention and authority, (e) strong commitment to school, (f) resilient personality traits (Borum et al., 2021).

ZERO-TOLERANCE POLICIES AND JUVENILE JUSTICE

Your school has a zero-tolerance policy for offenses such as skipping school, out of uniform and arguing with a teacher that would be better handled in other ways. You worry the school's approach is criminalizing offenses that should be handled by the school or parents/guardians. Whenever you bring up your concerns, administrators also point out the data indicating the school is being more successful academically and behaviorally since the inception of zero tolerance. What do you do?

Points to Consider

Zero-tolerance policies were falling rapidly out of favor only to be revived by recent tragedies such as the Oxford High School shooting in 2021. In a January 2022 survey, 55.4% of the school counselors responding said their school has a formal zero-tolerance policy for violent behavior (Stone, 2022d). Zero-tolerance policies shift the focus of discipline away from the school setting and into the juvenile justice system, resulting in negative and mostly unintended consequences for the students, families and communities they are designed to protect (American Psychological Association Zero Tolerance Task Force, 2008; Hirschfield, 2018). Educators are grappling with the daunting task of preventing school violence by adding security devices, searches and controversial zero-tolerance policies. Tran, a Texas honor student jailed for truancy, is one such example of zero tolerance gone awry. Tran's parents/guardians left her to care for her two siblings. Tran worked two jobs and kept up with a demanding academic load. Judge Lanny Moriarty was not sympathetic to Tran's situation. He focused on the overall prevalence of truancy cases and requested Tran suffer the consequences of her actions like other students would. After all, Judge Moriarty stated, "One night [in jail] is not a death sentence" (CBS Atlanta Staff, 2012, p.1). Although this is an extreme zero-tolerance case, it points to some of the controversy when educators shift discipline to the courts.

The school-to-prison pipeline is a much researched and considered area as the fear is the educational system is starting to look more like the criminal justice system. Student transgressions, once handled by a principal or a parent, are now being handled by prosecutors and the police. The Civil Rights Project at Harvard University, Opportunities Suspended: The Devastating Consequence of Zero Tolerance and School Discipline, found zero-tolerance policies "are derailing students from an academic track in schools to a future in the juvenile justice system." Many of the arrests are for minor infractions, such as arguing (not fighting), and some are absurd such as the two New Jersey elementary school students who were arrested and charged with terrorism for playing cops and robbers with paper guns. "Criminal behavior such as murder, serious violence or the sale or possession of illicit drugs, should be subjected to criminal charges, as they were even before zero tolerance became the watchword" (Allen, 2004, pp. 6-7).

The Anne Arundel, Md., School District's six-tier discipline system appeared to be much more reasonable than that of a zero-tolerance policy but not after it was interpreted to mean that a 7-year-old boy who nibbled his toaster pastry into the shape of a gun had committed a tier-three offense and was punished by suspension. This disciplinary action was for Maryland's Sen. Jennings "the last straw," and he introduced legislation that would prohibit the suspensions of young children for imaginary guns, pictures of guns or objects resembling a gun but serving another purpose (St. George, 2013).

Putting students into the juvenile justice system as a result of the school's zero tolerance is questionable, as the statistics regarding repeat offenders are grim. According to the Office of Juvenile Justice and Delinquency Prevention, "There is no data on the national recidivism rate for juveniles. Such a rate would not have much meaning since juvenile justice systems vary so much across states" (OJJDP, 2012, p.1). The Council of State Governments (CSG) Justice Center is a nonprofit, nonpartisan organization representing state officials in all three branches of government to develop research and policies that increase public safety. A 2015 CSG report compiled data from the 39 states that do track recidivism in order to compare the reported state statistics. The study found that juveniles were far more likely than adults to re-offend after release across all states. The highest reported recidivism rate for juvenile offenders was 76% within three years, and 84% within five years. When these juvenile offenders reach adulthood, the numbers are equally high. Doyle and Brown, MIT researchers, analyzed data on 30,000 juvenile offenders who had been involved in the Illinois juvenile justice system (2015). Their study found that 40% of juvenile offenders were incarcerated in an adult prison for reoffending by the time they turned 25. The study also found that juvenile offenders are unlikely to finish high school, severely limiting the types of jobs these prior offenders can get, which in turn can lead them back into the prison cycle (2015).

The Southern Poverty Law Center (2020) estimates 48,000 youth are in juvenile facilities. The Southern Poverty Law Center points to some promising community-based support programs in states with high rates of children entering the juvenile justice system or dropping out of school. These projects have sought to reduce the number of children in the juvenile justice system and provide adequate community-based alternatives. States including Alabama, California, Florida, Illinois, Michigan, Missouri, New York, Ohio and others have invested in these community-based supports and have significantly reduced the number of youth in detention or placement facilities and allowed them to continue their education in their community (2020). New York City began its Close to Home (C2H) initiative, which transferred custody of NYC youth from the state to the city. This allowed youth throughout the state to be placed in nonsecure and limited-secure placements in their community, and they could receive their education through New York City Department of Education's District 79. In the 2016--17 school year, 91% of the youth placed in facilities through C2H passed their courses, and 93% of middle school youth were promoted one grade level.

MENTAL HEALTH LAWS SENDING STUDENTS TO HOSPITALS

One of your five-year-old students diagnosed with autism had a breakdown today, kicking and screaming and unable to be constrained. This student has done this before, but his mother comes and is able to calm him. Today, however, the administration is asking the school resource officer to hospitalize the child under the Baker Act, making this the third student this week to be sent to a psychiatric hospital. This is going to be so traumatic for this child and his mother. You worry administration may be overusing the Baker Act. Are your concerns valid?

Points to Consider

The Treatment Advocacy Center has details regarding how all 50 states handle involuntary treatment for mental health issues. States vary, but most statutes allow children to be held involuntarily in psychiatric hospitals or wards. In Florida, for example, the Baker Act is the mental health law allowing school resource officers and other designated people to have a child who is exhibiting extreme behavior to be transported to a hospital for a psychiatric evaluation. During the 2019–2020 school year, 37,000 students in Florida were hospitalization using the Baker Act. A 2021 report by the Southern Poverty Law Center, the Florida Chapter of the American Academy of Pediatrics, Florida Student Power Network, The Florida Council Against Sexual Violence, Florida's Children First and Legal Aid of Palm Beach County they found that children as young as five have been handcuffed, placed into the back of police cars and transported to hospitals, to be held for up to 72 hours without parental consent.

The Baker Act is not a tool to use unless a person poses a "serious threat of death or bodily harm to themselves or others" or if the behavior is "caused by a developmental disability" such as autism (Southern Poverty Law Center, 2021). The law has a specific intent and is not a discipline or behavior management tool. "The Baker Act has effectively created a second pipeline that is pushing thousands of Black and brown children and children with disabilities out of schools and foster care facilities each year," said Bacardi Jackson, managing attorney for the the Southern Poverty Law Center's Florida office and senior supervising attorney for its children's rights practice group. The report also suggests some core reforms specifically for Florida, but the reforms are applicable wherever a mental health law is being overused:

- Requiring schools to intervene on behalf of children with individualized education programs to prevent law enforcement from wrongfully using the Baker Act on students with disabilities
- Providing robust training in schools, residential facilities and law enforcement on de-escalation methods and the Baker Act's narrow criteria for involuntary examination
- Requiring consent by parents and guardians before the Baker Act is initiated
- Fully integrating mobile crisis teams, telehealth services and credentialed school psychologists and social workers to help de-escalate and stabilize children experiencing crises and determine whether to initiate an examination under the Baker Act
- Allow parents/guardians or medical professionals to transport children to psychiatric facilities or other nontraumatic crisis stabilization units to reduce trauma
- Allow medical providers, not police, to make the decision to hold children in psychiatric facilities, often overnight, until they can see a physician.

MIRANDA WARNING AND STUDENTS IN SCHOOLS

You are working with a student when the police and administration detain the student for alleged sexual assault of a fellow student. They allowed you to accompany the student to a conference room, where the police began to question him. He was not read his Miranda rights, and now you wonder if you should have spoken up on his behalf. Was he entitled to Miranda protection?

Points to Consider

"A student is not entitled to a Miranda warning prior to being questioned by school authorities" (Alexander & Alexander, 2018, p.117). However, school police officers when working for the municipal government must give students their Miranda rights when questioning them about behavior or activities that could lead to criminal charges (*N.C. v Commonwealth of Kentucky*, 396 S.W. 3d 852 2013). When police question students in schools without a parent/guardian or legal counsel present, there is a considerable imbalance in power. Students are mandated to attend school, and, once there, they are expected to move about the school with permission only and to obey school officials. This lack of freedom can equate to being in custody for the purposes of Miranda rights. Prior to police interrogation, people in custody must be read their right to remain silent and to have legal counsel. If the student doesn't feel free to refuse or end the questioning of a police officer, the student is essentially in custody. Given minors' developmental levels, they are considered more vulnerable, and in the case of minors, judges have considered not only their physical custody for Miranda purposes but whether they were psychologically coerced.

There is considerable agreement among law scholars that students should be treated as if they are in custody and entitled to Miranda rights, and anything said prior to students' complete understanding and competence to give consent to waive their rights should not be used against them. "If school administrators rather than police officers are handling the questioning, they do not need to provide Miranda warnings unless they are working for or with law enforcement. However, the authority of school administrators can make the situation feel coercive" (Justia, 2019). Even if a student waives the right to remain silent, a judge may still question whether incriminating evidence can be admitted due to minors' vulnerability, their emotional state, their intellectual ability and/or how likely they were to be intimidated by the situation (Justia, 2019).

Scholars argue that the adolescent brain is more vulnerable to shows of authority. The nature of the school environment includes consequences for noncompliance, which can include criminal charges, thus resulting in an inherently coercive environment, which requires the adults in the school to protect students' rights. The Supreme Court's acceptance of these adolescent brain development studies in *Roper v. Simmons*, *Graham v. Florida* and *J.D.B. v. North Carolina* demonstrates that the courts understand that vulnerable adolescents need special protections, because adolescents are more likely to falsely confess, make immature decisions and have a strong propensity to comply with authority (Emory-Law, 2019).

The effort to prevent further violence will elude school officials unless they implement research-based policies addressing the power of confidentiality, methods for anonymous reporting and the impact of including students as vital links in violence prevention.

CODE OF SILENCE

A student in your school was caught carrying a gun that discharged, injuring another student. A number of students gave convincing details indicating they had seen the gun but chose not to notify school officials. The principal has asked you to participate on a committee to recommend policies and practices to encourage students to report weapons, violence and bullying. What policies and procedures do you hope will emerge from this committee?

Points to Consider

The tragic events of November 2021 at Oxford High School is but another example of rumors, hearsay and social media threats not finding their way to school authorities. Oxford senior Treshan Bryant told *The Washington Post* that he stayed home the day of the Oxford High School shootings because he had heard rumors about somebody planning to "shoot up" the school. "That puts a lot of fear into a kid," (Jackson, 2021). In nearly every case of reported school violence, students saw warning signs in advance but did not report what they saw to adults because of peer pressure, fear of retaliation and absence of a sense of personal responsibility to help keep their school safe (Pollack et al., 2008). In many cases of school violence, there are other students who are peripherally involved. This chapter's introduction discussed research that clearly points to the fact that attackers almost always share their plans for violence with peers, friends and classmates, who chose not to report the information to authorities (Pollack et al., 2008). Worth reiterating is the point that bystanders are most likely to report threats of violence when they have positive relationships with adults in the school, believe the threats to be serious and feel school officials will take the information seriously and address the threats immediately (Pollack et al., 2008).

Anonymous reporting is a communication system whereby students can report concerns about violence through a mechanism that does not require them to reveal their identity. This manner of revealing potentially incriminating information enables students to report to a school counselor or other trusted adult crimes, harassment or violence without fear of being hurt by angry students or being labeled an outsider or one who discloses information to adults (Payne & Elliott, 2011). One such system implemented in Colorado, Safe2Tell, purports to have prevented an estimated 28 planned school attacks from 2004–2011 and has had a positive impact on other student concerns as well, such as self-mutilation, drug and alcohol abuse and potential suicide events (Payne & Elliott, 2011). During the 2019–2020 school year, Safe2Tell received 20,822 tips, with the top five being suicide threats, drugs, bullying, school complaints and threats. Of those 20,822 tips, only 2% were nonactionable false tips. Programs such as Safe2Tell create opportunities to get students and staff involved in creating a safe learning environment.

High school students enrolled in a three-week college seminar at Yale University persuasively argued that students, rather than adults, are key to curbing violence in school (Stone & Isaacs, 2002b). Dozens of high school students contended their peers are more aware than adults of the different elements of a school's potentially dangerous social landscape: the cliques, gangs, aggressive students, isolated brooders, victims, perpetrators, weapon carrier, etc. Respondents reported they believed they should be allowed to anonymously alert adults, in a variety of ways, about potential acts of violence or problems they had observed or heard about, including acts of bullying, weapons on campus, gang activity, pending fights and sexual harassment (Stone & Isaacs, 2002b). Respondents advocated for a democratic, intergenerational partnership to address school violence (Stone & Isaacs, 2002b). Schools nationwide are implementing policies and programs aimed at encouraging students to report potentially dangerous students (Payne & Elliott, 2011). The school counselor's role of being the recipient of critical information will be far less complicated with a policy or guideline to help protect minors while also respecting the inherent rights of parents/guardians and the larger society. A school culture whereby students know they can and should report threats and suspicious activity with the expectation that their identity will not be revealed and their confidences will be respected should be established. In a survey, 249 ASCA members responded.

My school has an anonymous reporting system that protects the identity of students who report their peers for having a weapon or planning a violent act, crime or harassment.
Yes *48.6%*
No. *39%*
Unsure *12.4%*
(Stone, 2022d)

CONFIDENTIALITY BALANCED AGAINST COMMUNITY PROTECTION

You are exchanging journal entries with a student who needs help with his impulse control and disruptive behavior. The student has problems with authority and wrote in the journal he would hurt a particular teacher, "but I know I cannot do that." Later in class, this student shouted threats on this same teacher's life. The police were called, and they searched his belongings and found and read the journal, pausing and discussing the entry about the teacher. Even though the student qualified the threat as something he knew he could not do, the principal came to you concerned you had not reported this journal entry. Should you have reported the contents of the journal to the administration?

Points to Consider

Yes, you absolutely should have reported this. The protection of the school community always supersedes confidentiality. In the real case, the school counselor also took the journal off the principal's desk and refused to give it back, telling the principal it was her journal and it was confidential and could not be used against the student. The journal was needed to substantiate the potential for this student to be dangerous. The fact that a particular teacher was named as a target is an actual threat, and even a vague threat such as, "Teachers can be horrible to kids and no wonder some students want to hurt teachers," should not be kept confidential. This is a discipline issue. In the actual case, the journal was discovered in the course of investigating a very real and lethal-sounding threat, and it is the prudent school counselor who does not hinder the investigation.

The ASCA position statement The School Counselor and Confidentiality (2018b) reminds school counselors they have an ethical and professional responsibility to protect private information received through confidential relationships with students. However, student confidentiality pales, and school counselors' responsibilities heighten, when a student confides in them or they learn through other means a student may be a danger to others.

WARNING POTENTIAL VICTIMS

During a counseling session with Raymond, he threatens Stephan, another student with violence. What are your legal and ethical obligations in this situation? Do you inform the administration? Do you notify Stephan and/or his parents/guardians or Raymond's parents/ guardians?

Points to Consider

Run, don't walk to the administration and tell them everything you know, and allow them to do their job of protecting the school community. It is not your place to call Stephan's or Raymond's parents, but it is your duty to warn by telling the administration. A school counselor's duty to warn potential victims arises from the court case *Tarasoff v. Board of Regents of California* (1976). Posenjit Poddar killed Tatiana Tarasoff in 1969. Two months earlier, in a University of California hospital at Berkeley, Poddar had advised his psychologist, Dr. Moore, of his intention to kill Tarasoff. Tarasoff's parents/guardians filed a lawsuit charging negligence, with the claim that Moore had a duty to warn Tarasoff and her parents/guardians of the impending danger. The crux of the case was whether or not Moore had a duty to warn. The California Supreme Court ruled the psychologist-patient relationship is a special one and, as such, requires the duty to warn. The California court stated that the potential danger to Tarasoff outweighed the psychologist's obligation of confidentiality to his client.

A member of the general public who sees something dangerous has a moral duty, but not always a legal duty, to warn a potential victim. However, due to the special relationship school counselors have with their students, they are required by law to exercise the same skill, knowledge and care other members of their profession would demonstrate under similar circumstances (Hays et al., 2009). Since the *Tarasoff* ruling, a number of state courts have sought to limit or expand the scope of a duty to warn on the part of professionals. Some state legislatures have enacted laws granting greater privilege. Court cases that have followed *Tarasoff* have both broadened and narrowed the strength of the ruling. *McIntosh v. Milano* (1979), the first case decided after the *Tarasoff* decision, more broadly held the practitioner's obligations "to protect the welfare not only of the client as in *Tarasoff* but also of the community." In *Boynton v. Burglass* (1991), a court in Florida completely rejected the *Tarasoff* ruling. The court based its rejection of a duty to protect on its belief in the inexact science of psychiatry and the near-impossible task of predicting violence. The exact limits of the duty to warn from the *Tarasoff* case are uncertain and are context dependent. Regardless, school counselors know health and safety supersedes confidentiality, and administrators must be apprised of potential harm so they can act to protect potential victims (ASCA, 2019c).

All states have statutory obligations to breach confidentiality if there is bullying to report. For example, a New Hampshire statute explains that if not met, this duty may give rise to criminal liability on the part of the school counselor under N.H.R.S.A. 193-D:6. (New Hampshire Regulatory Statutes Act, 2004). Foreseeability is a critical consideration in cases where school officials are accused of negligence. Foreseeability means "a reasonably prudent person could foresee injuries" (Terando, 2011). In a case involving a student who was shot by a classmate on an unsupervised sidewalk near school grounds, the court found the school liable. The court held that the school had a duty to "take reasonable steps to protect students from harm that may befall them," a duty stemming from "increasingly foreseeable risks to children at school as well as the special relationship between student and school that exists due to the compulsory nature of education" (*Durant v. Los Angeles Unified School District* (2003)).

In Raymond's case, a breach of confidentiality is necessary because Stephan is vulnerable, and you have a "special legal relationship" to protect her. An administrator or law enforcement official should be responsible for notifying Stephan's parents/guardians of the threat, if such notification is deemed necessary.

SEXTING AS CRIMINAL BEHAVIOR

Adam, a 17-year-old student, distributed a nude picture of his ex-girlfriend to everyone in his contact list. Must you report this to your administration? To the police?

Points to Consider

Absolutely. Bullying is illegal, and revenge sexting is illegal in most states. Twenty-five states address minors sexting in state law (Hinduja & Patchin, 2018). According to the Cyberbullying Research Center, 26 states have sexting laws, and 25 of those laws address minors sending the information. Most states are working toward lesser penalties for teen sexting by leaving adult child pornography laws unchanged and creating new offenses with less severe penalties for minors who sext. For example, a Nevada law treats the first instance of sexting by a minor as a noncriminal offense. States that have adopted sexting laws have made distinctions based on the age of the sender and receiver. Revenge sexting, in which a receiver forwards a sender's sex text to hurt the sender, is carrying varying degrees of felony charges in most states. It is difficult for these charges to stick.

Before states made changes to laws that did not consider close-in-age relationships or the age of the minor, minors were treated like adults regarding sexting. The Supreme Court's pornography ruling is 34 years old, and today's teen behavior of cyber-distribution wasn't even a possibility when deciding the definition of pornography. What Adam faces is really in a category by itself, and the current legal framework is often not the appropriate one to judge his actions. Adam's behavior is not defensible, as he did a terrible thing designed to wound and humiliate. However, his actions were those of about 12% of teens who forward a sex text without consent (Madigan et al., 2018), not those of a pedophile who exploits and sexually abuses children. This same study found that one in seven youths send sexts, and one in four receive them (Madigan et al., 2018). Adam's behavior is not on the same level as a child molester, and states are removing them from pedophile lists and preventing them from being there in the first place. See Chapter 12 Bullying, Cyberbullying and Sexting for a more in-depth discussion.

DATE RAPE AND STATE LAWS

A distraught Whitney tells you there are pictures of her unconscious and being hauled upstairs by Roger and Clyde, and for three days, she has endured the sneering of Roger and his friends in the hallways "as they smugly march around with their worlds intact" while "I die a little more inside each day." She explains she only remembers sipping on a beer. She begs you not to tell anyone, especially her parents/guardians. What is the school counselor's advocacy and legal role?

Points to Consider

Date rape is not a legal term but a commonly used term to define forcible sexual contact during a voluntary social engagement in which a person does not intend to engage in sexual activities and resists the contact. Date rape is sexual assault, which is defined as any type of unwanted physical contact with a sexual organ and may include aggressive, sexually suggestive statements. Sexual assault may also occur between persons of the same gender. A widely publicized date rape of a 16-year-old unconscious girl by two high school football stars helped galvanize national outrage because of the abundance of evidence on social media. Trent Mays, 17, and Ma'lik Richmond, 16, were sentenced to two years and one year respectively in the state juvenile system. Outrage followed these light sentences, and Richmond served just 10 months and Mays 22 months before both went on to play college football. Mays' sentence was twice as long because he distributed a nude image of a minor. Social media spurred the initial prosecution, and text messages and cell phone pictures provided the evidence for the prosecution as scores of teens traded pictures of the assault. A 2019 documentary, "Roll Red Roll," revisited the rape and the code of silence to which many our students often adhere.

Under many states' laws, the penalties for sexual assault are severe and may include incarceration, significant fines, psychiatric treatment and paying restitution to the victim. In addition, a person convicted of sexual assault may be required to register as a sex offender. In most states, you can be charged with first-degree sexual assault or rape if you forced sexual intercourse or had sexual intercourse with someone who was unable to give legal consent. It is not a legal defense if the victim and perpetrator knew each other or were on a date together or had previously had sexual contact. Laws vary by state, but in the majority of states, a victim who is intoxicated is incapable of giving legal consent. Date rape drugs (rohypnol, gamma-hydroxybutyrate or GHB, ketamine) cause unconsciousness and, in some cases, death. Using these drugs on somebody is a federal crime with a possible 20-year sentence.

State statutes vary regarding date rape. Indiana specifically addresses drugging victims and raping and classifies it as a Class A felony carrying the most severe penalties for rape, along with rape with deadly force.

In the busy lives of school counselors, there are those "drop-everything-and-attend" moments, and this is one of those times. You are required by law to act quickly to prevent possible future victims, to protect the school from legal liability and to provide support for Whitney. Whitney needs help to come to terms with the fact that she was not responsible but was a victim of a federal and a state crime that has to be reported.

The anti-rape defenses of perpetrators must show affirmative consent. There must be a clear understanding that a partner is enthusiastically participating and able to give consent. The perpetrator's attorney will try to forward a defense that this is a case of regret, not rape. The new normal is it does not matter if the student's drinking was self-induced; the pertinent question is if the student was able to consent to sex. The course of action is clear. The school counselor has to report a rape to administration, who must report it to law enforcement and notify parents/guardians. The law does not give us discretion. If the state statute says it is rape if the individual is incapacitated, then child abuse has been committed. Peer-on-peer abuse is often handled differently than statutory rape. Child protective services can be a resource with regard to age difference, statutory rape and peer-on-peer abuse. Always report sexual harassment and sexual violence to your administration when placed on notice that a rape has occurred.

DATING VIOLENCE AND CONFIDENTIALITY

Lynette and Derrick are students in your school. Her friends describe Lynette as being abused by her boyfriend. From what her friends can deduct from the one-sided conversations they hear, Derrick dominates and terrorizes Lynette. Her friends tell you when they tried to get Lynette to drop Derrick, Lynette reported back to them that he slapped her in the face, told her he would decide when and if they broke up and he pushed her so hard into the lockers as to leave an imprint of the locker on her back. You reach out to Lynette, and she begs you to stay out of it or things will get worse." As Lynette's school counselor, what is your next step?

Points to Consider

You must report the dating violence to the school administration. School counselors are required by Title IX to report dating violence to school officials, who have to take steps to investigate if both students are in the same school, which may mean a hostile environment for the alleged victim. If Lynette requests confidentiality, school officials cannot agree. Title IX considers it as deliberate indifference if a school official knows of sexual harassment and does not report it. In 2021, the U.S. Department of Education, Office for Civil Rights started a review of the previous administration's approach to sexual harassment of students. Changes are likely under President Biden's administration. Regardless, in law now and unlikely to change, once Lynette confides she is being harassed or abused, this constitutes "notice," triggering the school counselor's legal requirement under Title IX to report the harassment.

Confidentiality presents a difficult dilemma for school counselors when federal and ethical guidelines tell them they must act. Supporting and protecting Lynette will be an ongoing process made more complicated by the fact that Derrick will know or suspect she told, and retaliation is Lynette's biggest fear. Even if we can protect victims from taunts or physical abuse, students know we cannot protect them from social isolation and the other cruelties that follow when students make serious allegations against their peers. Despite the fact that the Office for Civil Rights states school officials "should tell any complainants that Title IX prohibits retaliation and that school officials will not only take steps to prevent retaliation but also take strong responsive action if it occurs," school counselors know how important it is to many of their students that their confidentiality not be breached, especially to the perpetrator.

Breaching a student's confidence will often discourage reporting dating violence. As an advocate, school counselors try to work with administration to minimize the additional trauma an investigation could have on student victims. The school counselor's role is to encourage administration to act as the federal law allows, evaluating Lynette's request "in the context of responsibility to provide her with a safe environment." Administration has a responsibility to both parties involved. Not only do school officials owe Lynette support, but if Derrick remains in the school, educators still owe him loyalty and support to teach him how to become a productive citizen and how to have healthy relationships.

Chapter 11 Sexual Harassment contains expanded and detailed information on dating violence and educators' response under Title IX.

In a Position to Know: A School Counselor Educator Speaks

The case presented at the beginning of the chapter is revisited here and answered by a school counselor educator. Compare her answer with your own approach.

SUPPORTING A SAFE AND RESPECTFUL SCHOOL CLIMATE

Your student, Beth, came into your office with a letter from her best friend, Jane. In the letter, Jane was descriptive about the violence she wanted to inflict upon another girl, Samantha, who had "stolen her boyfriend." You know Jane fairly well and believe she would not act on her angry words. However, a threat was made. Do you have to tell the administrator? This information was supposed to be confidential.

Yes, you must tell the administration. Just as you would always call in child abuse, you would always tell administration about a direct or veiled threat on someone's life. Evaluating the level of intent and lethality is complicated since there are many factors for effectively conducting a threat assessment. In the scenario above, defending Jane by espousing that she wouldn't do anything would not hold up in court if some violence were to occur. In the school setting, one person in the system shouldn't shoulder the burden of all threat assessments. Adequate assessment includes many steps and involves a team approach for appropriate implementation.

Today's fast-paced culture requires district policy and an assessment protocol to responsibly evaluate the nature and danger of a student threat. An intentional and methodical plan to evaluate threat level and immediacy of the threat should be one of the components of threat assessment. In an assessment process, it is important to use a practical, well-thought-out, research-based protocol that will protect educators and students alike. Although the courts encourage educators to take threats seriously, they also ask education personnel to act reasonably. Legal vulnerability is present when the school personnel cannot demonstrate that reasonable care was taken in preventing school violence. In the court case of *Lovell v. Poway Unified School District* (1996), documentation of the steps that were used to determine a "true threat" classification may be valuable. It is important in this process to use guiding principles of threat assessment to evaluate a "true threat."

Whether it is an actual assessment, which requires a rigid protocol, or another type of assessment procedure, it's important to document the process. Identifying risk factors is a vital part of the process. Although risk factors don't always predict violence, research supports that as the volume of risk factors escalates so does the level of violence potential. In these difficult and emotional situations, it is important to follow established procedures and consider the needs of the at-risk individual, while keeping the needs and safety of those being threatened in balance. Both sides, Jane and Samantha, deserve your best and most ethical knowledge, decision-making and problem-solving skills in the ongoing effort to create a safe school.

– Rhonda Williams Ed.D., LPC, NCC, associate professor,
University of Colorado at Colorado Springs

Making Connections

1. Zero tolerance is a controversial topic in education, with some contending it is the only fair way to allocate discipline and curtail violence and others finding it does not work. Develop your position on zero tolerance by researching and writing a paper on the subject.

2. You have been told three students are planning to fight just off school grounds that afternoon. This is one of those dreaded days when all administrators are out of the building, and you are the principal designee for the day. What do you do?

3. Due to the recent increase in school violence, your principal has decided threat assessments are needed for those students who are multiple offenders in victimizing others. As a school counselor, what, if any, role would you serve in doing threat assessments?

4. Discuss duty to warn and the limits of duty to warn as you understand them. Do some additional research to find a case in your state that has ruled on a counselor's duty to warn. What does your state say about counselors' obligations regarding duty to warn?

5. Due to the increase of dating violence in your school, what policies can you develop to tackle issues that may arise?

Chapter 13 Quiz

1) Dating violence is a form of sexual harassment and discrimination under Title IX of the Education Amendments of 1972. The Office for Civil Rights, an arm of the U.S. Department of Education governing Title IX, expects educators to:
   a. Only attend to dating violence if the violence spills over into the school
   b. Turn dating violence over to the police and step away from any investigation so as not to taint the police investigation
   c. Only address sexual violence by calling the student's parent/guardian if the student is under 18 years of age
   d. Attend to dating violence even when the assault occurs off campus if it creates a hostile school environment for the victim
   e. Provide a grievance procedure only if the police are not involved

2) Best practices for creating a safer, more respectful school climate include all but which of the following:
   a. Provide a student-centered approach recognizing both adult and student participants as the most important method of resolving these issues
   b. Highlight the importance of students and adults working together, and allow students to educate adults in areas adults are often not aware of such as social cruelty
   c. Provide opportunity for students to anonymously report situations that create a hostile or dangerous school environment
   d. Enact a zero-tolerance policy, which means students are suspended or expelled when they contribute to an unsafe environment
   e. Assist as many students as possible to engage in meaningful intervention and interactions that make them feel connected to the school

3) If you are exchanging journal entries with a student who needs help with his impulse control and disruptive behavior, best practice would be to
   a. Assure the student ahead of time that you will be the only one to ever read the journal entries
   b. Assure the student that you will not read what is written and that it will be private thoughts for the student's eyes only
   c. Respond once a month to the student
   d. Report immediately to administrators if a student writes threatening statements in a journal
   e. Investigate any threats a student writes in a journal to determine if there is any need to report them or if they are empty threats

4) The court case *Tarasoff v. Board of Regents of California* is important because:
   a. It was the first negligence lawsuit against a school counselor
   b. The crux of the case was the establishment of a duty to warn when a counselor knows someone is in harm's way
   c. The general public has a moral and legal duty to warn a potential victim
   d. It was determined that the scope of the *Tarasoff* ruling cannot be limited or expanded
   e. It was determined that the duty to protect is an inexact science of psychiatry and the near-impossible task of predicting violence cannot place a duty on another to warn

5) Foreseeability in court cases involving negligence means:
   a. The ability to understand children's developmental levels
   b. The ability to understand the interrelatedness between education and future economic opportunities
   c. The ability to understand the admissions process for special education
   d. The duty to see that students attend school
   e. The reasonably competent person should have been able to foresee danger or injuries

Key Terms

Anonymous reporting
Bystander
Code of silence
Date rape drugs
Dating violence
Duty to warn
Gang violence
Historical risk factors
Identifiability of the victim
Mediation
Office for Civil Rights
Peer-on-peer aggression
Physical aggression
Protective risk factors
Rape
Recidivism rate
Risk factors
Safe school zone
School violence
Sexually hostile environment
Sexual violence
Social risk factors
Special relation
Statutory obligation
Threat assessments
True threat
Verbal aggression
Violent propensities
Zero tolerance

Legal and Ethical Advocacy

Objectives

By the time you have completed this chapter, you should be able to:

- Explain the ethical standards relating to advocacy for all students
- Define the philosophy of social justice in a school counseling program
- Use the freedoms of your First Amendment rights to advocate for marginalized students
- Understand the role of the school counselor as an impactful and astute advocate
- Understand the role of the school counselor as systems change agent
- Describe how a school counselor's behavior promotes equity and opportunities for all students
- Develop plans to responsibly challenge the institutional barriers denying equal access and prohibiting success for all students

Ethical Standards Addressed in This Chapter

Professionalism means knowing your professional association's standards and adhering to them. The ASCA Ethical Standards for School Counselors (2022b) most relevant to this chapter follow, but the entire document is directly related to the ethics of advocacy. You can review the full text at *www.schoolcounselor.org*.

School counselors:

- Support all students and their development by actively working to eliminate systemic barriers or bias impeding student development. (A.1.c).
- Provide culturally responsive instruction and appraisal and advisement to students. (A.1.d).
- Advocate for equitable, anti-oppressive and anti-bias policies and procedures, systems and practices, and provide effective, evidence-based and culturally sustaining interventions to address student needs. (A.1.j.)
- Actively work to establish a safe, equitable, affirming school environment in which all members of the school community demonstrate respect, inclusion and acceptance. (A.10.b).
- Collaborate with parents/guardians when appropriate and strive to establish consistent, constructive two-way communication in their preferred language to ensure students' needs are met. (A.10.d).

- Understand and advocate for all students' right to be treated in a manner that honors and respects their identity and expression, including but not limited to race, gender identity, gender expression, sexual orientation, language and ability status, and to be free from any form of discipline, harassment or discrimination based on their identity or expression. (A.10.e).
- Advocate for the equitable right and access to free, appropriate public education for all youth in which students are not stigmatized or isolated based on race, gender identity, gender expression, sexual orientation, language, immigration status, juvenile justice/court involvement, housing, socioeconomic status, ability status, foster care, transportation, special education, mental health and/or any other exceptionality or special need. (A.10.f).
- Advocate for access to and inclusion in opportunities (e.g., Advanced Placement, International Baccalaureate, gifted and talented, honors, dual enrollment) in which students are not stigmatized, isolated or excluded based on race, gender identity, gender expression, sexual orientation, language, immigration status, juvenile justice/court involvement, housing, socioeconomic status, ability, foster care, transportation, special education, mental health and/or any other exceptionality or special need. (A.10.g).
- Actively advocate for systemic and other changes needed for equitable participation and outcomes in educational programs when disproportionality exists regarding enrollment in such programs by race, gender identity, gender expression, sexual orientation, language, immigration status, juvenile justice/court involvement, housing, socioeconomic status, ability, foster care, transportation, special education, mental health and/or any other exceptionality or special need. (A.10.h).

Introduction

This topic of this chapter is daunting to try and put into a few pages. There are many wonderful resources on legal and ethical advocacy; seek them out, as no one book can do justice to the enormity and importance of our role as social justice advocate.

The ASCA National Model (2019a) provides a road map to help school counselors implement ethical, data-informed programs with management, delivery and assessment at their heart and center. School counselors solidify their position as important players in their school's mission through the ASCA National Model assessment component. Assessment allows the school counselor to determine the school counseling program's effectiveness, inform design and delivery improvements, and highlight the benefit students receive because of the program. The ASCA National Model promises to make a significant difference in closing any information, opportunity and intervention gaps that exist through the delivery and assessment components.

If all students are to realize brighter futures, the ethical and legal school counselor will need to take up the charge to promote a social justice agenda (Martin, 2002). Ethical school counselors act intentionally and strategically to increase each student's opportunity to participate fully in the economic and social rewards of our society (Stone & Martin, 2004). The ethical school counselor acts as an advocate, providing support and encouraging students to challenge their future by tackling the barriers hindering their success. (Kohli et al., 2017; LaForett & DeMarco, 2020; Levy et al., 2020; Steward, 2019)

Problems individuals face can often be traced to the systems in which they live, work and play. This includes schools, families, social agencies, neighborhoods and many others (Stone & Dahir, 2004; Stone & Martin, 2004). Embracing a social justice agenda requires school counselors to "possess the awareness, knowledge and skill to intervene not only at the individual level but at the systemwide level" (Lee & Park, 2013, p. 9). School counselors must not be passive members but active change agents with specific roles as advocates and leaders in their school system. Social justice advocacy is now an expected facet of counseling interventions in which school counselors can enact social change (Ratts & Greenleaf, 2018; Wilder, 2018). The practice of counseling is more complete and effective when the school counselor is educated and abreast of research and effective methods for aiding student success. Although school counselors do not have complete decision-making power, they can advise and advocate for equitable systems and models, particularly for ethnic minority students (Shure et al., 2019). Ethical school counselors advocate for students by ensuring college and career readiness, uncovering equity gaps and analyzing data to see whose opportunities are being stratified. Thus, school counselors become change agents who help bridge the gap between schools and students.

School counselors who couple the ethical imperative of social justice with an understanding of the issues affecting equity and opportunity can help change systems that continue to adversely stratify opportunities. As Steve Schneider, school counselor says, "Our mantra needs to include embracing our imperfections so that they don't prevent us from being helpful" (personal communication March 2020). School counselors can influence attitudes and beliefs regarding equitable practices, provide attention to equity and access issues and provide resources designed to improve opportunities (Martin, 2004; Stone & Martin, 2004). Learn the rules so you know how to break them properly. This maxim may seem like a contradiction or outright dishonorable practice on the part of the legal and ethical school counselor, and its use here is partly tongue-in-cheek, but there are system barriers that stratify students' opportunities and advocates learn to negotiate these barriers in a politically astute way.

Getting Started: What Would You Do?

The following two cases are answered for you at the end of this chapter by school counselors and a counselor educator. Before you read their responses, decide how you would approach these dilemmas.

PARENT VS. STUDENT ASPIRATIONS

Aarlyn has been a dedicated student throughout high school. She has built a transcript that will easily get her into any state university. You call Aarlyn in for a college/career advising session, and she informs you her parents are not allowing her to pursue higher education. She explains she is needed to take over the family's business, which is conducted on the first floor of the building where they live. Aarlyn says she will not abandon her family's needs, and after graduation, she will obey her parents' wishes so her father and mother can work fewer hours. She says her place is to care for a family that has always cared for her. She admits it is hard to let go of her dreams for higher education, chokes back tears, mumbles an excuse and quickly leaves your office. What, if anything, could you do?

DIFFICULT BUT NECESSARY CONVERSATIONS ABOUT RACE

Your district has chosen the book by Anastasia Higginbotham, "Not My Idea: A Book About Whiteness" for its fourth- and fifth-grade students. A parent is raging to you that the book violates civil rights as the book says, "Whiteness is a bad deal" and depicts "whiteness" as a pact with the devil. The parent describes the book as morally reprehensible. You research the book. What did you find?

Working Through Case Studies

STATUS QUO AND ETHICAL BEHAVIOR

The school district has a policy that one indicator, such as a 3.5 GPA, cannot be used to deny students admission into advanced, honors or advanced placement (AP) courses. You agree and believe GPA is often not a determinant of ability but simply a matter of who turned in homework. You are willing to give this new criterion an honest push and hope your colleagues will also. What might you say to your colleagues who are against this change?

Points to Consider

The ethical standards of the school counseling profession issue school counselors a directive: to envision a better world for students and to seek ways to make that vision a reality. If the vision is ethical, it seeks to challenge the institutional and environmental barriers, such as criteria for admission into rigorous courses and other system barriers impeding student success (Stone, 1998).

Ethical school counselors make certain they create advantages for students by challenging the status quo and questioning the rules and regulations denying a level playing field for all students. Access to advanced coursework is a predictor of future economic opportunities and allows students to choose from the widest array of postsecondary opportunities (ASCA, 2022d; Stone & Dahir, 2004).

Ethical standards change as students' and schools' needs change. School counselors cannot cling to the traditional roles of school counseling, and their ethics have changed as well to strengthen the call for school counselors to be social justice advocates, ferreting out systemic barriers limiting students' opportunities. The social justice imperative first appeared in the standards in 2004, and in 2022 has become even stronger. The language of the standards clearly defines the school counselor's role as a catalyst for change. The notion of social change, in whatever capacity is necessary to help students reach their maximum development, lies at the heart of the school counselor's role.

Moreover, students have the right to be supported when choosing a program of study and to have the safety nets to be able to fulfill their dreams. Providing educational and career planning from elementary school to graduation will present students with quality postsecondary opportunities and help close the information gap (ASCA, 2022d). Productive adults come to self-awareness and self-understanding not by walking smooth roads but by trial and error (Valickas, Raišienė, & Rapuano, 2018).

There are so many unalterable factors in students' lives causing them hurt and harm. School counselors cannot change the parents/guardians of those students who do not have security and comfort, give them a loving home or establish optimal conditions for them during their time away from school. Although school counselors cannot give to every child what they would seek for their own children, they can offer every child optimum opportunity in school. School counselors can fervently influence the school environment, so students have equitable access to rigorous course work (ASCA, 2022; ASCA, 2020; Atkins & Oglesby, 2019; Kendi, 2019).

EQUITABLE OPPORTUNITIES

Given the demographics of your high school, your Asian, Caucasian and higher-socioeconomic students are always overrepresented in advanced academic programs, and students of color and students on free and reduced lunch are underrepresented in rigorous coursework. Conversely, students of color are overrepresented in disciplinary actions. Do you have an ethical responsibility in course enrollment patterns?

Points to Consider

Data-informed school counseling and ethical action are agreeable and faithful companions. The ethical imperative outlined in the ASCA Ethical Standards for School Counselors (2022b) underscores that the advocacy is not just desirable; it is required. Always at the ready to take up the charge to promote a social justice agenda, the ethical school counselor helps students from all ethnicities, cultures, classes, socioeconomic levels, genders and sexual identities to realize brighter futures.

Ethical action requires examining critical data elements that are the key indicators of the many factors schools address on a daily basis. Critical data elements include attendance, promotion, suspensions, graduation and postsecondary-going rates, as well as standardized test results, discipline incidents and course-taking patterns. By using data, school counselors can accurately present the current situation of student challenges and accomplishments in all of the key areas that are publicly displayed. Using data to tell the story identifies the needs of the students in the school counselor's caseload.

Data paints a vivid picture of a school and its students. It's a graphic representation of the successes and failures of our systems and provides the roadmap to areas that need our ethical intervention. Examining data reveals the school- and systemwide challenges affecting opportunity, such as participation in the advanced academic program. Data helps school counselors identify and eliminate any school policies or practices stratifying certain demographic groups' opportunities and allows the school counselor to set data goals to quantify positive change. Data helps the ethical school counselor identify, illuminate and eradicate the disparities in who is accessing rigorous courses and programs.

A 2021 analysis of enrollment data for gifted programs collected by the Office for Civil Rights found disproportionality across demographics of race/ethnicity, English-language learners and students with disabilities regardless of efforts by policy makers to address these issues through cultural-bias training or state policies requiring screening all students (List & Dykeman, 2021). The hard facts of national economic security illustrate that all students regardless of racial, gender or economic backgrounds have to participate fully in educational opportunities for excellence. Does your school mimic the problem? School counselors as systemic change agents can determine if the problem exists in their school and take proactive steps toward equity in opportunities.

An August 2020 Office of Special Education infographic continues to show the trend of overrepresentation of Black students in special education. Black students are disproportionately identified as emotionally disturbed. Rates of classifying Black students as having emotional disturbances is twice the national average (OSED, 2020). This problem of the over-identification of Black youth is not new. In 2001, the U.S. House of Representatives Committee on Education and the Workforce held a special hearing concerning the level of incidence of Black boys being placed in special education. Considering that only 27% of Black male special education students graduate from high school, the overuse of special education as an intervention is a systemic problem. Many students could avoid special education placement with better interventions and different interactions. School counselors can implement strategies such as small groups, individual counseling, classroom instruction, parent contact, community resources, schoolwide behavior management programs, etc., to have an impact on the over-identification of Black students for emotional disturbance.

Challenging the status quo is not only an ethical imperative but also a legal one. The legal system is based on the premise that every citizen should be given consideration without fear or favor. NAACP branches across the country have filed a number of legal complaints, including one against New York City Public Schools. The New York NAACP along with a broad coalition of New York organizations challenged the admissions process at New York's specialized high schools. New York City's Department of Education responded with a new program that admits some students to specialized high schools based on criteria other than exam scores, which then faced a backlash from Asian parents who felt their children were being overlooked by the new process (Veiga, 2019). Elite public schools and programs, which provide key pathways to college, are among the most segregated in the nation.

Participation in advanced coursework means access to greater opportunities. Using the results of analyzed data, the ethical school counselor can illuminate and challenge the status quo and question the rules and regulations denying advanced courses for all students. When examining rigorous coursework, findings indicate that only 10% of Black eighth-grade students and 18% of Latino eighth-grade students are enrolled in algebra 1 despite being 15% and 25% of the population respectively. A similar pattern exists for enrollment in Advanced Placement courses, which are only enrolled by 9% of Black and 21% of Latino high school students despite representing 15% and 25% of the population respectively. (Patrick, Socal, & Morgan 2020).

Researchers are continually updating findings that show the school-to-prison pipeline does exist (Bacher-Hicks et al, 2021). There is a causal link between students who experience strict school discipline and being arrested or incarcerated as an adult. Exclusionary practices in school influence criminal activity in adulthood. "Our findings show that early censure of school misbehavior causes increases in adult crime – that there is, in fact, a school-to-prison pipeline… . Any effort to maintain safe and orderly school climates must take into account the clear and negative consequences of exclusionary discipline practices for young students, and especially young students of color, which last well into adulthood" (Bacher-Hicks et al., 2021, p.1). In this study, students are 3.2 percentage points more likely to have been arrested if coming from strict middle schools and 2.5 percentage points more likely to be incarcerated as adults. "The impacts are significantly more predictive for Black and Hispanic boys who attended strict middle schools" (Bacher-Hicks, 2021). This is but one of dozens of research reports. When advocating for restorative justice practices vs. suspension and expulsion, bring in the research illustrating the human cost to underscore the urgency for change.

EDUCATING VS. DIRECTING

Kimberly, one of your seniors, comes to you and requests your help with her application to Harvard. You are forced to explain that it is the policy of school administration that only the top five students in each graduating class can apply to an Ivy League school. What do you do?

Points to Consider

The New York Times article "Amid Policy Confusion, Senior Is Allowed to Apply to Harvard" (Herszenhorn, 2004) describes how a Brooklyn, N.Y., public high school senior was told she could not apply to Harvard. Kimberly Cummins was ranked 11 out of 400 in her senior class, with a solid academic and extracurricular activity record, but her school only allowed the top five students to apply to an Ivy League school. Shocked, Kimberly's older sister rallied her fellow NYU law school students to raise the issue with school and government officials and advocacy groups. Kimberly was allowed to apply. This represents an extreme case, but what about the numerous policies existing in schools today that defer dreams when there is no savvy advocate to question and challenge them?

In March 2020, *Inside Higher Ed* posted an article describing an unnamed private school that limits its seniors to nine college applications (Jaschik, 2020). The College Board says, "There is no magic number, but five to eight applications are usually enough to ensure that a student is accepted into a suitable institution (depending, of course, on the individual student's record and circumstances). This number should be made up of a combination of 'safety,' 'probable' and 'reach' colleges" (College Board, 2022). Arbitrary policies with arbitrary numbers need broad and generous exceptions so no one student is disadvantaged. As a student advocate, school counselors must inspect and critique the many school policies that may disadvantage students and advocate for needed change.

Basic to self-direction and autonomy is students' right to understand the full weight and meaning their decisions, as well as the interrelatedness between what the students do in school and their future economic opportunities. Each person has the right to receive the information and support needed to move toward self-direction and self-development and affirmation within one's group identities, with special care being given to students who have historically not received adequate educational services, e.g., students of color, students living at low socioeconomic status, students with disabilities and students from nondominant-language backgrounds (ASCA, 2019e; 2022a; 2022h). Kimberly had the right to try. It is unthinkable for school officials, whose mission it is to promote a student's self-direction and autonomy, to deny her the right to try.

COLLEGE COUNSELING: IS WHAT YOU SAY WHAT STUDENTS HEAR?

You have tried very hard to be a school counselor who helps students stretch and strive to meet their goals, never ever to squelch their dreams. However, a student's father says you told his child she could not get into Harvard. You are horrified that this is what the student heard, as this is not what you chose to convey. You now wonder if what you said actually conveyed some implicit bias on your part, or did the student just misunderstand when you asked her to choose a safety and match schools. How did this happen?

Points to Consider

Ketanji Brown Jackson, U.S. Supreme Court nominee, was told by her school counselor to "lower her sights" when she wanted to apply to Harvard University (Norris, 2022). Michelle Obama also stated that her high school counselor implied she should not aspire to Princeton, where her older brother went to college. Here are two amazing women of color who have expressed how the profession failed them. Jim Jump, a college admissions counselor, stated in an *Inside HigherEd* piece, "Counseling is above all about helping students make decisions about their future, and that is a noble calling, one damaged and perhaps even destroyed by the allegations against "that" counselor. The perceptions from Jackson ... should lead to serious self-reflection for all of us. I'm hoping there is another side to the story, that the truth is more nuanced... . I hope that Ketanji Brown Jackson's and Michelle Obama's guidance counselors were misunderstood, that they were guilty not of limited vision but of knowing too much" (Jump, 2022, n.p.1).

When students aspire to a particular college or university and their profile is way off the mean profile for the university, can the school counselor help them understand the realities of the college admissions process without somehow dampening their aspirations? First of all, maybe the approach should be to withhold any judgment on a student's admissions chances. After all, for every average student profile advertised, there are many exceptions to the profile, and who really knows which students might be among those exceptions. Students may process your words of caution as discouragement and a lack of faith in them. Students have a right to try; even if they fail, it is better that they tried than to go through life regretting. Maybe reframing advice to students when talking about adding a safety school and a match school to their application, such as encouraging multiple applications. "Ketanji Brown Jackson's memory of her interaction with her guidance counselor should cause all of us to think about the messages we send to students. We need to be aware of our implicit biases, and we need to work constantly to communicate both effectively and sensitively" (Jump, 2022, n.p.).

STUDENT-DRIVEN OR DATA-DRIVEN: NO DIFFERENCE

There is a heightened push for school counselors to use data in their work. Some school counselors are resisting and have a slogan, "student-driven not data-driven." You believe disaggregated data can help you be more intentional in supporting all students. What do you say to the naysayers?

Points to Consider

Data is necessary to see whose opportunities are stratified. Achieving the best results for students requires school counselors to regularly examine data. Without disaggregated data, it is all just a guess as to whether the strategies and interventions school counselors have put into place are making a difference and advancing students.

Ethnic minority students and low-income students are less likely to be placed in college preparatory or high-ability courses. The Status and Trends in the Education of Racial and Ethnic Groups report states, "disparities in the educational participation and attainment of different racial/ethnic groups in the United States are well-documented. For instance, the gap between white and Hispanic students in school readiness has narrowed, but the gap between white and Black students showed less movement" (U.S. Department of Education and National Center for Educational Statistics, 2019, p.1). School practices and procedures sometimes adversely limit students' opportunities, and using disaggregated data, the school counselor can determine who is being left out of the success equation.

ADVOCACY ROLE IN CELEBRATING DIVERSITY

You are trying to do lessons on diversity in a conservative school district. You have assessed the prevailing community temperature and are determining your course of action. You recognize you have limits of your First Amendment rights, but you also know ASCA has provided you with tools you can legally use to raise your students' awareness and celebration of diversity. What are those tools?

Points to Consider

The ASCA Ethical Standards state, "All students have the right to equitable access to school counselors who support students from all backgrounds and circumstances and who advocate for and affirm all students regardless of but not limited to ethnic/racial identity; nationality; age; social class; economic status; abilities/disabilities; language; immigration status; sexual orientation; gender identity and gender expression; family type; religious/spiritual identity; and living situations, including emancipated minor status, wards of the state, homelessness or incarceration" (ASCA, 2022b, Preamble). School should always be a place where students feel celebrated and safe mentally and physically.

In the effort to deliver a supportive curriculum and help all students celebrate each other, school counselors are trying to find ways in a divisive national, state and school district climate to foster support. We have all seen the increase in ugliness at school board meetings around Critical Race Theory. It is one thing to stand alone, but when you have parents and community on your side (ASCA, 2022g) and your national association's curriculum that sets the standards and norms for the profession, you have a stronger base to forward a diversity agenda. The ASCA National Model (2019a) demands classroom instruction, data-informed behaviors, collaboration with the school community around teaching diversity and creating a safe, respectful school climate for all. ASCA's expectation is that school counselors include diversity training for the students in their charge. Using a school board sanctioned curriculum is the safest way to deliver any controversial topic. topic. Even if the ASCA National Model has not been formally blessed by the school board, you are still on much more solid ground than, for example, the mathematics teacher to convey messages of diversity because this is part of your curriculum as defined at the highest level of school counselor associations. Unlike the mathematics teacher, who may have a line or two in their standards about being a purveyor of a safe, respectful school climate centered around the acceptance and celebration of diversity, it is in every word of the school counselors' expectations. The use of one's curriculum provides a shield from unwarranted attacks that the school counselor is being political (ASCA, 2022c).

ASCA Student Standards: Mindsets & Behaviors for Student Success: School counselors have specific standards in the form of mindsets and behaviors around diversity that they must help students meet. The ASCA Student Standards: Mindsets & Behaviors for Student Success (2019a) specifically give the school counselor the imperative to forward diversity training for students. A conversation with administration around your obligation toward the mindsets and behaviors will go a long way should parents feel the counselor is being political. Leaving the principal unaware of what you are doing in the classroom leaves them unarmed to defend your work should they start to get parent complaints. Following are just a few of the mindsets and behaviors that give school counselors a solid base on which to stand in forwarding a curriculum around the celebration of diversity such as:

- B-SS 2. Positive, respectful and supportive relationships with students who are similar to and different from them
- B-SS 4. Empathy
- B-SS 6. Effective collaboration and cooperation skills
- B-SS 7. Leadership and teamwork skills to work effectively in diverse groups
- B-SS 10. Cultural awareness, sensitivity and responsiveness

ASCA Ethical Standards for School Counselors: The ASCA Ethical Standards (2022b) are used in every court case involving a school counselor to inform the courts about the standard of care for the profession. The ASCA Ethical Standards (2022b) provide a solid platform on which every school counselor can stand in honoring and forwarding diversity. Practically every line of the ethical standards requires the celebration and promotion of diversity and, therefore, is a school counselor's most powerful tool in advocacy work. Excerpted here are just a few that apply but every line of the standards supports diversity work.

- A.1.c. Support all students and their development by actively working to eliminate systemic barriers or bias impeding student development.
- A.10.f. Advocate for the equal right and access to free, appropriate public education for all youth, in which students are not stigmatized or isolated based on their housing status, disability, foster care, special education status, mental health or any other exceptionality or special need.

Position Statements: Further evidence and another tool for diversity work are the position statements, almost all of which address diversity. An excerpt from the ASCA position statements on eliminating racism and bias (2020e) help school counselors demonstrate they are required to develop and implement programs promoting equity. School counselors work to help close opportunity, attainment, information and intervention gaps in their schools, districts and communities.

Written School Board Policy and Unwritten District Practice: Understand the temperature of the district with regard to valuing diversity. Where is the evidence in school board policy and mission statements that the district values diversity? What programs and practices are in place that support the school counselor's role in forwarding the celebration of diversity? If the evidence is not there, school counselors work for but do not wait for needed change.

In a politically astute way, move forward with diversity work while keeping your finger on the pulse of who is opposing your work. Avoid creating a substantial disruption to the educational process. If you are a public-school educator, you are a governmental employee, and you are not allowed to interrupt the learning process. Support marginalized groups in a nonpolitical way. For example, stress black lives matter as a necessary anti-racist message if the Black Lives Matter organization is considered political in your school community.

Focus on equity not equality. When people say, "Why pick out one group over another when all lives matter?" it is because school counselors must promote equity not equality and needs are not equal. As Damien Sweeney, Kentucky State Department of Education, explained in a recent webinar, "When one house is on fire, that's the fire we put out, not the house next door, which isn't on fire." It is appropriate to stress one group over another group at different times of crises.

Find entry points in the effort to celebrate diversity. If not us, then who? If not now, then when? The time is right. Know your First Amendment rights and obligations, and use your ASCA tools to exercise those rights so you can advantage all students in your charge.

EQUITY OF SERVICES

You love being a school counselor, especially for a select group of students that you believe have tremendous potential and are destined to make a considerable contribution to society. It is this group of students that receives most of your time and attention. You schedule this select group to have the best teachers and provide frequent academic advising sessions. Is your behavior ethical?

Points to Consider

This case is blatant unethical practice, but often the stratification of services is without malevolent or deliberate intent. School counselors are so outnumbered that there are certain students to whom they give more attention than others, and some students they rarely or never see. The struggle is to reach as many students as they can, not just the top 5% or the most at-risk 5% of the student population. Reaching all students is not easy. Ethical behavior requires school counselors to grapple with equitable service delivery (Ratts & Greenleaf,

2017). All students need support but especially those without strong advocates. Reaching the total student body is the focus of the ASCA National Model (2019a).

ADVOCATING LEGALLY AND ETHICALLY

In your latest survey, 78% of your students indicated in the latest survey that they would like to go to college, continuing with 44% of them identifying finances as their biggest obstacle. Finley is one of your students with the odds stacked against him, as his financial challenges are greater than just the costs associated with a college education. He feels an obligation to continue to help his younger siblings financially. He is ineligible for an especially lucrative scholarship that would make the difference for him because he does not quite have the required 3.5 GPA. With one keystroke in the student information system, you could bump his B grade in physical education to an A. Does the end justify the means?

Points to Consider

Advocate, advocate, advocate, but do so legally and politically astutely. Help Finley find the right approach to talk to the PE teacher about extra credit to raise his B grade. If his self-advocacy fails, perhaps there is another teacher you and/or Finley can approach about extra work to raise his grade. Call the scholarship funders, and ask for an exception to the 3.5 GPA. Turn Finley into his own advocate in looking for scholarships, and continue your efforts on his behalf in this endeavor. Falsifying records is the superhighway to losing your job and is never an option legally or ethically. Show Finley how to use advocacy muscle. The joy that comes from making the impossible possible for Finley is tainted when done illegally, and Finley may well pay the price if the lie is discovered, as happened to former Auburn running back Jovon Robinson. The NCAA ruled him ineligible to play at Auburn when it was discovered that his high school counselor made "substantial changes" to his grades. The school counselor admitted her part and resigned. Robinson and several coaches came under scrutiny but were never implicated. Regardless of the prize the school counselor was trying to help Robinson attain, she hurt him. The end is never a justification to falsify records; don't do it. Do all you can to make magic for each and every student on your caseload, as these are the moments that feed our professional souls. In the court of public opinion Robinson had a long road back, and the school counseling profession took quite a hit with this high-profile case.

CULTURALLY SUSTAINING SCHOOL COUNSELING PROGRAMS AND ETHICAL ACTION

When you look at the disaggregated demographic data for your school population and compare the data to the demographics of program and/or course assignments, two pieces of data jump out at you. There is an overrepresentation of certain ethnic groups in the emotionally handicapped class and an underrepresentation of certain ethnic groups in the advanced classes. What is the ethical response of the ethical school counselor?

Points to Consider

ASCA's Ethical Standards for School Counselors (2022) preamble and many of the ethical standards discuss the ethical responsibility to develop a culturally sustaining school counseling program that affirms and advocates for every student. School counselors provide rigorous action with political astuteness. Political astuteness for school counselors is absolutely essential to ensure our effectiveness in advocating for students, but the political velvet glove sometimes needs to encase the iron fist to move stubborn system barriers. Don't be afraid to pressure, battle, fight, bargain, collaborate, discuss, navigate, instigate, employ, fulfill, broker, carry out, engage and negotiate on behalf of brighter futures for the students in your charge. School counselors can be political while still persisting toward necessary changes. Each day that a culturally incompetent, broken system is allowed to operate is another day that hundreds of students emotionally, intellectually and/or physically are pushed out of the school system. Time is not on our side. The ASCA Ethical Standards (2022b) raise the urgency and demand for advocacy results.

Challenging the status quo is not only an ethical imperative, but also a legal one. The legal system is based on the premise that every citizen should be given consideration without fear or favor. Law is the minimum, and standards are aspirational. School counselors' ethical standards promote equity over equality, which means school counselors hold themselves to a higher standard ethically than the legal standard of fair and equal. Providing what is needed is not a one-size-fits-all approach. The ASCA National Model (2019a) uses data to identify and advocate for these over- or underrepresented groups, promote equitable policies and encourage students to address administration when they feel an inequity is present. School counselors' ethical obligation includes fostering a safe environment for student feedback. If students feel uncomfortable expressing their concerns, it is likely there is also a lack of cultural sensitivity at the school.

The definition of cultural responsiveness can be found in any publication on the subject, all of which speak to being able to be effective with students from cultures other than one's own and the ability to understand within-group differences that make each student unique. However, this definition remains hollow without action. Knowledge of cultural responsiveness without action is empty rhetoric. Many can espouse eloquently on cultural responsiveness, but look behind people's words to see if their words are matched by their deeds.

Access to advanced coursework is a predictor of future economic opportunities and allows students to choose from the widest array of postsecondary opportunities. Using the results of analyzed data, the culturally sensitive school counselor can illuminate and then eradicate equity gaps. School counselors challenge the status quo and question the rules and regulations denying equity for all students. Students have the right to understand the full weight and meaning of their program of study and to have the safety nets to stretch and strive to encourage them to challenge themselves.

Political astuteness always at the ready, the ethically competent and culturally sensitive school counselor will take up the charge to promote a social justice agenda to help all students from all ethnicities, cultures, classes, socioeconomic levels, genders, sexual identities, abilities, etc. to realize brighter futures. School counselors are in an influential position to help students learn to negotiate through the systems in which they must move. School counselors strive daily to offer every child optimum opportunity in school, fervently influencing the school environment so students have equitable access to rigorous coursework.

EDUCATIONAL OPPORTUNITIES FOR STUDENTS WHO ARE UNDOCUMENTED

You have students who are undocumented who dream of higher education but seem to have no avenue for support. What is the situation for education beyond high school for undocumented students and how can you help?

Points to Consider

Scores of students who are undocumented consider the United States as their own, but because of the state laws enacted following the U.S. Supreme Court case of *Plyler v. Doe* (1982), many of these students face considerable hardship in funding a higher education. Despite decades of trying to enact federal immigration reform to create educational pathways for students who are undocumented, federal legislation has yet to materialize. Until the federal government passes immigration reform, each state will remain as the primary determiner of the options available to students who are undocumented. *Plyler v. Doe* gives pre-K–12 students who are undocumented the right to public education. However, higher education remains a barrier, as states have figured out how to exclude or include higher education as a viable option. The DREAM Act would allow students who are undocumented access to higher education with the same financial support other students enjoy, but despite several attempts it has failed to pass.

The Deferred Action for Childhood Arrivals (DACA) program implemented in 2012 gives certain students who are undocumented the opportunity to obtain temporary legal status (American Immigration Council, 2016). The Trump administration discontinued accepting new applications until the Supreme Court said its action were illegal. The Biden administration reinstated DACA but currently it remains under a federal judge's order that DACA is illegal (U.S. Citizenship & Immigration Services, 2021). Therefore, affordability is still out of reach for most students who are undocumented as they cannot apply for the Free Application for Federal Student Aid (FAFSA). Some states allow undocumented residents of their state to pay in-state tuition rates for college. See *https://www.uleadnet.org/* and *www.ncsl.org/research/immigration/tuition-benefits-for-immigrants.aspx* for more information about your state's status on students who are undocumented.

As a school counselor, there are a number of ways you can help students who are undocumented realize their postsecondary education dreams. Students who are undocumented face legal, financial and social stressors in addition to barriers to postsecondary education. Let students know you are a safe place for students who are undocumented to seek help and advice. Currently many students who are undocumented are fearful about revealing their undocumented status to outsiders. Students may have been taught from the time they are little to keep this information to themselves. Spread the word among the student population that you provide a safe place (ASCA, 2019e).

Become the school's authority on your state's stance on higher education financial assistance for students who are undocumented. Seek consultation and ask questions until you are certain you have the whole story for your state's position on supporting students who are undocumented so you can advise students and their parents of the financial options afforded them by the state, state university system and private colleges. Seek community support, private scholarships and any other source of funding that may be available regardless of a student's immigration status. Be specific with college information they can use given their undocumented status.

Seek resources these students' broader needs as well. They may also have compounding problems such as poverty, homelessness, fear their parents will be deported and/or awareness that some people consider them a pariah and unwelcome in this country. Pair students who are undocumented with other students. For example, the Posse Foundation, founded in 1989, is an example of a successful organization in this area. Students are grouped together to support each other.

DACA youth are protected from deportation and are allowed to work. DACA does not provide a path for permanent residency or citizenship, but DACA status is renewal. To be eligible for DACA, children must qualify under each category below:

- You were under 31 years old as of June 15, 2012.
- You first came to the United States before your 16th birthday.
- You have lived continuously in the United States from June 15, 2007, until the present.
- You were physically present in the United States on June 15, 2012, and at the time you apply.
- You came to the United States without documents before June 15, 2012, or your lawful status expired as of June 15, 2012.
- You are currently studying, or you graduated from high school or earned a certificate of completion of high school or GED or have been honorably discharged from the Coast Guard or Armed Forces of the United States.
- You haven't been convicted of a felony, certain significant misdemeanors, or three or more misdemeanors of any kind. Consult with an attorney about any contact you have had with law enforcement or immigration authorities.

(Retrieved from *http://undocu.berkeley.edu/legal-supportoverview/what-is-daca/* and *https://www.uscis.gov/humanitarian/consideration-deferred-action-childhood-arrivals-daca*)

ASCA has given us guidance on the role of the school counselor, including:

- "Advocating for the rights of all students, including students who are undocumented, by ensuring students are not barred from education based on foreign birth certificates, lack of a Social Security number or a home language other than English
- Supporting students who are undocumented by helping them gain access to an equitable education that meets their needs and prepares them for postsecondary access, if necessary (e.g., referrals for ELL services, special education services and medical treatment)
- Working with community partners and leveraging resources to provide support in keeping families intact, if possible, while supporting students who are separated from a parent due to deportation

- Ensuring schools are a safe haven for students who are undocumented and will not divulge confidential information to any outside agencies without proper legal documentation
- Providing counseling intervention and social/emotional support for students affected by immigration stressors, including assessment of possible trauma that they may have experienced
- Keeping abreast of current policies and practices of postsecondary institutions regarding access for students who are undocumented
- Advocating against the practice of separating children from their families at U.S. borders
- Maintaining a database of community resources to support referrals in assisting families with various challenges related to issues surrounding undocumented status, including recovery associated with trauma resulting from separation" (ASCA, 2018a)

In a Position to Know: A School Counselor Educator and a School Counselor Speak

The two cases presented at the beginning of the chapter are revisited here and answered by practicing school counselors. Compare their answers with your own approach.

PARENTS'/GUARDIANS' VS . STUDENT'S ASPIRATIONS

Aarlyn has been a dedicated student throughout high school. She has built a transcript that will easily get her into any state university. You call Aarlyn in for a college/career advising session, and she informs you her parents are not allowing her to pursue higher education. She explains she is needed to take over the family's business, which is conducted on the first floor of the building where they live. Aarlyn says she will not abandon her family's needs, and after graduation, she will obey her parents' wishes so her father and mother can work fewer hours. She says her place is to care for a family that has always cared for her. She admits it is hard to let go of her dreams for higher education, chokes back tears, mumbles an excuse and quickly leaves your office. What, if anything, could you do?

Within the atmosphere of the large urban high school with its diverse student population, school counselors meet many challenges. In addition to academic matters, there are cultural and social issues that one anticipates in school counseling work, and there are unexpected and surprising situations that arise as well. These less-than-ordinary cases can challenge our ready responses and demand thoughtful, original solutions. Here, too, outside the boundaries within which we usually work, we are confronted with perhaps more ethical concerns.

As school counselors we naturally ask, doesn't Aarlyn deserve the chance to make a better life for herself, and possibly her family, if she were to attend college? From our perspective, if we do nothing, we see her future as limited. Aren't we obligated to help her recognize her broader options within the expectations of her family? It is a delicate matter demanding that we balance cultural sensitivity and ethical responsibility.

The school counselor's ethical responsibility is to advocate for Aarlyn by allowing her to make an informed choice about her future. The ethical standards for school counselors state that students have the right to understand the full magnitude and meaning of educational choices and how those choices will affect future opportunities.

To permit Aarlyn simply to accept her fate would be wrong. That would amount to giving up on her without any concern for her development and self-direction. The school counselor's role is critical. An idea or suggestion, a plan or question can alter a young person's vision of the future. In the case of Aarlyn, the meetings the school counselor holds with her must accomplish several things. They must affirm her worth as a student who would be valued by a college. They must acknowledge her culture and duty to her parents, and they should encourage her to be open to other possibilities that maximize her potential. The meetings cannot push her away through lack of understanding or coercion on the school counselor's part.

An attempt should be made to invite Aarlyn's parents to join us for an informational meeting, but Aarlyn's insistence against that idea, perhaps because of language barriers, takes that step out of the process. Without the parents' participation, the school counselor must beware of exerting too much pressure on Aarlyn. The school counselor's responsibility is to constantly remind Aarlyn that her parents' values and beliefs are not in question, but that her own nascent college aspirations are also valuable and worth exploring.

My goal would be to assure Aarlyn there might be practical solutions that satisfy her parents' expectations as well as her own desire for an education. These solutions might involve choosing a part-time university program close to home or perhaps weekend college classes or some online classes. Literally opening up college catalogs and reading about courses and designing an imaginary schedule of classes would be appropriate. I might emphasize the need to start off slowly, devoting time to the family business with the hope that more classes could be taken later. The important point to emphasize for her is that by taking some college classes, she would not be forsaking her parent's wishes, nor would she be sacrificing her own.

Aarlyn needs to see how the choices she makes in the present, to reject college or accept it in a limited way, will affect her in the near future. Should she go to college as I have counseled, her future may be more successful. Who knows? Perhaps her parents will recognize their daughter has profited from college, and they will be more supportive. Perhaps some other factor will change the equation altogether, and Aarlyn will be permitted to choose her path freely. The school counselor helps to point the student down the road or helps draw the map. The rest is up to her.

To advocate on Aarlyn's behalf means to defy knee-jerk responses. Helping her involves the school counselor's dedication to advocate for and affirm Aarlyn's right to an education, offered with compassion for her struggle and an application of ethical principles. All work toward one end: Aarlyn makes her decision in the most informed and respected manner.
– Robert Weiss, retired high school counselor, John F. Kennedy High School, New York, N.Y.

DIFFICULT BUT NECESSARY CONVERSATIONS ABOUT RACE

Your district has chosen the book by Anastasia Higginbotham, "Not My Idea: A Book About Whiteness" for its fourth- and fifth-grade students. A parent is raging to you that the book violates civil rights as the book says, "Whiteness is a bad deal" and depicts "whiteness" as a pact with the devil. The parent describes the book as morally reprehensible. You research the book. What did you find?

I did some research on the book in question in this actual case, and everything I learned came back positive. This book is promoted by Common Sense Media, and I listened to it in its entirety on YouTube. "Whiteness is a bad deal" and "whiteness" as a pact with the devil came from the end of the book where there are activities. On the very next page, the author says, "You can be white without signing onto 'whiteness.'" The book also highlights white people who have been actively involved in the civil rights movement and emphasizes that the white girl in the story is not at fault for white supremacy and has the power to do something about it. From my perspective, the book does not tell children their skin color is akin to evil. I am not sure how this book is "discriminating," nor do I find it morally reprehensible or exploitative.

That being said, I have done a lot of reflection, questioning my own biases, and personal work, including reading anti-racist books, attending webinars, listening to podcasts and watching shows to increase my understanding of the problem and what I can do to promote change. Conversations around race are hard to have. Not everyone is ready for these hard conversations, but it is time we start having them. I do appreciate the school counselor's sensitivity to parents' concerns. I am quite sure there will be pushback. This book can only do harm if the person reading it makes white people out to be evil. Let's not forget that Black and brown children have been exposed to racist literature and history for centuries in their schooling.

– *Wendy D. Rock, Ph.D., LPC-S, NCC, NCSC, Assistant Professor of Counseling, Southeastern Louisiana University*

Making Connections

1. Your school only encourages students who are likely to score a three or above to take the AP exam. District administrators compare AP test results for schools, and it is widely understood that it is considered a black mark against you if you have too many students in your caseload scoring below a three. Many high schools in the district, including yours, consider it best to covertly select students to take the AP exam and gingerly dissuade others from it. Are there any legal or ethical obligations involving this practice by your school district? With fellow professionals, discuss or debate the following positions:
   - Is it ethical to limit the students who can take the AP test so the school can enhance its standing and test scores?
   - Regardless of AP exam results, students always benefit by taking the AP exam.
   - Other test scores, such as the state test, are likely to be positively affected by students taking AP exams.

- If students know at the beginning of the school year they will be expected and supported to take the AP exam, these efforts will encourage the student to prepare for the exam more actively.
- School counselors do not narrow opportunities that might possibly lead to scholarship dollars or college credit for certain courses.

2. Discuss your beliefs about how an equitable and ethical school counseling program can serve all students. Describe the characteristics and behaviors of a systemic change agent. Discuss a time when you exhibited these characteristics.

3. Discuss ways a school counselor who is committed to equity for all students might avoid spending too much time with students who are among the top 5% of the class and those who are in the lowest 5% of the class.

4. Review the ASCA Ethical Standards for School Counselors (2022b), and identify which ethical standard dealing with equity is the most difficult to attain and maintain. Why?

5. Consider the student population in your building. Are some students marginalized in achieving an equitable education? What first step can you take to begin to remedy the situation?'

Chapter 14 Quiz

1) Ethical school counselors strive to make a difference for students in closing the information, opportunity and achievement gaps through which ASCA National Model pillar?
   a. Foundation
   b. Accountability
   c. Management
   d. Delivery
   e. Assessments

2) When working with students whose own future aspirations are unaligned with their parents'/guardians' aspirations for their future, which approach adheres to your role as an ethical school counselor?
   a. Insist the student invites the parents/guardians to participate in an informational meeting with intentions to persuade them to change their mind.
   b. Empower students to independently take charge of their own future by disregarding parents'/guardians' own wishes and pursue personal ambitions.
   c. Advocate for the student by researching educational options, including exploring practical solutions, to allow the student to make an informed decision.
   d. Evade liability by refraining from working with students whose future ambitions are unaligned with parents'/guardians' future ambitions.
   e. Work with the student to create an action plan to pursue future aspirations.

3) Ethical school counselors advocate intentionally and strategically by:
   a. Providing equitable service delivery
   b. Challenging the status quo and serving as a social-justice advocate
   c. Providing educational and career planning to help close the information gap
   d. Influencing the school environment so students can have equitable access to rigorous course work
   e. All of the above

4) To analyze a school counseling program's efficacy and to evaluate whose opportunities are stratified, ethical school counselors can utilize what key element?
   a. Intervention plans
   b. Research
   c. Competency data
   d. Disaggregated data
   e. Empirical evidence

5) When working with marginalized students, best practices include:
   a. Advocating for effective school-based preventions and interventions with an understanding of the issues affecting equity
   b. Monitoring and expanding personal multicultural and social-justice advocacy awareness, knowledge and skills to be an effective culturally sustaining school counselor
   c. Working with stakeholders and community resources to improve educational outcomes
   d. Identifying federal and state resources available to help marginalized students
   e. All of the above

Key Terms

Advocacy
Challenging the status quo
Cultural responsiveness
Deferred Action for Childhood Arrivals (DACA)
Dream Act
Entrenched inequities
Equal access
Equity and opportunity for all students
Marginalized students
Social justice
Social change agent
Cultural sensitivity
Culturally sustaining school counseling

Conclusion

We are our ethical standards. We have professionalized ourselves by assigning core ethical characteristics that distinguish us from all other professions. Our special skills, competence and application of knowledge have guided the development of ethical standards, just as our ethical standards guide the acquisition of new knowledge. This symbiotic relationship requires continual vigilance if we are to stay informed and current.

We perform our school counseling role in an institution that both empowers and hinders our efforts to be legal and ethical. The personal and social/emotional aspects of education compound the legal complexities. I hope one of the primary objectives of this book was accomplished, namely to demystify some of these complexities that have an impact on school counselors' daily work. If you found this book to be user-friendly and if it helped you gain a better understanding of the law and the practical application of your ethical standards, then another primary objective of the book was met.

Unlike public education systems in most countries, the system in the United States is decentralized, so that there are very few one-size-fits-all laws prevailing in every state and affecting every school counselor. Laws and legal precedents that govern school counselors are dependent on 50 different states, each with its own approach to the educational process. Federal legislation and Supreme Court decisions can give the bottom-line directive regarding some educational issues, but there are really few legal imperatives that can be uniformly applied to all school counselors; we have more exceptions than rules established by the variation in philosophies, perspectives, school law and community standards.

References

A Better Child. (n.d.). *How do online predators work?* http://www.a-better-child.org/page/784785

Adams, M., Bell, L. A., & Griffin, P. (2007). *Teaching for diversity and social justice* (2nd ed.). CRC Press.

Adams v. School Board of St. John's County, 3 F.4th 1299 (11th Cir. 2021). https://media.ca11.uscourts.gov/opinions/pub/files/201813592.op2.pdf

Adedokun, L. (2016, May 11). *How healthcare access in high schools can reduce teen pregnancy rates.* Doris Duke Charitable Foundation. https://www.ddcf.org/news--insights/insights/how-healthcare-access-in-high-schools-can-reduce-teen-pregnancy-rates/

Aizer, A., & Doyle, J. J., Jr. (2015). Juvenile incarceration, human capital, and future crime: Evidence from randomly assigned judges. *The Quarterly Journal of Economics, 130*(2), 759–803. https://doi.org/10.1093/qje/qjv003

Akos, P., Bastian, K. C., Domina, T., & de Luna, L. M. M. (2019). Recognized ASCA Model Program (RAMP) and student outcomes in elementary and middle schools. *Professional School Counseling, 22*(1). https://doi.org/10.1177/2156759X19869933

Akos, P., Schuldt, H., & Walendin, M. (2009) School counselor assignment in secondary schools. *Professional School Counseling, 13*(1), 23–29. https://doi.org/10.1177/2156759X0901300101

Alaska statute, § 47.10.011–47.10.015 (2008).

Albers v. Breen, 346 Ill. App. 3d 799, 806 N.E.2d 667 (4th Dist. 2004).

Alexander, K., & Alexander, M. D. (2018). *The law of school, students and teachers* (6th ed.). West Academic Publishing.

Alexander, K., & Alexander, M. D. (2019). *American public school law* (9th ed.). Thomson West.

Allen, J. L. (2021). The typology and content of parent-gay son communication about sexual identity: A qualitative content analysis. *Journal of Gay and Lesbian Social Services, 33*(4), 533–560. https://doi.org/10.1080/10538720.2021.1900011

Allen, Z. (2004). Schools against kids: 'Zero tolerance' policies criminalize students, youth of color hardest hit. *The Independent.* http://www.indypendent.org/2004/02/04/schools-against-kids-zero-tolerance-policies-criminalize-students-youth-color-hardest-hit

American Academy of Child & Adolescent Psychiatry. (2006, January). *Gay, lesbian and bisexual adolescents.* http://www.aacap.org/cs/root/facts_for_families/gay_lesbian_and_bisexual_adolescents

American Academy of Pediatrics. (2021, October). *A declaration from the American Academy of Pediatrics, American Academy of Child and Adolescent Psychiatry and Children's Hospital Association.* https://www.aap.org/en/advocacy/child-and-adolescent-healthy-mental-development/aap-aacap-cha-declaration-of-a-national-emergency-in-child-and-adolescent-mental-health/

American Association of University Women. (2011). *Crossing the line: Sexual harassment at school.* Author. https://www.aauw.org/resources/research/crossing-the-line-sexual-harassment-at-school/

American Bar Association. (n.d.). Center on Children and the Law. http://www.americanbar.org/groups/child_law.html

American Bar Association. (2004). Rights and responsibilities of parents. *American Bar Association Family Legal Guide* (3rd ed.). https://openlibrary.org/books/OL7585936M/American_Bar_Association_Family_Legal_Guide_Third_Edition

American Civil Liberties Union. (n.d.). *Legislation affecting LGBT rights across the country.* https://www.aclu.org/legislation-affecting-lgbtq-rights-across-country

American Civil Liberties Union. (2003a, April 8). *ACLU sues Arkansas school district to guarantee gay student's right to be "out" at school.* https://www.aclu.org/press-releases/aclu-sues-arkansas-school-district-guarantee-gay-students-right-be-out-school

American Civil Liberties Union. (2003b, July 17). *ACLU secures sweeping changes in Arkansas school district.* https://www.aclu.org/press-releases/aclu-secures-sweeping-changes-arkansas-school-district

American Civil Liberties Union. (2005, December 1). *Federal judge rules that high schools cannot out lesbian and gay students.* https://www.aclu.org/press-releases/federal-judge-rules-high-schools-cannot-out-lesbian-and-gay-students

American Civil Liberties Union. (2006, December 12). *Trial for Orange County teen 'outed' by principal concludes.* https://www.aclu.org/press-releases/trial-orange-county-teen-outed-principal-concludes

American Civil Liberties Union. (2007, September 25). *Nguon v. Wolf: Case profile.* http://www.aclu.org/lgbt-rights/nguon-v-wolf-case-profile

American Civil Liberties Union. (2008a, May 13). *Federal judge rules that students can't be barred from expressing support for gay people.* https://www.aclu.org/press-releases/federal-judge-rules-students-cant-be-barred-expressing-support-gay-people

American Civil Liberties Union. (2008b, July 30). *Okeechobee, FL high school gay-straight alliance wins groundbreaking federal lawsuit.* https://www.aclu.org/press-releases/okeechobee-fl-high-school-gay-straight-alliance-wins-groundbreaking-federal-lawsuit

American Civil Liberties Union. (2009a, May 18) *High school student takes on anti-gay harassment—and wins.* https://www.aclu.org/press-releases/high-school-student-takes-anti-gay-harassment-and-wins

American Civil Liberties Union. (2009b, July 20). *Gillman v. Holmes County School District case profile.* https://www.aclu.org/cases/gillman-v-holmes-county-school-district

American Civil Liberties Union. (2009c, July 20). *Morrison v. Boyd Co. Board of Education case profile.* https://www.aclu.org/cases/morrison-v-boyd-co-board-education

American Civil Liberties Union. (2011a, July 1). *Sweeping anti-bullying settlement announced following federal investigation into teen suicide.* https://www.aclu.org/press-releases/bush-signs-sweeping-law-enforcement-bill

American Civil Liberties Union. (2011b, December 8). *Sturgis v. Copiah County School District.* https://www.aclu.org/cases/lesbian-and-gay-rights/sturgis-v-copiah-county-school-district (2019, August 5). *Seth's Law (AB9)—Your right to not be bullied at school.* https://www.aclusocal.org/en/seths-law

American Counseling Association. (2012). *Practitioner's guide to ethical decision making.* https://www.counseling.org/docs/ethics/practitioners_guide.pdf?sfvrsn=2

American Counseling Association. (2014). *Code of ethics and standards of practice.* https://www.counseling.org/resources/aca-code-of-ethics.pdf

American Immigration Council. (2016). *Public education for immigrant students: Understanding Plyler v. Doe.* https://www.americanimmigrationcouncil.org/research/plyler-v-doe-public-education-immigrant-students

American Immigration Council. (2021, March 16). *The Dream Act: An overview.* https://www.americanimmigrationcouncil.org/research/dream-act-overview

American Mental Health Counselors Association. (2020). *AMHCA code of ethics.* https://www.amhca.org/HigherLogic/System/DownloadDocumentFile.ashx?DocumentFileKey=24a27502-196e-b763-ff57-490a12f7edb1&forceDialog=0

American Psychological Association. (2008). Are zero tolerance policies effective in the schools? An evidentiary review and recommendations. *American Psychologist, 63*(9), 852–862. https://doi.org/10.1037/0003-066X.63.9.852

American Psychological Association. (2021). *APA guidelines for psychological practice with sexual minority persons.* https://www.apa.org/about/policy/psychological-sexual-minority-persons.pdf

American School Counselor Association. (n.d.). *ASCA position statements.* https://www.schoolcounselor.org/Standards-Positions/Position-Statements/ASCA-Position-Statements

American School Counselor Association. (2017). The School Counselor and Student Safety and the Use of Technology. Alexandria, VA: Author

American School Counselor Association. (2018a). *Condemned the separation of children and families at U.S. borders.* Alexandria, VA: Author

American School Counselor Association. (2018b). The school counselor and confidentiality. *ASCA position statements.* Alexandria, VA: Author

American School Counselor Association. (2018c). The school counselor and prevention of sexually transmitted infections. *ASCA position statements.* Alexandria, VA: Author

American School Counselor Association. (2019a). *ASCA National Model: A Framework for School Counseling Programs* (4th ed.). Alexandria, VA: Author

American School Counselor Association. (2019b). The school counselor and discipline. *ASCA position statements.* Alexandria, VA: Author

American School Counselor Association. (2019c). The school counselor and prevention of school-related gun violence. *ASCA position statements.* Alexandria, VA: Author

American School Counselor Association. (2019d). The school counselor and safe schools and crisis response. *ASCA position statements.* Alexandria, VA: Author

American School Counselor Association. (2019e). The school counselor and working with students experiencing issues surrounding undocumented status. *ASCA position statements.* Alexandria, VA: Author

American School Counselor Association. (2020a). *ASCA standards for school counselor preparation programs.* Alexandria, VA: Author

American School Counselor Association. (2020b). The school counselor and group counseling. *ASCA position statements.* Alexandria, VA: Author

American School Counselor Association. (2020c). The school counselor and student mental health. *ASCA position statements.* Alexandria, VA: Author

American School Counselor Association. (2020d). The school counselor and suicide risk assessment. *ASCA position statements.* Alexandria, VA: Author

American School Counselor Association. (2020e). *Standards in practice: Eliminating racism and bias in schools: The school counselor's role.* Alexandria, VA: Author

American School Counselor Association. (2021a). *ASCA research report: State of the profession 2020.* Alexandria, VA: Author

American School Counselor Association. (2021b). The school counselor and annual performance appraisal. *ASCA position statements.* Alexandria, VA: Author

American School Counselor Association. (2021c). The school counselor and child abuse and neglect prevention. *ASCA position statements.* Alexandria, VA: Author

American School Counselor Association. (2021d). The school counselor and credentialing and licensure. *ASCA position statements.* Alexandria, VA: Author

American School Counselor Association. (2021e). The school counselor and multitiered systems of support. *ASCA position statements.* Alexandria, VA: Author

American School Counselor Association. (2021f). *School counselor roles & ratios.* Alexandria, VA: Author

American School Counselor Association. (2022a). *Anti-racism resources.* Alexandria, VA: Author

American School Counselor Association. (2022b). *ASCA ethical standards for school counselors.* Alexandria, VA: Author

American School Counselor Association. (2022c). The school counselor and character education. *ASCA position statements.* Alexandria, VA: Author

American School Counselor Association. (2022d). The school counselor and college access professionals. *ASCA position statements.* Alexandria, VA: Author

American School Counselor Association. (2022e). The school counselor and LGBTQ+ youth. *ASCA position statements.* Alexandria, VA: Author

American School Counselor Association. (2022f). The school counselor and promotion of safe schools through conflict resolution and bullying/harassment prevention. *ASCA position statements.* Alexandria, VA: Author

American School Counselor Association. (2022g). The school counselor and school-family-community partnerships. *ASCA position statements.* Alexandria, VA: Author

American School Counselor Association. (2022h). The school counselor and students with disabilities. *ASCA position statements.* Alexandria, VA: Author

American School Counselor Association. (2022i). The school counselor and transgender/nonbinary youth. *ASCA position statements.* Alexandria, VA: Author

American School Counselor Association. (2022j). The school counselor and trauma-informed practice. *ASCA position statements.* Alexandria, VA: Author

American Sikh Council. (2022). https://americansikhcouncil.org/

Ametrano, I. M. (2014). Teaching ethical decision making: Helping students reconcile personal and professional values. *Journal of Counseling & Development*, 92(2), 154–161. https://doi.org/10.1002/j.1556-6676.2014.00143.x

Amy Hestir Student Protection Act. Senate Bill 54 (2011).

Anderson, M., & Jiang, J. (2018a, November 18). *Teens, friendships and online groups.* Pew Research Center. https://www.pewresearch.org/internet/2018/11/28/teens-friendships-and-online-groups/

Anderson, M., & Jiang, J. (2018b, May 31). *Teens, social media and technology 2018*. Pew Research Center. https://www.pewresearch.org/internet/2018/05/31/teens-social-media-technology-2018/

Andrews and Beard Education Law Report. (2008). Teacher terminated for religious conduct has no title VII claim. *Andrews and Beard Education Law Report*, *3*(2), 5.

Applebome, P. (2009, March 7). Grades fixed: An allegation shocks no one. *The New York Times*. http://www.nytimes.com/2009/03/08/nyregion/08towns.html?_r=0

Arndt, A., Lovato, D., Mendez, S., Scott, M., & Tygret, J. (2020). The need for collaboration: Experiences and perceptions of preservice principals and school counselors. *Journal of Counselor Preparation & Supervision, 13*(4). https://digitalcommons.sacredheart.edu/jcps/vol13/iss4/3/

Arnold v. Board of Education of Escambia County, 880 F. 2d 305 (Ala. 1989).

Ash, P. (2019). Children are different: Liability issues in working with suicidal and dangerous youths. *FOCUS*, *17*(4), 355–359. https://doi.org/10.1176/appi.focus.20190018

Assistant Secretary for Public Affairs. (2019, December 5). *Cyberbullying tactics*. https://www.stopbullying.gov/cyberbullying/cyberbullying-tactics

Assistant Secretary for Public Affairs. (2021, October 6). *Federal laws*. https://www.stopbullying.gov/resources/laws/federal

Association for Specialists in Group Work. (2008, June). *Best practice guidelines 2007 revisions*.

Association for Specialists in Group Work. (2012, March). *Multicultural and social justice competence principles for group workers*. https://static1.squarespace.com/static/55cea634e4b083e448c3dd50/t/55d3f911e4b0ac443 3ebd4 cd/1439955217809/ASGW_MC_SJ_Priniciples_Final_ASGW.pdf

Association for Specialists in Group Work (2021). *ASGW guiding principles for group work*. https://asgw.org/wp-content/uploads/2021/07/ASGW-Guiding-Principles-May-2021.pdf

Association of American Educators. (n.d.). *AAE code of ethics for educators*. http://aaeteachers.org/images/pdfs/aaecodeofethicsforeducators.pdf

Associated Press. (1980, May 31). Six police protect homosexual, date at school's prom. *Eugene Register-Guard*. http://news.google.com/newspapers?nid=1310&dat=19800531&id=-a5hAAAAIBAJ&sjid=3OEDAAAAIBAJ&pg=4621,9325617

Associated Press. (2012a, May 24). Ohio school shooter to be tried as an adult. *CBS News*.

Associated Press. (2012b, June 5). Antigay-shirt ban illegal, group says. *The New York Times*. https://www.nytimes.com/2012/06/06/nyregion/aclu-says-antigay-shirt-ban-at-connecticut-school-was-illegal.html

Associated Press. (2012c, September 26). Morning-after pills available at 13 NYC public schools. *USA Today*. https://www.csmonitor.com/The-Culture/Family/2012/0926/Birth-control-NYC-schools-dispensing-morning-after-pill-to-girls

Associated Press. (2013, February 26). Seth Groody, Connecticut teen, has anti-gay t-shirt approved by high school. *Huffington Post*. https://h8discrimin8tion.blogspot.com/2013/02/seth-groody-connecticut-teen-has-anti.html

Atkins, R., & Oglesby, A. (2019). *Interrupting racism: Equity and social justice in school counseling*. Routledge.

Auxier, B., & Anderson, M. (2021, April 7). *Social media use in 2021*. Pew Research Center. https://www.pewresearch.org/internet/2021/04/07/social-media-use-in-2021/

Baab v. Medina City Schools Bd. of Edn, 28969 (Ohio-510 February 13, 2019). https://law.justia.com/cases/ohio/ninth-district-court-of-appeals/2019/28969.html

Baca, M. E. (2012, March 6). Anoka-Hennepin School District settles bullying lawsuit. *StarTribune: Newspaper of the Twin Cities* (Minneapolis, MN). https://www.startribune.com/local/north/141427303.html?page=1&c=y

Bacher-Hicks, A., Billings, S., & Deming, D. (2021). Proving the school-to-prison pipeline: Stricter middle schools raise the risk of adult arrests. *Education Next, 21*(4). https://www.educationnext.org/journal/vol-21-no-4/

Bain, A. L., & Podmore, J. A. (2020). Challenging heteronormativity in suburban high schools through "surplus visibility": Gay-straight alliances in the Vancouver city-region. *Gender, Place & Culture*, *27*(9), 1223–1246. https://doi.org/10.1080/0966369X.2019.1618798

Bakker, D., Kazantzis, N., Rickwood, D., & Rickard, N. (2016). Mental health smartphone apps: Review and evidence-based recommendations for future developments. *JMIR Mental Health*, *3*(1), e7. https://doi.org/10.2196/mental.4984

Baldwin, D., & Kaufman, M. (2002, March 9). *The Laramie project* [motion picture]. Home Box Office (HBO).

Balingit, M. (2016, December). Parents of Virginia teen who committed suicide sue school counselor. *The Washington Post.* https://www.washingtonpost.com/local/education/parents-of-teen-who-committed-suicide-sue-school-counselor/2016/12/03/f417bfae-b975-11e6-a677-b608fbb3aaf6_story.html?utm_term=.546acc3ac496

Bardick, A., Bernes, K., McCulloch, A., Witko, K., Spriddle, J., & Roest, A. (2004). Eating disorder intervention, prevention, and treatment. *Professional School Counseling*, *8*(2), 168–175. https://hdl.handle.net/10133/1180

Barr v. Lafron. (2020). https://caselaw.findlaw.com/us-6th-circuit/1235080.html

Baskin, J. S., Zeigler, B., & Negron, F. M. (2022). *Blurred lines: A new view of off-campus student speech* [webinar]. COSA School Law Seminar 2021. https://zoom.us/rec/play/3aW_g7sZTEWE983u-75WPd2AopGu1Mpm01q4GewEKZL9b67YcRuZuiNUeY5KmpPDj3XVVAgkqt6uO6Gq.4ekGGHSV9z2psp6w?continueMode=true&_x_zm_rtaid=zrhN_cqeRSyykKg1cJVNJg.1643212559057.64bd08da36ef81daa23b290aad5230bb&_x_zm_rhtaid=917

Belanger v. Nashua, New Hampshire, School District, 856 F. Supp. 40 (1994).

Bellotti v. Baird, 443 U.S. 622 (1979).

Berger, C. (2018). Bringing out the brilliance: A counseling intervention for underachieving students. *Professional School Counseling*, *17*(1). https://doi.org/10.1177/2156759X0001700102

Berman, A. L. (2017). Risk factors proximate to suicide and suicide risk assessment in the context of denied suicide ideation. *Suicide and Life-Threatening Behavior*, *48*(3), 340–352. https://doi.org/10.1111/sltb.12351

Bethel School District No. 403 v. Fraser, 478 U.S. 675, 106 S. Ct. 3159 (1986).

Betters-Bubon, J., Goodman-Scott, E., & Bamgbose, O. (2021). School counselor educators' reactions to changes in the profession: Implications for policy, evaluation, and preparation. *Journal of School-Based Counseling Policy and Evaluation, 3*(2), 40–50. https://doi.org/10.25774/gkr1-j228

Bhatt, S., Vinh, T., & Shaw, L. (2003, September 20). Accusations bring wave of support for Franklin trio. *The Seattle Times*. nwsource.com/archive/?date=20030920&slug=grades20m0

Bidell, M. P. (2011). School counselors and social justice advocacy for lesbian, gay, bisexual, transgender, and questioning students. *Journal of School Counseling*, *9*(10). http://jsc.montana.edu/articles/v9n10.pdf

Bird, J. D. P., Kuhns, L., & Garofalo, R. (2012). The impact of role models on health outcomes for lesbian, gay, bisexual, and transgender youth. *Journal of Adolescent Health*, *50*(4), 353-357. https://doi.org/10.1016/j.jadohealth.2011.08.006

Blokhuis, J., Feldman, J., Imber, N., & Van Geel, T. (2020) *Education law* (6th ed). Routledge.

Blum, R., Resnick, M., & Stark, T. (1990). Factors associated with the use of court bypass by minors to obtain abortions. *Family Planning Perspectives*, *22*(4), 158–160. https://pubmed.ncbi.nlm.nih.gov/2226746

Board of Education of Tonica Community High School District v. Adelbert E. Sickley, 479 N.E.2d 1142 (Ill. 1985).

Bogust v. Iverson, 102 N.W.2d 228 (Wis. 1960).

Bolton, A., Gandevia, S., & Newell, B. R. (2021). Appropriate responses to potential child abuse: The importance of information quality. *Child Abuse & Neglect*, *117*, 105062. https://doi.org/10.1016/j.chiabu.2021.105062

Bonvento v. Board of Public Instruction of Palm Beach County, 194 So. 2d 605 (Fla. 1967).

Borba, M. (2016). *Unselfie: Why empathetic kids succeed in our all-about-me world.* Touchstone.

Borum, R., Lodewijks, H. P. B., Bartel, P. A., & Forth, A. E. (2021). *The structured assessment of violence risk in youth (SAVRY)*, 438–461. Routledge/Taylor & Francis Group.

Boston 25 News. (2017, February 3). *Teacher suspended after rescinding recommendation letter, says students.* http://www.fox25boston.com/news/teacher-suspended-after-rescinding-recommendation-letter-says-students/490359833

Boyd, D. (2011, December 12). Four difficult questions regarding bullying and youth suicide. *Digital Media and Learning Research Hub*. http://dmlcentral.net/ blog/danah-boyd/four-difficult-questions-regarding-bullying-and-youth-suicide

Boyland, L. G., Geesa, R. L., Lowery, K. P., Quick, M. M., Mayes, R. D., Kim, J., Elam, N. P., & McDonald, K. M. (2019). Collaborative principal-school counselor preparation: National standards alignment to improve training between principals and school counselors. *International Journal of Educational Leadership Preparation*, *14*(1), 188–205.

Boynton v. Burglass, 590 So. 2d 446, 448–49 (Florida Dist. Ct. App. 1991).

Brandenburg v. Ohio, 395 U.S. 444 (1969).

Brassil, G. R. (2021, March 11). How some states are moving to restrict transgender women in sports. *The New York Times*. https://www.nytimes.com/2021/03/11/sports/transgender-athletes-bills.html

Bridges, K. (2019). *Critical race theory: A primer.* Pegasus Press.

Brown, T., Armstrong, S. A., Bore, S., & Simpson, C. (2017). Using an ethical decision-making model to address ethical dilemmas in school counseling. *Journal of School Counseling*, *15*(13). http://jsc.montana.edu/articles/v15n13.pdf

Brown v. Compton Unified School District, 68 Cal. App. 4th 114; 80 Cal. Rptr. 2d 171 (Cal. App. 1998).

Bryan, J. A., Young, A., Griffin, D., & Holcomb-McCoy, C. (2017). Leadership practices linked to involvement in school–family–community partnerships. *Professional School Counseling, 21*(1). https://doi.org/10.1177/2156759x18761897

Bryan, J., Day-Vines, N., Griffin, D., & Moore-Thomas, C. (2012). The disproportionality dilemma: Patterns of teacher referrals to school counselors for disruptive behavior. *Journal of Counseling & Development*, *90*(2), 177–190. https://doi.org/10.1111/j.1556-6676.2012.00023.x

Bully Police USA. (2022). *State anti bullying laws*. http://www.bullypolice.org/

Bureau of Labor Statistics (2019). 44.6 percent of high school dropouts were employed in August 2019. https://www.bls.gov/opub/ted/2019/44-6-percent-of-high-school-dropouts-and-72-3-percent-of-college-graduates-employed-in-august-2019.htm

Burpee v. Burton, 45 Wis. 150, 30 Am. Rep. 706 (1878).

C.A. v. William Hart Union High Sch. Dist., No. S188982 (Cal. Mar. 8, 2012). California Education Code § 49602 (2004).

C1.G. v. Siegfried. (2022, January 21). Cato Institute. https://www.cato.org/legal-briefs/c1g-v-siegfried

Camlin v. Beecher Community School District, App. 3d 1013; 791 N.E.2d 127 (2003).

Capital-Gazette Communications, Inc. (2004, October 19). http://www.capitalgazette.com/

Capuzzi, D. (2002). Legal and ethical challenges in counseling suicidal students. *Professional School Counseling*, 6(1), 36–46. https://doi.org/10.1177/2156759X0601000203

Cardi, J., & Green, M. (2008). Duty wars. *Southern California Law Review*, *81*, 672–733. Duty Wars - Article by W. Jonathan Cardi & Michael D. Green – Southern California Law Review

Carey, J. C., Martin, I., Harrington, K., & Trevisan, M. S. (2019). Competence in program evaluation and research assessed by state school counselor licensure examinations, *Professional School Counseling*, 22(1), 1–11. https://doi.org/10.1177/2156759X18793839

Carney, J. M., & Scott, H. L. (2012). Eating issues in schools: Detection, management, and consultation with allied professionals. *Journal of Counseling & Development*, *90*(3), 290–297. https://doi.org/10.1002/j.1556-6676.2012.00037.x

Carr, T. (2003, October 24). School forming death talk protocol. *Record-Eagle* (Traverse City, MI), 1–2. https://www.record-eagle.com

Carroll v. Rondout Valley Central School District, Ulster County, New York (1999).

Castillo, Paul D. (2021, June 28). Victory for transgender student, supreme court declines to hear bathroom dispute. *Lambda Legal*. https://www.lambdalegal.org/blog/us_20210628_scotus-declines-to-hear-transgender-bathroom-dispute

CBS Atlanta staff. (2012, May 25). *Texas honor student jailed for missing too much school*.

Centers for Disease Control and Prevention. (2016). Understanding teen dating violence. *Fact Sheet*. https://www.cdc.gov/violenceprevention/pdf/teen-dating-violence-factsheet-a.pdf

Centers for Disease Control and Prevention. (2017). Key statistics from the national survey of family growth. *National Survey of Family Growth, S Listing*. https://www.cdc.gov/nchs/nsfg/key_statistics/s.htm#sexeducation

Centers for Disease Control and Prevention. (2019). Youth risk behavior surveillance—United States, 2019. *Surveillance Summaries. Morbidity and Mortality Weekly Report, 2019 69(SS-01).* https://www.cdc.gov/mmwr/ind2020_su.html

Centre for Suicide Prevention. (2002). No-suicide contracts: A review of the findings from the research. *SEIC Alert #49.*

Cerrito, J. A., & Behun, R. J. (2020, December 9). Online career guidance systems for PK-12 school students: Compliments to a comprehensive school counseling program. *Education at the Intersection of Globalization and Technology.* https://www.intechopen.com/chapters/74356

Chang, C., & Pearman, C. (2018). Instant reminder: The impact of e-communication on first year college students. *International Journal of Technology in Teaching and Learning.* https://eric.ed.gov/?id=EJ1211992

Chen, E. C., Budianto, L., & Wong, K. (2010). Professional school counselors as social justice advocates for undocumented immigrant students in group work. *Journal for Specialists in Group Work, 35*(2), 255–261. ERIC - EJ893109 - Professional School Counselors as Social Justice Advocates for Undocumented Immigrant Students in Group Work, Journal for Specialists in Group Work, 2010-Sep

Child Abuse Prevention and Treatment Act, 42 U.S.C. 5101 *et seq.* (2019).

Child and Parental Rights Campaign, Inc. (2022). https://childparentrights.org/

Childhood Domestic Violence Association. (2014/02/10). *10 Startling domestic violence statistics.* http://cdv.org/2014/02/10-startling-domestic-violence-statistics-for-children/

Child Protective Services Act, Wyoming Code. § 14-3-2(1999).

Child Trends. (2015). *Oral sex behaviors among teens: Indicators on children and youth.* https://www.childtrends.org/wp-content/uploads/2013/12/95_Oral_ Sex_1.pdf

Child Welfare Information Gateway. (2010). *Infant safe haven laws: Summary of state laws.* http://www.childwelfare.gov/systemwide/laws_policies/statutes/safehaven.cfm

Child Welfare Information Gateway. (2019a). *Long-term consequences of child abuse and neglect.* https://www.childwelfare.gov/pubPDFs/long_term_consequences.pdf

Child Welfare Information Gateway. (2019b). *What is child abuse and neglect? Recognizing the signs and symptoms.* https://www.childwelfare.gov/pubPDFs/whatiscan.pdf

Child Welfare Information Gateway. (2020). *Parental substance use as child abuse.* https://www.childwelfare.gov/pubPDFs/parentalsubuse.pdf

Child Welfare Information Gateway. (2021a). *Child witness to domestic violence.* https://www.childwelfare.gov/pubPDFs/witnessdv.pdf

Child Welfare Information Gateway. (2021b). *Domestic violence: A primer for child welfare professionals.* https://www.childwelfare.gov/pubPDFs/domestic_violence.pdf

Cholewa, B., Goodman-Scott, E., Warren, J. M., & Hull, M. F. (2020). School counselor consultation preparation: A national study. *Counselor Education and Supervision, 59*(1), 46–58. https://doi.org/10.1002/ceas.12165

CNN Wire Staff. (2010, July 20). *Mississippi school pays damages to lesbian teen over prom dispute.* http://www.webcitation.org/5woNLWDDr

Colarossi, N. (2022, March 8). Education secretary slams Florida's 'Don't Say Gay' bill as 'hateful.' *Newsweek.* https://www.msn.com/en-us/news/us/education-secretary-slams-floridas-dont-say-gay-bill-as-hateful/ar-AAUO1Ax?ocid=uxbndlbing

College Board. (2016). *College advising essential* (vol. 1). https://counselorworkshops.collegeboard.org/pdf/college-advising-essentials-booklet-contents-web.pdf

College Board. (2022, March 5). *How many applications are enough?* https://professionals.collegeboard.org/guidance/applications/how-many

Colín v. Orange Unified School District, 83 F. Supp. 2d 1135 (C.D.Cal. 2000).

Chipman v. Grant County School District. 30 F. Supp. 2d 975 (1998).

Commonwealth v. Allen, 980 S.W.2d 278 (Ky. 1998).

Connick v. Myers, 461 U.S. 138, 146 (1983).

Copeland, W. E., Wolke, D., Angold, A., & Costello, E. J. (2013). Adult psychiatric outcomes of bullying and being bullied by peers in childhood and adolescence. *JAMA Psychiatry*, *70*(4), 419. https://doi.org/10.1001/jamapsychiatry.2013.504

Cordero, K., & Carlisle, V. (2019) *Banning conversion therapy on minors: A guide for creating tribal and state legislation.* American Bar Association Commission on Sexual Orientation and Gender Identity. https://www.americanbar.org/groups/diversity/sexual_orientation/publications/equalizer/2019-july/aba-conversion-therapy-legislative-guide/.html

Corey, G., Corey, M. S., Corey, C., & Callanan, R. (2018b). *Issues and ethics in the helping professions* (10th ed.). Cengage Learning.

Corey, M., Corey, G., & Corey, C. (2018a). *Groups: Process and practice* (10th ed.). Cengage Learning.

Cornell Law School. (2022). Privity. Legal Information Institute. https://www.law.cornell.edu/wex/privity

Craig v. Rich Township High Sch. Dist., No. 12-7581 (N.D. Ill. Feb. 19, 2013).

Crehan, A. (n.d.). Professional distance: Defining it, maintaining it managing it. *Centre for Applied Philosophy and Public Ethics* (Working Paper No. 2002/6). http://www.cappe.edu.au/docs/working-papers/CorboCrehan1.pdf

Cuff v. Grossmont Union High School, 221 Cal. App. 4th 582 (2013).

Cullitan, C. M. (2011). Please don't tell my mom! A minor's right to informational privacy. *Journal of Law of Education*, *40*(3), 417–460.

Curran, C. (2017). The law, policy, and portrayal of zero tolerance school discipline: Examining prevalence and characteristics across levels of governance and school districts. *Sage Journals, 33*(2), 319–349. https://doi.org/10.1177/0895904817691840

Curran, F. C. C. (2019, February 14). Just what are 'zero tolerance' policies—and are they still common? *UMBC Magazine*. https://magazine.umbc.edu/just-what-are-zero-tolerance-policies-and-are-they-still-common-in-americas-schools/

Cyberbullying Research Center. (n.d.). *Sexting laws across America*. https://cyberbullying.org/sexting-laws

Czyz, E. K., Horwitz, A. G., Yeguez, C. E., Ewell Foster, C. J., & King, C. A. (2018). Parental self-efficacy to support teens during a suicidal crisis and future adolescent emergency department visits and suicide attempts. *Journal of Clinical Child & Adolescent Psychology*, *47*(sup1). https://doi.org/10.1080/15374416.2017.1342546

D.T. v. Christ, No. CV-20-00484-TUC-JAS (D. Ariz. Aug. 5, 2021).

Freeman (2022, February 27). *Marbletown Elementary School students organize No Place for Hate event*. https://www.dailyfreeman.com/2022/02/27/marbletown-elementary-school-students-organize-no-place-for-hate-event/

Davis v. Monroe County Board of Education et al., 120 F.3d 1390. (Supreme Court, May 24, 1999).

Day, J. K., Fish, J. N., Grossman, A. H., & Russell, S. T. (2020). Gay-straight alliances, inclusive policy, and school climate: LGBTQ youths' experiences of social support and bullying. *Journal of Research on Adolescence*, *30*(suppl. 2), 418–430. https://doi.org/10.1111/jora.12487

Decker, J. R., Lewis, M. M., Shaver, E. A., Blankenship-Knox, A. E., & Paige, M. A. (2017). *The principal's legal handbook* (6th ed.). Education Law Association. Cleveland.

De Fina, D. (2020). Staff and student/parent friendship on social media: Some guidance and suggestions for schools. *School Governance*. https://www.schoolgovernance.net.au/news/staff-and-student-parent-friendship-on-social-mediasome-guidance-and-suggestions-for-schools

Department of Justice & U.S. Attorney's Office, Southern District of West Virginia. (2019, May 17). *Former high school counselor sentenced for mail fraud scheme* [Press release]. https://www.justice.gov/usao-sdwv/pr/former-high-school-counselor-sentenced-mail-fraud-scheme-inflating-daughters-grades

Doe v. Anoka-Hennepin School District No. 11, No. 11-cv-01999 (D. Minn. March 6, 2012).

Doe v. Blandford, 402 Mass. 831, 835, 525 N.E.2d 403 (2000).

Doe v. Coleville School District, WL 554430 (E.D. Wash. Feb. 21, 201.

Doe v. Fournier, WL 591669 (D. Mass. Feb. 22, 2012).

Doe v. Yunits, 15 Mass. L. Rep. 278; 2001 Mass. Super. LEXIS 327.

Doe and Doe v. Greendale Baptist Church and Academy, 327 F.3d 492 (Wisconsin 2003).

Doyle, R. L., & Fite, P. J. (2021). Indicators of suicidal outcomes among 6- to 12-year-old treatment seeking youth. *Child Psychiatry & Human Development*. https://doi.org/10.1007/s10578-021-01162-1

Drescher J. (2015). Out of DSM: Depathologizing homosexuality. *Behavioral Sciences*, *5*(4), 565–575. https://doi.org/10.3390/bs5040565

Duggan, M. (2017). *Online harassment 2017*. Pew Research Center. https://www.pewresearch.org/internet/2017/07/11/online-harassment-2017/

Duhaime's Online Legal Dictionary (n.d.). http://www.duhaime.org/dictionary/dict-c.aspx

Durant v. Los Angeles Unified School District, Court of Appeal of California, 2nd Appellate District, Div. 8, B155739 (2003).

Duval County Public Schools. (2017). *Student Code of Conduct 2016–2017*. Jacksonville, FL: Author.

Education World. (2022). *Stop tolerating zero tolerance*. https://www.educationworld.com/a_issues/issues303.shtml

Eckholm, E. (2011, September 13). Eight suicides in two years at Anoka-Hennepin School District. *The New York Times*. https://www.nytimes.com/2011/09/13/us/13bullysidebar.html?r=0

Eckholm, E. (2012, November 28). Gay 'conversion therapy' faces test in courts. *The New York Times*. https://www.nytimes.com/2012/11/28/us/gay-conversion-therapy-faces-tests-in-courts.html

Eisel v. Board of Education of Montgomery County, 324 Md. 376, 597 A. 2d 447 (Md Ct. App. 1991).

Elam, N. P, Geesa, R. L., Mayes, R. D., & McConnell, K. R. (2020). Improving school counselor efficacy through principal-counselor collaboration: A comprehensive literature review. *Mid-Western Educational Researcher*, *32*(2). https://www.mwera.org/MWER/volumes/v32/issue2/V32n2-McConnell-FEATURE-ARTICLE.pdf

Elias, M. (2007, February 11). Gay teens coming out earlier to peers and family. *USA Today*. http://usatoday30.usatoday.com/news/nation/2007-02-07-gay-teens-cover_x.htm

Eng, J. (2011, December 8). No tuxes or dresses for senior portraits after school settles lawsuit with lesbian. *NBC News*. http://usnews.nbcnews.com/_news/2011/12/08/9304669-no-tuxes-or-dresses-for-senior-portrait-after-school-settles-lawsuit-with-lesbian

Equal Access Act, 20 U.S.C. § 4071-74 (1984). *Title 20–Education, Chapter 52–Education for economic security, Subchapter VIII–Equal access.* www.justice.gov/crt/about/cor/byagency/ed4071.php

Equal Rights Advocates. (2022). *Sexual assault & sexual harrassment.* https://www.equalrights.org/issue/equality-in-schools-universities/sexual-harassment/

Erford, B. T. (2015). *Transforming the school counseling profession* (4th ed.). Pearson.

Erford, B. T. (2019). *Group work: Process an application* (2nd. ed.). Pearson Merrill.

Espelage, D. L., Basile, K. C., De La Rue, L., & Hamburger, M. E. (2015). Longitudinal associations among bullying, homophobic teasing, and sexual violence perpetration among middle school students. *Journal of Interpersonal Violence, 30*(14), 2541–2561. https://doi.org/10.1177/0886260514553113

Espelage, D. L., Hong, J. S., Rinehart, S., & Doshi, N. (2016). Understanding types, locations, and perpetrators of peer-to-peer sexual harassment in U.S. middle schools: A focus on sex, racial, and grade differences. *Children and Youth Services Review, 71*(C), 174–183. https://doi.org/10.1016/j.childyouth.2016.11.010

Ettinghoff, E. (2014). Outed at school: Student privacy rights and preventing unwanted disclosures of sexual orientation. *Loyola of Los Angeles Law Review.* https://paperity.org/p/82994362/outed-at-school-student-privacy-rights-and-preventing-unwanted-disclosures-of-sexual

Evancho et al. v. Pine-Richard School District et al, No.2:2016cv01537 (W.D. Pa. 2017). http://www.law.justia.com/cases/federal/district-courts/pennsylvania/pawdce/2:2016cv01537/233720/76/

Family Educational Rights and Privacy Act, 20 U.S.C.§1232g (1974).

Federal Bureau of Investigation. (n.d.). *The school shooter: A quick reference guide.* https://www.hsdl.org/?view&did=727626

FindLaw. (2016). *Teachers and social media: Rights and responsibilities.* https://www.findlaw.com/education/teachers-rights/teachers-and-social-media-rights-and-responsibilities.html

FindLaw. (2018, November 30). *Negligence and the 'reasonable person.'* https://www.findlaw.com/injury/accident-injury-law/standards-of-care-and-the-reasonable-person.html

Finnerty, S., Luke, M., & Duffy, J. T. (2019). A grounded theory of experiential group training of school counselors to engage in psychoeducational group lessons with first-in-family students. *The Journal for Specialists in Group Work, 44*(2), 99–117. https://doi.org/10.1080/01933922.2019.1599476

Fischer, A. J., & Bloomfield, B. S. (2020). Using technology to maximize engagement and outcomes in family–school partnerships. In S. A. Garbacz, *Establishing family-school partnerships in school psychology: Critical skills* (1st ed., 174–197). Foundations of School Psychology Research and Practice. Taylor & Francis. https://doi.org/10.4324/9781138400382-9

Fischer, L., & Sorenson, G. P. (1996). *School law for counselors, psychologists, and social workers* (3rd ed.). Pearson Longman.

Florida Bar. (2022). *Consumer pamphlet: A civil case or a criminal case?* https://www.floridabar.org/public/consumer/tip001/

Florida Statute. § 39.201-1a. (2012).

Florida Statute. § 1014.06 Parents Bill of Rights.

Focus on the Family. (2010, November 6). *New focus on day of truth: Now "day of dialogue."*

Forester-Miller, H., & Davis, T. (1996). *A practitioner's guide to ethical decision making.* https://www.counseling.org/docs/ethics/practitioners_guide.pdf?sfvrsn=2

Fossey, R., & Zirkel, P. (2004). Student suicide in the wake of Eisel. *Texas Wesleyan Law Review*, *10*(2), 403–439.

Fowler v. Szostek, 905 S.W.2d 336, 342 (Tex. App. 1995).

Franklin, J. C., Ribeiro, J. D., Fox, K. R., Bentley, K. H., Kleiman, E. M., Huang, X., Musacchio, K. M., Jaroszewski, A. C., Chang, B. P., & Nock, M. K. (2017). Risk factors for suicidal thoughts and behaviors: A meta-analysis of 50 years of research. *Psychological Bulletin*, *143*(2), 187–232. https://doi.org/10.1037/bul0000084

Franklin v. Gwinnett County Public Schools, Supreme Court of the United States, 1992. 503 U.S. 60, 112 S. Ct. 1028.

Frederique, N. (2020). What do the data reveal about violence in schools? *National Institute of Justice Journal.* https://nij.ojp.gov/topics/articles/what-do-data-reveal-about-violence-schools

Fricke v. Lynch, 491 F. Supp. 381; 1980 U.S. Dist. LEXIS 11770.

Frye, S. (2022, February 23). *Charges stand as Crumbley parents hearing concludes, case moves forward.* Oakland Press. https://www.theoaklandpress.com/2022/02/23/watch-live-crumbley-parents-in-court-again/

G. G. v. Gloucester County School Board. Ct. App. Virginia. No. 15-2056 (4th Cir. 2016).

Gable. K. (2016, January 20). *West Allegheny middle school parents pursuing possible lawsuit over anti-bullying program.* https://larryelder.com/2016/01/20/west-allegheny-middle-school-parents-pursuing-possible-lawsuit-over- anti-bullying-program/

Gammon v. Edwardsville Community Unit School District, 82 Ill. App. 3d 586 (1980).

Garcetti v. Ceballos, 547 U.S. 410 (2006).

Gavin, I., & Zirkel, P. (2008). An outcome analysis of school employee-initiated litigation: A comparison of 1977-81 and 1997-2001 decisions. *West's Education Law Reporter, 232*, 19–36.

Gay, Lesbian & Straight Education Network. (2017). *SCOTUS' decision on G.G. Case.*– https://www.glsen.org/article/SCOTUS-Decision-on-G.G.Case.

Geesa, R. L., Mayes, R. D., Lowery, K. P., Boyland, L. G., Quick, M. M., Kim, J., Elam, N. P., & McDonald, K. M. (2020). Increasing partnerships in educational leadership and school counseling: a framework for collaborative school principal and school counselor preparation and support. *International Journal of Leadership in Education,* 1–24. https://doi.org/10.1080/13603124.2020.1787525

Gerrity, E., & Folcarelli, C. (2008). Child traumatic stress: *What every policymaker should know.* National Center for Child Traumatic Stress.

Gender Recognition Act. Ca. Civ. Proc. Code § 1277.5 (2017). https://leginfo.legislature.ca.gov/faces/billTextClient.xhtml?bill_id=201720180SB179

Gender Spectrum. (2015). *Schools in transition: A guide for supporting transgender students in K-12 schools.* https://www.hrc.org/resources/schools-in-transition-a-guide-for-supporting-transgender-students-in-k-12-s

George, J. (2021). *A lesson on critical race theory.* https://www.americanbar.org/groups/crsj/publications/human_rights_magazine_home/civil-rights-reimagining-policing/a-lesson-on-critical-race-theory/

Gillander Gådin, K., & Stein, N. (2019). Do schools normalise sexual harassment? An analysis of a legal case regarding sexual harassment in a Swedish high school. *Gender and Education*, *31*(7), 920–937. https://doi.org/10.1080/09540253.2017.1396292

Gillborn, D. (2008). *Racism and education: Coincidence or conspiracy.* Routledge.

Gillman v. Holmes County School District, 567 F. Supp. 2d 1359, 1362 (N.D. Fla. 2008).

Gilly, N. R. (2020, April 4). *Text messaging between school counselors and students: An exploratory study*. Arcadia University. https://scholarworks.arcadia.edu/cgi/viewcontent.cgi?article=1026&context=grad_etd

Givhan v. Western Line Consolidated School District, 439 U.S. 410 (1979).

GLSEN. (n.d.). *Pronouns: A resource supporting transgender and gender nonconforming (GNC) educators and students.* https://www.glsen.org/sites/default/files/GLSEN%20Pronouns%20Resource.pdf

GLSEN. (2017). *SCOTUS' decision on G.G. Case.* https://www.glsen.org/article/SCOTUS-Decision-on-G.G.Case

GLSEN. (2019a). *Developing LGBTQ-inclusive classroom resources.* https://www.glsen.org/sites/default/files/2019-11/GLSEN_LGBTQ_Inclusive_Curriculum_Resource_2019_0.pdf

GLSEN. (2019b). Supporting safe and healthy schools for lesbian, gay, bisexual, transgender, and queer students. *A national survey of school counselors, social workers, and psychologists.* https://www.glsen.org/research/supporting-safe-and-healthy-schools-national-survey-mental-health-providers

GLSEN. (2019c). *The 2019 national school climate survey.* https://www.glsen.org/sites/default/files/2021-04/NSCS19-FullReport-032421-Web_0.pdf

GLSEN. (2020). *Model local education agency policy on transgender and nonbinary students.* https://www.glsen.org/activity/model-local-education-agency-policy-on-transgender-nonbinary-students

GLSEN. (2021a). *Day of silence.* https://www.glsen.org/day-of-silence

GLSEN. (2021b). *Gender affirming and inclusive athletics participation.* https://www.glsen.org/activity/gender-affirming-inclusive-athletics-participation

Goin, M. (2003). The suicide-prevention contract: A dangerous myth. *Psychiatric News, 38*(14), 3.

Goldberg, D. (2021). The war of critical race theory. *Boston Review* https://bostonreview.net/race-politics/david-theo-goldberg-war-critical-race-theory

Gonzaga Univ. v. Doe, 536 U.S. 273 (2002) 143 Wash. 2d 687, 24 P.3d 390.

Gonzalez v. Sch. Bd. of Okeechobee County, 571 F. Supp. 2d 1257, 1267 (S.D. Fla. 2008).

Goodman-Scott, E., Betters-Bubon, J., Olsen, J., & Donohue, P. (2020). *Making MTSS work*. American School Counselor Association.

Goodman-Scott, E., Upton, A. W., & Neuer Coburn, A. A. (2021). District-level school counseling supervisors' experiences and perceptions hiring school counselors. *Professional School Counseling, 24*(1b). https://doi.org/10.1177/2156759x20965179

Goodrich, K. M., Kingsley, K. V. & Sands, H. C. (2020). Digitally responsive school counseling across the ASCA national model. *International Journal for the Advancement of Counseling.* https://doi.org/10.1007/s10447-020-09396-9

Google. (2021). *Privacy & Security Center.* https://edu.google.com/why-google/privacy-security/

Grant v. Board of Trustees of Valley View School District, No 365-U, 676 N.E.2d 705 (Ill. App. Ct. 1997).

Grigentyte, G., & Lesinskiene, S. (2018). Prevalence and characteristics of sexual harassment among high school students: a pilot study. *Clinical Research Trials 4.* https://doi.org/10.15761/CRT.1000228

Grossman v. South Short Public School District, 507 F.3d 1097 (7th Cir. 2007).

Gruenke v. Seip, 225 F.3d 290 (3rd Cir. 2000).

Grossman, A. H., Park, J. Y., Frank, J. A., & Russell, S. T. (2021). Parental responses to transgender and gender nonconforming youth: Associations with parent support, parental abuse, and youths' psychological adjustment. *Journal of Homosexuality, 68*(8), 1260–1277. https://doi.org/10.1080/00918369.2019.1696103

Guttmacher Institute. (2021, December). *Parental involvement in minors' abortions.* https://www.guttmacher.org/state-policy/explore/parental-involvement-minors-abortions

Guttmacher Institute. (2022, January). *Minors access to contraceptive services.* Retrieved February 1, 2022, from https://www.guttmacher.org/state-policy/explore/minors-access-contraceptive-services

H. L. v. Matheson, 450 U.S. 398 (1981).

Hatzenbuehler, M., & Keyes K. (2013). Inclusive anti-bullying policies and reduced risk of suicide attempts in lesbian and gay youth. *Journal of Adolescent Health 53*(1), S21–S26. https://doi.org/10.1016/j.jadohealth.2012.08.010

Hamilton v. Vallejo City Unified School District. WL 1677123 (2009).

Hansen, M. C., Joseph, A. A., Wilcox, S. M., & Hnilica, R. J. (2020). Keeping race at the center of school discipline practices and trauma-informed care: An interpersonal framework. *Children & Schools, 42*(3), 161–170. https://doi.org/10.1093/cs/cdaa013

Hartung, C., Hendry, N. A., Albury, K., Johnston, S., & Welch, R. (2022). Teachers of Tiktok: Glimpses and gestures in the performance of professional identity. *Media International Australia.* https://doi.org/10.1177/1329878X211068836

Hasselbacher, L. A., Dekleva, A., Tristan, S., & Gilliam, M. L. (2014). Factors influencing parental involvement among minors seeking an abortion: A qualitative study. *American Journal of Public Health 104,* 2207–2211. https://doi.org/10.2105/AJPH.2014.302116

Hassouneh, N. A., & Alzoubi, A. F. (2019). The impact of modern technology on providing counseling services in light of some variables. *Journal of Education and Learning.* https://doi.org/10.5539/jel.v8n2p132

Havlik, S. A., Malott, K., Yee, T., DeRosato, M., & Crawford, E., (2019). School counselor training in professional advocacy: The role of the counselor educator. *Journal of Counselor Leadership and Advocacy,* 6(1), 71–85. https://doi.org/10.1080/2326716X.2018.1564710

Hawkins, D. (2016, September 30). A teen took a gun to his middle school. The school counselor talked him out of killing his teachers and a cop. *The Washington Post.* https://www.washingtonpost.com/news/morning-mix/wp/2016/09/30/a-teen-brought-a-gun-to-his-middle-school-this-counselor-talked-him-out-of-killing-teachers-and-a-cop/

Hays, D. G., Craigen, L. M., Knight, J., Healey, A., & Sikes, A. (2009). Duty to warn and protect against self-destructive behaviors and interpersonal violence. *Journal of School Counseling,* 7(11), 1–30. http://jsc.montana.edu/articles/v7n11.pdf

Heatherington, L., & Lavner, J. (2008). Coming to terms with coming out: Review and recommendations for family systems-focused research. *Journal of Family Psychology,* 22(3), 329–343. https://doi.org/10.1037/0893-2300.22.3.329

Heise, B., York, A., & Thatcher, B. (2016). Child suicide screening methods: Are we asking the right questions? A review of the literature and recommendations for Practice. *The Journal for Nurse Practitioners,* 12(6). https://www.npjournal.org/article/S1555-4155(16)00063-5/fulltext

Henshaw, S., & Kost, K. (1992). Parental involvement in minors' abortion decisions. *Family Planning Perspectives,* 24(5), 196–207, 213. https://pubmed.ncbi.nlm.nih.gov/1426181

Herlihy, B., & Corey, G. (2015). *ACA ethical standards casebook* (7th ed.). American Counselor Association.

Herszenhorn, D. (2004, October 16). Amid policy confusion, senior is allowed to apply to Harvard. *The New York Times.* https://www.nytimes.com/2004/10/16/nyregion/amid-policy-confusion-senior-is-allowed-to-apply-to-harvard.html

Hill v. Independent School District No 25 of Adair County 25 decided. (2002, September 6).

Hill, C., & Kearl, H. (2011). Crossing the line: *Sexual harassment at school.* American Association of University Women. http://www.aauw.org/ research/crossing-the-line/

Hinduja, S. (2016). *Revenge porn research, laws, and help for victims.* Cyberbullying Research Center. http://cyberbullying.org/revenge-porn-research-laws-help-victims

Hinduja, S. (2020, January 16). *It is time to teach safe sexting.* Cyberbullying Research Center. https://cyberbullying.org/it-is-time-to-teach-safe-sexting

Hinduja, S., & Patchin, J. (2018). *State sexting laws.* Cyberbullying Research Center. https://cyberbullying.org/state-sexting-laws.pdf

Hinduja, S. & Patchin, J. W. (2021). *Cyberbullying identification, prevention, and response.* Cyberbullying Research Center. https://cyberbullying.org/Cyberbullying-Identification-Prevention-Response-2019.pdf

Hirschfield, P. J. (2018). The role of schools in sustaining juvenile justice system inequality. *The Future of Children, 28,* 11–36. https://www.jstor.org/stable/26641545e

Hixenbaugh, M. (2021, January 22). *A viral video forced a wealthy Texas town to confront racism.* https://www.nbcnews.com/news/us-news/viral-video-forced-wealthy-texas-suburb-confront-racism-silent-majority-n1255230

Hobbs v. County of Moore, 267 N.C. 665, 149 S.E.2d 1 (1966).

Hoffman, J. (2009, November 6). Can a boy wear a skirt to school? *The New York Times.* http://www.nytimes.com/2009/11/08/fashion/08cross. html?pagewanted=all

Holland, K., Jones, C., Vivolo-Kantor, A., Idaikkadar, N., Zwald, M., & Hoots, B. (2021). Trends in US emergency department visits for mental health, overdose, and violence outcomes before and during the COVID-19 pandemic. *JAMA Psychiatry* https://jamanetwork.com/journals/jamapsychiatry/fullarticle/2775991

Holman, L. F., Nelson, J., & Watts, R. (2019). Organizational variables contributing to school counselor burnout: An opportunity for leadership, advocacy, collaboration, and systemic change. *The Professional Counselor, 9*(2), 126–141. https://doi.org/10.15241/lfh.9.2.126

Holt v. Bellflower Unified School District, Court of Appeal of California, Second Appellate District, Division Eight 2002 Cal. App. Unpublished. LexisNexis 6135. (2002, June 28).

Huber, S. (2018, January 23). *A term explained—"code of conduct and ethics".* https://www.security-ligue.org/news?tx_news_pi1%5Baction%5D=detail&tx_news_pi1%5Bcontroller%5D=News&tx_news_pi1%5Bnews%5D=27&cHash=ecabb2c67c34f77f32e04be82077f5ee

Hudson, D. (2020). *First amendment scholar gathered that happened in the month of June 2020.* https://www.freedomforum.org/2020/06/29/controversial-social-media-posts-by-public-school-employees-raise-interesting-free-speech-questions/

Hudson, D. L. H. (2021, July 6). Mahanoy Area School District v. B.L. (2021). *The First Amendment Encyclopedia.* https://mtsu.edu/first-amendment/article/1947/mahanoy-area-school-district-v-b-l

Huffington Post. (2012, January 17). *Online student speech appeals rejected by Supreme Court.*

Hughes v. Stanley County School Board, 594 N.W.2d 346 (S.D. 1999).
Human Rights Campaign, 2018. *LGBTQ+ youth report.* Author. https://assets2.hrc.org/files/assets/resources/2018-YouthReport-0514-Final.pdf
Hutchings, T. (2017, February 28). *Protecting the profession—professional ethics in the classroom.* https://www.ets.org/s/proethica/pdf/real-clear-articles.pdf
Huss, S., Bryant, A., & Mulet, S. (2008). Managing the quagmire of counseling in a school: Bringing the parents onboard. *Professional School Counseling, 11*(6), 362–367. https://doi.org/10.1177/2156759X0801100602
Hustler Magazine, Inc. v. Falwell, 485 U.S. 46 (1988).
iKeepSafe. (2022). *California student privacy certified.* https://ikeepsafe.org/certification/cspc/#:~:text=Earning%20the%20iKeepSafe%20CSPC%20asserts,Rights%20Amendment%20(%E2%80%9CPPRA%E2%80%9D)
Illinois Revised Statute. (1977). Ch. 122, par. 24-12, n1.
Independent College Counselors and Educational Consultants. (2014). *Statement of principles of good practice.* https://www.iecaonline.com/PDF/IECA_Principles_of_Good_Practice.pdf
Indiana Code Ann. § 31-33 (2004).
Individuals with Disabilities Education Act. (1990). 20 U.S.C. 1400-1485.
Individuals with Disabilities Education Improvement Act of 2004. (2004). 20 U.S.C. §1400.
Institute of Educational Sciences. (2021, September). *September 2021 school pulse panel.* https://ies.ed.gov/schoolsurvey/2021SeptemberSPP/
interACT (2021). *FAQ: What is intersex?* https://interactadvocates.org/faq/
International Centre for Missing and Exploited Children. (2017). *Online grooming of children for sexual purposes: Model legislation and global review.* https://www.icmec.org/wp-content/uploads/2017/09/Online-Grooming-of-Children_FINAL_9-18-17.pdf
Isaac, K. (2021). Where does the bizarre hysteria about 'critical race theory' come from? Follow the money! *Inside Higher Ed.* https://www.insidehighered.com/blogs/just-visiting/guest-blog-where-does-bizarre-hysteria-about-%E2%80%98critical-race-theory%E2%80%99-come-follow
Isaacs, M., & Stone, C. (2001). Confidentiality with minors: Mental health counselor's attitudes toward breaching or preserving confidentiality. *Journal of Mental Health Counseling, 23*(4), 342–356. https://eric.ed.gov/?id=EJ634427
Iyer, N. N., & Baxter-MacGregor, J. (2010). Ethical dilemmas for the school counselor: balancing student confidentiality and parent's right to know. *NERA Conference* Proceedings 2010 (Paper 15). https://opencommons.uconn.edu/cgi/viewcontent.cgi?article=1017&context=nera_2010
Jackson, J. (2021, December 1). Some students stayed home ahead of Oxford school shooting due to online threats. *Newsweek.* https://www.newsweek.com/some-students-stayed-home-ahead-oxford-school-shooting-due-online-threats-1654913
Jackson, L. (2021, August 18). What is critical race theory? And how to learn more about the issue dividing school districts across the country. *The New York Times.* https://www.nytimes.com/2021/07/09/podcasts/the-daily-newsletter-critical-race-theory.html
Jacob, S., Decker, D. M., & Lugg, E. T. (2022). *Ethics and law for school psychologists* (7th ed.). John Wiley & Sons.

James, S. (2008, July 16). Young teens openly express sexuality; LGBT pre-teens proud, not safe. *ABC News Online*. http://abcnews.go.com/Health/Sex/story?id=5381271&page=1#.T5W3UBwg1DQ

James Madison University. (2008). *Sexual harassment*. http://www.jmu.edu/assaultprev/Harassment.shtml

Jane Doe v. Unified School District, School Counselor, and Elementary School Principal, 255 F. Supp. 2d 1251 (D. Kan. 2003).

Jaschik, S. (2020, March 2). How to limit college applications. *Inside Higher Ed*. https://www.insidehighered.com/admissions/article/2020/03/02/private-high-school-limits-its-students-college-applications-nine

JC ex rel. RC v. Beverly Hills Unified School, 711 F. Supp. 2d 1094 (2010).

Johnson, M. (2010, July 7). Southern belle: Constance McMillen's suit over the prom is winning over the South. *Slate*. http://www.slate.com/articles/double_x/doublex/2010/07/southern_belle.html

Johnson, S. F. (2021, September 28). *Schools have diminished authority to restrict student speech on social media*. Concord Law School. https://www.concordlawschool.edu/blog/news/scotus-rules-student-speech-social-media/

Jonsson, P. (2010, March 11). Constance McMillen takes fight over same-sex prom date to court. *The Christian Science Monitor*. http://www.csmonitor.com/USA/

Joyner, C. (2010, March 11). Miss. prom canceled after lesbian's date request. *USA Today*. http://www.webcitation.org/5okMbDs7o

J.S. v. Blue Mountain Sch. Dist., No. 08-4138 (3d Cir. Jun. 13, 2011).

Julig, C. (2021, October 10). Cherry Creek student expelled for anti-Semitic Snapchat appeals lost free speech ruling. *Sentinel*. https://sentinelcolorado.com/news/metro/cherry-creek-student-expelled-for-anti-semitic-snapchat-appeals-lost-free-speech-ruling/

Jump, J. (2022, March 7). Ethical college admissions: Could that be me? *Inside Higher Ed*. https://www.insidehighered.com/admissions/views/2022/03/07/column-raises-question-college-counselor-opinion

Kaiser Family Foundation. (2018). *Abstinence education programs: Definition, funding, and impact on teen sexual behavior*. https://www.kff.org/womens-health-policy/fact-sheet/abstinence-education-programs-definition-funding-and-impact-on-teen-sexual-behavior/

Kaltiala-Heino, R., Lindberg, N., Fröjd, S., Haravuori, H., & Marttunen, M. (2019). Adolescents with same-sex interest: Experiences of sexual harassment are more common among boys. *Health Psychology and Behavioral Medicine*, *7*(1), 105–127. https://doi.org/10.1080/21642850.2019.1598864

Kamisugi, K. (2016). East County NAACP sues Antioch Unified School District for violating agreement on civil and disability rights. *Equal Justice Society*. https://equaljusticesociety.org/2016/07/06/lawsuit-vs-antioch-schools/

Kampf, A., McSherry, B., Ogloff, J., & Rothschild, A. (2010). *Confidentiality for mental health professionals: A guide to ethical and legal principles*. Australian Academic Press.

Kaplan, D. (2006). The end of clear and imminent danger. *Counseling Today*. https://ct.counseling.org/2006/01/ct-online-ethics-update/

Kaplan, L. (1996). Outrageous or legitimate concerns: What some parents are saying about school counseling. *The School Counselor, 43*(3), 165–170. https://eric.ed.gov/?id=EJ530366

Karnowski, S. (2012, March 6). Anoka-Hennepin School District settles lawsuits over gay bullying, gender neutral policy. *The Huffington Post.* http://www.huffingtonpost.com/2012/03/06/minn-school-district-sett_n_1323791.html

Katner, D. R. (2020). Delayed responses to child sexual abuse, the Kavanaugh confirmation hearing, and eliminating statutes of limitation for child sexual abuse cases. *American Journal of Criminal Law, 47*(1), 1–45. https://www.proquest.com/scholarly-journals/delayed-responses-child-sexual-abuse-kavanaugh/docview/2481921832/se-2?accountid=14690

Katz, C., & Fallon, B. (2021). Protecting children from maltreatment during COVID-19: Struggling to see children and their families through the lockdowns. *Child Abuse & Neglect, 116,* 105084. https://10.1016/j.chiabu.2021.105084

Katz, C., Priolo Filho, S. R., Korbin, J., Bérubé, A., Fouché, A., Haffejee, S., Kaawa-Mafigiri, D., Maguire-Jack, K., Muñoz, P., Spilsbury, J., Tarabulsy, G., Tiwari, A., Thembekile Levine, D., Truter, E., & Varela, N. (2021). Child maltreatment in the time of the COVID-19 pandemic: A proposed global framework on research, policy and practice. *Child Abuse & Neglect, 116,* 104824. https://doi.org/10.1016/j.chiabu.2020.104824

Kearney, C., Akos, P., Domina, T., & Young, Z. (2021). Student-to-school counselor ratios: A meta-analytic review of the evidence. *Journal of Counseling & Development, 99*(4), 418–428. https://doi.org/10.1002/jcad.12394

Kendi, I. X. (2019). *How to be an anti-racist.* One World. One World - How to Be an Antiracist - Hardcover

Killen v. Independent School Dist. No. 706, 547 N.W.2d 113, 117 (Minn. App. 1996).

Kiracofe, N., & Wells, L. (2007). Mandated disciplinary counseling on campus: Problems and possibilities. *Journal of Counseling & Development, 85*(3), 259–269. https://doi.org/10.1002/j.1556-6678.2007.tb00473.x

King, K. A., & Smith, J. (2000). Project SOAR: A training program to increase school counselors' knowledge and confidence regarding suicide prevention and intervention. *Journal of School Health, 70,* 402–407. http://doi.org/10.1111/j.1746-1561.2000.tb07227.x.

King-White, D., Kurt, L., & Seck, M. (2019). A qualitative study of online school counselors' ethical practices in K-12 schools. *Journal of Counselor Practice.* https://doi.org/10.22229/aqs1012019

Kitchener, K. S. (1984). Intuition, critical evaluation and ethical principles: The foundation for ethical decisions in counseling psychology. *Counseling Psychologist, 12*(3), 43–55. https://doi.org/10.1177/0011000084123005

Kjaran, J. I., & Jóhannesson, I. S. (2013). Manifestations of heterosexism in Icelandic upper secondary schools and the responses of LGBT students. *Journal of LGBT Youth, 10*(4), 351–372. https://doi.org/10.1080/19361653.2013.824373

Klein, A., & Golub, S. (2016). *Family rejection as a predictor of suicide attempts and substance misuse among transgender and gender nonconforming adults.* https://doi.org/10.1016/j.jaac.2020.08.300

Klump v. Nazareth Area Sch. Dist., 425 F. Supp.2d 622 (E.D. Pa., 2006).

Kohli, R., Pizarro, M., & Nevárez, A. (2017). The "new racism" of K-12 schools: Centering critical research on racism. *Review of Research in Education, 41*(1), 182–202. https://doi.org/10.3102/0091732X16686949

Komo Staff & News Services. (2003, November 25). Grade tampering investigation at Franklin High ends. *Komo News.*

Koocher, G. P. (2008). Ethical challenges in mental health services to children and families. *Journal of Clinical Psychology, 64*(5), 601–612. https://doi.org/10.1002/jclp.20476

Koschoreck, J. W., & Tooms, A. K. (2009). *Sexuality matters: Paradigms and policies for educational leaders.* Rowman & Littlefield.

Kraft, W. (2012, December 10). *Resolution of Julea Ward case leaves program, policies intact at Eastern Michigan University.* http://www.emich.edu/univcomm/ releases/release.php?id=1355161741

Kramer, S. (2011, May 20). 'Coming out': Gay teenagers, in their own words. *The New York Times.* https://www.nytimes.com/2011/05/23/us/23out.html

Kraut, M. E. (2020). *Children and grooming/online predators.* Child Crime Prevention & Safety Center. https://childsafety.losangelescriminallawyer.pro/children-and-grooming-online-predators.html

Kumar, A., & Epley, N. (2020). It's surprisingly nice to hear you: Misunderstanding the impact of communication media can lead to suboptimal choices of how to connect with others. *Journal of Experimental Psychology: General.* https://doi.org/10.1037/xge0000962

LaForett, D. R., & De Marco, A. (2020). A logic model for educator-level intervention research to reduce racial disparities in student suspension and expulsion. *Cultural Diversity and Ethnic Minority Psychology, 26*(3), 295–305. https://doi.org/10.1037/cdp0000303

Lambda Legal. (2012). *Amicus brief of parents, families and friends of lesbians and gays ("PFLAG"), Gay, Lesbian and Straight Education Network ("GLSEN"), affirmations, and Ruth Ellis Center in support of defendant-appellee for affirmance, Ward v. Wilbanks, 667 F.3d 727* (2012). https://www.lambdalegal.org/in-court/legal-docs/ward_mi_20110211_amicus-pflag-et-al

Lambda Legal. (2014, July 23). *Lambda legal resolves lawsuit against Desoto County schools on behalf of lesbian student.* https://www.lambdalegal.org/news/fl_20140723_hatcher-lawsuit-resolved

Lambda Legal. (2017, August 1). *Lambda legal lawsuit forces end to school district anti-transgender bathroom policy.* https://www.lambdalegal.org/news/pa_20170801_pine-richland-settlement

Lambda Legal. (2020, September 25). *Adams v. The School Board of St. Johns County, Florida.* https://www.lambdalegal.org/in-court/cases/fl_adams-v-school-board-st-johns-county

Lambda Legal. (2021a, May 26). *B.P.J. v. West Virginia State Board of Education.* https://www.lambdalegal.org/in-court/cases/jackson_wv_20210526_complaint

Lambda Legal. (2021b, November). *L.E. v. Lee.* https://www.lambdalegal.org/in-court/cases/le-v-lee

Lambda Legal. (2022). *Lambda Legal and ACLU ask Texas appeals court for new order blocking the state from investigating families of transgender youth.* https://www.lambdalegal.org/blog/abbott_tx_20220317_ll-aclu-ask-appeals-court-for-new-order-blocking-the-state-frominvestigating-families-of-transgender-youth

LaMorte, M. W. (2001). *School law.* Allyn & Bacon.

Landstrom v. Illinois Department of Children and Family Services, 892 F.2d 670 (7th Cir. 1990).

Large, M., Galletly, C., Myles, N., Ryan, C. J., & Myles, H. (2017). Known unknowns and unknown unknowns in suicide risk assessment: evidence from meta-analyses of aleatory and epistemic uncertainty. *BJPsych Bulletin*, *41*(3), 160–163. https://doi.org/10.1192/pb.bp.116.054940

Lawson, B. (2012). Hammad Memon trial could be several months away due to mental evaluations, schedule conflict. *The Huntsville Times*. https://www.al.com/breaking/2012/05/hammad_memon_trial_could_be_se.html

Lee, C. C., & Park, D. (2013). A conceptual framework for counseling across cultures. In C. C. Lee (Ed.), *Multicultural issues in counseling: New approaches to diversity* (4th ed). American Counseling Association.

Leenaars, A. A., & Wenckstern, S. (1999). Suicide prevention in schools: The art, thc issues, and the pitfalls. *Crisis*, *20*(3), 132–142. https://doi.org/10.1027//0227-5910.20.3.132

Legal Aid of Palm Beach County (2021). *Costly and cruel: How misuse of the Baker Act harms 37,000 Florida children each year.* https://www.aclu.org/issues/juvenile-justice/juvenile-justice-school-prison-pipeline

Legal Information Institute. (2022). Intentional infliction of emotional distress (IIED). https://www.law.cornell.edu/wex/intentional_infliction_of_emotional_distress

Lehmuth v. Long Beach Unified Sch. Dist. , 53 Cal.2d 544.

Leitsinger, M. (2012, April 19). $4.2 million settlement for student paralyzed by bully. *NBC News*. https://www.nbcnews.com/news/world/4-2-million-settlement-student-paralyzed-bully-flna724597

Levy, I. P., & Adjapong, E. S. (2020). Toward culturally competent school counseling environments: Hip-hop studio construction. *The Professional Counselor*, *10*(2), 266–284. http://doi.org/10.15241/ipl.10.2.266

Levy, I. P., & Lemberger-Truelove, M. E. (2021). Educator-counselor: A nondual identity for school counselors. *Professional School Counseling*. https://doi.org/10.1177/2156759X211007630

Lezner v. Shaw and Gresham School District, 156 Wis. 2d 466; 458 N.W.2d 388; 1990 Wisc. App. LEXIS 357 (April 17, 1990).

Li, Q. (2007). New bottle but old wine: A research of cyberbullying in schools. *Computers in Human Behavior, 23*, 1777–1791. https://doi.org/10.1016/j.chb.2005.10.005

List, A. & Dykeman, C. (2021) Disproportionalities in gifted and talented education enrollment rates: An analysis of the U.S. civil rights data collection series. *Preventing School Failure: Alternative Education for Children and Youth*, *65*(2), 108–113. https://doi.org/10.1080/1045988X.2020.1837061

Listenbee, R., et al., (2012). *Report of the Attorney General's National Task Force on Children Exposed to Violence*. U.S. Department of Justice. http://www.justice.gov/defendingchildhood/cev-rpt-full.pdf

Littlejohn v. School Board of Leon County. (N.D. Florida 2021). https://tallahasseereports.com/wp-content/uploads/2021/10/Complaint-As-Filed-101821.pdf

Lobron, A. (2007). Easy out. *The Boston Globe*. http://www.boston.com/bostonglobe/magazine/articles/2007/11/11/easy_out/?page=full

Losen, D. J., & Martinez, T. E. (2013, April 8). *Out of school and off track: The overuse of suspensions in American middle and high schools*. Civil Rights Project. https://civilrightsproject.ucla.edu/resources/projects/center-for-civil-rights-remedies/school-to-prison-folder/federal-reports/out-of-school-and-off-track-the-overuse-of-suspensions-in-american-middle-and-high-schools

Lovell v. Poway Unified School District, 90 F.3d 367 (9th Cir. 1996).

Ludeke, M. (2009). Transgender youth. *Principal Leadership*, *10*(3), 12–16.

Luke, M., Goodrich, K. M., & Gilbride, D. D. (2013). Intercultural Model of Ethical Decision Making: Addressing worldview dilemmas in school counseling. *Counseling and Values*, *58*(2), 177–194. https://doi.org/10.1002/j.2161-007x.2013.00032.x

Madigan, S., Ly, A., Rash, C. L., Van Ouytsel, J., & Temple, J. R. (2018). Prevalence of multiple forms of sexting behavior among youth: A systematic review and meta-analysis. *JAMA Pediatrics*. https://doi.org/10.1001/jamapediatrics.2017.5314

Mallory, C., Brown, T. N. T., & Conron, K. J. (2019). Conversion therapy and LGBT youth. *The Williams Institute*. https://williamsinstitute.law.ucla.edu/wp-content/uploads/Conversion-Therapy-Update-Jun-2019.pdf

Marsh, J. (2013, January 22). Hildebran Elementary School child pornography teacher sex abuse: Additional federal civil rights lawsuit filed. *ChildLaw Blog*. http://www.childlaw.us/2013/01/hildebran-elementary-school-ch.html

Martin, J., Hamilton, B., Osterman, M., & Driscoll, A. (2021). Births: Final data for 2019. *National Vital Statistics Report, 70*(2):1–50. https://doi.org/10.15620/cdc:100472

Martin, P. J. (2002). Transforming school counseling: A national perspective. *Theory into Practice*, *41*, 148–153. https://doi.org/10.1207/s15430421tip4103_2

Martin, P. W. (2020). *Basic legal citation*. Cornell School of Law. https://www.law.cornell.edu/citation/2-200

Martinez, G., Abma, J., & Copen, C. (2010). Educating teenagers about sex in the United States. *NCHS Data Brief, no. 44*. National Center for Health Statistics.

Martinez, G. M., Abma, J. C. (2020). Sexual activity and contraceptive use among teenagers aged 15–19 in the United States, 2015–2017. *NCHS Data Brief, no. 366*. National Center for Health Statistics. https://www.cdc.gov/nchs/products/databriefs/db366.htm

Mattise, J. (2021, August 30). 20 states sue over Biden admin school, work LGBTQ protections. *AP News*. https://apnews.com/article/sports-business-us-supreme-court-c462bcdd2ef65573712a916177e1ca32

Massachusetts Department of Elementary and Secondary Education. (2013). *Guidance for Massachusetts public schools: Creating a safe and supportive school environment, nondiscrimination on the basis of gender identity.* https://www.doe.mass.edu/sfs/lgbtq/genderidentity.html

Massachusetts State Ethics Commission. (1997, June 24). Sansone, Casper Charles Docket No. 566 G.L. c. 268B, s.4(a). http://www.mass.gov/ethics/opinions-and-rulings/enforcement-matters/enf-section-23/section-23-s-z/casper-sansone-da.html

Mayer, K. H., Garofalo, R., & Makadon, H. J. (2014). Promoting the successful development of sexual and gender minority youths. *American Journal of Public Health*, *104*(6), 976–981. https://doi.org/10.2105/ajph.2014.301876

McAndrews, Tobin. (2001). Zero Tolerance Policies. *ERIC Digest, 146*. https://files.eric.ed.gov/fulltext/ED451579.pdf

McIntosh v. Milano, 403 A.2d 500 (NJ, 1979).

McKean, A. J. S., Pabbati, C. P., Geske, J. R., & Bostwick, J. M. (2018). Rethinking lethality in youth suicide attempts: First suicide attempt outcomes in youth ages 10 to 24. *Journal of the American Academy of Child & Adolescent Psychiatry*, *57*(10), 786–791. https://doi.org/10.1016/j.jaac.2018.04.021

McKinney-Vento Homeless Assistance Act. (2001). 42 USC §§11431–11435. http://www2.ed.gov/programs/homeless/legislation.html

McLaughlin, J. (2010). Crime and punishment: Teen sexting in context. *Penn State Law Review, 115*(1), 135–181. https://ideas.dickinsonlaw.psu.edu/cgi/viewcontent.cgi?article=3953&context=dlra

McMillen v. Itawamba County School District, et al., 702 F.Supp.2d 699 (2010); 2010 U.S. Dist. LEXIS 27589.

Medley, S. (2021). *Shayna Medley discusses the impact of Texas abortion ban on LGBTQ+ rights*. Skadden Foundation. https://www.skaddenfellowships.org/news-and-stories/2021/11/shayna-medley-discusses-the-impact-of-texas-abortion-ban-on-lgbtq-rights

Meinick, R. (2020). *Analyzing the Department of Education's final Title IX rules on sexual misconduct*. Brookings. https://www.brookings.edu/research/analyzing-the-department-of-educations-final-title-ix-rules-on-sexual-misconduct

Meyer v. Nebraska, 262 U.S. 390, 399-401 (1923).

Michaels, N. L., & Letson, M. M. (2021). Child maltreatment fatalities among children and adolescents 5–17 years old. *Child Abuse & Neglect, 117*, 105032. https://doi.org/10.1016/j.chiabu.2021.105032

Michigan State Board of Education. (MSBE, 2016). *State Board of Education statement and guidance on safe and supportive learning environments for lesbian, gay, bisexual, transgender, and questioning (LGBTQ) students*. http://www.michigan.gov/documents/mde/Item_B_SBE_Statement_and_Guidance_on_LGBTQ_515608_7.pdf

Mikell v. School Administrative Unit No. 33 972 A. 2d 1050, 158 NH 723 - NH: Supreme Court (2009).

Miller et al. v. Skumanick, Court of Appeals 3d Cir. 3:09cv540 (PA 2010). Miller v. Mitchell, 598 F.3d 139 (2010).

Mills College School of Education. (2020, November 23). *Practices & policies for implementing restorative justice in schools*. https://online.mills.edu/blog/restorative-justice-in-schools/

Montana Code, Ann., Ch. 9, § 305 (2007).

Morrison v. Board of Education, 2006 U.S. Dist. LEXIS 6373 (E.D. Ky. Feb. 17, 2006).

Moyer, S. M., Sullivan, R. J., & Growcock, D. (2012). When is it ethical to inform administrators about student risk-taking behaviors? Perceptions of school counselors. *Professional School Counseling, 15*(3), 98–109. https://doi.org/10.1177/2156759X1201500303

Mozaffar, N., Burdick, K., McInerney, M., Moon, K., Dunn, K., Burke, S. C., & Goldstein, N. E. (2020). *Credit overdue: How states can mitigate academic credit transfer problems for youth in the juvenile justice system*. Southern Poverty Law Center. https://www.splcenter.org/sites/default/files/credit_overdue.pdf

Murthy, V. H. (2021). *Protecting youth mental health: The U.S. Surgeon General's advisory*. U.S. Department of Health and Human Services. https://www.hhs.gov/about/news/2021/12/07/us-surgeon-general-issues-advisory-on-youth-mental-health-crisis-further-exposed-by-covid-19-pandemic.html

Nabozny v. Podlesny, 92 F. 3d 446 (7th Cir. 1996).

National Association for College Admission Counseling. (2019). *State of college admission*. https://www.nacacnet.org/globalassets/documents/publications/research/2018_soca/soca2019_all.pdf

National Association for College Admission Counseling. (2021). *Pulse on college admission full report.* https://www.nacacnet.org/news--publications/Research/pulse-on-college-admission-may-june-2021/pulse-on-college-admission-full-report/

National Association of School Psychologists. (n.d.). *Preventing youth suicide: Tips for parents and educators.* https://www.nasponline.org/resources/crisis_safety/suicideprevention.aspx

National Association of Secondary School Principals (2008). Expression rights of public school employees and students. *A legal memorandum, 8*(4). https://www. nasp.org/portals/0/content/58255.pdf

National Association of Social Workers. (2021, February 19). *Highlighted revisions to the code of ethics.* https://www.socialworkers.org/About/Ethics/Code-of-Ethics/Highlighted-Revisions-to-the-Code-of-Ethics

National Center for Education Statistics. (2020). *Number of virtual schools, total state enrollment, total virtual school enrollment, and virtual school enrollment as a percentage of state total enrollment: School year 2019–20.* https://nces.ed.gov/ccd/tables/201920_Virtual_Schools_table_3.asp

National Center for Homeless Education. (2020). *National overview.* https://profiles.nche.seiservices.com/ConsolidatedStateProfile.aspx

National Center for Lesbian Rights. (n.d.) *Vlaming v. West Point School Board.* https://www.nclrights.org/our-work/cases/vlaming-v-west-point-school-board/

National Center for Lesbian Rights & GLSEN. (n.d.) *Expensive reasons why safe schools laws and policies are in your district's best interest.* support.nclrights.org/site/DocServer/PlanningWithPurpose_Web.pdf?docID=6121

National Child Abuse and Neglect Data System (NCANDS). (2019). *National Data Archive on Child Abuse and Neglect.* https://www.ndacan.acf.hhs.gov/datasets/dataset-details.cfm?ID=237

National Coalition for the Homeless. (2017). *LGBTQ homelessness.* https://nationalhomeless.org/wp-content/uploads/2017/06/LGBTQ-Homelessness.pdf

National Conference of State Legislators. (2016). *Teenage pregnancy.* https://www.ncsl.org/research/health/teen-pregnancy-prevention.aspx

National Conference of State Legislatures. (2021, March 1). *Tuition benefits for immigrants.* https://www.ncsl.org/research/immigration/tuition-benefits-for-immigrants.aspx#:~:text=Seventeen%20state%20legislatures%E2%80%94California%2C%20Colorado,benefits%20for%20certain%20unauthorized%20immigrant

National Education Association. (2006). *Strengthening the learning environment: A school employee's guide to lesbian, gay, bisexual, and transgender issues* (2nd ed.).

National Human Trafficking Hotline. (n.d.) *Recognizing the signs.* https://humantraffickinghotline.org/human-trafficking/recognizing-signs

National Institute on Drug Abuse. (2021). *Percentage of adolescents reporting drug use decreased significantly in 2021 as the COVID-19 pandemic endured.* https://www.drugabuse.gov/news-events/news-releases/2021/12/percentage-of-adolescents-reporting-drug-use-decreased-significantly-in-2021-as-the-covid-19-pandemic-endured

National PTA. (2016). *Position statement: positive school discipline.* https://www.pta.org/home/advocacy/ptas-positions/Individual-Position-Statements/Position-Statement-Positive-School-Discipline

National School Boards Association. (2011, November 10). *Sua Sponte: NSBA files amicus brief urging Supreme Court to provide guidance on off-campus online speech.* https://www.nsba.org/Advocacy/Legal-Advocacy/Legal-Briefs-and-Guides

National School Boards Association. (2020a). *Protections for LGBTQ Employees and Students after Bostock v. Clayton County.* https://www.nsba.org/-/media/NSBA/File/nsba-protections-for-lgbtq-employees-and-students-guide-2020.pdf

National School Boards Association. (2020b, September). *The key work of school boards* (4th ed.).

National Women's Law Center (2017). *Stopping school pushout for girls who are pregnant or parenting.* https://nwlc.org/wp-content/uploads/2017/04/Final_nwlc_Gates_PregParenting.pdf

National Women's Law Center. (2021, April 2). *100 school districts: A call to action for school districts across the country to address sexual harassment through inclusive policies and practice.* https://nwlc.org/resource/100-school-districts-a-call-to-action-for-school-districts-across-the-country-to-address-sexual-harassment-through-inclusive-policies-and-practices/

National Women's Law Center. (2022, March 2). *NWLC joins ACLU amicus brief in support of student survivors.* https://www2.ed.gov/about/offices/list/ocr/docs/202107-qa-titleix.pdf

NBC News (2019). Oakland Educators Accused of Falsifying Transcripts to Boost Students' Grades and Graduation Rates. Retrieved on April 12, 2022 from https://www.nbcbayarea.com/news/local/oakland-high-school-accused-of-falsifying-transcripts-to-boost-students-grades/1959637/

NBC News. (2020, October 30). *Lori Loughlin begins 2-month prison sentence in college admissions scandal.* https://www.nbcnews.com/news/us-news/lori-loughlin-begins-2-month-prison-sentence-college-admissions-scandal-n1245434

Neem, J. N. (2017). *Democracy's schools: The rise of public education in America.* Johns Hopkins University Press.

Neighmond, P. (2020, May 17). Home but not safe, some LGBTQ young people face rejection from families in lockdown. *National Public Radio.* https://www.npr.org/sections/health-shots/2020/05/17/856090474/home-but-not-safe-some-lgbtq-young-people-face-rejection-from-families-in-lockdo

New Hampshire Regulatory Statutes (2004). H.R.S.A. 193-F:3(II).

Newman, B. M., & Newman, P. R. (2012). *Development through life: A psychological approach* (11th ed). Wadsworth Cengage Learning.

Newport Academy (2021). *The most dangerous apps for teenagers.* https://www.newportacademy.com/resources/well-being/dangerous-apps-for-teens/

New York City Department of Education. (2022). *Reproductive health: Connecting Adolescents to Comprehensive Healthcare Program (CATCH).* https://www.schools.nyc.gov/school-life/health-and-wellness/staying-healthy/other-health-topics

New York Times. (2003, July 18). National briefing | South: Arkansas: Gay student settles suit. *The New York Times.* https://www.nytimes.com/2003/07/18/us/national-briefing-south-arkansas-gay-student-settles-suit.html

Nguon v. Wolf, 517 F. Supp. 2d 1177 (C.D. Cal. 2007).

Nicholson v. Williams, 205 F.R.D. 92 (E.D. NY 2001).

No Child Left Behind Act of 2001, 20 U.S.C. § 6301 (2002).

Nolo (2021). Standard of care. *Nolo legal dictionary.* https://www.nolo.com/dictionary/standard-of-care-term.html

Norris, M. L. (2022, February 28). Opinion: The maddeningly limited vision of Ketanji Brown Jackson's guidance counselor. *The Washington Post.* https://www.washingtonpost.com/opinions/2022/02/28/ketanji-brown-jackson-guidance-counselor/

North Carolina Gen. Stat. § 8-53.4 (2004).

North Dakota Century Code § 31-01-06.1 (2003).

Numngern, P. (2017). *The concurrent liability in contract and tort under U.S. and English law: To what extent plaintiff is entitled to recover for damages under tort claim?* Maurer School of Law, Indiana University. https://www.repository.law.indiana.edu/cgi/viewcontent.cgi?article=1047&context=etd

O'Brien, J. (2020, August 20). 'Get over yourselves': High school counselor can't get job back after Facebook comment goes viral. *Legal Newsline.* https://legalnewsline.com/stories/549197526-get-over-yourselves-high-school-counselor-can-t-get-job-back-after-facebook-comment-goes-viral

O'Connor, S. D., & Supreme Court of the United States. (1987). *U.S. Reports: United States v. Kozminski, 487 U.S. 931.* Library of Congress. https://www.loc.gov/item/usrep487931/

Oehrtman, P. (2018). *School counselors and intra/interprofessional collaboration: A grounded theory study on school counselors' utilization of intra/interprofessional collaboration and its perceived impact on student success.* ProQuest Dissertations Publishing.

Office of Juvenile Justice and Delinquency Prevention. (2012). *Aftercare.* http://www.ojjdp.gov/mpg/progTypesAftercare.aspx

Office of Special Education. (2020). *OSEP fast facts: Black or African American children with disabilities.* U.S. Department of Education. https://sites.ed.gov/idea/osep-fast-facts-black-or-african-american-children-with-disabilities-20/

Otto v. Boca Raton, 9:18-cv-80771-RLR (D.C. 2017).

Owasso Independent School Dist. v. Falvo, 534 U.S. 426 (2002) 233 F.3d 1203.

Pacer v. White, 2006 U.S. Dist. LEXIS 47955.

Page, Petitioner v. Rotterdam-Mohonasen Central School District et al., respondents, Supreme Court of New York, 109 Misc. 2d 1049; 441 N.Y.S. 2d 323 (June 3, 1981).

Paradice, D. (2017). An analysis of U.S. school shooting data (1840-2015). *Education, 138*(2), 135–144.

Parents against abuse in school v. Williamsport Area School District, 594 A.2d 796 (Pa. Commw. Ct. 1991).

Parents for Privacy v. Barr, No. 18-35708 (9th Cir. 2020).

Parker v. Hurley, 514 F.3d 87; 2008 U.S. App. LEXIS 2070.

Parrott, J. (2001, July 9). Are advisors risking lawsuits for misadvising students? *The Mentor: An Academic Advising Journal, 3.* https://journals.psu.edu/mentor/article/view/61720

Patrick, K., Socal, A. R., & Morgan, I. (2020). Inequities in advanced coursework. *The Education Trust.* https://edtrust.org/resource/inequities-in-advanced-coursework

Payne, S. T., & Elliott, D. S. (2011). Safe2Tell®: An anonymous, 24/7 reporting system for preventing school violence. *New Directions for Youth Development, 129,* 103–111. https://doi.org/10.1002/yd.390

Petrowski, N., Cappa, C., Pereira, A., Mason, H., & Daban, R. A. (2021). Violence against children during COVID-19: Assessing and understanding change in use of helplines. *Child Abuse & Neglect*, 116, 104757. https://10.1016/j.chiabu.2020.104757

Peterson, C., Florence, C., & Klevens, J. (2018). The economic burden of child maltreatment in the United States, 2015. *Child Abuse & Neglect*, *86*, 178–183. https://doi.org/10.1016/j.chiabu.2018.09.018

Pew Research Center. (2021). *The state of online harassment*. https://www.pewresearch.org/internet/2021/01/13/the-state-of-online-harassment/

PFLAG. (2005). *From our house to the schoolhouse*. pflag.org/page.aspx?pid=358

Picarella v. Terrizzi, 893 F. Supp. 1292 (Pa. 1995).

Pickering v. Board of Education, 391 US Supp. 563 (1968).

Plyler v. Doe, 457 US 202 (1982).

Polaris Project. (2022). *The Polaris Project*. https://www.thepolarisproject.org/

Pollack v. Cruz 296 So. 3d 453 (Fla. Dist. Ct. App. 2020).

Pollack, W. S., Modzelesky, W., & Rooney, G. (2008). *Prior knowledge of potential school-based violence: Information students learn may prevent a targeted attack*. U.S. Secret Service and U.S. Department of Education. http://www.secretservice.gov/ntac/bystander_study.pdf

Port Washington Teachers' Association v. Board of Education of the Port Washington Union Free School District, 361 F. Supp. 2d 69, 81 (E.D.N.Y. 2005).

Pottiger, M. (2022, February 21). Here's what you need to know about critical race theory. *Chicago Defender*. https://chicagodefender.com/heres-what-you-need-to-know-about-critical-race-theory-2/

Potoczniak, D., Crosbie-Burnett, M., & Saltzburg, N. (2009). Experiences regarding coming out to parents among African American, Hispanic, and White gay, lesbian, bisexual, transgender, and questioning adolescents. *Journal of Gay & Lesbian Social Services*, *21*(2–3), 189–205. https://doi.org/10.1080/10538720902772063

Protection of Pupil Rights Amendment Statute: 20 U.S.C. § 1232h. Regulations: 34 CFR Part 98.

Prasath, P. R., Lindinger-Sternart, S., & Duffey, T. L. (2021). Counselors as organizational leaders: Exploring parallels of servant leadership and professional counseling. *Journal of Counselor Leadership and Advocacy*, *8*(2), 146–156. https://doi.org/10.1080/2326716X.2021.1904460

Primary & Secondary Sources. (2012). *Journal of Law and Education*, *41*(1), 223–235.

Prober, M. (2005). Please don't tell my parents. *Brooklyn Law Review*, *71*(1), 557–587. https://brooklynworks.brooklaw.edu/blr

Prosser, W. (1971). *The law of torts*. West Publishing Co.

Public Justice. (2019). *Jury verdicts and settlements in bullying cases*. https://www.publicjustice.net/wp-content/uploads/2019/04/2019.04.22-Spring-2019-Edition-Bullying-Verdicts-and-Settlements-Final-1.pdf

Pullen Sansfaçon, A., Temple-Newhook, J., Suerich-Gulick, F., Feder, S., Lawson, M. L., Ducharme, J., Ghosh, S., Holmes, C., & Stories of Gender-Affirming Care Team (2019). The experiences of gender diverse and trans children and youth considering and initiating medical interventions in Canadian gender-affirming speciality clinics. *The International Journal of Transgenderism, 20*(4), 371–387. http://jeunestransyouth.ca/wp-content/uploads/2019/11/Parents-Journey-CIHR-care-and-acceptance-final-accepted-manuscript.pdf

Quilloin v. Walcott, 434 U.S. 246 (1978).

Rammell, J. (2020). An uncertain balance: Student privacy rights in a dangerous world. *New Mexico Law Review*, *50*(2), 223–234. https://digitalrepository.unm.edu/nmlr/vol50/iss2/3

Rankin v. McPherson, 483 U.S. 378 (1987).

Ratts, M. J., & Greenleaf, A. T. (2017). Multicultural and social justice counseling competencies: A leadership framework for professional school counselors. *Professional School Counseling, 21*(1b). https://doi.org/10.1177/2156759X18773582

Ratts, M. J., & Greenleaf, A. T. (2018). Counselor–advocate–scholar model: Changing the dominant discourse in counseling. *Journal of Multicultural Counseling & Development, 46*(2), 78–96. https://doi.org/10.1002/jmcd.12094

Ray, R. & Gibbons, A., 2021. *Why are states banning critical race theory?* Brookings. https://www.brookings.edu/blog/fixgov/2021/07/02/why-are-states-banning-critical-race-theory/

Reid, K. (2001, May 2). Iowa's high court holds counselors liable. *Education Week*. http://www.edweek.org/ew/articles/

Remley, T. P., Jr., & Herlihy, B. (2019). *Ethical, legal, and professional issues in counseling* (6th ed.). Pearson.

Repa, B. K. (2012, February). Bullycide prompts new law. *California Lawyer*. http://www.callawyer.com/Clstory.cfm?eid=920434

Rich, A. (2017, February 17). *Quote of the day*. https://www.idlehearts.com/1700554/when-someone-with-the-authority-of-a-teacher-say-describes-the-world

Richardson v. Braham, 125 Neb. 142, 249 N.W. 557 (1933).

Ricker v. Board of Education of Millard County School District, 16 Utah 2d 106, 396 P.2d 416 (1964).

Roberts, A. L., Rosario, M., Corliss, H. L., Koenen, K. C., & Austin, S. B. (2012). Childhood gender nonconformity: A risk indicator for childhood abuse and posttraumatic stress in youth. *Pediatrics, 129*(3), 410–417. https://doi.org/10.1542/peds.2011-1804

Roberts, G. (2003, December 4). Franklin counselors play down district reprimand. *Seattle Post-Intelligencer.* http://www.seattlepi.com/local/article/Franklin-counselors-play-down-district-reprimand-1131370.php#ixzz289R5bZZp

Robers, S., Zhang, J., & Truman, J. (2020). *Indicators of school crime and safety: 2019* (NCES 2012-002/NCJ 236021). National Center for Education Statistics, U.S. Department of Education, and Bureau of Justice Statistics, Office of Justice Programs, U.S. Department of Justice. http://nces.ed.gov/pubsearch/pubsinfo.asp?pubid=2012002

Roche, R., Hutchison, B., & Lemberger-Truelove, M. E. (2020). Historicity in advocating student-within-environment: Being a socially just school counselor. *The Journal of Humanistic Counseling, 59*(3), 173–187. https://doi.org/10.1002/johc.12143

Rodriguez, C. M., Lee, S. J., Ward, K. P., & Pu, D. F. (2021). The perfect storm: Hidden risk of child maltreatment during the COVID-19 pandemic. *Child Maltreatment, 26*(2), 139–151. https://10.1177/1077559520982066

Rogers v. Christina School Dist., 2012 WL 1415623, at *6 (Del.Super., Jan. 18, 2012).

Rogers v. Christina Sch. Dist., C.A. No. N10C-07-060 JRJ (Del. Super. Ct. Jan. 18, 2012).

Rowell, L. L., McBride, M. C., & Nelson-Leaf, J. (1996). The role of the school counselor in confronting peer sexual harassment. *The School Counselor, 43*(3), 196–207. http://www.jstor.org/stable/23901878

Ruiz, M., Peters, M. L., & Sawyer, C. (2018) Principals' and counselors' lens of the school counselor's role. *Journal of Professional Counseling: Practice, Theory & Research, 45*(1), 1–16. https://doi.org/10.1080/15566382.2019.1569321

Rusert, T., McLaughlin, J., Rasich, M., & Reeves, C. (2022). *RECs that change lives.* National Association for College Admission Counseling. https://www.nacacnet.org/news--publications/journal-of-college-admission/recs-that-change-lives/

Ryan, C., Huebner, D., Diaz, R. M., & Sanchez, J. (2009). Family rejection as a predictor of negative health outcomes in white and Latino lesbian, gay and bisexual young adults. *Pediatrics, 123*(1), 346–352. http://pediatrics.aappublications.org/content/123/1/346.full

Sabella, R. A. (2021, March 1). *Resources and downloads.* https://www.guardingkids.com/

Sabella, R. A., & Isaacs, M. (2018). Tech access, privacy and literacy. *Colorado School Counselor Association.* https://www.schoolcounselor.org/newsletters/december-2018/tech-access,-privacy-and-literacy?st=CO

Sain v. Cedar Rapids Community School District, 626 N.W. 2nd 115 (Iowa 2001).

Sallay, D., & Vance, A. (2020, March 27). *FAQs: The protection of pupil rights amendment.* https://studentprivacycompass.org/faqs-ppra/

Sanchez, R. (2000). District, parents settle over abortion. *Philly.com.*

Sanders, T. (2010, April 14). Clay school counselor's employer not told about student-sex probe before hiring. *Jacksonville News.*

Sanger, C., & Willemsen, E. (1992). Minor changes: Emancipating minors in modern times. *University of Michigan Journal of Law Reform, 25*, 239–355.

Sarla, G. S. (2020). Texting or calling: A comparison. *Journal of Open Source Developments*, 7(2), 18–21.

Savage, T. A., & Harley, D. A. (2009). A place at the blackboard: Including lesbian, gay, bisexual, transgender, intersex, and queer/questioning issues in the education process. *Multicultural Education, 16*(4), 2–9. https://doi.org/10.1080/00918369.2015.1112583

Savitz-Romer, M., Rowan-Kenyon, H. T., Nicola, T. P., Alexander, E., & Carroll, S. (2021). When the kids are not alright: School counseling in the time of COVID-19. *American Educational Research Association.* https://doi.org/10.1177/23328584211033600

Sawchuk, S. (2021). What is critical race theory and why is it under attack? *Education Week.* https://www.edweek.org/leadership/what-is-critical-race-theory-and-why-is-it-under-attack/2021/05

Scheidegger, K. (2008, May 5). "Exonerated," not necessarily innocent. *Crime and Consequences.* https://www.crimeandconsequences.com/crimblog/2008/05/exonerated-not-necessarily-inn.html

Scott, E. (2001). The legal construction of adolescence. *Hofstra Law Review, 29*(547), 547598. http://www.hofstra.edu/PDF/law_lawrev_esscott.pdf

Scott v. Stevens Point Area Public School District, 650 N.W.2d 560 (Wisconsin 2003).

Schott v Wenk. 136 S.Ct. 792. (2016).

SCOTUS blog. (2017). *Gloucester County School Board v. GG.* http://www.scotusblog.com/case-files/cases/gloucester-county-school-board-v-g-g/

Seelye, K. Q. (2018, May 07). M.I.T. is not responsible for student's suicide, court rules. *The New York Times.* https://www.nytimes.com/2018/05/07/us/mit-student-suicide-lawsuit.html

Sensoy, G., & Ikiz, F. E. (2019, May). *Ethics in school counseling: 20 years.* Presented at 1st International Science, Education, Art, & Technology Symposium. Dokuz Eylul University, Izmir.

Seth's Law of 2012, California Assembly Bill (AB) 9, Cal. Stat. Ch. 723 (2012)

Severson, K. (2012, October 14). Christian group finds gay agenda in an anti-bullying day. *The New York Times*. https://www.nytimes.com/2012/10/15/us/seeing-a-homosexual-agenda-christian-group-protests-an-anti-bullying-program.html

Shah, N. (2012, October 18). Conservative group pressures schools to nix 'Mix-It-Up' Day. *Education Week's blogs: Rules for Engagement*. http://blogs.edweek.org/edweek/rulesforengagement/2012/10/conservative_group_pressures_schools_to_nix_mix-it-up_day.html

Sheth, D. Shapiro, I., & Berry, T. (2021). *C1.G. v. Siegfried*. Cato Institute. https://www.cato.org/legal-briefs/c1g-v-siegfried

Shore Regional High School Board of Education v. P.S., No. 03-3438 (3d Cir. August 20, 2004).

Shure, L., West-Olatunji, C., & Cholewa, B. (2019). Investigating the relationship between school counselor recommendations and student cultural behavioral styles. *Journal of Negro Education, 88*(4), 454–466. https://doi.org/10.7709/jnegroeducation.88.4.0454

Silver, J., Simons, A., & Craun, S. (2018). A study of the pre-attack behaviors of active shooters in the United States between 2000–2013. Federal Bureau of Investigation, U.S. Department of Justice.

Simons, J. D., Brian, H., & Bahr, M. W. (2017). School counselor advocacy for lesbian, gay, and bisexual students: Intentions and practice. *Professional School Counseling*. https://doi.org/10.5330/1096-2409-20.1a.29

Singh, C. K. S., Singh, T. S. M., Abdullah, N. Y., Moneyam, S., Ismail, M. R., Ong, E. T., Karupayah, T., Chenderan, K., Singh, M. K. R., & Singh, J. K. S. (2020). Rethinking English language teaching through telegram, whats app, google classroom and zoom. *Systematic Reviews in Pharmacy*, *11*(11), 45–54. https://doi.org/10.31838/srp.2020.11.9

Sink, C., Edwards, C., & Eppler, C. (2012). *School based group counseling*. Brooks/Cole.

Skiba, R. J., Arredondo, M. I., & Williams, N. T. (2014, November 30). More than a metaphor: the contribution of exclusionary discipline to a school-to-prison pipeline, equity and excellence in education. *Equity & Excellence in Education*. 47(4), 546–564. https://doi.org/10.1080/10665684.2014.958965

Solomon, J. (2012, August 30). Counselor at Jovon Robinson's high school wouldn't say why she changed a player's grade. *The Birmingham News*. http://www.al.com/sports/index.ssf/2012/08/counselor_at_jovon_robinsons_h.html

Southern Poverty Law Center (2021). Costly and cruel: How misuse of the Baker Act harms 37,000 Florida children each year. https://www.splcenter.org/sites/default/files/com_special_report_baker_act_costly_and_cruel.pdf

Smead, R. (1995). *Skills and techniques for group work with children and adolescents*. Research Press.

Smith, M., Robinson, L., & Sega, J. (2012). Helping someone with an eating disorder. *HelpGuide*. http://www.helpguide.org/mental/eating_disorder_self_help.htm

Smith v. The School Board of Orange County, Court of Appeals of Florida, 5th District, 642 So. 2d 577; 1994 Fla. August 12, 1994.

Snyder v. Millersville, WL 5093140 (ED Pa 2008).

Snyder v. Phelps, 562 U.S. 443 (2011).

South Dakota Code § 19-13-21.1, Rule 508.1 (2003).

Southern Poverty Law Center, the Florida Chapter of the American Academy of Pediatrics, Florida Student. (2008). Spanierman v. Hughes, 576 F.Supp.2d 292.

Sparks, S. D. (2022, February 1). Bullying dropped as students spent less time in in-person classes during pandemic. *Education Week.* https://www.edweek.org/leadership/bullying-dropped-as-students-spent-less-time-in-in-person-classes-during-pandemic/2022/01

St. George, D. (2011). Suicide turns attention to Fairfax discipline procedures. *The Washington Post.* https://www.washingtonpost.com/local/education/suicide-turns-attention-to-fairfax-discipline-procedures/2011/02/14/AB9UtxH_story.html

St. George, D. (2013). Appeal for Maryland 7-year-old suspended for nibbling pastry into shape of a gun. *The Washington Post.* http://articles.washingtonpost.com/2013-03-14/local/37711264_1_anne-arundel-schools-spokesman-pastry-gun

Stadler, H. A. (1986). Making hard choices: Clarifying controversial ethical issues. *Counseling & Human Development, 19*, 1–10.

Stadler, H. A. (1990). Confidentiality. In B. Herlihy & I. B. Golden (Eds.), *AACD ethical standards-casebook* (4th ed., 102–110). American Association for Counseling and Development.

Steeg, S., Quinlivan, L., Nowland, R., Carroll, R., Casey, D., Clements, C., Cooper, J., Davies, L., Knipe, D., Ness, J., O'Connor, R. C., Hawton, K., Gunnell, D., & Kapur, N. (2018, April 25). Accuracy of risk scales for predicting repeat self-harm and suicide: A multicentre, population-level cohort study using routine clinical data. *BMC Psychiatry BioMed Central.* https://bmcpsychiatry.biomedcentral.com/articles/10.1186/s12888-018-1693-z

Steele, T. (2016). Counseling: Meeting student needs online. In J. Scarborough & R. Ravaglia (Eds.), *Perspectives from the disciplines.* CSLI Publications. https://web.stanford.edu/group/cslipublications/cslipublications/site/1575867400.shtml

Steele, T., Stone, C., & Nuckolds, G. (2017, March). *School counselors and cyberspace survey* [Unpublished manuscript].

Stevens, H. (2019, October 1). A 16-year-old boy died by suicide after his intimate messages to another boy were made public. What some experts say parents need to know about sexting. *Chicago Tribune.* https://www.chicagotribune.com/columns/heidi-stevens/ct-heidi-stevens-tuesday-channing-smith-suicide-intimate-texts-1001-20191001-ngtjty6jpfdhxcyiv662ucts2q-story.html

Steward, D. L. (2019). Envisioning possibilities for innovations in higher education research on race and ethnicity. *Journal Committed to Social Change on Race and Ethnicity, 5*(1), 7–32. https://journals.shareok.org/jcscore/article/download/74/50/

Stone, C. (2002). Negligence in academic advising and abortion counseling: Courts rulings and implications. *Professional School Counselor: Special Issue on Legal and Ethical Issues in School Counselor, 6*(1). Negligence in academic advising and abortion counseling: courts rulings and implications. (Special issue: legal and ethical issues in school counseling). - Free Online Library

Stone, C. (2003a). Counselors as advocates for lesbian, gay, and bisexual youth: A call for equity and action. *Journal of Multicultural Counseling and Development, 31*(2), 143–155. https://doi.org/10.1002/j.2161-1912.2003.tb00539.x

Stone, C. (2003b). Leadership and advocacy in personal/social development: Sexual harassment. In R. Perusse & G. Goodnough (Eds.), *Leadership and advocacy in school counseling* (1st ed., 353–377). Brooks/Cole.

Stone, C. (2005). *Steps: Solutions to ethical problems in schools* [Conference presentation]. National High School Coaches Association. https://nhsca.wildapricot.org/resources/Documents/Steps%20rev.pdf

Stone, C. (2017a, April). *Bullying and cyberbullying* [Unpublished raw data].
Stone, C. (2017b, February). *School counselors and individual and group counseling survey* [Unpublished raw data].
Stone, C. (2017c, February). *School counselors and negligence and obligations to the courts survey* [Unpublished raw data].
Stone, C. (2017d, February). *School counselors and professionalism* [Unpublished raw data].
Stone, C. (2017e, March). *School counselors and sexually active students* [Unpublished raw data].
Stone, C. (2020, May 1). Issues and lessons emerging from COVID-19. *ASCA School Counselor*. https://www.schoolcounselor.org/Magazines/May-June-2020/Issues-and-Lessons-Emerging%C2%A0-from-COVID-19
Stone, C. (2021a). School counselors and individualized educational program [Unpublished raw data].
Stone, C. (2021b). *Protection of Pupil Rights Amendment (PPRA) survey* [Unpublished raw data].
Stone, C. (2021c) *Whiplash in Title IX*. American School Counselor Association. https://www.schoolcounselor.org/Magazines/November-December-2020/Whiplash-in-Title-IX
Stone, C. (2022a, January). *School counselors and child abuse survey* [Unpublished raw data].
Stone, C. (2022b, February). *School counselors and Family Educational Rights and Privacy Act survey* [Unpublished raw data].
Stone, C. (2022c, January). *School counselors advocating for LGBTQ students* [Unpublished raw data].
Stone, C. (2022d, January). *Threats of violence* [Unpublished raw data].
Stone, C., & Dahir, C. (2004). *School counselors and accountability: A measure of student success*. Merrill Prentice-Hall.
Stone, C., & Glicksteen, S. B. (2012, December). *American School Counselor Association members weigh in on Ward v. Wilbanks* [Unpublished manuscript].
Stone, C., & Glicksteen, S. B. (2022, March). *School counselors and LGBT* [Unpublished manuscript].
Stone, C., & Isaacs, M. (2002a). Confidentiality with minors: The effects of Columbine on counselor attitudes regarding breaching confidentiality. *The Journal of Educational Research, 96*(2), 140–150.
Stone, C., & Isaacs, M. (2002b). Involving students in violence prevention: Anonymous reporting and the need to promote and protect confidences. *National Association of Secondary School Principals Bulletin, 86*(633), 54–65. https://doi.org/10.1177/019263650208663305
Stone, C., & Martin, P. (2004). School counselors using data driven decision making. *ASCA School Counselor, 41*(3), 10–17. https://www.schoolcounselor.org/Magazines/May-June-2004/Equity-of-Services-and-Dual-Relationships
Stone, C., Rock, W, & Steele, T. (2020 March 23). *Ethical considerations: School counseling in a virtual setting* (pt. 1) [Webinar]. American School Counselor Association.
Stone, C., & Zirkel, P. A. (2010). School counselor advocacy: When law and ethics may collide. *Professional School Counseling, 13*(4), 244–247. https://doi.org/10.1177/2156759X1001300405

Stone, C., & Zirkel, P. (2012). Student suicide: Legal and ethical implications. *ASCA School Counselor, 49*(5), 24–30.

Strear, M. M. (2017). Forecasting an inclusive future: School counseling strategies to deconstruct educational heteronormativity. *Professional School Counseling, 20*(1a). https://doi.org/10.5330/1096-2409-20.1a.47

Sturgis, C. (2011, December 8). My name is Ceara Sturgis, and I am not a troublemaker. *ACLU Blog of Rights.* https://www.aclu.org/blog/lgbtq-rights/lgbtq-youth/wear-dress-or-else

Substance Abuse and Mental Health Services Administration. (2019). *Ready, set, go, review: Screening for behavioral health risk in schools.* Office of the Chief Medical Officer. https://www.samhsa.gov/sites/default/files/ready_set_go_review_mh_screening_in_schools_508.pdf

Sugg v. Albuquerque Public School District, 988 P.2d 311 (NMCA; 1999).

Suler, J. (2004). The online disinhibition effect. *CyberPsychology & Behavior, 7,* 321–326.

Surprenant, K. S., (2020, March 30). *FERPA and virtual learning during COVID-19.* U.S. Department of Education, Student Privacy Policy Office Privacy Technical Assistance Center. https://studentprivacy.ed.gov/sites/default/files/resource_document/file/FERPAandVirtualLearning.pdf

Swedo, E., Idaikkadar, N., Leemis, R., Dias, T., Radhakrishnan, L., & Stein Z. (2020). Trends in U.S. emergency department visits related to suspected or confirmed child abuse and neglect among children and adolescents aged <18 years before and during the COVID-19 pandemic—United States, January 2019–September 2020. *Morbidity and Mortality Weekly Report, 69*(49),1841–1847. https://www.cdc.gov/mmwr/volumes/69/wr/mm6949a1.htm

Swinton, D. C. (2005). Criminal liability, failure to report child abuse, and school personnel: An examination of history, policy and caselaw. *Education Law & Policy Forum, 1,* 1–28. http://www.educationlawconsortium.org/forum/2005/papers/swinton.pdf

Tarasoff v. Board of Regents of California, 551 P.2d 334 (Cal.1976).

Terando, J. J. (2011, March). Defining the scope of a school's duty to supervise students. *Los Angeles Lawyer.* www.lacba.org

Texas Family Code § 261.201 (2015).

Texas Statute Pen Code § 21.12. https://www.statutes.legis.state.tx.us/docs/pe/htm/pe.21.htm

Texas v. Johnson, 491 US 397 (1989).

Theoharis, M. (2020, September 8). Teen sexting. *Criminal Defense Lawyer.* https://www.criminaldefenselawyer.com/crime-penalties/juvenile/sexting.htm

Thomsen, J. (2019, August 12). *A look at the history of state school safety legislation in the last 2 decades* (Ed. note). https://ednote.ecs.org/a-look-at-the-history-of-state-school-safety-legislation-in-the-last-2-decades/

Tingley v. Ferguson, 3:21-cv-05359-RJB (W.D. Wash. Aug. 30, 2021).

Tinker v. Des Moines Independent Community School District (393 U.S. 503, 1969).

Tishler, C. L., Reiss, N. S., & Rhodes, A. R. (2007). Suicidal behavior in children younger than twelve: a diagnostic challenge for emergency department personnel. *Academic Emergency Medicine: Official Journal of the Society for Academic Emergency Medicine, 14*(9), 810–818. https://doi.org/10.1197/j.aem.2007.05.014

Title IX of the Education Amendments of 1972, 20 U.S.C. §§ 1681-1688 (1994).

Trevor Project. (n.d.). *Bullying and suicide risk among LGBTQ youth.* https://www.thetrevorproject.org/research-briefs/bullying-and-suicide-risk-among-lgbtq-youth/

Trevor Project (2021). *The Trevor Project's 2021 national survey on LGBTQ youth mental health.* https://www.thetrevorproject.org/wp-content/uploads/2021/05/The-Trevor-Project-National-Survey-Results 2021.pdf

Trice-Black, S., Riechel, M. E. K., & Shillingford, M. A. (2013). School counselors' constructions of student confidentiality. *Journal of School Counseling, 11*(12), 1–46. http://jsc.montana.edu/articles/v11n12.pdf

Trilling, D. (2020, October). Why is the UK government suddenly targeting critical race theory? *The Guardian.* https://www.theguardian.com/commentisfree/2020/oct/23/uk-critical-race-theory-trump-conservatives-structural-in

Tucker, C. J., Finkelhor, D., & Turner, H. (2021). Exposure to parent assault on a sibling as a childhood adversity. *Child Abuse & Neglect, 122.* https://doi.org/10.1016/j.chiabu.2021.105310

UNICEF. (2022, February). *Cyberbullying: What is it and how to stop it.* https://www.unicef.org/end-violence/how-to-stop-cyberbullying

Uniform Law Commission. (2012). *Marriage and Divorce Act, model summary.*

U.S. Citizenship and Immigration Services. (2021). *I-821D, Consideration of deferred action for childhood arrivals.* https://www.uscis.gov/i-821d

U.S. Constitution, Amendment XIV. (20 U.S.C. §§ 1681 et seq. (2006); 34 C.F.R. § 106.40).

U.S. Department of Education. (n.d.). *Protecting student privacy.* https://studentprivacy.ed.gov/content/ppra

U.S. Department of Education. (2021a). Federal Register Notice of Interpretation: Enforcement of Title IX of the Education Amendments of 1972 with Respect to Discrimination Based on Sexual Orientation and Gender Identity in Light of Bostock v. Clayton County. https://www2.ed.gov/about/offices/list/ocr/docs/202106-titleix-noi.pdf

U.S. Department of Education. (2021b). *Supporting transgender youth in school.* https://www2.ed.gov/about/offices/list/ocr/docs/ed-factsheet-transgender-202106.pdf

U.S. Department of Education. (2021c). *U.S. Department of Education Confirms Title IX Protects Students from Discrimination Based on Sexual Orientation and Gender Identity.* https://www.ed.gov/news/press-releases/us-department-education-confirms-title-ix-protects-students-discrimination-based-sexual-orientation-and-gender-identity

U.S. Department of Education. (2022). Statement from U.S. Secretary of Education Miguel Cardona on the Florida State Legislature's Parental Rights in Education Bill. https://www.ed.gov/news/press-releases/statement-us-secretary-education-miguel-cardona-florida-state-legislatures-parental-rights-education-bill

U.S Department of Education, Federal Student Aid Department. (2021). *Don't get scammed on your way to college.* https://studentaid.gov/sites/default/files/dont-get-scammed.pdf

U.S. Department of Education, Office for Civil Rights. (2013). *Supporting the academic success of pregnant and parenting students under Title IX of the Education Amendments of 1972.* https://www2.ed.gov/about/offices/list/ocr/docs/pregnancy.html#_Toc2

U.S. Department of Education National Center for Education Statistics. (2020). *School survey on crime and safety: 2017–18 Public-Use Data File User's Manual* https://nces.ed.gov/pubs2020/2020054.pdf

U.S. Department of Education, Office of Elementary & Secondary Education. (2021). *Office of Safe and Healthy Students.* https://www2.ed.gov/about/offices/list/oese/oshs/oshsprograms.html

U.S. Department of Education, Student Privacy Policy Office. (2021). *A Parent's Guide to FERPA*. https://studentprivacy.ed.gov/resources/ferpa-general-guidance-parents

U.S. Department of Health and Human Services. (2019). *Child maltreatment*. Administration for Children and Families, Administration on Children, Youth and Families, Children's Bureau. https://www.acf.hhs.gov/sites/default/files/documents/cb/cm2019.pdf

U.S. Department of Health and Human Services. (2021a). *2.1A.1 CAPTA. Assurances and requirements, access to child abuse and neglect information, confidentiality.* https://www.acf.hhs.gov/cwpm/public_html/programs/cb/laws_policies/laws/cwpm/policy_dsp.jsp?citID=67

U.S. Department of Homeland Security. (2004). *Threat assessment in schools: A guide to managing threatening situations and to creating safe school climates*. http://www2.ed.gov/admins/lead/safety/edpicks.jhtml?src=In

U.S. Department of Justice. (2017, January 6). *Key legislation*. https://www.justice.gov/humantrafficking/key-legislation

U.S. Department of Justice. (2021). *Types of educational opportunities discrimination*. https://www.justice.gov/crt/types-educational-opportunities-discrimination

U.S. Department of Justice. (2022). *Dating violence*. https://www.justice.gov/ovw/dating-violence

U.S. Government Accountability Office. (2021). *Child welfare: Pandemic posed challenges, but also created opportunities for agencies to enhance future operations*. https://www.gao.gov/assets/gao-21-483.pdf

U.S. Secret Service. (2019). *Protecting America's schools: A U.S. Secret Service analysis of targeted school violence*. National Threat Assessment Center. https://www.secretservice.gov/sites/default/files/2020-04/Protecting_Americas_Schools.pdf

Valickas, A., Raišienė, A. G., & Rapuano, V. (2019). Planned happenstance skills as personal resources for students' psychological wellbeing and academic adjustment. *Sustainability, 11*(12), 3401. https://doi.org/10.3390/su11123401

Van der Bijl, C. (2018). Parental criminal responsibility for the misconduct of their children: A consideration. *Potchefstroom Electronic Law Journal, 21*(1), 1–21. https://doi.org/10.17159/1727-3781/2018/v21i0a1685

Veazey, K. (2012, August 30). Counselor wouldn't tell Memphis city schools why she changed player's grade. *The Commercial Appeal*. http://www.commercialappeal.com/news/2012/aug/30/counselor-wouldnt-tell-memphis-city-schools- why/

Veiga, C. (2019, January 18). Four takeaways from New York City's response to discrimination charges in specialized high schools lawsuit. *Chalkbeat*. https://ny.chalkbeat.org/2019/1/18/21106575/four-takeaways-from-new-york-city-s-response-to-discrimination-charges-in-specialized-high-schools-l

Villanueva v. San Marcos Consolidated Independent School Dist., Fifth Circuit, 07–19-2007. (2007). *AnyLaw*. https://www.anylaw.com/case/villanueva-v-san-marcos-consolidated-independent-school-dist/fifth-circuit/07-18-2007/74TnPmYBTlTomsSBwMq_

Villines, Z. (2021, March 15). What to know about internalized homophobia. *Medical News Today*. https://www.medicalnewstoday.com/articles/internalized-homophobia

Volokh, E. (2008, July 28). *Suppressions of homosexuality-related speech*. http://www.volokh.com/posts/1217288105.shtml

Wachter Morris, C. A., Wester, K. L., Jones, C. T., & Fantahun, S. (2021). School counselors and unified educator–counselor identity: A data-informed approach to suicide prevention. *Professional School Counseling, 24*(1b). https://doi.org/10.1177/2156759X211011909

Walsh, M. (2016). *Supreme court declines to take up case on mandatory reporters of child abuse.* http://blogs.edweek.org/edweek/school_law/2016/01/supreme_court_declines_to_take_2.html

Walsh v. Tehachapi Unified School District, 827 F. Supp. 2d 1107; 2011 U.S. Dist. LEXIS 125175.

Wang, K., Chen, Y., Zhang, J., & Oudekerk, B. A. (2020). *Indicators of school crime and safety: 2019* (NCES 2020-063/NCJ 254485). National Center for Education Statistics, U.S. Department of Education, and Bureau of Justice Statistics, Office of Justice Programs. U.S. Department of Justice. https://nces.ed.gov/pubs2020/2020063.pdf

Warbelow, S., Avant, C., & Kutney, C. (2020). *State Equality Index.* Human Rights Campaign Foundation. https://www.hrc.org/resources/state-equality-index

Ward v. Wilbanks, 667 F.3d 727 (2012).

Warner v. St. Bernard Parish School Board, 99 F.Supp.2d 748 (2000).

Watanabe, T. (2014). L.A. Unified fired lawyer who said girl could consent to sex with teacher. *Los Angeles Times.* hhttps://www.latimes.com/local/education/la-me-lausd-attorney-20141115-story.html

Welfel, E. R. (2016). *Ethics in counseling and psychotherapy* (6th ed.). Brooks/Cole.

WFTV Eyewitness News Report. (2016, August 11). Brevard County mental health counselor arrested for not reporting alleged abuse, police say. *U.S. News.* http:// www.wftv.com/news/local/brevard-county-mental-health-counselor-arrested-for-not- reporting-alleged-abuse-police-say/421553473

White County High School Peers v. White Co. School D, Civil Action No. 2:06-CV-29-WCO, (N.D. Ga. Jul. 14, 2006).

Wilder, C. (2018). Promoting the role of the school counselor. *Journal of Professional Counseling: Practice, Theory & Research, 45*(2), 60–68. https://doi.org/10.1080/15566382.2019.1646085

Williams, C., & Householder, M. (2021, December 14). Michigan school district sets new safety plan after shooting. *U.S. News.* https://www.usnews.com/news/us/articles/2021-12-14/parents-of-suspect-in-michigan-school-shooting-due-in-court

Williams Institute. (2017, February 22). *Media advisory: Fact sheet on guidance protecting over 350,000 transgender youth and young adults from discrimination.* https://williamsinstitute.law.ucla.edu/research/transgender-issues/media-advisory-fact- sheet-on-guidance-protecting-over-350000-transgender-youth-and-young-adults-from-discrimination/

Willis, S. P. (2004). Iowa school counselors had better get it right! *Iowa Law Review, 89,* 1093.

Winter, G. (2004, July 8). Wooing of guidance counselors is raising profiles and eyebrows. *The New York Times.* http://www.nytimes.com/2004/07/08/us/wooing-of-guidance-counselors-is-raising-profiles-and-eyebrows.html?pagewanted=all&src=pm

Wisconsin v. Yoder, 406 U.S. 205, 231-233 [**1172] (1972).

Wong, K. P., Bonn, G., Tam, C. L., & Wong, C. P. (2018). Preferences for online and/or face-to-face counseling among university students in Malaysia. *Frontiers in Psychology, 9.* https://doi.org/10.3389/fpsyg.2018.00064

Woodlock v. Orange Ulster B.O.C.E.S., 2006 WL 1738014 (S.D.N.Y. 2006).

Woodlock v. Orange Ulster B.O.C.E.S., 281 F. App'x. 66 (2d Cir. 2008).

Wooledge, S. (2012, March 11). Major victory in Anoka-Hennepin school district bullying lawsuit. *Daily Kos*. https://www.dailykos.com/stories/2012/03/11/1072927/-Major-victory-in-Anoka-Hennepin-school-district-bullying-lawsuit

Worden, L. (2012, March 8). State Supreme Court: Hart District can be held liable in molestation case. *SCV News*.com. http://scvnews.com/2012/03/08/state-supreme-court-hart-district-liable-in-2007-molestation/

Wu, S., Lin, T.-C., & Shih, J.-F. (2017). Examining the antecedents of online disinhibition. *Information Technology & People*. https://doi.org/10.1108/ITP-07-2015-0167

Wyke v. Polk County School Board, 137 F.3d 1292 (11th Cir. 1997).

Wyke v. Polk County School Bd., 898 F. Supp. 852 (M.D. Fla. 1995)

Wykes, S.L. (2005). Parents settle suit for alleged bullying by their children: Father faults them and school district for the two years of taunts his son endured. *San Jose Mercury News*. http://www.chron.com/disp/story.mpl/nation/3397491.html

Wyoming Mental Health Professions Practice Act, Wyoming Code § 33-38-113 (2004).

Young, E. L., Allen, M., & Ashbaker, B. Y. (n.d.). *Sexual harassment*. National Association of School Psychologists. http://www.nasponline.org/educators/ Sexual%20Harassment.pdf

Zamstein v. Marvasti, 240 Conn. 549, 692 A.2d 781 (1997).

Zapal, H. (2021, March 3). *State-by-state differences in sexting laws. Bark Parental Control App*. Bark. https://www.bark.us/blog/state-by-state-differences-in-sexting-laws/

Zirkel, P. (2001a). Ill advised. *Phi Delta Kappan, 83*, 98–99. https://doi.org/10.1177/003172170108300119

Zirkel, P. (2001b). A pregnant pause? *Phi Delta Kappan, 82*(7), 557–558. https://doi.org/10.1177/003172170108200717

Zirkel, P. (2001/2002, December/January). Decisions that have shaped U.S. education. *Principal Leadership, 59*, 6–12.

Zirkel, P. (2019). Liability for student suicide: An updated empirical analysis of the case law. *Communiqué, 48*(1), 1, 28, 30–31. https://eric.ed.gov/?q=law&ff1=subLegal+Responsibility&id=EJ1224882

Zirkel, P. (2020). An updated primer of special education law. *Teaching Exceptional Children, 52*(4), 261–265. https://doi.org/10.1177/0040059919878671

Zongrone, A. D., Truong, N. L., & Kosciw, J. G. (2020). *Erasure and resilience: The experiences of LGBTQ students of color, Latinx LGBTQ youth in U.S. schools* (17–18). GLSEN. https://www.glsen.org/research/latinx-lgbtq-students

Court Cases

D

E

F

G

H

J

K

L

M

N

O

P

Q

R

S

T

W

Z

Subject Index

A

B

C

D

E

F

G

H

I

L

M

N

O

P

R

S

T

Z

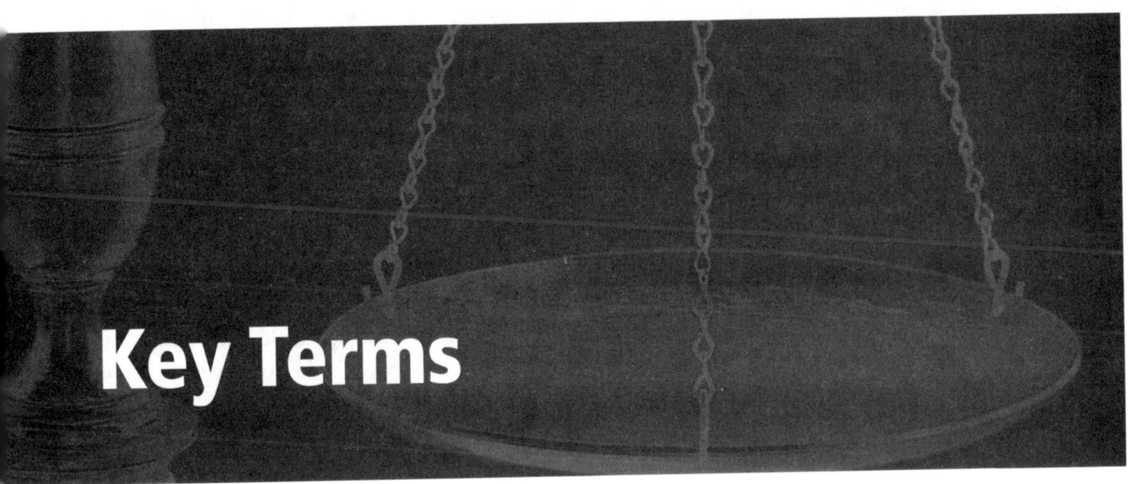

Key Terms

Abortion: termination of a pregnancy and expulsion of an embryo or fetus.

Addressing a known danger: a situation that is obviously harmful or has the potential for harm and, therefore, requires school officials to respond in a particular way.

Adversely stratified education opportunities: education opportunities that are unfavorably arranged in a school, especially unequal opportunities for historically disadvantaged students such as minority and low income students.

Advocacy: intervening on behalf of a particular student or group of students.

Age of Consent: the age minors can legally engage in sexual activity; age of consent varies from state to state.

***Amici Curiae* brief:** a legal opinion, testimony or learned treatise filed by a friend of the court who is neither defendant not plaintiff as a way to introduce concerns about the broader legal effects of a court decision that is not dependent solely on the parties directly involved in the case. For example, the American School Counselor Association has been *Amicus Curiae* (friend of the court) in *Amici Curiae* briefs involving cyber bullying.

Anonymous reporting: reporting of a situation without revealing the identity of the reporter; it is an effort to protect the identity of informants to encourage student reporting of dangerous situations in schools.

Anorexia: a disorder characterized by fear of becoming fat and refusal of food, leading to debility and even death.

ASCA Aspects: monthly publication by the American School Counselor Association. Each issue includes information about new projects, events, resources and more from ASCA.

ASCA SCENE: a networking site that is a professional meeting place for school counseling professionals to share and learn from each other.

Assigned sex: the sex that is assigned to an infant at birth.

Autonomy: promoting students' ability to choose their own direction.

Beneficence: promoting good for others. Ideally, counseling contributes to the growth and development of the student.

Biological sex: The condition or character of being female or male; the physiological, functional, and psychological differences that distinguish the female and the male.

Bisexuality: relating to or characterized by a tendency to direct sexual desire toward both sexes.

Blogs: a Web site that contains an online personal journal with reflections, comments, and often hyperlinks provided by the writer.

Breach: violation of the duty owed, such as confidentiality. Whether or not a breach occurred is based on reasonableness and the standard of care.

Breach of trust: a betrayal of a person's trust; breach of a student's confidence.

Bulimia: a serious eating disorder that is characterized by compulsive overeating usually followed by self-induced vomiting or laxative or diuretic abuse, and is often accompanied by guilt and depression.

Bystander: a person who observes a conflict, bullying, or other unacceptable behavior either minor or serious but the Bystander knows that the behavior is destructive or likely to make a bad situation worse but does not react positively.

Bullycide: term used to describe children/teens who were victims of bullying and became so emotionally distressed that they committed suicide.

Bullying: verbal or physical aggression demonstrated in words, actions or social exclusion intended to specifically hurt or harm another; the most common form of school violence.

Case law: laws pronounced by the courts.

Case notes: sole-possession records that act as memory aids or professional opinion or observation for the creator. They are to be kept separate from education records but may become education records when they are 1) shared with others in verbal or written form, 2) include information other than professional opinion or personal observations and/or 3) are made accessible to others.

Causal connection: connection between the school counselor's breach of duty and the injury the student suffered.

Challenging the status quo: stimulating change in conditions that are already established or currently in existence.

Child abuse: physical or psychological mistreatment of a child by his or her parents, guardians or other adults.

Child maltreatment: general term used to describe all forms of child abuse and neglect.

Child neglect: lack of care that risks or causes harm to a child, including lack of food, clothing, supervision or medical attention.

Child Protective Services: a constituted authority and agency in the state providing protection from harm to children and providing services to meet the needs of the child and family.

Chronological level: the level at which a student has reached based on actual age.

Cisgender: an individual whose gender self-perception matches the sex they were assigned at birth.

Civil law: the set of rules governing relations between persons.

Civil wrong: a wrong against another person that causes physical, emotional or monetary damage and for which the plaintiffs can seek compensation.

Classroom lessons: leading, advising and informing students on appropriate topics in a classroom setting.

Clear and imminent danger: now known as serious and foreseeable harm is a known or perceived harm to a student or others that has a risk of danger resulting in damage, injury and/or death if an action is not taken. School counselors consider in context their obligation to breach confidentiality and inform parents and administrators if a student indicates a serious and foreseeable harm to himself/herself or others.

Code of silence: a condition in effect when a person opts to withhold what is believed to be vital or important information voluntarily or involuntarily.

Common law: judge-made law based on legal precedents developed over hundreds of years; also referred to as the "body of general rules prescribing social conduct" and "unwritten" law.

Community standards: written and unwritten standards of behavior for a community, school counselors adhere to the written and unwritten prescribed behavioral norms of the community while working responsibly to change those standards that are detrimental to students.

Confidentiality in group counseling: confidentiality cannot be guaranteed in a group; school counselors use extraordinary care when putting young people together in groups where highly sensitive and personal materials may be disclosed.

Consequences: a result of a particular action or condition.

Constitutional law: consists of two major categories: criminal law and civil law.

Contraceptives: the deliberate prevention of conception or impregnation by any of various drugs, techniques, or devices; birth control.

Corporal punishment: deliberate infliction of pain intended as a disciplinary action or punishment; used in judicial, domestic and/or education settings.

Counselors' values: the ethical, moral, doctrinal, ideological, and social intrinsic beliefs and actions that influences all aspects of the school counselor's role.

Court of Appeals: a court having jurisdiction to review the actions of an inferior court (such as trial court) but not having the power to hear a legal action initially.

Court order: an order requiring a person to do a specified act, such as producing material or appearing in court. The government has the right to obtain a person's information by court order.

Criminal law: a crime against society; criminal law can be categorized as either a felony or a misdemeanor.

Cross-tabulate data: displays the joint distribution of two or more variables.

Cultural Competence: the ability to understand, appreciate, and interact with persons from cultures and/or different belief systems other than one's own.

Custodial parent: a term used for the parent having primary physical custody of a child.

Cyberbullying: the use of cell phones, instant messaging, e-mail, chat rooms or social networking sites such as Facebook and Twitter to harass, threaten or intimidate someone.

Cyberspace: the online world of computer networks and the Internet.

Cyber-speech: speech on the Internet or in cyberspace (especially in discussions of free speech).

Dangerous school climate: atmosphere of a school that is unsafe or unwelcoming for one or more students; atmosphere of harassment, violence, crime and/or bullying.

Data warehousing: a database that is used for reporting and data analysis.

Date rape drugs: controlled substances administered surreptitiously (as in a drink) to induce an unconscious or sedated state in a potential date rape victim.

Dating violence: the perpetration or threat of an act of violence by at least one member of an unmarried couple on the other member within the context of dating or courtship.

Dear Colleague Letter: April 2011 discussion by the Office for Civil Rights regarding Title IX's requirements related to student-on-student sexual harassment, including sexual violence, and explains schools' responsibility to take immediate and effective steps to end sexual harassment and sexual violence.

Defamation: injuring a person's character or reputation by false or malicious statements.

Defendant: the person against whom a legal action is brought. School counselors become defendants in cases such as academic advising and/or failure to report child abuse.

Deferred Action for Childhood Arrivals (DACA): eligible immigrant youth who came to the US as a child are protected from deportation. DACA does not provide a path to permanent residency of citizenship. Once a child receives DACA, that status is valid for two years and is eligible for renewal.

Deliberate indifference: intentional, unresponsiveness or lack of concern.

Deposition: testimony under oath, especially a statement by a witness that is written down or recorded for use in court at a later date.

Developmental level: a student's maturity level based on problem solving ability, competence, maturity and does not necessarily correlate to chronological age.

Developmentally delayed: maturity, behavior and competency level that is below that person's chronological level.

Digital footprint: the trail, traces or "footprints" that people leave online such as forum registration, e-mails and attachments, uploading videos or digital images.

Directory information: basic public information about a student such as name, address, telephone number, date and place of birth, etc.

Discriminatory harassment: is verbal or physical conduct that demeans or shows hostility, or aversion, toward an individual because of his/her race, color, religion, gender, national origin, age, disability, or because of retaliation for engaging in protected activity.

Disinhibition effect: pertains to cyberspace interactions and is a loosening (or complete abandonment) of social restrictions and inhibitions that would otherwise be present in normal face-to-face interactions.

Dogmatic solution: a black-and-white answer to a problem, without examining multiple perspectives in the context of a situation.

Domestic violence: assaultive and/or coercive behaviors, including physical, sexual, and psychological as well as economic coercion, that adults or adolescents use against their intimate partners.

Dream Act: introduced in 2001, aimed to provide a pathway to citizenship for undocumented, current, former, and future undocumented high school graduates and GED recipients a pathway to U.S. citizenship through college or the armed services.

Dual relationship: a relationship where professional distance is violated and impairs a school counselor's objectivity and increases the risk of harm to the student (e.g., counseling one's family members, close friends or associates).

Duces tecum: a Latin term meaning "you shall bring with you;" a court order issued by a clerk of court, justice of the peace, notary public or lawyer, usually signed by a lawyer; a lawyer signed subpoena.

Due process hearing: procedures or steps the school district and parents must take to settle disagreement.

Duty of care: a legal requirement that a person act toward others and the public with watchfulness, attention, caution and prudence.

Duty to warn: obligation to notify members involved in a potential harmful or dangerous situation; school counselors have a duty to warn parents if serious and foreseeable harm is perceived from a student.

Education for All Handicapped Children Act of 1975: this act requires all public schools accepting federal funds to provide equal access to education and one free meal a day for children with physical and mental disabilities.

Educational malpractice: a comparison between the acceptable standard of care for the school counseling profession and the specific act or conduct claimed to be malpractice.

Emotional harm: intentional infliction to a person's ability to think, reason or have feelings, such as cruel acts or statements, intimidation, rejection and indifference.

Entrenched inequities: established injustice or unfairness.

Equal access: providing opportunities, rights, and privileges by all people or groups, especially those who have historically been disadvantaged such as minority and low-income individuals.

Equal Access Act: a United States federal law passed in 1984 to compel federally funded secondary schools to provide equal access to extracurricular clubs. Lobbied for by religious groups who wanted to ensure students the right to conduct Bible study programs during lunch and after school, it has become an essential right in students' efforts to form Gay-Straight Alliances (GSA) clubs.

Equity and opportunity for all students: access to rights, privileges, opportunities and social institutions by all students or groups, especially those who have historically been disadvantaged such as minority and low-income students.

Ethical standards: guidelines developed by ASCA, used to clarify the standard of behavior and responsibility of all school counselors regardless of ASCA membership to students, parents, colleagues, the profession, the community and to themselves.

Ethics: agreed-upon values, norms, customs and mores that have withstood the test of time; provide a general framework for professional conduct.

Every Student Succeeds Act (ESSA): December 10, 2015, the ESSA reauthorized the Elementary and Secondary Education Act of 1965. The ESSA increases state authority on standards, assessments and interventions.

Ex-gay ministry: Christian ministries specializing in helping homosexually oriented persons change their sexual orientation or live as a heterosexual.

Expert witness: a person called to testify because he or she has a recognized competence in an area.

Facebook: a social networking website launched in 2004 with over 1 billion active users.

Falsifying student records: fraudulently altering a student's education record with or without a reasonable cause or authorization.

Family Educational Rights and Privacy Act (FERPA): federal legislation governing education records and dictating how all maintained information regarding a student will be handled and disseminated for the protection of students and their families.

Family Policy Compliance Office: an arm of the US Department of Education who administers the Family Education Rights and Privacy Act.

Federal court: litigation court for cases involving citizens of several states and cases involving federal statutes.

Federal law: a bill that makes it through both the House and the Senate and goes to the President who takes action by signing it into law, letting it become law without a signature or vetoing it.

Federal Statutes: laws passed by legislature and enacted by Congress.

Forcible Rape: sexual intercourse/contact without the lawful consent of the victim. In a forcible rape, the victim is prevented from resisting the sexual act because of the offender's use of force or threats of physical violence.

Foreseeable harm: a reasonable person would be able to predict or expect the ultimately harmful result of their actions.

Gang violence: criminal and non political acts of violence committed by a group of people who regularly engage in criminal activity against innocent people.

Gay-Straight Alliance Club: a student club in schools for the support of gay, lesbian, bisexual and transgender youth and their straight friends.

Gender binary: the concept that there are only two genders, male and female, and that everyone must be one or the other. Also implies the assumption that gender is biologically determined.

Gender expression: all of the external characteristics and behaviors that are socially defined as either masculine or feminine, such as dress, grooming, mannerisms, speech patterns and social interactions. It is a range of physical, mental, and behavioral characteristics distinguishing between masculinity and femininity.

Gender identity: a person's innate, deeply felt psychological identification as male or female, which may or may not correspond to the person's body or designated sex at birth (meaning what sex was originally listed on a person's birth certificate).

Gender nonconforming: behavior or gender expression that does not conform to dominant gender norms.

Gender spectrum: the concept that gender exists beyond a simple "male/female" binary model, but instead exists on an infinite continuum.

GLSEN: a national group of parents, students, teachers and others that wish to put an end to discrimination based on sexual orientation and gender identity/expression in K-12 schools.

Governmental immunity: protection from civil or tort liability while engaged in school functions of a governmental nature.

Group counseling sessions: counseling multiple members at the same time based on mutual needs and goals of the members; counselors avoid putting young people together in groups where highly sensitive and personal materials may be disclosed.

Guardian *ad litem*: a guardian appointed by a court to represent a minor unable to represent himself or herself.

Heterosexism: a belief that male-female sexuality is the only natural or moral mode of sexual behavior.

Historical Risk Factors: issues in a student's family that are dysfunctional behaviors or medical, social, or psychological problems that may contribute to an individual's risk of having those same problems.

Homophobia: fear of or prejudice against homosexuality or homosexual individuals.

Hostile environment: involves student-on-student sexual harassment, in which a student feels school is not a safe place.

Identifiability of the victim: the ability or inability to recognize the victim and/or perpetrator in a sexual harassment case.

Immune from liability: incapable of being held legally responsible.

Immunity: exemption from performing duties that the law generally requires other citizens to perform or from a penalty or burden that the law generally places upon other citizens.

In loco parentis: Latin term for "in place of parent" in which the person or entity acts as a parent with respect to the care, supervision and discipline of a child. School counselors act *in loco parentis* with minors in a school setting.

Individual with Disabilities Education Act: federal legislation for Exceptional Student Education (ESE) administered by the Office of Special Education, which spells out parents' and students' rights with regards to ESE records.

Informed consent: counselee chooses to enter a counseling relationship after being given direct information about the purposes, goals, techniques, rules of procedure and limits of confidentiality in which he or she may receive counseling.

Injury suffered: harm an individual suffered such as injury, lost scholarship or death.

Institutional standards: written and unwritten standards in which members of that institution must behave consistently and ethically within its parameters, while working to change those standards that are detrimental to its members.

Intersex: an individual displaying sexual characteristics of both male and female.

Intervening, superseding cause: breaks the line of causation from the wrongful act to the injury suffered and does not render liability.

Isms: an oppressive and especially discriminatory attitude or belief

Jessica Logan Act: Ohio cyberbullying law in honor of a student who committed suicide after being severely cyberbullied over a sextext she sent to her boyfriend.

Judicial bypass: a process by which minors can get state approval to have an abortion without parental consent or notification in states requiring parental involvement.

Justice: providing equal treatment to all people regardless of age, sex, race, ethnicity, disability, socioeconomic status, cultural background, religion or sexual orientation.

Lambda Legal: a nongovernmental organization devoted to promoting the legal rights of gays, lesbians, bisexuals, transgender and people with HIV or AIDS, through impact litigation, education and public policy work.

Laws: the minimum standard society will tolerate; used to codify a value or set of values. Laws and their interpretations differ from one geographic location to another.

Legal status of minors: generally under the age of 18 children are legally unable to make decisions on their own behalf.

Legitimate educational interest: Family Educational Rights and Privacy Act (FERPA) allows an educators to access education records for the purpose of performing appropriate tasks within their job description to provide a service or benefit to the student or to the student's family.

Liability: accountability to another party or to the state, that can be enforced through damages or criminal punishment.

List-servers: a special usage of email that allows for widespread distribution of information to many Internet users.

Loyalty: staying connected with students and being available to them to the extent possible.

Maintaining student records: keeping, organizing and updating student education records in compliance with FERPA.

Malicious, willful and intentional torts: occurs when one acts in a determined way and harms another; not an error but deliberate.

Malpractice: improper or unethical conduct by a professional that results in injury, damage or loss.

Mandated reporter: a person who is required by law to report suspected child abuse to proper authorities under penalty of criminal charges.

Marginalized students: a social phenomenon by which the needs of certain groups are ignored and often classified as insignificant or of lower status; likely to be subjected to multiple layers of discrimination.

McKinney Vento Homeless Assistance Act: funds local, regional, and state homeless assistance programs, amended October 1, 2016 by Every Student Succeeds Act, to strengthen that ability for homeless children and youth experiencing homelessness to enroll, attend, and succeed in school.

Mediation: an attempt to bring about a peaceful settlement or compromise between disputants through the objective intervention of a neutral party.

Ministerial: a duty that is plainly laid out and requires no discretion.

Missouri's Facebook Statute: addresses teacher's use of electronic communications with students.

Monitoring your competence: ASCA's Ethical Standards for School Counselors outlines seven major practices school counselors should engage in to ensure they are adhering to the standard of care expected of school counselors.

Moral Principles: the counseling profession's moral conduct is to act with beneficence, and nonmalefience, treat students with loyalty and justice, and to promote their autonomy.

Multiculturalism: the preservation of different cultures or cultural identities within a unified society, as a state or nation.

MySpace: a social networking site that allows its users to create blogs, upload videos and photos, and design profiles to showcase their interests and talents.

Negligence: civil liability if a school counselor is found to owe a duty to another person, breaches that duty and causes damages to another person.

No harm contract: an agreement that the individual signing the contract will not commit suicide.

Non-binary: describes any gender identity which does not fit the male and female binary.

Noncustodial parent: term used for the parent who has physical custody of a child for a lesser amount of time than the custodial parent. Typically the child does not reside with the noncustodial parent except when that parent exercises his or her visitation rights.

Nonmaleficence: avoiding doing harm to students and families.

Office for Civil Rights: the arm of the federal government requiring compliance with anti-discrimination policies and practices for school districts.

Opacity of law: sometimes it takes a court to interpret the meaning of a statute that on face value could be interpreted in different ways.

Over discipline: nonaccidental injury usually at the hands of a child's parents that goes beyond the boundaries of reasonable punishment into maltreatment (abuse or neglect).

Parental permission: written or unwritten consent from a parent or guardian for a student to participate in services such as small-group counseling.

Parents, Family and Friends of Lesbians and Gays (PFLAG): an organization whose mission it is to promote the health and well-being of gay, lesbian, bisexual and transgendered persons and their families and friends.

Peer-on-peer aggression: hostility between peers that includes teasing, harassment, verbal aggression and bullying.

Personal bias: a subjective preference or behavior based on personal values and beliefs.

Physical aggression: hostile or abusive behavior toward another person or group.

Physical and emotional safety: an atmosphere or condition free from physical or emotional harm.

Plaintiff: a person or party who initiates a lawsuit.

Planned Parenthood: health service organization providing reproductive health care and sexual health information to men, women and teens.

Potential courses of action: possible strategies or procedures.

Precedent: a court decision that serves as a guide or direction on how to decide future cases with similar facts or legal questions.

Prevailing community standards: written and unwritten standards in which the community and those who work in it must behave consistently and ethically within its parameters, while working to change those standards that are detrimental to its members.

Privacy rights of minors: privileges given to the parents of a minor student to make critical decisions regarding disclosure of personal information.

Privileged communication: a creature of statute that pertains to court testimony. Students in some states can render school counselors incapable of breaching their confidential conversations in court or the breach can only happen under certain conditions such as the student is in danger.

Privity: having an interest in a transaction, contract or legal action to which one is not a party but where the interest arises out of a relationship to one of the parties of the legal action.

Process of discovery: practice in which the attorneys may require an oral or written deposition; written interrogatories requiring written responses to questions; certain documents or materials; a request to submit a listing of facts that are not in dispute; and/or physical or mental examination of one of the parties of the lawsuit.

Professional communication: choosing words judiciously and in an effort to maintain optimal communication with those who have the "need to know."

Professional distance: the appropriate familiarity and closeness that a school counselor engages in with students and their family members.

Professionalism: internal motivation to perform at the level of practice representing the ideals of the profession. For school counselors, professionalism is used to maintain a school counselor's standing with peers, teachers, staff members, administrators, parents and students and adhering to local, state and federal laws, school board policy, ethical standards and community standards.

Protection of Pupil Rights Amendment: provides protective rights to parents in regards to their students taking surveys. It requires written parental consent prior to administering ED-funded surveys.

Protective Risk Factors: research on supportive conditions, internal traits, resources that make youth more resistant to victimization and perpetration and decreases the likelihood that a young person will become violent or engage in criminal activity.

Qualified privilege: permits persons in positions of authority or trust to make statements or relay or report statements that would be considered slander and libel if made by anyone else.

Queer: an umbrella identity term encompassing lesbian, questioning people, gay men, bisexuals, non-labeling people, transgender folks, and anyone else who does not strictly identify as heterosexual.

Questioning: someone who is exploring their sexual identity.

***Quid pro quo* harassment:** involves providing a student with a need or want contingent on the provision of sexual acts such as a better grade.

Rape: unlawful sexual intercourse or any other sexual penetration, with or without force, and without the consent of the victim.

Real threat: a danger that can be validated with evidence of a written threat, the presence of a weapon or other indicators that point to serious intent to harm.

Reasonableness: a person acting within the standard of care and taking necessary precautions.

Reasonable suspicion: the standard that requires a school counselor to report child abuse. The notion that a child is being abused or neglected as certainty is not required.

Recidivism rate: the rate at which repeated relapse into criminal or delinquent behavior occurs.

Relational aggression: bullying or other forms of harm caused through damage to one's social status.

Reparative therapy: psychotherapy aimed at eliminating homosexual desires, also known as conversion therapy.

Revenge porn: sexually explicit portrayal of one or more people that is distributed without their consent via any medium.

Risk factors: characteristics, conditions, or behaviors, that increase the possibility of disease or injury.

Safe haven law: a law that allows birth mothers to leave their newborns at hospitals, fire stations, or police stations anonymously, with no legal repercussions. Each state sets the outside age limit to which this law applies.

Safe Schools Coalition: partnership of organizations that seek to promote tolerance in schools by providing resources for students, parents and schools.

Safe school zone: established parameters around schools and school activities, e.g, 1000 feet from a school or 100 feet from a school bus stop. If a crime is committed within those parameters state law may impose increased penalties.

School board policy: guidelines or procedure developed by the school board relating to issues that may hinder the education process that all schools in the district must follow.

School climate: the quality and character of school life based on patterns of students', parents' and school personnel's experience of school life, teaching and learning practices, and organizational structures.

School culture: patterns of meaning or activity (norms, values, beliefs, relationships, rituals, traditions, myths, etc.) shared in varying degrees by members of a school community.

School violence: encompasses a wide range of violent activities including physical fights, threats, destruction, robbery, harassment, dating violence, molestation, rape, bullying, hostile or threatening remarks, assault with or without weapons and gang violence.

Screening member: assessing usually through interviews, the suitability of students for their appropriateness and commitment to participate in small groups.

Self-direction: a course that is guided by oneself; autonomous action.

Separation of power: each division of government functions freely within the area of its responsibility.

Sexting: the act of sending sexually explicit messages and/or photographs, primarily between mobile phones.

Sexual harassment: conduct that is sexual in nature or related to the gender of the person. The behavior occurs in an unequal relationship where one person has more power over another and the behavior is unsolicited or unwelcome.

Sexual harassment policy: a procedure protecting all students from sexual harassment.

Sexual minority: a group whose sexual identity, orientation or practices differ from the majority of the surrounding society.

Sexual orientation: the focus of a person's desires, fantasies and feelings; the gender(s) that one is primarily oriented toward.

Sexual violence: any sexual act that is perpetrated against someone's will.

Sexually active students: students who are intimate in a sexual way such as touching someone's genitals, oral sex or intercourse.

Sexually Hostile Environment: created when conduct is sufficiently serious that it interferes with or limits a student's ability to participate in or benefit from the school's program.

Slander: oral defamation; the speaking of false and malicious words that injure another person's reputation, business or property rights.

Slut-shaming: is the deliberate act of impugning a woman's character in sexual terms in order to embarrass, humiliate, intimidate, degrade or shame her for actions or behaviors that are a normal part of female sexuality.

Social bullying: is deliberate, repetitive and aggressive social behavior intended to hurt others. Sometimes referred to as relational bullying, involves hurting someone's reputation or relationships.

Social change agent: a representative in a position to affect and bring about change in schools regarding unequal procedures, policies and regulations.

Social justice: promotion of equity for all people and groups in schools to give special care to those who historically have not received adequate educational opportunities.

Social risk factors: the absence of support from family, friends, community that offers youth both emotional and physical resources that may protect them to achieve better outcomes. Research shows that the presence of one or more positive and significant individuals in a child's life may act as a buffer against negative outcomes.

Special relation: a legal existing connection such as *in loco parentis*.

Standard of care: what the reasonably competent professional would do; following laws, ethical standards and school board policies.

State court: a system that includes the court of last resort such as state supreme courts, intermediate appellate courts, courts of general jurisdiction and courts of limited jurisdiction or small-claims courts.

State legislature: provides the basis for public school law, interprets the laws, and gives school boards authority to create their own rules and regulations.

State statutes: laws issued by the state.

Statute of limitations: a law which sets the maximum period which one can wait before filing a lawsuit.

Statutory obligation: a responsibility passed into law by a unit of federal, state or local governments.

Statutory rape: adults, usually 18 years or older, who have a sexual relationship with a minor of a certain age; the age of both the victim and the perpetrator are variable depending on the state.

STEPS Solutions To Ethical Problems in Schools: a nine-step model adapted from the seven-step, American Counseling Association Ethical Decision Making Model addressing the emotional influence of a problem and considering chronological and developmental appropriateness as well as parental rights.

Student-on-student sexual harassment: one student is harassed by another student and doesn't feel safe in that environment, also known as hostile environment.

Subpoena: a Latin term meaning "under penalty"; a court order requiring the recipient to perform a specified act such as appearing in court to answer questions about something he or she has witnessed or heard or producing records as evidence. There are penalties if a person fails to respond to a subpoena.

Suicide Assessment: an assessment used to evaluate a student's risk of attempting suicide.

Teacher-on-student sexual harassment: a student is harassed by a teacher; typically a teacher gives a better grade or favor in exchange for a sexual act, also known as *quid pro quo*.

Technologically literate: the ability of an individual, working independently and with others, to responsibly, appropriately and effectively use technology tools to access, manage, integrate, evaluate, create and communicate information.

Teenage pregnancy: defined as a teenage girl, usually within the ages of 13-19 becoming pregnant.

Testimony: declarations, spoken or written, offered in a legal case or deliberative hearing.

Threat Assessments: set of investigative and operational techniques that can be used to identify, assess, and manage the risks of targeted violence and its potential perpetrators.

Threat of harm: activities, conditions or persons that place a child at risk of harm.

Title IX of Educational Amendment of 1972: federal law that requires educational institutions to maintain policies, practices and programs that do not discriminate against anyone based on sex.

Tolerance for ambiguity: acceptance and open-mindedness of situations that will not contain clear-cut solutions.

Transgender: applies to a variety of individuals, behaviors, and groups involving tendencies to vary from culturally conventional gender roles. It is the state of one's self-identification as woman, man, neither or both not matching one's assigned sex. Transgender does not imply any specific form of sexual orientation.

Transgender man: describes the trajectory of a person who is changing or has changed their body and lived gender role from a birth-assigned female to an affirmed male.

Transgender woman: describes the trajectory of a person who is changing or has changed their body and lived gender role from a birth-assigned male to an affirmed female.

Trauma informed practice: the recognition and understanding that trauma can be a barrier to student success and the ability to provide the appropriate support.

True threat: a threatening communication that can be prosecuted under the law.

Twitter: a very popular instant messaging system that lets a person send brief text messages up to 140 characters in length to a list of followers.

Unalterable factors: aspects of a student's life that are stable and difficult to change that may cause harm.

Unconditional Positive Regard: a term coined by the humanist Carl Rogers, that promotes basic acceptance and support of a person regardless of what the person says or does.

Uniform Child Custody Jurisdiction Act: designed to deter interstate parental kidnapping and promote uniform jurisdiction and enforcement provisions in interstate child-custody and visitation cases.

Uniform Marriage Act: procedure followed by many states when deciding custody, which encourages custodial decisions in part to favor the parent that is most likely to keep the other parent involved in the child's life.

Uninterrupted Scholars Act: a provision of the Family Educational Rights and Privacy Act of 1974 that child care agencies that are working on foster care cases to have access to education records without written parental consent.

USA Patriot Act: a response to the terrorist attacks of September 11th, it significantly reduces restrictions in law enforcement agencies' gathering of intelligence and immigration authorities in detaining and deporting immigrants suspected of terrorism-related acts.

Value-laden counseling: a caution for school counselors to be objective and not to impose their beliefs or infringe on a parent's right to be the guiding voice in their child's life in issues rooted in religion or ethnicity such as abortion.

Verbal aggression: hostile or abusive language used toward another person or group.

Vested with rights: having the legal rights of ownership.

Video conferencing: the holding of a conference among people at remote locations by means of transmitted audio and video signals.

Violent propensities: tendencies to act in a violent manner.

Viral: relating to or involving an image, video, or piece of information, etc., that is circulated rapidly and widely from one internet user to another.

Virtual: an image, video, advertisement, etc. that is circulated rapidly on the internet.

Webinar: short for web-based seminar, a presentation, lecture, workshop or seminar that is transmitted over the web.

Willful and Wanton Disregard: used in negligence law to describe extreme carelessness or indifference to safety.

Witnesses: school counselors act as witnesses for the court usually in cases of child custody, child abuse or disciplinary action.

Written interrogatories: written responses to questions required under the process of discovery.

Zero tolerance: a strict approach to rule enforcement that states absolutely no deviation will be allowed.

ABOUT THE AUTHOR

Carolyn Stone, Ed.D., is a professor of counselor education at the University of North Florida, where she teaches and researches in the area of legal and ethical issues for school counselors and school counselors' impact on opportunity, information and achievement gaps. Prior to becoming a school counselor educator in 1995, she spent 22 years with the Duval County Public Schools in Jacksonville, Fla., where she served as a middle school teacher, elementary and high school counselor and supervisor of guidance for 225 school counselors. The University of North Florida bestowed its highest honor on Stone by naming her the 2016 Distinguished Professor. Stone was the 2006 president of the American School Counselor Association (ASCA) and is in her 20th year as their Ethics Committee chair. She has written the only book exclusively for school counselors on legal and ethical issues. Stone was awarded the Mary Gerke Lifetime Achievement Award by ASCA in 2010 and the Bob Myrick Lifetime Achievement Award by the Florida School Counselor Association in 2012. She is a past president of the Florida Counseling Association and the Florida Association of Counselor Educators and Supervisors. Stone has delivered more than 500 workshops in all 50 states and 23 countries. She has authored six books, dozens of journal articles and serves the courts as an expert witness in cases involving school counselors. Her professional path in elementary and high school counseling, middle school teaching, supervisor of guidance for one of the nation's largest school district and school counselor educator has prepared her with first-hand experience and understanding of the professional world of school counselors.